Lecture Notes in Computer Science 4797

Commenced Publication in 1973
Founding and Former Series Editors:
Gerhard Goos, Juris Hartmanis, and Jan van Leeuwen

Marcelo Arenas Michael I. Schwartzbach (Eds.)

Database Programming Languages

11th International Symposium, DBPL 2007
Vienna, Austria, September 23-24, 2007
Revised Selected Papers

Springer

Volume Editors

Marcelo Arenas
Pontificia Universidad Católica de Chile
Departamento de Ciencia de la Computacion
Vicuna Mackenna 4860, Edificio San Agustin, 7820436 Macul, Santiago, Chile
E-mail: marenas@ing.puc.cl

Michael I. Schwartzbach
University of Aarhus, Department of Computer Science
Aabogade 34, 8200 Aarhus N, Denmark
E-mail: mis@brics.dk

Library of Congress Control Number: Applied for

CR Subject Classification (1998): H.2, H.3, E.2, D.3.3, H.4

LNCS Sublibrary: SL 3 – Information Systems and Application, incl. Internet/Web and HCI

ISSN 0302-9743
ISBN-10 3-540-75986-7 Springer Berlin Heidelberg New York
ISBN-13 978-3-540-75986-7 Springer Berlin Heidelberg New York

Springer is a part of Springer Science+Business Media

springer.com

Printed in Germany

Typesetting: Camera-ready by author, data conversion by Scientific Publishing Services, Chennai, India
Printed on acid-free paper SPIN: 12181230 06/3180 5 4 3 2 1 0

Preface

This volume contains the proceedings of the 11th International Symposium on Database Programming Languages (DBPL 2007), held in Vienna, Austria, on September 23–24, 2007. DBPL 2007 was one of 15 meetings co-located with VLDB (the International Conference on Very Large Data Bases).

DBPL continues to present the very best work at the intersection of database and programming language research. The proceedings include a paper based on the invited talk by Wenfei Fan and the 16 contributed papers that were selected by the program committee from 41 submissions. Every submission was reviewed by at least three members of the program committee. In addition, the program committee sought the opinions of additional referees, selected because of their expertise on particular topics. The final selection of papers was made during the last week of July.

We would like to thank all of the authors who submitted papers to the conference, and the members of the program committee for their excellent work. The program committee did not meet in person, but carried out extensive discussions during the electronic PC meeting. We are grateful to Andrei Voronkov for his EasyChair system that made it so easy to manage these discussions.

Finally, we would also like to thank Christoph Koch and Gavin Bierman for their assistance and sound counsel, and the organizers of VLDB 2007 for taking care of the local organization of DBPL.

September 2007

Marcelo Arenas
Michael I. Schwartzbach

Organization

Program Co-chairs

Marcelo Arenas	Pontificia Universidad Católica de Chile, Chile
Michael I. Schwartzbach	University of Aarhus, Denmark

Program Committee

Sihem Amer-Yahia	Yahoo! Research, USA
Marcelo Arenas	Pontificia Universidad Católica de Chile, Chile
Paolo Atzeni	Università Roma Tre, Italy
Pablo Barcelo	Universidad de Chile, Chile
Andrea Cali	Free University of Bozen-Bolzano, Italy
Alin Deutsch	University of California, San Diego, USA
Jan Hidders	University of Antwerp, Belgium
Anastasios Kementsietsidis	University of Edinburgh, UK
Wim Martens	Universität Dortmund, Germany
Maarten Marx	Universiteit van Amsterdam, The Netherlands
Erik Meijer	Microsoft, USA
Frank Neven	Hasselt University, Belgium
Benjamin Pierce	University of Pennsylvania, USA
Mukund Raghavachari	IBM Watson, USA
Michael I. Schwartzbach	University of Aarhus, Denmark
Helmut Seidl	Technische Universität München, Germany
Jérôme Siméon	IBM Watson, USA
Dan Suciu	University of Washington, USA
Wang-Chiew Tan	University of California, Santa Cruz, USA
Stijn Vansummeren	Hasselt University, Belgium
Limsoon Wong	National University of Singapore, Singapore

External Referees

Alexandru Berlea
Luca Cabibbo
Alessandro Campi
James Cheney
Nate Foster
Wouter Gelade
Mauricio Hernandez
Tadeusz Litak
Davide Martinenghi
Nicola Onose
Jorge Pérez
Christopher Re
Balder ten Cate
Yannis Velegrakis

Table of Contents

Invited Talk

XML Publishing: Bridging Theory and Practice 1
Wenfei Fan

Algorithms

Efficient Algorithms for the Tree Homeomorphism Problem 17
Michaela Götz, Christoph Koch, and Wim Martens

Datalog Programs over Infinite Databases, Revisited 32
Sara Cohen, Joseph (Yossi) Gil, and Evelina Zarivach

XML Query Languages

A Methodology for Coupling Fragments of XPath with Structural Indexes for XML Documents 48
George H.L. Fletcher, Dirk Van Gucht, Yuqing Wu, Marc Gyssens, Sofía Brenes, and Jan Paredaens

Conjunctive Query Containment over Trees 66
Henrik Björklund, Wim Martens, and Thomas Schwentick

A Better Semantics for XQuery with Side-Effects 81
Giorgio Ghelli, Nicola Onose, Kristoffer Rose, and Jérôme Siméon

Inconsistency Handling

Repairing Inconsistent XML Write-Access Control Policies 97
Loreto Bravo, James Cheney, and Irini Fundulaki

On the Consistent Rewriting of Conjunctive Queries Under Primary Key Constraints 112
Jef Wijsen

Data Provenance

Relational Completeness of Query Languages for Annotated Databases 127
Floris Geerts and Jan Van den Bussche

Provenance as Dependency Analysis 138
James Cheney, Amal Ahmed, and Umut A. Acar

Emerging Data Models

A Theory of Stream Queries 153
Yuri Gurevich, Dirk Leinders, and Jan Van den Bussche

Querying Structural and Behavioral Properties of Business Processes 169
Daniel Deutch and Tova Milo

Efficient Evaluation of `HAVING` Queries on a Probabilistic Database 186
Christopher Ré and Dan Suciu

Type Checking

Succinctness of Pattern-Based Schema Languages for XML 201
Wouter Gelade and Frank Neven

Analysis of Imperative XML Programs 216
Michael G. Burke, Igor Peshansky, Mukund Raghavachari, and Christoph Reichenbach

Efficient Inclusion for a Class of XML Types with Interleaving and Counting 231
Giorgio Ghelli, Dario Colazzo, and Carlo Sartiani

Towards Practical Typechecking for Macro Tree Transducers 246
Alain Frisch and Haruo Hosoya

Author Index 261

XML Publishing: Bridging Theory and Practice

Wenfei Fan*

University of Edinburgh and Bell Laboratories

Abstract. Transforming relational data into XML, as known as *XML publishing*, is often necessary when one wants to exchange data residing in databases or to create an XML interface of a traditional database. This paper aims to provide an overview of recent advances in XML publishing. We present a notion of publishing transducers recently developed for studying the expressive power and complexity of XML publishing languages. In terms of publishing transducers we then characterize XML publishing languages being used in practice. In addition, we address dynamic aspects of XML publishing, namely, incremental maintenance and update management of XML views published from relational data.

1 Introduction

While most data is currently residing in relational databases, it is increasingly common for one to exchange the data in XML format, or to build an XML interface of the databases. This highlights the need for transforming relational data into XML, as known as *XML publishing of relational data.*

In response to the need, a variety of XML publishing languages have been developed [2,3,15,26], and are rapidly being introduced into commercial products [18,21,24]. An XML publishing language is essentially a view definition language, for specifying XML views of relational data. Just like their relational counterparts, associated with XML publishing languages are a number of fundamental questions in connection with their complexity and expressiveness. These questions are not only of theoretical interest, but are also important in practice for both users and designers of XML publishing languages. Given a host of XML publishing languages, a user wants to decide which one to choose: is an XML view expressible in certain languages but not definable in others? Which language is "better" than others when it comes to evaluation cost? To support recursively-defined XML views in a publishing language, database vendors may want to know whether or not certain high-end DBMS features are a must: is it necessary to upgrade the DBMS to support linear recursion of SQL'99?

This paper aims to provide a synergy between theory and practice by answering these questions for XML publishing languages supported by commercial products or research prototype systems: SQL/XML of IBM DB2 XML Extender [18] and Oracle 10g XML DB [24], FOR-XML and XSD of SQL Server 2005 [21], DAD of DB2 XML Extender, DBMS_XMLGEN of XML DB, as well as XPERANTO [26], TreeQL

* Supported in part by EPSRC GR/S63205/01, GR/T27433/01, EP/E029213/1 and BBSRC BB/D006473/1.

M. Arenas and M.I. Schwartzbach (Eds.): DBPL 2007, LNCS 4797, pp. 1–16, 2007.

of SilkRoute [15,2], and ATG of PRATA [3]. We evaluate these languages in terms of their expressive power and complexity, by leveraging a notion of publishing transducers recently proposed in [13]. We characterize these languages in terms of various classes of publishing transducers, for which the complexity bounds and expressive power have been established in [13].

Another aim of the paper is to promote the study of dynamic aspects of XML publishing. Since XML publishing actually defines XML views of relational data, for all the reasons that the incremental update and view update problems are important for database views, efficient incremental maintenance and update management also deserve a full treatment for XML publishing. Unfortunately we are aware of the support of this functionality only in research prototype systems (*e.g.*, PRATA [6,11]), but currently not in any of the commercial systems.

The remainder of the paper is organized as follows. In Section 2, we discuss various dichotomies for assessing XML publishing languages. In Section 3 we present XML publishing transducers and give an account of results about their complexity bounds and expressive power. In Section 4 we characterize the XML publishing languages mentioned above in terms of publishing transducers. In Section 5, we address the incremental update and view update problems for XML publishing. Finally, we identify open research issues in Section 6.

2 XML Publishing

An XML document is typically modeled as a node-labeled, ordered, unranked tree. Given a relational schema R, XML publishing is to define an XML view, *i.e.*, a mapping τ such that for any instance I of R, $\tau(I)$ is an XML tree.

Example 1. Consider a relational schema R_0 (with keys underlined): course(cno, title, type), prereq(cno1, cno2). A database instance D_0 of R_0 maintains course data classified into "regular" and "project" *type*, and a relation *prereq* in which a tuple *(c1, c2)* indicates that *c2* is an *immediate prerequisite* of *c1*. Note that the transitive closure of *prereq* gives the prerequisite hierarchy of the courses.

One may want to define the following XML views of the relational database:

(1) As depicted in Fig. 1(a), view τ_1 is a tree of depth two, containing the list of all courses in D_0 that do not have DB as its immediate prerequisite, *i.e.*, for any such *course* c, (c, c') is not in *prereq* if the title of c' is DB.

(2) As shown in Fig. 1(b), view τ_2 contains the list of all courses in D_0. Under each course c are its *title* and the list of *cno*'s of its immediate prerequisites, followed by an element *next-level* under which are the immediate prerequisites of the *cno* children of c, and so on, until all the prerequisites of c are listed.

(3) As depicted in Fig. 1(c), view τ_3 is a tree of depth two, containing the list of all courses in D_0. Below each *course* c is its *cno*, followed by the list of all the *cno*'s that appear in the prerequisite *hierarchy* of c.

(4) As shown in Fig. 1(d), view τ_4 is an XML tree that is required to conform to the DTD d_0 below (the definition of elements whose type is PCDATA is omitted):

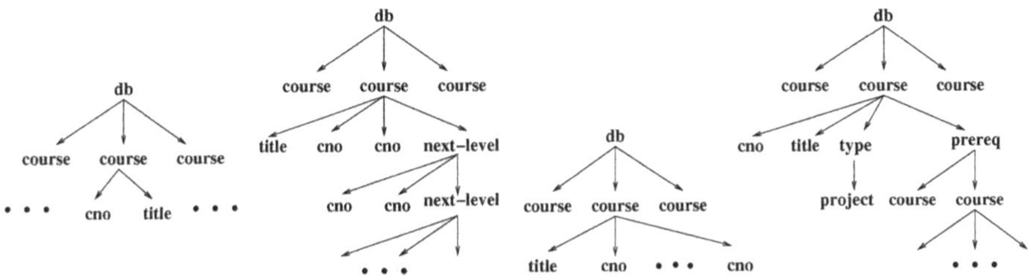

(a) XML view τ_1 (b) XML view τ_2 (c) XML view τ_3 (d) XML view τ_4

Fig. 1. Example XML publishing

```
<!ELEMENT db      (course*)>
<!ELEMENT course  (cno, title, type, prereq)>
<!ELEMENT type    (regular | project)>
<!ELEMENT prereq  (course*)>
<!ELEMENT regular (empty)>   /* similarly for project */
```

We may find it difficult to express (1) τ_1 in XSD of SQL Server 2005 [21], RDB_mapping of IBM DB2 XML Extender [18] and TreeQL [2], (2) τ_2 in any language except ATG [3], (3) τ_3 in any language except DBMS_XMLGEN of Oracle 10g XML DB [24] and ATG, and (4) τ_4 in any language except ATG to guarantee the conformance to D_0. However we are not sure whether it is because we do not know the languages well enough, or due to the limitations of the languages. □

To answer this question we study a variety of factors that may impact the expressive power of an XML publishing language. A publishing language typically specifies the behaviors of a middleware controller with a limited query interface to relational sources. An XML view defined in such a language builds an output tree top-down starting from the root: at each node it issues queries to a relational database I, generates the children of the node using the query results, and iteratively expands the subtrees of those children inductively. It may (implicitly) store intermediate query results in registers associated with nodes and pass the information downward to control subtree generation [2,3,18,21,24,26]. It may also allow *virtual* tree nodes [2,3] that will be removed from the output tree to express, *e.g.,* XML entities. In addition, it may be recursively defined, capable of generating XML trees for which the depth cannot be determined at compile time. Finally, it may encode a DTD to guarantee that the output trees conform to the predefined DTD. These motivate us to consider the following dichotomies:

– CQ, FO vs. FP: the relational query language in which queries on relational data are expressed. We consider conjunctive queries (CQ), first-order queries (FO) and (inflationary) fixpoint queries (FP). For example, view τ_1 requires an FO query and cannot be expressed in languages with CQ queries only.

- Relation vs. tuple: registers that store intermediate results. Some languages store a finite *relation* in a register while others allow a single *tuple*. View τ_2 is definable only in languages that support relation registers.
- Virtual vs. normal: the types of nodes. Languages may or may not allow *virtual* nodes that will be removed from the output tree. In a language that does not support FP (*e.g.*, SQL'99), view τ_3 is definable only if virtual nodes are allowed, by making the *next-level* nodes of τ_2 virtual.
- Recursive vs. nonrecursive: whether or not views can be recursively defined. For example, τ_2 and τ_4 are recursively defined: the depth of a *course* sub-tree in these views is determined by its prerequisite hierarchy in D_0.
- DTD-directed or not: whether or not output XML trees are guaranteed to conform to a predefined DTD. In practice, XML publishing is often directed by a type, typically a DTD, as shown by τ_4. A community or industry agrees on a certain DTD, and subsequently all members of the community create XML views of their relational data that conform to the predefined DTD [2].

Different combinations of these parameters yield a spectrum of XML publishing languages with quite different expressive power and complexity.

3 Publishing Transducers

We now present publishing transducers introduced in [13], which allow us to characterize the complexity and expressive power of existing XML publishing languages, as well as their equivalence and separation.

3.1 Definition of Publishing Transducers

Let R be a relational schema, $\mathcal{L}$ a relational query language, and Σ a set of XML tags. A publishing transducer is a finite state machine that, given a database instance I of R, generates an XML tree with elements labeled with tags in Σ, *top-down* starting from the root. To do this, with each element labeled $a \in \Sigma$ in the XML tree, it associates a register Reg_a, storing intermediate result as a relation of a fixed arity. At each a-node v, the transducer extracts data from the underlying database I and the intermediate result in Reg_a, via a query in $\mathcal{L}$, and spawns the children of v using the data. This is directed by a transduction rule, which is uniquely determined by the tag a and the current state of the machine. In contrast to tree recognizers (see [16]) and the automata for querying XML [22,23], which operate on an *existing tree* and either accept the tree or select a set of nodes from the tree, a publishing transducer does not take a tree as input; instead, it builds a *new XML tree* based on the data from a relational source.

Definition 1. *A* publishing transducer *for a relational schema R is defined to be $\tau = (Q, \Sigma, q_0, \delta)$, where Q is a finite set of* states*; Σ is a finite alphabet of* tags*; q_0 is the* start state *associated with the root tag $r \in \Sigma$; and δ is a finite set of* transduction rules*: for each $(q, a) \in Q \times \Sigma$, there is a unique rule*

$$(q, a) \quad \rightarrow \quad (q_1, a_1, \phi_1(\bar{x}_1; \bar{y}_1)), \ldots, (q_k, a_k, \phi_k(\bar{x}_k; \bar{y}_k)).$$

Here $k \geq 0$, $a_1, \ldots, a_k$ are distinct tags in Σ, $(q_i, a_i) \in Q \times \Sigma$ for $i \in [1, k]$, and $\phi_i \in \mathcal{L}$ is a relational query from R and Reg_a to Reg_{a_i}. □

We next give basic properties and the semantics of publishing transducers.

Deterministic. A publishing transducer is deterministic: for each $(q, a) \in Q \times \Sigma$, there is a unique transduction rule, except that for the start state q_0, for which only the rule for (q_0, r) is defined. Furthermore, (a) q_0 and r do not appear in the right-hand side of any rule; (b) *text* is a special "tag" in Σ, and the right-hand side of the rule for $(q, \textit{text})$ is empty, *i.e.*, *text* nodes do not have any children.

Tuple vs. relation register. The $\mathcal{L}$ query $\phi_i(\bar{x}_i; \bar{y}_i)$ extracts data from I and Reg_a. The result of the query is grouped by attributes $\bar{x}_i$, yielding sets of tuples. For each set S_j, a distinct a_i child is created, carrying S_j as the content of its register Reg_{a_i}. These a_i children are ordered based on an implicit ordering on the domain of data. When $|\bar{y}_i| = 0$, *i.e.*, when the result is grouped by the entire tuple, each register Reg_{a_i} holds a *single* tuple and is thus a *tuple register.*

Transduction. Initially, τ constructs a tree t consisting of a single node labeled (q_0, r) with an empty register. At each step, τ expands t by *simultaneously* operating on the leaf nodes of t. At each leaf u labeled (q, a), τ generates new nodes by finding the rule for (q, a) from δ, issuing queries $\phi_1(\bar{x}_1; \bar{y}_1), \ldots, \phi_k(\bar{x}_k; \bar{y}_k)$ embedded in the rule to the database I and the register $\mathsf{Reg}_a(u)$ associated with u. For each $i \in [1, k]$, the a_i children and their associated register Reg_{a_i} are produced as described above. These yield the children of u characterized by a regular expression $a_1^* \ldots a_k^*$. The transformation proceeds until a stop condition is satisfied at all the leaf nodes. A stop condition is one of the following.

1. There is a node v on the path from the root to u such that v and u have the *same* state q, tag a, and $Reg_a(v) = Reg_a(u)$. Since the subtree rooted at u is uniquely determined by $q, a, Reg_a(u)$ and I, this asserts that the tree t will not expand at u if the expansion *adds no new information* to the tree.
2. The query $\phi_j(\bar{x}_j; \bar{y}_j)$ evaluates to empty for all $i \in [1, k]$.
3. The right-hand side of the rule for (q, a) is empty. This is particularly the case for $a = \textit{text}$, for which u carries a string representation of $Reg_a(u)$.

These conditions ensure the termination of the transformation.

When the tree cannot be expanded further, *i.e.*, all leaf nodes satisfy a stop condition, an XML tree is generated by removing all registers and states from t. It is the output of the transducer τ, denoted by $\tau(I)$. We use $\tau(R)$ to denote the set of all XML trees generated by τ when I ranges over all instances of R.

Example 2. We define a publishing transducer $\tau_1 = (Q_1, \Sigma_1, q_0, \delta_1)$ to generate the view of Fig. 1(a), where $Q_1 = \{q_0, q\}$, $\Sigma_1 = \{\textit{db}, \textit{course}, \textit{cno}, \textit{title}, \textit{text}\}$, and the root tag is *db*. The transduction δ_1 is defined as follows:

$\delta_1(q_0,\ db) \quad = (q, course,\ \phi_1(n, t;\ \emptyset))$, where
$\phi_1(n,t) = \exists t_p\ (course(n,t,t_p) \wedge \neg\exists n_1, t_1, t_{p1}\ (prereq(n,n_1) \wedge course(n_1,t_1,t_{p1}) \wedge t_1 = \text{'DB'}))$

$\delta_1(q,\ course) \ = (q, cno,\ \phi_2(n;\emptyset)),\ \ (q, title,\ \phi_3(t;\emptyset)),$ where
$\phi_2(n) = \exists t\ \mathsf{Reg}_c(n,t)$, and $\phi_3(t) = \exists n\ \mathsf{Reg}_c(n,t)$,

$\delta_1(q, cno) = (q, text, \phi_4(n))$, where $\phi_4(n) = \mathsf{Reg}_n(n)$ (similarly for $\delta_1(q, title)$)

$\delta_1(q, text) = .$ (empty right-hand side.)

Here registers Reg_c and Reg_n are associated with *course* and *cno* nodes, respectively. These are tuple registers: in each query $\phi(\bar{x};\bar{y})$ in δ_1, $|\bar{y}| = 0$.

Given a database I_0 of schema R_0, τ_1 generates an XML tree as follows. First, it creates the root of a tree t labeled with $(q_0,\ db)$. It then evaluates query ϕ_1 on I, and for each tuple (*cno, title*) in the result of the query, it expands the tree by spawning a *course* child of the root, carrying the tuple in its register Reg_c. For each *course* node, it generates its *cno* and *title* children by extracting relevant attribute from the tuple in Reg_c via queries ϕ_2 and ϕ_3, respectively, which in turn have a single *text* child carrying the attribute as PCDATA. The transformation stops at the *text* nodes (stop condition 3 above). Finally, it outputs an XML tree by striking out states and registers associated with the nodes in t. □

Recursive transducers. Define the *dependency graph* G_τ of τ as follows. For each $(q,a) \in Q \times \Sigma$ there is a unique node $v(q,a)$ in G_τ, and there is an edge from $v(q,a)$ to $v(q',a')$ iff (q',a') is on the right-hand side of the rule for (q,a). We say that the transducer τ is *recursive* iff there is a cycle in G_τ.

Example 3. To generate the XML view of Fig. 1(b), we define a publishing transducer $\tau_2 = (Q_2, \Sigma_2,\ q_0,\ \delta_2)$, where the transduction δ_2 is defined as follows:

$\delta_2(q_0,\ db) \quad = (q, course,\ \psi_1(n, t;\ \emptyset))$, where $\psi_1(n,t) = \exists t_p\ course(n,t,t_p)$

$\delta_2(q,\ course) \ = (q, title,\ \psi_2(t;\emptyset)),\ (q, cno,\ \psi_3(n;\emptyset)),\ (q, next\text{-}level,\ \psi_4(\emptyset;\ n)),$ where
$\psi_2(t) = \exists n\ \mathsf{Reg}_c(n,t)$, $\psi_3(n_1) = \exists n, t(\mathsf{Reg}_c(n,t) \wedge prereq(n,n_1))$

$\delta_2(q, next\text{-}level) = (q, cno,\ \psi_5(n;\emptyset)),\ (q, next\text{-}level,\ \psi_5(\emptyset;\ n))$

where ψ_4 is identical to ψ_3 except that its result is put in a single relation ($|\bar{x}| = 0$ in ψ_4) as the content of register Reg_{nl} of the *next-level* node; in other words, Reg_{nl} is a *relation register* while Reg_n associated with *cno* is a *tuple register*; ψ_5 is the same as ψ_3 except that Reg_{nl} is used instead of Reg_c. In contrast to τ_1, τ_2 is *recursively defined*: in its dependency graph there is an edge from $v(q, next\text{-}level)$ to itself. On an instance I_0 of R_0 the transformation of τ_2 terminates due to stop condition 2, in any practical setting where no course is a prerequisite of itself. □

Virtual vs. normal nodes. To incorporate virtual nodes we generalize transducers to be of the form $\tau = (Q, \Sigma, q_0, \delta, \Sigma_e)$, where Σ_e is a designated subset of Σ and $r \notin \Sigma_e$, referred to as the *virtual tags* of τ; and Q, Σ, q_0, δ are the same as in Definition 1. On a relational database I the transducer τ behaves the same as a normal transducer, except that the XML tree $\tau(I)$ is obtained as follows. For each node v in t, if v is labeled with a tag in Σ_e, we *shortcut* v by replacing v with the children of v, *i.e.*, treating these children nodes as children of the

Table 1. Complexity of decision problems (S: relation or tuple; O: normal or virtual)

Classes	Equivalence	Emptiness	Membership
PT(FP, S, O)	undecidable	undecidable	undecidable
PT(FO, S, O)	undecidable	undecidable	undecidable
PT(CQ, tuple, normal)	undecidable	PTIME	Σ_2^p-complete
PT(CQ, relation, normal)	undecidable	PTIME	undecidable
PT(CQ, S, virtual)	undecidable	NP-complete	undecidable
PT_{nr}(FO, O, normal)	undecidable	undecidable	undecidable
PT_{nr}(CQ, tuple, normal)	Π_3^p-complete	PTIME	Σ_2^p-complete
PT_{nr}(CQ, tuple, virtual)	Π_3^p-complete	NP-complete	Σ_2^p-complete

parent of v, and removing v from the tree. The process continues until no node in the tree is labeled with a tag in Σ_e.

Example 4. The XML view of Fig. 1(c) can be generated by a publishing transducer $\tau_3 = (Q_2, \Sigma_2, q_0, \delta_2, \{\mathit{next\text{-}level}\})$, which is identical to τ_2 given in Example 3 except that here *next-level* is treated as a virtual tag. □

Different classes. We denote by $\mathrm{PT}(\mathcal{L}, S, O)$ various classes of publishing transducers. Here $\mathcal{L}$ indicates the relational query language in which queries embedded in the transducers are defined, ranging over CQ, FO and FP, all with equality '=' and inequality $\neq$. *Store* S is either *relation* or *tuple*, indicating that the trees induced by the transducers are with relation or tuple registers, respectively. As mentioned earlier, transducers with tuple registers are a special case of those with relation registers, *i.e.*, when $|\bar{y}_i| = 0$ in each query $\phi_i(\bar{x}_i; \bar{y}_i)$. *Output* O is either *normal* or *virtual*, indicating whether a transducer allows virtual nodes or not. We denote by $\mathrm{PT}_{nr}(\mathcal{L}, S, O)$ the subclass of $\mathrm{PT}(\mathcal{L}, S, O)$ consisting of all *nonrecursive* transducers. For instance, the transducers τ_1, τ_2 and τ_3 given in Examples 2, 3 and 4 are in PT_{nr}(FO, tuple, normal), PT(CQ, relation, normal) and PT(FO, relation, virtual), respectively (τ_3 is also in PT_{nr}(FP, tuple, normal)).

3.2 Complexity and Expressiveness of Publishing Transducers

Complexity. A natural question is: does a publishing transducer for a relational schema R always terminate on all instances of R? This is answered in [13]: For any publishing transducer τ defined for schema R and for any database I of R, the transformation of τ on I always terminates, and its worst-case data-complexity is (a) EXPTIME if τ is in $\mathrm{PT}(\mathcal{L}, S, O)$ and S is tuple, (b) 2EXPTIME if τ is in $\mathrm{PT}(\mathcal{L}, S, O)$ and S is relation, (c) PTIME if τ is in $\mathrm{PT}_{nr}(\mathcal{L}, S, O)$ no matter whether S is tuple or relation, where $\mathcal{L}$ ranges over CQ, FO and FP, and O is either normal or virtual. This tells us that while the presence of relation registers and recursion may complicate the transformation, relational query language $\mathcal{L}$ and virtual nodes have no impact on the worse-case data complexity.

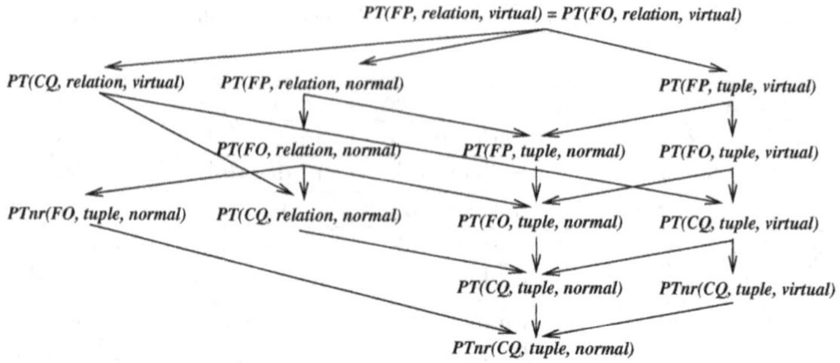

Fig. 2. Containment of various classes of XML publishing transducers

Classical decision problems associated with transducers include the following. For a class PT($\mathcal{L}$, S, O) of publishing transducers,

(i) the *membership problem* is to determine, given an XML tree t and a transducer τ in this class, whether or not there is a database I such that $t = \tau(I)$;

(ii) the *emptiness problem* is to decide, given τ in this class, whether there is an instance I such that $\tau(I)$ is a nontrivial tree with more than one node;

(iii) the *equivalence problem* is to determine, given two transducers τ_1 and τ_2 in the class defined for *the same schema* R, whether or not $\tau_1(I) = \tau_2(I)$ for all instances I of R, *i.e.*, they produce the same trees on all the instances of R.

The analyses of these problems may tell a user, at compile time, whether or not a publishing transducer makes sense (emptiness), whether an XML tree of particular interest can be generated by a transducer (membership), and whether a transducer can replaced by a more efficient one (equivalence).

Matching upper and lower bounds are established in [13] for various classes of publishing transducers, and are summarized in Table 1.

Expressive power. A class $\mathrm{PT}(\mathcal{L}_1, S_1, O_1)$ is *contained in* $\mathrm{PT}(\mathcal{L}_2, S_2, O_2)$, denoted by $\mathrm{PT}(\mathcal{L}_1, S_1, O_1) \subseteq \mathrm{PT}(\mathcal{L}_2, S_2, O_2)$, if for any τ_1 in $\mathrm{PT}(\mathcal{L}_1, S_1, O_1)$ defined for a relational schema R, there exists τ_2 in $\mathrm{PT}(\mathcal{L}_2, S_2, O_2)$ for the same R such that $\tau_1(I) = \tau_2(I)$ for all instances I of R. The two classes are *equivalent* in expressive power, denoted by $\mathrm{PT}(\mathcal{L}_1, S_1, O_1) = \mathrm{PT}(\mathcal{L}_2, S_2, O_2)$, if $\mathrm{PT}(\mathcal{L}_1, S_1, O_1) \subseteq \mathrm{PT}(\mathcal{L}_2, S_2, O_2)$ and $\mathrm{PT}(\mathcal{L}_2, S_2, O_2) \subseteq \mathrm{PT}(\mathcal{L}_1, S_1, O_1)$. A class $\mathrm{PT}(\mathcal{L}_1, S_1, O_1)$ is *properly contained in* $\mathrm{PT}(\mathcal{L}_2, S_2, O_2)$ if $\mathrm{PT}(\mathcal{L}_1, S_1, O_1) \subseteq \mathrm{PT}(\mathcal{L}_2, S_2, O_2)$ but $\mathrm{PT}(\mathcal{L}_1, S_1, O_1) \neq \mathrm{PT}(\mathcal{L}_2, S_2, O_2)$.

Containment. A containment hierarchy on various classes of publishing transducers is developed in [13], and is shown in Fig. 2. The containment is proper except that PT(FO, tuple, virtual) = PT(FP, tuple, virtual) if PTIME = NLOGSPACE. Figure 2 tells us that SQL'99 does not increase expressive power over SQL to a publishing language that supports virtual nodes, recursion and relation registers.

DTD conformance. It is known [23] that a set of unranked trees is regular iff it is MSO definable, and that a set of trees is MSO definable iff it is the set of trees recognized by a specialized DTD [25].

A DTD d' over Σ is defined by a set of rules of the form $a \to \alpha$, where a is a tag in Σ and α is a regular expression over Σ. An XML tree t conforms to d' iff for each a-element v in t, the list of the labels of the children of v is a word in α. A *normalized* DTD is a DTD in which for every rule $a \to \alpha$, α is defined as either $a_1, \ldots, a_k$ (concatenation), or $a_1 | \ldots | a_k$ (disjunction) or a_1^* (Kleene closure), where a_i is an element type. It is known that every DTD can be converted to an equivalent normalized DTD in linear time [5].

A *specialized* DTD d over Σ is a triple (Σ', d', g), where $\Sigma \subseteq \Sigma'$, g is a mapping $\Sigma' \mapsto \Sigma$, and d' is a DTD over Σ'. A tree t conforms to d if there exists a Σ'-tree t' that satisfies d' and moreover, $t = g(t')$. We denote by $L(d)$ the set of all Σ-trees conforming to d. A (specialized or normal) DTD d is said to be definable in PT($\mathcal{L}$, S, O) if there exists a publishing transducer τ in the class defined for some relational schema R such that $L(d) = \tau(R)$.

It is shown [13] that every specialized DTD over Σ is definable in PT(FO, tuple, virtual), and every normalized DTD is definable in PT(FO, tuple, normal). However, there exist normal DTDs that are not definable in PT(CQ, relation, virtual). This tells us that when $\mathcal{L}$ is FO or FP, PT($\mathcal{L}$, S, virtual) is capable of defining all specialized DTDs, and thus all regular unranked trees and MSO definable trees. In addition, PT($\mathcal{L}$, tuple, normal) can define normalized DTDs. In contrast, PT(CQ, S, O) does not have sufficient power to express even DTDs.

Example 5. Recall DTD D_0 from Example 1, which is normalized. One can define τ_4 in PT(FO, tuple, normal) to generate views of the form shown in Fig. 1(d) that are guaranteed to conform to D_0. While it is trivial to enforce rules defined with concatenation and Kleene closure in D_0, *e.g., db, course, prereq*, to enforce the rule *type* $\to$ *regular* | *project*, we need to make sure that each *type* node has either a *regular* or a *project* child, but not both. This can be checked by a Boolean FO query φ. If φ is true τ_4 uses the transduction below for *type* nodes:

$$\delta_4(q, \mathit{type}) = (q, \mathit{regular}, \varphi_1(t_p; \emptyset)), (q, \mathit{project}, \varphi_2(t_p; \emptyset))$$
$$\text{where } \varphi_1(t_p) = \exists n, t\ \mathit{course}(n, t, t_p) \wedge \mathsf{Reg}_c(n) \wedge t_p{=}\text{‘regular’};\ /\text{*similarly for } \varphi_2\text{*}/$$

Otherwise (φ is false) τ_4 produces a default XML tree that conforms to D_0. □

4 XML Publishing Languages in Practice

We are now ready to assess the expressive power of XML publishing languages being used in practice, in terms of various classes of publishing transducers.

SQL/XML is an SQL extension for XML, by incorporating XML publishing functions: XMLELEMENT, XMLATTRIBUTE, XMLFOREST, XMLCONCAT, XMLAGG and XMLGEN. For instance, τ_1 of Example 2 can be defined in SQL/XML as follows:

```
SELECT XMLELEMENT {NAME "course", XMLFOREST {c.cno AS "cno", c.title AS "title"}}
FROM course c
WHERE NOT EXISTS (SELECT c'.cno   FROM course c', prereq p
                  WHERE p.cno1 = c.cno AND p.cno2 = c'.cno AND c'.title = 'DB')
```

SQL/XML has essentially the same expressive power as PT_{nr}(FO, tuple, normal). It cannot express XML views τ_2, τ_3 and τ_4 given earlier. It has been introduced into commercial products, including IBM XML Extender [18] and Oracle 10g XML DB [24]. The publishing language of XPERANTO [26] has the same expressive power as SQL/XML.

DBMS_XMLGEN is a PL/SQL package supported by Oracle 10g XML DB [24]. It extends SQL/XML by supporting SQL'99 and a function newContextFormHierarchy, which, in combination of CONNECT BY PRIOR of SQL'99, is capable of expressing recursive XML views. For example, the following defines a recursive XML view that contains the list of all courses; under each course c are the cno and title of c followed by the hierarchy of the prerequisite courses of c.

```
DBMS_XMLGEN.newContextFormHierarchy{
  SELECT XMLELEMENT {NAME "course", XMLFOREST {c.cno AS "cno", c.title AS "title"}},
  FROM course c
  CONNECT BY PRIOR course.cno = prereq.cno1}
```

DBMS_XMLGEN allows neither virtual nodes nor relation registers. It cannot define τ_2 or guarantee specialized DTD conformance. Furthermore, it does not have stop condition and thus cannot guarantee termination. If the stop condition is imposed, XML views definable in DBMS_XMLGEN are in PT(FP, tuple, normal).

FOR-XML and XSD are supported by SQL Server 2005 [21]. FOR-XML extends SQL as follows: it extracts data from a relational source via an SQL query, and organizes the data into a hierarchical XML view with nested FOR-XML constructs. For example, τ_1 can be defined with FOR-XML as follows:

```
SELECT c.cno AS "cno", c.title AS "title"
FROM course c
WHERE NOT EXISTS (SELECT c'.cno   FROM course c', prereq p
                  WHERE p.cno1 = c.cno AND p.cno2 = c'.cno AND c'.title = 'DB')
FOR XML PATH('course'), ROOT('db')
```

FOR-XML supports neither recursive XML views, virtual nodes nor relation registers. It has essentially the same expressive power as PT_{nr}(FO, tuple, normal).

XSD specifies an XML view by annotating a (nonrecursive) schema, which associates elements and attributes with tables and table columns, respectively. Given a relational source, the annotated XSD constructs an XML tree by populating elements and attributes with tuples and values from their corresponding tables and columns, respectively. Information is passed via parent-child key-based joins. For example, the annotated XSD below generates a view that contains the list of all courses; under each course are its *cno*, *title* followed by a list of *prereq* elements, which consists of the *cno*'s of all immediate prerequisite courses:

```
<xsd:annotation>
  <xsd:appinfo>
    <sql:relationship name="prereq" parent="course"  parent-key="course.cno"
                                    child="prereq"  child-key="prereq.cno1"/>
  </xsd:appinfo>
<xsd:element name="course" sql:relation = "course">
   <xsd:complexType> <xsd:sequence>
     <xsd:element name="cno" sql:relation = "course.cno"> </xsd:element>
     <xsd:element name="title" sql:relation = "course.title"> </xsd:element>
     <xsd:element name="prereq" sql:relationship="prereq" maxOccurs="unbounded"/>
  </xsd:sequence> </xsd:complexType> </xsd:element>
</xsd:annotation>
```

All XSD views are nonrecursive and are expressible in PT_{nr}(CQ, tuple, normal).

DAD (Document Access Definition) of IBM DB2 XML Extender [18] supports SQL_MAPPING and RDB_MAPPING, which are similar to FOR-XML and XSD despite different syntax, and are contained in PT_{nr}(FO,tuple,normal) and PT_{nr}(CQ,tuple,normal), respectively. For example, the FOR-XML and XSD views given above can be expressed in SQL_MAPPING and RDB_MAPPING, respectively:

```
SQL_mapping:
<SQL_stmt> SELECT c.cno AS "cno", c.title AS "title"
           FROM course c
           WHERE NOT EXISTS (SELECT c'.cno  FROM course c', prereq p
                  WHERE p.cno1 = c.cno AND p.cno2 = c'.cno AND c'.title = 'DB')
</SQL_stmt>
<element_node name="course" multi_occurrence="yes">
  <element_node name="cno"> <text_node> <column name="cno"/></text_node>
  </element_node>                ... /*similarly for <element_node name="title">*/
</element_node>
```

```
RDB_mapping:
<element_node name="db">
  <rdb_node> <table name="course"/> <table name="prereq"/>
             <condition>course.cno=prereq.cno1</condition> </rdb_node>
  <element_node name="course" multi_occurrence="yes">
   ... /* <element_node name="cno"> and <element_node name="title">*/
   <element_node name="prereq" multi_occurrence="yes"> <text_node> <rdb_node>
     <table name="prereq"/><column name="cno2"/> </rdb_node> </text_node>
   </element_node> </element_node> </element_node>
```

TreeQL was proposed for publishing middleware SilkRoute [15]. Its abstraction [2] is precisely PT_{nr}(CQ, tuple, virtual): it defines an XML view by annotating the nodes of a tree template of a fixed depth with CQ queries, and supports virtual tree nodes and tuple-based information passing (tuple registers).

ATG (Attribute Transformation Grammar) was proposed in [3] and revised in [6], as the language of XML publishing middleware PRATA. An ATG defines an XML view based on a normalized DTD, by associating each element type a with an inherited attribute (register) $\$a$, and annotating its DTD production $a \to \alpha$ with a set of relational queries, one for each sub-element type b in the regular expression α, specifying how to compute $\$b$ and populate the b

children of an a element. It supports recursive DTDs and thus recursive XML views, as well as virtual nodes to cope with XML entities. It provides a DTD-directed method to define XML views, such that the views are guaranteed to conform to a predefined DTD. For example, view τ_4 given earlier is defined in ATG as follows, which guarantees the view to conforms to DTD D_0 of Example 1:

db → *course**
  $course = SELECT cno, title, type FROM course
course → *cno, title, type, prereq*
  $prereq = SELECT cno FROM *$course*; similarly for *$cno*, *$title* and *$type*
type → *regular* | *project*
  $regular = SELECT cno FROM *$type* WHERE type='regular';
  $project = SELECT cno FROM *$type* WHERE type='project';
prereq → *course**
  $course = SELECT c.cno, c.title, c.type FROM prereq p, $prereq cp, course c
    WHERE cp.cno = p.cno1 AND p.cno2 = c.cno;

ATG of [3] is essentially PT(FO,relation,virtual) and can express views τ_1–τ_4.

XQuery [9] is a Turing-complete XML query language and can express arbitrary XML views. In practice one typically does not need the expressive power of XQuery and thus should not be penalized by the evaluation cost of full-fledged XQuery. In contrast to ATG, XQuery neither guarantees DTD conformance, nor provides any guidance on how to define an XML view that typechecks.

5 Dynamic Aspects

In many applications including mediation, archiving and Web site management, large XML documents may need to be *exported* from relational sources and *maintained*, rather than being "disposed". Just like their relational counterparts, there are two practical problems associated with XML views published from relational data: *the incremental update problem* and *the view update problem*.

Incremental publishing. Given a publishing transducer τ defined on a relational schema R, an instance I of R, the XML view $t = \tau(I)$, and changes ΔI to I, *incremental XML publishing* is to compute XML changes Δt to t such that $t \oplus \Delta t = \tau(I \oplus \Delta I)$. As an example, recall the XML view of Fig. 1(d) published from database I_0 by the transducer τ_4 of Example 5. When I_0 is updated by, *e.g.*, ΔI consisting of the insertion of tuples into *prereq* followed by deletion of tuples from *course*, certain *course* subtrees of Fig. 1(d) have to be changed. Incremental publishing is to compute the XML change Δt in response to I_0.

In contrast to recomputing the new view $\tau(I \oplus \Delta I)$ from scratch, incremental publishing can, in principle, improve performance substantially by applying only the changes Δt to the old view t. The need for this is evident in practice: as PRATA experienced with applications of European Bioinformatics Institute [10], recomputing the entire new view may be quite costly: it may take hours for large XML views. In contrast, relational changes ΔI are often small, and a small ΔI typically incurs only small XML changes Δt. Incremental XML publishing is to efficiently compute Δt by minimizing unnecessary recomputation.

One approach for incremental XML publishing is to push incremental computation to the underlying relational DBMS, along the same lines as implementations of XML publishing middleware [3,15,26]. However, several practical issues hamper the applicability of this *reduction* approach. For example, for recursive XML views the reduction approach depends on incremental update of materialized views defined using SQL'99 recursion. However, few DBMS's support SQL'99, and none supports incremental maintenance of SQL'99 views. In addition, if the queries embedded in a transducer are even mildly complex, the combined queries to be pushed down to DBMS may become extremely complex. They may not be effectively optimized by all DBMS, even for non-recursive publishing mappings.

In light of this, we outline an incremental publishing technique developed for PT(CQ,tuple,virtual) in [6]. It requires the lowest common denominator of DBMS functionality: neither SQL'99 nor incremental maintenance. The technique can be extended to other publishing transducers and languages mentioned earlier.

(1) *External storage.* For any instance I of schema R, a publishing transducer τ on R induces a function ST that, given a tag a, a state q and a value v of Reg_a, $\mathsf{ST}(a, q, v)$ returns a *unique* subtree in $t = \tau(I)$, rooted at a node tagged a and carrying v in its register. Leveraging this *subtree property*, we can store t using (i) a hash index H in which each entry $(a, q, \mathsf{id}(v), p)$ identifies a node in t, along with a pointer p to its subtree in S to be given below, where $\mathsf{id}(v)$ is the unique and compact representation of v, computed by a Skolem function; (ii) a subtree pool S consisting of entries $(a, q, \mathsf{id}(v), L)$, where L is a list of H entries to all the children of the node identified by $(a, q, \mathsf{id}(v))$. This allows us to store an XML view as a DAG, which may take exponentially less space than t.

(2) *Algorithm.* Given ΔI, one can compute XML updates Δt as follows.

(Step 1) Compute E^+ and E^-, the set of edges to be inserted into and deleted from t, respectively. Here each edge is identified by a pair of H-entries. This can be done as follows. (i) For each pair (q, a, q', b) of (state, tag) pairs, define an SQL query $Q_{(q,a,q',b)}$ as the union of queries ψ that appear in a τ rule $(q, a) \rightarrow \ldots (q', b, \psi)$. (ii) Compute the incremental version $\Delta Q_{(q,a,q',b)}$ of $Q_{(q,a,q',b)}$ in response to ΔI, by capitalizing on incremental techniques for SQL queries such as the counting method of [17]. (iii) Evaluate $\Delta Q_{(q,a,q',b)}$ for all involved tags (a, b) to find E^+ and E^-. Note that *neither* $Q_{(q,a,q',b)}$ *nor* $\Delta Q_{(q,a,q',b)}$ is recursive.

(Step 2) Update the hash index H and the subtree pool S with E^+ and E^-, by modifying the L filed of those relevant S entries.

(Step 3) For each newly inserted node in E^+, generate its subtree if its subtree does not have an entry in S. Only this phase involves recursive computation.

(Step 4) Clean up H and S by removing "dangling" entries, by a garbage collection procedure that runs in the background.

This algorithm avoids unnecessary recomputation by reusing subtrees in S at various levels of granularity. It guarantees that each distinct subtree of the new view is computed *at most once.*

View updates. As opposed to incremental publishing, *the view update problem* in connection with XML publishing can be stated as follows. Given a publishing transducer τ defined on a relational schema R, an instance I of R, the XML view $t = \tau(I)$, and XML updates Δt on t, it is to compute *relational updates* ΔI such that $t \oplus \Delta t = \tau(I \oplus \Delta I)$. That is, the relational changes ΔI, when propagated to XML via τ, yield the desired XML updates Δt on the view t. XML updates can be expressed in terms of XPath. For example, one may want to pose U = *insert* CS240 *into course[cno=*'CS650'*]//course[cno=*'CS450'*]/prereq* on the XML view of Fig. 1(d); in response to this we want to find tuples ΔI_0 to insert into the underlying database I_0 such that $I_0 \oplus \Delta I_0$ yields the updated XML view.

The update problem is already hard for relational views. Indeed, given view updates, it is likely that there may not exist updates on the underlying source without introducing side effects, or there must exist multiple source updates (see, *e.g.*, [1]). Commercial relational DBMS's do not provide sophisticated view-update functionality. In particular, few complexity bounds are known even for relational view updates (see [8,12] for recent work in this line of research).

When it comes to XML views published from relational data, the update problem is far more intriguing. In addition to the complications encountered in relational views, it introduces a number of new challenges. First, these XML views may be recursively defined, and are required to conform to a predefined schema. Second, XML updates may be recursive themselves (*e.g.*, descendant-or-self axis in XPath). Third, the semantics of XML view updates has to revised. For example, the XML update U given above attempts to add CS240 as a prerequisite of only those CS450 nodes below CS650. However, CS450 may appear elsewhere in the tree. The subtree property given above tells us that there is a *unique* CS450 subtree. Thus either all occurrences of CS450 should take CS240 as a prerequisite or none of them does. Commercial XML publishing products, *e.g.*, Microsoft SQL Server 2005 [21], provide at best extremely limited view update functionality.

Algorithm. An approach to tackling the view update problem has been developed in [11] for PT(CQ, tuple, virtual). It allows both XML views and updates to be recursively defined, and adopts a revised notion of side effects of XML view updates based on the subtree property. It compresses the XML view t into a DAG, using the same external storage as in the setting of incremental publishing, and derives a set V of relational views defined as edge queries $Q_{(q,a,q',b)}$ given above. Note that V is a set of union of CQ queries. Given an XML update expression U_X posed on t, one can compute the relational updates ΔI as follows.

(Step 1) Validate $U_X(t)$ *w.r.t.* a predefined DTD of the XML view (if any), and reject U_X if $U_X(t)$ violates the DTD.

(Step 2) Translate U_X to an update expression U_V on the relational view V.

(Step 3) Translate U_V to an update expression U_R on the source I, if it exists.

(Step 4) Update the underlying database I using U_R and the relational views V using U_V, if U_R exists, otherwise report side effects to the user and reject U_X.

Step 3 may fail, *i.e.*, the XML view t is found *not updatable* by U_X, as for its relational counterparts. Furthermore, heuristic algorithms are necessary for Step 3 as the view update problem is intractable for the relational views V.

6 Concluding Remarks

The primary goal of the paper is to provide an overview of recent advances in XML publishing and a synergy between theory and practice. It is by no means a comprehensive survey: a number of related articles are not referenced due to the space constraint (see [20] for a recent survey). It is worth mentioning that XML publishing differs from recent work on data exchange (see [19] for a survey) in that XML publishing focuses on transformations from relations to XML defined in terms of mappings with embedded relational queries, rather than relation-to-relation or XML-to-XML mappings derived from source-to-target constraints.

Below we highlight some open research issues. One topic concerns XML integration: in contrast to XML publishing, it is to define a mapping from multiple distributed relational sources to XML documents. Along the same lines as XML publishing, the expressive power and complexity of XML integration languages deserve a full treatment. These are, however, more intriguing than their counterparts for XML publishing. In particular, to cope with dependencies on various sources, *two-way* transducers are required in contrast to *top-down* XML publishing transducers, as indicated by the language proposed in [4] for XML integration. In addition, other issues that arise in practice, such as information preservation required by data migration [7], make the study more complicated.

Another issue is about XML shredding, *i.e.*, for storing XML data in relations. A publishing transducer τ can be treated as a relational query [13]: fixing a designated output tag a_o, we can define the output of $\tau(I)$ on a database I as a *relation*: the union of all $\mathsf{Reg}_{a_o}(v)$ for all nodes v labeled a_o in the tree. Similarly one can define an *XML shredding automaton* that has XML queries embedded in it, operates on *existing XML trees* and returns *a set of tuples* to add to a database. In contrast to publishing transducers, an XML shredding automaton outputs a *relation* instead of an XML tree. Based on this an XML shredding language has been given in [14]. XML shredding automata can be used to characterize the expressive power and complexity of XML shredding languages found in practice.

Much more needs to be done for the view update problem associated with XML views published from relational data. To our knowledge no previous work has considered view update management for publishing transducers defined with relational queries beyond CQ, *e.g.*, PT(FO, relation, virtual).

References

1. Abiteboul, S., Hull, R., Vianu, V.: Foundations of Databases. Addison-Wesley, Reading (1995)
2. Alon, N., Milo, T., Neven, F., Suciu, D., Vianu, V.: Typechecking XML views of relational databases. TOCL 4 (2003)

3. Benedikt, M., Chan, C., Fan, W., Rastogi, R., Zheng, S., Zhou, A.: DTD-directed publishing with attribute translation grammars. In: Bressan, S., Chaudhri, A.B., Lee, M.L., Yu, J.X., Lacroix, Z. (eds.) CAiSE 2002 and VLDB 2002. LNCS, vol. 2590, Springer, Heidelberg (2003)
4. Benedikt, M., Chan, C.Y., Fan, W., Freine, J., Rastogi, R.: Capturing both type and integrity constraints in data integration. In: SIGMOD (2003)
5. Benedikt, M., Fan, W., Geerts, F.: XPath satisfiability in the presence of DTDs. In: PODS (2005)
6. Bohannon, P., Choi, B., Fan, W.: Incremental evaluation of schema-directed XML publishing. In: SIGMOD (2004)
7. Bohannon, P., Fan, W., Flaster, M., Narayan, P.: Information preserving XML schema embedding. In: VLDB (2005)
8. Buneman, P., Khanna, S., Tan, W.: On propagation of deletions and annotations through views. In: PODS (2002)
9. Chamberlin, D., et al.: XQuery 1.0: An XML Query Language. W3C Working Draft (June 2001), `http://www.w3.org/TR/xquery`
10. Choi, B., Fan, W., Jia, X., Kasprzyk, A.: A uniform system for publishing and maintaining XML data. In: VLDB (2004) Demo
11. Choi, B., Gao, C., Fan, W., Viglas, S.: Updating recursive XML views. In: ICDE (2007)
12. Cong, G., Fan, W., Geerts, F.: Annotation propagation revisited for key preserving views. In: CIKM (2006)
13. Fan, W., Geerts, F., Neven, F.: Expressiveness and complexity of XML publishing transducers. In: PODS (2007)
14. Fan, W., Ma, L.: Selectively storing XML data in relations. In: Bressan, S., Küng, J., Wagner, R. (eds.) DEXA 2006. LNCS, vol. 4080, Springer, Heidelberg (2006)
15. Fernandez, M., Kadiyska, Y., Suciu, D., Morishima, A., Tan, W.C.: SilkRoute: A framework for publishing relational data in XML. TODS 27(4), 438–493 (2002)
16. Gécseg, F., Steinby, M.: Tree languages. In: Handbook of Formal Languages, vol. 3, Springer, Heidelberg (1996)
17. Gupta, A., Mumick, I.S., Subrahmanian, V.S.: Maintaining views incrementally. In: SIGMOD (1993)
18. IBM. DB2 XML Extender, `www-3.ibm.com/software/data/db2/extended/xmlext/`
19. Kolaitis, P.G.: Schema mappings, data exchange, and metadata management. In: PODS (2005)
20. Krishnamurthy, R., Kaushik, R., Naughton, J.: XML-SQL query translation literature: The state of the art and open problems. In: Xsym (2003)
21. Microsoft. XML support in microsoft SQL server 2005 (2005), `msdn.microsoft.com/library/en-us/dnsql90/html/sql2k5xml.asp/`
22. Neven, F.: On the power of walking for querying tree-structured data. In: PODS (2002)
23. Neven, F., Schwentick, T.: Query automata over finite trees. TCS 275(1-2), 633–674 (2002)
24. Oracle. Oracle Database 10g Release 2 XML DB Whitepaper, `http://www.oracle.com/technology/tech/xml/xmldb/index.html`
25. Papakonstantinou, Y., Vianu, V.: Type inference for views of semistructured data. In: PODS (2000)
26. Shanmugasundaram, J., Shekita, E., Barr, R., Carey, M., Pirahesh, B.L.H., Reinwald, B.: Efficiently publishing relational data as XML documents. VLDB J. 10(2-3), 133–154 (2001)

Efficient Algorithms for the Tree Homeomorphism Problem

Michaela Götz[1], Christoph Koch[1], and Wim Martens[2,⋆]

[1] Saarland University
Saarbrücken, Germany
{goetz,koch}@infosys.uni-sb.de
[2] University of Dortmund
Dortmund, Germany
wim.martens@udo.edu

Abstract. Tree pattern matching is a fundamental problem that has a wide range of applications in Web data management, XML processing, and selective data dissemination. In this paper we develop efficient algorithms for the tree homeomorphism problem, i.e., the problem of matching a tree pattern with exclusively transitive (descendant) edges. We first prove that deciding whether there is a tree homeomorphism is LOGSPACE-complete, improving on the current LOGCFL upper bound. As our main result we develop a practical algorithm for the tree homeomorphism decision problem that is both space- and time efficient. The algorithm is in LOGDCFL and space consumption is strongly bounded, while the running time is linear in the size of the data tree. This algorithm immediately generalizes to the problem of matching the tree pattern against all subtrees of the data tree, preserving the mentioned efficiency properties.

1 Introduction

Tree patterns are a simple query language for tree-structured data. They are at the heart of several widely-used Web languages such as XPath and XQuery [4]. As a consequence, they form part of a number of typing mechanisms such as XML Schema, and of Web Programming Languages. They have also been used as query languages in their own right, for example for expressing subscriptions in publish-subscribe systems [1,5,6,13].

The general tree pattern matching problem considered in the literature is the problem of finding a mapping between two node-labeled trees which is, in a sense, a cross of a subtree homomorphism and a homeomorphism. In this paper we consider a clean and important special case of the tree pattern embedding problem that we call the *tree homeomorphism problem*. The question we consider is whether there is a mapping θ from the nodes of the first tree, the *tree pattern*

⋆ This work was supported by a scholarship of the FWO-Vlaanderen that permitted Wim Martens to visit the Technical University of Vienna in January–February, 2005.

M. Arenas and M.I. Schwartzbach (Eds.): DBPL 2007, LNCS 4797, pp. 17–31, 2007.

Table 1. Time and space consumption for algorithms solving the tree homeomorphism matching problem. Here *depth*(·) and *branch*(·) denote the depth and maximal branching factor of a tree, respectively.

	time	space	streaming
Yannakakis 1981 [19]	$O(\|Q\| \cdot \|D\| \cdot depth(D))$	$O(depth(Q) \cdot \|D\|)$	no
Gottlob et al. 2002 [10]	$O(\|Q\| \cdot \|D\|)$	$O(\|Q\| \cdot \|D\|)$	no
Olteanu et al. 2004 [16]	$O(\|Q\| \cdot \|D\| \cdot depth(D))$	$O(\|Q\| \cdot depth(D) + \|D\|)$	yes
Bar-Yossef et al. 2005 [3]	$O(\|Q\| \cdot \|D\|)$	$O(\|Q\| \cdot \log \|D\| + cand_D)$	yes
Ramanan 2005 [17]	$O((\|Q\| + depth(D)) \cdot \|D\|)$	$O(\|Q\| \cdot depth(D) + cand_D)$	yes
Our bottom-up algorithm	$O(\|Q\| \cdot \|D\| \cdot depth(\|Q\|))$	$O(depth(D) \cdot branch(D))$	no
Our LOGSPACE algorithm	$poly(\|Q\| + \|D\|)$	$O(\log(\|Q\| + \|D\|))$	no

or *query*, to the nodes of the second tree, the *data tree*, such that if node y is a child of x in the first tree, then $\theta(y)$ is a *descendant* of $\theta(x)$ in the second tree. We also consider the *tree homeomorphism matching problem*: finding *all* nodes v of the data tree such that there is such a tree homeomorphism with v the image of the root node of the pattern tree. This problem of selecting all nodes whose subtrees match the tree pattern has frequent application in XML and Web query processing [1,10].

While this problem is of immediate practical relevance and a substantial number of papers have studied complexity and efficient algorithms for tree pattern matching, the precise complexity of both the general tree pattern matching problem and the tree homeomorphism problem are open; they are both known to be in LOGCFL and LOGSPACE-hard [11].The former can be immediately concluded from earlier results on the complexity of the acyclic conjunctive queries [12] and the positive navigational fragment of XPath [11], both much stronger languages. The latter is a direct consequence of the fact that reachability in trees is LOGSPACE-complete [8].

Much work has been dedicated to developing efficient algorithms for finding matches of tree patterns and tree homeomorphisms. Certain algorithms aim at processing the data tree as a stream (i.e., in a single scan) [5,6,13,15,9,16,2,3,17]. For this case a number of lower bound results have been obtained using mechanisms from communication complexity [2,3,14]. It is basically known that streaming algorithms for even simple tree patterns consume space proportional to the size of the data tree in the worst case. Table 1 lists algorithms for the tree homeomorphism matching problem together with bounds on their running time and space consumption. Here D is the data tree and Q is the tree pattern. We assume a random access machine model with unit cost for reading and writing integers. Some of the algorithms presented support generalizations of the tree homeomorphism problem but where a better bound is known for the tree homeomorphism problem, it is shown. Some of the streaming algorithms [3,17] use a notion of candidate node sets $cand_D$ which depends on the algorithm and which can be of size close to $|D|$ in the worst case. The algorithm of [3] makes the assumption of so-called non-recursive data trees, in which no two nodes such that one is a descendant of the other may have the same label. Finally, streaming algorithms such as [15] focus on being able to process SAX-events in constant time, at the cost of an exponential preprocessing step.

In this paper we study the tree homeomorphism (matching) problem. We establish a tight complexity characterization and develop an algorithm for the node-selection problem (shown at the bottom of Table 1) that is both time- and space efficient. In detail, the technical contributions of this paper are as follows.

- We first develop a top-down algorithm for the tree homeomorphism problem that is in LOGDCFL.[1]
- From this we develop a proof that the problem is LOGSPACE-complete, improving on the LOGCFL upper bound from [11].
- As our main result we develop a bottom-up LOGDCFL algorithm for computing all solutions of the tree homeomorphism problem which is both time and space efficient. This is a rather difficult algorithm and the correctness proof is involved. The algorithm runs in time $O(|D| \cdot |Q| \cdot \mathit{depth}(Q))$ and employs a stack of depth bounded by $\mathcal{O}(\mathit{depth}(D) \cdot \mathit{branch}(D))$.

  The algorithm may be of relevance in practical implementations. Indeed, in most Web or XML applications, the data tree is *much* larger than the tree pattern yet its depth is rather small. It can be observed that ours is the only algorithm in Table 1 — and to the best of our knowledge, in existence — that can guarantee a space bound that does not contain the size, but only depth and branching factor, of the data tree as a term. At the same time the algorithm admits a good time bound.

  Furthermore, the algorithm is of relevance in theory as well. It is a first step in classifying the complexity of positive Core XPath with child and descendant axis, which is probably the most widely used XPath fragment in practice. Its precise complexity, however, is unknown.
- In some applications (e.g., for certain XML data trees), a few nodes can have a very large number of children. Our algorithm can be made to run in space $O(\mathit{depth}(D) \cdot \log(\mathit{branch}(D)))$ with the same time bound if we assume the data tree to be in a ranked form that can be obtained by a LOGSPACE linear-time preprocessing algorithm. Given that ours is an offline algorithm it means little loss of generality to assume that data trees are kept in a database in this preprocessed form.

The paper presents these result basically in the order given here. Because of space limitations, some proofs had to be omitted.

2 Definitions

By $\mathbb{N}$ we denote the set of strictly positive integers. By Σ we denote a finite alphabet. The set of *unranked Σ-trees*, denoted by $\mathcal{T}_\Sigma$, is the smallest set of strings over Σ and the parenthesis symbols "(" and ")" which contains the

[1] For our purposes, it is enough to know that LOGDCFL is characterized by deterministic logspace bounded pushdown automata which run in polynomial time [18].

empty string and, for each $a \in \Sigma$ and $w \in (\mathcal{T}_\Sigma)^*$, contains $a(w)$. So, a tree is either ε (empty) or is of the form $a(T_1 \cdots T_n)$ where each T_i is a tree. In the tree $a(T_1 \cdots T_n)$, the subtrees $T_1, \ldots, T_n$ are attached to the root labeled a. When we write a tree as $a(T_1 \cdots T_n)$, we tacitly assume that every T_i is a non-empty tree. Moreover, we write a rather than $a()$. Notice that there is no a priori bound on the number of children of a node in a Σ-tree; such trees are therefore *unranked.* A *hedge* H is a finite sequence $T_1 \cdots T_n$ of trees. Hence, the set of *unranked* Σ*-hedges*, denoted by $\mathcal{H}_\Sigma$, equals $(\mathcal{T}_\Sigma)^*$. When we write a hedge as $T_1 \cdots T_n$, we tacitly assume that every T_i is a non-empty tree. In the sequel, whenever we say tree or hedge, we always mean Σ-tree or Σ-hedge, respectively. We will slightly abuse terminology and use the term "tree" to also refer to a hedge consisting of one tree, and we use the term "hedge" to also refer to the union of trees and hedges. We assume familiarity with terms such as *child, parent, descendant, ancestor, leaf, root, first child, last child, first sibling*, and *last sibling.*

For a hedge H, the *set of nodes* or *domain* of H, denoted by $\mathrm{Dom}(H)$, is the subset of $\mathbb{N}^*$ inductively defined as follows: *(i)* if $H = \varepsilon$, then $\mathrm{Dom}(H) = \emptyset$; *(ii)* if $H = a$, then $\mathrm{Dom}(H) = \{1\}$; *(iii)* if $H = a(T_1 \cdots T_n)$, where each $T_i \in \mathcal{T}_\Sigma - \{\varepsilon\}$, then $\mathrm{Dom}(H) = \{1\} \cup \bigcup_{i=1}^{n} \{1iu \mid 1u \in \mathrm{Dom}(T_i)\}$; and *(iv)* if $H = T_1 \cdots T_n$ with $n \geq 2$ and each $T_i \in \mathcal{T}_\Sigma - \{\varepsilon\}$, then $\mathrm{Dom}(H) = \{iu \mid 1u \in \mathrm{Dom}(T_i)\}$. The label of node u in the tree or hedge H, denoted by $\mathrm{lab}^H(u)$, is defined as follows: *(i)* if $H = a$ and $u = 1$, then $\mathrm{lab}^H(u) = a$; *(ii)* if $H = a(T_1 \cdots T_n)$ and $u = 1iv$ with $i \in \{1, \ldots, n\}$, then $\mathrm{lab}^H(u) = \mathrm{lab}^{T_i}(1v)$; and *(iii)* if $H = T_1 \cdots T_n$ with $n \geq 2$ and $u = iv$ with $i \in \{1, \ldots, n\}$, then $\mathrm{lab}^H(u) = \mathrm{lab}^{T_i}(1v)$.

By $|H|$, we denote the number of nodes in a hedge H. The *depth* of a node u in hedge H, denoted by $\mathrm{depth}^H(u)$, is 1 when $u \in \mathbb{N}$ and $1 + \mathrm{depth}(v)$ when $u = vi$ and $i \in \mathbb{N}$. The *height* of a node u in hedge H, denoted by $\mathrm{height}^H(u)$, is 1 when u is a leaf and $\max(\mathrm{height}^H(u1), \ldots, \mathrm{height}^H(uk)) + 1$ when u has $k > 0$ children. By $\mathrm{subtree}^H(u)$, we denote the subtree of H rooted at node u. In the remainder of the paper, we usually leave H implicit when H is clear from the context.

The Tree Homeomorphism Problem. A *tree pattern query* (with descendant edges) Q is an unranked tree over the alphabet $\Sigma \uplus \{*\}$. In the following, we use the terms *data tree* or *data hedge* to refer to ordinary Σ-trees and Σ-hedges. Given a data hedge H, a node $u \in \mathrm{Dom}(H)$, and a tree pattern query Q, we say that H *matches* Q *at node* u, denoted by $H \models^u Q$, if one of the following holds:

- $H = a$, $Q = a$ or $Q = *$, and $u = 1$;
- $H = a(T_1 \cdots T_n)$, $Q = a$ or $Q = *$, and $u = 1$;
- $H = a(T_1 \cdots T_n)$, $T_i \models^{1v} Q$, and $u = 1iv$, for some $i \in \{1, \ldots, n\}$;
- $H = T_1 \cdots T_n$, $T_i \models^{1v} Q$, and $u = iv$, for some $i \in \{1, \ldots, n\}$;
- $H = a(T_1 \cdots T_n)$, $Q = x(Q_1 \cdots Q_m)$, $u = 1$, $x \in \Sigma \uplus \{*\}$, $a \models x$, and, for every $k = 1, \ldots, m$, there exists an $i_k \in \{1, \ldots, n\}, u_k \in \mathrm{Dom}(T_{i_k})$, such that $T_{i_k} \models^{u_k} Q_k$.

Notice that the ordering of children in our tree pattern queries does not matter. This corresponds to the well known semantics of XPath queries with descendant

Algorithm 1. Tree pattern matching with descendant axes: Top-down algorithm MATCH

MATCH (DNode d, QNode q)
2: **if** d matches q **then**
  return $\forall$ child q_c of q $\exists$ child d_c of d: MATCH(d_c,q_c)
4: **else** ▷ q not matched yet, try d's children
  return $\exists$ child d_c of d: MATCH(d_c,q)
6: **end if**

axes [7]. In the following, we abbreviate by $H \models Q$ that $H \models^u Q$ for some $u \in \text{Dom}(H)$. Alternatively, we say that H *matches* Q.

In this paper, we are interested in the following problems. Given a data tree T and a tree pattern query Q, the *tree homeomorphism problem* consists of deciding whether $T \models Q$. Furthermore, we are interested in *computing all answers* for the tree homeomorphism problem, that is, computing all nodes $u \in \text{Dom}(T)$ such that $T \models^u Q$. We refer to the latter problem as *tree homeomorphism matching.*

We assume that trees are stored on tape as a set of records; one for each node. Each record contains a pointer to its first child, last child, parent, previous sibling, and next sibling.

In the remainder of the paper, we assume a fixed data tree D and a fixed query tree Q for ease of presentation. We will refer to nodes of D and Q as *data nodes* and *query nodes*, respectively.

3 A Top-Down Algorithm

This section provides a simple top-down algorithm for the tree homeomorphism matching problem. The core of this top-down algorithm lies in a simple procedure that decides, given a data node d and a query node q, whether subtree(d) $\models$ subtree(q).

3.1 A Top-Down LOGDCFL Algorithm

Algorithm 1 describes the procedure MATCH to test whether subtree(d) $\models$ subtree(q). It is straightforward to prove that MATCH is indeed correct.

Lemma 1. MATCH *is correct. That is, given a data node d and a query node q,* MATCH *returns true iff subtree(d) $\models$ subtree(q).*

We can turn the procedure in Algorithm 1 into an algorithm TOP-DOWN-MATCH for the tree homeomorphism matching problem as follows. First, we need a procedure EXACT-MATCH that, given a data node d and query node q, decides whether subtree(d) $\models^1$ subtree(q). This is easy: EXACT-MATCH only differs from MATCH in l.5, where it just returns false. Given a data node d and the root q_{root} of the query tree, TOP-DOWN-MATCH now simply iterates over all the data nodes and returns every data node d for which EXACT-MATCH(d, q_{root}) returns true. From this construction and from the correctness of MATCH, it is now immediate that TOP-DOWN-MATCH is correct as well.

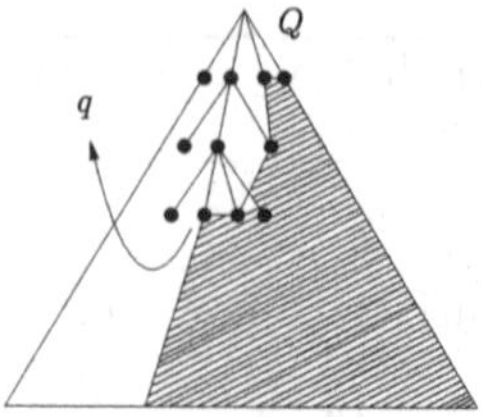

Fig. 1. Illustration of the remainder of q in Q

Time and Space Complexity. It can be shown quite directly that the time complexities of MATCH and EXACT-MATCH are in $\mathcal{O}(|\text{subtree}(d)| \cdot |\text{subtree}(q)|)$. As TOP-DOWN-MATCH simply calls EXACT-MATCH for every data node, we immediately have the following result.

Proposition 2. *The running time of* TOP-DOWN-MATCH *is in* $\mathcal{O}(|D|^2 \cdot |Q|)$. *Moreover,* TOP-DOWN-MATCH *makes* $\mathcal{O}(|D|^2 \cdot |Q|)$ *comparisons between a data node and a query node.*

It is immediate from our implementation of the algorithm that it can be executed by a deterministic logarithmic space bounded auxiliary pushdown automaton (see, e.g., [18]). Moreover, by Proposition 2, this auxiliary pushdown automaton runs in polynomial time. It follows from [18] that the tree homeomorphism matching problem is in LOGDCFL. As the maximum recursion depth of Algorithm 1 is $\mathcal{O}(\text{depth}(D))$, this renders the algorithm quite space-efficient, but the running time being quadratic in the size of the data tree, and the many unnecessary comparisons between query and data nodes are quite unsatisfactory. In the next section, we show how these issues can be resolved by turning to a bottom-up approach.

3.2 A LOGSPACE Procedure

While the top-down algorithm does not seem to be well-suited for efficiently computing *all* nodes u for which $D \models^u Q$, it is quite useful for *deciding* whether $D \models Q$, from a complexity theory point of view. Indeed, as we will exhibit, a modified version of MATCH can decide in LOGSPACE whether $D \models Q$. To this end, we assume the *left-to-right pre-order* ordering on nodes in trees and hedges in the remainder of this section. In particular, for every node u with k children in a hedge H, we have that $u < u1 < u2 < \cdots < uk$. For a node u, we denote by $u + 1$ the next node in the depth first, left-to-right traversal.

We argue how to transform Algorithm 1 into a LOGSPACE algorithm that decides whether $D \models Q$. Intuitively, the LOGSPACE algorithm processes the data and query trees in a top-down manner, just like Algorithm 1, and it processes the children of a node from left to right. The essential difference, however, lies in a backtracking procedure. When, for example, Algorithm 1 matches a leaf q of the query tree onto some data node d, then it uses the recursion stack to discover the data node onto which q's parent was matched in the data tree and tries to match

Algorithm 2. LOGSPACE decision procedure: Top-down algorithm L-MATCH. We assume left-to-right preordering on trees.

```
L-MATCH (DNode d, QNode q)
if d matches q, and both d and q have children then
    return L-MATCH (d + 1,q + 1)
else if d does not match q and d has a child then
    return L-MATCH (d + 1, q)
else if d matches q and q is a leaf then
    if q is maximal in Q then return true  ▷ none of q's ancestors has a right sib.
    else
        d' ← BACKTRACK(d, q + 1)      ▷ node onto which q + 1's parent was matched
        return L-MATCH (d' + 1, q + 1)
    end if
else                          ▷ d is a leaf and (d does not match q or q is not a leaf)
    if d is maximal in D then return false
    end if
    while q has a parent do
        d' ← BACKTRACK(d, q)            ▷ node onto which q's parent was matched
        if d' is an ancestor of d + 1 then return L-MATCH (d + 1, q)
        else q ← q.parent
        end if
    end while
    return L-MATCH (d + 1, q)
end if
```

q's next sibling in some subtree of that data node. Instead of using this recursion stack, the LOGSPACE algorithm enters a subprocedure BACKTRACK(d, q) that *recomputes* d'. In particular, BACKTRACK(d, q) computes the highest possible node d'' on the path from D's root to d, such that the path from D's root to d'' matches the path from Q's root to q's parent. The crux of the algorithm is that this is *correct*, i.e., $d'' = d'$; and that BACKTRACK(d, q) can be performed using only logarithmic space on a Turing Machine. BACKTRACK(d, q) stores d and q on tape and goes to the roots of the query and data tree. It then matches the path to d with the path to q in a greedy manner. The crux of executing BACKTRACK(d, q) using logarithmic space lies in the following. If we arrive at a node u in D (resp., Q), we have to be able to determine the child of u that lies on the path to d (resp. q). To this end, we first store d (resp., q) in a temporary variable v. We now determine v's parent by scanning the input tape (i.e., we search a node with a child-pointer to v) and we overwrite v with v's parent. We continue following the parent relation in this fashion until we find u, at which point we return the value of v, which is a child of u.

We present the LOGSPACE algorithm in Algorithm 2. For ease of presentation, we have written the algorithm as a recursive procedure, but it can be implemented to only use logarithmic space. This can be seen by observing Algorithm 2: every recursive call to L-MATCH is a return-statement, so the algorithm does not change when the recursion stack is not used at all.

Let, for a query node q, the *remainder of q in Q* be the subhedge of Q consisting of the nodes $\{q' \mid q \leq q' \leq q_{\max}\}$, where $q_{\max}$ is the maximal query nodes w.r.t. the depth-first left-to-right ordering. We illustrate the remainder of q in Q in Figure 1. Given a data node d and a query node q, the algorithm first tries to match the remainder of q in Q consistently with what has already been matched in D (lines 2–11). If this fails, it either returns false (line 13), or enters a backtracking procedure (lines 15–21).

Lemma 3. *Algorithm 2 is correct. That is, given the roots d and q of a data D and query tree Q, Algorithm 2 decides whether $D \models Q$. Moreover, Algorithm 2 only uses logarithmic space.*

Theorem 4. *The tree homeomorphism problem is LOGSPACE-complete.*

4 The Bottom-Up Algorithm

Although the previously presented top-down algorithms for tree homeomorphism matching are quite space-efficient, their time complexity is quite high and they involve quite a lot of recomputing of already obtained matchings, which is unsatisfactory. We therefore turn to a bottom-up matching approach which has the property that *no* obtained matchings between the data and query tree need to be recomputed, which leads to a better time complexity of the overall algorithm.

Before presenting the bottom-up algorithm for the tree homeomorphism matching problem in detail, we need to introduce several formal notions. As in the previous section, we first present an algorithm for the tree homeomorphism problem and then show how to change it into an algorithm for the tree homeomorphism matching problem.

In the present section, we assume the *left-to-right post-order* ordering on nodes in trees and hedges. In particular, for every node u with k children in a hedge H, we have that $u1 < u2 < \cdots < uk < u$. For a node u, we denote by $u+1$ the next node in the left-to-right postorder traversal. Hence, when we, e.g., use terminology such as "largest" and "smallest", we always assume the left-to-right post ordering. In this section, we also assume that XML documents are stored on tape in left-to-right postorder (or, alternatively, together with a left-to-right postorder index), which allows a random-access machine model to verify the left-to-right post-order ordering in constant time. For technical purposes, we also assume two dummy nodes in every tree and hedge: nil and ∞. The node nil is such that nil+1 is the smallest node in the hedge, and the node ∞ is defined as the successor of the largest node of the hedge. Given two nodes $h_{\text{from}} \leq h_{\text{until}}$ in a hedge H, we denote by the interval $[h_{\text{from}}, h_{\text{until}}]$ the subhedge of H consisting only of the nodes $\{v \mid h_{\text{from}} \leq v \leq h_{\text{until}}\}$. The notion of such an interval in a tree is illustrated in Figure 2(a). Here, the interval $[h_{\text{from}}, h_{\text{until}}]$ is the striped area in the tree. Given a hedge H and a node $h \in \text{Dom}(H)$, we denote by $\text{subhedge}^H(h)$ the subhedge $[h_{\text{from}}, h]$, where h_{from} is the smallest descendant of h's leftmost sibling according to the left-to-right postorder ordering. We illustrate this notion in Figure 2(b).

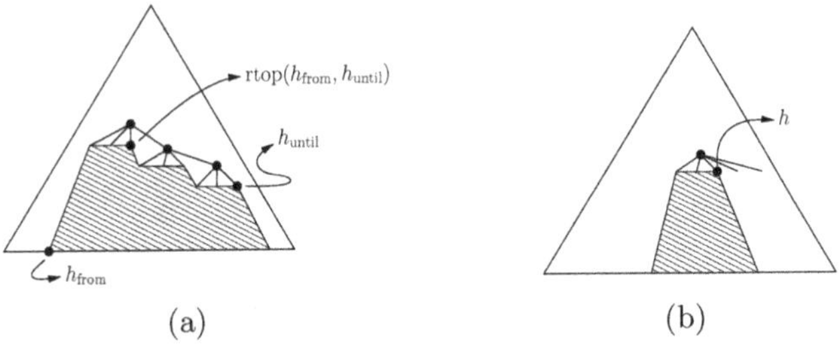

Fig. 2. Illustration of a hedge interval and RTOP (left) and of subhedge$^H(h)$ (right)

When H is a data hedge or a tree pattern query, we refer to $[h_{\text{from}}, h_{\text{until}}]$ as a data or query hedge interval, respectively. We extend the semantics of tree pattern matching to hedges as follows. Let $Q_1 \cdots Q_n$ be a query hedge interval $[q_{\text{from}}, q_{\text{until}}]$ and $D_1 \cdots D_m$ be a data hedge interval $[d_{\text{from}}, d_{\text{until}}]$. We say that $[d_{\text{from}}, d_{\text{until}}]$ matches $[q_{\text{from}}, q_{\text{until}}]$, denoted by $[d_{\text{from}}, d_{\text{until}}] \models [q_{\text{from}}, q_{\text{until}}]$, if, for every Q_i, $i = 1, \ldots, n$, there exists a D_j, $j = 1, \ldots, m$, such that $D_j \models Q_i$.

Before presenting the intuition about the bottom-up tree homeomorphism algorithm, we describe an auxiliary procedure RTOP, which, given two nodes h_{from} and h_{until}, returns the rightmost node among the topmost nodes in the interval $[h_{\text{from}}, h_{\text{until}}]$. More formally, RTOP$(h_{\text{from}}, h_{\text{until}})$ is the node u such that depth(u) is minimal and u is larger than every other node v in $[h_{\text{from}}, h_{\text{until}}]$ with depth(u) = depth(v). This notion is illustrated in Figure 2(a). Furthermore, in order to simplify the presentation of the algorithm, we define RTOP$(h_{\text{from}}, h_{\text{until}}) = \infty$ if $h_{\text{from}} > h_{\text{until}}$. Notice that RTOP can easily be computed in time linear in the depth of the tree and in logarithmic space by traversing the path from h_{until} to the query root and comparing the previous siblings of nodes on the path with h_{from} w.r.t. the left-to-right post-ordering. Indeed, assume that $h_{\text{from}} \leq h_{\text{until}}$. Let u be the highest ancestor of h_{until} that has a previous sibling s such that $s \geq h_{\text{from}}$. If no such u exists, then rtop$(h_{\text{from}}, h_{\text{until}})$ is h_{until}. Otherwise, rtop$(h_{\text{from}}, h_{\text{until}})$ is s.

We first present an algorithm for *deciding* whether $D \models Q$ and show later how it can be extended to an algorithm for the tree homeomorphism matching problem. The main procedure of our algorithm is called TMATCH. Given a data node d and query nodes q_{from} and q_{until}, TMATCH returns the largest query node q in the interval $[q_{\text{from}}, q_{\text{until}}]$ such that subtree$^D(d)$ matches $[q_{\text{from}}, q]$ if q exists; and $q_{\text{from}} - 1$ otherwise. Hence, if d is the root of D, and q_{from} and q_{until} are the leftmost leaf and the root of Q, respectively, then $D \models Q$ if and only if TMATCH returns q_{until}.

TMATCH uses an auxiliary procedure called HMATCH, which, given a data node d and query nodes q_{from} and q_{until}, returns the largest node q in the interval $[q_{\text{from}}, q_{\text{until}}]$ such that subhedge$^D(d)$ matches $[q_{\text{from}}, q]$ if q exists; and $q_{\text{from}} - 1$ otherwise.

We start by explaining the operation of TMATCH, which is presented in Algorithm 3. Given a data node d and query nodes q_{from} and q_{until}, TMATCH first

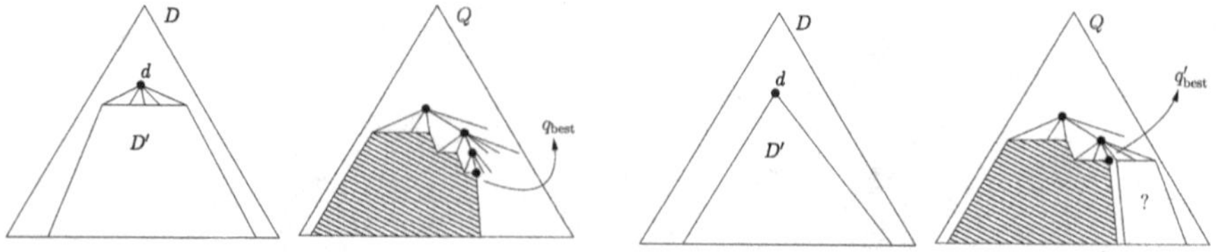

(a) Operation of TMATCH: recursive call of HMATCH.

(b) Operation of TMATCH: recursive call of TMATCH.

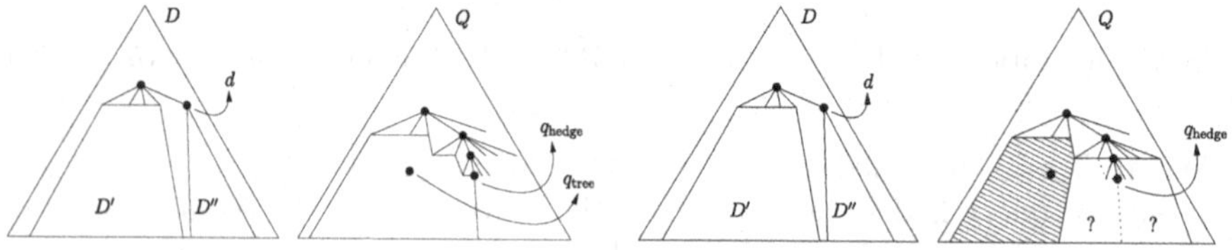

(c) Operation of HMATCH: first recursive calls of TMATCH and HMATCH.

(d) Operation of HMATCH: a subsequent recursive call of TMATCH, trying to improve q_{tree}.

Fig. 3. Illustrations of the tree homeomorphism algorithm

starts by recursively calling HMATCH with the same query nodes for the sub-hedge D' of D defined by d's last child, yielding result q_{best} (see Figure 3(a)). In the remainder of TMATCH, we essentially want to test how q_{best} can be improved when we also consider the node d in addition to D'. One particular interesting case is when q_{best} is a last sibling and its parent has the same label as d. In this case, we can at least improve our best query node to q_{best}'s parent which we call here q'_{best}. Furthermore, it is possible that q'_{best} is not yet the best query node we can obtain. In particular, we still need to test which part of the hedge defined by $[q'_{\text{best}}+1, q'_{\text{best}}.\text{lastSibling}]$ can be matched in the subtree below d (see Figure 3(b)). The largest node that is obtained in this manner is the node that TMATCH should return.

We now explain the operation of HMATCH, which is presented in Algorithm 4. Essentially, given d, q_{from}, and q_{until}, HMATCH starts by recursively calling itself with the same query nodes on the hedge defined by the previous sibling of d (i.e., D' in Figure 3(c)), yielding q_{hedge}, and by calling TMATCH with the same query nodes on the subtree under d itself (D'' in Figure 3(c)), yielding q_{tree}. The remainder of HMATCH consists of iteratively improving q_{tree} and q_{hedge}. That is, while it is possible that D' and D'' yield small values of q_{tree} and q_{hedge}, their concatenation can give rise to a much larger part of the query that can be matched. Essentially, this is due to the fact that the matching of tree pattern queries is *unordered*. For example, it can occur that we need to match a certain first sibling in D', a second one in D'', a third one again in D' and so on. Hence, the procedure HMATCH alternates between finding best matches in D' and D'' until it reaches a fixpoint.

Algorithm 3. Tree pattern matching: function TMATCH.

```
TMATCH (DNode d, QNode q_from, QNode q_until)
if d is a leaf then q_best ← q_from − 1
else q_best ← HMATCH(d.lastChild, q_from, q_until)
end if
if q_best + 1 ≤ q_until and d matches q_best + 1 then
    q_best ← q_best + 1
    if q_best + 1 ≤ q_best.lastSib then
        return TMATCH(d, q_best + 1, q_best.lastSib)
    else return q_best
    end if
else return q_best
end if
```

However, we need to take care in how this fixpoint is computed. One possible case is illustrated in Figure 3(d). This particular case builds further on the situation in Figure 3(c). Here, we try to improve q_{tree} by starting the TMATCH procedure again for the node d, but now only with the part of the query marked with question marks. The case where q_{tree} is larger than q_{hedge} is dual and not illustrated here.

Example 5. Figure 4(a) and 4(b) illustrate an example for the bottom up algorithm. For brevity, we denote TMATCH and HMATCH with TM and HM, respectively. The first calls of TM and HM demonstrate the basic recursive structure of our algorithm: TM on a node d calls HM on the rightmost child of d. HM on a node d returns TM of d if that node is a first sibling; or performs a divide-and-conquer technique by calling HM on the left sibling of d and TM on d itself (as in the function call $\text{HM}(d_4, q_1, q_5)$). Further recursive calls to TM or HM are then needed to maximize the part of the query that can be matched.

The simplest function call in the example that performs such further recursive calls is the call $\text{HM}(d_2, q_1, q_5)$, which starts by computing $q_{\text{hedge}} = \text{HM}(d_1, q_1, q_5)$ and $q_{\text{tree}} = \text{TM}(d_2, q_1, q_5)$. As can be seen in Figure 4(b), $q_{\text{hedge}} = \text{nil}$. The call $\text{TM}(d_2, q_1, q_5)$ is more successful, because d_2 and q_1 are both labeled with a. In general, it might be possible that q_2 and further nodes can be matched in subtree(d_2). The function call $\text{TM}(d_2, q_2, q_4)$ checks that possibility. (For sure, q_1 and q_5 cannot both be matched on d_2, which is why we restrict the query tree interval by q_4.) But q_2 is not labeled with a so the return value of the two TM calls is q_1. After this initial phase, $\text{HM}(d_2, q_1, q_5)$ tries to improve q_{tree} and q_{hedge} iteratively. It calls $\text{HM}(d_1, q_2, q_4)$ and improves q_{hedge} to be q_2, because q_2 and d_1 are both labeled with b. Further improvements fail as there is no c-labeled node in the subhedge of d_2.

A similar iterative improvement is illustrated by $\text{HM}(d_3, q_1, q_5)$. Observe that we try to improve q_{tree} here and call $\text{TM}(d_4, q_2, q_4)$ and $\text{TM}(d_4, q_3, q_3)$. Only the latter call yields an improvement. But we cannot omit the former one: if subtree(d_4) would match subtree(q_4), then the former call would yield q_4 and the latter call would yield q_3. As we want our algorithm to return the largest

---

Algorithm 4. Tree pattern matching: function HMATCH.

HMATCH (DNode d, QNode q_{from}, QNode q_{until})

14: **if** d is a first sibling **then return** TMATCH(d, q_{from}, q_{until})
    else
16:    $q_{hedge} \leftarrow$ HMATCH(d.prevSib, q_{from}, q_{until})
      $q_{tree} \leftarrow$ TMATCH(d, q_{from}, q_{until})
18:    **loop**
        if $q_{hedge} = q_{tree}$ **then return** q_{hedge}
20:        **else if** $q_{tree} < q_{hedge}$ **then**
            rtop $\leftarrow$ RTOP($q_{tree} + 1$, q_{hedge})
22:            **while** rtop $< \infty$ and $q_{hedge} <$ rtop.lastSib **do**
                $q_{tree} \leftarrow$ TMATCH(d, rtop+1, rtop.lastSib)
24:                rtop $\leftarrow$ RTOP($q_{tree} + 1$, q_{hedge})
            end while
26:            **if** $q_{tree} \leq q_{hedge}$ **then return** q_{hedge}
        end if
28:        **else**
            rtop $\leftarrow$ RTOP($q_{hedge} + 1$, q_{tree})
30:            **while** rtop $< \infty$ and $q_{tree} <$ rtop.lastSib **do**
                $q_{hedge} \leftarrow$ HMATCH(d.prevSib, rtop + 1, rtop.lastSib)
32:                rtop $\leftarrow$ RTOP($q_{hedge} + 1$, q_{tree})
            end while
34:            **if** $q_{hedge} \leq q_{tree}$ **then return** q_{tree}
        end if
36:        **end if**
    end loop
38: **end if**

---

query node such that the interval ending with it can be matched the result of the former call would have been the relevant one in that case.

Correctness. The main technical difficulty of the paper is proving that TMATCH is correct. Due to space limitations, the proof has been omitted.

Lemma 6. *Let D be a data tree and let Q be a query tree. TMATCH is correct, that is, given the root node d of D, the smallest and largest node q_{from} and q_{until} of Q, respectively, TMATCH returns q_{until} iff $D \models Q$.*

We now argue how TMATCH can be modified to a procedure TMATCH-ALL, that computes *all* data nodes u such that $D \models^u Q$. In order to compute *all* the matches, we add a test to l.9 of TMATCH. That is, before returning q_{best}, we test whether q_{best} is the root of Q, and we output d if it is. Now we return $q_{best} - 1$, as if the query root was not matched. Furthermore, TMATCH-ALL recursively calls TMATCH-ALL and HMATCH-ALL instead of TMATCH and HMATCH. Here HMATCH-ALL is the same as HMATCH, except that it recursively calls TMATCH-ALL and HMATCH-ALL instead of HMATCH and TMATCH.

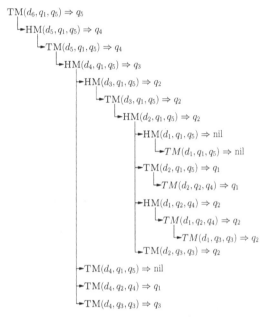

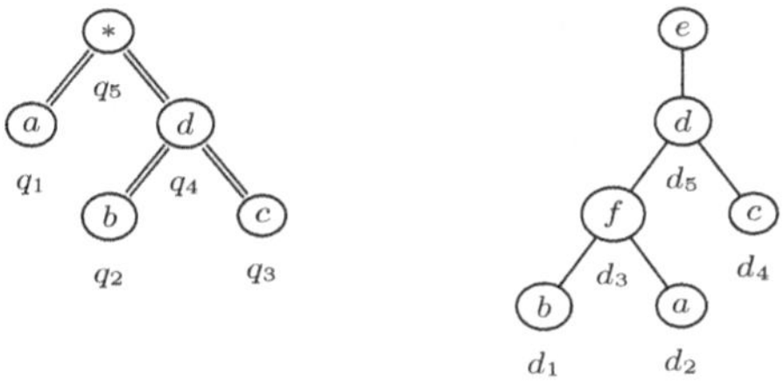

(a) Query tree (left) and data tree (right) of Example 5

```
TM(d6, q1, q5) ⇒ q5
└─HM(d5, q1, q5) ⇒ q4
   └─TM(d5, q1, q5) ⇒ q4
      └─HM(d4, q1, q5) ⇒ q3
         ├─HM(d3, q1, q5) ⇒ q2
         │  └─TM(d3, q1, q5) ⇒ q2
         │     └─HM(d2, q1, q5) ⇒ q2
         │        ├─HM(d1, q1, q5) ⇒ nil
         │        │  └─TM(d1, q1, q5) ⇒ nil
         │        ├─TM(d2, q1, q5) ⇒ q1
         │        │  └─TM(d2, q2, q4) ⇒ q1
         │        ├─HM(d1, q2, q4) ⇒ q2
         │        │  └─TM(d1, q2, q4) ⇒ q2
         │        │     └─TM(d1, q3, q3) ⇒ q2
         │        └─TM(d2, q3, q3) ⇒ q2
         ├─TM(d4, q1, q5) ⇒ nil
         ├─TM(d4, q2, q4) ⇒ q1
         └─TM(d4, q3, q3) ⇒ q3
```

(b) Function calls of HMATCH (HM) and TMATCH (TM) of Example 5.

Fig. 4. Illustrations for Example 5

The following theorem can be proved:

Theorem 7. *Let d be the root node of D and let q_{from} be the smallest and q_{root} be the largest node of Q, respectively.* TMATCH-ALL *is correct, that is,* TMATCH-ALL(d, q_{from}, q_{until}) *outputs the data nodes u such that $D \models^u Q$.*

Proof (Sketch). It follows directly from our additional test and the correctness of TMATCH that $D \models^u Q$ for all the nodes u that TMATCH-ALL outputs.

It remains to prove that, if $D \models^u Q$, then TMATCH-ALL outputs u. Towards a contradiction, assume that there is an u such that $D \models^u Q$, but u was not reported by TMATCH-ALL. By an easy induction it can be shown that for every data node d_0 in D there is a call TMATCH-ALL for d_0's subtree and Q. In particular, there was a call TMATCH-ALL$(u, q_{\mathrm{from}}, q_{\mathrm{root}})$. Since this call did not output u, it follows that u must have children and that HMATCH-ALL(u.lastChild, q_{from}, q_{root}) $< q_{\text{root}} - 1$, (because otherwise q_{root} and u would have been compared and u would have been written to the output). In general, we have that HMATCH-ALL(d, q_1, q_2)=min (HMATCH(d, q_1, q_2), q_{root} −1).

It follows that HMATCH-ALL(u.lastChild, q_{from}, q_{root}) = HMATCH(u.last Child, q_{from}, q_{root}).

If we now call TMATCH($u, q_{\text{from}}, q_{\text{root}}$), it calls HMATCH($u$.lastChild, q_{from}, q_{root}), which yields again a value less than $q_{\text{root}} - 1$. Therefore, the return value of TMATCH($u, q_{\text{from}}, q_{\text{root}}$) is less than q_{root}. But we assumed that subtree(u) $\models Q$, which contradicts the correctness of TMATCH proved in Lemma 6. □

Time and Space Complexity. First, we need to show that our algorithm determines in PTIME whether $D \models Q$. Notice that the naïve manner of computing the running time of TMATCH gives rise to only an exponential upper bound. Indeed, define *(i)* $T(N)$ as the running time of TMATCH on d, q_{from}, and q_{until}, where subtree(d) and $[q_{\text{from}}, q_{\text{until}}]$ have N nodes in total, and *(ii)* $H(N)$ as the running time of HMATCH on d, q_{from}, and q_{until}, where subhedge(d) and $[q_{\text{from}}, q_{\text{until}}]$ have N nodes in total. Then, we have that $T(2) \leq p(N)$ for a polynomial p, $T(N) \leq p(N) + H(N-1) + T(N-1)$, and $H(N) \leq T(N) + X(N)$, where $X(N) \geq 0$. Hence, $T(N) \leq 2^{N-1}$, which is obviously not sufficient.

We therefore employ a slightly more sophisticated approach in the following Lemma.

Lemma 8. *Given the root node of a data tree D, and the smallest and largest query nodes and of a query tree Q, respectively,* TMATCH *runs in time* $\mathcal{O}(|D| \cdot |Q| \cdot depth(Q))$. *Moreover,* TMATCH *makes* $\mathcal{O}(|D| \cdot |Q|)$ *comparisons between a data node and a query node.*

The depth(Q) factor in the complexity of TMATCH is due to the calls to rtop in HMATCH, and the computation of the successors of query nodes.

Theorem 9. TMATCH-ALL(D, Q) *runs in time* $\mathcal{O}(|D| \cdot |Q| \cdot depth(Q))$. *Moreover,* TMATCH-ALL *makes* $\mathcal{O}(|D| \cdot |Q|)$ *comparisons between a data node and a query node.*

Currently, the maximum recursion depth of TMATCH-ALL is $\mathcal{O}(\text{depth}(D) \times \text{branch}(D))$, where branch($D$) is the maximum number of children a node in D has. We have the branch(D) factor because HMATCH($d, q_{\text{from}}, q_{\text{until}}$) calls HMATCH($d$.prevSib, q_{from}, q_{until}). However, this bound can be improved using a simple preprocessing step: we can turn D into a binary tree D_{bin} by inserting intermediate levels of special nodes between each data node and its children. By doing so, D only grows linearly in size and the depth only grows by a factor of log(branch(D)).

As Q only uses descendant axes, we have that $D \models^u Q$ iff $D_{\text{bin}} \models^u Q$.[2] When this preprocessing step is carried out, our algorithm still has $\mathcal{O}(|D||Q|\text{depth}(Q))$ time complexity, but the recursion/stack depth is improved to $\mathcal{O}(\text{depth}(D) \cdot \log(\text{branch}(D)))$.

[2] Under the assumption that the new dummy nodes do not match $*$, which can be trivially incorporated in the algorithm.

References

1. Altinel, M., Franklin, M.: Efficient filtering of XML documents for selective dissemination of information. In: Proc. VLDB, pp. 53–64 (2000)
2. Bar-Yossef, Z., Fontoura, M., Josifovski, V.: On the memory requirements of XPath evaluation over XML streams. In: Proc. PODS, pp. 177–188 (2004)
3. Bar-Yossef, Z., Fontoura, M., Josifovski, V.: Buffering in query evaluation over XML streams. In: Proc. PODS (2005)
4. Bruno, N., Srivastava, D., Koudas, N.: Holistic twig joins: Optimal XML pattern matching. In: Proc. SIGMOD, pp. 310–321 (2002)
5. Chan, C.Y., Fan, W., Felber, P., Garofalakis, M.N., Rastogi, R.: Tree pattern aggregation for scalable XML data dissemination. In: Bressan, S., Chaudhri, A.B., Lee, M.L., Yu, J.X., Lacroix, Z. (eds.) CAiSE 2002 and VLDB 2002. LNCS, vol. 2590, pp. 826–837. Springer, Heidelberg (2003)
6. Chan, C.Y., Felber, P., Garofalakis, M.N., Rastogi, R.: Efficient filtering of XML documents with XPath expressions. In: Proc. ICDE, pp. 235–244 (2000)
7. Clark, J., DeRose, S.: XML Path Language (XPath). Technical report, World Wide Web Consortium (November 1999), `http://www.w3.org/TR/xpath`
8. Cook, S.A., McKenzie, P.: Problems complete for deterministic logarithmic space. J. Algorithms 8, 385–394 (1987)
9. Diao, Y., Altinel, M., Franklin, M.J., Zhang, H., Fischer, P.: Path sharing and predicate evaluation for high-performance XML filtering. ACM Trans. Database Syst. 28(4), 467–516 (2003)
10. Gottlob, G., Koch, C., Pichler, R.: Efficient algorithms for processing XPath queries. ACM Trans. Database Syst. 30(2), 444–491 (2005)
11. Gottlob, G., Koch, C., Pichler, R., Segoufin, L.: The complexity of XPath query evaluation and XML typing. J. ACM 52(2), 284–335 (2005)
12. Gottlob, G., Leone, N., Scarcello, F.: The complexity of acyclic conjunctive queries. J. ACM 48(1), 431–498 (2001)
13. Green, T.J., Gupta, A., Miklau, G., Onizuka, M., Suciu, D.: Processing XML streams with deterministic automata and stream indexes. ACM Trans. Database Syst. 29(4), 752–788 (2004)
14. Grohe, M., Koch, C., Schweikardt, N.: Tight lower bounds for query processing on streaming and external memory data. In: Caires, L., Italiano, G.F., Monteiro, L., Palamidessi, C., Yung, M. (eds.) ICALP 2005. LNCS, vol. 3580, Springer, Heidelberg (2005)
15. Gupta, A., Suciu, D.: Stream processing of XPath queries with predicates. In: Proc. SIGMOD, pp. 419–430 (2003)
16. Olteanu, D., Furche, T., Bry, F.: An evaluation of regular path expressions with qualifiers against XML streams. In: Williams, H., MacKinnon, L.M. (eds.) Key Technologies for Data Management. LNCS, vol. 3112, pp. 31–44. Springer, Heidelberg (2004)
17. Ramanan, P.: Evaluating an XPath query on a streaming XML document. In: Proc. COMAD 2005, pp. 41–52 (2005)
18. Sudborough, I.H.: Time and tape bounded auxiliary pushdown automata. In: Gruska, J. (ed.) Mathematical Foundations of Computer Science 1977. LNCS, vol. 53, pp. 493–503. Springer, Heidelberg (1977)
19. Yannakakis, M.: Algorithms for acyclic database schemes. In: Proc. VLDB, pp. 82–94 (1981)

Datalog Programs over Infinite Databases, Revisited
(Extended Abstract)

Sara Cohen, Joseph (Yossi) Gil, and Evelina Zarivach

Technion—Israel Institute of Technology

Abstract. This paper's revisit of infinite relational databases, a model traditionally perceived as purely theoretical, was sparked by a concrete implementation setting, and the results obtained here were used in a practical database problem. In the course of implementing a database system for querying Java software, we found that the universe of Java code can be effectively modeled as an infinite database. This modeling makes it possible to distinguish between queries which are "open-ended," that is, whose result may grow as software components are added into the system, and queries which are "closed," in that their result does not change as the software base grows. Further, closed queries can be implemented much more efficiently than open queries. Achievements include an algorithm for distinguishing between these two kinds of queries (we assume that queries are written in Datalog), and an algorithm to generate an efficient evaluation scheme of closed queries, which is a generalization of Vieille's famous QSQR algorithm for top-down evaluation of Datalog programs. A by-product of this work is a rather terse and elegant representation of QSQR.

1 Introduction

Usually, a database contains relations of finite size. However, there are natural settings which can be better modeled by infinite databases, over which a set of finiteness constraints is defined. In this paper we are interested in the safety problem, which is one of most fundamental issues related to DATALOG [2] programs over infinite relations. We say that a DATALOG program is *safe*, if it yields a finite result over all databases which satisfy some given finiteness constraints. Instead of studying the safety problem directly, we consider the *weak safety* and *termination* properties. Intuitively, a program (i) is weakly safe if it yields a finite answer for all finite applications of its rules and, (ii) terminates if every sequence of rule applications eventually ceases to yield new results.

To motivate our study of infinite databases, we describe below three different scenarios which involve (some degree of) inherent infiniteness of the database.

Function Symbols. Classically, infinite databases were first introduced as an abstraction that allow programs with function symbols to be modeled as function-free programs over infinite relations. As an intuitive example, consider the following DATALOG program which contains two function symbols:

$$\mathsf{q}(\mathsf{x}+1) \leftarrow \mathsf{p}(\mathsf{x}). \qquad\qquad \mathsf{q}(\mathsf{x}) \leftarrow \mathsf{q}(\sqrt{\mathsf{x}}), \mathsf{p}(\mathsf{x}).$$

M. Arenas and M.I. Schwartzbach (Eds.): DBPL 2007, LNCS 4797, pp. 32–47, 2007.

As [12] showed, this program can be abstractly modeled as follows, where succ and sqrt are infinite relations.

$$\mathsf{q}(y) \leftarrow \mathsf{p}(x), \mathsf{succ}(x, y). \qquad \mathsf{q}(x) \leftarrow \mathsf{q}(y), \mathsf{p}(x), \mathsf{sqrt}(x, y).$$

Finiteness constraints were introduced in [12] to model known characteristics of the function symbols, such that for each x, there are finitely many y such that sqrt(x, y) holds.

Open-World Software. Recently, the interest in infinite databases has been sparked by additional scenarios, e.g., as a formal model of a database of an open-world software or of other relations that may be spread across the Web. Open-world software is infinite in the sense that it is constantly growing, and thus, cannot be completely explored at any moment in time. For example, given a class C, there may be an unbounded number of program classes that *inherit* from C, that *call a method* from C, or that *have as a data member* an instance of C. Thus, querying in the open-world software scenario is naturally modeled as querying over infinite relations. This specific domain also gives rise to finiteness constraints, e.g., a class may inherit only from a finite number of classes.

Our study of infinite databases was motivated by JTL [3], a new DATALOG based system for making queries over software, which uses infinite relations as its data model. As an example of the usefulness of this paradigm for querying JAVA software, consider the following JTL query, which finds (i) all public interfaces or (ii) all public interfaces or classes that extend an abstract class or interface.

```
public [extends T, T abstract | interface];
```

The DATALOG program equivalent to the above is as follows.

$$\mathsf{q}(x) \leftarrow \mathsf{public}(x), \mathsf{p}(x). \qquad \mathsf{p}(x) \leftarrow \mathsf{interface}(x).$$
$$\mathsf{p}(x) \leftarrow \mathsf{extends}(x, y), \mathsf{abstract}(y).$$

Note that public, interface, abstract and extends are EDB predicates. Although this program is nonrecursive, it is also possible to express recursive constraints in JTL.

Even in an open-environment, finiteness constraints have a natural manifestation. For example, the transitive closure of a "uses" relationship between programs is assumed to be bounded. In other words, the programming model is such that, it is unknown which classes may be using a given class, and in general, the number of these classes is unbounded. However, the list of classes that the given class uses, directly or indirectly, is bounded, and must be available to the compiler at compile time. (This assumption is critical, as it allows a program to be compiled and executed by dynamically loading required components.)

Access Constraints. Infinite databases can also be used as an abstraction for computation that is highly inefficient. Consider, for example, a predicate tree(x, y), which holds pairs of parent-child node ids in a tree structure. It may be the case that given a value for x, it is easy to compute all values for y (since we have forward pointers), yet given a value for y, it is very inefficient to compute x (if we do not store backward pointers). Such constraints have been modeled in the past as *access constraints* (sometimes called *binding patterns*) and the rewriting problem for queries with access constraints has been extensively studied, e.g., [4, 9, 5]. An alternative modeling of such scenarios is to consider tree as an infinite relation, with a finiteness constraint that specifies the manner(s) in which it can be efficiently accessed.

Due to lack of space we do not discuss the exact similarities and differences between these two alternative models. However, it is of interest to note that our results shed some light on problems related to querying with access constraints. For example, our algorithm for implication of finiteness constraints can be adapted to imply access constraints over IDB predicates, when given access constraints over the EDB predicates.

Related Work. The problem of deciding safety (i.e., finiteness of results) of a DATALOG program has been extensively studied. Safety of recursive DATALOG programs without function symbols, but with negation, is known to be undecidable [11, 15]. Safety is also undecidable for DATALOG programs with functions symbols [14]. This latter result motivated [12] to abstractly model DATALOG programs with function symbols as function-free programs over infinite relations. [12] also introduced finiteness constraints to model known characteristics of function symbols.

The safety problem for DATALOG programs over infinite relations, with finiteness constraints, was studied in [13]. In particular, [13] showed that safety can be reduced to a combination of two properties: *weak safety* (i.e., finiteness of results for every finite number of rule applications) and termination. They presented a method to determine weak safety, and showed that termination is undecidable. For monadic programs, [13] proved that safety can be determined in polynomial time.

Several stronger notions than safety have also been studied for programs over infinite relations. *Supersafety* was considered in [6, 7] and shown to be decidable. Supersafety is a sufficient, but not necessary, condition for safety. Intuitively, supersafety requires finiteness of results in all fix-point models, whereas safety requires finiteness of results only in the least fix-point model. The *strong safety* variant was studied in [8]. Basically, a program is strongly safe if all intermediate rules (and not only the goal predicate) yield finite results. For a special case, [8] showed how to evaluate all results for a strongly safe program, using a bottom-up computation. One of the requirements in [8] is that each rule can be computed in a left-to-right ordering of its atoms, such that the variables in a specific atom are bounded by those appearing to its left. Our results can also be used to check such properties of rules.

Contributions. This paper presents new results on the safety problem for DATALOG programs over infinite relations. Our four main contributions can be summarized as follows. *First*, we present an algorithm (Sections 4 and 5) to determine finiteness constraints on IDB predicates defined in a DATALOG program based on the finiteness constraints defined on the EDB predicates. Our algorithm finds all finiteness constraints that must hold on the IDB after any finite number of rule applications. This result is useful in itself since it gives us insight on the characteristics of the IDB predicates, which can be important for developing query computation algorithms, such as the type in [8]. *Second*, we present an alternative characterization, based on this algorithm, of DATALOG programs which are *weakly safe* (Sec. 6). *Third*, the termination problem in also considered (Sec. 7). Our EDB predicates can be binary (as opposed to the monadic predicates considered in [13]). We decide termination when the database is *founded* which is natural, in particular, in the software model. *Fourth*, a characterization of DATALOG programs which can be evaluated even if they require in their evaluation partial exploration of infinite values is presented (Sec. 8). (This is the case if the program needs to check e.g., if a given class has at least one class that inherits from it.) An actual evaluation algorithm, based on the famous Vieille's [16, 17] query-subquery top-down evaluation technique is presented in Sec. 9. (We believe that our presentation of the algorithm is a bit more elegant and easy to understand than the original formulation.)

2 Preliminaries

This section briefly reviews the basic syntax and semantics of positive, recursive DATALOG programs, which are evaluated over a possibly infinite database. This review is necessary in order to introduce the notation that we will be using throughout the paper.

Syntax. Relations in DATALOG are represented by *predicates*, and are abstractly denoted with p and q. We use $\mathrm{ar}(p)$ to denote the arity of the predicate p. When discussing concrete examples of predicates, we will use the sanserif font, e.g., members, parent. For a predicate p, we denote by $p_1, p_2, \ldots$ its positions.

Let $\mathbb{V}$ be an enumerable set of *variable* symbols and $\mathbb{D}$ be an enumerable set of *constant* symbols. We shall use lower-case letters from the end of the Latin alphabet, i.e., x, y, z, etc., to denote variables and upper-case bold letters to denote sets of variables **X**, **Y**, **Z**. Constants are quoted, e.g., 'Moses', 'Isaac', etc. *Terms* are either constants or variables and are denoted t, t_1, t_2, etc.

An *atom* a is of the form $p(t_1, \ldots, t_n)$ where p is a predicate symbol of arity n and each t_i is a term. We use $\mathrm{pred}(a)$ to denote the predicate of a and we use $\mathrm{ar}(a)$ as a shorthand notation for $\mathrm{ar}(\mathrm{pred}(a))$. For an atom a, we denote by $t_i(a)$ a term which appears at position i. Terms which are mapped to a constant are said to be *bound*; other terms are *free*. In parent(x, 'Moses'), the first term is free while the second is bound. A *fact* is a ground atom, i.e., an atom in which all arguments are bound. For example, parent('Amram', 'Moses') is a fact. The phrase *p-fact* refers to a fact a such that $\mathrm{pred}(a) = p$.

Let $\mathbf{vars}(a)$ (respectively $\mathbf{consts}(a)$) denote the set of all variables (respectively constants) appearing in atom a. Let $\mathbf{terms}(a) = \mathbf{vars}(a) \cup \mathbf{consts}(a)$, i.e., $\mathbf{terms}(a)$ is the set of all the terms appearing in the atom a. An *assignment* is a function $\mu : \mathbb{V} \to \mathbb{D}$. By applying an assignment μ to an atom a, one derives a $\mathrm{pred}(a)$-fact.

A *rule* r has the form $p(t_1, \ldots, t_k) \leftarrow a_1, \ldots, a_n$, where $p(t_1, \ldots, t_k)$ is the *head* of r, and $a_1, \ldots, a_n$ is the *body* of r. We use the overloaded notation $\mathrm{pred}(r)$ to denote the predicate of the head of r. If $p = \mathrm{pred}(r)$, we say that r *defines* p. We overload the notations $\mathbf{vars}(r)$, $\mathbf{consts}(r)$ and $\mathbf{terms}(r)$ to represent all the variables, constants and terms(respectively) appearing in rule r. For $i = 1, 2, \ldots$, let $\mathbf{terms}_i(r)$ be the ith element of $\mathbf{terms}(r)$ in some enumeration of this set.

A DATALOG *program* Π is a *finite* collection of rules, with a designated predicate, called the *goal*. We use $\mathbf{consts}(\Pi)$ to denote the set of constants appearing in any rule of Π, i.e., $\mathbf{consts}(\Pi) = \bigcup_{r \in \Pi} \mathbf{consts}(r)$. We distinguish between two kinds of predicates that appear in a program: (i) extensional database (*EDB*) predicates, denoted $\mathbf{edb}(\Pi)$, which are predicates that do not occur in the head of any of the

r_1: heir(x, y) ← extends(x, y).
r_2: heir(x, y) ← extends(x, z), heir(z, y).
r_3: class_cousins(x, y, z) ← extends(x, x′), extends(x′, z), extends(y, y′), extends(y′, z).
r_4: heirs(x, u, v) ← heir(x, u), heir(x, v), not_eq(u, v).
r_5: multi(x, y) ← heirs(x, u, v), class_cousins(u, v, y), dependant(x, y).
r_6: q(x, y) ← multi(x, y), heir('Bill', x), extends(w, 'Bill').

Fig. 1. A DATALOG program

program's rules, and (ii) intensional database (*IDB*) predicates (all other predicates), denoted $\mathbf{idb}(\Pi)$. By convention, we use q to denote the goal of a program. We always require that $q \in \mathbf{idb}(\Pi)$.

Semantics. A *database* $\mathcal{D}$ is a possibly *infinite* set of facts. To be exact, for each EDB predicate p, the database $\mathcal{D}$ may contain infinitely many p-facts; $\mathcal{D}$ usually does not contain any facts for the IDB predicates. The *result* of applying a rule r to a database $\mathcal{D}$ is defined in the standard fashion. Informally, the semantics of a rule is "If the body atoms are true then so is the head atom." To make the semantics precise, we consider a set $\mathcal{F}$ that contains facts for the EDB (and possibly for the IDB) predicates. Such sets are intermediate values during the evaluation of a program on a database. Then, an application of a rule r: $p(t_1, \ldots, t_k) \leftarrow a_1, \ldots, a_n$ to $\mathcal{F}$ produces a set of facts denoted $r(\mathcal{F})$, such that *(1)* every fact in $\mathcal{F}$ is in $r(\mathcal{F})$, and *(2)* if μ is an assignment that satisfies the body of r (i.e., $\mu(a_i) \in \mathcal{F}$, for all i), then also $\mu(p(t_1, \ldots, t_k)) \in r(\mathcal{F})$.

For a sequence $\boldsymbol{r}$ of rules, let $\boldsymbol{r}(\mathcal{F})$ denote the set of all facts obtained by applying the rules in $\boldsymbol{r}$ in sequence to $\mathcal{F}$, i.e., if $\boldsymbol{r}$ is empty, then $\boldsymbol{r}(\mathcal{F}) = \mathcal{F}$. Otherwise, $\boldsymbol{r} = \boldsymbol{r}'r$, where $\boldsymbol{r}'$ is a sequence and r is a rule, in which case $\boldsymbol{r}(\mathcal{F}) = r(\boldsymbol{r}'(\mathcal{F}))$. The notation $\Pi^i(\mathcal{F})$ will stand for the union of all $\boldsymbol{r}(\mathcal{F})$, where $\boldsymbol{r}$ is a sequence of at most i rules selected from Π. Also, let $\Pi^\infty(\mathcal{F}) = \bigcup_{i \geq 0} \Pi^i(\mathcal{F})$.

If p is a predicate, then subscript p will be used to denote the restriction of a set of facts to p-facts only. Thus, $\Pi^i_p(\mathcal{F})$ is the set of p-facts in $\Pi^i(\mathcal{F})$, and $\boldsymbol{r}_p(\mathcal{F})$ is defined similarly. The *result* of applying Π to a database $\mathcal{D}$ is $\Pi^\infty_q(\mathcal{D})$ where q is Π's goal. Note that $\Pi^\infty_q(\mathcal{D})$ may be infinite if $\mathcal{D}$ is infinite.

For the purpose of illustration, Fig. 1 presents a simple DATALOG program, which will be used as the running example of this paper. The program is defined over extends, dependant and not_eq EDB predicates which are suitable for JAVA classes. In particular, a fact extends('c', 'p') states that module (e.g., a class or an interface) 'c' extends module 'p' and a fact dependant('a', 'b') represents a couple in which 'a' depends upon 'b'.

Expansion Rules. We will find it convenient to summarize the application of a rule sequence in a sequence of *expansion* rules, i.e., rules which involve only EDB predicates. We will use γ to denote a single expansion rule and Γ to denote a set of expansion rules. Fac. 1 is well known, and follows, e.g., from [10].

Fact 1. *For every finite sequence of rules* $\boldsymbol{r}$ *and every predicate* p *there exists a finite set of expansion rules* Γ*, which uses only the constants occurring in the rules of* $\boldsymbol{r}$*, such that for all databases* $\mathcal{D}$*,* $\boldsymbol{r}_p(\mathcal{D}) = \bigcup_{\gamma \in \Gamma} \gamma_p(\mathcal{D})$.

In our running example, applying τ_1 and then τ_4 is the shortest sequence of rule applications that generates heirs-facts. The expansion rule for this sequence is

$$\mathsf{heirs}(\mathtt{x},\mathtt{u},\mathtt{v}) \leftarrow \mathsf{extends}(\mathtt{x},\mathtt{u}), \mathsf{extends}(\mathtt{x},\mathtt{v}), \mathsf{not\_eq}(\mathtt{u},\mathtt{v}). \tag{2.1}$$

Similarly, one sequence that yields a multi-fact, is by applying first τ_1 and τ_4 (to obtain heirs-facts), then τ_3 (to obtain class_cousins-facts), and finally τ_5. The corresponding expansion rule is similar to (2.1), but a bit longer

$$\begin{aligned}\mathsf{multi}(\mathtt{x},\mathtt{y}) \leftarrow\ & \mathsf{extends}(\mathtt{x},\mathtt{u}), \mathsf{extends}(\mathtt{u},\mathtt{u}'), \mathsf{extends}(\mathtt{u}',\mathtt{y}), \mathsf{dependant}(\mathtt{x},\mathtt{y}),\\ & \mathsf{extends}(\mathtt{x},\mathtt{v}), \mathsf{extends}(\mathtt{v},\mathtt{v}'), \mathsf{extends}(\mathtt{v}',\mathtt{y}), \mathsf{not\_eq}(\mathtt{u},\mathtt{v}).\end{aligned} \tag{2.2}$$

Recall that the result of applying a program Π, with goal q, to a database $\mathcal{D}$ is $\Pi_q^{\infty}(\mathcal{D})$. It follows from Fac. 1 that there exists an infinite series of expansion rules $\gamma^1, \gamma^2, \ldots$ defining q such that

$$\Pi_q^{\infty}(\mathcal{D}) = \bigcup_{i=1}^{\infty} \gamma_q^i(\mathcal{D}). \tag{2.3}$$

Henceforth, we shall tacitly assume that the head atom of any rule r does not contain any variable $\mathtt{v} \in \mathbf{vars}(r)$ more than once and does not contain constants. No generality is lost. Rules can always be brought to this form without changing their semantics by introduction of auxiliary variables and by using the infinite EDB predicate $\mathsf{eq}(\mathtt{x},\mathtt{y})$ which holds whenever $\mathtt{x} = \mathtt{y}$. For example, rule $\mathsf{a}(\mathtt{x},\mathtt{x},\mathtt{y},\text{'Ben'}) \leftarrow \mathsf{a}(\mathtt{x},\text{'Dan'},\mathtt{z})$. will be transformed to $\mathsf{a}(\mathtt{x},\mathtt{w},\mathtt{y},\mathtt{u}) \leftarrow \mathsf{a}(\mathtt{x},\text{'Dan'},\mathtt{z}), \mathsf{eq}(\mathtt{w},\mathtt{x}), \mathsf{eq}(\mathtt{u},\text{'Ben'})$.

3 The Safety Problem

In this section we present a theory of *finiteness constraints* which is crucial to the analysis of the problem that we research. Informally, the problem is:

> *Given a* DATALOG *program and restrictions over its database, decide whether the result of a program is finite for any infinite database that meets the restrictions.*

One should understand that when there are no constraints on the database, nothing meaningful can be stated about the program's semantics. Even a simple DATALOG program, such as $\mathsf{moses\_son}(\mathtt{x}) \leftarrow \mathsf{parent}(\text{'Moses'},\mathtt{x})$ can deduce an infinite number of facts for the moses_son predicate when no restrictions are imposed on parent predicate.

Consider, on the other hand, a case in which we restrict the set of parent-facts in the database such that for any 'c' $\in \mathbb{D}$, the set $\{\mathtt{x} \mid \mathsf{parent}(\text{'c'},\mathtt{x})\}$ is finite. Under this restriction, we can conclude that the above program deduces only finitely many facts to its goal. To express such restrictions, we use *finiteness constraints*, as defined in [12].

Definition 2. *Let p be a predicate. Then,* $\mathbf{pos}(p)$ *is the set of symbols* $\{p_1, \ldots, p_{\mathrm{ar}(p)}\}$, *and a* finiteness constraint *(*constraint *for short) of p is an expression of the form* $\mathbf{x} \rightsquigarrow \mathbf{y}$, *where* $\mathbf{x}, \mathbf{y} \subseteq \mathbf{pos}(p)$.

A set of fact $\mathcal{F}$ satisfies constraint $\mathbf{x} \rightsquigarrow \mathbf{y}$ if the search for p-facts in $\mathcal{F}$ with some fixed assignment to positions $\mathbf{x}$, yields only a finite variety of combinations of values for positions $\mathbf{y}$. More formally,

Definition 3. *Let $\sigma = \mathbf{x} \rightsquigarrow \mathbf{y}$ be a constraint on predicate p and $\mathcal{F}$ be a set of facts. Then, $\mathcal{F} \models \sigma$ (read $\mathcal{F}$* satisfies *σ) if the set*

$$\{b[\mathbf{y}] \mid b \in \mathcal{F} \textit{ and } \mathrm{pred}(b) = p \textit{ and } b[\mathbf{x}] = a[\mathbf{x}]\}$$

is finite for every p-fact $a \in \mathcal{F}$. If C is a set of constraints, then $\mathcal{F} \models C$ if $\mathcal{F} \models \sigma$ for all $\sigma \in C$.

As an example, consider the predicate intersect, in which a fact intersect('c1', 'c2', 'p') states that 'c1' and 'c2' are two distinct circles intersecting at a point 'p'. Then, (infinite) set of all facts about intersections of distinct circles in the plane satisfies the constraint $\{\mathsf{intersect}_1, \mathsf{intersect}_2\} \rightsquigarrow \{\mathsf{intersect}_3\}$, since there are at most two points in which such circles intersect. This set does not satisfy any other constraints.

Remark 1. Using constraints it is possible to state that the number of p-facts, for some predicate p, must be finite. Formally, this is written as $\emptyset \rightsquigarrow \mathbf{pos}(p)$.

Remark 2. Note that finiteness constraints are a somewhat weaker version of functional dependencies. Not surprisingly, Armstrong's axioms also characterize finiteness constraints for EDB predicates [12].

Let $\mathfrak{C}(\mathcal{F})$ denote the set of *all* constraints that set $\mathcal{F}$ satisfies. It is easy to show that the set of constraints satisfied by the intersection of finitely many sets is equal to the intersection of the constraints of the sets, or more formally, $\mathfrak{C}(\mathcal{F}_1 \cup \cdots \cup \mathcal{F}_n) = \mathfrak{C}(\mathcal{F}_1) \cap \cdots \cap \mathfrak{C}(\mathcal{F}_n)$. (Unfortunately, this fact does not hold for infinite sequences.)

After defining the notion of finiteness constraints, we are ready to formally state the central problem of the research. For the purpose of the following definitions, let Π be a fixed DATALOG program, and let predicate q be its goal. Also let C be a set of constraints. Then, the main problem of this paper is to determine whether the set $\Pi_q^\infty(\mathcal{D})$ is finite whenever $\mathcal{D} \models C$, i.e., to decide whether a given program is *safe* or not.

Definition 4. *Program Π is* safe *if $\Pi_q^\infty(\mathcal{D})$ is finite whenever $\mathcal{D} \models C$.*

The safety problem can be reduced to two problems [13]: **(i)** the *weak safety* problem, which is to decide whether any finite sequence of program rule applications yields a finite number of facts to its goal, and **(ii)** the *termination* problem, which is to decide whether there is a finite number of rule applications after which no new facts are added to the program's goal. Formally,

Definition 5. *We say that Π is* weakly safe *with respect to C if the set $\Pi_q^n(\mathcal{D})$ is finite for all $n \geq 0$ whenever $\mathcal{D} \models C$.*

Definition 6. *We say that Π is* terminating *with respect to C if there exists $n \geq 0$ such that $\Pi_q^\infty(\mathcal{D}) = \Pi_q^n(\mathcal{D})$ whenever $\mathcal{D} \models C$.*

It is well known that a program Π is safe iff it is both weakly safe and terminating [13]. It is also known [13] that the weak safety problem is complete for exponential time. However, no algorithm has been shown to, given a program, deduce all constraints for the IDB predicates that follow from the constraints on the EDB predicates, for all finite applications of the program rules. Such an algorithm is the topic of Sec. 4 and of Sec. 5. This algorithm is interesting of itself, since it proves that the finite implication problem for constraints is decidable. It is also useful as an alternative method for determining weak safety (see Sec. 6) and as a skeleton for query evaluation.

4 Single Rule Constraints Implication

Let r be a rule, and $\mathcal{C}$ be a set of constraints. This section is concerned with the constraints that can be inferred from $\mathcal{C}$ on the output of a single application of r.

Definition 7. *Let σ be a constraint on* pred(r). *Then, $\mathcal{C} \models_r \sigma$ ($\mathcal{C}$* implies *σ in r) if for every set of facts $\mathcal{F}$, the set $r(\mathcal{F})$ satisfies σ whenever $\mathcal{F} \models \mathcal{C}$.*

Intuitively, $\mathcal{C} \models_r \sigma$ means that if all constraints of $\mathcal{C}$ hold prior to an application of r, then σ holds after a single application of r. Let $\mathcal{C}_r$ denote the set of all constraints implied by $\mathcal{C}$ with respect to rule r, i.e., $\mathcal{C}_r = \{\sigma \mid \mathcal{C} \models_r \sigma\}$.

Consider, for example, rule τ_3 in the running example. Assume that the constraints set for the running example is $\mathcal{C}$ as follows:

$$\mathcal{C} = \{\{\mathsf{extends}_1\} \rightsquigarrow \{\mathsf{extends}_2\}, \{\mathsf{dependant}_1\} \rightsquigarrow \{\mathsf{dependant}_2\}\}. \quad (4.1)$$

Then the set of constraints of τ_3 is $\mathcal{C}_{\tau_3}$, which contains $\{\mathsf{class\_cousins}_1\} \rightsquigarrow \{\mathsf{class\_cousins}_3\}$ and $\{\mathsf{class\_cousins}_2\} \rightsquigarrow \{\mathsf{class\_cousins}_3\}$.

Now, a *rule constraint* (or a *causation*) is an expression of the form $\mathbf{X} \rightsquigarrow \mathbf{Y}$ where $\mathbf{X}, \mathbf{Y} \subseteq \mathbf{terms}(r)$. For example, $\{\mathsf{x}\} \rightsquigarrow \{\mathsf{z}\}$ is a causation of the rule τ_3 defined in Fig. ??.

Inference in the context of rule r, must be done in terms of r's vocabulary, that is the set $\mathbf{terms}(r)$. We introduce mechanisms for vocabulary translation: For a p-atom a, we introduce a function $\mathsf{t2p}_a(\cdot)$ which given a set of terms of a, returns the corresponding set of p-positions, e.g., for $a = \mathsf{p}(\mathsf{x}, \text{`B'}, \mathsf{y}, \mathsf{x}, \text{`B'}, \mathsf{y})$, we have $\mathsf{t2p}_a(\{\mathsf{x}, \text{`B'}\}) = \{\mathsf{p}_1, \mathsf{p}_2, \mathsf{p}_4, \mathsf{p}_5\}$. Function $\mathsf{p2t}_a(\cdot)$ is simply $\mathsf{t2p}_a{}^{-1}(\cdot)$. Also, for p-rule r with head atom h, define function $\mathsf{t2p}_r(\mathbf{X})$, for $\mathbf{X} \subseteq \mathbf{terms}(r)$, as $\mathsf{t2p}_h(\mathbf{X} \cap \mathbf{terms}(h))$, that is, convert to p-positions only terms occurring in the head. Function $\mathsf{p2t}_r(\cdot)$ is simply $\mathsf{p2t}_h(\cdot)$.

To define the semantics of a causation $\sigma = \mathbf{X} \rightsquigarrow \mathbf{Y}$, we construct a (predicate-) constraint $\sigma' = \mathsf{t2p}_{r'}(\mathbf{X}) \rightsquigarrow \mathsf{t2p}_{r'}(\mathbf{Y})$ where rule r' is constructed from r by selecting p', a fresh predicate symbol not occurring in r, and letting r' be the p'-rule identical to r except that all members of $\mathbf{terms}(r)$ occur in its head term, i.e., the bodies of r' and r are the same, and the head of r' is $h' = p'(\mathbf{terms}_1(r), \ldots, \mathbf{terms}_k(r))$, where $k = |\mathbf{terms}(r)|$. We write $\mathcal{C} \models_r \sigma$ (read $\mathcal{C}$ *implies* σ in rule r), or simply $\mathcal{C} \models \sigma$ (read $\mathcal{C}$ *implies* σ) when the rule is clear from context, iff $\mathcal{C} \models_{r'} \sigma'$.

The notion of *closure*, which will be defined next, is useful when inferring causations of a rule. Informally, a closure of terms set $\mathbf{X}$ consists of all the $\mathbf{terms}(r)$ which are implied by $\mathbf{X}$.

Definition 8. *The* closure *of a set* $\mathbf{X} \subseteq \mathbf{terms}(r)$ *with respect to* $\mathcal{C}$ *and* r*, denoted* $\mathbf{X}^{+}_{\mathcal{C},r}$*, is the largest set* $\mathbf{Y} \subseteq \mathbf{terms}(r)$ *such that* $\mathcal{C} \models_r \mathbf{X} \rightsquigarrow \mathbf{Y}$.

For example, if $\mathcal{C} = \{\{\mathsf{extends}_1\} \rightsquigarrow \{\mathsf{extends}_2\}\}$, and the rule is given by τ_3 in the running example, then $\{\mathtt{y}\}^{+}_{\mathcal{C},\tau_3} = \{\mathtt{y}, \mathtt{y}', \mathtt{z}\}$.

Lemma 1. *There exists a polynomial-time algorithm which, given a rule* r*, a set* $\mathcal{C}$*, and a set* $\mathbf{X} \subseteq \mathbf{vars}(r)$*, computes* $\mathbf{Y} = \mathbf{X}^{+}_{\mathcal{C},r}$.

Proof. Initially, $\mathbf{Y} \leftarrow \mathbf{X}$. For all $\sigma \in \mathcal{C}$ and all atoms $a \in \mathbf{body}(r)$, if $\sigma = \mathbf{u} \rightsquigarrow \mathbf{v}$ and $\mathsf{p2t}_a(\mathbf{u}) \subseteq \mathbf{Y}$, then add $\mathsf{p2t}_a(\mathbf{v})$ to $\mathbf{Y}$. Iterate until $\mathbf{Y}$ ceases to change.

The straightforward version of the closure algorithm runs in quadratic time in the size of the input ($\mathcal{C}$, $\mathbf{X}$ and $\mathbf{vars}(r)$): There are at most $|\mathbf{vars}(r)|$ iterations (each iteration increases $\mathbf{Y}$ by one argument in the worst case). In each iteration, all constraints in $\mathcal{C}$ are examined. There also exists a linear time algorithm for the closure computation [1].

The closure procedure is used in Alg. 1 which computes the set $\mathcal{C}_r$ of constraints implied by $\mathcal{C}$ in r.

Algorithm 1. r_constraints(r, $\mathcal{C}$)

Return $\mathcal{C}_r$ for rule r and constraints set $\mathcal{C}$.

1: **let** $\mathcal{C}_r \leftarrow \emptyset$
2: **let** $\mathbf{H} \leftarrow \mathbf{terms}(\mathrm{head}(r))$
3: **For all** $\mathbf{X} \subseteq \mathbf{H}$ **do** // *Find which variables are bound by* $\mathbf{X}$
4: **For all** $\mathbf{Y} \subseteq \mathbf{X}^{+}_{\mathcal{C},r}$ **do** // *Adjust the result according to Def. 7*
5: $\mathcal{C}_r \leftarrow \mathcal{C}_r \cup \{\mathsf{t2p}_r(\mathbf{X}) \rightsquigarrow \mathsf{t2p}_r(\mathbf{Y})\}$
6: **return** $\mathcal{C}_r$

The main loop of the algorithm, i.e., lines 3–5, is performed for all the subsets of variables appearing in the head term. For each such subset $\mathbf{X}$ the algorithm computes its closure $\mathbf{X}^{+}$. Now, since $\mathbf{X} \rightsquigarrow \mathbf{X}^{+}_{\mathcal{C},r}$ holds, it remains to translate this constraint (and subconstraints of it) to constraints over $\mathrm{pred}(r)$.

Lemma 2. *Alg. 1 correctly computes the set* $\mathcal{C}_r$ *in time* $2^m O(n^2)$*, where* $m = \mathrm{ar}(\mathrm{pred}(r)) + 1$ *and* n *is the length of* $\mathbf{vars}(r)$ *and* $\mathcal{C}$.

5 Program Wide Constraints Implication

Now that the means for inferring constraints within a single rule are established, we are ready to study the more interesting problem, i.e., inference of constraints with respect to an entire DATALOG program Π. In doing so, we will need to take into account the effects of multiple applications of the same rule, the fact that an IDB may be defined by more than one rule, and that the definition of different IDBs may be mutually recursive.

In this section let $\mathcal{C}$ be a fixed set of constraints on the extensional predicates of Π and let $\mathcal{D}$ be a database, i.e., a set of p-facts, where $p \in \mathbf{edb}(\Pi)$.

Definition 9. *Let* $p \in \mathbf{idb}(\Pi)$ *and let* σ *be a constraint on* p*. We say that* $\mathcal{C}$ implies σ*, denoted* $\mathcal{C} \models \sigma$*, if* $\Pi^n_p(\mathcal{D})$ *satisfies the constraint* σ *for all* $n \geq 0$ *whenever* $\mathcal{D} \models \mathcal{C}$.

Remark 3. The implication considered in this paper is *finite implication*, i.e., a constraint is implied if it holds in all finite number of rule applications. Deciding which constraints hold after infinitely many applications, allows one to decide termination, and is therefore undecidable.

Henceforth, we shall assume that $\mathcal{D}$ satisfies $\mathcal{C}$. Let $\mathcal{C}_p$ the set of all the implied constraints over $p \in \mathbf{idb}(\Pi)$, i.e., all constraints $\mathbf{x} \rightsquigarrow \mathbf{y}$, where $\mathbf{x}, \mathbf{y} \subseteq \mathbf{pos}(p)$ and $\mathcal{C} \models \mathbf{x} \rightsquigarrow \mathbf{y}$. Let $\mathcal{C}_\Pi$ denote the set of all the constraints on IDB predicates of Π.

Observe that if no facts are established for a certain predicate p, i.e., no p-facts exist in $\mathcal{F}$, then $\mathcal{F}$ satisfies *any* constraint $\sigma = \mathbf{x} \rightsquigarrow \mathbf{y}$, where $\mathbf{x}, \mathbf{y} \subseteq \mathbf{pos}(p)$, This is precisely the circumstances for all $p \in \mathbf{idb}(\Pi)$, when program Π starts. The set $\mathcal{F}$ will continue to satisfy σ if no rule defining p will ever generate facts that violate σ.

Algorithm 2. program_constraints($\Pi, \mathcal{C}$)

Given a program Π, and a set $\mathcal{C}$ of constraints over its extensional predicates, return $\mathcal{C}_\Pi$.

1: **For all** $p \in \mathbf{idb}(\Pi)$ **do** // *find IDB candidate constraints*
2:     **let** $\mathcal{P}_p \leftarrow \{\mathbf{x} \rightsquigarrow \mathbf{y} \mid \mathbf{x}, \mathbf{y} \subseteq \mathbf{pos}(p)\}$
3: **let** $\mathcal{C}_\Pi \leftarrow \mathcal{C} \cup \bigcup_{p \in \mathbf{idb}(\Pi)} \mathcal{P}_p$ // *add candidates to* $\mathcal{C}_\Pi$
4: **Repeat** // *Invalidate constraints until each* $\mathcal{P}_p$ *is reduced to* $\mathcal{C}_p$
5:     **For all** $p \in \mathbf{idb}(\Pi)$ **do** // *refine* $\mathcal{P}_p$ *as implied by* $\mathcal{C}_\Pi$
6:         **For all** $\alpha \in \Pi$, $\mathrm{pred}(\alpha) = p$ **do** // *examine all p-rules*
7:             **let** $\mathcal{C}_\alpha \leftarrow$ r_constraints($\alpha, \mathcal{C}_\Pi$)
8:             $\mathcal{C}_\Pi \leftarrow \mathcal{C}_\Pi \setminus \mathcal{P}_p$ // *forget all p-constraints regarding p*
9:             $\mathcal{P}_p \leftarrow \mathcal{P}_p \cap \mathcal{C}_\alpha$ // *remove constraints not preserved by* α
10:            $\mathcal{C}_\Pi \leftarrow \mathcal{C}_\Pi \cup \mathcal{P}_p$ // *revive p-constraints preserved by* α
11: **until** no changes in $\mathcal{C}_\Pi$
12: **return** $\mathcal{C}_\Pi$

These observations are employed in Alg. 2 which uses a fixed point evaluation strategy for computing $\mathcal{C}_\Pi$. Alg. 2 maintains the set $\mathcal{P}_p$ of constraints for every intensional predicate $p \in \Pi$. Initially, the algorithm assumes that all the constraints are satisfied by the set $\mathcal{F}$ of p-facts (line 2). Then, the algorithm iteratively eliminates the constraints which are definitely not satisfied by $\mathcal{F}$ until a fixed point is reached. In particular, a constraint σ is in $\mathcal{C}_p$, if σ is implied (in a steady state) by all the rules defining p. One can show that Alg. 2 indeed computes $\mathcal{C}_\Pi$, albeit in exponential time.

6 Deciding Weak Safety

In this section we present the theorem which decides the weak safety problem.

Theorem 1. *Let* Π *be a* DATALOG *program, and let* q *be its goal. Then,* Π *is* weakly safe *iff* $\mathcal{C} \models \emptyset \rightsquigarrow \mathbf{pos}(q)$.

Proof. If Π is weakly safe, then according to Def. 5, $\Pi_q^n(\mathcal{D})$ is finite for all $n \geq 0$ whenever $\mathcal{D} \models \mathcal{C}$. The above is possible only if $\mathcal{C} \models \emptyset \rightsquigarrow \mathbf{pos}(q)$.

Conversely, assume that $\mathcal{C} \models \emptyset \rightsquigarrow \mathbf{pos}(q)$. Then, by Def. 9, the set $\mathcal{F}_n = \Pi_q^n(\mathcal{D})$ satisfies $\emptyset \rightsquigarrow \mathbf{pos}(q)$ for all $n \geq 0$ whenever $\mathcal{D} \models \mathcal{C}$. Finally, according to Def. 3 it follows that the set $\{a \mid a \in \mathcal{F}_n \wedge \mathrm{pred}(a) = q\}$ is finite for all $n \geq 0$. □

Consider, for example, the following DATALOG program, which computes all direct or indirect super classes of 'ArrayList':

$$\mathsf{heir}(x, y) \leftarrow \mathsf{extends}(x, y). \qquad \mathsf{superclass}(x) \leftarrow \mathsf{heir}(\text{'ArrayList'}, x).$$
$$\mathsf{heir}(x, y) \leftarrow \mathsf{extends}(x, z), \mathsf{heir}(z, y).$$

Suppose that $\mathcal{C} = \{\{\mathsf{extends}_1\} \rightsquigarrow \{\mathsf{extends}_2\}\}$ is satisfied by the input database of the above program. Alg. 2 deduces that $\{\mathsf{heir}_1\} \rightsquigarrow \{\mathsf{heir}_2\}$ holds and so is $\emptyset \rightsquigarrow \{\mathsf{superclass}_1\}$, i.e., any finite number of rule applications deduces finitely many superclass-facts. It follows that the above program is weakly safe.

Remark 4. Thm. 1 establishes that $\mathcal{C}_\Pi$ can be used to decide weak safety. But, since weak safety EXP-time complete [13], it is no wonder that our algorithm for computing $\mathcal{C}_\Pi$ is exponential.

7 Deciding Termination

If a program is weakly safe, then any finite number of rule applications contributes a finite number of facts to the program semantics. However, the semantics of weakly safe program may include an unbounded number of facts, since in general, the number of rule applications is unbounded. Indeed, Sagiv and Vardi [13] showed that the independent problem of termination is undecidable, without being able to produce an algorithm for determining termination in the case that weak safety is known, or conversely, to prove that no such algorithm exists.

This section sets conditions, common in tasks of processing software, which exclude the situation that a program is weakly safe yet not terminating.Specifically, we show that every weakly safe program is also terminating whenever the database is *founded.*

Definition 10. *A database $\mathcal{D}$ satisfying a set of constraints $\mathcal{C}$ is* founded *if all EDB predicates are binary, and there are only finitely many distinct elements in every infinite sequence $\ell_1, \ell_2, \ldots$ in which every consecutive pair ℓ_i, ℓ_{i+1}, $i \geq 1$ satisfies at least one of the following:* (i) *$p(\ell_i, \ell_{i+1})$ holds for some EDB predicate p and $\{p_1\} \rightsquigarrow \{p_2\} \in \mathcal{C}$ or* (ii) *$p(\ell_{i+1}, \ell_i)$ holds for some EDB predicate p and $\{p_2\} \rightsquigarrow \{p_1\} \in \mathcal{C}$.*

Consider the database which represents relations between programming units. Such database contains relations such as "inherits", "calls" etc. It is obvious to see that this database is founded, since the number of units used by a certain programming module must be finite (otherwise the compilation process will never end).

Now we are ready to state the central theorem of this section.

Theorem 2. *Let $\mathcal{D}$ be a founded database satisfying the set of constraints $\mathcal{C}$. Then, if Π is weakly safe, then it is also terminating over $\mathcal{D}$.*

The theorem can be made a bit more general, dealing with unary EDB predicates. To simplify the presentation, we omit this generalization.

Henceforth assume that Π is indeed weakly safe with regards to $\mathcal{C}$ and $\mathcal{D}$ is founded. To prove the theorem we first write the yield of q-facts of every possible sequence of rule applications as a set of expansion rules defining q (as in (2.3)).

In the running example, an expansion rule that corresponds to the shortest sequence of rule applications that may generate a q-fact is obtained by adding two atoms to the body of expansion rule (2.2):

$$\begin{aligned}\mathsf{q}(\mathrm{x},\mathrm{y}) \leftarrow\ & \mathsf{extends}(\mathrm{x},\mathrm{u}), \mathsf{extends}(\mathrm{u},\mathrm{u}'), \mathsf{extends}(\mathrm{u}',\mathrm{y}),\\ & \mathsf{extends}(\mathrm{x},\mathrm{v}), \mathsf{extends}(\mathrm{v},\mathrm{v}'), \mathsf{extends}(\mathrm{v}',\mathrm{y}),\\ & \mathsf{not\_eq}(\mathrm{u},\mathrm{v}), \mathsf{dependant}(\mathrm{x},\mathrm{y}), \mathsf{extends}(\text{'Bill'},\mathrm{x}), \mathsf{extends}(\mathrm{w},\text{'Bill'}).\end{aligned} \tag{7.1}$$

Fix an enumeration of these rules, $\gamma^1, \gamma^2, \ldots$.

The proof is carried out by showing that the set $\bigcup_{i=1}^{\infty} \left(\gamma^i(\mathcal{D}) \setminus \mathcal{D}\right)$ is finite. We show in fact that there is a finite set of representative rules (which are not necessarily expansion rules) $\gamma^{i_1}, \ldots, \gamma^{i_k}$, such that for every expansion rule γ^i there is a representative rule γ^j, where $j \in \{i_1, \ldots, i_k\}$ such that $\gamma^i(\mathcal{D}) \subseteq \gamma^j(\mathcal{D})$. Thm. 2 now follows from the observation that each such $\gamma^j(\mathcal{D}) \setminus \mathcal{D}$ is finite when Π is weakly safe.

8 Computability

Having shown that every weakly safe program defined over founded database is safe, it is only natural to ask how such programs may be evaluated. This section presents our computational model and discusses which programs may be computed in it.

For the reminder of the article we assume that the database $\mathcal{D}$ is founded, and hence all EDB predicates are binary. Let $\mathcal{D}$ be a founded database and p be a binary predicate. Then, similarly to [12], we assume that given constants (c, c'), one can determine in finite time whether $p(c, c') \in \mathcal{D}$. Also, if $\{p_1\} \rightsquigarrow \{p_2\}$ (resp. $\{p_2\} \rightsquigarrow \{p_1\}$), then given a constant c, it is also possible to find in finite time all constants c' such that $p(c, c') \in \mathcal{D}$ (resp., $p(c', c) \in \mathcal{D}$). Further, if $\emptyset \rightsquigarrow \{p_1\}$ (resp. $\emptyset \rightsquigarrow \{p_2\}$), then we can find in finite time all constants c, such that there exists a c' for which $p(c, c') \in \mathcal{D}$ (resp. $p(c', c) \in \mathcal{D}$). However, in the absence of constraints, one cannot find in finite time all constants c' such that $p(c, c') \in \mathcal{D}$, (nor respectively, $p(c', c) \in \mathcal{D}$).

It may first seem that if a program is safe, then it is also *computable*, i.e., there exists an evaluation algorithm, using this computational model, which computes its result in finite time. In this section we prove that safety is a necessary but not a sufficient requirement for computability of a DATALOG program and present a theorem which settles the computability problem for founded programs. Then, Sec. 9 presents an evaluation algorithm for safe programs.

To see that safe programs are not necessarily computable, consider the following program Π, which is aimed to find all the superclasses y on which superclass 'Bill' depends.

$$\begin{aligned}&\tau_1\colon\ \mathsf{superclasses}(\mathrm{x},\mathrm{y}) \leftarrow \mathsf{extends}(\mathrm{w},\mathrm{x}), \mathsf{extends}(\mathrm{z},\mathrm{y}).\\ &\tau_2\colon\ \mathsf{dep\_superclasses}(\mathrm{x},\mathrm{y}) \leftarrow \mathsf{dependant}(\mathrm{x},\mathrm{y}), \mathsf{superclasses}(\mathrm{x},\mathrm{y}).\\ &\tau_3\colon\ \mathsf{q}(\mathrm{y}) \leftarrow \mathsf{dep\_superclasses}(\text{'Bill'},\mathrm{y}).\end{aligned} \tag{8.1}$$

Then, $C_\Pi = \{\{\mathsf{dep\_superclasses}_1\} \rightsquigarrow \{\mathsf{dep\_superclasses}_2\}, \emptyset \rightsquigarrow \{\mathsf{q}_1\}\}$ can be inferred with the supposition that **extends** and **dependant** predicates satisfy constraints as in (4.1). Since this set includes $\emptyset \rightsquigarrow \{q_1\}$ in C_Π, we have (Thm. 1) that this program is weakly safe. Also, since $\mathcal{D}$ is founded, it is also terminating by Thm. 2. Nevertheless, it is impossible to compute its output, because for any assignment μ to $\mathbb{D}$ and an atom $t = \mathsf{superclasses}(\mathrm{x}, \mathrm{y})$ it is undecidable whether $\mu(t)$ holds. The difficulty here is that the evaluation process must find a subclass of x and a subclass of y to prove that x and y are indeed superclasses. Now, if the evaluation algorithm does find such subclasses, it can conclude that $\mathsf{superclasses}(\mathrm{x}, \mathrm{y})$ holds. But, what should the algorithm do if it does *not* find any subclasses of x?

Missing such evidence may be due to the fact that x indeed does not have subclasses. Still, lack of evidence, could be a result of evaluation procedure's failure to explore the infinite database. In the software interpretation, it could be that a software engineer, in a very remote galaxy, has implemented a class that inherits from x, but the evaluation algorithm did not have sufficient resources to find this inheriting class.

If one is willing to permit similar existential queries in the algorithm, then any program which is terminating can also be evaluated in practice. The following definition however is designed to preclude such queries from DATALOG programs.

Definition 11. *Predicate* p *is* variable-bound *if for every rule* $r \in \Pi$ *defining* p *with head* h *it holds that* $C_\Pi \models_r \mathbf{vars}(h) \rightsquigarrow \mathbf{terms}(r)$.

For example, predicate dep_superclasses in example (8.1) is variable-bound, while predicate superclasses is not. Note that the definition implies that every EDB predicate is (trivially) variable-bound.

The above definitions lead to the next theorem, whose proof is provided by the evaluation algorithm described in the next section.

Theorem 3. *A program* Π *is* computable *if* (i) *it is safe and* (ii) *every predicate* p *appearing in it is variable-bound.*

9 A Top-Down Evaluation Algorithm

This section describes a top-down algorithm for query evaluation. The heart of our algorithm is in function idb_eval (Alg. 3), whose parameters include a predicate p, and a subquery expressed as a relation (in the relational algebra sense) Q, defining a possibly partial assignment to the positions of p, i.e., $\mathbf{schema}(Q) \subseteq \mathbf{pos}(p)$ (where $\mathbf{schema}(Q)$ is the schema of Q). The function answers the subquery by returning a relation whose columns are those columns in $\mathbf{pos}(p)$ which are finitely constrained by $\mathbf{schema}(Q)$ and whose tuples are computed from the tuples of Q by these finiteness constraints.

For each of the rules defining the predicate, function idb_eval calls function rule_eval (Alg. 4), which in its turn, calls function atom_eval (Alg. 5) for each of the atoms in the rule. If the atom's predicate is an EDB, then atom_eval invokes edb_eval; otherwise, it recursively calls idb_eval.

Even simple rules such as $\mathsf{anc}(\mathrm{x}, \mathrm{y}) \leftarrow \mathsf{anc}(\mathrm{x}, \mathrm{z}), \mathsf{anc}(\mathrm{z}, \mathrm{y})$, typical to transitive closure computation, may cause a naive implementation of idb_eval to recurse indefinitely. To guard against this predicament, the algorithm passes through the recursive calls variable $\mathbf{X}$, which stores in it all "open queries" in the recursion stack. Variable $\mathbf{X}$ is implemented as an associative array of relations. For each positions set $\mathbf{q}$, s.t. $\mathbf{q} \subseteq \mathbf{pos}(p)$

Algorithm 3. idb_eval(p, Q, $\mathbf{X}$)

1: **let** $\mathbf{q} \leftarrow$ **schema**(Q) // *elicit the pattern of this query*
2: **let** $Q' \leftarrow Q \setminus \mathbf{X}[\mathbf{q}]$ // *restrict interest to queries not in cache*
3: $\mathbf{X}[\mathbf{q}] \leftarrow \mathbf{X}[\mathbf{q}] \cup Q'$ // *record remaining queries in cache*
4: **let m** be the maximal set s.t. $\mathbf{q} \rightsquigarrow \mathbf{m} \in \mathcal{C}_\Pi$ // **m** *is the schema of the answer relation*
5: **If** $Q' \neq \emptyset$ **then** // *queries remained for execution*
6:     **Repeat** // *exercise all rules until no new answers are found*
7:         **For all** $r \in \Pi$ such that $\text{pred}(r) = p$ **do** // *try rule* r
8:             **let** $T \leftarrow$ rule_eval(r, p2t$_r(Q')$, $\mathbf{X}$)
9:             $\mathbf{M}[\mathbf{q}] \leftarrow \mathbf{M}[\mathbf{q}] \cup \pi_{\mathbf{m}}$t2p$_r(T)$
10:     **until** no changes in $\mathbf{M}$
11: **return** $\mathbf{M}[\mathbf{q}] \bowtie Q$ // *restrict global answer set to queries in* Q

---

and p is an IDB predicate, $\mathbf{X}[\mathbf{q}]$ is a relation with schema $\mathbf{q}$ containing all subqueries whose pattern is $\mathbf{q}$ which are on the recursion stack. At its 2nd line, idb_eval restricts its interest to new such queries. At line 3, the function records the currently executing queries in $\mathbf{X}$.

Thus, the call to idb_eval that starts the evaluation process is with parameters: q (the program goal), I (the relation with no columns and a single, empty, tuple), and initialization of all entries in $\mathbf{X}$ to an empty relation.

In addition to $\mathbf{X}$, the algorithm maintains a similarly organized *global* array $\mathbf{M}$ for results memoization, except that the schema of $\mathbf{M}[\mathbf{q}]$ is $\mathbf{m}$, where $\mathbf{m}$ is the maximal set such that $\mathbf{q} \rightsquigarrow \mathbf{m}$. The main loop of idb_eval (lines 6–10) uses the results of calls to rule_eval to extend, as long as this is possible, relation $\mathbf{M}[\mathbf{q}]$. The function result is obtained by restricting $\mathbf{M}[\mathbf{q}]$ (which records *all* queries of pattern $\mathbf{q}$ that the algorithm *ever* executed) to answers of queries in Q; this is carried out by the natural join operation in line 11.

In order to delegate its work to function rule_eval, function idb_eval must translate the query Q', which is formulated in terms of positions in p, to the list of symbolic variables that rule r expects. To this end, we use an overloaded version of function p2t$_r$ (invoked at line 8), which returns its input relation with renamed columns as per the head of rule r. The reverse translation of rule_eval's return value, is carried out by the call to (an overloaded version of) function t2p$_r$, at line 9. This line also projects the return value into the schema $\mathbf{m}$.

Algorithm 4. rule_eval(r, Q, $\mathbf{X}$)

1: $Q \leftarrow Q \bowtie \mathit{CONSTS}_r$
2: **Repeat**
3:     **For all** $a \in$ **body**(r) **do**
4:         $Q \leftarrow Q \bowtie$ atom_eval(a, $\pi_a Q$, $\mathbf{X}$)
5: **until** no changes in Q
6: **return** $\pi_{\text{head}(r)} Q$

Algorithm 5. atom_eval(a, Q, $\mathbf{X}$)

1: **let** $p \leftarrow \text{pred}(a)$
    // *elicit the predicate of this atom*
2: **let** $P \leftarrow$ t2p$_a(Q)$ // *bound terms of* a
3: **let** $A \leftarrow \begin{cases} \text{edb\_eval}(p, P) & \text{if } p \in \mathbf{edb}(\Pi) \\ \text{idb\_eval}(p, P, \mathbf{X}) & \text{otherwise} \end{cases}$
4: **return** p2t$_a(A)$

Line 9 of rule_eval begins the computation of a subquery with respect to a rule, by augmenting the given subquery with the values of constants used in the rule: variable $CONSTS_r$ denotes the relation whose column names are simply **consts**(r), while its single tuple consists also of these constants. The recursive call to atom_eval is preceded by a projection to the variables (and constants) used in the atom. We assume that the operator π ignores columns in projection schema which do not exist in the projected relation. Hence, the projection succeeds even if Q does not contain all terms of the current atom. (In particular, if Q does not contain any term of a, a no-columns relation containing the empty tuple is returned.) A projection to terms in the rule head is applied before the function is returned.

Function atom_eval is rather straightforward; note however that the call to functions that evaluate a predicate require a change of vocabulary, before and after the call.

Our algorithm differs from that of Vieille's [16, 17], due to the differences in the setting, e.g., our computation model is restrictive and our programs are evaluated over an infinite database. A full comparison of these algorithms, as well as a proof of correctness, is omitted, due to lack of space.

10 Conclusion

In this paper we studied the weak safety and termination problems (and thereby, also the safety problem) for recursive DATALOG programs over infinite databases. We presented an algorithm that computes all constraints for IDB predicates that are (finitely) implied by the constraints on the EDB predicates and the rules of a given program. We also showed that weak safety guarantees termination if the database is founded, a natural property in many models. Finally, for safe programs we presented an elegant evaluation algorithm that computes the goal predicate in a top-down manner, using sideways information passing.

In the future, we intend to extend our algorithm to deal with additional classes of programs that are not necessarily founded. We also intend to study the effect of negation on the problems considered in this paper.

References

1. Beeri, C., Bernstein, P.A.: Computational problems related to the design of normal form relational schemas. ACM Trans. Database Syst. 4(1), 30–59 (1979)
2. Ceri, S., Gottlob, G., Tanca, L.: Logic programming and databases. Springer, New York (1990)
3. Cohen, T., Gil, J.Y., Maman, I.: JTL—the Java tools language. In: OOPSLA 2006 (2006)
4. Deutsch, A., Ludäscher, B., Nash, A.: Rewriting queries using views with access patterns under integrity constraints. Theoretical Comp. Sci. 371(3), 200–226 (2007)
5. Florescu, D., Levy, A.Y., Manolescu, I., Suciu, D.: Query optimization in the presence of limited access patterns. In: SIGMOD 1999 (1999)
6. Kifer, M., Ramakrishnan, R., Silberschatz, A.: An axiomatic approach to deciding query safety in deductive databases. In: PODS 1988 (1988)
7. Kifer, M.: On the decidability and axiomatization of query finiteness in deductive databases. J. ACM 45(4), 588–633 (1998)
8. Krishnamurthy, R., Ramakrishnan, R., Shmueli, O.: A framework for testing safety and effective computability of extended datalog. In: ICMD 1988 (1988)
9. Li, C., Chang, E.Y.: On answering queries in the presence of limited access patterns. In: Van den Bussche, J., Vianu, V. (eds.) ICDT 2001. LNCS, vol. 1973, Springer, Heidelberg (2000)

10. Maier, D., Ullman, J.D., Vardi, M.Y.: On the foundations of the universal relation model. ACM Trans. Database Syst. 9(2), 283–308 (1984)
11. Paola, R.D.: The recursive unsolvability of the decision problem for the class of definite formulas. J. ACM 16(2), 324–327 (1969)
12. Ramakrishnan, R., et al.: Safety of recursive Horn clauses with infinite relations. In: PODS 1987 (1987)
13. Sagiv, Y., Vardi, M.Y.: Safety of Datalog queries over infinite databases. In: PODS 1988 (1988)
14. Shmueli, O.: Decidability and expressiveness aspects of logic queries. In: PODS 1987 (1987)
15. Vardi, M.: The decision problem for database dependencies. Inf. Process. Lett. 12(5), 251–254 (1981)
16. Vieille, L.: Recursive axioms in deductive databases: The Query/Subquery approach. In: 1st Int. Conf. on Expert Database Syst. (1986)
17. Vieille, L.: Recursive query processing: The power of logic. Theoretical Comp. Sci. 69(1), 1–53 (1989)

A Methodology for Coupling Fragments of XPath with Structural Indexes for XML Documents

George H.L. Fletcher[1], Dirk Van Gucht[2], Yuqing Wu[2], Marc Gyssens[3], Sofía Brenes[2], and Jan Paredaens[4]

[1] Washington State University, Vancouver
gfletcher@acm.org
[2] Indiana University, Bloomington
{vgucht,yuqwu,sbrenesb}@cs.indiana.edu
[3] Hasselt University and Transnational University of Limburg
marc.gyssens@uhasselt.be
[4] University of Antwerp
jan.paredaens@ua.ac.be

1 Introduction

Supporting efficient access to XML data using XPath [3] continues to be an important research problem [6, 12]. XPath queries are used to specify node-labeled trees which match portions of the hierarchical XML data. In XPath query evaluation, indices similar to those used in relational database systems – namely, value indices on tags and text values – are first used, together with structural join algorithms [1, 2, 19]. This approach turns out to be simple and efficient. However, the structural containment relationships native to XML data are not directly captured by value indices.

To directly capture the structural information of XML data, a family of structural indices has been introduced. DataGuide [5] was the first to be proposed, followed by the 1-index [13], which is based on the notion of bi-simulation among nodes in an XML document. These indices can be used to evaluate some path expressions accurately without accessing the original data graph. Milo and Suciu [13] also introduced the 2-index and T-index, based on similarity of pairs (vectors) of nodes. Unfortunately, these and other early structural indices tend to be too large for practical use because they typically maintain too fine-grained structural information about the document [9, 16].

To remedy this, Kaushik et al. introduced the $A(k)$-index which uses a notion of bi-similarity on nodes relativized to paths of length k [10]. This captures localized structural information of a document, and can support path expressions of length up to k. Focusing just on local similarity, the $A(k)$-index can be substantially smaller than the 1-index and others.

Several works have investigated maintenance and tuning of the $A(k)$ indices. The $D(k)$-index [15] and $M(k)$-index [8] extend the $A(k)$-index to adapt to query workload. Yi et al. [18] developed update techniques for the $A(k)$-index and 1-index. Finally, the integrated use of structural and value indices has been

M. Arenas and M.I. Schwartzbach (Eds.): DBPL 2007, LNCS 4797, pp. 48–65, 2007.

explored [11], and there have also been investigations on covering indices [9, 16] and index selection [14, 17].

The introduction of structural indices for XML data has lead to significant improvements in the performance of XPath query evaluation. As was demonstrated empirically, the performance benefits of these indices are most dramatic when queries "match" the index definitions [10]. To date, however, there lacks a formal understanding of this notion of queries matching indices. This leads to some fundamental questions about using structural indices in query evaluation:

1. For which fragments of XPath are particular structural indices *ideally* suited?
2. For these fragments, how are its expressions efficiently evaluated with the index?
3. Can the answers to these questions be bootstrapped to provide general techniques for evaluation of arbitrary XPath expressions?

In this paper, we present a methodology for investigating such questions and apply it to the important special case of the $A(k)$-indices. For question (1), we begin by noting that the $A(k)$-index of a document induces a partitioning on its nodes. Recently, an approach has been proposed for considering partitioning XML documents based on notions of query indistinguishability of nodes and paths, relative to particular fragments of XPath [7]. If we apply this approach to show that there exists a fragment of XPath which induces a partition identical to the $A(k)$-partition, then we can speak of an "ideal" match between the index and this fragment. Given this ideal coupling, we can then turn to a principled investigation of questions (2) and (3). A main contribution of this paper is the identification of such a fragment of XPath.

Before going into the technical details of the various steps we take in our methodology, we illustrate the general approach with a simple example coming from relational databases. Note that the results in this example are well-known, and as such do not add to the results of this paper.

1.1 A Motivating Example

Consider the B^+-tree index on a column A of a relation R [4]. Clearly, this index induces a partition on the tuples of R: tuples t_1 and t_2 in R will be in the same partition block[1] if and only if $t_1(A) = t_2(A)$. We will call this partition the *B^+-tree-partition* on column A of R, and denote it as $\mathsf{Btree}(A, R)$. (For emphasis, observe that a B^+-tree *index* on A of R is different than the $\mathsf{Btree}(A, R)$*-partition*. The first is a tree data structure, whereas the second is a partition on R.)

Next, consider the relational algebra, and in particular its sub-algebra consisting of the *range queries*. In this example, we focus on such queries as they are specified on attribute A of R. We will denote this class of queries by $\mathsf{RangeQ}(A, R)$. Its queries are of the form $\sigma_{((a_1 \leq A \leq a_2) \texttt{ or } \cdots \texttt{ or } (a_{2n-1} \leq A \leq a_{2n}))}(R)$.[2]

The $\mathsf{RangeQ}(A, R)$ algebra defines a partition on R, called the $\mathsf{RangeQ}(A, R)$-*partition* of R, and is defined as follows: tuples t_1 and t_2 in R are placed in the

[1] "Block" stands for an element of a partition, not be confused with a block on a disk.

[2] For simplicity, we will assume that all the a_i values occur in the A-column of R.

same block of the $\mathsf{RangeQ}(A,R)$-partition if for *any* query Q in $\mathsf{RangeQ}(A,R)$, $t_1 \in Q(R)$ if and only if $t_2 \in Q(R)$. In other words, t_1 and t_2 can not be distinguished by any query in $\mathsf{RangeQ}(A,R)$, i.e., either t_1 and t_2 are both in $Q(R)$, or they are both not in $Q(R)$. An important property of the $\mathsf{RangeQ}(A,R)$-partition is that for each query $Q \in \mathsf{RangeQ}(A,R)$, their exists a subset of blocks in the partition such that $Q(R)$ is the union of these blocks.

A natural question that arises now is to ask if the Btree-partition and the RangeQ-partition are the same. It should come as no surprise that this is indeed the case. This is captured in the following theorem.

Theorem 1. [Btree-RangeQ **Coupling Theorem**] *Let R be a relation and let A be one of its attributes. The* $\mathsf{Btree}(A,R)$*-partition and the* $\mathsf{RangeQ}(A,R)$*-partition are the same.*

Proof. We give a proof of this statement, not because it is difficult, but because its structure reveals the strategy that we will follow to prove an analogous theorem for the XML case (Theorem 4).

1. Let tuples t_1 and t_2 be in the same block of the $\mathsf{Btree}(A,R)$-partition. Then, by definition, $t_1(A) = t_2(A)$. Consider now an arbitrary range query Q. Then clearly, if $t_1(A)$ (and therefore also $t_2(A)$) is in the range of Q then t_1 and t_2 are both in $Q(R)$, but if $t_1(A)$ is not in the range of Q, then they are both not in $Q(R)$. Consequently, t_1 and t_2 are in the same block of the $\mathsf{RangeQ}(A,R)$-partition.
2. Let tuples t_1 and t_2 be in different blocks of the $\mathsf{Btree}(A,R)$-partition. Then, by definition, $t_1(A) \neq t_2(A)$. Let $a = t_1(A)$. Then the range query $\mathtt{label}_a := \sigma_{A=a}(R)$ has t_1 in its result, but not t_2. Thus t_1 and t_2 are in different blocks of the $\mathsf{RangeQ}(A,R)$-partition, and the proof is done.

An immediate consequence of Theorem 1 is that each range query evaluated on R is equal to the union of a family of blocks of the $\mathsf{Btree}(A,R)$-partition.

Theorem 2. [Btree-RangeQ **Block-Union Theorem**] *Let R be a relation, let A be one of its attributes, and let $Q \in$* $\mathsf{RangeQ}(A,R)$*. Then there exists a class $\mathcal{B}_Q$ of partition blocks of the* $\mathsf{Btree}(A,R)$*-partition such that* $Q(R) = \bigcup_{B\in\mathcal{B}_Q} B$.

Note that the Btree-RangeQ Block-Union Theorem can provide guidance and insight in the processing of queries in richer relational fragments.

In the second part of the proof of Theorem 1, observe that the range query $\mathtt{label}_a$ has the property that it uniquely identifies the block of the $\mathsf{RangeQ}(A,R)$-partition consisting of the tuples of R that are indistinguishable from t_1 by any query in $\mathsf{RangeQ}(A,R)$. We will call the query $\mathtt{label}_a$, a *labeling query* and its defining a-value a *label*. Now as a consequence of Theorem 2 we have that evaluating a range query $Q \in \mathsf{RangeQ}(A,R)$ can be done by forming a union of such labeling expressions applied to R.

Theorem 3. [Btree-RangeQ **Label-Union Theorem**] *Let R be a relation and A one of its attributes. Then for each query $Q \in$* $\mathsf{RangeQ}(A,R)$*, there is a set of labeling queries $\mathcal{L}_Q \subseteq$* $\mathsf{RangeQ}(A,R)$ *such that* $Q(R) = \bigcup_{\mathtt{label}\in\mathcal{L}_Q} \mathtt{label}(R)$.

Obviously, in practice we do not want to evaluate the labeling queries `label` $\in \mathcal{L}_Q$ directly on R, but rather we would want a data structure that stores each result $\texttt{label}(R)$. If such a data structure supports efficient look-up of the tuples in the partition block associated with each labeling expression `label`, then evaluating Q can be done by simply streaming out these tuples. Of course, such a data structure is the B^+-tree index. So, in a formal sense we have shown that range queries match ideally with B^+-tree indexes, which of course is a well-known fact.

1.2 Paper Overview

We proceed as in this motivating example, for structural indices and the XPath query language. Specifically:

- We introduce the family of $P(k)$-partitions, which are derivatives of the family of $A(k)$-partitions. It turns out that this new class of partitions is fundamental for establishing the results which follow.
- We then introduce a family of upward XPath algebras, $\mathscr{U}(k)$, and show that the $P(k)$-partition and the partition induced by the $\mathscr{U}(k)$ algebra are the same. As a consequence of this we have that the evaluation of a $\mathscr{U}(k)$ query is equal to the union of some blocks of the $P(k)$-partition.
- Based on this result, we then develop guidelines for the use of a $P(k)$-partition in the evaluation of general XPath queries.
- Following this, we show that for each block in the $P(k)$-partition a labeling expression in $\mathscr{U}(k)$ can be constructed which uniquely identifies the block. Thus, we conclude that each query in $\mathscr{U}(k)$ can be rewritten as the union of some $\mathscr{U}(k)$ block labeling expressions.

These results indicate research directions into new data structures to support efficient evaluation of general XPath queries.

2 Coupling Indices and XPath Fragments

In this section, we set out to apply the methodology described in the motivating relational example to the XML case.

2.1 The XML Data Model

We begin by introducing the document data model that will be used in this paper. Our data model is a simplified version of the XML data model wherein we view a document as a labeled tree.

Definition 1. *A document D is a 4-tuple (V, Ed, r, λ), with V the finite set of nodes, $Ed \subseteq V \times V$ a tree of parent-child edges, $r \in V$ the root, and $\lambda\colon V \to \mathcal{L}$ a node-labeling function into a countably infinite set of labels $\mathcal{L}$.*

Given a document, it is useful to introduce the concept of its paths. We define the set of *paths* of a document D, denoted $\mathsf{Paths}(D)$, as the set $V \times V$. So, for us a path is not a sequence of nodes, but rather a pair. This makes

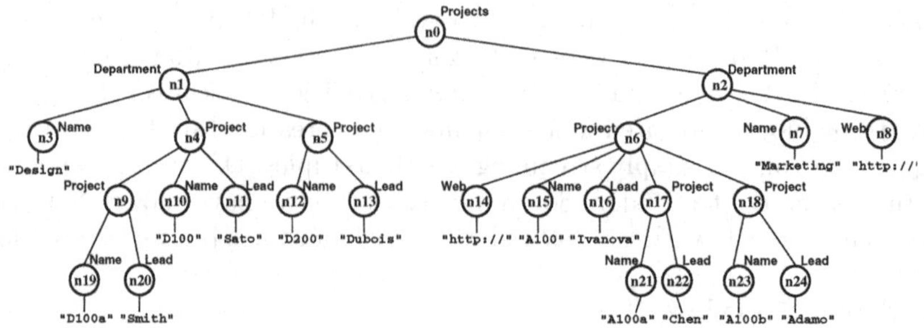

Fig. 1. An XML document. For reference, non-leaf nodes are given unique IDs.

sense however, since a pair of nodes $(n, m) \in \mathsf{Paths}(D)$ identifies the unique path from node n to node m in D. The set of *downward-paths*, $\mathsf{DownPaths}(D)$, consists of the paths (n, m) where n is an ancestor of m. Similarly, the set of *upwards-paths*, $\mathsf{UpPaths}(D)$, consists of the paths (n, m) where n is a descendant of m. Furthermore, for $k \in \mathbb{N}$, $\mathsf{DownPaths}(D, k)$ ($\mathsf{UpPaths}(D, k)$) are those paths in $\mathsf{DownPaths}(D)$ (in $\mathsf{UpPaths}(D)$, respectively) of length at most k. For example, in document D of Figure 1 the path (n_1, n_1) is a member of both $\mathsf{DownPaths}(D, 0)$ and $\mathsf{UpPaths}(D, 0)$, the paths (n_1, n_1), (n_1, n_4), and (n_1, n_9) are in $\mathsf{DownPaths}(D, 2)$, and their corresponding inverse paths (n_1, n_1), (n_4, n_1), and (n_9, n_1) are in $\mathsf{UpPaths}(D, 2)$. The paths (n_9, n_{12}) and (n_1, n_{19}) are in neither $\mathsf{DownPaths}(D, 2)$ nor $\mathsf{UpPaths}(D, 2)$.

2.2 The $A(k)$-Partition of a Document

Given a labeled semi-structured document[3] and a natural number k, Kaushik et al. [10] introduced the $A(k)$*-index* for this document.

The index is built on the partition induced by a certain bi-similarity equivalence relation on the nodes in the document. When specialized to a document, as defined here, the definition of this bi-similarity equivalence is as follows.

Definition 2. *Let* $D = (V, Ed, r, \lambda)$ *be a document,* $n_1, n_2 \in V$*, and let* $k \in \mathbb{N}$*. We say that* n_1 *and* n_2 *are* $A(k)$-equivalent *in* D*, denoted* $n_1 \equiv_{A(k)} n_2$*, if*

1. $\lambda(n_1) = \lambda(n_2)$*; and*
2. *if* $k \geq 1$ *then*
   (a) n_1 *has a parent in* D *if and only if* n_2 *has a parent in* D*; and*
   (b) if n_1 *has parent* p_1 *and* n_2 *has parent* p_2*, then* $p_1 \equiv_{A(k-1)} p_2$*.*

We call the partition induced by $\equiv_{A(k)}$ *on* V *the* $A(k)$-partition *of* D*.*

A more intuitive reading of this definition is that nodes n_1 and n_2 belong to the same block of the $A(k)$-partition, if the label sequences associated with their

[3] A semi-structured document does not need to be a tree. In particular, it is possible that a node has multiple parents.

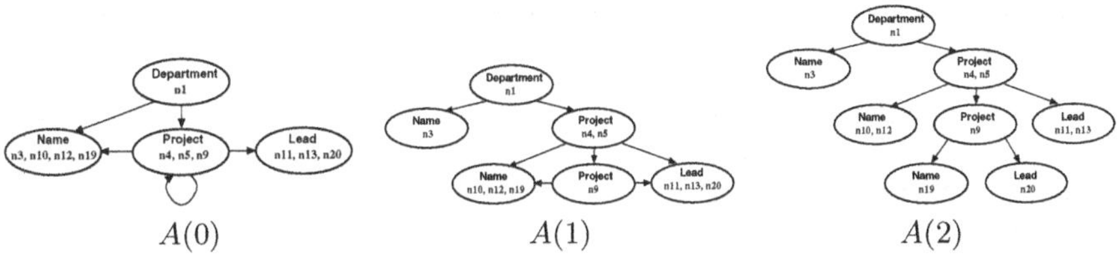

Fig. 2. $\boldsymbol{A(k)}$-indices ($\boldsymbol{k = 0, 1, 2}$) associated with their corresponding $\boldsymbol{A(k)}$-partitions for the "Design" Department sub-tree in the document of Figure 1

incoming paths in D of length at most k are the same. Also note that the $A(k+1)$-partition of a document is a refinement of the $A(k)$-partition.

Example 1. Figure 2 illustrates (ignoring for now the edges between the blocks), for $k = 0, 1$, and 2, the $A(k)$-partition of the Design Department sub-tree rooted at node n_1 in the document of Figure 1.

Following Kaushik et al. [10], the $A(k)$-*index* of a document D is a *graph* wherein each node is a block of the $A(k)$-partition of D, and an edge exists from a block B_1 to a block B_2 if there exists a parent-child edge in D from a node in B_1 to a node in B_2. So, the $A(k)$-index can be thought of as a representation of the $A(k)$-partition and how its blocks can be related in accordance with the document D. The $A(k)$-indexes for $k = 0, 1, 2$ are visualized in Figure 2 on the Design Department sub-tree of the document of Figure 1. Note that if k is equal to the height of the document, then the $A(k)$-index corresponds to the 1-index proposed by Milo and Suciu [13] and the strong DataGuide proposed by Goldman and Widom [5].

2.3 The $P(k)$-Partition of a Document

The $A(k)$-partitions of a document D are partitions on its *nodes*. We will need another family of partitions, the $P(k)$-partitions, which, rather than being defined on nodes, are defined on the sets $\mathsf{UpPaths}(D, k)$, i.e., the sets of *upward-paths* of D of length at most k. As we will see, the $P(k)$-partitions are more fundamental than the $A(k)$-partitions for developing our results.

Definition 3. *Let D be a document, let $k \in \mathbb{N}$, and let (n_1, m_1) and (n_2, m_2) be two paths in* $\mathsf{UpPaths}(D, k)$. *We say that (n_1, m_1) and (n_2, m_2) are $P(k)$-*equivalent, *denoted $(n_1, m_1) \equiv_{P(k)} (n_2, m_2)$, if*

1. $n_1 \equiv_{A(k)} n_2$; *and*
2. $\mathtt{length}(n_1, m_1) = \mathtt{length}(n_2, m_2)$.[4]

We call the partition induced by $\equiv_{P(k)}$ on $\mathsf{UpPaths}(D, k)$ *the* $P(k)$-partition *of D.*

[4] As should be clear, $\mathtt{length}(n, m)$ denotes the length of the path in D from node n to node m.

Example 2. Consider the sub-tree D' in the document of Figure 1 rooted at n_4. For $k = 0, 1$, we have that

1. the $P(0)$-partition on D' is the set $\{[(n_{19}, n_{19}), (n_{10}, n_{10})], [(n_{20}, n_{20}), (n_{11}, n_{11})], [(n_9, n_9), (n_4, n_4)]\}$; and
2. the $P(1)$-partition on D' is the set $\{[(n_{19}, n_{19}), (n_{10}, n_{10})], [(n_{20}, n_{20}), (n_{11}, n_{11})], [(n_9, n_9)], [(n_4, n_4)], [(n_{19}, n_9), (n_{10}, n_4)], [(n_{20}, n_9), (n_{11}, n_4)], [(n_9, n_4)]\}$.
   Notice that the block $[(n_9, n_9), (n_4, n_4)]$ of the $P(0)$-partition is split into two blocks of the $P(1)$-partition, namely $[(n_9, n_9)]$ and $[(n_4, n_4)]$. This is because $n_9 \equiv_{A_0} n_4$, but $n_9 \not\equiv_{A_1} n_4$.

Finally, we wish to observe that when k is equal to the height of a document D, then the $P(k)$-partition corresponds to the partitions induced by the 2-index on D proposed by Milo and Suciu [13].

2.4 The XPath-Algebra

We next present an algebraization [7] of the logical navigational core of XPath [6] which we adopt in this paper and define the paths and nodes-semantics of expressions in this algebra.

Definition 4. *The* XPath-algebra *consists of the primitives* $\varepsilon, \emptyset, \ell, \downarrow,$ *and* $\uparrow$ *together with the operations on expressions* $E_1 \diamond E_2$, $E_1[E_2]$, $E_1 \cup E_2$, $E_1 \cap E_2$, *and* $E_1 - E_2$. *Given a document* $D = (V, Ed, r, \lambda)$, *the* semantics *of an XPath-algebra expression* E *on* D, *denoted* $E(D)$, *is a subset of* $\mathsf{Paths}(D)$. *The semantics for each primitive and each operation is given in Table 1.*

Table 1. The XPath-Algebra Path-Semantics

$$
\begin{aligned}
\varepsilon(D) &= \{(n,n) \mid n \in V\} & E_1 \cup E_2(D) &= E_1(D) \cup E_2(D)\\
\emptyset(D) &= \emptyset & E_1 \cap E_2(D) &= E_1(D) \cap E_2(D)\\
\ell(D) &= \{(n,n) \mid m \in V \text{ and } \lambda(n) = \ell\} & E_1 - E_2(D) &= E_1(D) - E_2(D)\\
\downarrow(D) &= Ed & &\\
\uparrow(D) &= Ed^{-1} & &\\
E_1 \diamond E_2(D) &= \{(n,m) \mid \exists w\colon (n,w) \in E_1(D) \,\&\, (w,m) \in E_2(D)\} & &\\
E_1[E_2](D) &= \{(n,m) \in E_1(D) \mid \exists w\colon (m,w) \in E_2(D)\} & &
\end{aligned}
$$

The XPath-algebra semantics reflects a “global” perspective of expressions being evaluated on an entire document. There is also a “local” semantic perspective, in which expressions are viewed as working at a particular node, as follows.

Definition 5. *Let* E *be an XPath-algebra expression and let* $D = (V, Ed, r, \lambda)$ *be a document. For* $n \in V$, *the* local semantics *of* E *on* D *at* n, *denoted* $E(D)(n)$, *is the set* $\{m \in V \mid (n,m)) \in E(D)\}$.

Consider the XPath query `/Projects/Department/Project[./Project]` that retrieves all the projects of departments that have a sub-project. When applied to the document D of Figure 1, this query returns the set of nodes $\{n_4, n_6\}$. An XPath-algebra expression corresponding to this query can be formulated as `Projects` $\diamond \downarrow \diamond$ `Department` $\diamond \downarrow \diamond$ `Project`[$\downarrow \diamond$ `Project`]. According to the semantics of the XPath-algebra, the global semantics of this expression on D is the set of paths $\{(n_0, n_4), (n_0, n_6)\}$ whereas its local semantics at the root node n_0 is the set of nodes $\{n_4, n_6\}$, which, as intended, corresponds to the result set of the original XPath query.

2.5 Linking the $P(k)$-Partition to the XPath Algebra

The $A(k)$-indexes were introduced to support efficient evaluation of certain path queries on XML documents. As was demonstrated empirically on a benchmark of queries, the performance benefits of these indexes were most dramatic when the queries "matched" the index definitions [10]. However, in that paper the concept of queries matching indexes was not formalized. A main theme of this paper is that we can indeed formalize this concept. More specifically, in the remainder of this section we identify a class $\mathcal{U}(k)$ of sub-algebras of the XPath-algebra whose queries ideally match up with the $P(k)$-partitions (and as such with the $A(k)$ indexes). The central idea behind this formalization comes from showing that the $P(k)$-partitions are identical to the partitions induced on the document by the $\mathcal{U}(k)$ algebras. These language induced partitions are defined using equivalence relations that define a pair of paths equivalent when they can not be distinguished by the queries of the sub-algebras. i.e., they are either both in the answer of a query, or they are both not. Intuitively, such pairs are always processed together during query evaluation.

In the following two sections, we define the $\mathcal{U}(k)$ sub-algebras and show how the $P(k)$-partitions are identical to partitions induced by these algebras.

2.6 The $\mathcal{U}(k)$-Algebras and Their Associated $\mathcal{U}(k)$-Partitions

In the example of Section 1.1, we considered the class of RangeQ relational queries and introduced the notion of RangeQ-partitions. In this section, we define the $\mathcal{U}(k)$ XPath-algebras, and then, in analogy with this example, define the associated $\mathcal{U}(k)$-partitions.

Definition 6. *We recursively define the* upward-k XPath algebras, $\mathcal{U}(k)$ *for each* $k \in \mathbb{N}$, *as follows. (Notice that the* $\downarrow$ *primitive can not be used in expressions of these algebras).*

1. $\mathcal{U}(0)$ *is the set of XPath-algebra expressions without occurrences of the "*$\downarrow$*" and "*$\uparrow$*" primitives.*
2. *For* $k \geq 1$, $\mathcal{U}(k)$ *is the smallest set of expressions satisfying*
   (a) if $E \in \mathcal{U}(k-1)$, *then* $E \in \mathcal{U}(k)$;
   (b) $\uparrow \in \mathcal{U}(k)$;

(c) *if* $E_1 \in \mathscr{U}(k)$ *and* $E_2 \in \mathscr{U}(k)$*, then* $E_1 \star E_2 \in \mathscr{U}(k)$*, for* $\star = \cup, \cap, -$*; and*

(d) *if* $E_1 \in \mathscr{U}(k_1)$ *and* $E_2 \in \mathscr{U}(k_2)$*, and* $k_1 + k_2 \leq k$*, then* $E_1 \diamond E_2 \in \mathscr{U}(k)$ *and* $E_1[E_2] \in \mathscr{U}(k)$*.*

Example 3. As an example of $\mathscr{U}(k)$ expressions, note that `Name` $\diamond \uparrow \diamond$ `Project` $\diamond \uparrow \diamond$ `Project` is in $\mathscr{U}(2)$ but not in $\mathscr{U}(1)$, the expression $\uparrow \diamond$ `Department` is in $\mathscr{U}(1)$ but not in $\mathscr{U}(0)$, and the combined expression `Name` $\diamond \uparrow \diamond$ `Project` $\diamond \uparrow \diamond$ `Project`[$\uparrow \diamond$ `Department`] is in $\mathscr{U}(3)$ but not in $\mathscr{U}(2)$.

The following useful proposition about the $\mathscr{U}(k)$-algebras can be shown by a simple inductive argument.

Proposition 1. *Let* D *be a document,* $k \in \mathbb{N}$*, and* $E \in \mathscr{U}(k)$*. Then* $E(D) \subseteq \mathsf{UpPaths}(D, k)$*.*

We are now ready to define the partitions associated with the $\mathscr{U}(k)$-algebras. Proposition 1 motivates us defining these partitions on $\mathsf{UpPaths}(D, k)$, just as with the $P(k)$-partitions. In the next section we will then show that it is these partitions that are identical with the $P(k)$-partitions.

Recall from the relational example, that we associated the RangeQ query language with the RangeQ-partition. This partition was defined such that each of its blocks grouped those tuples in a relation that could not be distinguished by the queries in RangeQ. We define the partitions associated with the $\mathscr{U}(k)$-algebras analogously.

Definition 7. *Let* $D = (V, Ed, r, \lambda)$ *be a document, and* $k \in \mathbb{N}$*. We say two paths* (n_1, m_1) *and* (n_2, m_2) *in* $\mathsf{UpPaths}(D, k)$ *are* $\mathscr{U}(k)$-equivalent*, denoted* $(n_1, m_1) \equiv_{\mathscr{U}(k)} (n_2, m_2)$*, if for any expression* E *in* $\mathscr{U}(k)$*, it is the case that* $(n_1, m_1) \in E(D)$ *if and only if* $(n_2, m_2) \in E(D)$*. We call the partition induced by* $\equiv_{\mathscr{U}(k)}$ *on* $\mathsf{UpPaths}(D, k)$ *the* $\mathscr{U}(k)$-partition *of* D*.*

2.7 The Coupling of P(k) and $\mathscr{U}(k)$

We establish a coupling theorem for the $P(k)$ and $\mathscr{U}(k)$ partitions, in analogy to Theorem 1, as follows.

Theorem 4. [**Coupling Theorem**] *Let* D *be a document and* $k \in \mathbb{N}$*. The* $P(k)$*-partition of* D *and the* $\mathscr{U}(k)$*-partition of* D *are the same.*

Proof. (Sketch) Compared to the proof that shows that the Btree-partition and the RangeQ-partition are the same, the proof of Theorem 4 is considerably more involved. Nevertheless, the proof follows the same strategy. First, we show that if two paths (n_1, m_1) and (n_2, m_2) in $\mathsf{UpPaths}(D, k)$ are in the same block of the $P(k)$-partition, then they are also together in a block of the $\mathscr{U}(k)$-partition. In particular, we show by induction that for each expression $E \in \mathscr{U}(k)$, it is the case that $(n_1, m_1) \in E(D)$ if and only if $(n_2, m_2) \in E(D)$. The proof of this fact is given in the Appendix. Second, we show that if (n_1, m_1) and (n_2, m_2) are in two different blocks of the $P(k)$-partition, then they are also in two different blocks of the $\mathcal{U}(k)$-partition. This is shown by constructing an expression $\texttt{label} \in \mathcal{U}(k)$ such that $(n_1, m_1) \in \texttt{label}(D)$, but $(n_2, m_2) \notin \texttt{label}(D)$. The expression `label` is of independent interest since it can be shown that it uniquely identifies (i.e., labels) the block of the $\mathcal{U}(k)$-partition of which (n_1, m_1) is a member. More precisely, $\texttt{label}(D)$ consists of exactly those paths in $\mathsf{UpPaths}(D, k)$ that can not be distinguished from (n_1, m_1) by the $\mathcal{U}(k)$-algebra. Section 4 is devoted to the existence and the construction of `label`.

As an immediate consequence, each $\mathcal{U}(k)$ query evaluated on a document D is equal to the union of a family of blocks of the $P(k)$-partition of D.

Theorem 5. [Block-Union Theorem] *Let D be a document, $k \in \mathbb{N}$, and $Q \in \mathcal{U}(k)$. Then there exists a class $\mathcal{B}_Q$ of partition blocks of the $P(k)$-partition of D such that $Q(D) = \bigcup_{B \in \mathcal{B}_Q} B$.*

In analogy with Theorem 2, the Block-Union Theorem provides insight into the processing of general XPath-algebra queries, as we see next.

3 XPath Query Evaluation with $P(k)$-Partitions

The results of Section 2 speak to answering $\mathcal{U}(k)$ queries directly using the $P(k)$-partition structure. In this section we consider the evaluation of general XPath algebra expressions and show how the results of Section 2 concerning the coupling between the $\mathcal{U}(k)$ and $P(k)$-partitions can be utilized in this case. Given an XPath expression and a $P(k)$-partition, the main idea is to identify its $\mathcal{U}(k)$ sub-expressions or those that are easily converted to $\mathcal{U}(k)$ expressions using rewrite rules. For each such expression, we are then guaranteed by the Block-Union Theorem that its value is the union of an appropriate set of blocks of the $P(k)$-partition. If we then have a method to quickly identify and return partition blocks, we will have an efficient way of evaluating these expressions. We return to this issue in the next section. In this section, we focus on the development of general techniques for using $P(k)$-partitions in the evaluation of arbitrary XPath algebra expressions.

3.1 Evaluating Upward Expressions

If our given XPath expression is in fact a member of $\mathcal{U}(k)$ then no decomposition is necessary. However, if we consider a $\mathcal{U}(j)$ expression of the form $E = A_1 \diamond \uparrow \diamond \ldots \diamond \uparrow \diamond A_j$ where $j > k$, then such a query is not directly supported by the $P(k)$-partition. Nevertheless, we can decompose it into sub-expressions that are in $\mathcal{U}(k)$. For example, consider the $P(2)$-partition available and the expression $E_1 = A_1 \diamond \uparrow A_2 \diamond \uparrow \diamond A_3 \diamond \uparrow \diamond A_4$ in $\mathcal{U}(4)$, then E_1 contains sub-expressions $F_1 = A_1 \diamond \uparrow \diamond A_2 \uparrow \diamond A_3$, and $F_2 = A_3 \diamond \uparrow \diamond A_4$ which are both in $\mathcal{U}(2)$. As such, they can be directly evaluated using the $P(2)$-partition as $E_1(D) = F_1(D) \bowtie F_2(D)$.

3.2 Evaluating Downward Expressions

In practice, most XPath expressions use navigation just along the parent-child ($\downarrow$) axis. Consider the XPath sub-algebra $\mathscr{D}$ which is defined as the set of all XPath expressions in which the $\uparrow$ primitive does not appear (and the $\mathscr{D}(k)$ algebras defined analogously to the $\mathscr{U}(k)$ algebras). For such queries, we cannot directly utilize the Block-Union Theorem. However, we can convert downward navigation into upward navigation by using a technique which we will refer to as "inverting expressions." We will illustrate this technique on downward expressions with and without predicate operations. For this discussion, we consider downward expressions to be in the $\mathscr{D}(k)$-algebra which is defined in complete analogy with $\mathscr{U}(k)$, except that the $\downarrow$ primitive is permitted, but not the $\uparrow$ primitive.

Downward Expressions without Predicates. Downward expressions without predicates can be "inverted" into expressions in corresponding upward expressions without predicates using the rewrite rules shown in Table 2.

So, given a downward expression $E \in \mathscr{D}(k)$ without predicates, we can rewrite E into E^{-1} which is in $\mathscr{U}(k)$ and also has no predicates. We can then obtain $E(D)$ by first computing $E^{-1}(D)$ and then considering its inverted result. Now since E^{-1} is an expression in $\mathscr{U}(k)$, we can directly apply the evaluation techniques for $\mathscr{U}(k)$ expressions discussed above.

Table 2. Inversion Rewrite Rules for $\mathscr{D}$

$E \rightarrow E^{-1}$
$\epsilon \rightarrow \epsilon$
$\emptyset \rightarrow \emptyset$
$\downarrow \rightarrow \uparrow$
$\hat{\lambda} \rightarrow \hat{\lambda}$
$E_1 \cup E_2 \rightarrow E_1^{-1} \cup E_2^{-1}$
$E_1 \cap E_2 \rightarrow E_1^{-1} \cap E_2^{-1}$
$E_1 - E_2 \rightarrow E_1^{-1} - E_2^{-1}$
$E_1 \diamond E_2 \rightarrow E_2^{-1} \diamond E_1^{-1}$.

Downward Expressions with Predicates. Now consider the evaluation of downward algebra expressions wherein predicate operations occur. A simple example is the expression $E_2 = \downarrow[\downarrow]$. Applied to a document, E_2 evaluates to the document's parent-child pairs for children that have at least one child themselves. As above, to evaluate E_2 on a document D, we could consider the concept of inverting E_2 into an expression $E_2^{-1} \in \mathscr{U}(2)$ such that $E_2(D) = (E_2^{-1}(D))^{-1}$. This approach does not work here because the inversion rules in Table 2 do not extend to include the predicate operation. In fact, we can construct a document D_2 such that for *each* expression $F \in \mathscr{U}(2)$, $E_2(D_2) \neq F(D)^{-1}$.

Clearly E_2 is equivalent to the XPath-algebra expression $\downarrow \diamond \downarrow \diamond \uparrow$.[5] Notice that this expression is neither a downward nor an upward expression. However its sub-expression $G_1 = \downarrow \diamond \downarrow$ is in $\mathscr{D}(2)$ and its sub-expression $G_2 = \uparrow$

[5] Incidentally, it can be shown that each expression in the $\mathscr{D}(k)$ algebra can be converted into an alternating composition of $\mathscr{D}(k)$ and $\mathscr{U}(k)$ expressions all of which do **not** use predicates.

is in $\mathscr{U}(1)$. Using the inversion technique described in Section 3.2 applied to G_1, the evaluation of $E_2(D)$ can be accomplished by computing the relation $(G_1^{-1}(D))^{-1} \bowtie G_2(D)$, and, as indicated in this section, the evaluations of $G_2(D) = \uparrow (D)$ and $G_1^{-1}(D) = \uparrow \diamond \uparrow (D)$ can be done by utilizing the Block-Union Theorem for the $P(2)$ and $P(1)$-partitions respectively.

Given that the selectivity of a longer path is no larger than that of short sub-paths of the path, evaluating G_1 reduces the search space to the minimum that can be obtained on such a chain expression. Starting from any given node, upward navigation in an XML data tree, unlike downward navigation, has one and only one route to follow, which is to reach its parent. Therefore, it is reasonable to claim that the result of $G_1^{-1}(D)$ is substantially smaller than that of $G_2(D)$, and the $\bowtie$ operation can be further optimized by $G_1^{-1}(D)$ followed by an upward navigation.

We will now consider a slightly more complicated downward expression $E_3 \in \mathscr{D}(3)$ which retrieves information about leaders of projects that have a sub-project: $E_3 = \texttt{Department} \diamond \downarrow \diamond \texttt{Project}[\downarrow \diamond \texttt{Project}] \diamond \downarrow \diamond \texttt{Lead}$. E_3 can be represented as an expression pattern tree, as illustrated in Figure 3(a). The shaded node can be interpreted as the "answer" of E_3.

Assume that the $P(2)$-partition is available. Then, as shown in Figure 3(b), there are two natural chains of length 2 present in the pattern tree of E_3: G_1 and G_2. There are also natural chains of length 1 as shown in Figure 3(c): G_3, G_4, and G_5.

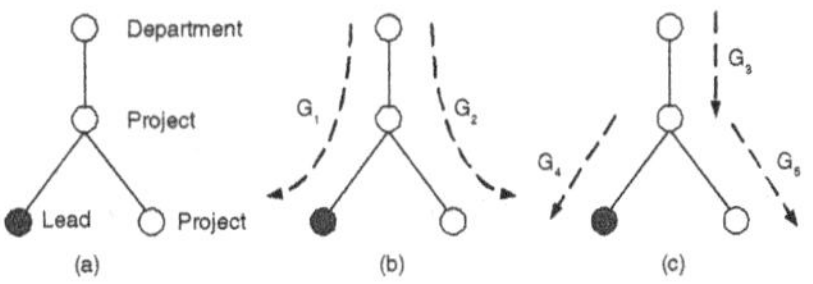

Fig. 3. Chain pattern tree for E_3

Using G_1, G_2, and G_4, the expression E_3 is equivalent to the expression H_1 defined as follows: $H_1 = ((G_1 \diamond \uparrow) \cap (G_2 \diamond \uparrow)) \diamond G_4$, and therefore, for a document D, $E_3(D)$ can be computed as follows:

$$E_3(D) = \begin{pmatrix} ((G_1^{-1}(D))^{-1} \bowtie \uparrow (D)) \\ \cap \\ ((G_2^{-1}(D))^{-1} \bowtie \uparrow (D)) \end{pmatrix} \bowtie (G_4^{-1}(D))^{-1}.$$

All sub-expressions in this transformed expression of E_3 are in $\mathscr{U}(2)$, and hence, as already discussed, can be evaluated using the Block-Union Theorem for $P(2)$.

Now assume that only the $P(1)$-partition is available. In this case, the longest path expressions that can take advantage of the partitions are those of length at most 1. Such expressions are G_3, G_4 and G_5. Using these sub-expressions, E_3 is equivalent with the expression H_2 defined as follows:

$$H_2 = (((G_3 \diamond G_4) \diamond \uparrow) \cap ((G_3 \diamond G_5) \diamond \uparrow)) \diamond G_4.$$

We have just observed how the Block-Union Theorem assists in the evaluation of XPath expressions. However, if we want to make efficient utilization of these ideas, we will need techniques for quickly identifying the $P(k)$-partition blocks associated with a query. We turn to this issue in the following section.

4 Labeling $P(k)$-Partition Blocks

In Section 2 we investigated the *semantic* relationship between $\mathscr{U}(k)$-equivalence and the $P(k)$-partition. There is also an alternative *syntactic* characterization of this relationship which is critical in identifying the $P(k)$-partition blocks used in evaluating a query. In particular, we have that evaluation of a $\mathscr{U}(k)$ query on a document D can be done by forming a union of partition block labeling expressions applied to D, similarly to Theorem 3 for the range queries.

Theorem 6. **[Label-Union Theorem]** *Let D be a document and $k \in \mathbb{N}$. Then for each query $Q \in \mathscr{U}(k)$, a set of labeling queries $\mathcal{L}_Q \subseteq \mathscr{U}(k)$ can be constructed such that $Q(D) = \bigcup_{\mathtt{label} \in \mathcal{L}_Q} \mathtt{label}(D)$.*

The Label-Union Theorem is a crucial syntactic link between $P(k)$-partitions and the semantics of $\mathscr{U}(k)$ expressions, and is an immediate corollary of Theorem 5 and the following result.

Proposition 2. *Let D be a document and $k \in \mathbb{N}$. For each block B of the $P(k)$-partition of D, an expression $\mathtt{label}_B \in \mathscr{U}(k)$ can be constructed such that for each pair $(n, m) \in \mathsf{UpPaths}(D, k)$ it is the case that $(n, m) \in B$ if and only if $(n, m) \in \mathtt{label}_B(D)$.*

We now proceed with the proof of Proposition 2. First, we define in two steps the labeling expressions for partition blocks. Then, we make precise the relationship of these expressions to the partition blocks.

Step 1: Ancestor Path Expressions.

Definition 8. *Let $D = (V, Ed, r, \lambda)$ be a document, $k \in \mathbb{N}$, and $n \in V$. Let the* k-ancestor label path *of n be the list of labels $L_0, \dots, L_\ell$ of the nodes on the path from n up towards the root node r, of length $\ell = \min\{k, \mathsf{length}(n, r)\}$. For $i \leqslant k$, the ith* k-ancestor label expression *of n is the $\mathscr{U}(k)$ expression $\mathrm{L}_{k,n,i}$ defined in Figure 4.*[6]

$$\mathrm{L}_{k,n,i} = \begin{cases} L_0 \diamond \uparrow \diamond L_1 \diamond \cdots \diamond \uparrow \diamond L_i [\uparrow \diamond L_{i+1} \diamond \cdots \diamond \uparrow \diamond L_\ell] & \text{if } i < \ell \\ L_0 \diamond \uparrow \diamond L_1 \diamond \cdots \diamond \uparrow \diamond L_\ell \diamond \uparrow^{i-\ell} & \text{if } i \geqslant \ell \end{cases}$$

Fig. 4. The ith k-ancestor label expression of node n having k-ancestor label path $L_0, \dots, L_\ell$

We observe that all members of a $P(k)$ partition block share a k-ancestor label expression. Namely, for a block B, all elements share the expression $\mathrm{L}_{k,n,\mathsf{length}(n,m)}$, where (n, m) is any member of block B. This observation follows directly from the definition of $P(k)$-equivalence and Definition 8.

[6] Where $\uparrow^0 = \varepsilon$ and for $i > 0$, $\uparrow^i = \underbrace{\uparrow \diamond \cdots \diamond \uparrow}_{i \text{ times}}$.

Example 4. Consider the $P(1)$-partition of the small document in Figure 5, wherein each node has label A:

$$\{[(n_a, n_a)], [(n_b, n_b), (n_c, n_c)], \\ [(n_c, n_b), (n_b, n_a)]\}.$$

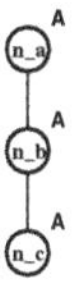

Fig. 5. Three-node document

As noted above, we can associate with each block in this partition an $\mathtt{L}_{1,n,\mathsf{length}(n,m)}$ expression, for any element (n, m) in the block, as in Figure 6.

Note, however, that ancestor label expressions do *not* necessarily uniquely identify particular $P(k)$ blocks.

Partition Block	Expression
$[(n_a, n_a)]$	$\mathtt{L}_{1,n_a,0} = \mathtt{A}$
$[(n_b, n_b), (n_c, n_c)]$	$\mathtt{L}_{1,n_b,0} = \mathtt{A}[\uparrow \diamond \mathtt{A}]$
$[(n_c, n_b), (n_b, n_a)]$	$\mathtt{L}_{1,n_b,1} = \mathtt{A} \diamond \uparrow \diamond \mathtt{A}$

Fig. 6. Ancestor label expressions

Example 5. Continuing Example 4, we note that expression $\mathtt{L}_{1,n_a,0} = \mathtt{A}$ for block $[(n_a, n_a)]$ evaluates on the document D as $\mathtt{A}(D) = \{(n_a, n_a), (n_b, n_b), (n_c, n_c)\}$, and hence does not uniquely identify its block. This is due to the fact that $\mathtt{L}_{1,n_a,0}$ is not selective enough. In particular, all blocks, with 1-ancestor label expressions having as a *prefix* expression $\mathtt{L}_{1,n_a,0}$, will also appear in the evaluation of $\mathtt{L}_{1,n_a,0}$. For example, the 1-ancestor labeling expression $\mathtt{A}[\uparrow \diamond \mathtt{A}]$ for block $[(n_b, n_b), (n_c, n_c)]$ has as a prefix the 1-ancestor labeling expression A for block $[(n_a, n_a)]$, and therefore both blocks appear in the evaluation of A. We pursue a remedy for this problem in the next step.

Step 2: Partition Labeling Expressions. To tighten up ancestor label expressions, we need two tools. To compare these expressions, we introduce the following notion of expression prefixes.

Definition 9. *Let D be a document, $i, k \in \mathbb{N}$, $i \leqslant k$, and m and n be nodes in D. For i^{th} k-ancestor label expressions $\mathtt{L}_{k,m,i}$ and $\mathtt{L}_{k,n,i}$, we denote by $\mathtt{L}_{k,m,i} \prec \mathtt{L}_{k,n,i}$ that the k-ancestor label path of node m is a* prefix *of the k-ancestor label path of node n.*

Example 6. In Example 5, we observed that $\mathtt{L}_{1,n_a,0} \prec \mathtt{L}_{1,n_b,0}$.

Relationship to Partition Blocks. To precisely single out blocks of a $P(k)$-partition, we introduce the following class of expressions derived from the $\mathtt{L}_{k,n,i}$ expressions above. The trick is to eliminate all spurious node pairs introduced from blocks with prefixing ancestor label expressions.

Definition 10. *Let $D = (V, Ed, r, \lambda)$ be a document and let $k \in \mathbb{N}$. Then the* k-partition labeling expression *for (n, m), with $(n, m) \in \mathsf{UpPaths}(D, k)$, is the $\mathscr{U}(k)$ expression $\mathtt{label}_{k,(n,m)} = \mathtt{L}_{k,n,l} - \bigcup_{n' \in V \ \& \ \mathtt{L}_{k,n,l} \prec \mathtt{L}_{k,n',l}} \mathtt{L}_{k,n',l}$, where $l = \mathsf{length}(n, m)$.*

Example 7. Since $\mathtt{L}_{1,n_a,0} \prec \mathtt{L}_{1,n_b,0}$, as we observed in Example 6, we have that $\mathtt{label}_{1,(n_a,n_a)} = \mathtt{L}_{1,n_a,0} - \mathtt{L}_{1,n_b,0} = \mathtt{A} - \mathtt{A}[\uparrow \diamond \mathtt{A}]$, and clearly this expression evaluated on document D of Figure 5 gives us precisely the $P(1)$-partition block for pair (n_a, n_a), namely $\mathtt{label}_{1,(n_a,n_a)}(D) = [(n_a, n_a)]$, as desired.

By construction of partition labeling expressions, it is easy to see that for a given block B of a $P(k)$-partition of document D, each $(n, m) \in B$ has the same label. Furthermore, by an examination of the definition of $\mathtt{label}_{k,(n,m)}$, it is straightforward to show that it is indeed the case that $(n, m) \in \mathtt{label}_{k,(n,m)}(D)$. In other words, we have that for each block B, an expression $\mathtt{label}_B \in \mathscr{U}(k)$ can be constructed such that $\mathtt{label}_B(D) = B$, completing the proof of Proposition 2. These are precisely the labeling expressions of Theorem 6.

5 Towards Indexes: *A*(*k*)-Based, or *P*(*k*)-Based?

In Section 3, we argued that many XPath queries can be evaluated by (1) discovering appropriate blocks of $P(k)$-partitions and (2) assembling these blocks, typically through unions and joins, into the final answer. Step (1) was accomplished through decomposition and inversion techniques. Relative to a $P(k)$-partition, these techniques yield expressions in $\mathscr{D}(k)$ and $\mathscr{U}(k)$ without predicate operations. Through the Label-Union Theorem developed in Section 4, we know that these expressions can be associated with label expressions, which are syntactic objects that identify the relevant blocks. Thus, to develop an index structure to support these evaluations, we need a data structure that organizes these label expressions and their associated partition blocks in a way that allows fast look up. Given the simplicity of the labeling expressions, this is entirely feasible. In fact, we are currently implementing such a index structure, and plan to report on its performance. One of the potential drawbacks of such an index structure is that it can be large: for a given k, its size is $O(k|V|)$ where V is the set of nodes of the document. However, we believe that in practice, storing such indexes will only be necessary for small k values, and as such their size is nearly linear in the size of the document.

Of course, it is also possible to develop indexes that are based on the $A(k)$-partitions. In fact, the $A(k)$-index introduced by Kaushik et al. [10] is an example of this. This index has several very desirable properties: (1) its size is $O(|V|)$ and (2) for expressions in $\mathscr{U}(k)$ without predicates wherein exactly k "$\uparrow$" primitives occur, simple navigations through the index yield their results. However, it has also some significant limitations. For example, consider an expression without predicates in $\mathscr{U}(j)$, $j > k$, that utilizes j "$\uparrow$" primitives. Such an expression can be written in the form $E_1 \diamond E_2$ where $E_1 \in \mathscr{U}(k)$ and $E_2 \in \mathscr{U}(j-k)$. Now the $A(k)$-index can determine the set of nodes that are the result of evaluating E_1 on the document. However now, starting from these nodes, E_2 is to be evaluated, and this can only be done by accessing and navigating the original document tree. (Notice that an index based on the $P(k)$-partitions does not suffer from this problem because it never requires extra navigation in the document.) A very similar problem occurs with expressions that have predicates. Consider an expression in $\mathscr{U}(j)$ of the form $E_1[E_2]$, where $E_1 \in \mathscr{U}(k)$ and $E_2 \in \mathscr{U}(j-k)$. Again, the $A(k)$-index can support E_1 well and retrieve the set of nodes that are the result of its evaluation. But again, to process the predicate $[E_2]$, it is necessary to navigate the original document. (Notice, again, that the $P(k)$-based indexes do not suffer from this problem.)

From this discussion, we conclude that for many reasons, $P(k)$-based indexes are to be preferred over $A(k)$-based indexes, especially when only small k's are sufficient.

6 Future Directions

In this paper, we take a fresh step towards establishing connections between the theoretical study of query languages and engineering research on the design and implementation of XML database systems. These connections hinge on a new methodology for coupling *index*-induced partitions and *language*-induced partitions of an XML document. To take full advantage of the $P(k)$-partitions introduced here and their block labeling expressions, we next need a data structure that is capable of locating all partition blocks based on label look-up, and in which the partition blocks that participate in the evaluation of a query are stored close to each other and can be located with a minimum number of label look-ups. Currently, we are focusing efforts towards the development of a data structure which satisfies these requirements.

References

[1] Al-Khalifa, S., et al.: Structural joins: A primitive for efficient XML query pattern matching. In: ICDE (2002)

[2] Bruno, N., et al.: Holistic twig joins: optimal XML pattern matching. In: SIGMOD (2002)

[3] Clark, J., DeRose, S. (eds.): XML path language (XPath) version 1.0. `http://www.w3.org/TR/XPATH`

[4] Comer, D.: The Ubiquitous B-Tree. ACM Comput. Surv. 11(2), 121–137 (1979)

[5] Goldman, R., Widom, J.: Dataguides: Enabling query formulation and optimization in semistructured databases. In: VLDB, pp. 436–445 (1997)

[6] Gottlob, G., Koch, C., Pichler, R.: Efficient Algorithms for Processing XPath Queries. ACM Trans. Database Syst. 30(2), 444–491 (2005)

[7] Gyssens, M., et al.: Structural Characterizations of the Semantics of XPath as Navigation Tool on a Document. In: ACM PODS, pp. 318–327. ACM Press, New York (2006)

[8] He, H., Yang, J.: Multiresolution indexing of XML for frequent queries. In: IEEE ICDE, IEEE Computer Society Press, Los Alamitos (2004)

[9] Kaushik, R., et al.: Covering indexes for branching path queries. In: SIGMOD (2002)

[10] Kaushik, R., et al.: Exploiting local similarity for efficient indexing of paths in graph structured data. In: IEEE ICDE, IEEE Computer Society Press, Los Alamitos (2002)

[11] Kaushik, R., et al.: On the integration of structure indexes and inverted lists. In: ACM SIGMOD, ACM Press, New York (2004)
[12] Koch, C.: Processing queries on tree-structured data efficiently. In: ACM PODS, pp. 213–224. ACM Press, New York (2006)
[13] Milo, T., Suciu, D.: Index structures for path expressions. In: Beeri, C., Bruneman, P. (eds.) ICDT 1999. LNCS, vol. 1540, pp. 277–295. Springer, Heidelberg (1998)
[14] Moro, M.M., et al.: Tree-pattern queries on a lightweight XML processor. In: VLDB (2005)
[15] Qun, C., Lim, A., Ong, K.W.: D(k)-index: An adaptive structural summary for graph-structured data. In: SIGMOD (2003)
[16] Ramanan, P.: Covering indexes for XML queries: Bisimulation - simulation = negation. In: Aberer, K., Koubarakis, M., Kalogeraki, V. (eds.) Databases, Information Systems, and Peer-to-Peer Computing. LNCS, vol. 2944, Springer, Heidelberg (2004)
[17] Runapongsa, K., Patel, J.M., Bordawekar, R., Padmanabhan, S.: XIST: An XML index selection tool. In: Bellahsène, Z., Milo, T., Rys, M., Suciu, D., Unland, R. (eds.) XSym 2004. LNCS, vol. 3186, pp. 219–234. Springer, Heidelberg (2004)
[18] Yi, K., He, H., Stanoi, I., Yang, J.: Incremental maintenence of XML structural indexes. In: ACM SIGMOD, pp. 491–502. ACM Press, New York (2004)
[19] Zhang, C., et al.: On supporting containment queries in relational database management systems. In: SIGMOD (2001)

Appendix

Structural Characterizations of $\mathscr{U}(k)$ Indistinguishability

We prove the following fact needed in establishing Theorem 4: on a fixed document, for each $k \geqslant 0$ it is the case that $P(k)$-equivalence (of node pairs) implies indistinguishability in the $\mathscr{U}(k)$ algebra (of node pairs).

Lemma A. *Let $D = (V, Ed, r, \lambda)$ be a document, $k \in \mathbb{N}$, and n_1, m_1, $n_2 \in V$ with m_1 is an ancestor of n_1 and $\mathsf{length}(n_1, m_1) \leq k$. If $n_1 \equiv_{A(k)} n_2$, then there exists $m_2 \in V$ such that m_2 is an ancestor of n_2 and $(n_1, m_1) \equiv_{P(\mathsf{length}(n_1,m_1))} (n_2, m_2)$.*[7] *Furthermore, $m_1 \equiv_{A(k-\mathsf{length}(n_1,m_1))} m_2$.*

Proof. By induction on k. For the base case, $k = 0$, clearly $m_1 = n_1$ and $\lambda(n_1) = \lambda(n_2)$. The statement holds for $m_2 = n_2$.

For $k \geq 1$, we can assume that the statement holds for $k - 1$. If $n_1 \equiv_{A(k)} n_2$, then either (1) both n_1 and n_2 have no parents, or (2) they both have parents p_1 and p_2, respectively, such that $p_1 \equiv_{A(k-1)} p_2$ (by definition of $A(k)$ equivalence). In case (1), clearly $m_1 = n_1$ and the statement holds for $m_2 = n_2$. In case (2), $\mathsf{length}(p_1, m_1) \leq k - 1$, and by the definition of $A(k)$ equivalence, $p_1 \equiv_{A(k-1)} p_2$. By the induction hypothesis, there exists an ancestor m_2 of p_2 such that $(p_1, m_1) \equiv_{P(\mathsf{length}(p_1,m_2))} (p_2, m_2)$ and $m_1 \equiv_{A(k-1-\mathsf{length}(p_1,m_1))} m_2$. It readily follows that $(n_1, m_1) \equiv_{P(\mathsf{length}(n_1,m_1))} (n_2, m_2)$ and $m_1 \equiv_{A(k-\mathsf{length}(n_1,m_1))} m_2$.

---

[7] And even stronger, $(n_1, m_1) \equiv_{P(k)} (n_2, m_2)$.

Proposition A. *Let $D = (V, Ed, r, \lambda)$ be a document, $k \in \mathbb{N}$, $E \in \mathscr{U}(k)$, and $n_1, m_1, n_2, m_2 \in V$ such that m_1 is an ancestor of n_1 and m_2 is an ancestor of n_2, and $(n_1, m_1) \equiv_{P(k)} (n_2, m_2)$. If $(n_1, m_1) \in E(D)$, then $(n_2, m_2) \in E(D)$, and vice versa.*

Proof. First observe that it follows from $E \in \mathscr{U}(k)$ and $(n_1, m_1) \in E(D)$ that $\mathsf{length}(n_1, m_1) \leq k$, by Proposition 1.

The proof is by induction on k. The base case, $k = 0$, follows straightforwardly from the definition of $P(0)$-equivalence and a simple structural induction on expressions in $\mathscr{U}(0)$. Now assume that $k \geq 1$, and that the statement holds for $0, 1, 2, \ldots, k-1$. The proof goes by structural induction on expressions in $\mathscr{U}(k)$. Thus, let $E \in \mathscr{U}(k)$.

- $E \in \mathscr{U}(k-1)$. The statement holds by the induction hypothesis.
- $E = \uparrow$. If $(n_1, m_1) \in \uparrow (D)$, then m_1 is the parent of n_1. Since $(n_1, m_1) \equiv_{P(k)} (n_2, m_2)$, it follows in particular that m_2 is the parent of n_2. We conclude that $(n_2, m_2) \in \uparrow (D)$.
- $E = E_1 \cup E_2$, for E_1 and $E_2 \in \mathscr{U}(k)$. Suppose $(n_1, m_1) \in E(D)$. Then $(n_1, m_1) \in E_1(D)$ or $(n_1, m_1) \in E_2(D)$. Without loss of generality, assume $(n_1, m_1) \in E_1(D)$. Then by structural induction, $(n_2, m_2) \in E_1(D)$, and we conclude $(n_2, m_2) \in E(D)$.
- $E = E_1 \cap E_2$ or $E = E_1 - E_2$, for E_1 and $E_2 \in \mathscr{U}(k)$. Similar to the previous case.
- $E = E_1 \diamond E_2$, for $E_1 \in \mathscr{U}(k_1)$ and $E_2 \in \mathscr{U}(k_2)$, such that $k_1 + k_2 \leq k$. Suppose $(n_1, m_1) \in E(D)$. Then there is a node $w_1 \in V$ such that $(n_1, w_1) \in E_1(D)$ and $(w_1, m_1) \in E_2(D)$. By Lemma 1, $\mathsf{length}(n_1, w_1) \leq k_1$ and $\mathsf{length}(w_1, m_1) \leq k_2$. By Lemma A, there is a node $w_2 \in V$ such that $(n_1, w_1) \equiv_{P(\mathsf{length}(n_1, w_1))} (n_2, w_2)$, and $w_1 \equiv_{A(k - \mathsf{length}(n_1, w_1))} w_2$. Since, $k_2 \leq k - \mathsf{length}(n_1, w_1)$, by Lemma A, a node $m' \in V$ exists with $(w_1, m_1) \equiv_{P(\mathsf{length}(w_1, m_1))} (w_2, m')$.

  By $(n_1, w_1) \equiv_{P(\mathsf{length}(n_1, w_1))} (n_2, w_2)$, and $(w_1, m_1) \equiv_{P(\mathsf{length}(w_1, m_1))} (w_2, m')$, it is (definitions of $\equiv_{P(k_1)}$ and $\equiv_{P(k_2)}$) that $\mathsf{length}(n_2, w_2) = \mathsf{length}(n_1, w_1)$ and $\mathsf{length}(w_2, m') = \mathsf{length}(w_1, m_1)$.

  Consequently, $\mathsf{length}(n_2, m') = \mathsf{length}(n_1, m_1)$, and since m' is the unique ancestor at this length, we conclude that $m' = m_2$. Thus $(w_1, m_1) \equiv_{P(k_2)} (w_2, m_2)$. By the induction hypothesis, we can conclude that $(n_2, w_2) \in E_1(D)$ and $(w_2, m) \in E_2(D)$ and thus $(n_2, m_2) \in E(D)$.
- $E = E_1[E_2]$, for $E_1 \in \mathscr{U}(k_1)$ and $E_2 \in \mathscr{U}(k_2)$, such that $k_1 + k_2 \leq k$. Similar to the previous case.

Conjunctive Query Containment over Trees*

Henrik Björklund, Wim Martens, and Thomas Schwentick

University of Dortmund

Abstract. The complexity of containment and satisfiability of conjunctive queries over finite, unranked, labeled trees is studied with respect to the axes *Child*, *NextSibling*, their transitive and reflexive closures, and *Following*. For the containment problem a trichotomy is presented, classifying the problems as in PTIME, coNP-complete, or Π_2^P-complete. For the satisfiability problem most problems are classified as either in PTIME or NP-complete.

1 Introduction

Conjunctive query containment for relational databases is one of the most thoroughly investigated problems in database theory. It is known to be essentially equivalent to conjunctive query evaluation and to Constraint Satisfaction in AI [9]. From the database point of view, the importance of conjunctive queries on relational structures lies in the fact that they correspond to the most widely used queries in practice. More precisely, they correspond to the select-from-where queries from SQL that only use "and" as a Boolean connective.

Recently, conjunctive queries over trees also attracted quite some attention [7]. It is somewhat surprising that they have not been studied earlier, as they arise very naturally in various settings, such as data extraction and integration, computational linguistics, and dominance constraints [7]. Moreover, unary and binary conjunctive queries over trees form a very natural fragment of XPath 2.0 [1], and therefore also of XQuery [2]. Indeed, unary and binary conjunctive queries over trees correspond to Core XPath without *negation* and *union* (see, e.g., [6]), but with *path intersection*, as introduced in XPath 2.0 (see, e.g., [8,13]). Gottlob et al. already showed that unary conjunctive queries over trees can be translated to XPath 1.0 queries, albeit with an exponential blow-up [7], and the above-mentioned Core XPath queries with path intersection can be translated into conjunctive queries by identifying variables. Hence, our complexity upper bounds transfer to positive Core XPath expressions with path intersection, but without union.

In this paper, we consider conjunctive query containment on trees. We mainly focus on Boolean containment of conjunctive queries, i.e., given two conjunctive queries P and Q, is $L(P) \subseteq L(Q)$, where $L(P)$ (resp., $L(Q)$) denotes the set of trees on which P (resp., Q) has a non-empty output. Conjunctive query containment over trees is a problem that needs to be solved for conjunctive query

* This work was supported by the DFG Grant SCHW678/3-1.

M. Arenas and M.I. Schwartzbach (Eds.): DBPL 2007, LNCS 4797, pp. 66–80, 2007.

Table 1. Complexities of Conjunctive Query Containment

	Child	*Child*$^+$	*Child**	*NextSibling*	*NextSibling*$^+$	*NextSibling**	*Following*
Child	in P	Π_2^P	Π_2^P	coNP	coNP	coNP	Π_2^P
Child$^+$		coNP	coNP	Π_2^P	Π_2^P	Π_2^P	Π_2^P
Child*			coNP	Π_2^P	Π_2^P	Π_2^P	Π_2^P
NextSibling				in P	coNP	coNP	Π_2^P
NextSibling$^+$					coNP	coNP	Π_2^P
NextSibling*						coNP	Π_2^P
Following							coNP

optimization. The latter is, for instance, important for XQuery engines, but is also relevant in the other settings mentioned above. Moreover, conjunctive query *satisfiability*, which we also study and which is a simplified form of containment, needs to be solved if one wants to decide well-definedness for important XQuery fragments [14]. There is a further relevant setting in which the set of trees under consideration is restricted by a schema and the containment question is asked relative to this schema. We give a brief overview of our results.

Containment. We obtain a similar classification as Gottlob et al. [7]. The most essential differences are that the PTIME membership results for conjunctive query evaluation translate to coNP membership results for containment and that NP-completeness results for evaluation translate to Π_2^P-completeness results for containment. The former translation is easy to obtain due to a polynomial size witness property for counter examples (Lemma 8). For the latter translation, we build on some of the NP lower bound reductions by Gottlob et al. for our Π_2^P lower bound proofs. They had to be significantly adapted, however, as unlike in the relational setting, conjunctive query containment on trees cannot be reduced in a straightforward manner to conjunctive query evaluation on a canonical model. Most of our complexity results on conjunctive query containment are summarized in Table 1. From the above mentioned polynomial size witness property and the results by Gottlob et al. [7], we can also conclude that containment is in coNP for the fragments CQ(*Child*, *NextSibling*, *NextSibling**, *NextSibling*$^+$), CQ(*Child**, *Child*$^+$), and CQ(*Following*). Combined with the results from the table, this gives us a complete trichotomy of the complexity of conjunctive query containment with respect to all sets of axes we consider.

Unfortunately, as we can see from the table, conjunctive query containment on trees is quite a hard problem. We only identify two tractable fragments, that is, CQ(*NextSibling*) and CQ(*Child*). For the latter fragment, PTIME membership is already non-trivial. All other combinations of axes are at least coNP-hard.

Satisfiability. Conjunctive query satisfiability can be seen as a simplification of the containment problem. Indeed, Q is satisfiable if and only if $L(Q) \not\subseteq L(\text{false})$. Our results on satisfiability are summarized in Table 2. Interestingly, we see here that the dichotomy drawn by the evaluation and the containment problem shifts.

Table 2. Complexities of Conjunctive Query Satisfiability

	Child	*Child*$^+$	*Child**	*NextSibling*	*NextSibling*$^+$	*NextSibling**	*Following*
Child	in P	NP [8]	NP	in P	in P	in P	NP
Child$^+$		in P	in P	?	?	?	?
Child*			in P	?	?	?	?
NextSibling				in P	NP	NP	NP
NextSibling$^+$					in P	in P	in P
NextSibling*						in P	in P
Following							in P

For the satisfiability problem, we obtain significantly more tractable fragments than for the containment problem. Some cases, however, still remain NP-hard.

We note that the NP lower bound for satisfiability of CQ(*Child*, *Child*$^+$) is already obtained by Hidders [8]. We prove it in an alternative manner in Theorem 26.

Containment with respect to a schema. It turns out that the complexity of the containment problem is (presumably) much higher if it is posed relative to a given schema which restricts the set of trees under consideration. A similar effect was observed before for XPath query containment [11]. More concretely, we show that deciding whether a conjunctive query only using *Child*-axes returns a non-empty output on each tree defined by a DTD is EXPTIME-hard. In fact, the conjunctive query in our proof can even be expressed as an XPath query using wildcards, predicates, and the axes *Child* and *Descendant*, thereby obtaining that XPath containment w.r.t. a DTD is EXPTIME-complete for XPath queries using *Child*, *Descendant*, predicates, and wildcards.

Related Work. Most of the related work has already been mentioned. We note, however, that conjunctive query containment has also been investigated for object-oriented database systems [3]. In particular, it is shown that conjunctive query containment is Π_2^P-complete. The classes of conjunctive queries studied in [3] are, however, incomparable to ours.

2 Preliminaries

2.1 Trees

By Σ we always denote a fixed but infinite set of labels. For a finite set S, we denote by $|S|$ the number of elements of S. The trees we consider are rooted, ordered, finite, labeled, unranked trees, which are directed from the root downwards. That is, we consider trees with a finite number of nodes and in which nodes can have arbitrarily many children. We view a tree t as a relational structure over a finite number of unary labeling relations $a(\cdot)$, where each $a \in \Sigma$, and binary relations *Child*$(\cdot,\cdot)$ and *NextSibling*$(\cdot,\cdot)$. Here, $a(u)$ expresses that u is a node with label a, and *Child*(u, v) (respectively, *NextSibling*(u, v)) expresses that v is a child (respectively, next sibling) of u.

Notice that, in contrast to standard practice, we have an infinite set of labels from which our (finite) trees can choose. This reflects how trees occur in an XML-context: an XML tree is a finite structure, but there is no restriction on how it should be labeled (if no schema is provided).

In addition to *Child* and *NextSibling*, we use their transitive closures (denoted $Child^+$ and $NextSibling^+$) and their transitive and reflexive closures (denoted $Child^*$ and $NextSibling^*$). We also use the *Following*-relation, which is inspired by XPath [4] and defined as

$$Following(u, v) = \exists x \exists y\, Child^*(x, u) \wedge NextSibling^+(x, y) \wedge Child^*(y, v).$$

We denote the set of nodes of a tree t by Nodes(t). We define the *size of* t, denoted by $|t|$, as the number of nodes of t. We refer to the above mentioned binary relations as *axes*.

2.2 Conjunctive Queries

Let $X = \{x, y, z, \ldots\}$ be a set of variables. A *conjunctive query* (CQ) over alphabet Σ is a positive existential first-order formula without disjunction over a finite set of unary predicates $a(x)$ where each $a \in \Sigma$, and the binary predicates *Child*, $Child^+$, $Child^*$, *NextSibling*, $NextSibling^+$, $NextSibling^*$, and *Following*. In this paper, we will mainly focus on Boolean satisfaction of conjunctive queries. We will therefore consider conjunctive queries without free variables. As our conjunctive queries do not contain free variables, we sometimes omit the existential quantifiers to simplify notation. For a conjunctive query Q, we denote the set of variables appearing in Q by Var(Q). We use CQ($R_1, \ldots, R_k$) or CQ($\mathcal{R}$) (where $\mathcal{R} = \{R_1, \ldots, R_k\}$) to denote the fragment of CQs that uses only the unary alphabet predicates and the binary predicates $R_1, \ldots, R_k$. We use the terminology on valuations of a query and query graphs from Gottlob et al. [7].

Definition 1. Let Q be a conjunctive query, and t a tree. A *valuation* of Q on t is a total function θ : Var(Q) $\rightarrow$ Nodes(t). A valuation is a *satisfaction* if it satisfies the query, that is, if every atom of Q is satisfied by the assignment. A tree t *models* Q ($t \models Q$) if there is a satisfaction of Q on t. The language $L(Q)$ of Q is the set of all trees that model Q.

We say that a tree t is a *minimal model* of Q if $t \models Q$ and the number of nodes in t is minimal among all trees in $L(Q)$.

The following example illustrates a conjunctive query.

Example 2. Consider the conjunctive query $Q = Child^+(x_1, x_2) \wedge Child^+(x_2, x_4) \wedge Child^+(x_1, x_3) \wedge Child^+(x_3, x_4) \wedge a(x_1) \wedge b(x_2) \wedge c(x_3) \wedge d(x_4) \wedge e(x_5)$. A tree t models Q if t has an a-labeled node u with a d-labeled descendant v such that the path from u to v contains a b-labeled node and a c-labeled node (in arbitrary order). Moreover, t must contain an e-labeled node somewhere.

Definition 3. Let Q be a conjunctive query over Σ with variables Var(Q). The query graph Q is the directed multigraph $G_Q = (V, E)$ with edge labels and node labels such that $V = \text{Var}(Q)$, node x is labeled a if and only if $a(x)$ is an atom in Q; and E contains the labeled directed edge $x \xrightarrow{R} y$ if and only if $R(x, y)$ is an atom in Q.

We assume familiarity with standard graph-related terminology such as *reachability*, *connected components*, etc. Subgraphs of G_Q correspond to subqueries of Q. We will sometimes slightly abuse the terminology by using graph-related concepts when talking about queries. Thus "variable x is reachable from variable y in Q" means that x is reachable from y in G_Q. Similarly, "maximal connected component of Q" means a subquery corresponding to a maximal connected component of G_Q.

For ease of readability, we often represent queries (or their query graphs) graphically. For example, the rightmost picture in Figure 2 represents the query

$$\mathit{Child}(x_1, x_2) \wedge \mathit{Child}(x_2, x_3) \wedge \mathit{Child}(x_2, x_4) \wedge b(x_3) \wedge c(x_4).$$

The following decision problems for conjunctive queries are the main topic of interest for this paper.

Definition 4

- Containment: Given two conjunctive queries P and Q, is $L(P) \subseteq L(Q)$?
- Satisfiability: Given a conjunctive query Q, is $L(Q) \neq \emptyset$?

The above problems are in a sense both instances of the containment problem. That is, satisfiability for Q is testing whether $L(Q) \nsubseteq L(\text{false})$.

As mentioned above, we consider conjunctive queries without free variables. This means that we only look at whether a tree models the query or not, and not at the whole set of satisfactions. One can also consider *k-ary conjunctive queries*, i.e., CQs with k free variables, returning a k-ary relation when evaluated on a tree. For two k-ary queries P and Q, *P is contained in Q* if, for every tree t, the relation returned by P is a subset of the relation returned by Q. Using a result of Miklau and Suciu [10], this problem reduces to containment for Boolean queries for all fragments that include the *Child*-axis. For instance, consider the left query $P(x_1, x_2, x_3)$ in Figure 1. By introducing, for each free variable x_i, a new variable x_i' and adding the atoms $\mathit{Child}(x_i, x_i') \wedge X_i(x_i')$ to the query, where X_i is a new label, the query P', depicted on the right of Figure 1, is obtained. It is now easy to see that, for two queries $P(\overline{x})$ and $Q(\overline{x})$[1] with k free variables, P is contained in Q if and only if $L(P') \subseteq L(Q')$, where P' and Q' are obtained by adding the atoms $\mathit{Child}(x_i, x_i') \wedge X_i(x_i')$ to P and Q, respectively. Indeed, the proof is analogous to the one in [10]. For satisfiability, it is of course immediate that the complexities are the same for 0-ary and k-ary queries.

2.3 Basic Properties

If t and t' are trees, h is a function from t to t', and $\mathcal{R}$ is a set of binary relations, we say that h is an *$\mathcal{R}$-homomorphism* if $h(u)$ is defined for every node u in t,

[1] We can assume w.l.o.g. that the free variables are the same in P and Q.

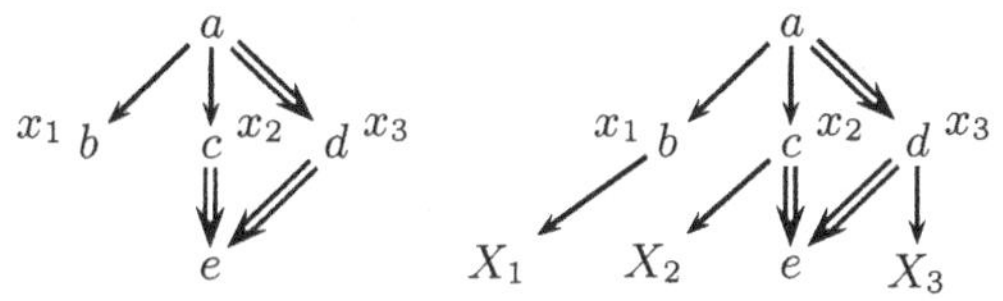

Fig. 1. How to reduce from k-ary queries to 0-ary queries

$a(u)$ in t implies $a(h(u))$ in t', for each $a \in \Sigma$, and $R(u, v)$ holds in t implies that $R(h(u), h(v))$ holds in t', for each $R \in \mathcal{R}$.

Observation 5. Let t be a tree and let $Q \in CQ(\mathcal{R})$ be a query such that $t \models Q$. If t' is a tree and there exists an $\mathcal{R}$-homomorphism $h : t \to t'$, then $t' \models Q$.

Observation 6. Conjunctive queries are monotonous, i.e., if $t \models Q$, for a tree t and a CQ Q, then $t' \models Q$ for all trees t' for which $t \subseteq t'$.

3 Containment

When we investigate whether query P is contained in query Q, i.e., $L(P) \subseteq L(Q)$, we will always assume that the graph of Q has only one maximal connected component. This is because P is contained in Q if and only if P is contained in every subquery of Q that corresponds to a maximal connected component.

3.1 PTIME Upper Bounds

Theorem 7. *Containment is in PTIME for CQ(Child) and CQ(NextSibling).*

Proof (Sketch). The proof for CQ(*NextSibling*) is straightforward: for testing whether $L(P) \subseteq L(Q)$, one can start by simplifying both queries, by applying the chase for the relation *NextSibling*(A, B) with functional dependencies $A \to B$ and $B \to A$ (i.e., *NextSibling*$(x, x_1) \wedge$ *NextSibling*(x, x_2) or *NextSibling*$(x_1, x) \wedge$ *NextSibling*(x_2, x) should not occur). Consequently, we have to test whether the chased query for Q can be embedded into the chased query for P.

The proof for CQ(*Child*) is tedious and too intricate to illustrate the main idea here. We just want to point out that the problem is not trivial. A naive algorithm would try to find an embedding of Q into P and accept iff it can be found. However, Figure 2 illustrates that not finding an embedding of Q into P does not imply that $L(P) \not\subseteq L(Q)$. □

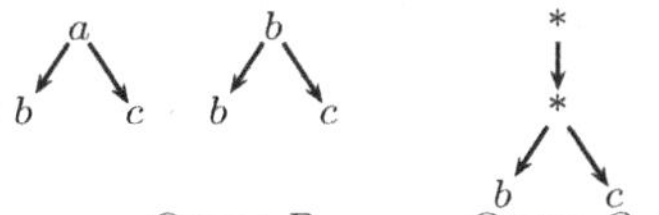

Fig. 2. Example for which $L(P) \subseteq L(Q)$ but Q cannot obviously be embedded into P. Every arrow denotes a *Child*-axis.

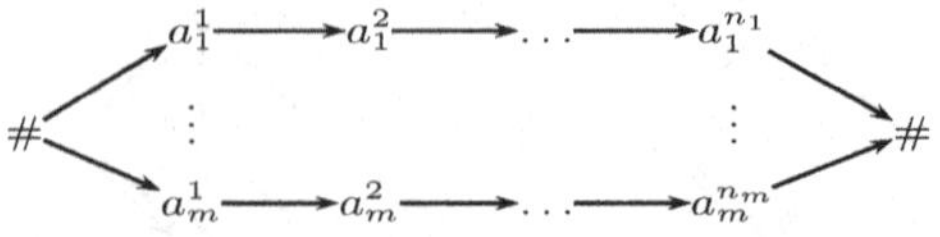

Fig. 3. Structure of query P in the proof of Theorem 10

3.2 coNP and Π_2^P Upper Bounds

We first show that if CQ P is not contained in CQ Q, then there is a polynomial size witness tree.

Lemma 8. *Let P and Q be conjunctive queries. If $L(P) \not\subseteq L(Q)$ then there exists a tree t such that $t \models P$, $t \not\models Q$, and $|t| \leq 2 \cdot |Var(P)| \cdot (|Var(Q)| + 4)$.*

The above lemma puts conjunctive query containment in Π_2^P. Indeed, for testing whether $L(P) \not\subseteq L(Q)$, the algorithm would guess a tree t_{small} of size at most $2 \cdot |\text{Var}(P)| \cdot (|\text{Var}(Q)| + 4)$, test in NP whether $t_{\text{small}} \models P$ and test in coNP whether $t_{\text{small}} \not\models Q$. As Gottlob et al. showed that conjunctive query evaluation is in PTIME for CQ(*Child*, *NextSibling*, *NextSibling**, *NextSibling*$^+$), CQ(*Child**,*Child*$^+$), and CQ(*Following*), the above algorithm gives us a coNP upper bound for containment for these fragments. We can therefore state the following theorem.

Theorem 9.

1. *Containment is in Π_2^P for CQs.*
2. *Containment is in coNP for CQ(Child*,Child$^+$), CQ(Following), and CQ(Child,NextSibling,NextSibling*,NextSibling$^+$).*

3.3 coNP Lower Bounds

For the coNP lower bounds, we will reduce from the complement of the SHORTEST COMMON SUPERSEQUENCE problem; or the SHORTEST COMMON SUPERSTRING problem, both of which are known to be NP-complete [12,5]. The SHORTEST COMMON SUPERSEQUENCE (respectively, SHORTEST COMMON SUPERSTRING) problem asks, given a set of strings S, and an integer k, whether there exists a string of length at most k which is a supersequence (respectively, superstring) of each string in S. Here, s is a supersequence of s_0 if s_0 can by obtained by deleting symbols from s, and s is a superstring of s_0 if s_0 can be obtained by deleting a prefix and a postfix of s.

Theorem 10. *Containment is coNP-hard for CQ(NextSibling$^+$), CQ(NextSibling*), CQ(Child$^+$), CQ(Child*), and CQ(Following).*

Proof. All cases can be proved by a reduction from SHORTEST COMMON SUPERSEQUENCE. Thereto, let S and k be an instance of SHORTEST COMMON SUPERSEQUENCE. We now define conjunctive queries P and Q such that $P \not\subseteq Q$ if and only if there exists a shortest common supersequence for S of length at most k. Thereto, let $S = \{s_1, \ldots, s_m\}$ where, for each $i = 1, \ldots, m$, $s_i = a_i^1 \cdots a_i^{n_i}$. Let # be a symbol not occurring in any string in S.

We first show how the proof works for *NextSibling*$^+$. The query P is defined as in Figure 3, where each arrow represents a *NextSibling*$^+$-axis and # and each a_i^j is a Σ-symbol. The query Q now essentially states that each tree must have a string of siblings with at least $k+1+2$ different nodes. Formally, we define Q as

$$NextSibling^+(x_1, x_2) \wedge \cdots \wedge NextSibling^+(x_{k+2}, x_{k+3}).$$

It is not difficult to see that $P \not\subseteq Q$ if and only if there exists a shortest common supersequence for S of length at most k. The proofs for *Child*$^+$and *Following* are completely analogous. For *Child**and *NextSibling**, we need to insert dummy #-symbols between all a_i^j labels in P, and adapt the query Q accordingly. □

The proof of the next theorem is in the same lines as the previous one, but this time we reduce from the Shortest Common Superstring problem. The essential difference is that P now does not contain the leftmost and rightmost #-labeled symbol in Figure 3, the arrows in Figure 3 now denote *NextSibling*-axes, and that all the a_j^i-labeled nodes are connected to a common parent by *Child*-axes.

Theorem 11. *Containment is coNP-hard for CQ(Child,NextSibling).*

3.4 Π_2^P Lower Bounds

The Π_2^P lower bounds in this section will all be obtained by a reduction from $\forall\exists$ positive 1-in-3 SAT, which is formally defined as follows. A set $C_1, \ldots, C_m$ of clauses is given, each of which has three Boolean variables from $\{x_1, \ldots, x_{n_x}\} \uplus \{y_1, \ldots, y_{n_y}\}$. No variable is negated. The question is whether, for every truth assignment for $\{x_1, \ldots, x_{n_x}\}$, there exists a truth assignment for $\{y_1, \ldots, y_{n_y}\}$ such that each C_i contains precisely one true variable.

The proof of the following lemma is analogous to the proof showing that positive 1-in-3 SAT is NP-complete.

Lemma 12. $\forall\exists$ *positive 1-in-3 SAT is* Π_2^P*-complete.*

Theorem 13. *Containment is* Π_2^P*-complete for CQ(Child, Child*$^+$*) and CQ(Child, Child***).*

Proof. We present a proof for CQ(*Child*, *Child*$^+$) and discuss in the end how to adapt it for CQ(*Child*, *Child**).

The proof is an adaptation of a proof by Gottlob et al., showing that the query complexity of evaluation for CQ(*Child*, *Child*$^+$) is NP-hard [7]. We reduce from $\forall\exists$ positive 1-in-3 SAT, which is Π_2^P-complete according to Lemma 12.

For the purposes of this proof, we will assume that each tree node can carry multiple labels. It can be modified to work for the standard definition of labeled trees, where each node has only one label.

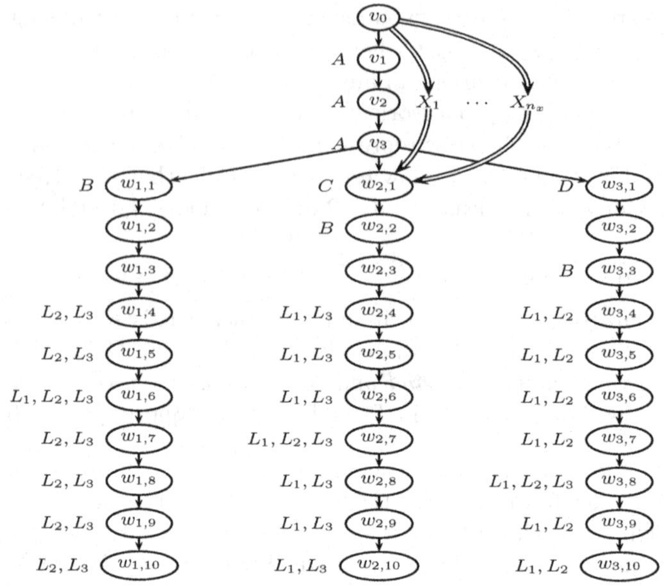

Fig. 4. Illustration of the definition of query P in the proof of Theorem 13

Let $\forall\overline{x}\exists\overline{y}C_1,\ldots,C_m$ be an instance of $\forall\exists$ positive 1-in-3 SAT, where $\overline{x} = \{x_1,\ldots,x_{n_x}\}$ and $\overline{y} = \{y_1,\ldots,y_{n_y}\}$. We may assume that no clause contains a particular literal more than once. Let Φ denote the formula

$$\forall\overline{x}\exists\overline{y}C_1,\ldots,C_m,C_{m+1},\ldots C_{m+n_x}.$$

Here, for each $i = 1,\ldots,n_x$, C_{m+i} denotes the clause (y_i', x_i, y_i''), where y_i' and y_i'' are new existentially quantified variables. It is easy to see that there is solution for the original formula if and only if there is one for Φ.

Let query P be defined as in Figure 4, where single lines represent the *Child* axis, double lines represent the *Child*$^+$ axis, and the symbols outside of nodes, as well as $X_1,\ldots X_{n_x}$, are labels.

For the query Q, we introduce variables a_i, b_i for each $i = 1,\ldots,m+n_x$ and in addition a variable $c_{k,l,i,j}$ whenever the k-th literal of C_i coincides with the l-th literal of C_j $(1 \leq j \leq m+n_x,\ i \neq j,\ 1 \leq k,l \leq 3)$.

The query Q consists of the following atoms:

- for each $i = 1,\ldots,m+n_x$, $A(a_i) \wedge B(b_i) \wedge \mathit{Child}^3(a_i,b_i)$;
- for each variable $c_{k,l,i,j}$, $L_k(c_{k,l,i,j}) \wedge \mathit{Child}^+(b_i,c_{k,l,i,j}) \wedge \mathit{Child}^{8+k+l}(a_j,c_{k,l,i,j})$; and,
- for each $i = m+1,\ldots,m+n_x$, $X_{i-m}(a_i)$.

This concludes the reduction for CQ(*Child*, *Child*$^+$). For CQ(*Child*, *Child**) we replace each pair of atoms $\mathit{Child}^+(v_0,X_i)$, $\mathit{Child}^+(X_i,w_{2,1})$ of P (for $1 \leq i \leq n_x$) with the pair $\mathit{Child}^*(v_1,X_i)$, $\mathit{Child}^*(X_i,v_3)$. In Q, we can simply replace *Child*$^+$ by *Child**. □

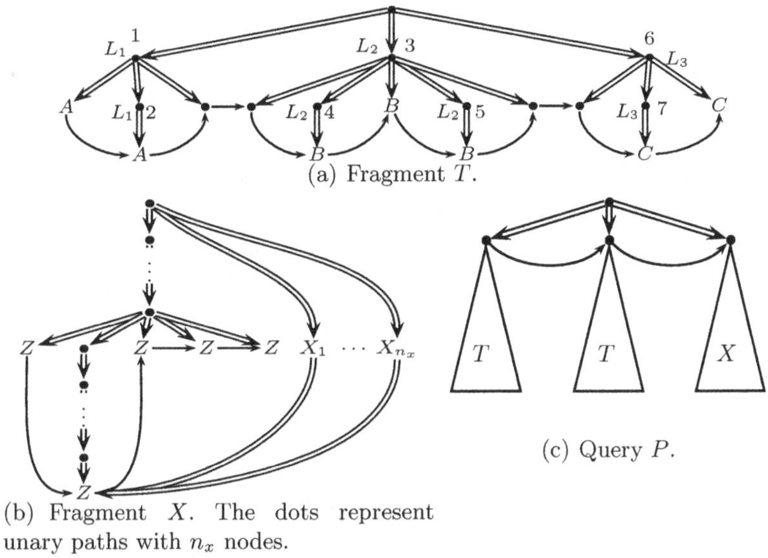

Fig. 5. Definition of query P in the proof of Theorem 15

Theorem 14. *Containment is* Π_2^P*-hard for CQ(Child, Following).*

Proof. We adapt the proof of Theorem 13 by simulating *Child*$^+$with *Child* and *Following*. To this end, we begin by equipping each of the variables u in query P defined in Figure 4 that has an outgoing *Child*$^+$-axes by two "dummy" children z_1 and z_2. These new variables are used nowhere else, and get the new label #. Now, whenever *Child*$^+(u, v)$ is used in one of the queries, we can replace it by

$$\mathit{Child}(u, z_1) \wedge \mathit{Child}(u, z_2) \wedge \mathit{Following}(z_1, v) \wedge \mathit{Following}(v, z_2).$$

It is now enough to note that all variables in the queries P and Q that have no specified label are required by the queries to have children. Thus none of them can bind to a node in one of the minimal models of the modified P query that is labeled by #. □

Theorem 15. *Containment is* Π_2^P*-hard for CQ(Child*$^+$*,Following).*

Proof (Sketch). Let $\forall\overline{x}\exists\overline{y}C_1, \ldots, C_m$ be an instance of $\forall\exists$ positive 1-in-3 SAT. Let $\overline{x} = \{x_1, \ldots, x_{n_x}\}$ and let $\overline{y} = \{y_1, \ldots, y_{n_y}\}$. We can assume that no clause contains a particular literal more than once.

We construct two queries, P and Q, over the labeling alphabet $\{A, B, C, L_1, L_2, L_3, X_1, \ldots, X_{n_x}, Z\}$ such that $P \subseteq Q$ if and only if $\forall\overline{x}\exists\overline{y}C_1, \ldots, C_m$ has a solution. The current proof builds further on a proof by Gottlob et al. that shows that the query complexity of evaluation for CQ(*Child*$^+$,*Following*) is NP-hard [7].

The construction of query P is illustrated in Figure 5. Here, every double-lined edge represents a *Child*$^+$-axis and every directed edge represents a *Following*-axis. For improved readability, we adopt the terminology of the proof by Gottlob

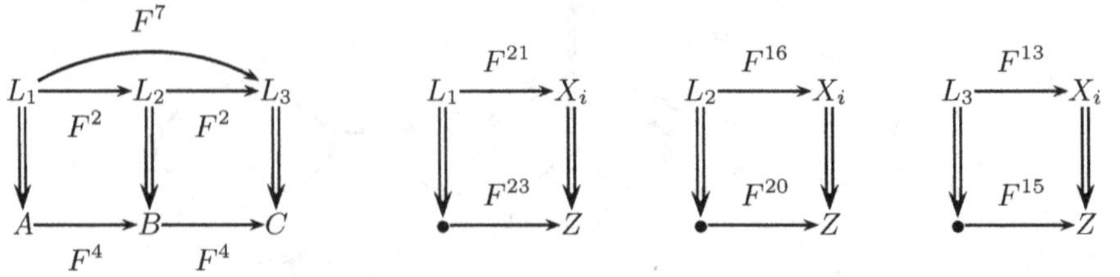

(a) The 1-in-3 gadget.

(b) The X-variable gadgets: varX$(1, i)$ (left), varX$(2, i)$ (middle), and varX$(3, i)$ (right).

Fig. 6. Gadgets for the definition of query Q in the proof of Theorem 15

et al.. That is, we will refer to the nodes labeled L_1, L_2, and L_3 in the *1-in-3 gadget* from Figure 6(a) by v_1, v_2, and v_3, respectively. Moreover, we annotate the query fragment T in Figure 5(a) with numbers from 1 to 7. We call the node 1 (resp., 3, 6) the *topmost position* of variable v_1 (resp., v_2, v_3).

Let t_{min} be a minimal model of fragment T from Figure 5(a). That is, t_{min} is essentially shaped as the structure given by the *Child*$^+$ axes in T. Gottlob et al. show that the following observation holds.

Observation 16 ([7]). Every satisfaction θ of the 1-in-3 gadget on t_{min} maps exactly one of the variables v_1, v_2, and v_3 to its topmost position.

Given a clause C, we interpret a satisfaction θ in which variable v_k is mapped to its topmost position as the selection of the k-th literal from C to be true. Hence, the 1-in-3 gadget would ensure that, on t_{min}, exactly one variable of clause C is selected and becomes true.

We now define the query P as in Figure 5(c). That is, P contains two copies of the fragment T, followed by a copy of the X-fragment from Figure 5(b). The ordering between the subqueries of P is enforced by *Following*-axes: the root of T's left copy has a *Following*-axis to the root of T's right copy, and root of T's right copy has a *Following*-axis to the root of the X-fragment.

Intuitively, the purposes of the different parts of the query P are as follows. The left copy of the T-fragment in P, together with the 1-in-3 gadget, is used to verify that the truth assignments we consider for $\overline{x}$ and $\overline{y}$ actually make one literal per clause of $\forall\overline{x}\exists\overline{y}C_1, \ldots, C_m$ true. The second copy of T in P is needed to ensure consistency of variable assignments between clauses: if we pick a variable to be true in one clause, that variable must be true in all clauses. Finally, the fragment X is used in P to generate all possible truth assignments for the $\overline{x}$-variables. Roughly, we interpret x_i as "false" if X_i appears in the upper unary path with n_x nodes and as "true" if X_i appears in the lower unary path with n_x nodes in Figure 5(b).

The query Q is defined much like the query in the proof of Gottlob et al., with the essential difference that we have to transfer the variable assignment that is generated in the X-fragment of P to the matching of L_1, L_2, and L_3 of the 1-in-3 gadget of Q onto the subtrees that satisfy the two copies of T in P. This will be taken care of by the X-assignment gadgets in Q, which are illustrated in Figure 6(b). □

Theorem 17. *Containment is Π_2^P-hard for CQ(Child*, Following).*

Proof. The proof for this case can be obtained from the proof of Theorem 15 by ensuring that, for each occurrence of $Child^+(x, y)$, x and y bear a different alphabet label in P. □

As *Following* can be defined in terms of *Child** and *NextSibling*$^+$, we immediately have the following corollary.

Corollary 18. *Containment is Π_2^P-hard for CQ(Child*, NextSibling$^+$).*

Theorem 19. *Containment is Π_2^P-hard for*
(1) CQ(Child, NextSibling),*
(2) CQ(Child,NextSibling*),*
(3) CQ(Child$^+$,NextSibling),
(4) CQ(Child$^+$,NextSibling$^+$), and
(5) CQ(Child$^+$,NextSibling).*

Proof. For each of these fragments, the proofs of Theorems 15 and 17 can be adapted by the same methods as in the article by Gottlob et al. [7]. For the fragments (2)–(5), we also need to adapt the query P, such that P accepts trees in which the T-fragments have the shape from the proof by Gottlob et al. This is, however, straightforward for each of the fragments. □

Theorem 20. *Containment is Π_2^P-hard for CQ(Following,NextSibling).*

The proof uses a modified version of the reduction from Theorem 15.

Theorem 21. *Containment is Π_2^P-hard for CQ(Following, NextSibling$^+$) and CQ(Following, NextSibling*).*

4 Satisfiability

We first note that a conjunctive query Q is satisfiable if and only if all its maximal connected components are satisfiable. We therefore assume in our proofs that Q has only one maximal connected component.

Proposition 22. *Satisfiability for CQs is in NP.*

Proof. It is easy to see that if a CQ is satisfiable, then it is satisfiable in a linear size tree. Indeed, let Q be a CQ and let t be a tree satisfying Q under valuation θ. Now let t' be the tree that

- contains the nodes of t onto which variables are matched by θ;
- contains, for each pair of variables $x \neq y$, the least common ancestor of $\theta(x)$ and $\theta(y)$;

- contains no other nodes; and
- preserves the descendant relation and document order (i.e., depth-first-left-to-right order) from t.

It is easy to see that t' contains less than $2 \cdot |\text{Var}(Q)|$ nodes and that t' models Q. Thus we can guess this tree, guess a satisfaction, and verify in polynomial time that all atoms are satisfied. □

4.1 PTIME Upper Bounds

Theorem 23. *Satisfiability is in PTIME for CQ(Child) and CQ(NextSibling).*

Proof. First, we apply the chase on the relations in Q, i.e., we compute equivalence classes $[x]$ of variables such that $[x]$ is the set of variables that must be mapped to the same tree node as x by any satisfaction of Q. For $Q \in CQ(\mathit{Child})$, we start with one class for each variable in Var(Q), and iteratively merge classes $[x]$ and $[y]$ if there are $x' \in [x]$, $y' \in [y]$, and a variable z such that there is are paths from x' to z and from y' to z in G_Q, both of equal length. For $Q \in CQ(\mathit{NextSibling})$ we do the same, with the addition that we also merge classes $[x]$ and $[y]$ if there are $x' \in [x]$, $y' \in [y]$, and z such that there are equal length paths from z to x' and from z to y'.

Once these classes are computed, we test whether Q contains a cycle on equivalence classes. If Q contains a cycle, it is unsatisfiable. Otherwise, we check whether there exist a class containing two variables x, y and $a \neq b$ such that $a(x)$ and $b(y)$ are both atoms of Q. If this is the case, Q is unsatisfiable. Otherwise it is satisfiable. □

Theorem 24. *Satisfiability is in PTIME for CQ(NextSibling$^+$,NextSibling*, Following) and CQ(Child$^+$,Child*).*

Proof. As in the proof of Theorem 23 we first check for cycles. However, unlike for Theorem 23, a query may have cycles of *Child**(resp., *NextSibling**) axes and still be satisfiable. On such cycles, there can be no variables x, y such that $a(x)$ and $b(y)$ are atoms, for $a \neq b$. We start by removing such (allowed) cycles by identifying all variables on the cycle. In the remainder of the proof, we assume that the query is cycle free.

For CQ(*NextSibling*$^+$,*NextSibling**,*Following*), we argue that if Q is satisfiable, then there is a tree t and a satisfaction θ for Q on t such that θ assigns all variables of Q to nodes of t which are all siblings of one another (i.e., in the same *siblinghood*). As a first step we note that, if Q is satisfiable, then Q', obtained by replacing all *NextSibling**-atoms of Q by *NextSibling*$^+$-atoms is also satisfiable. Indeed, if θ is a satisfaction of Q on tree t, *NextSibling*$^*(x, y)$ is an atom of Q, and $\theta(x) = \theta(y)$, we can modify t by inserting a new node between $\theta(x)$ and its left sibling (or at the beginning of the siblinghood if there is no left sibling), and modify θ by assigning x to the new node. After doing this for all such pairs x, y, the modified θ is a satisfaction of both Q and Q'.

Next, we note that any acyclic query Q in CQ(*NextSibling*$^+$,*Following*) induces a strict partial order on the variables. A topological sorting according to this partial order gives us a string of variables such that if *NextSibling*$^+(x, y)$ or *Following*(x, y) is an atom of Q, then x appears before y in the string. From such a string it is easy to construct a tree with a siblinghood that satisfies Q.

For CQ(*Child*$^+$, *Child**) we use the same arguments as for CQ(*NextSibling*$^+$, *NextSibling**, *Following*), except that instead of a siblinghood we use a tree that does not branch. □

Theorem 25. *Satisfiability is in PTIME for CQ(Child, NextSibling) and CQ(Child, NextSibling*$^+$*, NextSibling***).*

4.2 NP Lower Bounds

Theorem 26. *Satisfiability is NP-hard for*

(1) CQ(Child, Child$^+$*),*
(2) CQ(Child, Child**),*
(3) CQ(NextSibling, NextSibling$^+$*),*
(4) CQ(NextSibling, NextSibling**),*
(5) CQ(NextSibling, Following), and
(6) CQ(Child, Following).

The proof uses reductions from Shortest Common Supersequence.

5 Containment with Respect to a DTD

We abstract from Document Type Definitions (DTDs) as follows:

Definition 27. A *Document Type Definition (DTD)* is a triple $D = (\Sigma_f, d, s_d)$ where Σ_f is a finite subset of Σ, d is a function that maps Σ_f-symbols to regular expressions over Σ_f and $s_d \in \Sigma_f$ is the start symbol.

For ease of notation, we denote by $\text{lab}^t(u)$ the Σ-symbol a such that $a(u)$ appears in t. A tree t then *satisfies* D if *(i)* $\text{lab}^t(u) = s_d$ for the root u of t and, *(ii)* for every $u \in \text{Nodes}(t)$ with n children $u_1, \ldots, u_n$ from left to right, $\text{lab}^t(u_1) \cdots \text{lab}^t(u_n) \in L(d(\text{lab}^t(u)))$. By $L(d)$ we denote the set of trees satisfying d.

The main problem of interest of this section is *validity of a conjunctive query Q w.r.t. a DTD D*, that is, is $L(D) \subseteq L(Q)$? Notice that here, validity with respect to a DTD can also be seen as a form of containment of conjunctive queries with respect to a DTD. That is, $L(D) \subseteq L(Q)$ if and only if $(L(D) \cap L(\text{true})) \subseteq (L(D) \cap L(Q))$.

Theorem 28. *Validity with respect to DTDs is EXPTIME-hard for CQ(Child).*

6 Conclusions

We have determined the complexity of the containment problem for all sets of axes built from *Child*, *NextSibling*, their transitive, respectively reflexive and transitive, closures, and *Following*. The complexity of the satisfiability problem was pinpointed for most sets, but the cases involving transitive closures of *Child* and *NextSibling* (which we believe will be quite similar) are still open.

All these results were obtained in a schema-less setting. Since XML processing is mostly done with respect to a schema, this is far from the complete picture. As we show in Section 5, the presence of a schema dramatically increases the complexity. We have preliminary results for some combinations of schemas and axes, and intend to study this subject in more detail.

References

1. Berglund, A., Boag, S., Chamberlin, D., Fernández, M.F., Kay, M., Robie, J., Siméon, J.: XML Path Language (XPath) 2.0. Technical report, World Wide Web Consortium (January 2007), `http://www.w3.org/TR/xpath20/`
2. Boag, S., Chamberlin, D., Fernández, M.F., Florescu, D., Robie, J., Siméon, J.: Xquery 1.0: An XML query language. Technical report, World Wide Web Consortium (January 2007), `http://www.w3.org/TR/xquery/`
3. Chan, E.P.F., van der Meyden, R.: Containment and optimization of object-preserving conjunctive queries. Siam J. on Computing 29(4), 1371–1400 (2000)
4. Clark, J., DeRose, S.: XML Path Language (XPath) version 1.0. Technical report, World Wide Web Consortium (1999), `http://www.w3.org/TR/xpath/`
5. Gallant, J., Maier, D., Storer, J.A.: On finding minimal length superstrings. JCSS 20(1), 50–58 (1980)
6. Gottlob, G., Koch, C., Pichler, R., Segoufin, L.: The complexity of XPath query evaluation and XML typing. Journal of the ACM 52(2), 284–335 (2005)
7. Gottlob, G., Koch, C., Schulz, K.U.: Conjunctive queries over trees. Journal of the ACM 53(2), 238–272 (2006)
8. Hidders, J.: Satisfiability of XPath expressions. In: Lausen, G., Suciu, D. (eds.) DBPL 2003. LNCS, vol. 2921, pp. 21–36. Springer, Heidelberg (2004)
9. Kolaitis, P.G., Vardi, M.Y.: Conjunctive-query containment and constraint satisfaction. JCSS 61(2), 302–332 (2000)
10. Miklau, G., Suciu, D.: Containment and equivalence for a fragment of XPath. Journal of the ACM 51(1), 2–45 (2004)
11. Neven, F., Schwentick, T.: On the complexity of XPath containment in the presence of disjunction, DTDs, and variables. Logical Methods in Computer Science 2(3) (2006)
12. Räihä, K.J., Ukkonen, E.: The shortest common supersequence problem over binary alphabet is NP-complete. TCS 16(2), 187–198 (1981)
13. ten Cate, B., Lutz, C.: The complexity of query containment in expressive fragments of XPath 2.0. In: PODS 2007. 26th International Symposium on Principles of Database Systems, pp. 73–82 (2007)
14. Vansummeren, S.: On deciding well-definedness for query languages on trees. Journal of the ACM 54(4) (2007)

A Better Semantics for XQuery with Side-Effects

Giorgio Ghelli[1], Nicola Onose[2], Kristoffer Rose[3], and Jérôme Siméon[3]

[1] Università di Pisa
ghelli@di.unipi.it
[2] University of California, San Diego
nicola@cs.ucsd.edu
[3] IBM T. J. Watson Research Center
krisrose/simeon@us.ibm.com

Abstract. Formal semantics for XQuery with side-effects have been proposed in [13,16]. We propose a different semantics which is better suited for database compilation. We substantiate this claim by formalizing the compilation of XQuery extended with updates into a database algebra. We prove the correctness of the proposed compilation by mapping both the source language and the algebra to a common core language with list comprehensions and extensible tuples.

1 Introduction

Two semantics of XQuery. The use of list comprehensions to formalize database languages has been popular since the work of Trinder and Wadler [24], and that of Buneman et al [23,3]. More recently, the same approach has been used successfully by Fernandez et al. [11] to specify the semantics of XQuery. It notably relies on a notion of *normalization* that is now part of the XQuery Formal Semantics [7]. For instance, the following FLWOR expression applied to a variable *$d* containing the element `<doc><a>1</a><a>2</a></doc>`

```
for $x in $d/a
for $y in $d/a
where $x = $y
return ($x+$y)
```

is defined as being equivalent to the following expression in the target fragment of XQuery called the XQuery *core* (we use a different font for the core)

```
for $x in $d/a return
  for $y in $d/a return
    if ($x = $y) then ($x+$y) else ()
```

This approach has the benefit of relying on a small set of simple primitives which are well understood from functional programming, and support laws useful for optimization.

M. Arenas and M.I. Schwartzbach (Eds.): DBPL 2007, LNCS 4797, pp. 81–96, 2007.

Because of the importance of FLWOR expressions as a database primitive, most compilers do not rely on normalization, but instead compile into tuple-based algebras that support traditional database optimizations [19,18,21]. For instance, the above query is compiled in the following plan using the algebra of [21].

```
Map{#x+#y}
 (Select{#x = #y}
  (MapConcat
   {Map{[y:ID]}(TreeJoin[a](#d))}
   (Map{[x:ID]}(TreeJoin[a](#d)))))
```

This plan manipulates streams of tuples whose fields correspond to the variables in the source code. It first builds a stream of tuples [x:v], by applying tuple construction [x:ID] to each node resulting from the navigation TreeJoin[a](#d) (i.e, $\$d/a$). It then concatenates each [x:v] tuple which each of the [y:v] tuples built by the Map{[y:ID]}(TreeJoin[a](#d)) subplan, selects the tuples that satisfy #x = #y, and computes #x+#y once for each tuple. Algebraic equivalences can be applied to that plan to introduce a more efficient join operator.

Several extensions to XQuery involving side-effects have recently been proposed [6,13,4] by the research community, and are being considered by the W3C [5]. While the first proposals for side-effects relied on whole-program snapshot semantics [6], meaning that a piece of code could not observe its own effect, some consensus is emerging that allowing side-effects to be visible is a key feature for new XML applications [13,4,16,5]. Normalization and algebraic compilation coincide for a "pure" language such as XQuery 1.0. Unfortunately, in presence of visible side-effects, tuple based compilation and nested-for semantics diverge. Consider the following query, where `insert` exemplifies any visible side-effect.

```
for $x in $d/a
for $y in $d/a
where $x = $y
return (do insert <a>{$x+$y}</a> into $d)
```

The normalization approach, as used in [16,13], defines the query to be equivalent to the following core expression.

```
for $x in $d/a return
 for $y in $d/a return
  if ($x = $y) then (do insert <a>{$x+$y}</a> into $d) else ()
```

Hence, it first executes the internal **for** *\$y*... with *\$x* bound to the first a element, and then executes the same expression with *\$x* bound to the second a element. The first iteration inserts a new element a into *\$d*. Hence, in the second iteration *\$y* is bound to a different set of nodes. Instead, the tuple-building phase is protected from the effects of the `return` clause when the algebraic compilation is applied, as follows.

```
Map{Insert(<a>{#x+#y}</a>,#d)}
 (Select{#x = #y}
  (MapConcat
   {Map{[x:ID]}(TreeJoin[a](#d))}
   (Map{[y:ID]}(TreeJoin[a](#d)))))
```

One may argue which of the two semantics is better for the programmer. We observe that the informal, but normative, semantics for XQuery is actually defined in terms of a tuple stream, and mandates that the **return** clause is executed after the tuple-stream has been built and filtered [2]. We believe that the tuple-stream semantics is at least as natural as the nested-for semantics, and is better suited for optimization: in this example, the nested-for semantics requires the internal loop to be run on two different sequences, hence makes it impossible to use a join, while the tuple-stream semantics enables join optimization, which would produce the following plan.

```
Map{Insert(<a>{#x+#y}</a>,#d)}
 (Join{#x = #y}
  (Map{[x:ID]}(TreeJoin[a](#d)),
   Map{[y:ID]}(TreeJoin[a](#d))))
```

Scope of the paper. Our goal is to provide a list-comprehension based semantics for XQuery which enables the use of traditional tuple-based algebras for compilation and optimization. To this aim, we first formalize the tuple-stream semantics, by translating XQuery with updates into a target language with records which we call the *XQueryU core with tuples.* The result is still a nesting of for-expressions, which, in this case, are used to first build the tuple-stream, and to finally apply the return clause. For example, the code above is translated as follows, where *$environment* is a tuple-stream that only contains one context-tuple, [d:<doc><a>1</a><a>2</a></doc>].

```
for $t5 in
    for $t4 in
        for $t2 in
            (for $t0 in $environment
             return for $t1 in $d/a return [x:$t1]++ $t0)
        return for $t3 in $d/a return [y:$t3]++ $t2
    return if ($t4.x = $t4.y) then $t4 else ()
return (do insert element 'a' {$t5.x+$t5.y} into $t5.d)
```

The translation transforms variables into tuple fields, moves the outermost iteration in the innermost position and, most importantly, moves the filtering, reordering, and **return** phases at the end of the whole process, as required by the tuple-stream semantics. This formalization is not only a first step to our main theorem about the soundness of a database-like interpretation of tuple-stream semantics, but it also shows that the tuple-stream semantics admits, in a measure, the same advantages of the nested-for semantics, namely:

1. it admits a simple PL-style implementation, based on in-memory nested loops, with no need of going through algebraic compilation, for applications where a PL-style implementation may be useful.
2. it can be mapped down to a simple core language which is best suited for studies about semantics and types, as we will do in this paper.

We then formally define a database algebra for this language and a compilation function from XQuery with side-effects to the algebra, and we prove that the compilation implements the tuple-stream semantics. The target language and the algebra are typed, by a type system that keeps track of record access and concatenation. These type systems involve record concatenation and subtyping, which means that we have to address the well-known problem that these two mechanisms are incompatible for simple record types [14]. We have chosen an original solution for this old problem, based on *linearity* conditions which identify a sub-language where concatenation and simple subtyping safely coexist, and we show that this sub-language is indeed sufficient to interpret XQuery.

Related work. Design and semantics for database query languages based on comprehension were first introduced by [3,23,22]. This work notably led to the development of the Kleisli system which is probably the most advanced query language compiler based on functional techniques [25,8]. However, join optimization in Kleisli is not handled at the comprehension level, but remains internal to the compiler. So far, functional optimizations did not catch on as most database management system optimizers to this day rely on tuple-based algebras [1,20,19]. The recent emergence of languages which blend database and programming languages features [17,12,4,15] has created renewed interest in list comprehensions. We believe our work is the first to provide a list comprehension treatment of a tuple-based database algebra. The reconciliation of record subtyping with record concatenation has been the subject of a huge body of work [14]. The proposed approaches were mostly based on the addition of information about missing fields, or on the substitution of subtyping with parametric polymorphism. We instead use the simplest form of record types, but impose a linearity constraint on the code. Finally, the topic of optimization in the presence of side effects have received almost no attention so far. On notably exception is the work by Fegaras [9] which also relies on a monadic approach.

We first introduce the XQuery core with tuples (Section 2). We then introduce the source language XQueryU (Section 3) and its semantics, through a translation to the core. We finally define the typed second-order algebra (Section 4), the compilation of XQueryU into the algebra, and prove its correctness.

2 XQueryU Core with Tuples

In this section we define a core language with support for tuples, which we use to specify the semantics of both XQuery with updates and the corresponding algebra. This core language is based on the W3C XQuery core defined in [7].

Definition 2.1 (core syntax). Our core language has the following syntax, using e for *core expressions*, and s for XPath *steps*:

$$
\begin{aligned}
e ::= {} & \textbf{for } \$x \textbf{ in } e_1 \textbf{ return } e_2 \mid \textbf{order } \$x \textbf{ in } e_1 \textbf{ by } e_2 \\
& \mid \textbf{let } \$x := e_1 \textbf{ return } e_2 \mid \$x \mid \textbf{if } (e_1) \textbf{ then } e_2 \textbf{ else } e_3 \\
& \mid \ell \mid () \mid e_1, e_2 \mid \textbf{element } q\ \{e\} \mid \$x/s \mid f(e_1, \ldots, e_n) \\
& \mid [a_1 : e_1; \ldots; a_n : e_n] \mid \$x.a \mid e_1 \mathbin{+\!\!+} e_2 \mid \textbf{do insert } e_1 \textbf{ into } e_2 \mid \textbf{do delete } e
\end{aligned}
$$

$$
s ::= \textbf{child}::q \mid \textbf{descendant}::q \mid \ldots
$$

$\$x$ (and other $\$$-names) denotes *variables*, q denotes XML "qualified" *element names*, f denotes *function names*, a denotes *field names*, and ℓ denotes literals including numbers and strings; finally we have left the exact list of steps unspecified as our analysis does not depend on the specific steps. We allow the usual XPath/XQuery shorthands, in particular the **child**:: axis can be omitted, // abbreviates the **descendant**:: axis, and we will write certain built-in functions with traditional infix notation (such as $e_1 = e_2$ for equal(e_1, e_2)).

Our core differs from the W3C core [7] in three important ways: (1) it adds side-effects, in the form of two operations to update XML data in-place, which are executed immediately (2) it adds an explicit **order by** expression for sorting (a construction the W3C semantics does not specify), and (3) it adds *tuples* (*a.k.a. records*) which are finite mappings of field names to values: $[a_1 : e_1; \ldots; a_n : e_n]$ constructs a new tuple that maps each distinct field name a_i to the value of the corresponding e_i, $\$x.a$, extracts the value of the a field from the tuple value of $\$x$, and $e_1 \mathbin{+\!\!+} e_2$, constructs a new tuple with the combined fields from two existing tuples.

Since we use the core also as a target language for the algebra's semantics, we adopt record subtyping, *i.e.*, every tuple type specifies some fields that are guaranteed present, but more fields may be found in the typed value. This is notoriously incompatible with record concatenation: from $e_1 : [a : t]$ and $e_2 : [\ ]$ one cannot deduce that $e_1 \mathbin{+\!\!+} e_2 : [a : t]$, since e_2 may actually include an a field with an incompatible type. To solve the problem, we first adopt the following definition for the semantics of tuple concatenation for the case when the same field appears in both v_1 and v_2.

1. if $v_1.a = xv_1$ and $v_2.a = xv_2$ and xv_1 is different from xv_2, then $v_1 \mathbin{+\!\!+} v_2$ raises an error (informally "concatenation failure,");
2. if $v_1.a = xv = v_2.a$, then $v_1 \mathbin{+\!\!+} v_2$ associates a with xv.

We prove below that the translation of XQuery only generates well-typed *linear* core expressions (to be defined later), which never raise a concatenation failure. However, case (2) above must be allowed since it actually happens in the linear expressions that derive from XQuery translation.

Definition 2.2 (core semantics). The dynamic semantics of the core is defined by the judgment

$$\Sigma; \sigma \vdash e \Rightarrow v'; \sigma'$$

Σ is the dynamic environment mapping free variables of e to values (defined below). σ is a store mapping XML nodes *ids* to their value, and is used to support features such as node creation, node identity, backward navigation, and tree update. e is a core expression, v' the computed value, and σ' the resulting store. (The actual definition is standard, apart from tuple concatenation which we commented on above, and can be found in the Appendix.)

Values are partitioned into two classes, XML values xv and table values tv. XML values are sequences of XML items iv, while table values are sequences of tuples. In both cases we identify a single item, or tuple, with the corresponding sequence of one element.

Definition 2.3 (values). The values, relative to a store σ, are given by

$$\begin{aligned} v &::= xv \mid tv && \text{(value)} \\ xv &::= xv_1, xv_2 \mid () \mid iv && \text{(XML value)} \\ tv &::= tv_1, tv_2 \mid () \mid [a_1 : xv_1; \ldots; a_n : xv_n] && \text{(table value)} \\ iv &::= \ell \mid id \quad \text{with } id \in \sigma && \text{(item value)} \end{aligned}$$

where ℓ denotes literals. The fields of a tuple value are distinct and unordered.

The type system for the core should play two roles: (a) checking that predefined functions and operators are applied to arguments of the correct type, as it happens with the XQuery type system; (b) checking that tuple deconstruction and concatenation are correctly applied. Such a type system can be defined by enriching the XQuery type system with tuple types. To simplify the presentation, we follow here a much leaner approach, where all the types for the instances of the XQuery Data Model [10] are merged into *Item*, i.e. we focus on the (b) role only, since nothing is new, with respect to XQuery, on the (a) role. Similarly to values, types are partitioned into XML types xt and table types tt.

Definition 2.4 (types).

$$\begin{aligned} t &::= xt \mid tt && \text{(type)} \\ xt &::= \{xt\} \mid \mathit{Item} && \text{(XML type)} \\ tt &::= \{tt\} \mid [r] && \text{(table type)} \\ r &::= a : xt \mid r_1; r_2 \mid \epsilon && \text{(fields)} \\ \mathit{ft} &::= (t_1, \ldots, t_n) \to t && \text{(function type)} \end{aligned}$$

Tuple types are understood as follows:

- $[\epsilon]$ is the type of tuples with no fields, which we write $[]$.
- $[a : xt]$ is the type of tuples that map the field a to an XML value of type xt, and may be either defined or undefined on the other fields.
- $[r_1; r_2]$ is undefined if r_1 and r_2 map the same field name to two different types; otherwise, it is the intersection of types $[r_1]$ and $[r_2]$.

Hence, record fields are subject to the equalities $(r_1; r_2); r_3 = r_1; (r_2; r_3)$, $r_1; r_2 = r_2; r_1$, $a : xt; a : xt = a : xt$, and $r; \epsilon = r$, where $r_1 = r_2$ means that we identify them in every context (type equality, type rules, type semantics). Finally, since value sequences are flat, for any type t, $\{\{t\}\} = \{t\}$.

Definition 2.5 (core type semantics). The *semantics* of a type in a store, $\mathcal{T}[\![t]\!]_\sigma$, is defined as follows:

- $\mathcal{T}[\![Item]\!]_\sigma$ contains all node ids that are bound in σ, and all literal values;
- $\mathcal{T}[\![\{t\}]\!]_\sigma$ is the set of all finite sequences of elements of $\mathcal{T}[\![t]\!]_\sigma$; a single element of $\mathcal{T}[\![t]\!]_\sigma$ belongs to this set, and is equivalent to a singleton sequence;
- $\mathcal{T}[\![[a_1 : t_1; \ldots; a_n : t_n]]\!]_\sigma$ is the set of all functions that, for i in $1 \ldots n$, map a_i to an element of $\mathcal{T}[\![t_i]\!]_\sigma$; an element of $\mathcal{T}[\![[a_1 : t_1; \ldots; a_n : t_n]]\!]_\sigma$ may also be defined on any field name that is not specified in the type.
- $\mathcal{T}[\![(t_1, \ldots, t_n) \rightarrow t]\!]_\sigma$ is the set of all functions that, applied to n arguments in $\mathcal{T}[\![t_1]\!]_\sigma \ldots \mathcal{T}[\![t_n]\!]_\sigma$, return a value in $\mathcal{T}[\![t]\!]_\sigma$.

The fact that a tuple type does not give information about the fields that are not explicitly specified, and the fact that a single element is identified with a singleton sequence, lead to the following subtyping relation.

Definition 2.6 (subtyping). The *subtyping* relation $\leq:$ is the transitive homomorphic closure over types of the relation defined by

$$[r_1; r_2] \leq: [r_1] \qquad\qquad t \leq: \{t\}$$

Definition 2.7 (core typing). The judgment $\Gamma \vdash e : t$ holds iff it can be proved by the rules of Fig. 1, where:

1. Γ is a *type environment* which associates each free variable $\$x$ of e with a type $\Gamma(\$x)$, and each predefined function f with its function type $\Gamma(f)$.
2. $(\Gamma, \$x \mapsto t)$ denotes a new type environment where $\$x$ is assigned the type t instead of what it was in Γ; the empty type environment is written ().

We generalize the notions of typing to whole type environments: $\Sigma : \Gamma$ means that every variable bound by Σ is typed as specified by Γ, and $\mathcal{T}[\![\$x_1 : t_1; \ldots; \$x_n : t_n]\!]_\sigma$ is the set of all functions that, for i in $1 \ldots n$, map $\$x_i$ to an element of $\mathcal{T}[\![t_i]\!]_\sigma$.

Unfortunately, this type-system is not sound in general; for example, record concatenation fails in the two well-typed expressions below:

(1) [a:1] ++ [a:2]
(2) **let** *$x* := (**for** *$w* **in** (1,2) **return** [a:*$w*]) **return**
for *$y*₁ **in** *$x* **return for** *$y*₂ **in** *$x* **return** (*$y*₁ ++ *$y*₂)

However, the type-system *is* sound when we restrict the attention to a *linear* subset of the language. Informally, a closed core expression is linear if none of the following non-linearity conditions apply.

$$\frac{\Gamma \vdash e : t_1 \quad t_1 \leq: t_2}{\Gamma \vdash e : t_2}\text{(sub)} \qquad \frac{\Gamma(\$x) = t}{\Gamma \vdash \$x : t}\text{(var)} \qquad \frac{\Gamma \vdash e_1 : \{t_1\} \quad \Gamma \vdash e_2 : t_2 \quad \Gamma \vdash e_3 : t_2}{\Gamma \vdash \textbf{if } (e_1) \textbf{ then } e_2 \textbf{ else } e_3 : t_2}\text{(if)}$$

$$\frac{\Gamma \vdash e_1 : \{t_1\} \quad (\Gamma, \$x \twoheadrightarrow t_1) \vdash e_2 : t_2}{\Gamma \vdash \textbf{for } \$x \textbf{ in } e_1 \textbf{ return } e_2 : \{t_2\}}\text{(for)} \qquad \frac{\Gamma \vdash e_1 : \{t_1\} \quad (\Gamma, \$x \twoheadrightarrow t_1) \vdash e_2 : \{Item\}}{\Gamma \vdash \textbf{order } \$x \textbf{ in } e_1 \textbf{ by } e_2 : \{t_1\}}\text{(order)}$$

$$\frac{\Gamma \vdash e_1 : t_1 \quad (\Gamma, \$x \twoheadrightarrow t_1) \vdash e_2 : t_2}{\Gamma \vdash \textbf{let } \$x := e_1 \textbf{ return } e_2 : t_2}\text{(let)} \qquad \frac{}{\Gamma \vdash \ell : Item}\text{(literal)} \qquad \frac{}{\Gamma \vdash () : \{t\}}\text{(empty)}$$

$$\frac{\Gamma \vdash e_1 : \{t\} \quad \Gamma \vdash e_2 : \{t\}}{\Gamma \vdash e_1, e_2 : \{t\}}\text{(comma)} \qquad \frac{\Gamma \vdash e : \{Item\}}{\Gamma \vdash \textbf{element } q \, \{e\} : Item}\text{(element)} \qquad \frac{\Gamma \vdash \$x : Item}{\Gamma \vdash \$x/s : \{Item\}}\text{(step)}$$

$$\frac{\Gamma(f) = (\{xt_1\}, \ldots, \{xt_n\}) \rightarrow xt \quad \forall i \in 1..n\colon \Gamma \vdash e_i : \{xt_i\}}{\Gamma \vdash f(e_1, \ldots, e_n) : xt}\text{(fun)} \qquad \frac{\Gamma \vdash \$x : [a : xt]}{\Gamma \vdash \$x.a : xt}\text{(field)}$$

$$\frac{\forall i \in 1..n\colon \Gamma \vdash e_i : xt_i}{\Gamma \vdash [a_1 : e_1; \ldots; a_n : e_n] : [a_1 : xt_1; \ldots; a_n : xt_n]}\text{(tuple)} \qquad \frac{\Gamma \vdash e_1 : [r_1] \quad \Gamma \vdash e_2 : [r_2]}{\Gamma \vdash e_1 +\!\!+ \, e_2 : [r_1; r_2]}\text{(concat)}$$

$$\frac{\Gamma \vdash e : \{Item\}}{\Gamma \vdash \textbf{do delete } e : \{Item\}}\text{(delete)} \qquad \frac{\Gamma \vdash e_1 : \{Item\} \quad \Gamma \vdash e_2 : \{Item\}}{\Gamma \vdash \textbf{do insert } e_1 \textbf{ into } e_2 : \{Item\}}\text{(insert)}$$

Fig. 1. Type rules for the core

1. *double construction*: the presence of two distinct constructors for a field a is "non-linear" (case (1) above); double construction is only allowed in independent subexpressions, as in **if** ([a:1]) **then** [a:2] **else** [a:3].
2. *non-linear let-variables*: two distinct uses of a **let** variable are "non-linear" (like the occurrences of $x in case (2) above); as in the *double construction* case, double use is allowed in independent code branches.

The above definition is extended to pairs (Σ, e) formed by an expression and a dynamic environment that defines the free variables of e, so that the evaluation of a linear expression only involves linear (Σ, e) pairs. With these tools, we can prove the following theorem, which will allow us to prove that the semantics of any well-typed XQueryU or algebraic expression is always well-defined, despite the combined use of subtyping and record concatenation in the core.

Theorem 2.8 (soundness of typing). *For any expression e linear for $\Sigma : \Gamma$, type t such that $\Gamma \vdash e : t$, and store σ such that $\Sigma \in \mathcal{T}[\![\Gamma]\!]_{\sigma}$, there exist $v'; \sigma'$ such that $\Sigma; \sigma \vdash e \Rightarrow v'; \sigma'$ and $v' \in \mathcal{T}[\![t]\!]_{\sigma'}$.*

3 XQuery

We define here XQueryU, a minimal subset of XQuery with immediate updates.

Definition 3.1 (XQueryU syntax). XQueryU syntax consists of *expressions* E, where F denotes FLWOR expressions, and s denotes XPath steps.

$$E ::= F \mid () \mid E_1\texttt{,}E_2 \mid \$x \mid \texttt{if (}E_1\texttt{) then } E_2 \texttt{ else } E_3 \mid f\texttt{(}E_1\texttt{,}\ldots\texttt{,}E_n\texttt{)}$$
$$\mid \texttt{element } q \texttt{ \{}E\texttt{\}} \mid E\texttt{/}s \mid \ell \mid \texttt{do insert } E_1 \texttt{ into } E_2 \mid \texttt{do delete } E$$
$$F ::= \texttt{for } \$x \texttt{ in } E\ F \mid \texttt{let } \$x \texttt{ :=} E\ F \mid \texttt{where } E\ F \mid \texttt{order by } E\ F \mid \texttt{return } E$$

with the standard constraints that each FLWOR-expression must have at least one `for` or `let` clause, `where` clauses cannot be followed by `for` or `let` clauses, and `order by` clauses can only be followed by a `return` clause.

Definition 3.2 (XQuery semantics). The semantics of an XQueryU expression E is given by the translation $\mathcal{X}[\![E]\!]^{\varrho}_{\$t}$ defined in the following table, provided $\$t$ is a core variable of tuple type and ϱ is a mapping from XQueryU variables to core field names, which must map all free variables of E to fields defined by $\$t$.

Most of the XQueryU operators are mapped to the core by homomorphism. We use **do insert** as an example, and give the non-homomorphic cases:

$$\mathcal{X}[\![\texttt{do insert } E_1 \texttt{ into } E_2]\!]^{\varrho}_{\$t} = \textbf{do insert } \mathcal{X}[\![E_1]\!]^{\varrho}_{\$t} \textbf{ into } \mathcal{X}[\![E_2]\!]^{\varrho}_{\$t}$$
$$\mathcal{X}[\![\$x]\!]^{\varrho}_{\$t} = \$t.a \qquad \text{where } a = \varrho(\$x)$$
$$\mathcal{X}[\![E\texttt{/}s]\!]^{\varrho}_{\$t} = \textbf{for } \$dot \textbf{ in } (\mathcal{X}[\![E]\!]^{\varrho}_{\$t}) \textbf{ return } \$dot/s$$
$$\mathcal{X}[\![F]\!]^{\varrho}_{\$t} = \mathcal{X}^*[\![F]\!]^{\varrho}_{\$t} \qquad \text{where } \mathcal{X}^* \text{ is defined below}$$
$$\mathcal{X}^*[\![\texttt{for } \$x \texttt{ in } E\ F]\!]^{\varrho}_{e} = \mathcal{X}^*[\![F]\!]^{(\varrho,\$x\mapsto a)}_{e_1} \qquad \text{where } a \text{ is a fresh field name, and}$$
$$e_1 = \textbf{for } \$t \textbf{ in } e \textbf{ return for } \$v \textbf{ in } (\mathcal{X}[\![E]\!]^{\varrho}_{\$t}) \textbf{ return } \$t{+\!+}\,[a\!: \$v]$$
$$\mathcal{X}^*[\![\texttt{let } \$x \texttt{ :=} E\ F]\!]^{\varrho}_{e} = \mathcal{X}^*[\![F]\!]^{(\varrho,\$x\mapsto a)}_{e_1} \qquad \text{where } a \text{ is a fresh field name, and}$$
$$e_1 = \textbf{for } \$t \textbf{ in } e \textbf{ return } \$t{+\!+}\,[a\!: \mathcal{X}[\![E]\!]^{\varrho}_{\$t}]$$
$$\mathcal{X}^*[\![\texttt{order by } E\ F]\!]^{\varrho}_{e} = \mathcal{X}^*[\![F]\!]^{\varrho}_{\textbf{order } \$t \textbf{ in } e \textbf{ by } (\mathcal{X}[\![E]\!]^{\varrho}_{\$t})}$$
$$\mathcal{X}^*[\![\texttt{where } E\ F]\!]^{\varrho}_{e} = \mathcal{X}^*[\![F]\!]^{\varrho}_{\textbf{for } \$t \textbf{ in } e \textbf{ return if } (\mathcal{X}[\![E]\!]^{\varrho}_{\$t}) \textbf{ then } \$t \textbf{ else } ()}$$
$$\mathcal{X}^*[\![\texttt{return } E]\!]^{\varrho}_{e} = \textbf{for } \$t \textbf{ in } e \textbf{ return } (\mathcal{X}[\![E]\!]^{\varrho}_{\$t})$$

The most notable aspect of those rules is how the result of compilation for prior clauses in a FLWOR is passed as a parameter (as subscript) to the auxiliary $\mathcal{X}^*$ translation judgment.

$\mathcal{X}[\![E]\!]^{\varrho}_{\$t}$ is always well-defined, but it is only guaranteed to be well-typed in a specific static context, specified by Theorem 3.3 below. Informally, $\$t$ collects values for the free variables of E which is why ϱ must map these variables to field names of $\$t$. Similarly, in the helper translation $\mathcal{X}^*[\![F]\!]^{\varrho}_{e}$, e is an expression producing the tuple stream used to evaluate F, and ϱ maps the free variables of F to the field names of this tuple stream. To formalize these requirements we equip XQueryU with a type judgement, $\Gamma \vdash E : xt$, similar to the core typing of Def. 2.7, which we do not specify here for space reasons. We map type environments to tuple types by defining $\varrho(\$x_1{:}xt_1;\ldots;\$x_n{:}xt_n) = [\varrho(\$x_1){:}\{xt_1\};\ldots;\varrho(\$x_n){:}\{xt_n\}]$, where each xt_i is mapped to $\{xt_i\}$ (*i.e.*, to $\{Item\}$) because we map `let` into **for**, hence the core type system sometimes infers sequence types in places where XQueryU typing was more precise. This is also reflected in the statement of the type preservation theorem. It would be easy to have exact type preservation, using a finer type system for the core, but this paper is focused on the use of tuple types to map static environments, and the other typing aspects are kept minimal by design.

We can finally show that the translation of well-typed terms is well-typed and linear, hence, thanks to Theorem 2.8, it is always well defined.

Theorem 3.3 (type preservation). *If $\varrho(\Gamma)$ is well defined, then:*

$$\begin{array}{ll} \Gamma \vdash E : xt & \Rightarrow (\$t : \varrho(\Gamma)) \vdash \mathcal{X}[\![E]\!]^{\varrho}_{\$t} : \{xt\} \\ (\$t : tt) \vdash e : \{\varrho(\Gamma)\} \wedge \Gamma \vdash F : xt & \Rightarrow (\$t : tt) \vdash \mathcal{X}^{*}[\![F]\!]^{\varrho}_{e} : \{xt\} \end{array}$$

Theorem 3.4 (linearity). *For any E, ϱ, tv, where ϱ is defined on all free variables of E, and $tv = [\varrho(\$x_1) : xv_1; \ldots; \varrho(\$x_n) : xv_n]$ is defined on the whole image of ϱ, the term $\mathcal{X}[\![E]\!]^{\varrho}_{\$t}$ is linear with $(\$t \mapsto tv)$.*

Corollary 3.5 (XQueryU semantics). *For any $\Gamma, E, xt, \varrho, \sigma, tv$, if $\Gamma \vdash E : xt$, $\varrho(\Gamma)$ is defined, $tv = [\varrho(\$x_1) : xv_1; \ldots; \varrho(\$x_n) : xv_n]$ with $xv_i \in \mathcal{T}[\![\Gamma(x_i)]\!]_{\sigma}$, then there exist $v'; \sigma'$ such that $(\$t \mapsto tv); \sigma \vdash \mathcal{X}[\![E]\!]^{\varrho}_{\$t} \Rightarrow v'; \sigma'$ and $v' \in \mathcal{T}[\![t]\!]_{\sigma'}$.*

4 Algebra

We formally specify the semantics and type system for an existing nested-relational algebra for XQuery [18,21]. Most other database algebras are quite similar, so most of the treatment proposed here should apply quite directly to other relational or nested-relational algebras. From a functional programming perspective, database algebras are first order languages, where efforts are taken in order to avoid any manipulation of functions. For example, the projection operator from relational algebra, usually written $\pi_{\phi}R$, is similar to a map and applies ϕ to every element of R. However, traditional database algebras usually do not allow ϕ to be a function from tuples to tuples, but always use a variable-free syntax [20], which significantly simplifies the analysis and rewriting of algebraic terms. Algebras for object databases sometimes depart from this, since methods have to be formalized, and we have seen a drift towards higher-order algebras, where functions and lambda-binders play a role. XQuery seems to call for that approach, since the language is functional, and also because every expression is always evaluated with respect to an implicit context item, which means that every expressions denotes a function.

We propose a different approach that merges the advantages of binder-free syntax and the expressivity of higher-order. In our algebra, every term (or *plan*) denotes a first-order function, that yields a result when applied to a context tuple. Every n-ary algebra operator (with $n > 0$), such as Map or Select, denotes a second-order function, which yields a first-order plan when applied to first-order subplans. We will show how this approach gives all the expressive power we need, while avoiding the need for higher-order syntax and rewriting.

$$\frac{}{\mathsf{ID} : t \rightarrow t}\ (\text{ID}) \qquad \frac{}{\ell : t \rightarrow \mathit{Item}}\ (\text{Literal}) \qquad \frac{p : t \rightarrow xt}{[a : p] : t \rightarrow [a : xt]}\ (\text{Tuple}) \qquad \frac{}{\#a : [a : xt] \rightarrow xt}\ (\text{Field})$$

$$\frac{p_2 : t \rightarrow \{[r]\} \quad p_1 : [r] \rightarrow \{\mathit{Item}\}}{\mathsf{Select}\{p_1\}(p_2) : t \rightarrow \{[r]\}}\ (\text{Select}) \qquad \frac{p_2 : t \rightarrow \{[r]\} \quad p_1 : [r] \rightarrow \{\mathit{Item}\}}{\mathsf{OrderBy}\{p_1\}(p_2) : t \rightarrow \{[r]\}}\ (\text{OrderBy})$$

$$\frac{p_2 : t \rightarrow \{[r_2]\} \quad p_1 : [r_2] \rightarrow \{[r_1]\}}{\mathsf{MapConcat}\{p_1\}(p_2) : t \rightarrow \{[r_1; r_2]\}}\ (\text{MapConcat}) \qquad \frac{p_2 : t \rightarrow \{t'\} \quad p_1 : t' \rightarrow t''}{\mathsf{Map}\{p_1\}(p_2) : t \rightarrow \{t''\}}\ (\text{Map})$$

$$\frac{}{\mathsf{Empty}() : t \rightarrow \{\mathit{Item}\}}\ (\text{Empty}) \qquad \frac{p_1 : t \rightarrow \{\mathit{Item}\} \quad p_2 : t \rightarrow \{\mathit{Item}\}}{\mathsf{Sequence}(p_1, p_2) : t \rightarrow \{\mathit{Item}\}}\ (\text{Seq})$$

$$\frac{p : t \rightarrow \{\mathit{Item}\}}{\mathsf{TreeJoin}[s](p) : t \rightarrow \{\mathit{Item}\}}\ (\text{TreeJoin}) \qquad \frac{p_1 : t \rightarrow \{\mathit{Item}\} \quad p_2 : t \rightarrow u \quad p_3 : t \rightarrow u}{\mathsf{Conditional}(p_1, p_2, p_3) : t \rightarrow u}\ (\text{If})$$

$$\frac{\Gamma(f) = (t'_1, \ldots, t'_n) \rightarrow t' \quad p_1 : t \rightarrow t'_1 \quad \ldots \quad p_n : t \rightarrow t'_n}{\mathsf{Call}[f](p_1, \ldots, p_n) : t \rightarrow t'}\ (\text{Call})$$

$$\frac{p_1 : t \rightarrow \{\mathit{Item}\} \quad p_2 : t \rightarrow \{\mathit{Item}\}}{\mathsf{Insert}(p_1, p_2) : t \rightarrow \{\mathit{Item}\}}\ (\text{Insert}) \qquad \frac{p : t \rightarrow \{\mathit{Item}\}}{\mathsf{Delete}(p) : t \rightarrow \{\mathit{Item}\}}\ (\text{Delete})$$

$$\frac{p : t \rightarrow u \quad p : t^- \leq: t \quad p : u \leq: u^+}{p : t^- \rightarrow u^+}\ (\text{Sub})$$

Fig. 2. Type rules for the base algebra

Example 4.1. Consider the following XQuery expression:

```
for $x in $doc//a where $x/empno≥1 return $x
```

Database compilers compile this into a *query plan* similar to the following, denoting a function to be applied to a context tuple where the #doc field is defined.

```
Map{#x}(Select{TreeJoin[empno](#x) ≥1}
          (MapConcat{Map{[x:ID]}(TreeJoin[//a](#doc))}
                 (ID)))
```

To illustrate the first order nature of each operator, the same plan with explicit binders would look as follows.

```
λt0→ Map (λt1→ t1.x)
       (Select (λt2→ t2.x/empno ≥1)
              (MapConcat (λt3→ Map (λt4→ [x : t4]) (t3.doc//a))
                        (t0)))
```

Due to lack of space, we focus on a base algebra which contains only the algebraic operators that are needed for compilation, and we ignore the additional operators needed for optimization purposes.

Definition 4.2 (base algebra syntax). For unoptimized *query plans* we use the following basic syntax:

$$\begin{aligned} p ::= &\ \mathsf{ID} \mid \mathsf{Empty}() \mid \mathsf{Sequence}(p_1, p_2) \mid \ell \mid \mathsf{Element}[q](p) \\ &\mid \mathsf{Select}\{p_1\}(p_2) \mid \mathsf{OrderBy}\{p_1\}(p_2) \mid \mathsf{Map}\{p_1\}(p_2) \mid \mathsf{MapConcat}\{p_1\}(p_2) \\ &\mid \mathsf{TreeJoin}[s](p) \mid \mathsf{Conditional}(p_1, p_2, p_3) \mid \mathsf{Call}[f](p_1, \ldots, p_n) \\ &\mid [a{:}p] \mid \#a \mid \mathsf{Insert}(p_1, p_2) \mid \mathsf{Delete}(p) \end{aligned}$$

The semantics of the basic query plans is given in the following table, through a translation to the core. Every plan p denotes a core expression $\mathcal{A}\llbracket p\rrbracket_{\$t}$ with one free variable $\$t$ for the input tuple stream. Every algebraic plan receives an input value, and, with the only exception of the leaf operators $\#a$, ID, ℓ and Empty, does not operate on it, but passes it to the subplans enclosed in round brackets. Select, OrderBy, MapConcat and Map also apply their curly-brackets subplan to each value in the list returned by the round-brackets. Finally, the values returned by the subplans are acted upon.

$$\begin{aligned}
&\mathcal{A}\llbracket \mathsf{ID}\rrbracket_{\$t} = \$t \\
&\mathcal{A}\llbracket \mathsf{Sequence}(p_1, p_2)\rrbracket_{\$t} = (\mathcal{A}\llbracket p_1\rrbracket_{\$t}, \mathcal{A}\llbracket p_2\rrbracket_{\$t}) \\
&\mathcal{A}\llbracket \mathsf{Empty}()\rrbracket_{\$t} = () \\
&\mathcal{A}\llbracket \mathsf{Scalar}[\ell]()\rrbracket_{\$t} = \ell \\
&\mathcal{A}\llbracket \mathsf{Element}[q](p)\rrbracket_{\$t} = \textbf{element}\ q\ \{\mathcal{A}\llbracket p\rrbracket_{\$t}\} \\
&\mathcal{A}\llbracket \mathsf{Select}\{p_1\}(p_2)\rrbracket_{\$t} = \textbf{for}\ \$t_1\ \textbf{in}\ \mathcal{A}\llbracket p_2\rrbracket_{\$t} \textbf{return if}\ (\mathcal{A}\llbracket p_1\rrbracket_{\$t_1})\ \textbf{then}\ \$t_1\ \textbf{else}\ () \\
&\mathcal{A}\llbracket \mathsf{TreeJoin}[s](p)\rrbracket_{\$t} = \textbf{for}\ \$t_1\ \textbf{in}\ \mathcal{A}\llbracket p\rrbracket_{\$t} \textbf{return}\ \$t_1/s \\
&\mathcal{A}\llbracket \mathsf{Map}\{p_1\}(p_2)\rrbracket_{\$t} = \textbf{for}\ \$t_1\ \textbf{in}\ \mathcal{A}\llbracket p_2\rrbracket_{\$t} \textbf{return} \mathcal{A}\llbracket p_1\rrbracket_{\$t_1} \\
&\mathcal{A}\llbracket \mathsf{MapConcat}\{p_1\}(p_2)\rrbracket_{\$t} = \textbf{for}\ \$t_1\ \textbf{in}\ \mathcal{A}\llbracket p_2\rrbracket_{\$t} \textbf{return} \\
&\qquad\qquad\qquad\qquad\qquad\qquad \textbf{for}\ \$t_2\ \textbf{in}\ \mathcal{A}\llbracket p_1\rrbracket_{\$t_1} \textbf{return}\ \$t_1 +\!\!+ \$t_2 \\
&\mathcal{A}\llbracket \mathsf{OrderBy}\{p_1\}(p_2)\rrbracket_{\$t} = \textbf{order}\ \$t_1\ \textbf{in}\ \mathcal{A}\llbracket p_2\rrbracket_{\$t} \textbf{by} \mathcal{A}\llbracket p_1\rrbracket_{\$t_1} \\
&\mathcal{A}\llbracket \mathsf{Conditional}(p_1, p_2, p_3)\rrbracket_{\$t} = \textbf{if}\ (\mathcal{A}\llbracket p_1\rrbracket_{\$t})\ \textbf{then}\ \mathcal{A}\llbracket p_2\rrbracket_{\$t} \textbf{else}\ \mathcal{A}\llbracket p_3\rrbracket_{\$t} \\
&\mathcal{A}\llbracket \mathsf{Call}[f](p_1, \ldots, p_n)\rrbracket_{\$t} = f(\mathcal{A}\llbracket p_1\rrbracket_{\$t}, \ldots, \mathcal{A}\llbracket p_n\rrbracket_{\$t}) \\
&\mathcal{A}\llbracket [a : p]\rrbracket_{\$t} = [a : \mathcal{A}\llbracket p\rrbracket_{\$t}] \\
&\mathcal{A}\llbracket \#a\rrbracket_{\$t} = \$t.a \\
&\mathcal{A}\llbracket \mathsf{Insert}(p_1, p_2)\rrbracket_{\$t} = \textbf{do insert} \mathcal{A}\llbracket p_1\rrbracket_{\$t}\ \textbf{into}\ \mathcal{A}\llbracket p_2\rrbracket_{\$t} \\
&\mathcal{A}\llbracket \mathsf{Delete}(p)\rrbracket_{\$t} = \textbf{do delete}\ \mathcal{A}\llbracket p\rrbracket_{\$t}
\end{aligned}$$

Definition 4.3 (application of a plan). The notation $\mathcal{A}\llbracket p\rrbracket^{\sigma}_{v}$ denotes the value-store pair $v'; \sigma'$ such $\$t \mapsto v; \sigma \vdash \mathcal{A}\llbracket p\rrbracket_{\$t} \Rightarrow v'; \sigma'$. We will also use the same notation to denote just the value component v', when this is clear from the context.

Every plan has a first order type $t \to t'$, where t and t' are defined exactly as in Definition 2.4; the two type languages coincide since the semantics of the algebra is given through a translation to the core.

Definition 4.4 (algebra typing). The algebra type system is defined by the rules in Figure 2; subtyping is defined as in the core.

Notice that Γ is treated as a constant here (with just the built-in function signatures) hence is not propagated within the rules. Tuple concatenation plays a key role here as in the core (whereas the distinction between $\{t\}$ and t is only relevant for optimizations purposes that we do not consider here). Once more, we are able to combine record concatenation with record subtyping by adopting a linearity constraint. We say that the query plan p *builds* a field a if it contains a tuple constructor for a, *i.e.*, a subplan $[a : p']$. Linearity then means that, informally, every tuple field is only built in one specific point of the code.

Definition 4.5 (linearity). A plan p is *linear* if no field is built by two distinct tuple constructors inside p.

A plan p is *linear with a tuple type* $[a_1 : t_1; ...; a_n : t_n]$ or with a tuple sequence type $\{[a_1 : t_1; ...; a_n : t_n]\}$, if it is linear and no field among $a_1, \ldots, a_n$ is built by p. A piece of code p is linear with an XML type iff p is linear.

Definition 4.6 ($\pi_t(v)$). The projection $\pi_t(v)$ of a value v over a type t such that $v \in \mathcal{T}[\![t]\!]_\sigma$ is defined by cases on t, as follows. $\pi_{[a_1:t_1,\ldots,a_n:t_n]}(v)$ is a tuple that coincides with v on the fields $a_1, \ldots, a_n$, and is undefined on the others. $\pi_{\{tt\}}(v_1, \ldots, v_n)$ is equal to $\pi_{\{tt\}}(v_1), \ldots, \pi_{\{tt\}}(v_n)$. Finally, $\pi_{xt}(v) = v$.

We can now state the type soundness of the algebra. The theorem is not trivial, because it requires that the extra fields in the input tuple are removed by projection ($\pi_t(tv)$), but the thesis $v' \in \mathcal{T}[\![t']\!]_{\sigma'}$ does not exclude the presence of extra fields in the result. This means that the theorem cannot be proved directly by induction, but we need to resort on linearity to prove that the extra fields are actually harmless. In a sense, this theorem specifies that any optimizer that preserves types and linearity never needs to insert extra projections.

Theorem 4.7 (type soundness). *If $p : t \to t'$ and p is linear with t, then, for any σ and any tuple $tv \in \mathcal{T}[\![t]\!]_\sigma$, then $\mathcal{A}[\![p]\!]^\sigma_{\pi_t(tv)}$ is well defined, and, if $(v', \sigma') = \mathcal{A}[\![p]\!]^\sigma_{\pi_t(tv)}$, then $v' \in \mathcal{T}[\![t']\!]_{\sigma'}$.*

4.1 Compilation

We give now a formal definition of the algebraic compilation $\mathcal{C}[\![E]\!]^\varrho$ of an XQueryU expression E, in the table below. ϱ is a mapping from free variables in E to core field names, and a is a fresh field name in cases *for* and *let*.

$$
\begin{array}{ll}
\mathcal{C}[\![F]\!]^\varrho = \mathcal{C}^*[\![F]\!]^\varrho_{\mathsf{ID}} & \text{where } \mathcal{C}^* \text{ is defined below} \\
\mathcal{C}[\![\texttt{()}]\!]^\varrho = \mathsf{Empty()} & \\
\mathcal{C}[\![E_1\texttt{,}E_2]\!]^\varrho = \mathsf{Sequence}(\mathcal{C}[\![E_1]\!]^\varrho, \mathcal{C}[\![E_2]\!]^\varrho) & \\
\mathcal{C}[\![\$x]\!]^\varrho = \#a & \text{with } a = \varrho(\$x) \\
\multicolumn{2}{l}{\mathcal{C}[\![\texttt{if (}E_1\texttt{) then } E_2 \texttt{ else } E_3]\!]^\varrho = \mathsf{Conditional}(\mathcal{C}[\![E_1]\!]^\varrho, \mathcal{C}[\![E_2]\!]^\varrho, \mathcal{C}[\![E_3]\!]^\varrho)} \\
\mathcal{C}[\![f\texttt{(}E_1, \ldots, E_n\texttt{)}]\!]^\varrho = \mathsf{Call}[f](\mathcal{C}[\![E_1]\!]^\varrho, \ldots, \mathcal{C}[\![E_n]\!]^\varrho) & \\
\mathcal{C}[\![\texttt{element } q \texttt{ \{}E\texttt{\}}]\!]^\varrho = \mathsf{Element}[q](\mathcal{C}[\![E]\!]^\varrho) & \\
\mathcal{C}[\![E\texttt{/}s]\!]^\varrho = \mathsf{TreeJoin}[s](\mathcal{C}[\![E]\!]^\varrho) & \\
\mathcal{C}[\![\ell]\!]^\varrho_{\$t} = \ell &
\end{array}
$$

$$\mathcal{C}[\![\texttt{do insert}\, E_1 \,\texttt{into}\, E_2]\!]^{\varrho} = \mathsf{Insert}(\mathcal{C}[\![E_1]\!]^{\varrho})\mathcal{C}[\![E_2]\!]^{\varrho}$$
$$\mathcal{C}[\![\texttt{do delete}\, E]\!]^{\varrho} = \mathsf{Delete}(\mathcal{C}[\![E]\!]^{\varrho})$$

$$\mathcal{C}^*[\![\texttt{for}\,\$x\,\texttt{in}\, E\; F]\!]^{\varrho}_{p} = \mathcal{C}^*[\![F]\!]^{(\varrho,\$x \mapsto a)}_{p_1} \quad p_1 = \mathsf{MapConcat}\{\mathsf{Map}\{[a : \mathsf{ID}]\}(\mathcal{C}[\![E]\!]^{\varrho})\}(p)$$
$$\mathcal{C}^*[\![\texttt{order by}\, E\; F]\!]^{\varrho}_{p} = \mathcal{C}^*[\![F]\!]^{\varrho}_{p_1} \quad p_1 = \mathsf{OrderBy}\{\mathcal{C}[\![E]\!]^{\varrho}\}(p)$$
$$\mathcal{C}^*[\![\texttt{let}\,\$x := E\; F]\!]^{\varrho}_{p} = \mathcal{C}^*[\![F]\!]^{(\varrho,\$x \mapsto a)}_{p_1} \quad p_1 = \mathsf{MapConcat}\{[a : \mathcal{C}[\![E]\!]^{\varrho}]\}(p)$$
$$\mathcal{C}^*[\![\texttt{where}\, E\; F]\!]^{\varrho}_{p} = \mathcal{C}^*[\![F]\!]^{\varrho}_{p_1} \quad p_1 = \mathsf{Select}\{\mathcal{C}[\![E]\!]^{\varrho}\}(p)$$
$$\mathcal{C}^*[\![\texttt{return}\, E]\!]^{\varrho}_{p} = \mathsf{Map}\{\mathcal{C}[\![E]\!]^{\varrho}\}(p)$$

The compilation rules correspond strictly to those of [21] (except for some minor syntactic variations and the use of ϱ for explicit field naming). As in the rules that describe the semantics of XQueryU, the most interesting rules are those we have described with the helper function $\mathcal{C}^*[\![F]\!]^{\varrho}_{p}$, which compiles the "tail clauses" F of a FLWOR expression. Those rules are specified in the context of an operator p that generates the stream of tuples that are generated by the "head clauses" of the same FLWOR.

Example 4.8 (algebraic compilation). The example XQueryU from the "two semantics" part of the introduction compiles with the translation scheme to the algebraic expression in the "database algebra" part of the introduction. The following table shows how the application of $\mathcal{C}^*$ constructs the plan backwards:

i	F_i	$p_i = \mathcal{C}^*[\![F_i]\!]^{\cdots}_{\cdots}$
1	`for $a in` ... F_2	$\mathsf{Map}\{[\mathsf{a{:}ID}]\}(\ldots)$
2	`for $b in` ... F_3	$\mathsf{MapConcat}\{\mathsf{Map}\{[\mathsf{b{:}ID}]\}(\ldots)\}(p_1)$
3	`where` $\$a{=}\$b$ F_4	$\mathsf{Select}\{\#\mathsf{a}{=}\#\mathsf{b}\}(p_2)$
4	`return $a`	$\mathsf{Map}\{\#\mathsf{a}\}(p_3)$

The following theorem expresses the correctness of this compilation scheme, with respect to our semantics. Interestingly, the proof is done by merely applying a simple variant of the semantics provided in Section 4 to the result of compilation, and showing that it is *syntactically* equivalent to the semantics of the same query in the core. The variant is defined in the Appendix.

Theorem 4.9 (correctness). *For any environment Σ, stores σ, σ', XQueryU expression E, variable $\$t$, field name assignment ϱ defined for all free variables in E, and value v',*

$$\Sigma, \sigma \vdash \mathcal{A}[\![\mathcal{C}[\![E]\!]^{\varrho}]\!]_{\$t} \Rightarrow v, \sigma' \quad \textit{iff} \quad \Sigma, \sigma \vdash \mathcal{X}[\![E]\!]^{\varrho}_{\$t} \Rightarrow v, \sigma'$$

5 Conclusion

In this paper, we showed how the nested-for and the tuple-stream semantics for FLWOR expressions diverge in presence of side-effects. We have formalized the compilation process for XQuery extended with side effects into a database algebra, and we have shown that this compilation scheme is sound for the tuple-stream semantics. This formalization shows that the tuple-stream semantics admits a simple implementation, based on normalization and list comprehensions, along the lines of the traditional implementation of main-memory programming language iterators. We are currently investigating optimization of database languages with side-effects based on that framework.

Acknowledgements. We would like to thank Limsoon Wong for clarifying some details about optimization in Kleisli, and Mary Fernández for feedback on earlier drafts of this paper.

References

1. Astrahan, M.M., Blasgen, M.W., Chamberlin, D.D., Eswaran, K.P., Gray, J., Griffiths, P.P., Frank King III, W., Lorie, R.A., McJones, P.R., Mehl, J.W., Putzolu, G.R., Traiger, I.L., Wade, B.W., Watson, V.: System R: Relational approach to database management. ACM Transactions on Database Systems 1(2), 97–137 (1976)
2. Boag, S., Chamberlain, D., Fernández, M.F., Florescu, D., Robie, J., Siméon, J.: XQuery 1.0: An XML query language, W3C recommendation (2007)
3. Buneman, P., Libkin, L., Suciu, D., Tannen, V., Wong, L.: Comprehension syntax. SIGMOD Record 23(1), 87–96 (1994)
4. Chamberlain, D., Carey, M., Florescu, D., Kossmann, D., Robie, J.: XQueryP: Programming with XQuery. In: XIME-P (2006)
5. Chamberlain, D., Florescu, D., Robie, J.: XQuery scripting extension 1.0 requirements, W3C working draft (March 23, 2007), `http://www.w3.org/TR/2007/WD-xquery-sx-10-requirements-20070323/2007`
6. Chamberlain, D., Florescu, D., Robie, J.: XQuery Update Facility, W3C working draft (July 11, 2006) (2007)
7. Draper, D., Fankhauser, P., Fernández, M.F., Malhotra, A., Rose, K., Rys, M., Siméon, J., Wadler, P.: XQuery 1.0 and XPath 2.0 formal semantics, W3C recommendation (January 24, 2007) (2007)
8. Fegaras, L.: Query unnesting in object-oriented databases. In: SIGMOD Conference, pp. 49–60 (1998)
9. Fegaras, L.: Optimizing queries with object updates. J. Intell. Inf. Syst. 12(2-3), 219–242 (1999)
10. Fernández, M., Malhotra, A., Marsh, J., Nagy, M., Walsh, N.: XQuery1.0 and XPath 2.0 data model (xdm). W3C Recommendation (January 2007)
11. Fernández, M.F., Siméon, J., Wadler, P.: A semi-monad for semi-structured data. In: Van den Bussche, J., Vianu, V. (eds.) ICDT 2001. LNCS, vol. 1973, pp. 263–300. Springer, Heidelberg (2000)
12. Florescu, D., Grünhagen, A., Kossmann, D.: XL: An XML programming language for Web service specification and composition. In: International conference on World Wide Web, pp. 65–76 (May 2002)
13. Ghelli, G., Re, C., Siméon, J.: XQuery!: An XML query language with side effects. In: Grust, T., Höpfner, H., Illarramendi, A., Jablonski, S., Mesiti, M., Müller, S., Patranjan, P.-L., Sattler, K.-U., Spiliopoulou, M., Wijsen, J. (eds.) EDBT 2006. LNCS, vol. 4254, pp. 178–191. Springer, Heidelberg (2006)
14. Gunter, C.A., Mitchell, J.C.: Theoretical Aspects of Object-Oriented Programming. MIT Press, Cambridge (1994)
15. Harren, M., Raghavachari, M., Shmueli, O., Burke, M.G., Bordawekar, R., Pechtchanski, I., Sarkar, V.: Xj: facilitating xml processing in java. In: International conference on World Wide Web, pp. 278–287 (2005)

16. Hidders, J., Paredaens, J., Vercammen, R.: On the expressive power of xquery-based update languages. In: Amer-Yahia, S., Bellahsène, Z., Hunt, E., Unland, R., Yu, J.X. (eds.) XSym 2006. LNCS, vol. 4156, pp. 92–106. Springer, Heidelberg (2006)
17. The linq project. `msdn.microsoft.com/XML/linqproject`
18. May, N., Helmer, S., Moerkotte, G.: Nested queries and quantifiers in an ordered context. In: ICDE, pp. 239–250 (2004)
19. Moerkotte, G.: Building query compilers, draft manuscript (December 2005), `http://db.informatik.uni-mannheim.de/moer`
20. Ramakrishnan, R., Gehrke, J.: Database Management Systems. McGraw-Hill, New York (2000)
21. Re, C., Siméon, J., Fernández, M.F.: A complete and efficient algebraic compiler for XQuery. In: ICDE, p. 14 (2006)
22. Tannen, V.: Tutorial: Languages for collection types. In: PODS, pp. 150–154 (1994)
23. Tannen, V., Buneman, P., Wong, L.: Naturally embedded query languages. In: Hull, R., Biskup, J. (eds.) ICDT 1992. LNCS, vol. 646, pp. 140–154. Springer, Heidelberg (1992)
24. Trinder, P., Wadler, P.: Improving list comprehension database queries. In: Fourth IEEE Region 10 Conference (TENCON), pp. 186–192. IEEE Computer Society Press, Los Alamitos (1989)
25. Wong, L.: Kleisli, a functional query system. Journal of Functional Programming 10(1), 19–56 (2000)

Repairing Inconsistent XML Write-Access Control Policies

Loreto Bravo, James Cheney, and Irini Fundulaki

School of Informatics, University of Edinburgh, UK
{lbravo,jcheney,efountou}@inf.ed.ac.uk

Abstract. XML access control policies involving updates may contain security flaws, here called *inconsistencies*, in which a forbidden operation may be simulated by performing a sequence of allowed operations. This paper investigates the problem of deciding whether a policy is consistent, and if not, how its inconsistencies can be repaired. We consider policies expressed in terms of annotated DTDs defining which operations are allowed or denied for the XML trees that are instances of the DTD. We show that consistency is decidable in PTIME for such policies and that consistent partial policies can be extended to unique "least-privilege" consistent total policies. We also consider repair problems based on deleting privileges to restore consistency, show that finding minimal repairs is NP-complete, and give heuristics for finding repairs.

1 Introduction

Discretionary access control policies for database systems can be specified in a number of different ways, for example by storing access control lists as annotations on the data itself (as in most file systems), or using rules which can be applied to decide whether to grant access to protected resources. In relational databases, high-level policies that employ rules, roles, and other abstractions tend to be much easier to understand and maintain than access control list-based policies; also, they can be implemented efficiently using static techniques, and can be analyzed off-line for security vulnerabilities [7].

Rule-based, fine-grained access control techniques for XML data have been considered extensively for *read-only queries* [11,15,14,2,17,10]. However, the problem of controlling *write access* is relatively new and has not received much attention. Authors in [2,10,16] studied enforcement of write-access control policies following annotation-based approaches.

In this paper, we build upon the schema-based access control model introduced by Stoica and Farkas [19], refined by Fan, Chan, and Garofalakis [11], and extended to write-access control by Fundulaki and Maneth [13]. We investigate the problem of checking for, and repairing, a particular class of vulnerabilities in XML write-access control policies. An access control policy specifies which actions to allow a user to perform based on the syntax of the atomic update, not its actual behavior. Thus, it is possible that a single-step action which is explicitly forbidden by the policy can nevertheless be simulated by one or more allowed actions. This is what we mean by an *inconsistency*; a consistent policy is one in which such inconsistencies are not possible. We believe inconsistencies are an interesting class of policy-level security vulnerabilities since such policies allow users to circumvent the intended effect of the policy. The

M. Arenas and M.I. Schwartzbach (Eds.): DBPL 2007, LNCS 4797, pp. 97–111, 2007.

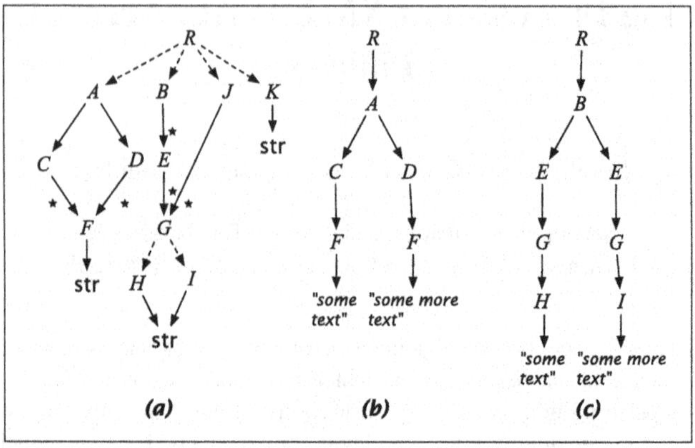

Fig. 1. DTD graph (a) and XML documents conforming to the DTD (b, c)

purpose of this paper is to define consistency, understand how to determine whether a policy is consistent, and show how to automatically identify possible repairs for inconsistent policies.

Motivating Example. We introduce here an example and refer to it throughout the paper. Consider the XML DTD represented as a graph in Fig. 1(a). A document conforming to this DTD has as root an R-element with a single child element that can either be an A, B, J or K-element (indicated with dashed edges); similarly for G. An A-element has one C and one D children elements. A B-element can have zero or more E children elements (indicated with $*$-labeled edges); similarly, E and J elements can have zero or more G children elements. Finally, F, H, I and K are text elements. Fig. 1(b) and (c) show two documents that conform to the DTD.

Suppose that a security policy *allows* one to *insert* and *delete* G elements and *forbids* one from replacing an H with an I element. It is straightforward to see that the forbidden operation can be simulated by first deleting the G element with an H child and then inserting a G element with an I child. There are different ways of fixing this inconsistency: either *(a)* to allow all operations below element G or *(b)* forbid one of the *insert* and *delete* operations at node G.

Now, suppose that the policy *allows* one to *replace* an A-element with a B-element and this with a J-element, but *forbids* the replacement of A with J elements. The latter operation can be easily simulated by performing a sequence of the allowed operations. As in the previous case, the repairs that one can propose are *(a)* to allow the forbidden replace operation or *(b)* forbid one of the allowed replace operations.

Our contributions. In this paper we consider policies that are defined in terms of *non-recursive structured* XML DTDs as introduced in [11] that capture without loss of generality more general non-recursive DTDs. We first consider *total* policies in which all allowed or forbidden privileges are explicitly specified. We define consistency for such policies and prove the correctness of a straightforward polynomial time algorithm for consistency checking. We also consider *partial* policies in which privileges may be omitted. Such a policy is consistent if it can be extended to a consistent total policy;

there may be many such extensions, but we identify a canonical *least-privilege* consistent extension, and show that this can be found in polynomial time (if it exists). Finally, given an inconsistent (partial or total) policy, we consider the problem of finding a "repair", or minimal changes to the policy which restore consistency. We consider repairs based on changing operations from allowed to forbidden, show that finding minimal repairs is NP-complete, and provide heuristic repair algorithms that run in polynomial time.

The rest of this paper is structured as follows: in Section 2 we provide the definitions for XML DTDs and trees. Section 3 discusses *i)* the atomic updates and *ii)* the access control policies that we are considering. Consistency is discussed in Section 4; Section 5 discusses algorithms for detecting and repairing inconsistent policies. We conclude in Section 6. Proofs of theorems and detailed algorithms can be found in the full version of the paper [4].

2 XML DTDs and Trees

We consider *structured* XML DTDs as discussed in [11]. Although not all DTDs are syntactically representable in this form, one can (as argued by [11]) represent more general DTDs by introducing new element types. The DTDs we consider here are 1-unambiguous as required by the XML standard [5].

Definition 1 (XML DTD). Let $\mathcal{L}$ be the infinite domain of labels. A DTD D is represented by (Ele, Rg, rt) where *i)* $Ele \subseteq \mathcal{L}$ is a finite set of *element types* *ii)* rt is a distinguished type in Ele called the *root type* and *iii)* Rg defines the element types: that is, for any $A \in Ele$, $Rg(A)$ is a regular expression of the form:

$$Rg(A) := \mathsf{str} \mid \epsilon \mid B_1, B_2, \ldots, B_n \mid B_1 + B_2 + \ldots + B_n \mid B_1*$$

where $B_i \in Ele$ are distinct, ",", "+" and "$*$" stand for *concatenation, disjunction* and *Kleene star* respectively, ϵ for the EMPTY element content and str for text values.

We will refer to $A \to Rg(A)$ as the *production rule* for A. An element type B_i that appears in the production rule of an element type A is called the *subelement* type of A. We write $A \leq_D B$ for the transitive, reflexive closure of the subelement relation.

A DTD can also be represented as a directed acyclic graph that we call *DTD graph.*

Definition 2 (DTD Graph). A DTD graph $G_D = (\mathcal{V}_D, \mathcal{E}_D, r_D)$ for a DTD $D = (Ele, Rg, rt)$ is a directed acyclic graph (DAG) where *i)* $\mathcal{V}_D$ is the set of nodes for the element types in $Ele \cup \{\mathsf{str}\}$, *ii)* $\mathcal{E}_D = \{(A, B) \mid A, B \in Ele$ and B is a subelement type of $A\}$ and *iii)* r_D is the distinguished node rt.

Example 1. The production rules for the DTD graph shown in Fig. 1 are:

$R \to A+B+J+K$	$D \to F*$	$G \to H+I$	$H \to \mathsf{str}$
$A \to C, D$	$B \to E*$	$J \to G*$	$I \to \mathsf{str}$
$C \to F*$	$E \to G*$	$F \to \mathsf{str}$	$K \to \mathsf{str}$

□

We model XML documents as *rooted unordered* trees with labels from $\mathcal{L} \cup \{\mathsf{str}\}$.

Definition 3 (XML Tree). An unordered XML tree t is an expression of the form $t = (N_t, E_t, \lambda_t, r_t, v_t)$ where *i)* N_t is the set of nodes *ii)* $E_t \subset N_t \times N_t$ is the set of edges, *iii)* $\lambda_t : N_t \to \mathcal{L} \cup \{\mathsf{str}\}$ is a labeling function over nodes *iv)* r_t is the root of t and is a distinguished node in N_t and *v)* v_t is a function that assigns a string value to nodes labeled with str.

We denote by $\mathsf{children}_t(n)$, $\mathsf{parent}_t(n)$ and $\mathsf{desc}_t(n)$, the children, parent and descendant nodes, respectively, of a node n in an XML tree t. The set $\mathsf{desc}^e_t(n)$ denotes the edges in E_t between descendant nodes of n. A node labeled with an element type A in DTD D is called an *instance* of A or an *A-element.*

We say that an XML tree $t = (N_t, E_t, \lambda_t, r_t, v_t)$ *conforms* to a DTD $D = (Ele, Rg, rt)$ at element type A if *i)* r_t is labeled with A (i.e., $\lambda_t(r_t) = A$) *ii)* each node in N_t is labeled with either an Ele element type B or with str, *iii)* each node in t labeled with an Ele element type B has a list of children nodes such that their labels are in the language defined by $Rg(B)$ and *iv)* each node in t labeled with str has a string value ($v_t(n)$ is defined) and is a leaf of the tree. An XML tree t is a valid instance of the DTD D if r_t is labeled with rt. We write $I_D(A)$ for the set of valid instances of D at element type A, and I_D for $I_D(rt)$.

Definition 4 (XML Tree Isomorphism). We say that an XML tree t_1 is isomorphic to an XML tree t_2, denoted $t_1 \equiv t_2$, iff there exists a bijection $h : N_{t_1} \to N_{t_2}$ where: *i)* $h(r_{t_1}) = r_{t_2}$ *ii)* if $(x, y) \in E_{t_1}$ then $(h(x), h(y)) \in E_{t_2}$, *iii)* $\lambda_{t_1}(x) = \lambda_{t_2}(h(x))$, and *iv)* $v_{t_1}(x) = v_{t_2}(h(x))$ for every x with $\lambda_{t_1}(x) = \mathsf{str} = \lambda_{t_2}(h(x))$.

3 XML Access Control Framework

3.1 Atomic Updates

Our updates are modeled on the XQuery Update Facility draft [8], which considers delete, replace and several insert update operations. A $\mathsf{delete}(n)$ operation will delete node n and all its descendants. A $\mathsf{replace}(n, t)$ operation will replace the subtree with root n by the tree t. A $\mathsf{replace}(n, s)$ operation will replace the text value of node n with string s. There are several types of insert operations, *e.g.*, $\mathsf{insert\ into}(n, t)$, $\mathsf{insert\ before}(n, t)$, $\mathsf{insert\ after}(n, t)$, $\mathsf{insert\ as\ first}(n, t)$, $\mathsf{insert\ as\ last}(n, t)$. Update $\mathsf{insert\ into}(n, t)$ inserts the root of t as a child of n whereas update $\mathsf{insert\ as\ first}(n, t)$ ($\mathsf{insert\ as\ last}(n, t)$) inserts the root of t as a first (resp. last) child of n. Update operations $\mathsf{insert\ before}(n, t)$ and $\mathsf{insert\ after}(n, t)$ insert the root node of t as a preceding and following sibling of n resp..

Since we only consider unordered XML trees, we deal only with the operation $\mathsf{insert\ into}(n, t)$ (for readability purposes, we are going to write $\mathsf{insert}(n, t)$). Thus, in what follows, we will restrict to four types of update operations: $\mathsf{delete}(n)$, $\mathsf{replace}(n, t)$, $\mathsf{replace}(n, s)$ and $\mathsf{insert}(n, t)$.

More formally, for a tree $t_1 = (N_{t_1}, E_{t_1}, \lambda_{t_1}, r_{t_1}, v_{t_1})$, a node n in t_1, a tree $t_2 = (N_{t_2}, E_{t_2}, \lambda_{t_2}, r_{t_2}, v_{t_2})$ and a string value s, the result of applying $\mathsf{insert}(n, t_2)$, $\mathsf{replace}(n, t_2)$, $\mathsf{delete}(n)$ and $\mathsf{replace}(n, s)$ to t_1, is a new tree $t = (N_t, E_t, \lambda_t, r_t, v_t)$ defined as shown in Table 1. We denote by $[\![op]\!](t)$ the result of applying update operation *op* on tree t.

Table 1. Semantics of update operations

	N_t	E_t	λ_t	r_t	v_t
$[\![\mathsf{insert}(n,t_2)]\!](t_1)$	$N_{t_1} \cup N_{t_2}$	$E_{t_1} \cup E_{t_2} \cup \{(n, r_{t_2})\}$	$\lambda_{t_1}(m), m \in N_{t_1}$ $\lambda_{t_2}(m), m \in N_{t_2}$	r_{t_1}	$v_{t_1}(m), m \in N_{t_1}$ $v_{t_2}(m), m \in N_{t_2}$
$[\![\mathsf{replace}(n,t_2)]\!](t_1)$	$N_{t_1} \cup N_{t_2}$ $\setminus \mathsf{desc}_{t_1}(n)$	$E_{t_1} \cup E_{t_2} \cup$ $\{(\mathsf{parent}_{t_1}(n), r_{t_2})\} \setminus$ $\mathsf{desc}^e_{t_1}(n)$	$\lambda_{t_1}(m)$, $m \in (N_{t_1} \setminus \{n\})$ $\lambda_{t_2}(m), m \in N_{t_2}$	r_{t_1}	$v_{t_1}(m)$, $m \in (N_{t_1} \setminus \{n\})$ $v_{t_2}(m), m \in N_{t_2}$
$[\![\mathsf{replace}(n,s)]\!](t_1)$	N_{t_1}	E_{t_1}	$\lambda_{t_1}(m), m \in N_{t_1}$	r_{t_1}	$v_{t_1}(m)$, $m \in (N_{t_1} \setminus \{n\})$ $v_{t_1}(n) = s$
$[\![\mathsf{delete}(n)]\!](t_1)$	$N_{t_1} \setminus \mathsf{desc}_{t_1}(n)$	$E_{t_1} \setminus \mathsf{desc}^e_{t_1}(n)$	$\lambda_{t_1}(m)$, $m \in (N_{t_1} \setminus \mathsf{desc}_{t_1}(n))$	r_{t_1}	$v_{t_1}(m)$, $m \in (N_{t_1} \setminus \mathsf{desc}_{t_1}(n))$

An update operation $\mathsf{insert}(n, t_2)$, $\mathsf{replace}(n, t_2)$, $\mathsf{replace}(n, s)$ or $\mathsf{delete}(n)$ is *valid* with respect to tree t_1 provided $n \in N_{t_1}$ and t_2, if present, does not overlap with t_1 (that is, $N_{t_1} \cap N_{t_2} = \emptyset$). We also consider *update sequences* $op_1; \ldots; op_n$ with the (standard) semantics $[\![op_1; \ldots; op_n]\!](t_1) = [\![op_n]\!]([\![op_{n-1}]\!](\cdots [\![op_1]\!](t_1)))$. A sequence of updates $op_1; \ldots; op_n$ is valid with respect to t_0 if for each $i \in \{1, \ldots, n\}$, op_{i+1} is valid with respect to t_i, where $t_1 = [\![op_1]\!](t_0)$, $t_2 = [\![op_2]\!](t_1)$, *etc.* The result of a valid update (or valid sequence of updates) exists and is unique up to tree isomorphism. We restrict attention to valid updates and sequences in the rest of the paper.

3.2 Access Control Framework

We use the notion of *update access type* to specify the access authorizations in our context. Our update access types are inspired from the XAcU^{annot} language discussed in [13]. Authors followed the idea of *security annotations* introduced in [11] to specify the access authorizations for XML documents in the presence of a DTD.

Definition 5 (Update Access Types). Given a DTD D, an *update access type* (*UAT*) defined over D is of the form $(A, \mathsf{insert}(B_1))$, $(A, \mathsf{replace}(B_1, B_2))$, $(A, \mathsf{replace}(\mathsf{str}, \mathsf{str}))$ or $(A, \mathsf{delete}(B_1))$, where A is an element type in D, B_1 and B_2 are subelement types of A and $B_1 \neq B_2$.

Intuitively, an *UAT* represents a set of *atomic update operations*. More specifically, for t an instance of DTD D, *op* an atomic update and uat an update access type we say that *op* matches uat on t (*op* $\mathsf{matches}_t$ uat) if:

$$\frac{\lambda_t(n) = A \quad t' \in I_D(B)}{\mathsf{insert}(n, t') \ \mathsf{matches}_t \ (A, \mathsf{insert}(B))} \qquad \frac{\lambda_t(n) = B \quad \lambda_t(\mathsf{parent}_t(n)) = A}{\mathsf{delete}(n) \ \mathsf{matches}_t \ (A, \mathsf{delete}(B))}$$

$$\frac{\lambda_t(n) = B, t' \in I_D(B'), \lambda_t(parent_t(n)) = A, B \neq B'}{\mathsf{replace}(n, t') \ \mathsf{matches}_t \ (A, \mathsf{replace}(B, B'))}$$

$$\frac{\lambda_t(n) = \mathsf{str}, \lambda_t(\mathsf{parent}_t(n)) = A}{\mathsf{replace}(n, s) \ \mathsf{matches}_t (A, \mathsf{replace}(\mathsf{str}, \mathsf{str}))}$$

It is trivial to translate our update access types to XAcU^{annot} security annotations. In this work we assume that the evaluation of an update operation on a tree that conforms to a DTD D results in a *tree that conforms to* D. It is clear then that each update access type only makes sense for specific element types. For our example DTD, the update access type $(A, \mathsf{delete}(C))$ is not meaningful because allowing the deletion of a C-element would result in an XML document that does not conform to the DTD, and therefore, the update will be rejected. Similar for $(R, \mathsf{delete}(A))$ or $(R, \mathsf{insert}(A))$. But, $(B, \mathsf{delete}(E))$ and $(B, \mathsf{insert}(E))$ are relevant for this specific DTD. The relation uat valid_in D, which indicates that an update access type uat is valid for the DTD D, is defined as follows:

$$\frac{Rg(A) := B_1^*}{(A, \mathsf{insert}(B_1)) \ \mathsf{valid\_in}\ D} \qquad \frac{Rg(A) := B_1*}{(A, \mathsf{delete}(B_1)) \ \mathsf{valid\_in}\ D}$$

$$\frac{Rg(A) := \mathsf{str}}{(A, \mathsf{replace}(\mathsf{str}, \mathsf{str})) \ \mathsf{valid\_in}\ D} \qquad \frac{Rg(A) := B_1 + \cdots + B_n, i, j \in [1, n] \quad i \neq j}{(A, \mathsf{replace}(B_i, B_j)) \ \mathsf{valid\_in}\ D}$$

We define the set of valid *UATs* for a given DTD D as $\mathsf{valid}(D) = \{uat \mid uat \ \mathsf{valid\_in}\ D\}$. A *security policy* will be defined by a set of *allowed* and *forbidden* valid *UATs*.

Definition 6. A security policy P defined over a DTD D, is represented by $(\mathcal{A}, \mathcal{F})$ where $\mathcal{A}$ is the set of *allowed* and $\mathcal{F}$ the set of *forbidden* update access types defined over D such that $\mathcal{A} \subseteq \mathsf{valid}(D)$, $\mathcal{F} \subseteq \mathsf{valid}(D)$ and $\mathcal{A} \cap \mathcal{F} = \emptyset$. A security policy is *total* if $\mathcal{A} \cup \mathcal{F} = \mathsf{valid}(D)$, otherwise it is *partial*.

Example 2. Consider the DTD D in Fig. 1 and the total policy $P = (\mathcal{A}, \mathcal{F})$ where $\mathcal{A}$ is:

$(R, \mathsf{replace}(A, B))$	$(R, \mathsf{replace}(B, J))$	$(R, \mathsf{replace}(J, K))$	$(R, \mathsf{replace}(K, J))$
$(R, \mathsf{replace}(K, B))$	$(C, \mathsf{insert}(F))$	$(C, \mathsf{delete}(F))$	$(D, \mathsf{insert}(F))$
$(D, \mathsf{delete}(F))$	$(F, \mathsf{replace}(\mathsf{str}, \mathsf{str}))$	$(B, \mathsf{insert}(E))$	$(B, \mathsf{delete}(E))$
$(E, \mathsf{insert}(G))$	$(E, \mathsf{delete}(G))$	$(G, \mathsf{replace}(I, H))$	$(J, \mathsf{insert}(G))$
$(J, \mathsf{delete}(G))$	$(D, \mathsf{insert}(F))$	$(D, \mathsf{delete}(F))$	$(H, \mathsf{replace}(\mathsf{str}, \mathsf{str}))$
$(I, \mathsf{replace}(\mathsf{str}, \mathsf{str}))$	$(K, \mathsf{replace}(\mathsf{str}, \mathsf{str}))$		

and $\mathcal{F} = \mathsf{valid}(D) \setminus \mathcal{A}$. On the other hand, $P = (\mathcal{A}, \emptyset)$ is a partial policy. □

The operations that are allowed by a policy $P = (\mathcal{A}, \mathcal{F})$ on an XML tree t, denoted by $[\![\mathcal{A}]\!](t)$, are the union of the atomic update operations matching each *UAT* in $\mathcal{A}$. More formally, $[\![\mathcal{A}]\!](t) = \{op \mid op \ \mathsf{matches}_t\ uat, \text{ and } uat \in \mathcal{A}\}$. We say that an update sequence $op_1; \ldots; op_n$ is allowed on t provided the sequence is valid on t and $op_1 \in [\![\mathcal{A}]\!](t)$, $op_2 \in [\![\mathcal{A}]\!]([\![op_1]\!](t))$, *etc.*[1] Analogously, the forbidden operations are $[\![\mathcal{F}]\!](t) = \{op \mid op \ \mathsf{matches}_t\ uat, \text{ and } uat \in \mathcal{F}\}$. If a policy P is *total*, its semantics is given by its allowed updates, i.e. $[\![P]\!](t) = [\![\mathcal{A}]\!](t)$. The semantics of a partial policy is studied in detail in Section 4.1.

4 Consistent Policies

A policy is said to be consistent if it is not possible to simulate a forbidden update through a sequence of allowed updates. More formally:

Definition 7. *A policy $P = (\mathcal{A}, \mathcal{F})$ defined over a DTD D is consistent if for every XML tree t that conforms to D, there does not exist a valid sequence of updates $op_1; \ldots; op_n$ that is allowed on t and a valid update $op_0 \in [\![\mathcal{F}]\!](t)$ such that:*

$$[\![op_1; \ldots; op_n]\!](t) \equiv [\![op_0]\!](t).$$

[1] Note that this is *not* the same as $\{op_1, \ldots, op_n\} \subseteq [\![\mathcal{A}]\!](t)$.

In our framework inconsistencies can be classified as: insert/delete and replace.

Inconsistencies due to *insert/delete* operations arise when the policy *allows* one to insert *and* delete nodes of element type A whilst *forbidding* some operation in some descendant element type of A. In this case, the forbidden operation can be simulated by first deleting an A-element and then inserting a new A-element after having done the necessary modifications.

There are two kinds of inconsistencies created by *replace* operations on a production rule $A \to B_1 + \cdots + B_n$ of a DTD. First, if we are allowed to replace B_i by B_j and B_j by B_k but not B_i by B_k, then one can simulate the latter operation by a sequence of the first two. Second, consider that we are allowed to replace some element type B_i with an element type B_j and vice versa. If some operation in the subtree of *either* B_i or B_j is forbidden, then it is evident that one can simulate the forbidden operation by a sequence of allowed operations, leading to an inconsistency.

We say that *nothing is forbidden below an element type* A in a policy $P = (\mathcal{A}, \mathcal{F})$ defined over D if for every B_i s.t. $A \leq_D B_i$ and every $(B_i, x) \in \mathsf{valid}(D)$, $(B_i, x) \notin \mathcal{F}$. If $A \to B_1 + \ldots + B_n$, then we define the *replace graph* $\mathcal{G}_A = (\mathcal{V}_A, \mathcal{E}_A)$ for a policy $P = (\mathcal{A}, \mathcal{F})$, where *i)* $\mathcal{V}_A$ is the set of nodes for $B_1, \ldots, B_n$ and *ii)* $(B_i, B_j) \in \mathcal{E}_A$ if there exists $(A, \mathsf{replace}(B_i, B_j)) \in \mathcal{A}$. Also, the set of *forbidden edges* of A, is $\mathcal{E}_A^F = \{(B_i, B_j) \mid (A, \mathsf{replace}(B_i, B_j)) \in \mathcal{F}\}$. We say that a graph $\mathcal{G} = (\mathcal{V}, \mathcal{E})$ is *transitive* if $(x, y), (y, z) \in \mathcal{E}$ then $(x, z) \in \mathcal{E}$. We write $\mathcal{G}_A^+$ for the transitive graph of $\mathcal{G}_A$. The following theorem characterizes policy consistency:

Theorem 1. *A policy $P = (\mathcal{A}, \mathcal{F})$ defined over DTD D is consistent if and only if for every production rule:*

1. *$A \to B*$ in D, if $(A, \mathsf{insert}(B)) \in \mathcal{A}$ and $(A, \mathsf{delete}(B)) \in \mathcal{A}$, then nothing is forbidden below B*
2. *$A \to B_1 + \cdots + B_n$ in D, if for every edge (B_i, B_j) in $\mathcal{G}_A^+$, $(B_i, B_j) \notin \mathcal{E}_A^F$, and*
3. *$A \to B_1 + \cdots + B_n$ in D, if for every $i \in [1, \ldots n]$, if B_i is contained in a cycle in $\mathcal{G}_A$ then nothing is forbidden below B_i.*

Proof (Sketch). The forward direction is straightforward, since if any of the rules are violated an inconsistency can be found, as sketched above. For the reverse direction, we first need to reduce allowed update sequences to certain (allowed) normal forms that are easier to analyze, then the reasoning proceeds by cases. A full proof is given in [4]. □

In the case of total policies, condition 2 in Theorem 1 amounts to requiring that the replace graph $\mathcal{G}_A$ is transitive (i.e., $\mathcal{G}_A = \mathcal{G}_A^+$).

Example 3. (example 2 continued) The total policy P is inconsistent because:

- $(E, \mathsf{insert}(G))$ and $(E, \mathsf{delete}(G))$ are in $\mathcal{A}$, but $(G, \mathsf{replace}(H, I)) \in \mathcal{F}$ (condition 1, Theorem 1),
- $(R, \mathsf{replace}(A, J))$, $(R, \mathsf{replace}(A, K))$ and $(R, \mathsf{replace}(B, K))$ are in $\mathcal{F}$ (condition 2, Theorem 1), and
- There are cycles in $\mathcal{G}_R$ involving both B and J, but below both of them there is a forbidden *UAT*, namely $(G, \mathsf{replace}(H, I))$ (condition 3, Theorem 1). □

It is easy to see that we can check whether properties 1, 2, and 3 hold for a policy using standard graph algorithms:

Proposition 1. *The problem of deciding policy consistency is in* PTIME.

We wish to emphasize that consistency is highly sensitive to the design of policies and update types. For example, we have consciously chosen to *omit* an update type $(A, \mathsf{replace}(B_i, B_i))$ for an element type A in the DTD whose production rule is either of the form $B*$ or $B_1 + \ldots + B_n$. Consider the case of a conference management system where a *paper* element has a $decision$ and a $title$ subelement. Suppose that the policy allows the author of the paper to *replace* a *paper* with another *paper* element, but forbids to change the value of the $decision$ subelement. This policy is inconsistent since by replacing a *paper* element by another with a different $decision$ subelement we are able to perform a forbidden update. In fact, the $\mathsf{replace}(paper, paper)$ can simulate any other update type applying below a *paper* element. Thus, if the policy forbids replacement of *paper* nodes, then it would be inconsistent to allow any other operation on $decision$ and $title$. Because of this problem, we argue that update type $(A, \mathsf{replace}(B_i, B_i))$ should not be used in policies. Instead, more specific privileges should be assigned individually, *e.g.*, by allowing replacement of the text values of $title$ or $decision$ element types.

4.1 Partial Policies

Partial policies may be smaller and easier to maintain than total policies, but are ambiguous because some permissions are left unspecified. An access control mechanism must either allow or deny a request. One solution to this problem (in accordance with the *principle of least privilege*) might be to deny access to the unspecified operations. However, there is no guarantee that the resulting total policy is *consistent*. Indeed, it is not obvious that a partial policy (even if consistent) has *any* consistent total extension. We will now show how to find consistent extensions, if they exist, and in particular how to find a "least-privilege" consistent extension; these turn out to be unique when they exist so they seem to be a natural choice for defining the meaning of a partial policy.

For convenience, we write $\mathcal{A}_P$ and $\mathcal{F}_P$ for the allowed and forbidden sets of a policy P; i.e., $P = (\mathcal{A}_P, \mathcal{F}_P)$. We introduce an *information ordering* $P \sqsubseteq Q$, defined as $\mathcal{A}_P \subseteq \mathcal{A}_Q$ and $\mathcal{F}_P \subseteq \mathcal{F}_Q$; that is, Q is "more defined" than P. In this case, we say that Q extends P. We say that a partial policy P is *quasiconsistent* if it has a consistent total extension. For example, a partial policy on the DTD of Figure 1 which allows $(B, \mathsf{insert}(E))$, $(B, \mathsf{delete}(E))$, and denies $(H, \mathsf{replace}(\mathsf{str}, \mathsf{str}))$ is not quasiconsistent, because any consistent extension of the policy has to allow $(H, \mathsf{replace}(\mathsf{str}, \mathsf{str}))$.

We also introduce a *privilege ordering* on total policies $P \leq Q$, defined as $\mathcal{A}_P \subseteq \mathcal{A}_Q$; that is, Q allows every operation that is allowed in P. This ordering has unique greatest lower bounds $P \wedge Q$ defined as $(\mathcal{A}_P \cap \mathcal{A}_Q, \mathcal{F}_P \cup \mathcal{F}_Q)$. We now show that every quasiconsistent policy has a *least-privilege* consistent extension $P^\dagger$; that is, $P^\dagger$ is consistent and $P^\dagger \leq Q$ whenever Q is a consistent extension of P.

Lemma 1. *If P_1, P_2 are consistent total extensions of P_0 then $P_1 \wedge P_2$ is also a consistent extension of P_0.*

Proof. It is easy to see that if P_1, P_2 extend P_0 then $P_1 \wedge P_2$ extends P_0. Suppose $P_1 \wedge P_2$ is inconsistent. Then there exists an XML tree t, an atomic operation $op_0 \in$

$[\![\mathcal{F}_{P_1 \wedge P_2}]\!](t)$, a sequence $\overline{op}$ allowed on t by $P_1 \wedge P_2$, such that $[\![op_0]\!](t) = [\![\overline{op}]\!](t)$. Now $\mathcal{A}_{P_1 \wedge P_2} = \mathcal{A}_{P_1} \cap \mathcal{A}_{P_2}$, so op_0 must be forbidden by either P_1 or P_2. On the other hand, $\overline{op}$ must be allowed by *both* P_1 and P_2, so $t, op_0, \overline{op}$ forms a counterexample to the consistency of P_1 (or symmetrically P_2). □

Proposition 2. *Each quasiconsistent policy P has a unique $\leq$-least consistent total extension $P^\dagger$.*

Proof. Since P is quasiconsistent, the set $S = \{Q \mid P \sqsubseteq Q, Q \text{ consistent}\}$ is finite, nonempty, and closed under $\wedge$, so has a $\leq$-least element $P^\dagger = \bigwedge S$. □

Finally, we show how to find the least-privilege consistent extension, or determine that none exists (and hence that the partial policy is not quasiconsistent). Define the operator $T : \mathcal{P}(\mathsf{valid}(D)) \to \mathcal{P}(\mathsf{valid}(D))$ as:

$$\begin{aligned} T(S) = S &\cup \{(C,x) \mid B \leq_D C, Rg(A) = B^*, \{(A, \mathsf{insert}(B)), (A, \mathsf{delete}(B))\} \subseteq S\} \\ &\cup \{(C,x) \mid B_i \leq_D C, Rg(A) = B_1 + \ldots + B_n, (B_i, B_i) \in \mathcal{G}_A^+(S)\} \\ &\cup \{(A, \mathsf{replace}(B_i, B_k)) \mid Rg(A) = B_1 + \ldots + B_n, (B_i, B_k) \in \mathcal{G}_A^+(S)\} \end{aligned}$$

where $\mathcal{G}_A^+(S)$ is the transitive graph of A for the partial policy S.

Lemma 2. *If $uat \in T(S)$ then for any valid operation op_0 matching uat on t there exists a valid sequence of operations $\overline{op}$ allowed on t by S such that $[\![op_0]\!](t) = [\![\overline{op}]\!](t)$.*

Theorem 2. *Let P be a partial policy. The following are equivalent: (1) P is quasiconsistent, (2) P is consistent (3) $T(\mathcal{A}_P) \cap \mathcal{F}_P = \emptyset$.*

Proof. To show (1) implies (2), if P' is a consistent extension of P, then any inconsistency in P would be an inconsistency in P', so P must be consistent. To show (2) implies (3), we prove the contrapositive. If $T(\mathcal{A}_P) \cap \mathcal{F}_P \neq \emptyset$ then choose $uat \in T(\mathcal{A}_P) \cap \mathcal{F}_P$. Choose an arbitrary tree t and atomic update op satisfying $op_0 \in [\![uat]\!](t)$. By Lemma 2, there exists a sequence $\overline{op}$ allowed by $\mathcal{A}_P$ on t with $[\![\overline{op}]\!](t) = [\![op_0]\!](t)$. Hence, policy P is inconsistent. Finally, to show that (3) implies (1), note that $(T(\mathcal{A}_P), \mathsf{valid}(D) \setminus T(\mathcal{A}_P))$ extends P and is consistent provided $T(\mathcal{A}_P) \cap \mathcal{F}_P = \emptyset$.

Indeed, for a (quasi-)consistent P, the least-privilege consistent extension of P is simply $P^\dagger = (T(\mathcal{A}_P), \mathsf{valid}(D) \setminus T(\mathcal{A}_P))$ (proof omitted). Hence, we can decide whether a partial policy is (quasi-)consistent and if so find $P^\dagger$ in PTIME.

5 Repairs

If a policy is inconsistent, we would like to suggest possible minimal ways of modifying it in order to restore consistency. In other words, we would like to find *repairs* that are as close as possible to the inconsistent policy.

There are several ways of defining these repairs. We might want to repair by changing the permissions of certain operations from allow to forbidden and vice versa; or we might give preference to some type of changes over others. Also, we can measure the minimality of the repairs as a minimal number of changes or a minimal set of changes under set inclusion.

Due to space restrictions, in this paper we will focus on finding repairs that transform *UATs* from *allowed* to *forbidden* and that minimize the number of changes. We believe that such repairs are a useful special case, since the repairs are guaranteed to be more restrictive than the original policy.

Definition 8. A policy $P' = (\mathcal{A}', \mathcal{F}')$ is a *repair* of a policy $P = (\mathcal{A}, \mathcal{F})$ defined over a DTD D iff: i) P' is a policy defined over D, ii) P' is consistent, and iii) $P' \leq P$.

A repair is *total* if $\mathcal{F}' = \mathsf{valid}(D) \setminus \mathcal{A}'$ and *partial* otherwise. Furthermore a repair $P' = (\mathcal{A}', \mathcal{F}')$ of $P(\mathcal{A}, \mathcal{F})$ is a *minimal-total-repair* if there is no total repair $P'' = (\mathcal{A}'', \mathcal{F}'')$ such that $|\mathcal{A}'| < |\mathcal{A}''|$ and a *minimal-partial-repair* if $\mathcal{F}' = \mathcal{F}$ and there is no partial repair $P'' = (\mathcal{A}'', \mathcal{F})$ such that $|\mathcal{A}'| < |\mathcal{A}''|$.

Given a policy $P = (\mathcal{A}, \mathcal{F})$ and an integer k, the total-repair (partial-repair) problem consists in determining if there exists a total-repair (partial-repair) $P' = (\mathcal{A}', \mathcal{F}')$ of policy P such that $|\mathcal{A} \setminus \mathcal{A}'| < k$. This problem can be shown to be NP-hard by reduction from the edge-deletion transitive-digraph problem [20].

Theorem 3. *The total-repair and partial-repair problem is* NP*-complete.*

If the DTD has no production rules of the type $A \rightarrow B_1 + \cdots + B_n$, then the total-repair problem is in PTIME.

5.1 Repair Algorithm

In this section we discuss a repair algorithm that finds a minimal repair of a total or partial policy. All the algorithms can be found in [4].

The algorithm to compute a minimal repair of a policy relies in the independence between inconsistencies *w.r.t.* insert/delete (Theorem 1, condition 1) and replace (Theorem 1, conditions 2 and 3) operations. In fact, a local repair of an inconsistency *w.r.t.* insert/delete operations will never solve nor create an inconsistency with respect to a replace operation and vice-versa. We will separately describe the algorithm for repairing the insert/delete inconsistencies and then the algorithm for the replace ones.

Both algorithms make use of the *marked DTD graph* $MG_D = (G_D, \mu, \chi)$ where μ is a function from nodes in $\mathcal{V}_D$ to {"+", "−"} and χ is a partial function from $\mathcal{V}_D$ to $\{\perp\}$. In a marked graph for a DTD D and a policy $P = (\mathcal{A}, \mathcal{F})$ *i)* each node in the graph is either marked with "+" (i.e., nothing is forbidden below the node) or with a "−" (i.e., there exists at least one update access type that is forbidden below the node). If, for nodes A and B in the DTD, *both* $(A, \mathsf{insert}(B))$ and $(A, \mathsf{delete}(B))$ are in $\mathcal{A}$ and $\mu(A) =$ "−", then $\chi(A) =$ "$\perp$". A marked graph is obtained from algorithm **markGraph** which takes as input a DTD graph and a policy P and traverses the DTD graph starting from the nodes with out-degree 0 and marks the nodes and edges as discussed above.

Example 4. Consider the graph for DTD D in Fig. 2(a) and policy $P = (\mathcal{A}, \mathcal{F})$, with $\mathcal{A}$ defined in Example 2. The result of applying **markGraph** to this DTD and policy is shown in Fig. 2(b). Notice that nodes B, E and J are marked with both a "−" and "$\perp$" since *i)* update access type $(G, \mathsf{replace}(H, I))$ is in $\mathcal{F}$ and *ii)* all insert and delete update access types for B, E and J are in $\mathcal{A}$. For readability purposes we do not show the multiplicities in the marked DTD graph. □

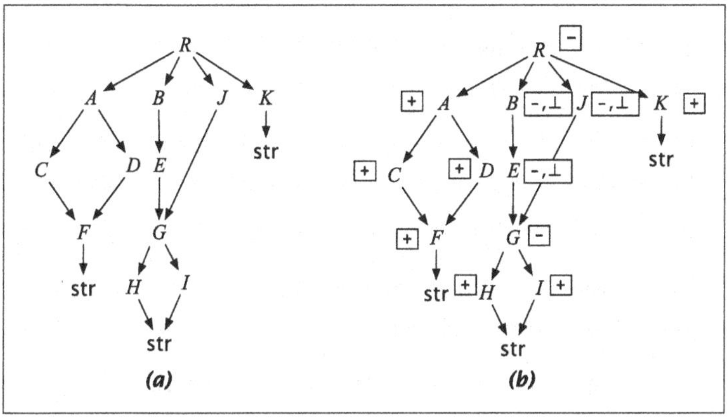

Fig. 2. DTD Graph (a) and Marked DTD Graph (b) for the DTD in Fig. 1

Repairing Inconsistencies for Insert and Delete Operations. Recall that if both the insert and delete operations are allowed at some element type and there is some operation below this type that is not allowed, then there is an inconsistency (see Theorem 1, condition 1). The marked DTD graph provides exactly this information: a node A is labeled with "$\perp$" if it is inconsistent w.r.t. *insert/delete* operations. For each such node and for the repair strategy that we have chosen, the inconsistency can be minimally repaired by removing either $(A, \mathsf{insert}(B))$ or $(A, \mathsf{delete}(B))$ from $\mathcal{A}$. Algorithm **InsDelRepair** in [4] takes as input a DTD graph G_D and a security policy $P = (\mathcal{A}, \mathcal{F})$ and returns a set of *UATs* to remove from $\mathcal{A}$ to restore consistency *w.r.t.* insert/delete-inconsistencies.

Example 5. Given the marked DTD graph in Fig. 2(b), it is easy to see that the *UATs* that must be repaired are associated with nodes B, J and E (all nodes are marked with "$\perp$"). The repairs that can be proposed to the user are to remove from $\mathcal{A}$ one *UAT* from each of the following sets: $\{(B, \mathsf{insert}(E)), (B, \mathsf{delete}(E))\}$, $\{(E, \mathsf{insert}(G)), (E, \mathsf{delete}(G))\}$ and $\{(J, \mathsf{insert}(G)), (J, \mathsf{delete}(G))\}$. □

Repairing Inconsistencies for Replace Operations. There are two types of inconsistencies related to replace operations (see Theorem 1, conditions 2–3): the first arises when some element type A is contained in some cycle and something is forbidden below it; the second arises when the replace graph $\mathcal{G}_A$ cannot be extended to a transitive graph without adding a forbidden edge in $\mathcal{E}_A^F$. In what follows we will refer to these type of inconsistencies as *negative-cycle* and *forbidden-transitivity*. By Theorem 3, the repair problem is NP-complete, and therefore, unless P = NP, there is no polynomial time algorithm to compute a minimal repair to the replace-inconsistencies. Our objective then, is to find an algorithm that runs in polynomial time and computes a repair that is not necessarily minimal.

Algorithm **ReplaceNaive** given in [4] traverses the marked graph MG_D and at each node, checks whether its production rule is of the form $A \rightarrow B_1 + \ldots + B_n$. If this is the case, it builds the replace graph for A, $\mathcal{G}_A$, and runs a modified version of the Floyd-Warshall algorithm [12]. The original Floyd-Warshall algorithm adds an edge (B, D) to the graph if there is a node C such that (B, C) and (C, D) are in the graph and (B, D) is not. Our modification consists on deleting either (B, C) or (C, D) if $(B, D) \in \mathcal{E}_A^F$, *i.e.*, if there is forbidden-transitivity. In this way, the final graph will satisfy condition 2 of Theorem 1. Also, if there are edges (B, C) and (C, B) and $\mu(C) =$ "–", *i.e.*, there is a negative-cycle, one of the two edges is deleted. Algorithm **ReplaceNaive** returns the set of edges to delete from each node to remove replace-inconsistencies.

Example 6. The replace graph $\mathcal{G}_G$ has no negative-cycles nor forbidden-transitivity, therefore it is not involved in any inconsistency. On the other hand, the replace graph $\mathcal{G}_R = (\mathcal{V}_R, \mathcal{E}_R)$, shown in Fig. 3(a) is the source of many inconsistencies. A possible execution of **ReplaceNaive** is: $(A, B), (B, J) \in \mathcal{E}_R$ but $(A, J) \in \mathcal{E}_R^F$, so (A, B) or (B, J) should be deleted, say (A, B). Now, (B, J), $(J, K) \in \mathcal{E}_R$ and $(B, K) \in \mathcal{E}_R^F$, therefore we delete either (B, J) or (J, K), say (B, J). Next, (K, J), $(J, K) \in \mathcal{E}_R$ and $\mu(J) =$ "–" in Fig. 2(b), therefore there is a negative-cycle and either (K, J) or (J, K) has to be deleted. If (K, J) is deleted, the resulting graph has no forbidden-transitivity nor negative-cycles. The policy obtained by removing $(R, \mathsf{replace}(A, B))$, $(R, \mathsf{replace}(B, J))$ and $(R, \mathsf{replace}(J, K))$ from $\mathcal{A}$ has no replace-inconsistencies. □

The **ReplaceNaive** algorithm might remove more than the necessary edges to achieve consistency: in our example, if we had removed edge (B, J) at the first step, then we would have resolved the inconsistencies that involve edges (A, B), (B, J) and (J, K).

An alternative to algorithm **ReplaceNaive**, that can find a solution closer to minimal repair, is algorithm **ReplaceSetCover** also given in [4]. This algorithm computes, using the Floyd-Warshall algorithm, the transitive closure of the replace graph $\mathcal{G}_A$ and labels each newly constructed edge e with a set of *justifications* $\mathcal{J}$. Each justification contains the sets of edges of $\mathcal{G}_A$ that were used to add e in $\mathcal{G}_A^+$. Also, if a node is found to be part of a negative-cycle, it is labeled with the justifications $\mathcal{J}$ of the edges in each cycle that contains the node. An edge or vertex might be justified by more than one set of edges. In fact, the number of justifications an edge or node might have is $O(2^{|\mathcal{E}_A|})$. To avoid the exponential number of justifications, **ReplaceSetCover** assigns at most $\mathfrak{J}$ justifications to each edge or node, where $\mathfrak{J}$ is a fixed number. This new labeled graph is then used to construct an instance of the minimum set cover problem (MSCP) [18]. The solution to the MSCP, can be used to determine the set of edges to remove from $\mathcal{G}_A$ so that none of the justifications that create inconsistencies are valid anymore. Because of the upper bound $\mathfrak{J}$ on the number of justifications, it might be the case that the graph still has forbidden-transitivity or negative-cycles. Thus, the justifications have to be computed once more and the set cover run again until there are no more replace inconsistencies.

Example 7. For $\mathfrak{J} = 1$, the first computation of justifications of **ReplaceSetCover** results in the graph in Fig. 3 (b) with the following justifications:

$$\mathcal{J}((A, J)) = \{\{(A, B), (B, J)\}\} \qquad \mathcal{J}((J, B)) = \{\{(J, K), (K, B)\}\}$$
$$\mathcal{J}((A, K)) = \{\{(A, B), (B, J), (J, K)\}\} \qquad \mathcal{J}(B) = \{\{(B, J), (J, K), (K, B)\}\}$$
$$\mathcal{J}((B, K)) = \{\{(B, J), (J, K)\}\} \qquad \mathcal{J}(J) = \{\{(J, K), (K, J)\}\}$$

Justifications for edges represent violations of transitivity. Justification for nodes represent negative-cycles. If we want to remove the inconsistencies, it is enough to delete one edge from each set in $\mathcal{J}$. □

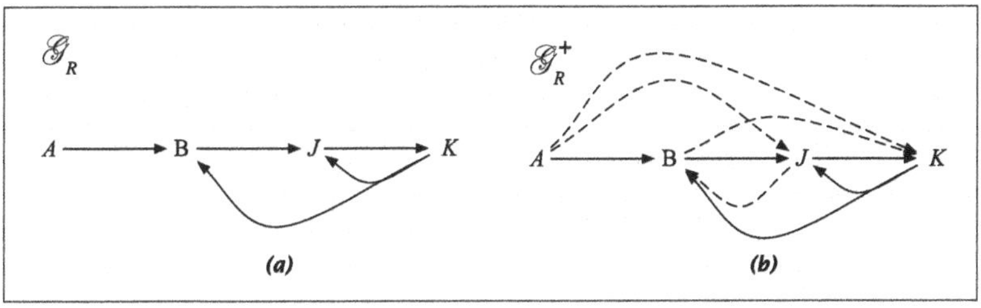

Fig. 3. Replace $\mathcal{G}_R$ (a) and Transitive Replace Graph $\mathcal{G}_R^+$(b)

The previous example shows that, for each element type A, replace-inconsistencies can be repaired by removing at least one edge from each of the justifications of edges and vertices in $\mathcal{G}_A^+$. It is easy to see that this problem can be reduced to the MSCP. An instance of the MSCP consists of a universe $\mathcal{U}$ and a set $\mathcal{S}$ of subsets of $\mathcal{U}$. A subset $\mathcal{C}$ of $\mathcal{S}$ is a set cover if the union of the elements in it is $\mathcal{U}$. A solution of the MSCP is a set cover with the minimum number of elements.

The set cover instance associated to $\mathcal{G}_A^+ = (\mathcal{V}_A, \mathcal{E}_A)$ and the set of forbidden edges $\mathcal{E}_A^F$, is $MSCP(\mathcal{G}_A^+, \mathcal{E}_A^F) = (\mathcal{U}, \mathcal{S})$ for i) $\mathcal{U} = \{s \mid s \in \mathcal{J}(e), e \in \mathcal{E}_A^F\} \cup \{s \mid s \in \mathcal{J}(V), V \in \mathcal{V}_A\}$, and ii) $\mathcal{S} = \bigcup_{e \in \mathcal{E}} \mathcal{I}(e)$ where $\mathcal{I}(e) = \{s \mid s \in \mathcal{U}, e \in s\}$. Intuitively, $\mathcal{U}$ contains all the inconsistencies, and the set $\mathcal{I}(e)$ the replace-inconsistencies in which an edge e is involved. Notice that in this instance of the MSCP, $\mathcal{U}$ is a set of justifications, therefore, $\mathcal{S}$ is a set of sets of justifications.

Example 8. The minimum set cover instance, $MSCP(\mathcal{G}_R^+, \mathcal{E}_R^F) = (\mathcal{U}, \mathcal{S})$, is such that $\mathcal{U} = \{\{(A,B),(B,J),(J,K)\}, \{(A,B),(B,J)\}, \{(B,J),(J,K)\}, \{(J,K),(K,B)\}, \{(J,K),(K,J)\}, \{(K,J),(J,K)\}, \{(B,J),(J,K),(K,B)\}\}$ and $\mathcal{S} = \{\mathcal{I}((A,B)), \mathcal{I}((B,J)), \mathcal{I}((J,K)), \mathcal{I}((K,J)), \mathcal{I}((K,B))\}$. The extensions of $\mathcal{I}$ are given in Table 2, where each column corresponds to a set $\mathcal{I}$ and each row to an element in $\mathcal{U}$. Values 1 and 0 in the table represent membership and non-membership respectively. A minimum set cover of $MSCP(\mathcal{G}_R^+, \mathcal{E}_R^F)$ is $\mathcal{C} = \{\mathcal{I}((B,J)), \mathcal{I}((J,K))\}$, since $\mathcal{I}((B,J))$ covers all the elements of $\mathcal{U}$ except for the element $\{(A,B), (B,J)\}$, which is covered by $\mathcal{I}((J,K))$. Now, using the solution from the set cover, we remove edges (B,J) and (J,K) from $\mathcal{G}_R$. If we try to compute the justifications once again, it turns out that there are no more negative-cycles and that the graph is transitive. Therefore, by removing $(R, \mathsf{replace}(B,J))$ and $(R, \mathsf{replace}(J,K))$ from $\mathcal{A}$, there are no replace-inconsistencies in node R. □

The set cover problem is MAXSNP-hard [18], but its solution can be approximated in polynomial time using a greedy-algorithm that can achieve an approximation factor of $\log(n)$ where n is the size of $\mathcal{U}$ [9]. In our case, n is $O(\mathfrak{J} \times |Ele|)$. In the ongoing example, the approximation algorithm of the set cover will return a cover of size 2. This is better than what was obtained by the **ReplaceNaive** algorithm. In order to decide which one is better, we need to run experiments to investigate the trade off between efficiency and the size of the repaired policy.

Algorithm **ReplaceRepair** will compute the set of *UATs* to remove from $\mathcal{A}$, by using either **ReplaceNaive** or **ReplaceSetCover** .

Table 2. Set cover problem

	$\mathcal{S}$				
$\mathcal{U}$	$\mathcal{I}((A,B))$	$\mathcal{I}((B,J))$	$\mathcal{I}((J,K))$	$\mathcal{I}((K,J))$	$\mathcal{I}((K,B))$
$\{(A,B),(B,J),(J,K)\}$	1	1	1	0	0
$\{(A,B),(B,J)\}$	1	1	0	0	0
$\{(B,J),(J,K)\}$	0	1	1	0	0
$\{(J,K),(K,B)\}$	0	0	1	0	1
$\{(J,K),(K,J)\}$	0	0	1	1	0
$\{(K,J),(J,K)\}$	0	0	1	1	0
$\{(B,J),(J,K),(K,B)\}$	0	1	1	0	1

Computation of a Repair. Algorithm **Repair** computes a new consistent policy $P' = (\mathcal{A}', \mathcal{F}')$ from $P = (\mathcal{A}, \mathcal{F})$ by removing from $\mathcal{A}$ the union of the *UATs* returned by algorithms **InsDelRepair** and **ReplaceRepair**. The algorithm is capable of computing total and partial repairs.

Theorem 4. *Given a total (partial) policy P, algorithm* **Repair** *returns a total (partial) repair of P.*

6 Conclusion

Access control policies attempt to constrain the actual operations users can perform, but are usually enforced in terms of syntactic representations of the operations. Thus, policies controlling update access to XML data may forbid certain operations but permit other operations that have the same effect. In this paper we have studied such *inconsistency* vulnerabilities and shown how to check consistency and repair inconsistent policies. This is, to our knowledge, the first investigation of consistency and repairs for XML write-access control policies. We also considered consistency and repair problems for partial policies which may be more convenient to write since many privileges may be left unspecified.

Cautis, Abiteboul and Milo in [6] discuss XML update constraints to restrict insert and delete updates, and propose to detect updates that violate these constraints by measuring the size of the modification of the database. This approach differs from our security framework for two reasons: a) we consider in addition to insert/delete also *replace* operations and b) we require that each operation in the sequence of updates does not violate the security constraints, whereas in their case, they require that only the input and output database satisfies them.

Minimal repairs are used in the problem of returning consistent answers from inconsistent databases [1]. There, a consistent answer is defined in terms of all the minimal repairs of a database. In [3] the set cover problem was used to find repairs of databases *w.r.t.* denial constraints.

There are a number of possible directions for future work, including running experiments for the proposed algorithms, studying consistency for more general security policies specified using XPath expressions or constraints, investigating the complexity of and algorithms for other classes of repairs, and considering more general DTDs.

Acknowledgments. We would like to thank Sebastian Maneth and Floris Geerts for insightful discussions and comments.

References

1. Arenas, M., Bertossi, L., Chomicki, J.: Consistent Query Answers in Inconsistent Databases. In: PODS, pp. 68–79. ACM Press, New York (1999)
2. Bertino, E., Ferrari, E.: Secure and Selective Dissemination of XML Documents. ACM TISSEC 5(3), 290–331 (2002)
3. Bertossi, L., Bravo, L., Franconi, E., Lopatenko, A.: Complexity and Approximation of Fixing Numerical Attributes in Databases Under Integrity Constraints. In: Bierman, G., Koch, C. (eds.) DBPL 2005. LNCS, vol. 3774, pp. 262–278. Springer, Heidelberg (2005)
4. Bravo, L., Cheney, J., Fundulaki, I.: Repairing Inconsistent XML Write-Access Control Policies (August 2007), `http://arxiv.org/abs/0708.2076`
5. Bray, T., Paoli, J., Sperberg-McQueen, C.M., Maler, E., Yergeau, F.: Extensible Markup Language (XML) 1.0 (Fourth Edition) (September 2006), `http://www.w3.org/TR/REC-xml/`
6. Cautis, B., Abiteboul, S., Milo, T.: Reasoning about XML Update Constraints. In: PODS, pp. 195–204 (2007)
7. Centonze, P., Naumovich, G., Fink, S.J., Pistoia, M.: Role-Based Access Control Consistency Validation. In: ISSTA, pp. 121–132. ACM Press, New York (2006)
8. Chamberlin, D., Florescu, D., Robie, J.: XQuery Update Facility. W3C Working Draft (July 2006), `http://www.w3.org/TR/xqupdate/`
9. Chvatal, V.: A Greedy Heuristic for the Set Covering Problem. Mathematics of Operations Research 4, 233–235 (1979)
10. Damiani, E., De Capitani di, S., Paraboschi, S., Samarati, P.: A Fine-grained Access Control System for XML Documents. ACM TISSEC 5(2), 169–202 (2002)
11. Fan, W., Chan, C.-Y., Garofalakis, M.: Secure XML Querying with Security Views. In: ACM SIGMOD, pp. 587–598. ACM Press, New York (2004)
12. Floyd, R.: Algorithm 97: Shortest path. Communications of the ACM 5(6), 345 (1962)
13. Fundulaki, I., Maneth, S.: Formalizing XML Access Control for Update Operations. In: SACMAT, pp. 169–174 (2007)
14. Fundulaki, I., Marx, M.: Specifying Access Control Policies for XML Documents with XPath. In: SACMAT, pp. 61–69 (2004)
15. Kuper, G., Massacci, F., Rassadko, N.: Generalized XML Security Views. In: SACMAT, pp. 77–84 (2005)
16. Lim, C.-H., Park, S., Son, S.H.: Access control of XML documents considering update operations. In: ACM Workshop on XML Security, pp. 49–59. ACM Press, New York (2003)
17. Murata, M., Tozawa, A., Kudo, M., Hada, S.: XML Access Control Using Static Analysis. ACM TISSEC 9(3), 290–331 (2006)
18. Papadimitriou, C.: Computational Complexity. Addison-Wesley, Reading (1994)
19. Stoica, A., Farkas, C.: Secure XML Views. In: IFIP WG 11.3, vol. 256, pp. 133–146. Kluwer, Dordrecht (2002)
20. Yannakakis, M.: Edge-Deletion Problems. SIAM Journal on Computing 10(2), 297–309 (1981)

On the Consistent Rewriting of Conjunctive Queries Under Primary Key Constraints

Jef Wijsen

Université de Mons-Hainaut, Mons, Belgium
jef.wijsen@umh.ac.be

Abstract. This article deals with the computation of consistent answers to queries on relational databases that violate primary key constraints. A repair of such inconsistent database is obtained by selecting a maximal number of tuples from each relation without ever selecting two distinct tuples that agree on the primary key. We are interested in the following problem: Given a Boolean conjunctive query q, compute a Boolean first-order (FO) query ψ such that for every database $\mathbf{db}$, ψ evaluates to true on $\mathbf{db}$ if and only if q evaluates to true on every repair of $\mathbf{db}$. Such ψ is called a consistent FO rewriting of q.

We use novel techniques to characterize classes of queries that have a consistent FO rewriting. In this way, we are able to extend previously known classes and discover new ones. Finally, we use an Ehrenfeucht-Fraïssé game to show the non-existence of a consistent FO rewriting for (the existential closure of) $R(\underline{x}, y) \wedge R(\underline{y}, c)$, where c is a constant and the first coordinate of R is the primary key.

1 Introduction

Consistent query answering (CQA) was introduced by Arenas et al. [1] and has gained considerable interest in recent years; see for example the invited talk by Chomicki [2]. The aim of CQA is to filter consistent information out of inconsistent databases. In technical terms, the repairs of an inconsistent database $\mathbf{db}$ are defined as the consistent databases that are maximally close to $\mathbf{db}$ according to some distance measure. If, as in this article, the constraints are primary keys, then it is natural to take as repairs the maximal consistent subsets of $\mathbf{db}$. Given a Boolean query q, the problem then is to decide whether q evaluates to true on every repair of $\mathbf{db}$.

We deal with conjunctive queries in this article. For a fixed Boolean conjunctive query q, $\mathsf{CQA}(q)$ is the following problem: On input of a not-necessarily-consistent database $\mathbf{db}$, decide whether q evaluates to true on every repair of $\mathbf{db}$. It is by now well known (see for example [2]) that $\mathsf{CQA}(q_1)$ is **coNP**-complete for the following Boolean query q_1

$$q_1 : \exists x \exists y \exists z (R(\underline{x}, z) \wedge S(\underline{y}, z)) \ ,$$

where primary key positions are underlined. On the other hand, $\mathsf{CQA}(q_2)$ is in **P** for the following query q_2 [3]

$$q_2 : \exists x \exists y \exists z (R(\underline{x}, z) \wedge S(\underline{z}, y)) \ .$$

M. Arenas and M.I. Schwartzbach (Eds.): DBPL 2007, LNCS 4797, pp. 112–126, 2007.

The different computational behavior arises because the "join" variable z (i.e. the variable common to both atoms) constitutes a primary key in the second query, but not in the first one.

Fuxman and Miller [3] showed that for every query q in some syntactically restricted class, called $\mathcal{C}_{forest}$, there exists a computable Boolean first-order (FO) query ψ such that for every database **db**, q evaluates to true on every repair of **db** if and and only if ψ evaluates to true on **db**. We call such ψ a consistent FO rewriting of q. Clearly, if q has a consistent FO rewriting ψ, then $\mathsf{CQA}(q)$ is in **P** (because ψ can be evaluated in polynomial time on any database). For the query q_2, a consistent FO rewriting is:

$$\psi_2 : \exists x \exists z'(R(\underline{x}, z') \wedge \forall z(R(\underline{x}, z) \rightarrow \exists y(S(\underline{z}, y)))) \ .$$

Intuitively, ψ_2 checks whether for all R-tuples with primary key value x, there exists a joining tuple in S.

Query rewriting is a clean and elegant approach to consistent query answering. This article presents a number of new results in this field; its main contributions can be summarized as follows:

1. We define the class of *rooted* queries and give a rewriting scheme that computes a consistent FO rewriting for *every* rooted query. The scheme consists of two non-procedural rewriting rules. The class of rooted queries includes $\mathcal{C}_{forest}$.
2. As the notion of rooted queries is a semantical one, the task then is to define syntactic restrictions on queries that guarantee "rootedness" (and hence guarantee applicability of our rewriting scheme). The advantage of our approach is that the notion of rootedness hides the syntactical intricacies that complicate FO rewriting.
   Rather than using Fuxman Miller (FM) join graphs, we use the join graphs defined by Beeri, Fagin, Maier and Yannakakis [4], called BFMY join graphs hereafter. This technique allows us to characterize new, previously unknown classes of queries with a consistent FO rewriting (some of which have cyclic FM join graphs, but acyclic BFMY join trees).
3. We pay special attention to queries with multiple occurrences of the same relation name, a class for which consistent FO rewriting was largely unexplored until now. For the query $q = \exists x \exists y \exists z(R(\underline{x}, z) \wedge R(\underline{y}, z) \wedge x \neq y)$, it is known that $\mathsf{CQA}(q)$ is in **P** but q has no consistent FO rewriting [5]. We show that the same holds for the query $q = \exists x \exists y(R(\underline{x}, y) \wedge R(\underline{y}, c))$, where c is a constant. This result is surprising, since the join variable y appears as primary key.

This article is organized as follows. The next section introduces the notations and terminology used throughout the article. In particular, the term "rule" will be used as a shorthand for "Boolean conjunctive query." Section 3 discusses related work. Section 4 defines the model-theoretic class of rooted rules. Section 5 gives a rewriting scheme that computes a consistent FO rewriting for any rooted rule. Section 6 characterizes classes of rooted rules in terms of BFMY join trees.

Section 7 shows that for the query $q = \exists x \exists y(R(\underline{x}, y) \wedge R(\underline{y}, c))$, $\mathsf{CQA}(q)$ is in **P** but q has no consistent FO rewriting. Section 8 concludes the article.

2 Notations and Terminology

A *symbol* is either a constant or a variable. Let $\boldsymbol{x}$ be a sequence of symbols. A *valuation of* $\boldsymbol{x}$ is a total mapping θ from symbols to symbols such that for every variable v that occurs in $\boldsymbol{x}$, $\theta(v)$ is a constant; if symbol s does not occur in $\boldsymbol{x}$ or if s is a constant, then $\theta(s) = s$. If $\boldsymbol{x}$ is a sequence of symbols, then $\mathsf{vars}(\boldsymbol{x})$ is the set of variables that occur in $\boldsymbol{x}$.

Key-equal atoms. A *database schema* is a finite set of *relation names*. Every relation name R has a unique *signature*, which is is a pair $[n, k]$ with $n \geq k \geq 1$: n is the *arity* of the relation name and the coordinates $1, 2, \ldots, k$ make up the *primary key*. If R is a relation name with signature $[n, k]$, then $R(s_1, \ldots, s_n)$ is an *R-atom* (or simply atom), where each s_i is a constant or a variable ($1 \leq i \leq n$). Such an atom is commonly written as $R(\underline{\boldsymbol{x}}, \boldsymbol{y})$ where $\boldsymbol{x} = s_1, \ldots, s_k$ and $\boldsymbol{y} = s_{k+1}, \ldots, s_n$. An atom is *ground* if it contains no variables. All constructs that follow are defined relative to a fixed database schema.

A *database* is a finite set I of ground atoms using only the relation names of the schema. Two ground atoms $R_1(\underline{\boldsymbol{a}_1}, \boldsymbol{b}_1), R_2(\underline{\boldsymbol{a}_2}, \boldsymbol{b}_2) \in I$ are *key-equal* if $R_1 = R_2$ and $\boldsymbol{a}_1 = \boldsymbol{a}_2$. We write $[\![R_1(\underline{\boldsymbol{a}_1}, \boldsymbol{b}_1)]\!]_I$ for the set containing each atom of I that is key-equal to $R_1(\underline{\boldsymbol{a}_1}, \boldsymbol{b}_1)$. This notation extends to subsets $J \subseteq I$: $[\![J]\!]_I = \bigcup\{[\![A]\!]_I \mid A \in J\}$.

Repair. A database I is *consistent* if it does not contain two distinct atoms that are key-equal. Thus, I is consistent if for every atom $A \in I$, $[\![A]\!]_I = \{A\}$. A *repair* J of a database I is a maximal (under set inclusion) consistent subset of I.

[Ordered] rules. As in [6, p. 41], the term *rule* will be used as a shorthand for *rule-based conjunctive query*. Moreover, all rules are understood to be Boolean.

A *rule* is a finite set $q = \{R_1(\underline{\boldsymbol{x}_1}, \boldsymbol{y}_1), \ldots, R_m(\underline{\boldsymbol{x}_m}, \boldsymbol{y}_m)\}$ of atoms. This rule is satisfied by a database I, denoted $I \models q$, if there exists a valuation θ of $\boldsymbol{x}_1\boldsymbol{y}_1 \ldots \boldsymbol{x}_m\boldsymbol{y}_m$ such that for each $i \in \{1, \ldots, m\}$, $R_i(\theta(\underline{\boldsymbol{x}_i}), \theta(\boldsymbol{y}_i)) \in I$.

We call q an *ordered rule* if the order in which the atoms are listed is significant. If q is ordered and $m \geq 1$, then $R_1(\underline{\boldsymbol{x}_1}, \boldsymbol{y}_1)$ is called the *head* of q, and $\{R_2(\underline{\boldsymbol{x}_2}, \boldsymbol{y}_2), \ldots, R_m(\underline{\boldsymbol{x}_m}, \boldsymbol{y}_m)\}$ the *tail*.

Consistently true. A rule q is *consistently true* in I, denoted $I \overset{*}{\models} q$, if for every repair J of I, $J \models q$. The problem $\mathsf{CQA}_S(q)$, where S is a database schema and q is a rule, is the complexity of (testing membership of) the set:

$$\mathsf{CQA}_S(q) = \{I \mid I \text{ is a database over } S \text{ and } I \overset{*}{\models} q\} .$$

Throughout this article, the schema S will be implicitly understood and therefore omitted.

Consistent FO rewriting. We say that a Boolean FO query ψ is a *consistent FO rewriting* of a rule q if for every database I, $I \models^{*} q$ if and only if $I \models \psi$.

3 Related Work

The repairs defined above are maximal consistent subsets of the original database. In the case of primary keys, it makes no difference whether maximality is expressed relative to set inclusion (as in [1]) or cardinality (as in [7]). Inserting new tuples is useless for restoring primary key violations. Tuple modifications, as proposed in [8], are not considered in this article.

The idea of consistent query rewriting first appeared in [1]. Fuxman and Miller [3] have made a number of breakthroughs in the consistent FO rewriting of rules under primary key constraints, which motivated the ConQuer system [9]. Their results have been generalized and extended to exclusion dependencies by Grieco et al. [10] and to unions of conjunctive queries by Lembo et al. [11].

Although Fuxman and Miller have extended their results to non-Boolean conjunctive queries later on [3], we will limit the discussion to Boolean queries here. Thus, all variables of a rule are understood to be implicitly existentially quantified. The definition of Fuxman Miller (FM) join graph first appeared in [12] and was slightly adapted in [3].

FM join graph. The *FM join graph* of a rule $q = \{R_1(\underline{\boldsymbol{x}_1}, \boldsymbol{y}_1), \ldots, R_m(\underline{\boldsymbol{x}_m}, \boldsymbol{y}_m)\}$ is an oriented graph (q, E) such that there is an edge from $R_i(\underline{\boldsymbol{x}_i}, \boldsymbol{y}_i)$ to $R_j(\underline{\boldsymbol{x}_j}, \boldsymbol{y}_j)$ if $i \neq j$ and $\mathsf{vars}(\boldsymbol{y}_i) \cap \mathsf{vars}(\boldsymbol{x}_j\boldsymbol{y}_j) \neq \{\}$.

Fig. 1 shows two FM join graphs; neither is a tree (the left graph has a vertex with two incoming edges).

Fuxman and Miller [12] give an algorithm that computes a consistent FO rewriting for any rule $q = \{R_1(\underline{\boldsymbol{x}_1}, \boldsymbol{y}_1), \ldots, R_m(\underline{\boldsymbol{x}_m}, \boldsymbol{y}_m)\}$ with the following properties:

1. $1 \leq i < j \leq m$ implies $R_i \neq R_j$. Thus, no relation name occurs more than once in q.
2. The FM join graph of q is a tree (or a forest); and
3. if there is an oriented edge from $R_i(\underline{\boldsymbol{x}_i}, \boldsymbol{y}_i)$ to $R_j(\underline{\boldsymbol{x}_j}, \boldsymbol{y}_j)$, then $\mathsf{vars}(\boldsymbol{x}_j) \subseteq \mathsf{vars}(\boldsymbol{y}_i)$.

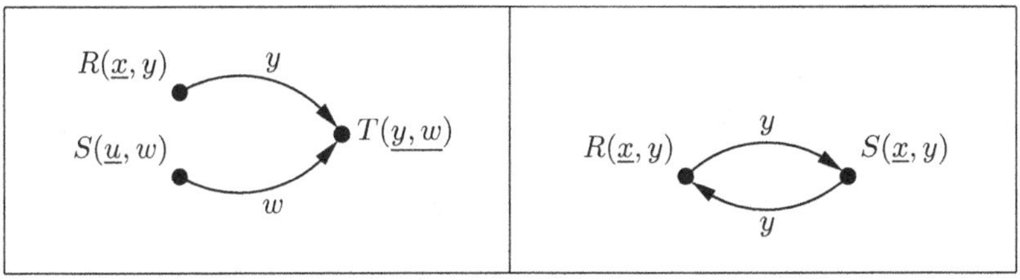

Fig. 1. FM join graphs of $\{R(\underline{x}, y), S(\underline{u}, w), T(\underline{y, w})\}$ and $\{R(\underline{x}, y), S(\underline{x}, y)\}$

This class of rules is called $\mathcal{C}_{tree}$ (or $\mathcal{C}_{forest}$). The class $\mathcal{C}^{+}_{tree}$, defined by Grieco et al. [10], omits the third condition.

Complexity results on consistent query answering for larger classes of constraints appear in [13,14]. Calì et al. [15] study query rewriting under key and inclusion dependencies in a larger context of data integration.

4 Rooted Rules

We define the model-theoretic notion of rooted rules. Rooted rules capture the following model-theoretic property which can be easily verified. An ordered rule q with head $R_1(\underline{\boldsymbol{x}_1}, \boldsymbol{y}_1)$ and tail q' is true in every repair of a database I if the following condition is satisfied:

> there exists a valuation θ of $\boldsymbol{x}_1$ such that (let $\theta(\boldsymbol{x}_1) = \boldsymbol{a}$) I contains an R_1-atom with primary key value $\boldsymbol{a}$ and for every such atom $R_1(\underline{\boldsymbol{a}}, \boldsymbol{b}) \in I$, there exists a valuation $\theta_{\boldsymbol{b}}$ of $\boldsymbol{x}_1\boldsymbol{y}_1$ such that $\theta_{\boldsymbol{b}}(\boldsymbol{x}_1\boldsymbol{y}_1) = \boldsymbol{ab}$ and $\theta_{\boldsymbol{b}}(q')$ is true in every repair of I that contains $R_1(\underline{\boldsymbol{a}}, \boldsymbol{b})$.

The above condition deals with all ways to repair multiple R_1-atoms with the same primary key value $\boldsymbol{a}$. There are two points to observe:

1. If such valuation θ exists, then $\theta(q)$ is also true in every repair of I.
2. Consistent truth of q is reduced to consistent truth of the shorter rule $\theta_{\boldsymbol{b}}(q')$.

The above condition is sufficient for $I \overset{*}{\models} q$. We now define the class of rooted rules as a semantically restricted class of rules satisfying this condition. Observation 1 leads to the notion of "reifiability" (Def. 1); observation 2 to a recursive definition of rooted rules (Def. 2). Proposition 1 then indicates that the class of rooted rules is of practical interest: it encompasses the class $\mathcal{C}_{forest}$, which contains many common, practical queries [12]. Moreover, as we will see later on, it covers relevant queries not in $\mathcal{C}_{forest}$, such as $\exists\boldsymbol{x}\exists\boldsymbol{y}(R(\underline{\boldsymbol{x}}, \boldsymbol{y}) \wedge S(\underline{\boldsymbol{x}}, \boldsymbol{y}))$, testing whether two relations have a nonempty intersection.

Definition 1. *Let q be a rule containing $R_i(\underline{\boldsymbol{x}_i}, \boldsymbol{y}_i)$. We call $R_i(\underline{\boldsymbol{x}_i}, \boldsymbol{y}_i)$* reifiable *in q if for every database I, if $I \overset{*}{\models} q$, then there exists a valuation θ of $\boldsymbol{x}_i$ such that $I \overset{*}{\models} \theta(q)$.*

Definition 2. *We define* rooted *ordered rules:*

1. *The empty rule is rooted.*
2. *The ordered rule $q = \{R_1(\underline{\boldsymbol{x}_1}, \boldsymbol{y}_1), \ldots, R_m(\underline{\boldsymbol{x}_m}, \boldsymbol{y}_m)\}$ with $m \geq 1$ is rooted if*
   (a) $R_1(\underline{\boldsymbol{x}_1}, \boldsymbol{y}_1)$ is reifiable in q; and
   (b) for each valuation θ of $\boldsymbol{x}_1\boldsymbol{y}_1$, the ordered rule $\theta(q')$ is rooted where q' is the tail of q. Here, $\theta(q')$ inherits its order from q, i.e. $\theta(q') = \{\theta(R_2(\underline{\boldsymbol{x}_2}, \boldsymbol{y}_2)), \ldots, \theta(R_m(\underline{\boldsymbol{x}_m}, \boldsymbol{y}_m))\}$, in that order.

The following proposition will serve in certain examples. It is subsumed by more general theorems to follow.

Proposition 1. *Let q be a rule.*

1. *If $|q| = 1$, then q is rooted.*
2. *If $q = \{R_1(\underline{\boldsymbol{a}}, \boldsymbol{y}_1), R_2(\underline{\boldsymbol{x}_2}, \boldsymbol{y}_2)\}$ and the primary key value $\boldsymbol{a}$ contains no variables, then q is rooted (possibly $R_1 = R_2$).*
3. *If $q \in \mathcal{C}_{forest}$ and the atoms of q are ordered in increasing depth of the FM join graph, then q is rooted.*

Lemma 1 shows that for every rooted rule q, $\mathsf{CQA}(q)$ is in **P**. The proof characterizes $\mathsf{CQA}(q)$ as the set of databases satisfying a property, called Property FO, which can be checked in polynomial time. As was to be expected, Property FO expresses the condition that motivated the definition of rootedness (see first paragraph of Section 4). Significantly, we will show in Section 5 that Property FO is first-order expressible, which thus gives us a consistent FO rewriting for any rooted rule.

Lemma 1. *For every rooted ordered rule q, $\mathsf{CQA}(q)$ is in* **P**.

Proof. Let $q = \{R_1(\underline{\boldsymbol{x}_1}, \boldsymbol{y}_1), \ldots, R_m(\underline{\boldsymbol{x}_m}, \boldsymbol{y}_m)\}$ be a rooted ordered rule. If $m = 0$, then the desired result is obvious. Next assume $m \geq 1$.

Let I be a relation such that $I \models^* q$. Since $R_1(\underline{\boldsymbol{x}_1}, \boldsymbol{y}_1)$ is reifiable in q, we can assume the existence of a valuation θ of $\boldsymbol{x}_1$ such that $I \models^* \theta(q)$. Assume w.l.o.g. that $\theta(\boldsymbol{x}_1) = \boldsymbol{a}$. Then, there exists an atom $R_1(\underline{\boldsymbol{a}}, \boldsymbol{b}') \in I$ such that every repair J of I contains exactly one atom of $[\![R_1(\underline{\boldsymbol{a}}, \boldsymbol{b}')]\!]_I$.

Let $R_1(\underline{\boldsymbol{a}}, \boldsymbol{b}) \in I$ be key-equal to $R_1(\underline{\boldsymbol{a}}, \boldsymbol{b}')$. Let J be a repair of I such that $R_1(\underline{\boldsymbol{a}}, \boldsymbol{b}) \in J$. Since $J \models \theta(q)$, it follows that there exists a valuation $\theta_{\boldsymbol{b}}$ of $\boldsymbol{x}_1\boldsymbol{y}_1$ such that $\theta_{\boldsymbol{b}}(\boldsymbol{x}_1) = \theta(\boldsymbol{x}_1) = \boldsymbol{a}$, $\theta_{\boldsymbol{b}}(\boldsymbol{y}_1) = \boldsymbol{b}$, and $J \models \theta_{\boldsymbol{b}}(q)$. Clearly, if J is a repair of I such that $R_1(\underline{\boldsymbol{a}}, \boldsymbol{b}) \in J$, then J is a repair of $(I \setminus [\![R_1(\underline{\boldsymbol{a}}, \boldsymbol{b}')]\!]_I) \cup \{R_1(\underline{\boldsymbol{a}}, \boldsymbol{b})\}$; and the inverse is also true. It follows $(I \setminus [\![R_1(\underline{\boldsymbol{a}}, \boldsymbol{b}')]\!]_I) \cup \{R_1(\underline{\boldsymbol{a}}, \boldsymbol{b})\} \models^* \theta_{\boldsymbol{b}}(q)$. Hence, if $I \models^* q$, then the following condition holds:

Property FO: for some atom $R_1(\underline{\boldsymbol{a}}, \boldsymbol{b}') \in I$, for every key-equal atom $R_1(\underline{\boldsymbol{a}}, \boldsymbol{b}) \in I$, there exists a valuation $\theta_{\boldsymbol{b}}$ of $\boldsymbol{x}_1\boldsymbol{y}_1$ such that $\theta_{\boldsymbol{b}}(\boldsymbol{x}_1\boldsymbol{y}_1) = \boldsymbol{ab}$ and

$$(I \setminus [\![R_1(\underline{\boldsymbol{a}}, \boldsymbol{b}')]\!]_I) \cup \{R_1(\underline{\boldsymbol{a}}, \boldsymbol{b})\} \models^* \theta_{\boldsymbol{b}}(q') \ , \tag{1}$$

where q' is the tail of q.

It is easy to see that the latter condition is also sufficient for $I \models^* q$. The crux is that $\theta_{\boldsymbol{b}}(q')$ is rooted by Def. 2. That is, we have reduced the test $I \models^* q$ to tests of the form $I' \models^* q'$ where $I' \subseteq I$ and $|q'| = |q| - 1$. For every query length, we have to test the existence of at most $|I|$ valuations. The overall complexity is $\mathcal{O}(|I|^m)$ where $m = |q|$. □

5 Consistent FO Rewriting of Rooted Rules

We show that if q is a rooted ordered rule, then we can construct a FO formula ψ_q that checks membership of $\mathsf{CQA}(q)$; that is, for every database I, $I \models^* q$ if and only if $I \models \psi_q$. The formula ψ_q is essentially nothing else than a first-order encoding of Property FO in the proof of Lemma 1.

To start with a simple example, consider the singleton rule $q = \{R_1(\underline{a}, b)\}$, which is obviously rooted because it contains no variables. To ease the technical treatment, we encode this rule as $R_1(\underline{x}, y) \wedge \varphi$ where $\varphi = (x = a) \wedge (y = b)$. The following formula starts encoding Property FO:

$$\exists x \exists y'(R_1(\underline{x}, y') \wedge \forall y(R_1(\underline{x}, y) \rightarrow \mathsf{Rewrite}(\varphi))) \ .$$

Intuitively, "for some atom $R_1(\underline{\boldsymbol{a}}, \boldsymbol{b}') \in I$" is encoded by $\exists x \exists y'(R_1(\underline{x}, y') \wedge \ldots)$, and "for every key-equal atom $R_1(\underline{\boldsymbol{a}}, \boldsymbol{b}) \in I$" is encoded by $\forall y(R_1(\underline{x}, y) \rightarrow \ldots)$. For a formula φ that contains only equality predicates, we will define $\mathsf{Rewrite}(\varphi) = \varphi$. The formula φ checks the correctness of the valuations in Property FO; in this example, x must be a, and y must be b:

$$\exists x \exists y'(R_1(\underline{x}, y') \wedge \forall y(R_1(\underline{x}, y) \rightarrow (x = a) \wedge (y = b))) \ .$$

A subtlety to note is that in Property FO, the $\models^*$ test for the tail query q', expressed by (1), is not with respect to I, but with respect to the database obtained from I by selecting $R_1(\underline{\boldsymbol{a}}, \boldsymbol{b})$ as the only representative of $[\![R_1(\underline{\boldsymbol{a}}, \boldsymbol{b}')]\!]_I$. However, since the tail query in this simple example contains only built-in predicates, its truth is database independent.

As a follow-up example, consider the rule $\{R_1(\underline{a}, y), R_2(\underline{x}, y)\}$, which is rooted by Proposition 1. Note incidentally that this rule has a cyclic FM join graph and hence does not belong to $\mathcal{C}_{tree}$. We will first write this rule as:

$$R_1(\underline{x_1}, y_1) \wedge R_2(\underline{x_2}, y_2) \wedge \varphi \text{ where } \varphi = (x_1 = a) \wedge (y_1 = y_2) \ .$$

We proceed as in the first example:

$$\exists x_1 \exists y_1'(R_1(\underline{x_1}, y_1') \wedge \forall y_1(R_1(\underline{x_1}, y_1) \rightarrow \mathsf{Rewrite}(R_2(\underline{x_2}, y_2) \wedge \varphi))) \quad (2)$$

Next, we have to distinguish two cases:

- If $R_2 \neq R_1$, then we can compute $\mathsf{Rewrite}(R_2(\underline{x_2}, y_2) \wedge \varphi)$ as before, because $R_2(\underline{x_2}, y_2) \wedge \varphi$ is true in every repair of I *that contains* $R_1(\underline{x_1}, y_1)$ if and only if $\mathsf{Rewrite}(R_2(\underline{x_2}, y_2) \wedge \varphi)$ is true in every repair of I:

$$\begin{aligned} &\mathsf{Rewrite}(R_2(\underline{x_2}, y_2) \wedge \varphi) \\ &\quad = \exists x_2 \exists y_2'(R_2(\underline{x_2}, y_2') \wedge \forall y_2(R_2(\underline{x_2}, y_2) \rightarrow (x_1 = a) \wedge (y_1 = y_2))) \end{aligned}$$

- On the other hand, if $R_2 = R_1$, then it becomes significant that the formula $\mathsf{Rewrite}(R_2(\underline{x_2}, y_2) \wedge \varphi)$ must be true in I if and only if the query tail $R_2(\underline{x_2}, y_2) \wedge \varphi$ is true in each repair of I *that contains* $R_1(\underline{x_1}, y_1)$. This yields two cases: if $x_2 \neq x_1$, then we proceed as before; if $x_2 = x_1$, then $R_2(\underline{x_2}, y_2)$ must be identified with $R_1(\underline{x_1}, y_1)$.

$$\begin{aligned} &\mathsf{Rewrite}(R_2(\underline{x_2}, y_2) \wedge \varphi) \\ &\quad = \exists x_2 \exists y_2'((x_2 \neq x_1) \wedge R_2(\underline{x_2}, y_2') \wedge \forall y_2(R_2(\underline{x_2}, y_2) \rightarrow (x_1 = a) \wedge (y_1 = y_2))) \\ &\qquad \vee \exists x_2 \exists y_2((x_2 = x_1) \wedge (y_2 = y_1) \wedge (x_1 = a) \wedge (y_1 = y_2)) \end{aligned}$$

In this particular example, the second disjunct is equivalent to simply $(x_1 = a)$ and is implied by the first disjunct. Hence, if $R_1 = R_2$, then the formula $\mathsf{Rewrite}(R_2(\underline{x_2}, y_2) \wedge \varphi)$ is equivalent to $(x_1 = a)$. When we substitute this result in formula (2), we find a formula equivalent to:

$$\exists x_1 \exists y_1' (R_1(\underline{x_1}, y_1') \wedge (x_1 = a)) \ .$$

To see that the latter formula correctly checks membership of $\mathsf{CQA}(q)$ where $q = \{R_1(\underline{a}, y), R_2(\underline{x}, y)\}$ and $R_1 = R_2$, notice that if $R_1 = R_2$, then q is equivalent to the rule $\{R_1(\underline{a}, y)\}$.

We now define our rewrite function. The function takes the form $\mathsf{Rewrite}_{q_1}(q_2 \wedge \varphi)$, where q_1 "remembers" the part of the query that has already been rewritten, so that atoms of q_2 can possibly be identified with atoms of q_1 (as in the above example). Note that the use of the separator $\wedge$ instead of a comma (,) is just for readability. Theorem 1 then shows that this rewriting scheme computes a consistent FO rewriting for every rooted rule.

Definition 3. *Let $q_1 \wedge q_2 \wedge \varphi$ be an ordered rule, written in the form where $q_1 \wedge q_2$ is constant-free and contains no two occurrences of the same variable; φ is a set of equalities involving variables occurring in $q_1 \wedge q_2$ and constants.*

1. $\mathsf{Rewrite}_{q_1}(\varphi) = \varphi$
2. $\mathsf{Rewrite}_{q_1}(R(\underline{\boldsymbol{x}}, \boldsymbol{y}) \wedge q_2 \wedge \varphi) =$

$$\begin{array}{l} \exists \boldsymbol{x} \exists \boldsymbol{y} (\bigvee_{R(\underline{\boldsymbol{v}}, \boldsymbol{w}) \in q_1} \mathsf{Rewrite}_{q_1}(q_2 \wedge \varphi \wedge (\boldsymbol{x} = \boldsymbol{v}) \wedge (\boldsymbol{y} = \boldsymbol{w}))) \\ \qquad\qquad\qquad\qquad \vee \\ \exists \boldsymbol{x} \exists \boldsymbol{y} (R(\underline{\boldsymbol{x}}, \boldsymbol{y}) \wedge \neg (\bigvee_{R(\underline{\boldsymbol{v}}, \boldsymbol{w}) \in q_1} (\boldsymbol{x} = \boldsymbol{v})) \\ \qquad\qquad \wedge \forall \boldsymbol{y} (R(\underline{\boldsymbol{x}}, \boldsymbol{y}) \rightarrow \mathsf{Rewrite}_{q_1 \cup \{R(\underline{\boldsymbol{x}}, \boldsymbol{y})\}}(q_2 \wedge \varphi))) \end{array}$$

It is understood that $\boldsymbol{x} = \boldsymbol{v}$ is a shorthand for $x_1 = v_1 \wedge \ldots \wedge x_k = v_k$, where $\boldsymbol{x} = \langle x_1, \ldots, x_k \rangle$ and $\boldsymbol{v} = \langle v_1, \ldots, v_k \rangle$. Likewise for $\boldsymbol{y} = \boldsymbol{w}$. Also, $\exists \boldsymbol{x}$ is a shorthand for $\exists x_1 \ldots \exists x_k$. The empty disjunction is false.

For example, the complete rewriting of the rule $\{R(\underline{a}, y), R(\underline{x}, y)\}$ now goes as follows. First, we write this rule in the form $R(\underline{x_1}, y_1) \wedge R(\underline{x_2}, y_2) \wedge (x_1 = a) \wedge (y_1 = y_2)$, as required by Def. 3. Next,

$$\begin{array}{l} \mathsf{Rewrite}_{\{\}}(R(\underline{x_1}, y_1) \wedge R(\underline{x_2}, y_2) \wedge (x_1 = a) \wedge (y_1 = y_2)) \\ = \exists x_1 \exists y_1 (R(\underline{x_1}, y_1) \wedge \forall y_1 (R(\underline{x_1}, y_1) \rightarrow \\ \qquad\qquad \mathsf{Rewrite}_{\{R(\underline{x_1}, y_1)\}}(R(\underline{x_2}, y_2) \wedge (x_1 = a) \wedge (y_1 = y_2)))) \end{array}$$

where

$$\begin{array}{l} \mathsf{Rewrite}_{\{R(\underline{x_1}, y_1)\}}(R(\underline{x_2}, y_2) \wedge (x_1 = a) \wedge (y_1 = y_2)) \\ = \exists x_2 \exists y_2 ((x_1 = a) \wedge (y_1 = y_2) \wedge (x_2 = x_1) \wedge (y_2 = y_1)) \\ \quad \vee \exists x_2 \exists y_2 (R(\underline{x_2}, y_2) \wedge (x_2 \neq x_1) \wedge \forall y_2 (R(\underline{x_2}, y_2) \rightarrow (x_1 = a) \wedge (y_1 = y_2))) \end{array}$$

Theorem 1. *Let $q \wedge \varphi$ be a rooted ordered rule written in the form required by Def. 3 (thus, q is constant-free and no variable occurs twice in q). For every database I, $I \stackrel{*}{\models} q \wedge \varphi$ if and only if $I \models \mathsf{Rewrite}_{\{\}}(q \wedge \varphi)$.*

Since the rewriting of a rule $q = R(\boldsymbol{x}, \boldsymbol{y}) \wedge q_2 \wedge \varphi$ contains rewritings of both $q_2 \wedge \varphi \wedge (\boldsymbol{x} = \boldsymbol{v}) \wedge (\boldsymbol{y} = \boldsymbol{w})$ and $q_2 \wedge \varphi$, its length can be exponential in the size of q. However, if no relation name occurs more than once, then the disjunction $\bigvee_{R(\underline{\boldsymbol{v}}, \boldsymbol{w}) \in q_1}(\ldots)$ is empty, resulting in a rewriting of polynomial length.

6 New Classes of Rules with a Consistent FO Rewriting

Now that we are able to compute a consistent FO rewriting for any rooted rule, we can shift our attention to characterizing classes of rooted rules. What is new is that we will not use the FM join graphs employed by others for characterizing classes of rules with a FO rewriting. Instead, we use the join graphs defined by Beeri et al. [4].

This section consists of four subsections. Subsection 6.1 defines the notion of BFMY join graph. After that, three subsections each contain a theorem introducing a new class of rooted rules. Subsections 6.2 and 6.3 cover rules where the same relation name can occur multiple times. We are not aware of already existing rewriting algorithms that can handle such rules. Subsection 6.4 then elaborates on the classes $\mathcal{C}_{tree}$ and $\mathcal{C}^{+}_{tree}$ defined in Section 3. Significantly, the rooted rules in Subsections 6.2 and 6.4 can have cyclic FM join graphs (but always have acyclic BFMY join trees). Again, we are not aware of already existing rewriting algorithms that can handle such rules.

6.1 BFMY Join Trees

The notion of join tree introduced by Beeri, Fagin, Maier, and Yannakakis [4] naturally extends to rules. The authors' initials will be used to distinguish with the FM join trees introduced by Fuxman and Miller [3]. Fig. 2 shows two BFMY join graphs; both are (undirected) trees. Compare with the FM join graphs of the same queries in Fig. 1.

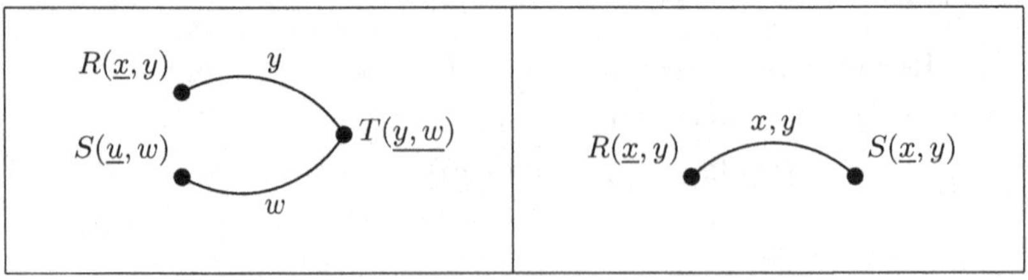

Fig. 2. BFMY join trees of $\{R(\underline{x}, y), S(\underline{u}, w), T(\underline{y, w})\}$ and $\{R(\underline{x}, y), S(\underline{x}, y)\}$

Definition 4. *A* BFMY join graph *of a rule q is an undirected graph $\tau = (q, E)$ such that*

1. *each edge $\{R_i(\underline{\boldsymbol{x}_i}, \boldsymbol{y}_i), R_j(\underline{\boldsymbol{x}_j}, \boldsymbol{y}_j)\}$ is labeled by $\mathsf{vars}(\boldsymbol{x}_i\boldsymbol{y}_i) \cap \mathsf{vars}(\boldsymbol{x}_j\boldsymbol{y}_j)$; and*
2. *for every pair $R_i(\underline{\boldsymbol{x}_i}, \boldsymbol{y}_i)$, $R_j(\underline{\boldsymbol{x}_j}, \boldsymbol{y}_j)$ of distinct nodes, for each variable $v \in \mathsf{vars}(\boldsymbol{x}_i\boldsymbol{y}_i) \cap \mathsf{vars}(\boldsymbol{x}_j\boldsymbol{y}_j)$, there is a path between $R_i(\underline{\boldsymbol{x}_i}, \boldsymbol{y}_i)$ and $R_j(\underline{\boldsymbol{x}_j}, \boldsymbol{y}_j)$ with the property that each edge label along the path includes v.*

A BFMY join tree *is an acyclic BFMY join graph.*

If q has a BFMY join tree, then any atom $R_i(\underline{\boldsymbol{x}_i}, \boldsymbol{y}_i)$ of q can be selected as the root of the tree, giving a directed BFMY join tree with root $R_i(\underline{\boldsymbol{x}_i}, \boldsymbol{y}_i)$.

6.2 No Variables in the Primary Key of the Root

Theorem 2 uses the construct of BFMY join tree to characterize a class of rooted ordered rules—and for which Theorem 1 thus provides a consistent FO rewriting. The class contains the rule shown in Fig. 3. The rule has four occurrences of the same relation name and the FM join graph (not shown) would contain an oriented edge from any node to any other node (and hence would not be a tree).

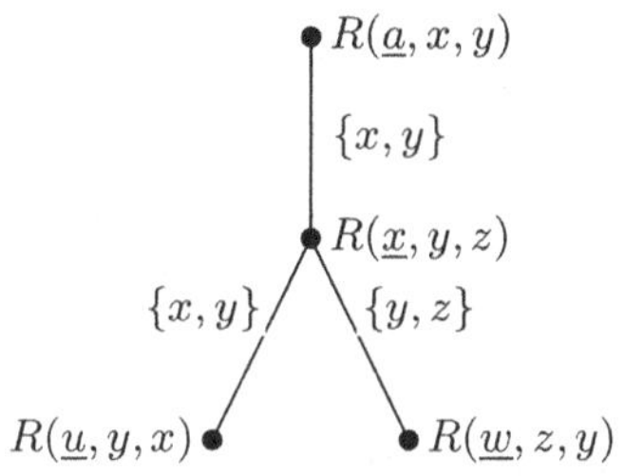

Fig. 3. BFMY join tree of $\{R(\underline{a}, x, y), R(\underline{x}, y, z), R(\underline{u}, y, x), R(\underline{w}, z, y)\}$

Theorem 2. *An ordered rule $q = \{R_1(\underline{\boldsymbol{x}_1}, \boldsymbol{y}_1), \ldots, R_m(\underline{\boldsymbol{x}_m}, \boldsymbol{y}_m)\}$ is rooted (and hence q has a consistent FO rewriting by Theorem 1) if it has a BFMY join tree with root $R_1(\underline{\boldsymbol{x}_1}, \boldsymbol{y}_1)$ such that*

1. *If $R_i(\underline{\boldsymbol{x}_i}, \boldsymbol{y}_i)$ is the parent of $R_j(\underline{\boldsymbol{x}_j}, \boldsymbol{y}_j)$, then $i < j$. Thus, the atoms in q appear in increasing depth.*
2. *$\mathsf{vars}(\boldsymbol{x}_1) = \{\}$. Thus, the primary key of the root node contains only constants.*
3. *If $R_i(\underline{\boldsymbol{x}_i}, \boldsymbol{y}_i)$ is the parent of $R_j(\underline{\boldsymbol{x}_j}, \boldsymbol{y}_j)$, then either $R_j(\underline{\boldsymbol{x}_j}, \boldsymbol{y}_j)$ is a leaf node or $\mathsf{vars}(\boldsymbol{x}_j) \subseteq \mathsf{vars}(\boldsymbol{x}_i\boldsymbol{y}_i)$.*

6.3 Single Relation Name

Theorem 3 characterizes another class of rooted rules in terms of BFMY join trees. A rule of this class is shown in Fig. 4. The FM join graphs of queries in this class are trees, but unlike the queries considered in [3], all atoms share the same relation name.

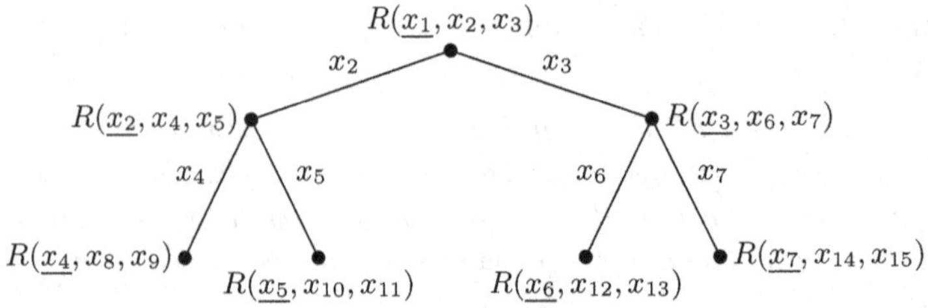

Fig. 4. BFMY join tree of a rule covered by Theorem 3

Theorem 3. *An ordered rule* $q = \{R(\underline{\boldsymbol{x}_1}, \boldsymbol{y}_1), \ldots, R(\underline{\boldsymbol{x}_m}, \boldsymbol{y}_m)\}$, *with a single relation name* R, *is rooted (and hence* q *has a consistent FO rewriting by Theorem 1) if it has a BFMY join tree with root* $R_1(\underline{\boldsymbol{x}_1}, \boldsymbol{y}_1)$ *such that*

1. *If* $R_i(\underline{\boldsymbol{x}_i}, \boldsymbol{y}_i)$ *is the parent of* $R_j(\underline{\boldsymbol{x}_j}, \boldsymbol{y}_j)$, *then* $i < j$.
2. *Every atom is constant-free and contains no two occurrences of the same variable.*
3. *Whenever* $R(\underline{\boldsymbol{x}_i}, \boldsymbol{y}_i)$ *and* $R(\underline{\boldsymbol{x}_j}, \boldsymbol{y}_j)$ *are internal nodes, then the subtree of depth* 1 *with root* $R(\underline{\boldsymbol{x}_i}, \boldsymbol{y}_i)$ *is the same up to a renaming of variables as the subtree of depth* 1 *with root* $R(\underline{\boldsymbol{x}_j}, \boldsymbol{y}_j)$.
4. *All leaf nodes are at the same depth.*
5. *For* $j \neq 1$, *the edge connecting* $R(\underline{\boldsymbol{x}_j}, \boldsymbol{y}_j)$ *to its parent has label* $\mathsf{vars}(\boldsymbol{x}_j)$.

Moreover, the theorem is no longer valid if one of these conditions is dropped.

6.4 No Duplicate Relation Names

The following theorem builds on the characterization of the classes $\mathcal{C}_{tree}$ [3] and $\mathcal{C}_{tree}^{+}$ [10]. No relation name can occur more than once (condition 2 in the theorem's statement) and the variables shared by two atoms must be part of the primary key of one of the atoms (condition 3.b). Our contribution lies in the weakening of the latter condition through an alternative (condition 3.a). The "intersection" query $\{R(\underline{x}, y), S(\underline{x}, y)\}$, for example, is covered by Theorem 4, but does not belong to $\mathcal{C}_{tree}^{+}$.

Theorem 4. *An ordered rule* $q = \{R_1(\underline{\boldsymbol{x}_1}, \boldsymbol{y}_1), \ldots, R_m(\underline{\boldsymbol{x}_m}, \boldsymbol{y}_m)\}$ *is rooted (and hence* q *has a consistent FO rewriting by Theorem 1) if it has a BFMY join tree with root* $R_1(\underline{\boldsymbol{x}_1}, \boldsymbol{y}_1)$ *such that:*

1. *If* $R_i(\underline{\boldsymbol{x}_i}, \boldsymbol{y}_i)$ *is the parent of* $R_j(\underline{\boldsymbol{x}_j}, \boldsymbol{y}_j)$, *then* $i < j$.
2. *If* $i \neq j$, *then* $R_i \neq R_j$. *Thus, no relation name occurs more than once in* q.
3. *If* $R_i(\underline{\boldsymbol{x}_i}, \boldsymbol{y}_i)$ *is the parent of* $R_j(\underline{\boldsymbol{x}_j}, \boldsymbol{y}_j)$, *then at least one of the following two conditions is true:*
   (a) $\mathsf{vars}(\boldsymbol{x}_j) \supseteq \mathsf{vars}(\boldsymbol{x}_i)$; *or*
   (b) $\mathsf{vars}(\boldsymbol{x}_j) \supseteq \mathsf{vars}(\boldsymbol{x}_i\boldsymbol{y}_i) \cap \mathsf{vars}(\boldsymbol{x}_j\boldsymbol{y}_j)$. *That is,* $\mathsf{vars}(\boldsymbol{x}_j)$ *is a superset of the label on the edge between* $R_j(\underline{\boldsymbol{x}_j}, \boldsymbol{y}_j)$ *and its parent.*

The rule $\{R(\underline{x}, y), S(\underline{u}, w), T(\underline{y, w})\}$ has a BFMY join tree (left graph of Fig. 2) but is not covered by Theorem 4, no matter which atom is selected as the root. On the other hand, the rule $\{R(\underline{x}, y), S(\underline{x}, y)\}$ (right graph of Fig. 2) is covered by the theorem and hence has a consistent FO rewriting. The latter rule is not in $\mathcal{C}_{tree}^{+}$ because its FM join graph is cyclic (right graph in Fig. 1).

It should be noticed here that Theorem 4 covers most, but not all queries in $\mathcal{C}_{tree}$ (or $\mathcal{C}_{tree}^{+}$). Proposition 2 states that each query $q \in \mathcal{C}_{tree}$ that is not covered by Theorem 4, must contain atoms that join only on their primary keys. Such a query q can encode a cyclic join, which has no BFMY join tree [4]. It should be clear, however, that atoms that join only on their primary keys pose no difficulties in consistent FO rewriting. For example, $q = \{R(\underline{x, y}, u_1), S(\underline{x, z}, u_2), T(\underline{y, z}, u_3)\}$ is in $\mathcal{C}_{tree}$ but has no BFMY join tree; it is easy to see that q itself is a consistent FO rewriting of q.

Proposition 2. *An ordered rule* $q = \{R_1(\underline{\boldsymbol{x}_1}, \boldsymbol{y}_1), \ldots, R_m(\underline{\boldsymbol{x}_m}, \boldsymbol{y}_m)\}$ *satisfies all conditions in Theorem 4 if*

1. $i \neq j$ *implies* $R_i \neq R_j$;
2. *the FM join graph of* q *is a tree and the atoms of* q *appear in increasing depth; and*
3. *for all* $i, j \in \{1, \ldots, m\}$, *if* $\mathsf{vars}(\boldsymbol{x}_i\boldsymbol{y}_i) \cap \mathsf{vars}(\boldsymbol{x}_j\boldsymbol{y}_j) \neq \{\}$, *then* $\mathsf{vars}(\boldsymbol{x}_i\boldsymbol{y}_i) \cap \mathsf{vars}(\boldsymbol{x}_j\boldsymbol{y}_j) \cap \mathsf{vars}(\boldsymbol{y}_i\boldsymbol{y}_j) \neq \{\}$. *Thus, if two atoms have variables in common, then at least one shared variable occurs at a non-key position in one of the atoms.*

7 $R(\underline{x}, y) \wedge R(\underline{y}, c)$ Has No Consistent FO Rewriting

We found in the literature no rewriting algorithms that produce consistent FO rewritings for rules with multiple occurrences of the same relation name. Theorems 2 and 3 seem to be the first positive results in this direction. We now argue that there is little hope to significantly extend these results.

Clearly, under the assumption $\mathbf{P} \neq \mathbf{NP}$, a rule q can have no consistent FO rewriting if $\mathsf{CQA}(q)$ is **coNP**-complete. We will now show that for the simple rule $q = \{R(\underline{x}, y), R(\underline{y}, c)\}$, where c is constant, $\mathsf{CQA}(q)$ is in $\mathbf{P}$ but q has no consistent FO rewriting. This may come as a surprise, because the join in this rule is foreign-key-to-primary-key, the rule has a BFMY join tree, and its FM join graph is a tree. The rule is not covered by Theorem 2 because no primary key is ground; it is not covered by Theorem 3 because it contains a constant. So it turns out that the double occurrence of the same relation name in a rule q easily leads to the non-existence of a consistent FO rewriting (even if $\mathsf{CQA}(q)$ is in $\mathbf{P}$).

Theorem 5. *Let* $q = R(\underline{x}, y), R(\underline{y}, c)$.

1. $\mathsf{CQA}(q)$ *is in* $\mathbf{P}$.
2. *There exists no Boolean FO query* ψ *such that for every database* I, $I \models^{*} q$ *if and only if* $I \models \psi$. *Thus,* q *has no consistent FO rewriting.*

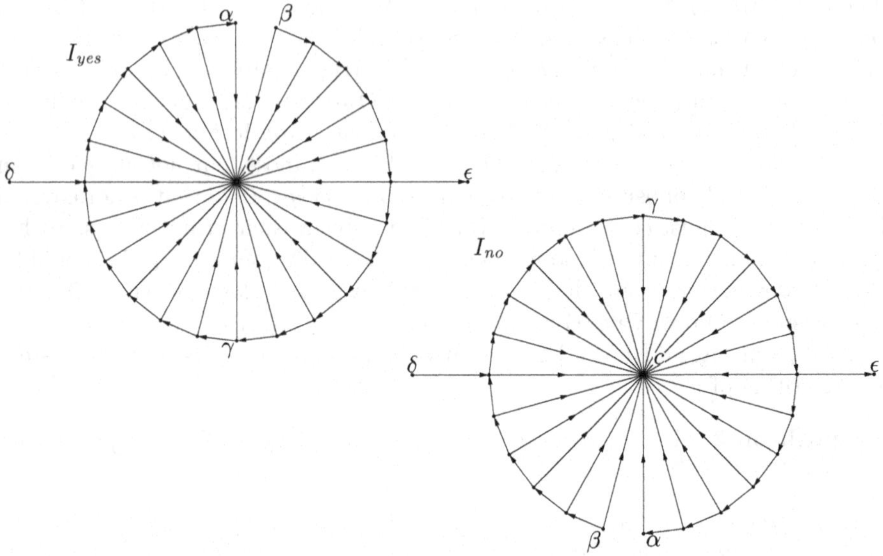

Fig. 5. $R(\underline{x}, y) \wedge R(\underline{y}, c)$ is consistently true in I_{yes}, but not in I_{no}

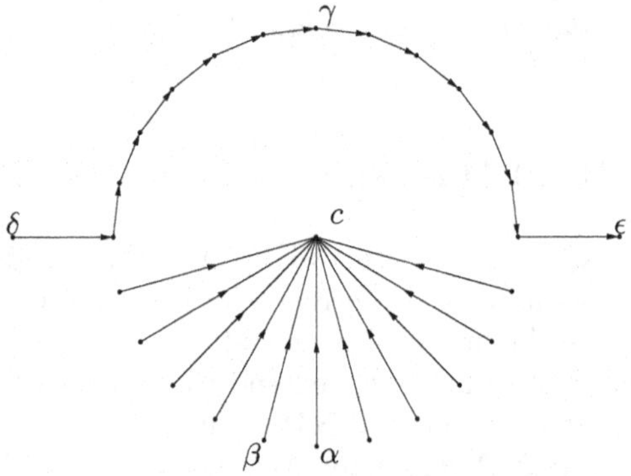

Fig. 6. Repair of I_{no} falsifying $R(\underline{x}, y) \wedge R(\underline{y}, c)$

Proof. For the first item, let I be a database. Construct a maximal sequence $C_0 \subsetneq C_1 \subsetneq C_2 \subsetneq \ldots$ where $C_0 = \{\}$ and for each $i > 0$, $C_i = C_{i-1} \cup \{b\}$ for some b such that $R(b, c) \in I$ and $\forall z((R(\underline{b}, z) \in I) \rightarrow (z \in C_{i-1} \cup \{c\}))$. Let C_m be the last element in this sequence. It can be shown that $I \overset{*}{\models} q$ if and only if $m \geq 1$ and $\exists x \exists y'((R(\underline{x}, y') \in I) \wedge \forall y((R(\underline{x}, y) \in I) \rightarrow (y \in C_m)))$. Obviously, $m \leq |I|$ and C_m can be computed in polynomial time.

For the second item, we use an Ehrenfeucht-Fraïssé game. Suppose there is a FO sentence ψ checking membership of $\mathsf{CQA}(q)$. Let d be the quantifier depth of

ψ. We exhibit a database $I_{yes} \models^* q$ and a database $I_{no} \not\models^* q$ such that I_{yes} and I_{no} are undistinguishable by Ehrenfeucht-Fraïssé games of length d. Consequently, I_{yes} and I_{no} are undistinguishable using sentences of quantifier depth d, a contradiction.

The databases I_{yes} and I_{no} are illustrated by the graphs in Fig. 5. Distinct vertices are distinct constants and an edge from a to b means that the atom $R(\underline{a}, b)$ is in the database. The vertex at the center is c. In every repair, no vertex can have more than one outgoing edge. Fig. 6 shows a repair of I_{no} that falsifies q, because no path of length 2 ends in c.

We sketch the winning strategy for Duplicator. At the ith move of Spoiler, if he or she picks a node close to γ on one graph, then Duplicator picks on the other graph the node at the same distance from γ and in the same direction (clockwise or counterclockwise). Likewise for α, β, δ, ϵ.

The graphs are taken sufficiently large so that the resulting subgraphs after d moves are isomorphic. Note, for example, that Spoiler cannot take advantage of the fact that there is an oriented path from δ to ϵ in I_{no}, but not in I_{yes}. To do so, Spoiler would have to exhibit an oriented path from δ to ϵ in I_{no}, which Duplicator could not do in I_{yes}. However, Spoiler cannot construct such a path because it requires choosing more than d nodes. □

8 Concluding Remarks

Our consistent FO rewriting scheme of Def. 3 is relatively simple compared to certain procedural rewriting algorithms found in the literature, and yet turns out to be widely applicable. We proved that this rewriting scheme yields a consistent FO rewriting for any rooted rule. This result allowed us to shift our attention from the syntactical intricacies of FO rewriting toward characterizing classes of rooted rules. This characterization was successful using BFMY join trees (rather than FM join trees used so far in the literature). Finally, we showed that the rule $\{R(\underline{x}, y), R(\underline{y}, c)\}$ has no consistent FO rewriting.

In this article, the target language of the rewriting scheme is first-order. The motivation for this is that target queries execute in polynomial time data complexity and can be easily encoded in SQL. Nevertheless, the proof of Theorem 5 suggests adding recursion to the target language.

The model-theoretic notion of rooted rules was engineered so as to capture the typical $\exists\forall$ quantifier alternation in consistent FO rewritings: the formula $\exists \boldsymbol{x} \exists \boldsymbol{y}' \forall \boldsymbol{y} (R(\underline{\boldsymbol{x}}, \boldsymbol{y}') \wedge (R(\underline{\boldsymbol{x}}, \boldsymbol{y}) \rightarrow \psi))$ expresses that ψ must hold no matter how we repair R-atoms that agree on the primary key $\boldsymbol{x}$. Two intriguing questions about rootedness are open for further research: First, does there exist a rule q such that q has a consistent FO rewriting but q is not rooted, no matter how its atoms are ordered? Second, is it decidable whether a given rule q is rooted?

References

1. Arenas, M., Bertossi, L.E., Chomicki, J.: Consistent query answers in inconsistent databases. In: Proc. 18th ACM Symp. on Principles of Database Systems, pp. 68–79. ACM Press, New York (1999)
2. Chomicki, J.: Consistent query answering: Five easy pieces. In: Schwentick, T., Suciu, D. (eds.) ICDT 2007. LNCS, vol. 4353, pp. 1–17. Springer, Heidelberg (2006)
3. Fuxman, A., Miller, R.J.: First-order query rewriting for inconsistent databases. J. Comput. Syst. Sci. 73(4), 610–635 (2007)
4. Beeri, C., Fagin, R., Maier, D., Yannakakis, M.: On the desirability of acyclic database schemes. J. ACM 30(3), 479–513 (1983)
5. Fuxman, A., Miller, R.J.: Towards inconsistency management in data integration systems. In: IIWeb 2003. Proc. of IJCAI-03 Workshop on Information Integration on the Web, pp. 143–148 (2003)
6. Abiteboul, S., Hull, R., Vianu, V.: Foundations of Databases. Addison-Wesley, Reading (1995)
7. Lin, J., Mendelzon, A.O.: Merging databases under constraints. Int. J. Cooperative Inf. Syst. 7(1), 55–76 (1998)
8. Wijsen, J.: Database repairing using updates. ACM Trans. Database Syst. 30(3), 722–768 (2005)
9. Fuxman, A., Fazli, E., Miller, R.J.: Conquer: Efficient management of inconsistent databases. In: SIGMOD 2005. Proc. of the ACM SIGMOD Int. Conf. on Management of Data, pp. 155–166. ACM Press, New York (2005)
10. Grieco, L., Lembo, D., Rosati, R., Ruzzi, M.: Consistent query answering under key and exclusion dependencies: Algorithms and experiments. In: CIKM 2005. Proc. 14th ACM Int. Conf. on Information and Knowledge Management, pp. 792–799. ACM Press, New York (2005)
11. Lembo, D., Rosati, R., Ruzzi, M.: On the first-order reducibility of unions of conjunctive queries over inconsistent databases. In: Grust, T., Höpfner, H., Illarramendi, A., Jablonski, S., Mesiti, M., Müller, S., Patranjan, P.-L., Sattler, K.-U., Spiliopoulou, M., Wijsen, J. (eds.) EDBT 2006. LNCS, vol. 4254, pp. 358–374. Springer, Heidelberg (2006)
12. Fuxman, A.D., Miller, R.J.: First-order rewriting for inconsistent databases. In: Eiter, T., Libkin, L. (eds.) ICDT 2005. LNCS, vol. 3363, pp. 337–351. Springer, Heidelberg (2004)
13. Calí, A., Lembo, D., Rosati, R.: On the decidability and complexity of query answering over inconsistent and incomplete databases. In: Proc. 22nd ACM Symp. on Principles of Database Systems, pp. 260–271. ACM Press, New York (2003)
14. Chomicki, J., Marcinkowski, J.: Minimal-change integrity maintenance using tuple deletions. Information and Computation 197(1-2), 90–121 (2005)
15. Calì, A., Lembo, D., Rosati, R.: Query rewriting and answering under constraints in data integration systems. In: Proc. 18th Int. Joint Conf. on Artificial Intelligence, pp. 16–21. Morgan Kaufmann, San Francisco (2003)

Relational Completeness of Query Languages for Annotated Databases

Floris Geerts[1,2] and Jan Van den Bussche[1]

[1] Hasselt University/Transnational University Limburg
[2] University of Edinburgh

Abstract. Annotated relational databases can be queried either by simply making the annotations explicitly available along the ordinary data, or by adapting the standard query operators so that they have an implicit effect also on the annotations. We compare the expressive power of these two approaches. As a formal model for the implicit approach we propose the color algebra, an adaptation of the relational algebra to deal with the annotations. We show that the color algebra is relationally complete: it is equivalent to the relational algebra on the explicit annotations. Our result extends a similar completeness result established for the query algebra of the MONDRIAN annotation system, from unions of conjunctive queries to the full relational algebra.

1 Introduction

Recently, much attention has been paid to annotated databases [10,4,2,5,8,7,6,3]. In querying annotated databases, there are two distinct approaches:

1. In *annotation propagation* [10,4,2,6,3], queries are directed primarily at the ordinary data, not the annotations: the latter are merely propagated to the query results. For example, when joining two relations, the annotations of two joined tuples would become annotations of the new joint tuple.
2. In *annotation querying* [8,7,5], queries can be directed to the annotations as well as to the ordinary data. For example, when joining two relations, two tuples might be considered joinable only if they have a common annotation. Such join queries are outside the scope of annotation propagation.

Of course, these two approaches are not competing; it is simply that in some applications we want annotation propagation, while in other applications we want to really query on the basis of annotations. As a matter of fact, annotation propagation can be precisely characterized [3] as that part of annotation querying that is invariant under arbitrary re-annotations, even those re-annotations that replace two different annotations by the same one.

In the present paper, we are concerned with full annotation querying, and here one can again distinguish two approaches: *explicit* and *implicit*.

1. In explicit querying, we simply make the annotations explicitly available along with the ordinary data; any standard query language can then be used

M. Arenas and M.I. Schwartzbach (Eds.): DBPL 2007, LNCS 4797, pp. 127–137, 2007.

to query the database. For example, suppose we want to join annotated relations $R(A, B)$ and $S(A, C)$ not only on their common A-attribute, but also on common annotations. Then we simply model R as a relation $R(A, B, N)$, where N is an extra column holding the annotations, and likewise model S as $S(A, C, N)$, and write in SQL:

```
select R.*, S.*
from R, S
where R.A=S.A and R.N=S.N
```

A similar feature is provided by the ANNOT operator of the pSQL language in DBNotes [5], where we would write:

```
select R.*, S.*
from R, ANNOT(R) N1, S, ANNOT(S) N2
where R.A=S.A and N1=N2
```

2. In implicit querying, which is more in the spirit of annotation propagation, annotations are not explicitly addressed in query formulations. Rather, the standard query operators are adapted so that they have an effect not only on the ordinary data but also on the annotations. For example, in the query algebra of MONDRIAN [8], one would write the above join query as

$$\mu\,\sigma_{R.A=S.A}(R \times S),$$

where
   - the Cartesian product operator $\times$ is adapted so as to keep, for each joint tuple $r \cup s \in R \times S$ with $r \in R$ and $s \in S$, two sets of annotations: the annotations that r already had in R, and the annotations that s already had in S;
   - the selection operator σ simply propagates these sets of annotations;
   - the new merge operator μ intersects the two sets of annotations.

A natural question now arises as to the relative expressiveness of explicit versus implicit annotation querying. This question was already addressed for the MONDRIAN query algebra, which has been shown to be equivalent to the positive relational algebra on explicit annotations [8]. In the present paper, we continue this investigation and extend it to the full relational algebra (as opposed to its positive fragment, which does not have the difference operator). Recall [1] that the relational algebra is much more powerful and complicated than its positive fragment. For instance, in the positive algebra only unions of conjunctive queries can be expressed, and containment and equivalence of queries is decidable; in the full relational algebra, all first-order logic definable queries can be expressed, and equivalence (let alone containment) is undecidable.

We will introduce *color relations* as a simple but general abstraction of annotated databases. A color relation is a standard database relation, where additionally every tuple is annotated by some set of "colors". Moreover, we will introduce the *color algebra (CA)*, an adaptation of the relational algebra to deal with color relations. CA is inspired by, but different from, the MONDRIAN query algebra. The operators of CA always produce color relations as output;

in particular, in CA one cannot compute intermediate results that explicitly relate the colors of different tuples. Nevertheless, we will prove that CA can still express any expression of the full relational algebra on explicit annotations, as long as the latter expression starts from color relations and finally ends up in color relations.

Our result, while answering a natural question, is mainly of theoretical interest. Yet, good theoretical underpinnings of new database management features, such as annotation, are important. We hope that the elegant formalism provided by our color algebra can serve as a guide to the understanding and design of annotation query languages.

2 Color Relations

Basically we assume as given an infinite set of *attributes*, an infinite set $\mathbb{D}$ of *data values*, and an infinite set $\mathbb{C}$ of *colors*. The sets $\mathbb{D}$ and $\mathbb{C}$ are disjoint; colors serve as an abstraction for annotation values.

1. A *relation schema* is a finite set R of attributes.
2. A *tuple* over R is a mapping $t\colon R \to \mathbb{D}$.
3. A *relation* over R is a finite set of tuples over R.
4. A *coloring* of a relation r is a subset r' of $r \times \mathbb{C}$, i.e., a set of tuple–color pairs where the tuples come from r, such that every tuple of r appears in r', i.e., every tuple of r gets at least one color.
5. We call r the *underlying relation* of r'. We agree that whenever we denote a coloring by a primed letter, the unprimed letter stands for the underlying relation.
6. Colorings of relations over R are also called *color relations over* R.
7. A *database schema* $\mathcal{S}$ consists of a finite set of relation variables x, each with an associated relation schema $\mathcal{S}(x)$.
8. A *color database* D over $\mathcal{S}$ consists of a set of color relations $D(x)$, one for each relation variable x of $\mathcal{S}$, such that $D(x)$ is a color relation over $\mathcal{S}(x)$.

We can view a color relation r' alternatively as a mapping r' from r to $2^{\mathbb{C}}$, as follows:

$$r'(t) = \{c \mid (t, c) \in r'\}.$$

Note that, since every tuple gets at least one color, $r'(t)$ is never empty. For any subset $s \subseteq r$, the restriction of the mapping r' to s, which we denote by $r'|_s$, is of course a coloring of s. We will use this observation in the following section.

Remark 1. In our data model, we restrict attention to the coloring of entire tuples. In annotation systems such as DBNotes [2,5], not just tuples in relations can be colored, but also individual components of these tuples. We can model this by multiple color relations, one for each attribute. The system MONDRIAN [8,7] even allows the coloring of arbitrary subsets of projections of a relation. Even more generally, one can consider annotations of arbitrary combinations of records and sets [3]. Such complex structures can always be decomposed in multiple flat relations, however, and since the focus of this paper is on expressive power, our model of color relations is sufficient.

3 The Color Algebra

We are familiar with the classical relational algebra operations on relations: union ($\cup$), difference ($-$), natural join ($\bowtie$), renaming (ρ), selection (σ), and projection (π). We now define a number of analogous operations on color relations. The result of these operations is again a color relation.

Let r' and s' be two color relations over the same relation scheme R.

Union: $r' \cup s'$ is the standard set-theoretic union. This is a coloring of $r \cup s$.
Tuple difference: $r' \boxminus s'$ equals $r'|_{r \setminus s}$. It is thus a coloring of $r \setminus s$.
Full difference: $r' - s'$ is the standard set-theoretic difference. It is a coloring not of $r \setminus s$, but of

$$(r \setminus s) \cup \{t \in r \cap s \mid r'(t) \not\subseteq s'(t)\}.$$

For the definition of the next two operations, s' no longer needs to be over the same relation scheme as r'.

Tuple join: $r' \boxtimes s'$ equals

$$\{(t_1 \cup t_2, c) \mid t_1 \cup t_2 \in r \bowtie s \text{ and } c \in r'(t_1) \cup s'(t_2)\}.$$

It is a coloring of $r \bowtie s$.
Full join: $r \bowtie s$ is defined in the same way as $r \boxtimes s$, except that now we take the intersection $r'(t_1) \cap s'(t_2)$ rather than the union. It is thus a coloring not of $r \bowtie s$, but of

$$\{t_1 \cup t_2 \in r \bowtie s \mid r'(t_1) \cap s'(t_2) \neq \emptyset\}.$$

Renaming: if $A \in R$ and B is an attribute not in R, then $\rho_{A/B}(r')$ equals

$$\{(\rho_{A/B}(t), c) \mid (t, c) \in r'\},$$

with $\rho_{A/B}(t) = t|_{R-A} \cup \{(B, t(A))\}$ the classical renaming of a tuple. It is thus a coloring of $\rho_{A/B}(r)$.
Selection: if $A, B \in R$, then $\sigma_{A=B}(r')$ equals $r'|_{\sigma_{A=B}(r')}$.
Color selection: if $k \geq 2$ is a natural number, then $\sigma_{\text{color} \geq k}(r')$ equals $r'|_u$, where

$$u = \{t \in r \mid |r'(t)| \geq k\},$$

with $|r'(t)|$ denoting the cardinality of $r'(t)$, i.e., the number of distinct colors of t in r'.
Projection: if $X \subseteq R$, then $\pi^{\text{c}}_X(r')$ equals

$$\{(t|_X, c) \mid (t, c) \in r'\}.$$

This concludes the definition of the operations of the *color algebra*, abbreviated CA.

Example 1. A simple example is the CA-expression

$$\pi^{\mathrm{c}}_{X}(x \bowtie \mathsf{green}),$$

where green is a constant relation (over attributes disjoint from x) consisting of a single "green"-colored tuple and X consists of the attributes in x. This expression returns all tuples in x that are colored 'green'; all colors of those tuples are returned as well.

For another example, the CA-expression

$$(x \bowtie (x \boxtimes y)) - (y \bowtie (x \boxtimes y))$$

applied to colored relations r' and s', returns joint tuples $t_1 \cup t_2$ from the natural join of the underlying relations r and s (with $t_1 \in r$ and $t_2 \in s$); these joint tuples are colored by the colors t_1 has in r', except for the colors t_2 has in s'. In particular, if t_1 has only colors that t_2 has too, then the joint tuple $t_1 \cup t_2$ is not returned at all, since in colored relations, each tuple must have at least one color.

As a final example, the expression

$$x - \sigma_{\mathrm{color} \geq 3}(x)$$

returns all tuples in x that have at most two colors.

Remark 2. We remark that most of the operators in CA are intuitive except for maybe the color selection $\sigma_{\mathrm{color} \geq k}$. This operator is necessary, however, to show the completeness of CA.

4 CA and the Relational Algebra

Let us reserve a special attribute *col* and agree that it is never used in the relation schemes of color relations. For any relation scheme R, we define the relation scheme $\bar{R} = R \cup \{col\}$. We can naturally view a color relation r over R as a relation over $\bar{R}$, as follows:

$$\{t \cup \{(col, c)\} \mid (t, c) \in r\}.$$

Conversely, any relation r over $\bar{R}$ can be viewed as a color relation as follows:

$$\{(t|_R, t(col)) \mid t \in r\}.$$

Beware that when we regard r as a *color* relation, it is a color relation over R, i.e., r's relation scheme is just R, because the color attribute is implicit in color relations. Indeed, this is exactly the main feature of the color algebra: that colors

Table 1. Simulation of CA by relational algebra. In the case of $x \boxminus y$, the R refers to the relation scheme of the color relations x and y; in the cases of $x \boxtimes y$ and $\sigma_{\mathrm{color} \geq k}(x)$, the R (S) refers to the relation scheme of the color relation x (y). Moreover, in the simulation of $\sigma_{\mathrm{color} \geq k}(x)$, the auxiliary attributes col_i are chosen such that they do not appear in R.

$x \cup y$	$x \cup y$
$x \boxminus y$	$(\pi_R(x) - \pi_R(y)) \bowtie x$
$x - y$	$x - y$
$x \boxtimes y$	$(x \bowtie \pi_S(y)) \cup (\pi_R(x) \bowtie y)$
$x \bowtie y$	$x \bowtie y$
$\rho_{A/B}(x)$	$\rho_{A/B}(x)$
$\sigma_{A=B}(x)$	$\sigma_{A=B}(x)$
$\sigma_{\mathrm{color} \geq k}(x)$	$\pi_{\bar{R}} \sigma_{\bigwedge_{i \neq j} col_i \neq col_j} (\rho_{col/col_1}(x) \bowtie \cdots \bowtie \rho_{col/col_k}(x))$
$\pi^{\mathrm{c}}_X(x)$	$\pi_{X \cup \{col\}}(x)$

are handled automatically. When we regard r as an ordinary relation, however, it is a relation over $\bar{R}$ and the color attribute becomes explicitly visible.

Under the view of color relations as ordinary relations, we can apply classical relational algebra operations to color relations, and consider relational algebra expressions with $\bar{R}$ as result relation scheme to be producing color relations over R. It then becomes apparent that the classical relational algebra can actually simulate the color algebra. The simulation is given in Table 1. The table shows the simulation of the individual operations; the simulation of more complex expressions can be obtained using composition.

More interestingly, the converse simulation holds as well: every operation on color relations that is definable in the relational algebra is already definable in CA. More formally, to every color database schema $\mathcal{S}$ we can associate the relational database schema $\bar{\mathcal{S}}$ which has precisely the same relation variables, but when relation variable x has relation scheme R in $\mathcal{S}$, then x has relation scheme $\bar{R}$ in $\bar{\mathcal{S}}$. We will establish:

Theorem 1. *For every relational algebra expression over $\bar{\mathcal{S}}$ whose result relation scheme is of the form $\bar{R}$ for some relation scheme R, there exists an equivalent CA-expression over $\mathcal{S}$.*

In proving this theorem, one cannot hope for a simple bottom-up syntax-directed translation from relational algebra to CA, such as we had with Table 1 for the other direction. For instance, consider in that table the line for $\sigma_{\mathrm{color} \geq k}(x)$, but now read from right to left. More generally, the challenge is how to deal with relational algebra expressions that produce relations as intermediate results that explicitly relate colors from different tuples in the database.

5 Simulation of the Relational Algebra by the Color Algebra

In this section, we prove our theorem. It is actually sufficient to do this for a restricted fragment of the relational algebra, which we call the color-typed relational algebra, denoted by RA^c. In order to define this fragment, we must first go from our one special color attribute *col* to an infinite set $\mathcal{C}$ of color attributes, and agree that these are, like *col*, never used in relation schemes of color relations. Of course we put $col \in \mathcal{C}$. The color-typed restriction now only lies in a condition imposed on selections and renamings. Specifically, if e is an expression, then $\sigma_{A=B}(e)$ and $\rho_{A/B}(e)$ are only allowed if either A and B are both color attributes, or are both not color attributes. Expressions of the form $e_1 \cup e_2$, $e_1 - e_2$, $e_1 \bowtie e_2$, or $\pi_X(e)$ can be constructed just like in the classical relational algebra.

A result on the first-order completeness of many-sorted logic [9] implies that every relational algebra expression over a database schema $\bar{\mathcal{S}}$ with result relation scheme of the form $\bar{R}$ can be expressed in RA^c. (We point out that this depends crucially on the disjointness of the universes $\mathbb{D}$ of data values and $\mathbb{C}$ of colors.) So, we indeed only have to prove the theorem for RA^c.

Our proof uses the technical notion of an *R-parameterized monadic database schema*, where R is a relation scheme. This is a relational database schema where every relation name has the same relation scheme $\bar{R}$. Equivalently, it can be viewed as a color database schema where every relation scheme has the same relation scheme R. Furthermore, an RA^c-expression f over such a schema is called *R-uniform* if it satisfies the following:

- f uses only renamings $\rho_{A/B}$ and selections $\sigma_{A=B}$ where A and B are color attributes;
- all projections π_X appearing in f satisfy $R \subseteq X$.

The intuition is that an R-uniform expression does not explicitly work with the attributes in R; these attributes are merely dragged along as parameters.

We now show that CA can simulate R-uniform RA^c, in the following sense:

Lemma 1. *Let f be an R-uniform* RA^c*-expression over the R-parameterized monadic database schema $\mathcal{S}$. Let S be the result relation scheme of f.*

- *If $S \cap \mathcal{C} = \emptyset$, i.e., $S = R$, then there exists a CA-expression* $\mathrm{sim}(f)$ *such that $f(D)$ equals the relation underlying* $\mathrm{sim}(f)(D)$*, for each color database D over $\mathcal{S}$.*
- *If $S \cap \mathcal{C} \neq \emptyset$, then for each equivalence relation E on $S \cap \mathcal{C}$, there exists a set* $\mathrm{sim}_E(f)$ *of mappings from $S \cap \mathcal{C}$ to CA, such that $f(D)$ equals*

$$\bigcup_{E} \bigcup_{\tau \in \mathrm{sim}_E(f)} \sigma_{\bigwedge_{(col',col'') \in E} col'=col''}$$

$$\sigma_{\bigwedge_{(col',col'') \notin E} col' \neq col''} \bowtie_{col' \in S \cap C} \rho_{col/col'}(\tau(col')(D))$$

Proof. Assume that $\mathcal{S}$ consists of the relation names $z_1, \ldots, z_n$. We begin by refining the classical correspondence between the relational algebra and the relational calculus (first-order logic, FO) to R-uniform RA^c. The corresponding fragment of FO, which we denote by FO_R^c, is obtained as follows. Let

$R = \{A_1, \ldots, A_m\}$. We use the A_j's, plus all color attributes, as first-order variables. The allowed atomic formulas are of two forms:

1. $z_i(A_1, \ldots, A_m, col')$ with $col' \in \mathcal{C}$. We abbreviate such formulas by $z_i(R, col')$.
2. $col' = col''$ with $col', col'' \in \mathcal{C}$.

The only variables that can be quantified are color attributes. It is then readily seen that R-uniform RA^{c} corresponds to FO^{c}_R under the active-domain semantics, with the understanding that, when evaluating a formula in a database D, the tuple of free variables $A_1, \ldots, A_m$ is only instantiated by R-tuples that actually appear in D.

We next apply the well-known quantifier elimination method for monadic first-order logic to FO^{c}_R. Concretely, this gives us that every FO^{c}_R formula can be written without quantifiers if we additionally allow predicates of the form $|z_\alpha(R)| \geq \ell$ in formulas, where $\ell \geq 1$ is a natural number, and α is a nonempty subset of $\{1, \ldots, n\}$. The meaning of such a predicate, for a given tuple t over R, is that $|z_\alpha(t)| \geq \ell$, where $z_\alpha(t)$ equals

$$\{t' \in \bigcup_i z_i \mid t'|_R = t \ \& \ \bigwedge_{i \in \alpha} t' \in z_i \ \& \ \bigwedge_{i \in \hat{\alpha}} t' \notin z_i\},$$

where $\hat{\alpha}$ abbreviates $\{1, \ldots, n\} - \alpha$.

Putting the quantifier-free formula in disjunctive normal form, and simplifying each conjunction, we obtain a disjunction of conjunctions of factors of the following possible forms:

- If $S \cap \mathcal{C} = \emptyset$, then each factor of the conjunction is of one of the following three forms:
  1. $|z_\alpha(R)| \geq 1$. This can be expressed in CA by $\bowtie_{i \in \alpha} z_i - \bigcup_{i \in \hat{\alpha}} z_i$.
  2. $|z_\alpha(R)| \geq \ell$ with $\ell \geq 2$. This can be expressed in CA by $\sigma_{\text{color} \geq \ell}(|z_\alpha(R)| \geq 1)$.
  3. $\neg(|z_\alpha(R)| \geq \ell)$. This can be expressed in CA by $\bigcup_i z_i \boxminus (|z_\alpha(R)| \geq \ell)$.
- If $S \cap \mathcal{C} \neq \emptyset$, then factors may additionally be of the following possible forms:
  4. $z_i(R, col')$ for some color attribute col'. This can be expressed in CA by z_i.
  5. $\neg z_i(R, col')$. This can be expressed in CA by $\bigcup_j z_j - z_i$.
  6. equalities and inequalities among color attributes.

Without loss of generality, we may assume that in each conjunction γ, the set of equalities and inequalities among color attributes is maximally consistent, involving all color attributes in $S \cap \mathcal{C}$. Such a maximally consistent set gives rise to an equivalence relation E_γ on the color attributes.

We now construct, for each conjunction γ, the following mapping τ from $S \cap \mathcal{C}$ to CA and put it in $\text{sim}_{E_\gamma}(f)$. For each color attribute col', we take the CA-expressions for all factors of types 1–3 above, and also take the CA-expressions for all factors of types 4–5 that concern the particular color attribute *col'*. If there are no such factors of types 4–5 for *col'*, then we add the CA-expression $\bigcup_{z \in \mathcal{S}} \pi_{\emptyset}(z)$. We conjoin all these CA-expressions using $\boxtimes$. The resulting CA-expression then equals $\tau(col')$. □

Our second lemma connects R-uniform expressions to general RA^{c}-expressions. Together with the first lemma, it establishes the theorem.

Lemma 2. *Let h be an* RA^{c}*-expression over $\bar{\mathcal{S}}$ with result relation scheme S, and let $R = S - \mathcal{C}$. Then there exist a natural number n; CA-expressions e_1, …, e_n, all with result relation scheme R; and an R-uniform* RA^{c}*-expression $f(z_1, \ldots, z_n)$, such that the composition $f(e_1, \ldots, e_n)$ is equivalent to h.*

Proof. By induction on the structure of e. If h is a relation name x, then $n = 1$; e_1 is x; and f is z_1.

If h is $h_1 \cup h_2$, by induction we have, for $j = 1, 2$, the natural number n_j, the sequence of CA-expressions $\boldsymbol{e^j} = e_1^j, \ldots, e_{n_j}^j$, and the RA^{c}-expression f_j. Then we put

$$\begin{aligned} n &:= n_1 + n_2 \\ e_1, \ldots, e_n &:= \boldsymbol{e^1}, \boldsymbol{e^2} \\ f &:= f_1(z_1, \ldots, z_{n_1}) \cup f_2(z_{n_1+1}, \ldots, z_n). \end{aligned}$$

The case where h is $h_1 - h_2$ is similar, but now f is $f_1 - f_2$.

If h is $h_1 \bowtie h_2$, we again begin by obtaining the ingredients for h_1 and h_2 by induction, as above. By Lemma 1, we can simulate f_1 and f_2 in CA. We now perform a case analysis based on how the result relation schemes S_1 and S_2 of h_1 and h_2 intersect with $\mathcal{C}$. There are four cases.

First, $S_1 \cap \mathcal{C} = \emptyset = S_2 \cap \mathcal{C}$. We put

$$\begin{aligned} n &:= 1 \\ e_1 &:= \mathrm{sim}(f_1)(\boldsymbol{e^1}) \boxtimes \mathrm{sim}(f_2)(\boldsymbol{e^2}) \\ f &:= \pi_R(z_1). \end{aligned}$$

Second, $S_1 \cap \mathcal{C} = \emptyset$ and $S_2 \cap \mathcal{C} \neq \emptyset$. Let us first introduce the following derived CA operator: $x \rhd y$ is an abbreviation for $x \bowtie (x \boxtimes y)$. Note that $r' \rhd s'$, for color relations r' and s', equals $\{(t_1 \cup t_2, c) \mid t_1 \cup t_2 \in r \bowtie s \;\&\; (t_1, c) \in r'\}$. Now in this case we take n to be the total number of expressions occurring in all sets $\mathrm{sim}_{E_2}(f_2)$, for all equivalence relations E_2 on $S_2 \cap \mathcal{C}$. For each of those expressions g, we form $g' := g(\boldsymbol{e^2}) \rhd \mathrm{sim}(f_1)(\boldsymbol{e^1})$, and all these expressions g' constitute the e_i's. Denoting the relation name corresponding to g' by z_g, we can then use the following expression for f:

$$\bigcup_{E_2} \bigcup_{\tau \in \mathrm{sim}_{E_2}(f_2)} \sigma_{\bigwedge_{(col', col'') \in E_2} col' = col''} \sigma_{\bigwedge_{(col', col'') \notin E_2} col' \neq col''} \mathop{\bowtie}_{col' \in S_2 \cap \mathcal{C}} \rho_{col/col'}(z_{\tau(col')}).$$

Third, $S_1 \cap \mathcal{C} = \emptyset$ and $S_2 \cap \mathcal{C} \neq \emptyset$. This case is symmetric to the previous case.

Fourth, $S_1 \cap \mathcal{C} \neq \emptyset \neq S_2 \cap \mathcal{C}$. In this case we use three kinds of CA-expressions:

1. $\tau_1(col')(\mathbf{e^1}) \ltimes \tau_2(col')(\mathbf{e^2})$, with $col' \in S_1 \cap S_2 \cap \mathcal{C}$, and $\tau_j \in \mathrm{sim}_{E_j}(f_j)$, for an equivalence relation E_j of $S_j \cap \mathcal{C}$, for $j = 1, 2$;
2. $\tau(col')(\mathbf{e^1}) \rhd \tau(col'')(\mathbf{e^2})$, with $col' \in (S_1 \cap \mathcal{C}) \setminus (S_2 \cap \mathcal{C})$ and $col'' \in S_2 \cap \mathcal{C}$, and τ_j as above;
3. $\tau(col'')(\mathbf{e^2}) \rhd \tau(col')(\mathbf{e^1})$, with $col'' \in (S_2 \cap \mathcal{C}) \setminus (S_1 \cap \mathcal{C})$ and $col' \in S_1 \cap \mathcal{C}$, and again τ_j as above.

So, n equals the total number of all possible CA-expressions of those three kinds. For all these expressions, which are all of the form $i \ltimes j$ or $i \rhd j$, the underlying R-parameterized monadic database schema has corresponding relation names $z_{i,j}$. The expression f then becomes:

$$\bigcup_{E_1} \bigcup_{E_2} \bigcup_{\tau_1} \bigcup_{\tau_2} \sigma_{\bigwedge_{(col',col'') \in E_1} col'=col''} \sigma_{\bigwedge_{(col',col'') \notin E_1} col' \neq col''}$$

$$\sigma_{\bigwedge_{(col',col'') \in E_2} col'=col''} \sigma_{\bigwedge_{(col',col'') \notin E_2} col' \neq col''}$$

$$\bigotimes_{col' \in S_1 \cap S_2 \cap \mathcal{C}} \rho_{col/col'}(z_{\tau_1(col'),\tau_2(col')})$$

$$\ltimes \bigotimes_{\substack{col' \in (S_1 \cap \mathcal{C}) \setminus (S_2 \cap \mathcal{C}) \\ col'' \in S_2 \cap \mathcal{C}}} \rho_{col/col'}(z_{\tau_1(col'),\tau_2(col'')})$$

$$\ltimes \bigotimes_{\substack{col'' \in (S_2 \cap \mathcal{C}) \setminus (S_1 \cap \mathcal{C}) \\ col' \in S_1 \cap \mathcal{C}}} \rho_{col/col'}(z_{\tau_2(col''),\tau_1(col')}).$$

If h is $\rho_{A/B}(h_1)$ with A and B not in $\mathcal{C}$, then we put $n := n_1$; $e_i := \rho_{A/B}(e_i^1)$; and $f := f_1$.

If h is $\rho_{col'/col''}(h_1)$ with $col', col'' \in \mathcal{C}$, then $n := n_1$; $e_i := e_i^1$; and $f := \rho_{col'/col''}(f_1)$.

If h is $\sigma_{A=B}(h_1)$ with A and B not in $\mathcal{C}$, then we put $n := n_1$; $e_i := \sigma_{A=B}(e_i^1)$; and $f := f_1$.

If h is $\sigma_{col'=col''}(h_1)$ with $col', col'' \in \mathcal{C}$, then $n := n_1$; $e_i := e_i^1$; and $f := \sigma_{col'=col''}(f_1)$.

Finally, if h is $\pi_X(h_1)$, then we simulate f_1 in CA according to Lemma 1. Now if the intersection of the result relation scheme S_1 of h_1 with $\mathcal{C}$ is empty, then we put $n := 1$; $e_1 := \pi^c_X(\mathrm{sim}(f_1)(\mathbf{e^1}))$; and $f := z_1$. If $S_1 \cap \mathcal{C} \neq \emptyset$, then we take n to be the total number of expressions occurring in all sets $\mathrm{sim}_E(f_1)$, for all equivalence relations E on $S_1 \cap \mathcal{C}$. For each of those expressions g, we form $g' := \pi_{X-\mathcal{C}}(g)(\mathbf{e^1})$, and all these expressions g' constitute the e_i's. Denoting the relation name corresponding to g' by z_g, we can then use the following expression for f:

$$\pi_X \bigcup_{E} \bigcup_{\tau \in \mathrm{sim}_E(f_1)} \sigma_{\bigwedge_{(col',col'') \in E} col'=col''} \sigma_{\bigwedge_{(col',col'') \notin E} col' \neq col''} \bigotimes_{col' \in S_1 \cap \mathcal{C}} \rho_{col/col'}(z_{\tau(col')}).$$

□

Acknowledgements

Floris Geerts is a postdoctoral researcher of the FWO Vlaanderen and is supported in part by EPSRC GR/S63205/01.

References

1. Abiteboul, S., Hull, R., Vianu, V.: Foundations of Databases. Addison-Wesley, Reading (1995)
2. Bhagwat, D., Chiticariu, L., Tan, W.-C., Vijayvargiya, G.: An annotation management system for relational databases. The VLDB Journal 14(4), 373–396 (2005)
3. Buneman, P., Cheney, J., Vansummeren, S.: On the expressiveness of implicit provenance in query and update languages. In: Schwentick, T., Suciu, D. (eds.) ICDT 2007. LNCS, vol. 4353, pp. 209–223. Springer, Heidelberg (2006)
4. Buneman, P., Khanna, S., Tan, W.-C.: On propagation of deletions and annotations through views. In: Proceedings 21st ACM Symposium on Principles of Database Systems, pp. 150–158. ACM Press, New York (2002)
5. Chiticariu, L., Tan, W.-C., Vijayvargiya, G.: DBNotes: A post-it system for relational databases based on provenance. In: Proceedings 2005 ACM SIGMOD International Conference on Management of Data, pp. 942–944. ACM Press, New York (2005)
6. Cong, G., Fan, W., Geerts, F.: Annotation propagation revisited for key preserving views. In: Proceedings 15th ACM International Conference on Information and Knowledge Management, pp. 632–641. ACM Press, New York (2006)
7. Geerts, F., Kementsietsidis, A., Milano, D.: iMONDRIAN: A visual tool to annotate and query scientific databases. In: Ioannidis, Y., Scholl, M.H., Schmidt, J.W., Matthes, F., Hatzopoulos, M., Boehm, K., Kemper, A., Grust, T., Boehm, C. (eds.) EDBT 2006. LNCS, vol. 3896, pp. 1168–1171. Springer, Heidelberg (2006)
8. Geerts, F., Kementsietsidis, A., Milano, D.: MONDRIAN: Annotating and querying databases through colors and blocks. In: Proceedings 22th International Conference on Data Engineering, p. 82 (10 pages). IEEE Computer Society Press, Los Alamitos (2006)
9. Van den Bussche, J., Cabibbo, L.: Converting untyped formulas into typed ones. Acta Informatica 35(8), 637–643 (1998)
10. Wang, Y.R., Madnick, S.E.: A polygen model for heterogeneous database systems: the source taging perspective. In: McLeod, D., Sacks-Davis, R., Schek, H. (eds.) Proceedings of the 16th International Conference on Very Large Data Bases, pp. 518–538. Morgan Kaufmann, San Francisco (1990)

Provenance as Dependency Analysis

James Cheney[1], Amal Ahmed[2], and Umut A. Acar[2,⋆]

[1] University of Edinburgh
[2] Toyota Technological Institute at Chicago

Abstract. Provenance is information recording the source, derivation, or history of some information. Provenance tracking has been studied in a variety of settings; however, although many design points have been explored, the mathematical or semantic foundations of data provenance have received comparatively little attention. In this paper, we argue that dependency analysis techniques familiar from program analysis and program slicing provide a formal foundation for forms of provenance that are intended to show how (part of) the output of a query depends on (parts of) its input. We introduce a semantic characterization of such *dependency provenance*, show that this form of provenance is not computable, and provide dynamic and static approximation techniques.

1 Introduction

Provenance is information about the origin, ownership, influences upon, or other *historical* or *contextual* information about an object. Such information has many applications, including evaluating integrity or authenticity claims, establishing the chain of custody of or responsibility for an object, detecting and repairing errors, and memoization and caching of the results of computations. Provenance is particularly important in scientific computation and recordkeeping, since it is considered essential for ensuring the repeatability of experiments and judging the scientific value of their results.

Provenance tracking has been studied in a variety of settings, including databases, file systems, and scientific workflows; indeed, many familiar systems provide simple forms of provenance, such as the timestamp and ownership metadata in file systems, system logs, and version control systems. Although a wide variety of design points have been explored [8,17,21], there is relatively little understanding of the relationships among techniques or of the design considerations that should be taken into account when developing or evaluating an approach to provenance. The mathematical or semantic foundations of data provenance have received comparatively little attention, with a few relatively recent exceptions [10,11,15,19].

Most prior approaches have invoked intuitive concepts such as *contribution*, *influence*, and *relevance* as motivation for their definitions of provenance. These intuitions seem adequate when considering monotone relational queries, but tend to break down when negation, grouping, or aggregation are considered. These intuitions have also motivated rigorous approaches to seemingly quite different problems, such as aiding debugging via *program slicing* [7,16,24], supporting efficient memoization and caching [2,4], and

⋆ Cheney was supported by EPSRC grant R37476. Acar was supported by an Intel gift.

M. Arenas and M.I. Schwartzbach (Eds.): DBPL 2007, LNCS 4797, pp. 138–152, 2007.

(a)

Protein			
ID	Name	MW	⋯
p_1	thioredoxin	**11.8**	⋯
p_2	flavodoxin	19.7	⋯
p_3	ferredoxin	12.3	⋯
p_4	ArgR	**−700**	⋯
p_5	CheW	18.1	⋯
⋮	⋮	⋮	⋮

EnzReact	
PID	RID
p_1	r_1
p_2	r_1
p_1	**r_2**
p_4	**r_2**
p_5	r_3
⋮	⋮

Reaction		
ID	Name	⋯
r_1	thia-phos + ATP = thi diphos + ADP	⋯
r_2	H_2O + an acyl phos → phos + a carboxylate	⋯
r_3	D-ribose-5-phosp = D-ribulose-5-phos	⋯
r_4	β-D-gluc-6-phos = fruct-6-phos	⋯
r_5	panteth 4′-phos + ATP = dephos-CoA + diphos	⋯
⋮	⋮	⋮

(b)

```
SELECT R.Name as Name, AVERAGE(P.MW) as AvgMW
  FROM Protein P, EnzymaticReaction ER, Reaction R
 WHERE P.ID = ER.ProteinID, ER.ReactionID = R.ID
GROUP BY R.Name
```

(c)

Name	AvgMW
thia-phos + ATP = thi diphos + ADP	15.75
H_2O + an acyl phos → phos + a carboxylate	*-338.2*
D-ribose-5-phosp = D-ribulose-5-phos	18.1
⋮	⋮

Fig. 1. Example (a) input, (b) query, and (b) output data; input field values relevant to *italicized* erroneous output value are highlighted in **bold**

improving program security using information flow analysis [20]. As Abadi et al. have argued [1], slicing, information flow, and several other program analysis techniques can all be understood in terms of dependence.

In this paper, we argue that these *dependency analysis* and *slicing* techniques familiar from programming languages provide a suitable foundation for an interesting class of provenance techniques. To illustrate our approach, consider the (realistic, but biologically inaccurate) input data shown in Figure 1(a) and the query in Figure 1(b) which calculates the average molecular weights of proteins involved in each reaction. The result of this query is shown in Figure 1(c).

Since the MW field contains the molecular weight of a protein, it is clearly an error for the italicized value in the result to be negative. To track down the source of the error, it would be helpful to know which parts of the input *contributed to*, or were *relevant to*, the erroneous part of the output. We can formalize this intuition by saying that a part of the output *depends on* a part of the input if a change to the input part may result in a change to the output part. This is analogous to program slicing [24], a debugging aid that identifies the parts of a *program* on which a program output depends.

In this example, the input field values that the erroneous output AvgMW-value depends on are highlighted in bold. The dependences include the two summed MW values and the ID fields which are compared by the selection and grouping query. These ID fields must be included because a change to any one of them could result in a change to the italicized output value—for example, changing the occurrence of p_4 in table EnzymaticReaction. On the other hand, the names of the proteins and reactions are *irrelevant* to the output AvgMW.

This example is simplistic, but the ability to concisely explain which parts of the input influence each part of the output is much more important if we consider a realistic database with perhaps tens or hundreds of columns per table and thousands or millions of rows. Moreover, dependence information can also be useful for a variety of other applications, including estimating the *quality* or *freshness* of data in a query result by aggregating timestamps or quality annotations on the relevant inputs.

In this paper, we argue that data dependence provides a solid semantic foundation for generalizing why-provenance, lineage, and similar techniques. We consider the full nested relational calculus with set difference, equality, grouping and aggregation operations, and functions on basic types. We consider annotation-propagating semantics for such queries and define a property called *dependency-correctness*, which, intuitively, means that the annotations produced by a query correctly show all parts of the output that may change if a part of the input is changed.

The structure of the rest of this paper is as follows. We briefly review the nested relational calculus in Section 2. We then introduce (in Section 3) the annotation-propagation model and define dependency-correctness. In Section 3.1 we describe a dynamic *provenance-tracking* semantics that is dependency-correct. We also (Section 3.2) introduce a type-based *provenance analysis* which is less accurate than provenance tracking, but can be performed statically; we also prove its correctness relative to dynamic provenance tracking. We discuss our results and a preliminary implementation in Section 3.3 and discuss related and future work and conclude in Sections 4–5. Full proofs of our main results are provided in a companion technical report [14].

2 Background

We assume some familiarity with the *nested relational calculus* (NRC) [13], which is closely related to *monad algebra* [22]. We consider multiset (or bag) collections rather than sets. The types and expressions of our variant of NRC are as follows:

$$\begin{aligned} \tau &::= \mathsf{bool} \mid \mathsf{int} \mid \tau_1 \times \tau_2 \mid \{\tau\} \\ e &::= x \mid \mathsf{let}\ x = e_1\ \mathsf{in}\ e_2 \mid (e_1, e_2) \mid \pi_i(e) \mid b \mid i \mid \neg e \mid e_1 \wedge e_2 \mid e_1 + e_2 \mid \mathsf{sum}(e) \\ &\quad \mid e_1 \approx e_2 \mid \mathsf{if}\ e_0\ \mathsf{then}\ e_1\ \mathsf{else}\ e_2 \mid \emptyset \mid \{e\} \mid e_1 \cup e_2 \mid e_1 - e_2 \mid \{e_2 \mid x \in e_1\} \mid \bigcup e \end{aligned}$$

Here, $i \in \mathbb{Z} = \{\ldots, -1, 0, 1, \ldots\}$ represents integer constants and $b \in \mathbb{B} = \{\mathsf{true}, \mathsf{false}\}$ denotes Boolean constants. The type $\{\tau\}$ describes *collections* of elements of type τ; in this paper, we consider collections to be *bags* (multisets). The bag operations include $\emptyset$, the constant empty bag; singletons $\{e\}$; bag union and difference; comprehension $\{e_2 \mid x \in e_1\}$; and flattening $\bigcup e$. By convention, we write $\{e_1, \ldots, e_n\}$ as syntactic sugar for $\{e_1\} \cup \cdots \cup \{e_n\}$. Finally, we include sum, a typical aggregation operation, which adds together all of the elements of a bag and produces a value; e.g.

$\mathsf{sum}\{1, 2, 3\} = 6$ (by convention, $\mathsf{sum}(\emptyset) = 0$). We syntactically distinguish between NRC's equality operation $\approx$ and mathematical equality $=$.

Types. Query language expressions can be typechecked using standard techniques. Contexts Γ are lists of pairs of variables and types $x_1 : \tau_1, \ldots, x_n : \tau_n$, where $x_1, \ldots, x_n$ are distinct. The rules for typechecking expressions are shown in Figure 2.

Semantics. We write $\mathcal{M}_{\mathsf{fin}}(X)$ for the set of all finite bags with elements drawn from X. The (standard) interpretation of base types as sets of values is as follows:

$$\mathcal{T}[\![\mathsf{bool}]\!] = \mathbb{B} = \{\mathsf{true}, \mathsf{false}\} \qquad \mathcal{T}[\![\tau_1 \times \tau_2]\!] = \mathcal{T}[\![\tau_1]\!] \times \mathcal{T}[\![\tau_2]\!]$$
$$\mathcal{T}[\![\mathsf{int}]\!] = \mathbb{Z} = \{\ldots, -1, 0, 1, \ldots\} \qquad \mathcal{T}[\![\{\tau\}]\!] = \mathcal{M}_{\mathsf{fin}}(\mathcal{T}[\![\tau]\!])$$

An environment γ is a function from variables to values. We define the set of environments matching context Γ as $\mathcal{T}[\![\Gamma]\!] = \{\gamma \mid \forall x \in dom(\Gamma).\gamma(x) \in \mathcal{T}[\![\Gamma(x)]\!]\}$.

Figure 3 gives the semantics of queries. Note that we overload notation for pair projection π_i and bag operations such as $\cup$ and $\biguplus$; also, if S is a bag of integers, then $\sum S$ is the sum of their values (taking $\sum \emptyset = 0$). It is straightforward to show that

Lemma 1. *If $\Gamma \vdash e : \tau$ then $\mathcal{E}[\![e]\!] : \mathcal{T}[\![\Gamma]\!] \to \mathcal{T}[\![\tau]\!]$.*

As discussed in previous work [13], the NRC can express a wide variety of queries including ordinary relational queries as well as grouping and aggregation. We do not consider incomplete information (`NULL` values). Additional primitive functions and relations such as average can also be added without difficulty (in fact, average is definable in our language). For example, using more readable named record, comprehensions, and patterns, the SQL query from the Figure 1(b) can be defined as

$$\mathsf{let}\ X = \{(r.Name, p.MW) \mid r \in R, er \in ER, p \in P, er.RID{=}r.ID, p.ID{=}er.PID\}\ \mathsf{in}$$
$$\{(n, \mathsf{average}\{mw \mid (n', mw) \in X, n = n'\}) \mid (n, \_) \in X\}$$

Additional examples are shown in Figure 4.

3 Annotations, Provenance and Dependence

We wish to define *dependency provenance* as information relating each part of the output of a query to a set of parts of the input on which the output part depends. Collection types such as sets and bags are unordered and lack a natural way to "address" parts of values, so we must introduce one. One technique (familiar from many program analyses as well as other work on provenance [10,23]) is to enrich the data model with *annotations* that can be used to refer to parts of the value. We can then infer provenance information from functions on annotated values by observing how such functions propagate annotations; conversely, we can define provenance-tracking semantics by enriching ordinary functions with annotation-propagation behavior. In this section, we show how to define dependency provenance in this way. In the next sections, we will show how to compute dynamic and static dependency provenance for NRC queries using annotations.

$$\boxed{\Gamma \vdash e : \tau}$$

$$\frac{x{:}\tau \in \Gamma}{\Gamma \vdash x : \tau} \quad \frac{\Gamma \vdash e_1 : \tau_1 \quad \Gamma, x{:}\tau_1 \vdash e_2 : \tau_2}{\Gamma \vdash \mathsf{let}\ x = e_1\ \mathsf{in}\ e_2 : \tau_2} \quad \frac{i \in \mathbb{Z}}{\Gamma \vdash i : \mathsf{int}} \quad \frac{\Gamma \vdash e_1 : \mathsf{int} \quad \Gamma \vdash e_2 : \mathsf{int}}{\Gamma \vdash e_1 + e_2 : \mathsf{int}}$$

$$\frac{\Gamma \vdash e : \{\mathsf{int}\}}{\Gamma \vdash \mathsf{sum}(e) : \mathsf{int}} \quad \frac{b \in \mathbb{B}}{\Gamma \vdash b : \mathsf{bool}} \quad \frac{\Gamma \vdash e_0 : \mathsf{bool} \quad \Gamma \vdash e_1 : \tau \quad \Gamma \vdash e_2 : \tau}{\Gamma \vdash \mathsf{if}\ e_0\ \mathsf{then}\ e_1\ \mathsf{else}\ e_2 : \tau} \quad \frac{\Gamma \vdash e : \mathsf{bool}}{\Gamma \vdash \neg e : \mathsf{bool}}$$

$$\frac{\Gamma \vdash e_1 : \mathsf{bool} \quad \Gamma \vdash e_2 : \mathsf{bool}}{\Gamma \vdash e_1 \wedge e_2 : \mathsf{bool}} \quad \frac{\Gamma \vdash e_1 : \tau_1 \quad \Gamma \vdash e_2 : \tau_2}{\Gamma \vdash (e_1, e_2) : \tau_1 \times \tau_2} \quad \frac{\Gamma \vdash e : \tau_1 \times \tau_2}{\Gamma \vdash \pi_i(e) : \tau_i}$$

$$\frac{\Gamma \vdash e_1 : \tau \quad \Gamma \vdash e_2 : \tau}{\Gamma \vdash e_1 \approx e_2 : \mathsf{bool}} \quad \frac{}{\Gamma \vdash \emptyset : \{\tau\}} \quad \frac{\Gamma \vdash e : \tau}{\Gamma \vdash \{e\} : \{\tau\}} \quad \frac{\Gamma \vdash e_1 : \{\tau\} \quad \Gamma \vdash e_2 : \{\tau\}}{\Gamma \vdash e_1 \cup e_2 : \{\tau\}}$$

$$\frac{\Gamma \vdash e_1 : \{\tau\} \quad \Gamma \vdash e_2 : \{\tau\}}{\Gamma \vdash e_1 - e_2 : \{\tau\}} \quad \frac{\Gamma \vdash e_1 : \{\tau_1\} \quad \Gamma, x{:}\tau_1 \vdash e_2 : \tau_2}{\Gamma \vdash \{e_2 \mid x \in e_1\} : \{\tau_2\}} \quad \frac{\Gamma \vdash e : \{\{\tau\}\}}{\Gamma \vdash \bigcup e : \{\tau\}}$$

Fig. 2. Well-formed query expressions

$$\begin{aligned}
\mathcal{E}[\![x]\!]\gamma &= \gamma(x) & \mathcal{E}[\![\mathsf{let}\ x = e_1\ \mathsf{in}\ e_2]\!]\gamma &= \mathcal{E}[\![e_2]\!]\gamma[x \mapsto \mathcal{E}[\![e_1]\!]\gamma] \\
\mathcal{E}[\![i]\!]\gamma &= i & \mathcal{E}[\![e_1 + e_2]\!]\gamma &= \mathcal{E}[\![e_1]\!]\gamma + \mathcal{E}[\![e_2]\!]\gamma \\
\mathcal{E}[\![\mathsf{sum}(e)]\!]\gamma &= \textstyle\sum \mathcal{E}[\![e]\!]\gamma & \mathcal{E}[\![b]\!]\gamma &= b \\
\mathcal{E}[\![\neg e]\!]\gamma &= \neg\mathcal{E}[\![e]\!]\gamma & \mathcal{E}[\![e_1 \wedge e_2]\!]\gamma &= \mathcal{E}[\![e_1]\!]\gamma \wedge \mathcal{E}[\![e_2]\!]\gamma \\
\mathcal{E}[\![(e_1, e_2)]\!]\gamma &= (\mathcal{E}[\![e_1]\!]\gamma, \mathcal{E}[\![e_2]\!]\gamma) & \mathcal{E}[\![\pi_i(e)]\!]\gamma &= \pi_i(\mathcal{E}[\![e]\!]\gamma) \\
\mathcal{E}[\![\emptyset]\!]\gamma &= \emptyset & \mathcal{E}[\![\{e\}]\!]\gamma &= \{\mathcal{E}[\![e]\!]\gamma\} \\
\mathcal{E}[\![e_1 \cup e_2]\!]\gamma &= \mathcal{E}[\![e_1]\!]\gamma \cup \mathcal{E}[\![e_2]\!]\gamma & \mathcal{E}[\![e_1 - e_2]\!]\gamma &= \mathcal{E}[\![e_1]\!]\gamma - \mathcal{E}[\![e_2]\!]\gamma \\
\mathcal{E}[\![\textstyle\bigcup e]\!]\gamma &= \textstyle\bigcup \mathcal{E}[\![e]\!]\gamma & \mathcal{E}[\![\{e \mid x \in e_0\}]\!]\gamma &= \{\mathcal{E}[\![e]\!]\gamma[x \mapsto v] \mid v \in \mathcal{E}[\![e_0]\!]\gamma\}
\end{aligned}$$

$$\mathcal{E}[\![\mathsf{if}\ e_0\ \mathsf{then}\ e_1\ \mathsf{else}\ e_2]\!]\gamma = \begin{cases} \mathcal{E}[\![e_1]\!]\gamma \text{ if } \mathcal{E}[\![e_0]\!]\gamma = \mathsf{true} \\ \mathcal{E}[\![e_2]\!]\gamma \text{ if } \mathcal{E}[\![e_0]\!]\gamma = \mathsf{false} \end{cases}$$

$$\mathcal{E}[\![e_1 \approx e_2]\!]\gamma = \begin{cases} \mathsf{true} \text{ if } \mathcal{E}[\![e_1]\!]\gamma = \mathcal{E}[\![e_2]\!]\gamma \\ \mathsf{false} \text{ if } \mathcal{E}[\![e_1]\!]\gamma \neq \mathcal{E}[\![e_2]\!]\gamma \end{cases}$$

Fig. 3. Semantics of query expressions

We define *annotated values (a-values)* v, *raw values (r-values)* w, and *multisets of annotated values* V as follows:

$$v ::= w^{\Phi} \qquad w ::= i \mid b \mid (v_1, v_2) \mid V \qquad V ::= \{v_1, \ldots, v_n\}$$

For us, annotations are *sets* $\Phi \subseteq$ Color of values from some atomic data type Color of *colors*. We often omit set brackets in the annotations, for example writing $w^{a,b,c}$ instead of $w^{\{a,b,c\}}$ and w instead of $w^{\emptyset}$. An a-value v is said to be *distinctly colored* if every part of it is colored with a singleton set $\{a\}$ and no color c is repeated anywhere in v.

For each type τ, we define the set $\mathcal{A}_0[\![\tau]\!]$ of annotated values of type τ as follows:

$$\begin{aligned}
\mathcal{A}_0[\![\mathsf{bool}]\!] &= \{b^{\Phi} \mid b \in \mathbb{B}\} & \mathcal{A}_0[\![\tau_1 \times \tau_2]\!] &= \{(v_1, v_2)^{\Phi} \mid v_1 \in \mathcal{A}_0[\![\tau_1]\!], v_2 \in \mathcal{A}_0[\![\tau_2]\!]\} \\
\mathcal{A}_0[\![\mathsf{int}]\!] &= \{i^{\Phi} \mid i \in \mathbb{Z}\} & \mathcal{A}_0[\![\{\tau\}]\!] &= \{V^{\Phi} \mid \forall v \in V. v \in \mathcal{A}_0[\![\tau]\!]\}
\end{aligned}$$

$$\begin{aligned}
\Pi_A(R) &= \{x.A \mid x \in R\} \\
\sigma_{A=B}(R) &= \bigcup\{\textsf{if } x.A = x.B \textsf{ then } \{x\} \textsf{ else } \emptyset \mid x \in R\} \\
R \times S &= \{(A : x.A, B : x.B, C : y.C, D : y.D, E : y.E) \mid x \in R, y \in S\} \\
\Pi_{BE}(\sigma_{A=D}(R \times S)) &= \{\textsf{if } x.A = y.D \textsf{ then } \{(B : x.B, E : y.E)\} \textsf{ else } \emptyset \mid x \in R, y \in S\} \\
R \cup \rho_{A/C,B/D}(\Pi_{CD}(S)) &= R \cup \{(A : y, C, B : y.D) \mid y \in S\} \\
R - \rho_{A/D,B/E}(\Pi_{DE}(S)) &= R - \{(A : y, D, B : y.E) \mid y \in S\} \\
\textsf{sum}(\Pi_A(R)) &= \textsf{sum}\{x.A \mid x \in R\} \\
\textsf{count}(R) &= \textsf{sum}\{1 \mid x \in R\}
\end{aligned}$$

Fig. 4. Example queries

Annotated environments $\widehat{\gamma}$ map variables to annotated values. We define the set of annotated environments matching context Γ as $\mathcal{A}_0[\![\Gamma]\!] = \{\widehat{\gamma} \mid \forall x \in dom(\Gamma).\widehat{\gamma}(x) \in \mathcal{A}_0[\![\Gamma(x)]\!]\}$.

We define an erasure function $|-|$, mapping a-values to ordinary values (and, abusing notation, also mapping r-values to ordinary values), as follows:

$$|i| = i \quad |b| = b \quad |(v_1, v_2)| = (|v_1|, |v_2|) \quad |\{V\}| = \{|v| \mid v \in V\} \quad |w^{\Phi}| = |w|$$

and an annotation extraction function $\|-\|$ which extracts the set of all colors mentioned anywhere in an a-value or r-value, defined by taking $\|w^{\Phi}\| = \Phi \cup \|w\|$ and

$$\|i\| = \emptyset \quad \|b\| = \emptyset \quad \|(v_1, v_2)\| = \|v_1\| \cup \|v_2\| \quad \|\{V\}\| = \bigcup\{\|v\| \mid v \in V\}$$

Two a-values are said to be *compatible* (written $v \cong v'$) if $|v| = |v'|$.

We now consider annotated functions (a-functions) $F : \mathcal{A}_0[\![\Gamma]\!] \to \mathcal{A}_0[\![\tau]\!]$ on a-values. Recall that we plan to define provenance for functions $f : \mathcal{T}[\![\Gamma]\!] \to \mathcal{T}[\![\tau]\!]$ by observing how a-functions transform annotations. For this to make sense, we first need to restrict attention to a-functions F whose behavior is consistent with that of some function f; that is, such that $\forall v \in \mathcal{A}_0[\![\Gamma]\!].f(|v|) = |F(v)|$. If this is the case, then we say that the a-function F is an enrichment of f; there can be at most one such f, so we sometimes write $|F|$ for f. Of course, many a-functions are not enrichments of any ordinary function: for example, suppose $F_0(1^a) = 1^a$ while $F_0(1^b) = 2^b$. It may be of interest to semantically characterize the a-functions that are enrichments of ordinary functions, by analogy with generic queries in relational databases and color-invariance in [10]; while this would be important for studying expressiveness, in this paper we simply restrict attention to a-functions F that are enrichments of ordinary functions, that is, for which $|F|$ exists.

Dependency-correctness. Intuitively, an a-function F is dependency-correct if its output annotations tell us how changes to parts of the input may affect parts of the output. First, we need to capture the intuitive notion of changing a value at a particular location:

Definition 1 (Equal except at c**).** *Two a-values* v_1, v_2 *are* equal except at c ($v_1 \equiv_c v_2$) *provided that they have the same structure except possibly at subterms labeled with* c*; this relation is defined as follows:*

$$\frac{d \in \mathbb{B} \cup \mathbb{Z}}{d \equiv_c d} \quad \frac{v_1 \equiv_c v_1' \quad v_2 \equiv_c v_2'}{(v_1, v_2) \equiv_c (v_1', v_2')} \quad \frac{v_1 \equiv_c v_1' \quad \cdots \quad v_n \equiv_c v_n'}{\{v_1, \ldots, v_n\} \equiv_c \{v_1', \ldots, v_n'\}} \quad \frac{w_1 \equiv_c w_2}{w_1^{\Phi} \equiv_c w_2^{\Phi}} \quad \frac{c \in \Phi_1 \cap \Phi_2}{w_1^{\Phi_1} \equiv_c w_2^{\Phi_2}}$$

Example 1. Consider the two a-environments:

$$\widehat{\gamma} = (\mathrm{R} : \{(1^{c_1}, 3^{c_2}, 5^{c_3})^{b_1}, \ldots\}^a, \mathrm{S} : \cdots)$$
$$\widehat{\gamma}' = (\mathrm{R} : \{(2^{c_1}, 3^{c_2}, 5^{c_3})^{b_1}, \ldots\}^a, \mathrm{S} : \cdots)$$

We have $\widehat{\gamma} \equiv_a \widehat{\gamma}'$, $\widehat{\gamma} \equiv_{b_1} \widehat{\gamma}'$, and $\widehat{\gamma} \equiv_{c_1} \widehat{\gamma}'$, assuming that the elided portions are identical. For distinctly-colored values, a color serves as an address uniquely identifying a subterm. Thus, $\equiv_c$ relates a distinctly-colored value to a value which can be obtained by modifying the subterm "at c"; that is, if we write v_1 as $C[v_1']$ where C is a context and v_1' is the subterm labeled with c in v_1, and $v_1 \equiv_c v_2$, then $v_2 = C[v_2']$ for some subterm v_2' labeled with c. Note that v_2' and v_2 need not be distinctly colored, and that $\equiv_c$ makes sense for arbitrary a-values, not just distinctly colored ones.

Definition 2 (Dependency-correctness). *An a-function $F : \mathcal{A}_0[\![\Gamma]\!] \to \mathcal{A}_0[\![\tau]\!]$ is dependency-correct if for any $c \in \mathsf{Color}$ and $\widehat{\gamma}, \widehat{\gamma}' \in \mathcal{A}_0[\![\Gamma]\!]$ satisfying $\widehat{\gamma} \equiv_c \widehat{\gamma}'$, we have $F(\widehat{\gamma}) \equiv_c F(\widehat{\gamma}')$.*

Example 2. Recall $\widehat{\gamma}, \widehat{\gamma}'$ as in the previous example. Suppose

$$F(\widehat{\gamma}) = \{(1^{c_1}, 3^{c_2}, 5^{c_3})^{b_1}\}^a .$$

Since $\widehat{\gamma} \equiv_{c_1} \widehat{\gamma}'$, we know that $F(\widehat{\gamma}) \equiv_{c_1} F(\widehat{\gamma}')$ so we can see that $F(\widehat{\gamma}')$ must be of the form

$$\{(s^{c_1}, 3^{c_2}, 5^{c_3})^{b_1}\}^a$$

for some $n \in \mathbb{Z}$. We do *not* necessarily know that n must be 2; this is not captured by dependency-correctness.

More generally, dependency-correctness tells us that for any c, we must have $F(\widehat{\gamma}) = C[v_1, \ldots, v_n]$ and $F(\widehat{\gamma}') = C[v_1', \ldots, v_n']$, where $C[-, \ldots, -]$ is a context not mentioning c and $v_1, \ldots, v_n, v_1', \ldots, v_n'$ are labeled with c. Thus, F's annotations tell us which parts of the output (i.e., $v_1, \ldots, v_n$) *may* change if the input is changed at c. Dually, they also tell us what part of the output (i.e., $C[-, \ldots, -]$) *cannot* be changed by changing the input at c.

Of course, dependency-correctness does not uniquely characterize the annotation behavior of a given F. It is possible for the annotations to be dependency-correct but *inaccurate*. For example we can always trivially annotate each part of the output with *every* color appearing in the input. This, of course, tells us nothing about the function's behavior. In general, the fewer the annotations present in the output of a dependency-correct F, the more they tell us about F's behavior. We therefore consider a function F to be *minimally annotated* if no annotations can be removed from F's output for any v without damaging correctness.

We say that a query e is *constant* if $[\![e]\!]\gamma = v$ for some v and every suitable γ.

$$(w^{\Phi})^{+\Phi_0} = w^{\Phi \cup \Phi_0} \qquad (i_1^{\Phi_1}) \mathbin{\widehat{+}} (i_2^{\Phi_2}) = (i_1 + i_2)^{\Phi_1 \cup \Phi_2}$$
$$\widehat{\neg}(b^{\Phi}) = (\neg b)^{\Phi} \qquad (b_1^{\Phi_1}) \mathbin{\widehat{\wedge}} (b_2^{\Phi_2}) = (b_1 \wedge b_2)^{\Phi_1 \cup \Phi_2}$$
$$\widehat{\pi}_i((v_1, v_2)^{\Phi}) = v_i^{+\Phi} \qquad (w_1^{\Phi_1}) \mathbin{\widehat{\cup}} (w_2^{\Phi_2}) = (w_1 \cup w_2)^{\Phi_1 \cup \Phi_2}$$
$$\widehat{\mathsf{cond}}(\mathsf{true}^{\Phi}, v_1, v_2) = v_1^{+\Phi} \qquad \widehat{\mathsf{cond}}(\mathsf{false}^{\Phi}, v_1, v_2) = v_2^{+\Phi}$$

$$\widehat{\sum}(\{v_1, \ldots, v_n\}^{\Phi}) = (v_1 \mathbin{\widehat{+}} \cdots \mathbin{\widehat{+}} v_n)^{+\Phi}$$
$$\widehat{\bigcup}\{v_1, \ldots, v_n\}^{\Phi} = (v_1 \mathbin{\widehat{\cup}} \cdots \mathbin{\widehat{\cup}} v_n)^{+\Phi}$$
$$\{v(x) \mid x \mathbin{\widehat{\in}} w^{\Phi}\} = \{v(x) \mid x \in w\}^{\Phi}$$
$$(w_1^{\Phi_1}) \mathbin{\widehat{-}} (w_2^{\Phi_2}) = \{v \in w_1 \mid |v| \notin |w_2|\}^{\Phi_1 \cup \|w_1\| \cup \Phi_2 \cup \|w_2\|}$$
$$v_1 \mathbin{\widehat{\approx}} v_2 = \begin{cases} \mathsf{true}^{\|v_1\| \cup \|v_2\|} & |v_1| = |v_2| \\ \mathsf{false}^{\|v_1\| \cup \|v_2\|} & |v_1| \neq |v_2| \end{cases}$$

Fig. 5. Auxiliary annotation-propagating operations

Proposition 1. *It is undecidable whether a Boolean NRC query is constant.*

Proof. Recall that query equivalence is undecidable for the (nested) relational calculus [3]; this holds even for queries $e(x), e'(x)$ over a single variable x. Given two such queries, consider the expression $\widehat{e} = e(x) \approx e'(x) \vee y$ (definable as $\neg(\neg(e(x) \approx e'(x)) \wedge \neg y)$). The result of this expression cannot be false everywhere since the disjunction is true for $y = \mathsf{true}$, so is $\widehat{e}$ is constant iff $[\![\widehat{e}]\!]v = \mathsf{true}$ for every v iff $e \equiv e'$.

Clearly, an annotation is needed on the result of a Boolean query if and only if the query is not a constant, so finding minimal annotations is undecidable. As a result, we cannot expect to be able to compute dependency-correct annotations with perfect accuracy. It is important to note, though, that dependency-tracking is hard even if we leave out the $e_1 - e_2$ or $e_1 \approx e_2$ operators. For example, we can reduce (coNP-hard) propositional validity problems to dependency-tracking for ordinary Boolean expressions or conditionals.

3.1 Dynamic Provenance Tracking

We now consider a *provenance tracking* approach in which we interpret each expressions e as dependency-correct a-functions $\mathcal{P}[\![e]\!]$. The definition of the provenance-tracking semantics is shown in Figure 6. Auxiliary operations are used to define $\mathcal{P}[\![-]\!]$; these are shown in Figure 5. In particular, note that we define $(w^{\Phi})^{+\Psi} = w^{\Phi \cup \Psi}$.

Many cases involving ordinary programming constructs are self-explanatory. Constants always have empty annotations: nothing in the input can affect them. Built-in functions such as $+, \wedge, \neg$ propagate all annotations on their arguments to the result. For a conditional $\mathsf{if}\ e_0\ \mathsf{then}\ e_1\ \mathsf{else}\ e_2$, the result is the result of evaluating e_1 or e_2, combined with the annotations of e_0. A constructed pair has an empty top-level annotation; in a projection, the top-level annotation of the pair is merged with that of the returned value.

The cases involving collection types deserve some explanation. The empty set is a constant, so has an empty top-level annotation. Similarly, a singleton set constructor has an empty annotation. For union, we take the union of the underlying bags (of annotated

$$
\begin{array}{rlrl}
\mathcal{P}[\![x]\!]\widehat{\gamma} &= \widehat{\gamma}(x) & \mathcal{P}[\![\mathsf{let}\ x = e_1\ \mathsf{in}\ e_2]\!]\widehat{\gamma} &= \mathcal{P}[\![e_2]\!]\widehat{\gamma}[x \mapsto \mathcal{P}[\![e_1]\!]\widehat{\gamma}] \\
\mathcal{P}[\![i]\!]\widehat{\gamma} &= i^{\emptyset} & \mathcal{P}[\![e_1 + e_2]\!]\widehat{\gamma} &= \mathcal{P}[\![e_1]\!]\widehat{\gamma} \mathbin{\widehat{+}} \mathcal{P}[\![e_2]\!]\widehat{\gamma} \\
\mathcal{P}[\![\mathsf{sum}(e)]\!]\widehat{\gamma} &= \widehat{\sum}\mathcal{P}[\![e]\!]\widehat{\gamma} & \mathcal{P}[\![b]\!]\widehat{\gamma} &= b^{\emptyset} \\
\mathcal{P}[\![\neg e]\!]\widehat{\gamma} &= \widehat{\neg}\mathcal{P}[\![e]\!]\widehat{\gamma} & \mathcal{P}[\![e_1 \wedge e_2]\!]\widehat{\gamma} &= \mathcal{P}[\![e_1]\!]\widehat{\gamma} \mathbin{\widehat{\wedge}} \mathcal{P}[\![e_2]\!]\widehat{\gamma} \\
\mathcal{P}[\![(e_1, e_2)]\!]\widehat{\gamma} &= (\mathcal{P}[\![e_1]\!]\widehat{\gamma}, \mathcal{P}[\![e_2]\!]\widehat{\gamma})^{\emptyset} & \mathcal{P}[\![\pi_i(e)]\!]\widehat{\gamma} &= \widehat{\pi}_i(\mathcal{P}[\![e]\!]\widehat{\gamma}) \\
\mathcal{P}[\![\emptyset]\!]\widehat{\gamma} &= \emptyset^{\emptyset} & \mathcal{P}[\![\{e\}]\!]\widehat{\gamma} &= \{\mathcal{P}[\![e]\!]\widehat{\gamma}\}^{\emptyset} \\
\mathcal{P}[\![e_1 \cup e_2]\!]\widehat{\gamma} &= \mathcal{P}[\![e_1]\!]\widehat{\gamma} \mathbin{\widehat{\cup}} \mathcal{P}[\![e_2]\!]\widehat{\gamma} & \mathcal{P}[\![e_1 - e_2]\!]\widehat{\gamma} &= \mathcal{P}[\![e_1]\!]\widehat{\gamma} \mathbin{\widehat{-}} \mathcal{P}[\![e_2]\!]\widehat{\gamma} \\
\mathcal{P}[\![\bigcup e]\!]\widehat{\gamma} &= \widehat{\bigcup}\, \mathcal{P}[\![e]\!]\widehat{\gamma} & \mathcal{P}[\![\{e \mid x \in e_0\}]\!]\widehat{\gamma} &= \{\mathcal{P}[\![e]\!]\widehat{\gamma}[x \mapsto v] \mid v \mathbin{\widehat{\in}} \mathcal{P}[\![e_0]\!]\widehat{\gamma})\} \\
\mathcal{P}[\![e_1 \approx e_2]\!]\widehat{\gamma} &= \mathcal{P}[\![e_1]\!]\widehat{\gamma} \mathbin{\widehat{\approx}} \mathcal{P}[\![e_2]\!]\widehat{\gamma} & \mathcal{P}[\![\mathsf{if}\ e_0\ \mathsf{then}\ e_1\ \mathsf{else}\ e_2]\!]\widehat{\gamma} &= \widehat{\mathsf{cond}}(\mathcal{P}[\![e_0]\!]\widehat{\gamma}, \mathcal{P}[\![e_1]\!]\widehat{\gamma}, \mathcal{P}[\![e_2]\!]\widehat{\gamma})
\end{array}
$$

Fig. 6. Provenance-tracking semantics

values) and fuse the top-level annotations. For comprehension, we leave the top-level annotation alone. For flattening $\bigcup e$, we take the lifted union ($\widehat{\bigcup}$) of the elements of e and add the top-level annotation of e. Similarly, $\widehat{\mathsf{sum}}(e)$ uses $\widehat{+}$ to add together the elements of e, fusing their annotations with that of e. For set difference, to ensure dependency correctness, we must conservatively include all of the colors present on either side in the annotation of the top-level expression. Similarly, for equality tests, we must include all of the colors present in either value in the result annotation.

Remark 1. Our approach to handling negation and equality is somewhat awkward since it may result in very large annotations. For example, consider $\{1^a, 2^b\}^c - \{1^d, 3^e\}^f$: clearly, changing any of the input locations a, b, c, d, e, f can cause the output to change. In contrast, other approaches such as lineage associate tuple $t \in R - S$ only with $t \in R$ and all tuples of S. This may seem more "accurate", but it is not dependency-correct. On the other hand, our approach can also be more "accurate" than lineage in the presence of negation; for example, in $\{1\} - \{\pi_1(x) \mid x \in S\}$, our approach will indicate that the output does not depend on the second components of elements of S, whereas the lineage of this query include all the records in S.

However, although our approach to negation and equality has pathological behavior in some cases, it does seem to provide useful provenance for typical queries. Developing more sophisticated forms of dependence that are better-behaved in the presence of negation or equality is an interesting area for future work.

Example 3. Consider an annotated input environment $\widehat{\gamma}$, shown in Figure 7(a), of schema $R : (A : \mathsf{int}, B : \mathsf{int}), S(C : \mathsf{int}, D : \mathsf{int}, E : \mathsf{int})$ (we use more compact relational schema notation with field names for readability). Figure 7(b) shows the provenance tracking semantics of the example queries from Figure 4. We write a_{123} as an abbreviation for a_1, a_2, a_3, etc. Note that in the count example query, the output depends on *no* individual of the input; we cannot change the number of elements of a multiset by changing field values. However, in a query such as $\mathsf{count}(\sigma_{A=B}(R))$, the result depends on all of the A and B fields.

These annotated results can easily be used to "highlight" the parts of the input that may be relevant to a part of the output, by examining the annotations appearing above the output part of interest. This is how the example in Figure 1 was constructed.

Note that equivalent expressions $e \equiv e'$ need not satisfy $\mathcal{P}[\![e]\!] \equiv \mathcal{P}[\![e']\!]$; for example, $x - x \equiv \emptyset$ but $\mathcal{P}[\![x - x]\!] \not\equiv \emptyset^{\emptyset}$.

(a)

$$\widehat{\gamma} = [R := \{(A:1^{a_1}, B:1^{b_1}), (A:1^{a_2}, B:2^{b_2}), (A:2^{a_3}, B:3^{b_3})\},$$
$$S := \{(C:1^{c_1}, D:2^{d_1}, E:3^{e_1}), (C:1^{c_2}, D:1^{d_2}, E:4^{e_2})\}]$$

(b)

$$\begin{aligned}
\mathcal{P}[\![\Pi_A(R)]\!]\widehat{\gamma} &= \{(A:1^{a_1}), (A:1^{a_2}), (A:2^{a_3})\} \\
\mathcal{P}[\![\sigma_{A=B}(R)]\!]\widehat{\gamma} &= \{(A:1^{a_1}, B:1^{b_1})\}^{a_1,b_1} \\
\mathcal{P}[\![R \times S]\!]\widehat{\gamma} &= \{(A:1^{a_1}, B:1^{b_1}, C:1^{c_1}, D:2^{d_1}, E:3^{e_1}), \\
&\quad (A:1^{a_1}, B:1^{b_1}, C:1^{c_2}, D:1^{d_2}, E:4^{e_2}), \ldots\} \\
\mathcal{P}[\![\Pi_{BE}(\sigma_{A=D}(R \times S))]\!]\widehat{\gamma} &= \{(B:1^{b_1}, E:4^{e_2}), (B:2^{b_2}, E:4^{e_2}), \\
&\quad (B:3^{b_3}, E:3^{e_1})\}^{a_{123},d_{12}} \\
\mathcal{P}[\![R \cup \rho_{A/C,B/D}(\Pi_{CD}(S))]\!]\widehat{\gamma} &= \{(A:1^{a_1}, B:1^{b_1}), (A:1^{a_2}, B:2^{b_2}), (A:2^{a_3}, B:3^{b_3}), \\
&\quad (A:1^{c_1}, B:2^{d_1}), (A:1^{c_2}, B:1^{d_2})\} \\
\mathcal{P}[\![R - \rho_{A/D,B/E}(\Pi_{DE}(S))]\!]\widehat{\gamma} &= \{(A:1^{a_1}, B:1^{b_2}), (A:1^{a_2}, B:2^{b_2})\}^{a_{123},b_{123},d_{12},e_{12}} \\
\mathcal{P}[\![\mathsf{sum}(\Pi_A(R))]\!]\widehat{\gamma} &= 4^{a_1,a_2,a_3} \qquad \mathcal{P}[\![\mathsf{count}(R)]\!]\widehat{\gamma} = 3
\end{aligned}$$

Fig. 7. (a) Annotated input environment (b) Examples of provenance tracking

We summarize the main results concerning $\mathcal{P}[\![-]\!]$ as follows:

Theorem 1. *If $\Gamma \vdash e : \tau$ then (1) $\mathcal{P}[\![e]\!] : \mathcal{A}_0[\![\Gamma]\!] \to \mathcal{A}_0[\![\tau]\!]$, (2) $|\mathcal{P}[\![e]\!]| = \mathcal{E}[\![e]\!]$, and (3) $\mathcal{P}[\![e]\!]$ is dependency-correct.*

3.2 Static Provenance Analysis

Although it can often be quite accurate, dynamic provenance seems expensive to compute and nontrivial to implement in a standard relational database system. Moreover, dynamic analysis cannot tell us anything about a query without looking at (annotated) input data. In this section we consider a *static provenance analysis* which statically approximates the dynamic provenance, but can be calculated more easily and without accessing the input.

We formulate the analysis as a type-based analysis; annotated types (a-types) $\widehat{\tau}$ and raw types (r-types) ω are defined as follows:

$$\widehat{\tau} ::= \omega^{\Phi} \qquad \omega ::= \mathsf{int} \mid \mathsf{bool} \mid \widehat{\tau} \times \widehat{\tau}' \mid \{\widehat{\tau}\}$$

We write $\widehat{\Gamma}$ for a typing context mapping variables to a-types. We lift the auxiliary a-value operations of erasure ($|\widehat{\tau}|$), annotation extraction ($\|\widehat{\tau}\|$), and compatibility ($\widehat{\tau}_1 \cong \widehat{\tau}_2$) to a-types in the obvious way.

We also define a "union" operation $\sqcup$ on compatible types as follows:

$$\omega_1^{\Phi_1} \sqcup \omega_2^{\Phi_2} = (\omega_1 \sqcup \omega_2)^{\Phi_1 \cup \Phi_2} \quad \mathsf{int} \sqcup \mathsf{int} = \mathsf{int} \quad \mathsf{bool} \sqcup \mathsf{bool} = \mathsf{bool}$$
$$(\widehat{\tau}_1 \times \widehat{\tau}_2) \sqcup (\widehat{\tau}_1' \times \widehat{\tau}_2') = (\widehat{\tau}_1 \sqcup \widehat{\tau}_1') \times (\widehat{\tau}_2 \sqcup \widehat{\tau}_2') \quad \{\widehat{\tau}\} \sqcup \{\widehat{\tau}'\} = \{\widehat{\tau} \sqcup \widehat{\tau}'\}$$

Finally, we write $\widehat{\tau} \sqsubseteq \widehat{\tau}'$ if $\widehat{\tau}' = \widehat{\tau} \sqcup \widehat{\tau}'$; this is essentially a subtyping relation.

$$\frac{}{\widehat{\Gamma} \vdash i : \mathsf{int}\ \&\ \emptyset} \quad \frac{\widehat{\Gamma} \vdash e_1 : \mathsf{int}\ \&\ \Phi_1 \quad \widehat{\Gamma} \vdash e_2 : \mathsf{int}\ \&\ \Phi_2}{\widehat{\Gamma} \vdash e_1 + e_2 : \mathsf{int}\ \&\ \Phi_1 \cup \Phi_2} \quad \frac{\widehat{\Gamma} \vdash e : \{\mathsf{int}^{\Phi_0}\}\ \&\ \Phi}{\widehat{\Gamma} \vdash \mathsf{sum}(e) : \mathsf{int}\ \&\ \Phi_0 \cup \Phi}$$

$$\frac{}{\widehat{\Gamma} \vdash b : \mathsf{bool}\ \&\ \emptyset} \quad \frac{\widehat{\Gamma} \vdash e : \mathsf{bool}\ \&\ \Phi}{\widehat{\Gamma} \vdash \neg e : \mathsf{bool}\ \&\ \Phi} \quad \frac{\widehat{\Gamma} \vdash e_1 : \mathsf{bool}\ \&\ \Phi_2 \quad \widehat{\Gamma} \vdash e_2 : \mathsf{bool}\ \&\ \Phi_2}{\widehat{\Gamma} \vdash e_1 \wedge e_2 : \mathsf{bool}\ \&\ \Phi_1 \cup \Phi_2}$$

$$\frac{\widehat{\Gamma} \vdash e_1 : \widehat{\tau}_1 \quad \widehat{\Gamma} \vdash e_2 : \widehat{\tau}_2}{\widehat{\Gamma} \vdash (e_1, e_2) : (\widehat{\tau}_1 \times \widehat{\tau}_2)\ \&\ \emptyset} \quad \frac{\widehat{\Gamma} \vdash e : \omega_1^{\Phi_1} \times \omega_2^{\Phi_2}\ \&\ \Phi}{\widehat{\Gamma} \vdash \pi_i(e) : \omega_i\ \&\ \Phi_i \cup \Phi}$$

$$\frac{\widehat{\Gamma} \vdash e_1 : \widehat{\tau}_1 \quad \widehat{\Gamma} \vdash e_2 : \widehat{\tau}_2 \quad \widehat{\tau}_1 \cong \widehat{\tau}_2}{\widehat{\Gamma} \vdash e_1 \approx e_2 : \mathsf{bool}\ \&\ \|\widehat{\tau}_1\| \cup \|\widehat{\tau}_2\|} \quad \frac{\widehat{\Gamma} \vdash e_0 : \mathsf{bool}\ \&\ \Phi_0 \quad \widehat{\Gamma} \vdash e_1 : \widehat{\tau}_1 \quad \widehat{\Gamma} \vdash e_2 : \widehat{\tau}_2 \quad \omega_1 \cong \omega_2}{\widehat{\Gamma} \vdash \mathsf{if}\ e_0\ \mathsf{then}\ e_1\ \mathsf{else}\ e_2 : (\widehat{\tau}_1 \sqcup \widehat{\tau}_2)^{+\Phi_0}}$$

$$\frac{}{\widehat{\Gamma} \vdash \emptyset : \{\widehat{\tau}\}\ \&\ \emptyset} \quad \frac{\widehat{\Gamma} \vdash e : \widehat{\tau}}{\widehat{\Gamma} \vdash \{e\} : \{\widehat{\tau}\}\ \&\ \emptyset} \quad \frac{\widehat{\Gamma} \vdash e_1 : \{\widehat{\tau}_1\}\ \&\ \Phi_1 \quad \widehat{\Gamma} \vdash e_2 : \{\widehat{\tau}_2\}\ \&\ \Phi_2 \quad \widehat{\tau}_1 \cong \widehat{\tau}_2}{\widehat{\Gamma} \vdash e_1 \cup e_2 : \{\widehat{\tau}_1 \sqcup \widehat{\tau}_2\}\ \&\ \Phi_1 \cup \Phi_2}$$

$$\frac{\widehat{\Gamma} \vdash e_1 : \{\widehat{\tau}_1\}\ \&\ \Phi_1 \quad \widehat{\Gamma} \vdash e_2 : \{\widehat{\tau}_2\}\ \&\ \Phi_2 \quad \widehat{\tau}_1 \cong \widehat{\tau}_2}{\widehat{\Gamma} \vdash e_1 - e_2 : \{\widehat{\tau}_1\}\ \&\ \|\{\widehat{\tau}_1\}^{\Phi_1}\| \cup \|\{\widehat{\tau}_2\}^{\Phi_2}\|} \quad \frac{\widehat{\Gamma} \vdash e : \{\{\widehat{\tau}\}^{\Phi_2}\}\ \&\ \Phi_1}{\widehat{\Gamma} \vdash \bigcup e : \{\widehat{\tau}\}\ \&\ \Phi_1 \cup \Phi_2}$$

$$\frac{\widehat{\Gamma} \vdash e_1 : \{\widehat{\tau}_1\}\ \&\ \Phi_1 \quad \widehat{\Gamma}, x{:}\widehat{\tau}_1 \vdash e_2 : \omega\ \&\ \Phi_2}{\widehat{\Gamma} \vdash \{e_2 \mid x \in e_1\} : \{\omega_2^{\Phi}\}\ \&\ \Phi_1} \quad \frac{x{:}\widehat{\tau} \in \widehat{\Gamma}}{\widehat{\Gamma} \vdash x : \widehat{\tau}} \quad \frac{\widehat{\Gamma} \vdash e_1 : \widehat{\tau}_1 \quad \widehat{\Gamma}, x : \widehat{\tau}_1 \vdash e_2 : \widehat{\tau}_2}{\widehat{\Gamma} \vdash \mathsf{let}\ x = e_1\ \mathsf{in}\ e_2 : \widehat{\tau}_2}$$

Fig. 8. Type-based provenance analysis

We interpret a-types $\widehat{\tau}$ as sets $\mathcal{A}[\![\widehat{\tau}]\!]$ of a-values. We interpret the annotations in a-types as upper bounds on the annotations in the corresponding a-values:

$$\begin{aligned} \mathcal{A}[\![\mathsf{int}]\!] &= \{i \mid i \in \mathbb{Z}\} & \mathcal{A}[\![\widehat{\tau}_1 \times \widehat{\tau}_2]\!] &= \{(v_1, v_2) \mid v_1 \in \mathcal{A}[\![\widehat{\tau}_1]\!], v_2 \in \mathcal{A}[\![\widehat{\tau}_2]\!]\} \\ \mathcal{A}[\![\mathsf{bool}]\!] &= \{b \mid b \in \mathbb{B}\} & \mathcal{A}[\![\{\widehat{\tau}\}]\!] &= \{V \mid \forall v \in V. v \in \mathcal{A}[\![\widehat{\tau}]\!]\} \\ \mathcal{A}[\![\omega^{\Phi}]\!] &= \{w^{\Psi} \mid \Psi \subseteq \Phi, w \in \mathcal{A}[\![\omega]\!]\} \end{aligned}$$

The syntactic operations $|-|$, $\|-\|$, $\sqsubseteq$ and $\sqcup$ correspond to appropriate semantic operations on sets of a-values. We note some useful properties of these operations:

Lemma 2. *1. If $v \in \mathcal{A}[\![\widehat{\tau}]\!]$ then $|v| \in \mathcal{T}[\![|\widehat{\tau}|]\!]$ and $\|v\| \subseteq \|\widehat{\tau}\|$.*
2. If $\widehat{\tau}_1 \sqsubseteq \widehat{\tau}_2$ then $\mathcal{A}[\![\widehat{\tau}_1]\!] \subseteq \mathcal{A}[\![\widehat{\tau}_2]\!]$ and $\|\widehat{\tau}_1\| \subseteq \|\widehat{\tau}_2\|$.
3. If $\widehat{\tau}_1 \sqcup \widehat{\tau}_2$ is defined then $\mathcal{A}[\![\widehat{\tau}_1 \sqcup \widehat{\tau}_2]\!] = \mathcal{A}[\![\widehat{\tau}_1]\!] \cup \mathcal{A}[\![\widehat{\tau}_2]\!]$ and $\|\widehat{\tau}_1 \sqcup \widehat{\tau}_2\| = \|\widehat{\tau}_1\| \cup \|\widehat{\tau}_2\|$.

The annotated typing judgment $\widehat{\Gamma} \vdash e : \widehat{\tau}$ (sometimes written $\widehat{\Gamma} \vdash e : \omega\ \&\ \Phi$ for readability, provided $\widehat{\tau} = \omega^{\Phi}$) extends the plain typing judgment shown in Figure 2.

Proposition 2. *The judgment $\Gamma \vdash e : \tau$ is derivable if and only if for any $\widehat{\Gamma}$ enriching Γ, there exists a $\widehat{\tau}$ enriching τ such that $\widehat{\Gamma} \vdash e : \widehat{\tau}$. Moreover, given $\Gamma \vdash e : \tau$, and $\widehat{\Gamma}$ enriching Γ, we can compute $\widehat{\tau}$ in polynomial time (by a simple syntax-directed algorithm).*

The correctness of the analysis is proved with respect to the provenance-tracking semantics. This property takes the form of a type-soundness theorem: we simply need to show that if the input environment $\widehat{\gamma}$ is well-formed at annotated context $\widehat{\Gamma}$ then the result $\mathcal{P}[\![e]\!]\widehat{\gamma}$ is well-formed at type $\widehat{\tau}$:

(a)

$$\widehat{\Gamma} = [R : \{(A : \mathsf{int}^a, B : \mathsf{int}^b)\}, S : \{(C : \mathsf{int}^c, D : \mathsf{int}^d, E : \mathsf{int}^e)\}]$$

(b)

$$\begin{array}{ll}
\widehat{\Gamma} \vdash \Pi_A(R) & : \{(A : \mathsf{int}^a)\} \\
\widehat{\Gamma} \vdash \sigma_{A=B}(R) & : \{(A : \mathsf{int}^a, B : \mathsf{int}^b)\}^{a,b} \\
\widehat{\Gamma} \vdash R \times S & : \{(A : \mathsf{int}^a, B : \mathsf{int}^b, C : \mathsf{int}^c, D : \mathsf{int}^d, E : \mathsf{int}^e)\} \\
\widehat{\Gamma} \vdash \Pi_{BE}(\sigma_{A=D}(R \times S)) & : \{(B : \mathsf{int}^b, E : \mathsf{int}^e)\}^{a,d} \\
\widehat{\Gamma} \vdash R \cup \rho_{A/C,B/D}(\Pi_{CD}(S)) & : \{(A : \mathsf{int}^{a,c}, B : \mathsf{int}^{b,d})\} \\
\widehat{\Gamma} \vdash R - \rho_{A/D,B/E}(\Pi_{DE}(S)) & : \{(A : \mathsf{int}^a, B : \mathsf{int}^b)\}^{a,b,d,e} \\
\widehat{\Gamma} \vdash \mathsf{sum}(\Pi_A(R)) & : \mathsf{int}^a \\
\widehat{\Gamma} \vdash \mathsf{count}(R) & : \mathsf{int}
\end{array}$$

Fig. 9. (a) Annotated input context (b) Examples of provenance analysis

Theorem 2. *If* $\widehat{\Gamma} \vdash e : \widehat{\tau}$ *then* $\mathcal{P}[\![e]\!] : \mathcal{A}[\![\widehat{\Gamma}]\!] \to \mathcal{A}[\![\widehat{\tau}]\!]$.

This theorem tells us that the annotations we obtain (statically) by provenance analysis over-approximate those obtained (dynamically) by provenance tracking provided the initial value $\widehat{\gamma}$ matches $\mathcal{A}[\![\widehat{\Gamma}]\!]$.

Example 4. Consider an annotated type context $\widehat{\Gamma}$, shown in Figure 9(a), where we have annotated field values A, B, C, D, E with colors a, b, c, d, e respectively. Figure 9(b) shows the results of static analysis for the queries in Figure 7. In some cases, the type information simply reflects the field names which are present in the output. However, the colors are not affected by renamings, as in $\rho_{A/C,B/D}$. Furthermore, note that (if we replace the colors a, b, c, d, e with color sets $\{a_1, a_2, a_3\}$, etc.) in each case the type-level colors over-approximate the value-level colors calculated in Figure 7.

Example 5. To illustrate how the analysis works in practice, we consider an extended example for a query that performs grouping and aggregation:

$$Q(R) = \{(\pi_1(x), \mathsf{sum}(G(x))) \mid x \in R\}$$

where we make the following abbreviations:

$$\begin{array}{l}
G(x) := \bigcup\{\mathsf{if}\ \pi_1(y) \approx \pi_1(x)\ \mathsf{then}\ \{\pi_2(y)\}\ \mathsf{else}\ \{\} \mid y \in R\} \\
\quad \widehat{\tau}_R := \mathsf{int}^a \times \mathsf{int}^b \quad \widehat{\Gamma} := R{:}\{\widehat{\tau}_R\} \\
\quad \widehat{\Gamma}_1 := \widehat{\Gamma}, x{:}\widehat{\tau}_R \qquad \widehat{\Gamma}_2 := \widehat{\Gamma}_1, y{:}\widehat{\tau}_R
\end{array}$$

We will derive $\widehat{\Gamma} \vdash Q(R) : \{\mathsf{int}^a \times \mathsf{int}^{a,b}\}$. The derivation illustrates how color a is propagated from the to both parts of the result type, while color b is only propagated to the second column.

First, we can reduce the analysis of Q to analyzing G as follows:

$$\dfrac{\widehat{\Gamma}\vdash R:\{\widehat{\tau}_R\} \qquad \dfrac{\dfrac{\widehat{\Gamma}_1\vdash x:\widehat{\tau}_R}{\widehat{\Gamma}_1\vdash \pi_1(x):\mathsf{int}^a} \quad \dfrac{\widehat{\Gamma}_1\vdash G(x):\{\mathsf{int}^b\}^a}{\widehat{\Gamma}_1\vdash \mathsf{sum}(G(x)):\mathsf{int}^{a,b}}}{\widehat{\Gamma}_1\vdash (\pi_1(x),\mathsf{sum}(G(x))):\mathsf{int}^a\times\mathsf{int}^{a,b}}}{\widehat{\Gamma}\vdash \{(\pi_1(x),\mathsf{sum}(G(x)))\mid x\in R\}:\{\mathsf{int}^a\times\mathsf{int}^{a,b}\}}$$

We next reduce the analysis of G to an analysis of the conditional inside G:

$$\dfrac{\dfrac{\widehat{\Gamma}_1\vdash R:\{\widehat{\tau}_R\} \quad \widehat{\Gamma}_2\vdash \mathsf{if}\ \pi_1(y)\approx\pi_1(x)\ \mathsf{then}\ \{\pi_2(y)\}\ \mathsf{else}\ \{\}:\{\mathsf{int}^b\}^a}{\widehat{\Gamma}_1\vdash \{\mathsf{if}\ \pi_1(y)\approx\pi_1(x)\ \mathsf{then}\ \{\pi_2(y)\}\ \mathsf{else}\ \{\}\mid y\in R\}:\{\{\mathsf{int}^b\}^a\}}}{\widehat{\Gamma}_1\vdash \bigcup\{\mathsf{if}\ \pi_1(y)\approx\pi_1(x)\ \mathsf{then}\ \{\pi_2(y)\}\ \mathsf{else}\ \{\}\mid y\in R\}:\{\mathsf{int}^b\}^a}$$

Finally, we can analyze the conditional as follows:

$$\dfrac{\dfrac{\dfrac{\overline{\widehat{\Gamma}_2\vdash y:\widehat{\tau}_R}}{\widehat{\Gamma}_2\vdash \pi_1(y):\mathsf{int}^a} \quad \dfrac{\overline{\widehat{\Gamma}_2\vdash y:\widehat{\tau}_R}}{\widehat{\Gamma}_2\vdash \pi_1(x):\mathsf{int}^a}}{\widehat{\Gamma}_2\vdash \pi_1(y)\approx\pi_1(x):\mathsf{bool}^a} \quad \dfrac{\dfrac{\overline{\widehat{\Gamma}_2\vdash y:\widehat{\tau}_R}}{\widehat{\Gamma}_2\vdash \pi_2(y):\mathsf{int}^b}}{\widehat{\Gamma}_2\vdash \{\pi_2(y)\}:\{\mathsf{int}^b\}} \quad \overline{\widehat{\Gamma}_2\vdash \{\}:\{\mathsf{int}\}}}{\widehat{\Gamma}_2\vdash \mathsf{if}\ \pi_1(y)\approx\pi_1(x)\ \mathsf{then}\ \{\pi_2(y)\}\ \mathsf{else}\ \{\}:\{\mathsf{int}^b\}^a}$$

3.3 Discussion

We have implemented a prototype interpreter for the NRC that performs ordinary typechecking and evaluation as well as provenance tracking and analysis. We used this implementation to construct the examples.

We chose to study provenance via the NRC because it is a clean and system-independent model; we believe our results can be specialized to common database implementations and physical operators without much difficulty. We have not yet investigated scaling this approach to large datasets. There are several apparent obstacles to implementing annotation-based provenance tracking in standard database systems that do not natively support annotation. Recent research has begun to address this problem [6,18] and we plan to investigate whether these techniques can be used to implement our approach.

Static provenance analysis is also more expensive than ordinary typechecking, but since the overhead is proportional only to the size of the *query*, not the (usually much larger) data, this seems acceptable. Moreover, static analysis may be useful in optimizing provenance tracking, for example by using the results of static analysis to avoid tracking annotations that are statically irrelevant to the output.

4 Related and Future Work

Slicing and other dependence analyses. Dependence tracking and analysis have been shown to be useful in many contexts [1] such as program slicing [7,16,24], memoization and caching [2,4], and information-flow security [20]. In program slicing [24], the goal is to identify a (small) set of program points whose execution contributes to the value of an output variable (or other observable behavior). This is analogous to our approach to provenance, except that provenance identifies relevant parts of the *input database*, not the *program* (i.e. query). Our approach is inspired by, and in some cases could be viewed as an adaptation of, these techniques to a database setting with collection types.

Provenance in databases. Most work on provenance in databases [23,15,11,12,10] has focused on identifying information that explains *why* some data is present in the output of a query (or view) or *where* some data in the output was copied from in the input. However, semantic characterizations of these intuitions have been elusive and difficult to generalize beyond monotone relational queries. Our work generalizes some of these techniques and provides clear semantic guarantees and qualitatively useful provenance information in the presence of grouping and aggregation.

Updates. Some recent work has generalized where-provenance to database updates [9,10], motivated by "curated" scientific databases that are updated frequently, often by (manual) copying from other sources. Our approach addresses an orthogonal issue; we plan to investigate dependency provenance for updates.

Workflow provenance. Provenance has also been studied in geospatial and scientific "grid" computation [8,17,21], particularly for *workflows* (visual programs written by scientists). At present, formal correctness criteria have not been identified for most of these approaches, but we believe it to be worthwhile to seek a foundation for workflow provenance using dependence analysis.

Annotations. Recent research on annotations, uncertainty, and incomplete information [6,5,18,19] is closely related to provenance. Green et al. [19] showed that relations with semiring-valued annotations generalize several variations of the relational model, including set, bag, probabilistic, and incomplete information models, and identified a relationship between free semiring-valued relations and why-provenance.

5 Conclusions

Provenance information that relates parts of the result of a query to "relevant" parts of the input is useful for many purposes, including judging the reliability of information based on the relevant sources and identifying parts of the database that may be responsible for an error in the output of a query. We have argued that the notion of *dependence*, familiar from program slicing, information flow security, and other analyses, provides a solid semantic foundation for understanding provenance for complex database queries. In this paper we introduced a semantic characterization of *dependency provenance*, showed that minimal dependency provenance is not computable, and presented approximate tracking and analysis techniques. We believe there are many promising directions for future work, including implementing efficient practical techniques, identifying more sophisticated and useful dependency properties, and studying dependency provenance in other settings such as update languages and workflows.

Acknowledgments. We wish to thank Peter Buneman and Stijn Vansummeren for helpful discussions on this work.

References

1. Abadi, M., Banerjee, A., Heintze, N., Riecke, J.G.: A core calculus of dependency. In: POPL, pp. 147–160. ACM Press, New York (1999)
2. Abadi, M., Lampson, B., Lévy, J.-J.: Analysis and caching of dependencies. In: ICFP, pp. 83–91. ACM Press, New York (1996)
3. Abiteboul, S., Hull, R., Vianu, V.: Foundations of Databases. Addison-Wesley, Reading (1995)
4. Acar, U.A., Blelloch, G.E., Harper, R.: Selective memoization. In: Proceedings of the 30th Annual ACM Symposium on Principles of Programming Languages, ACM Press, New York (2003)
5. Benjelloun, O., Sarma, A.D., Halevy, A.Y., Widom, J.: ULDBs: Databases with uncertainty and lineage. In: VLDB, pp. 953–964 (2006)
6. Bhagwat, D., Chiticariu, L., Tan, W.-C., Vijayvargiya, G.: An annotation management system for relational databases. VLDB Journal 14(4), 373–396 (2005)
7. Biswas, S.: Dynamic Slicing in Higher-Order Programming Languages. PhD thesis, University of Pennsylvania (1997)
8. Bose, R., Frew, J.: Lineage retrieval for scientific data processing: a survey. ACM Comput. Surv. 37(1), 1–28 (2005)
9. Buneman, P., Chapman, A., Cheney, J.: Provenance management in curated databases. In: SIGMOD 2006, pp. 539–550 (2006)
10. Buneman, P., Cheney, J., Vansummeren, S.: On the expressiveness of implicit provenance in query and update languages. In: Schwentick, T., Suciu, D. (eds.) ICDT 2007. LNCS, vol. 4353, pp. 209–223. Springer, Heidelberg (2006)
11. Buneman, P., Khanna, S., Tan, W.-C.: Why and where: A characterization of data provenance. In: Van den Bussche, J., Vianu, V. (eds.) ICDT 2001. LNCS, vol. 1973, pp. 316–330. Springer, Heidelberg (2000)
12. Buneman, P., Khanna, S., Tan, W.-C.: On propagation of deletions and annotations through views. In: PODS, pp. 150–158 (2002)
13. Buneman, P., Naqvi, S.A., Tannen, V., Wong, L.: Principles of programming with complex objects and collection types. Theor. Comp. Sci. 149(1), 3–48 (1995)
14. Cheney, J., Ahmed, A., Acar, U.: Provenance as dependency analysis. Technical Report arXiv:0708.2173v1, arXiv.org e-Print archive (2007)
15. Cui, Y., Widom, J., Wiener, J.L.: Tracing the lineage of view data in a warehousing environment. ACM Trans. Database Syst. 25(2), 179–227 (2000)
16. Field, J., Tip, F.: Dynamic dependence in term rewriting systems and its application to program slicing. Information and Software Technology 40(11–12), 609–636 (1998)
17. Moreau, L., Foster, I. (eds.): IPAW 2006. LNCS, vol. 4145. Springer, Heidelberg (2006)
18. Geerts, F., Kementsietsidis, A., Milano, D.: Mondrian: Annotating and querying databases through colors and blocks. In: ICDE 2006, p. 82 (2006)
19. Green, T.J., Karvounarakis, G., Tannen, V.: Provenance semirings. In: PODS, pp. 31–40. ACM Press, New York (2007)
20. Sabelfeld, A., Myers, A.: Language-based information-flow security. IEEE Journal on Selected Areas in Communications 21(1), 5–19 (2003)
21. Simmhan, Y., Plale, B., Gannon, D.: A survey of data provenance in e-science. SIGMOD Record 34(3), 31–36 (2005)
22. Wadler, P.: Comprehending monads. Mathematical Structures in Computer Science 2, 461–493 (1992)
23. Wang, Y.R., Madnick, S.E.: A polygen model for heterogeneous database systems: The source tagging perspective. In: VLDB, pp. 519–538 (1990)
24. Weiser, M.: Program slicing. In: ICSE, pp. 439–449. IEEE Press, Piscataway, NJ, USA (1981)

A Theory of Stream Queries

Yuri Gurevich[1], Dirk Leinders[2], and Jan Van den Bussche[2]

[1] Microsoft Research
gurevich@microsoft.com
[2] Hasselt University and Transnational University of Limburg
{dirk.leinders,jan.vandenbussche}@uhasselt.be

Abstract. Data streams are modeled as infinite or finite sequences of data elements coming from an arbitrary but fixed universe. The universe can have various built-in functions and predicates. Stream queries are modeled as functions from streams to streams. Both timed and untimed settings are considered. Issues investigated include abstract definitions of computability of stream queries; the connection between abstract computability, continuity, monotonicity, and non-blocking operators; and bounded memory computability of stream queries using abstract state machines (ASMs).

1 Introduction

Over the past few years in the database systems research community, much attention has been paid to query languages and query processing for data streams. We give just a few references here [15,5,6,14,7]; much more has been published. Stream queries are typically "continuous" in that their result must be continually updated as new data arrives: indeed, stream applications are "data-driven". Consequently, continuous stream queries must be computed in an incremental fashion, using so-called "non-blocking" operators. Relational algebra operators that are monotone are non-blocking; query operators that are not monotone, such as difference, or grouping and aggregation, are typically made non-blocking by restricting them to sliding windows.

The aim of this paper is to offer a theoretical framework that attempts to clarify various philosophical questions about stream queries. For instance, if streams are thought of as infinite, and arbitrary queries are modeled as functions from streams to streams, what does it mean for a query to be computable? Is computability the same concept as continuity? What is the precise connection between continuity and monotonicity? Can one give a formal definition of what it means for an arbitrary operator to be non-blocking?

Earlier work in this direction has already been reported by Arasu and Widom [3] and by Law, Wang and Zaniolo [12]. Our work has the following new features:

1. We distinguish from the outset between timed and untimed applications. In a timed setting, the timestamps in the output stream of some stream query are synchronized with the timestamps in the input stream; in an untimed setting, they are not. The usual applications mentioned in the data stream literature,

M. Arenas and M.I. Schwartzbach (Eds.): DBPL 2007, LNCS 4797, pp. 153–168, 2007.

such as stock quotes or sensors, are timed. Nevertheless, untimed streams also find applications, e.g., in audio or video streams, or Internet broadcasts, where the logical order among arriving packets is more important than precise timing information. More fundamentally, however, much of the theory of stream queries can already be developed on the more basic untimed level, viewing timed streams merely as a special case of untimed streams. Nonetheless, we will also identify some specific aspects of timed queries, in particular, their non-predicting nature (in a sense that will be made precise later).

2. Our formal definitions of abstract computable stream queries are grounded in the theory of type-2 effectivity (TTE) [16]. This is a well-established theory of computability on infinite strings (and much more, which we will not use here). The basic idea of TTE, strikingly analogous to the idea of continuous stream queries, is that arbitrary long finite prefixes of the infinite output can be computed from longer and longer finite prefixes of the infinite input. A basic insight from TTE is that computable functions on infinite strings are indeed "continuous", but now in the precise sense of mathematical topology. More specifically, under a natural metric on infinite strings (known as the Cantor metric), where two strings are closer the longer they agree on their prefixes, computable functions can be shown to be continuous in the standard mathematical sense of the word. Continuity is a useful property for it provides us with a principled way to prove that not just *any* function from streams to streams can be naturally considered to be a stream query.
3. Our theory is abstract in the sense that elements from a stream can come from an arbitrary universe, equipped with predicates and functions. In mathematical logic one speaks of a *structure*, and we will refer to the universe as the *background structure*. In particular, we do not concern ourselves with the encoding of stream elements as bitstrings (finite or infinite), or with Turing machine computations on those bitstrings, since those aspects are already well understood from the TTE. Consequently, our theory is very general, and computable stream queries will turn out to be the same thing as continuous functions from streams to streams (where we introduce a variant of the Cantor topology that accommodates finite as well as infinite streams).
4. We define a concrete computation model for stream queries, called "streaming ASM". Due to the abstract nature of our theory, streaming ASMs are naturally based on (sequential) Abstract State Machines [9,10]. Every computable stream query is computable by a streaming ASM with an appropriate background structure. Moreover, streaming ASMs allow us to prove impossibility results. Specifically, we focus on bounded memory machines: such machines can only remember a constant number of previously seen stream elements. Bounded memory machines are natural in the context of query processing; for example, any query operator that applies a sliding window (typical in streaming applications) is computable in bounded memory. Bounded memory evaluation of stream queries was already emphasized by Arasu et al. [1]. We will prove that there exist simple queries that are not bounded memory computable, one of the simplest being the query INTERSECT: finding the common elements in two interleaved streams.

The present paper is a companion to our paper with Grohe, Schweikardt, and Tyszkiewicz [8] on Finite Cursor Machines (FCM). There, we studied classical database query processing using a bounded number of one-way cursors over the database relations. Streaming ASMs are similar to FCMs, but a crucial difference is that a streaming ASM has only one cursor, and this cursor is manipulated by the stream rather than by the machine (recall the data-driven nature of streaming applications). So, FCMs are unrealistically powerful in the context of data streams, because they can control their own cursors, which is only realistic when the stream is fully given as a completed, finite input list. In particular, FCMs are certainly at least as powerful as streaming ASMs. Since we already know that the query INTERSECT mentioned above is not even computable by an FCM, it follows by a reduction that the query is also not computable by a streaming ASM. Yet, in this paper we will give a direct proof of this result, that is much simpler and thus provides more direct insight on the limitations of bounded memory stream processing. Moreover, we will see that there exist stream queries that are computable by an FCM, but not by a streaming ASM.

We must also note that Arasu et al. have already presented impossibility results for bounded memory evaluation of stream queries [1], which seem to encompass, for example, the result on the query INTERSECT which we prove in this paper. Their impossibility proofs, however, assume that stream elements are encoded in bits: they show, for instance, that INTERSECT cannot be computed in $o(n)$ bits of memory. Our proof shows how to perform such impossibility arguments on a level where elements can be stored in their entirety as abstract objects. Note that it is not so easy to reduce the abstract level to the bit level, because in $o(n)$ bits of memory we cannot simply encode on the fly all elements we encounter as binary numbers, and still remember whether we have already seen some element earlier. More generally, there seems to be a discrepancy in the mentioned paper [1] between the computation model assumed for the positive results, and that assumed for the negative results (that for the negative results appears weaker).

2 Abstract Computability

Basically, we assume a universe $\mathbb{U}$ of data elements. A *stream* is a possibly infinite sequence of data elements. The set of all streams is denoted by *Stream*, and the set of all finite streams is denoted by *finStream*. Thus *finStream* $\subseteq$ *Stream*. We denote the i-th element of a stream $\mathbf{s}$ by s_i.

Our model of streams is very abstract and thus very general.

Example 1. Consider measurements coming from sensors, where each entry is a pair of the form (i, m) with i a sensor identifier and m a measurement. Suppose, at each discrete time point t (with time points modeled by natural numbers), we collect all entries that arrived in the interval $(t-1, t]$. Then $\mathbb{U}$ would contain sets of entries as data elements.

In a setting where time points would be more fine-grained, so that at most one entry can arrive per clock tick, $\mathbb{U}$ would contain entries directly as data elements, plus possibly some dummy element to indicate no entry arrived. □

Mathematically, a *stream query* is simply a mapping from *Stream* to *Stream*. Not all such mappings make sense in the streaming context, however. To make formal which queries do make sense, we define the notion of *abstract computability*. Intuitively, a stream query $\mathcal{Q}$ is abstract computable if there exists a function K: *finStream* $\to$ *finStream* such that the result of $\mathcal{Q}$ can be obtained by concatenating the results of K applied to larger and larger prefixes of the input.

Formally, for any K as above, we define the function

$$\mathrm{Repeat}(K)\colon \mathbf{s} \mapsto \bigodot_{k=0}^{\mathrm{size}(\mathbf{s})} K(\mathbf{s}^{\leq k}) \quad \text{of type} \quad \mathit{Stream} \to \mathit{Stream},$$

where $\mathbf{s}^{\leq k}$ is the prefix of $\mathbf{s}$ of length k, and $\mathrm{size}(\mathbf{s})$ is the length of $\mathbf{s}$ in case $\mathbf{s}$ is finite, and ∞ in case $\mathbf{s}$ is infinite (in which case the index k ranges over all natural numbers). Here $\bigodot$ denotes concatenation. We now define:

Definition 2. *A query* $\mathcal{Q}$: *Stream* $\to$ *Stream is abstract computable if there exists a function* K *such that* $\mathcal{Q} = \mathrm{Repeat}(K)$. *We call* K *a kernel for* $\mathcal{Q}$.

The following example shows an abstract computable stream query:

Example 3. Let $\mathcal{Q}$ be the *running average* query, defined on streams of natural numbers and returning at each step the average value of the numbers arrived so far. The function returning $(\sum u_i)/n$ on input stream $u_1 \dots u_n$ (and returning the empty stream when the input is the empty stream) is a kernel for $\mathcal{Q}$. □

In connection to finite streams, we make the following two important observations:

1. The answer to an abstract computable query on an infinite stream can be finite.

   Example 4. Consider the query $\mathcal{Q}$ that returns all elements in the input stream satisfying a certain predicate P. On a stream with only a finite number of elements satisfying P, the result of $\mathcal{Q}$ will be finite. Note that this query $\mathcal{Q}$ indeed has a kernel: for example the function K that given a finite stream, returns its last element if it satisfies P, and returns the empty stream otherwise, is a kernel for $\mathcal{Q}$. □

2. *The answer to an abstract computable query on a finite stream must be finite.* Indeed, the result of K is always a finite stream and on a finite input stream, K is applied only a finite number of times. So, queries transforming finite streams into infinite streams will never be computable in our model. This is not a problem since our model is primarily meant to capture input-data-driven computations.

We note:

Proposition 5. *Abstract computable stream queries are closed under composition.*

3 Continuity

We will now see that abstract computability and continuity of stream queries coincide.

Recall from elementary calculus [4] that a real function $f\colon \mathbb{R} \to \mathbb{R}$ is called continuous if for all $x \in \mathbb{R}$, for every neighborhood around $f(x)$, there exists a neighborhood around x that is completely mapped into the neighborhood of $f(x)$. In order to generalize this definition of continuity to stream queries, we must first agree on a definition of neighborhood of a stream $\mathbf{s}$. In other words, we need to define a suitable topology on streams.

For infinite streams, there is a standard topology, known from computable analysis [16], called the Cantor topology. This topology arises from the following metric (distance function) on infinite streams:

$$d(\mathbf{s}, \mathbf{s}') = \begin{cases} 0 & \text{if } \mathbf{s} = \mathbf{s}', \\ 2^{-n} & \text{if } \mathbf{s} \neq \mathbf{s}' \text{ and } n = \min\{i \mid s_i \neq s_i'\}. \end{cases}$$

According to this topology, open balls around an infinite stream $\mathbf{s}$ are sets of the form $\mathbf{B}(\mathbf{p})$, with $\mathbf{p}$ some finite prefix of $\mathbf{s}$, defined as follows:

$$\mathbf{B}(\mathbf{p}) = \{\mathbf{s}' \text{ infinite stream} \mid \mathbf{p} \text{ is a prefix of } \mathbf{s}'\}.$$

In this paper, we generalize this notion of open ball to the setting of both finite and infinite streams, as follows:

Definition 6. *Let* $\mathbf{p} \in \mathit{finStream}$*. Then*

$$\mathbf{B}(\mathbf{p}) := \{\mathbf{s}' \in \mathit{Stream} \mid \mathbf{p} \textit{ is a prefix of } \mathbf{s}'\}.$$

Any set of the form $\mathbf{B}(\mathbf{p})$*, for some* $\mathbf{p} \in \mathit{finStream}$*, is called an open ball. Elements of* $\mathbf{B}(\mathbf{p})$ *are called continuations of* $\mathbf{p}$*.*

This notion of open ball gives rise to a topology on streams, and the notion of continuity then amounts to the following:

Definition 7. $\mathcal{Q}$: *Stream* $\to$ *Stream is continuous if for every open ball* $\mathbf{B}$*, the pre-image* $\mathcal{Q}^{-1}(\mathbf{B})$ *is a union (possibly infinite) of open balls.*

Remark 8. The Cantor metric described above has only been defined on infinite streams. One may wonder whether the topology on *Stream* given by Definition 6 can be given by some metric of that sort but applicable to finite as well as infinite streams. The answer is negative: metrizable topologies must be Hausdorff, and our topology is not. Indeed, an infinite stream $\mathbf{q}$ and a finite prefix $\mathbf{p}$ of $\mathbf{q}$ can not be separated as each open ball containing $\mathbf{p}$ contains $\mathbf{q}$. For basic background on topology, we refer to Hocking and Young [11].

Theorem 9. *Let* $\mathcal{Q}$ *be a stream query mapping finite inputs to finite outputs. Then* $\mathcal{Q}$ *is abstract computable if and only if* $\mathcal{Q}$ *is continuous.*

Proof. For the only-if direction let K be a kernel for $\mathcal{Q}$, i.e., $\mathcal{Q} = \text{Repeat}(K)$. Consider $\mathbf{X} := \mathbf{B}(\mathbf{p})$. Let $\mathbf{s}$ be a stream in $\mathcal{Q}^{-1}(\mathbf{X})$. Then, from some natural number ℓ on, we know that $\bigodot_{k=0}^{\ell} K(\mathbf{s}^{\leq k})$ starts with $\mathbf{p}$. Consider then the open ball $\mathbf{B}(s_1 \dots s_\ell)$. Every $\mathbf{s}' \in \mathbf{B}(s_1 \dots s_\ell)$ is mapped into $\mathbf{X}$. Indeed,

$$\mathcal{Q}(\mathbf{s}') = \bigodot_{k=0}^{\ell} K(\mathbf{s}^{\leq k}) \odot \bigodot_{k=\ell+1}^{\text{size}(\mathbf{s})} K(\mathbf{s}'^{\leq k})$$

clearly starts with $\mathbf{p}$. Thus, $\mathbf{s} \in \mathbf{B}(s_1 \dots s_\ell) \subseteq \mathcal{Q}^{-1}(\mathbf{X})$, as desired.

For the if-direction, we define a kernel K for $\mathcal{Q}$ as follows. $K(()) := \mathcal{Q}(())$, and $K(\mathbf{s}u) := \mathcal{Q}(\mathbf{s}u) - \mathcal{Q}(\mathbf{s})$, where the difference is to be interpreted as removing a prefix, so that $\mathcal{Q}(\mathbf{s}u) = \mathcal{Q}(\mathbf{s}) \odot K(\mathbf{s}u)$. Note that $\mathcal{Q}(\mathbf{s})$ and $\mathcal{Q}(\mathbf{s}u)$ are both finite.

For K to be well-defined, we must show that $\mathcal{Q}(\mathbf{s})$ is indeed a prefix of $\mathcal{Q}(\mathbf{s}u)$. Consider $\mathbf{X} = \mathcal{Q}^{-1}(\mathbf{B}(\mathcal{Q}(\mathbf{s})))$. By continuity, $\mathbf{X}$ is a union of open balls. Thus, there must be an open ball $\mathbf{B}(\mathbf{p})$ with $\mathbf{s} \in \mathbf{B}(\mathbf{p}) \subseteq \mathbf{X}$. Clearly, $\mathbf{p}$ must be a prefix of $\mathbf{s}$. But then also $\mathbf{s}u \in \mathbf{B}(\mathbf{p}) \subseteq \mathbf{X}$, and therefore $\mathcal{Q}(\mathbf{s}u) \in \mathbf{B}(\mathcal{Q}(\mathbf{s}))$. This means that $\mathcal{Q}(\mathbf{s})$ is a prefix of $\mathcal{Q}(\mathbf{s}u)$.

We now show that $\text{Repeat}(K) = \mathcal{Q}$ by showing that they have the same prefixes. By construction, $\text{Repeat}(K)$ coincides with $\mathcal{Q}$ on finite streams. Let $\mathbf{s} = s_1 s_2 \dots$ be an infinite stream and let $v_1 \dots v_j$ be an arbitrary prefix of $\text{Repeat}(K)(\mathbf{s})$. Let i be the smallest natural number such that $v_1 \dots v_j$ is a prefix of $\text{Repeat}(K)(s_1 \dots s_i) = \mathcal{Q}(s_1 \dots s_i)$. Since $\mathcal{Q}(\mathbf{s}) \in \mathbf{B}(\mathcal{Q}(s_1 \dots s_i))$, we have $v_1 \dots v_j$ also as a prefix of $\mathcal{Q}(\mathbf{s})$. We conclude that every prefix of $\text{Repeat}(K)(\mathbf{s})$ is also a prefix of $\mathcal{Q}(\mathbf{s})$.

For the other direction, let $v_1 \dots v_j$ be an arbitrary prefix of $\mathcal{Q}(\mathbf{s})$. By continuity, $v_1 \dots v_j$ is also a prefix of $\mathcal{Q}(s_1 \dots s_i)$ for some i. Since $\text{Repeat}(K)(s_1 \dots s_i) = \mathcal{Q}(s_1 \dots s_i)$, we have $v_1 \dots v_j$ also as a prefix of $\text{Repeat}(K)(s_1 \dots s_i)$, which by construction is itself a prefix of $\text{Repeat}(K)(\mathbf{s})$, as desired. □

Theorem 9 can be used to prove that there are simple stream queries that are not abstract computable.

Example 10. Consider the following query CHECK. Let $a, b \in \mathbb{U}$ and let $\mathbf{s}$ be a stream over $\mathbb{U}$. Then CHECK($\mathbf{s}$) is the stream (a) if b does not occur in $\mathbf{s}$; otherwise, CHECK($\mathbf{s}$) is the empty stream (). This query is not abstract computable; we prove that CHECK is not continuous. Consider the open ball $\mathbf{B}(a)$. Clearly, the empty stream () is in $\text{CHECK}^{-1}(\mathbf{B}(a))$. The only open ball that contains the empty stream is $\mathbf{B}(())$. This open ball, however, is not included into $\text{CHECK}^{-1}(\mathbf{B}(a))$. Indeed, $(b) \in \mathbf{B}(())$, but $\text{CHECK}(b) = () \notin \mathbf{B}(a)$. □

Remark 11. In connection to Theorem 9 we remark the following:

1. Suppose we would have extended the Cantor metric to finite (as well as infinite) streams in the obvious manner; in particular, if $\mathbf{s}$ is a finite prefix of $\mathbf{s}'$, but $\mathbf{s} \neq \mathbf{s}'$, then we define $d(\mathbf{s}, \mathbf{s}') = 2^{-(n+1)}$ with n the length of $\mathbf{s}$. In the resulting topology, abstract computable queries need no longer be continuous. A simple example is provided by the query $\mathcal{Q}$ from Example 4.

Let $\mathbb{U} := \{a, b\}$ and let P be true of a and false of b. Consider the open ball $\mathbf{B}$ containing only the empty stream (). Then $\mathcal{Q}$ maps the infinite stream $\mathbf{b}$ containing only b's into $\mathbf{B}$. Any open ball $\mathbf{B}(\mathbf{p})$ around $\mathbf{b}$, however, contains the stream $\mathbf{p}a$ which is not in $\mathcal{Q}^{-1}(\mathbf{B})$. Thus, $\mathcal{Q}$ is not continuous.

2. The qualification in Theorem 9 that $\mathcal{Q}$ must map finite inputs to finite outputs is important for the if-direction. Indeed, any constant query, that always outputs some fixed infinite stream, is continuous, but not abstract computable (precisely because it maps finite to infinite).

4 The Finite Case

Considering only finite streams makes the situation simpler. Define a finite stream query as a mapping from *finStream* to *finStream*. Define abstract computability of finite stream queries in the same way as for queries on *Stream*, and consider the topology on *finStream* induced by the topology on *Stream*, i.e., the open balls are now *finite* continuations of finite streams. We will use the notation $\mathbf{B}_{\text{fin}}(\mathbf{p})$ to denote the set of all finite continuations of the finite stream $\mathbf{p}$. We then indeed have:

Proposition 12. *A finite stream query is abstract computable if and only if it is continuous.*

In the finite case, there is also a third equivalent notion: monotonicity. A query $\mathcal{Q}$: *finStream* $\rightarrow$ *finStream* is called monotone if for all $\mathbf{s}, \mathbf{s}' \in$ *finStream*, $\mathbf{s} \sqsubseteq \mathbf{s}'$ implies $\mathcal{Q}(\mathbf{s}) \sqsubseteq \mathcal{Q}(\mathbf{s}')$, where $\sqsubseteq$ denotes the "prefix of" relation.

Proposition 13. *A finite stream query is continuous if and only if it is monotone.*

Proof. For the if-direction let $\mathcal{Q}$: *finStream* $\rightarrow$ *finStream* be monotone. Consider $\mathbf{X} := \mathbf{B}_{\text{fin}}(\mathbf{p})$. Let $\mathbf{s}$ be a stream in $\mathcal{Q}^{-1}(\mathbf{X})$. Then, $\mathbf{s} \in \mathbf{B}_{\text{fin}}(\mathbf{s}) \subseteq \mathcal{Q}^{-1}(\mathbf{X})$. Indeed, $\mathbf{s}' \in \mathbf{B}_{\text{fin}}(\mathbf{s})$ implies $\mathbf{s} \sqsubseteq \mathbf{s}'$, which by monotonicity implies $\mathcal{Q}(\mathbf{s}) \sqsubseteq \mathcal{Q}(\mathbf{s}')$. As $\mathcal{Q}(\mathbf{s})$ has $\mathbf{p}$ as a prefix, $\mathcal{Q}(\mathbf{s}')$ has $\mathbf{p}$ as a prefix too and thus $\mathcal{Q}(\mathbf{s}') \in \mathbf{X}$.

The only-if direction is proved by the argument already used in the proof of the if-direction of Theorem 9, where we showed that K is well-defined. Concretely, let $\mathcal{Q}$: *finStream* $\rightarrow$ *finStream* be continuous. Let $\mathbf{s} \sqsubseteq \mathbf{s}'$. Consider $\mathbf{X} := \mathcal{Q}^{-1}(\mathbf{B}_{\text{fin}}(\mathcal{Q}(\mathbf{s})))$. By continuity, $\mathbf{X}$ is a union of open balls. Thus, there must be an open ball $\mathbf{B}_{\text{fin}}(\mathbf{p})$ with $\mathbf{s} \in \mathbf{B}_{\text{fin}}(\mathbf{p}) \subseteq \mathbf{X}$. Clearly, $\mathbf{p}$ must be a prefix of $\mathbf{s}$. But then also $\mathbf{s}' \in \mathbf{B}_{\text{fin}}(\mathbf{p}) \subseteq \mathbf{X}$, and therefore $\mathcal{Q}(\mathbf{s}') \in \mathbf{B}_{\text{fin}}(\mathcal{Q}(\mathbf{s}))$. This means that $\mathcal{Q}(\mathbf{s}) \sqsubseteq \mathcal{Q}(\mathbf{s}')$. □

As a corollary we obtain the following equivalence already noted by Law, Wang and Zaniolo (LWZ), who referred to our notion of abstract computability as computability by a "nonblocking" operator:

Corollary 14 ([12]). *Let $\mathcal{Q}$ be a finite stream query. $\mathcal{Q}$ is computable by a nonblocking operator if and only if $\mathcal{Q}$ is monotone.*

The proof given by LWZ is slightly confusing. Their formalism is based on a notion of queries on finite streams that are computable by (not necessarily non-blocking) "operators". They fail to mention, however, that *any* query on finite streams is computable by such an operator.

5 Time

In some applications, the output stream is synchronized with the input stream. In such cases, we need an additional requirement on stream queries beyond mere abstract computability.

Example 15. Consider the following instance of the query from Example 4: the input is a stream of numbers (e.g., sensor readings) and the output consists of all readings below a certain threshold, say 0. In an "untimed" setting, where the original time points of the output readings are not required by the client of the query, we can simply formalize this stream query as being abstract computable with kernel function K_0 with $K_0(()) = ()$, and

$$K_0(\mathbf{s}u) = \begin{cases} u & \text{if } u < 0 \\ () & \text{otherwise.} \end{cases}$$

On the other hand, in a "timed" setting stream positions in the output are supposed to be synchronized with stream positions in the input [3,2]. In that case, the above formalization is inadequate, because, the 5th element of the output may well be, say, the 10th element of the input!

A more proper computation would be given by the function K_1 with again $K_1(()) = ()$, and now

$$K_1(\mathbf{s}u) = \begin{cases} u & \text{if } u < 0 \\ \text{NULL} & \text{otherwise.} \end{cases}$$

where NULL is an explicitly visible element denoting that the reading at this time point was not below 0. □

The above discussion motivates:

Definition 16. *A stream query Q is synchronous abstract computable (SAC) if $Q = \text{Repeat}(K)$ for some kernel K: finStream $\to$ finStream such that $K(()) = ()$ and every other $K(\mathbf{s})$ is of length one. We will call such kernel K a length-one kernel.*

SAC stream queries can be characterized by means of non-predicting queries. Here and below, $\mathbb{N}_0$ stands for the set of natural numbers without zero.

Definition 17. *A stream query Q is non-predicting if for all streams $\mathbf{s}$ and $\mathbf{s}'$ and for all $t \in \mathbb{N}_0$ such that $\mathbf{s}^{\leq t} = (\mathbf{s}')^{\leq t}$, we have $Q(\mathbf{s})_t = Q(\mathbf{s}')_t$.*

We note that non-predicting is part of the definition of "stream operator" by Arasu, Babu and Widom [3,2].

Proposition 18. *A stream query is SAC if and only if it is non-predicting.*

Proof. Let K be a length-one kernel for stream query $\mathcal{Q}$. Let $\mathbf{s}, \mathbf{s}' \in \mathit{Stream}$ and $t \in \mathbb{N}_0$ such that $\mathbf{s}^{\leq t} = (\mathbf{s}')^{\leq t}$. Then

$$\mathcal{Q}(\mathbf{s})_t = K(\mathbf{s}^{\leq t}) = K((\mathbf{s}')^{\leq t}) = \mathcal{Q}(\mathbf{s}')_t$$

and thus $\mathcal{Q}$ is non-predicting.

For the "if" direction, let $\mathcal{Q}$ be non-predicting. For each finite stream $\mathbf{p}$ of length t, define $\pi(\mathbf{p})$ as the infinite stream with $\pi(\mathbf{p})_i = p_i$ for $i \leq t$ and with $\pi(\mathbf{p})_i = p_t$ for $i > t$. Then the following function K is a length-one kernel for $\mathcal{Q}$. If $\mathbf{p}$ is a finite stream of length t then $K(\mathbf{p}) := \mathcal{Q}(\pi(\mathbf{p}))_t$.

Furthermore, for each stream $\mathbf{s}$ and any time instant t, define $\pi'(\mathbf{s}, t)$ as the infinite stream with $\pi'(\mathbf{s}, t)_i = s_i$ for $i \leq t$ and with $\pi'(\mathbf{s}, t)_i = s_t$ for $i > t$. We now prove that K is indeed as desired. Let $\mathbf{s}$ be a stream and let t be a time instant. Then

$$\mathcal{Q}(\mathbf{s})_t = \mathcal{Q}(\pi'(\mathbf{s}, t))_t = \mathcal{Q}(\pi(\mathbf{s}^{\leq t}))_t = K(\mathbf{s}^{\leq t}).$$

Here, the first equality follows from the fact that $\mathcal{Q}$ is non-predicting; the second equality follows from the definition of $\pi'(s, t)$; and the third equality follows from the definition of K. □

We also have:

Proposition 19. *SAC stream queries are closed under composition.*

6 Complexity Limitations

The definition of abstract computability does not impose any restriction on K: the function is not even required to be computable, neither in the classical sense nor in the sense of TTE. The results in the previous sections are thus very general.

To further study the limitations of streaming applications, however, such restrictions are necessary. Concretely, for a class $\mathcal{C}$ of functions from *finStream* to *finStream*, we say that a query $\mathcal{Q}$: *Stream* $\rightarrow$ *Stream* is *abstract computable modulo* $\mathcal{C}$ if $\mathcal{Q}$ has a kernel K in $\mathcal{C}$. The class $\mathcal{C}$ could for example be the class of functions computable in the classical sense or in the sense of TTE; or—as in the "streaming model of computation" [5]—$\mathcal{C}$ could be the class of functions incrementally computable in polylog space and in polylog time per data element.

In the next section, we will define several classes $\mathcal{C}$ of functions computable by a concrete model based on the Abstract State Machine (ASM) methodology [9], that we will call "streaming ASM" (sASM). We will study abstract computability modulo the classes $\mathcal{C}$ obtained by altering the computation power of the model.

7 Streaming ASMs

An abstract state machine (ASM) is a transition system whose states are many-sorted first-order structures. Transitions change the interpretation of some of the function and relation symbols—those in the *dynamic* part of the vocabulary—and leave the remaining symbols—those in the *static* part of the vocabulary—unchanged. The part of the structure that is never changed during state transitions, i.e., the structure over the static part of the vocabulary, is typically called the *background structure*. Transitions are described by simple rules that produce state updates which are "fired" simultaneously (if they are inconsistent, no update is carried out). A crucial property of the sequential ASM model is that in each transition only a limited part of the state is changed. The detailed definition of sequential ASMs is given in the Lipari guide [9].

We now describe the streaming abstract state machine (sASM) model.

The states: The base set of any state, i.e., the universe of the structure in the sense of logic, contains at least our universe $\mathbb{U}$ of data elements. We assume that $\mathbb{U}$ contains an element $\bot$.

The static functions and predicates on the base set include, but are not limited to, the functions and predicates defined on $\mathbb{U}$.

Each state of an sASM contains a finite number of dynamic functions on the base set. There are always the nullary dynamic function *in* and a number of nullary dynamic functions, called output registers, denoted by *out*, possibly with subscripts. The output registers and *in* take values in $\mathbb{U}$.

The names of the static and dynamic functions and predicates are collected in a vocabulary.

The program: A program for an sASM is a basic sequential program in the sense of ASM theory. Concretely, a basic update rule has the form: $f(t_1, \ldots, t_n) := t_0$ where f is a function name and $t_0, \ldots, t_n$ are terms in the vocabulary. To fire the basic update rule at a state $\mathcal{A}$, evaluate the terms $t_0, \ldots, t_n$ in $\mathcal{A}$ to elements $a_0, \ldots, a_n$ in the base set and then change the interpretation of f in $(a_1, \ldots, a_n)$ to a_0.

Update rules $r_1, \ldots, r_m$ can be combined to a new rule par $r_1 \ldots r_m$ endpar, the semantics of which is this: Fire rules $r_1, \ldots, r_m$ in parallel; if they are inconsistent then do nothing.

Furthermore, if r_1 and r_2 are rules and φ is a quantifier-free formula in the vocabulary, then if φ then r_1 else r_2 endif is also a rule. The semantics is obvious.

Now, an sASM program is just a single rule.

The run and the output: An sASM M that is set to work on a finite stream $\mathbf{s}$ starts in the state where all dynamic functions have the interpretation $\bot$, except for the function *in*: In the initial state, the function *in* contains the first element of the stream $\mathbf{s}$.

The run of M on $\mathbf{s}$ is the sequence of states obtained as follows: start from the initial state and fire (the rule of) M's program, in each step interpreting the function *in* as the next element in $\mathbf{s}$. The sASM halts when the end of $\mathbf{s}$ is reached. The interpretation of *in* is dynamic but it is controlled by the environment rather than by the machine; *in* is an *external* function.

We define the *final output of M on a finite stream* $\mathbf{s}$ as the stream obtained by concatenating the interpretations of the output registers in some predefined order when M has halted, and where $\bot$-elements are disregarded.

We now say that an sASM M computes a function $K\colon \mathit{finStream} \to \mathit{finStream}$ (meant as a kernel for a stream query) if for all finite streams $\mathbf{s}$, the final output of M on $\mathbf{s}$ equals $K(\mathbf{s})$. By K_M we denote the function K computed by M.

It is important to note that the final output of an sASM M on a stream $s_1 \dots s_{n+1}$ can be simply obtained by running M on the input $s_1 \dots s_n$ first, and then making one final step upon reading s_{n+1}. Consequently, on any stream $\mathbf{s}$ (finite or infinite), we can compute $\mathrm{Repeat}(K_M)(\mathbf{s})$ simply by continuously running M on $\mathbf{s}$, at each step producing the current output. We refer to $\mathrm{Repeat}(K_M)$ as the *stream query computed by M*.

Example 20. Recall Example 1. In the setting where $\mathbb{U}$ contains sets of entries, there could for example be a function defined on $\mathbb{U}$ that given a set of entries, returns the set of sensor identifiers that measured an alarmingly high value.

In the setting where $\mathbb{U}$ contains entries directly, there could for example be a predicate defined on $\mathbb{U}$ that checks whether an entry has an alarmingly high measurement and a function that given an entry, returns the sensor identifier of the entry. □

Example 21. Consider the sliding window join between two streams of tuples of natural numbers over the attributes $\{A, B\}$ and $\{C, D\}$, where the join condition is $B = C$. The output tuples have attributes $\{A, B, D\}$. The universe $\mathbb{U}$ then contains $\bot$, Tuple_{AB}, Tuple_{CD}, and Tuple_{ABD}, with Tuple_{AB} the set of tuples over the attributes $\{A, B\}$, and similarly for Tuple_{CD} and Tuple_{ABD}. The function $\mathit{join}_{B=C}\colon \mathit{Tuple}_{AB} \times \mathit{Tuple}_{CD} \to \mathit{Tuple}_{ABD}$ checks whether two tuples join on their B- and C-attributes and returns the joined tuple; the result is $\bot$ if the tuples do not join.

The output of the sliding window join depends on two streams, whereas streaming ASMs work on a *single* stream. Moreover, the output depends on the particular interleaving in which the streams arrive. By choosing an appropriate universe $\mathbb{U}$, however, we can represent the two input streams and their interleaving as a single stream.

Concretely, we extend the universe $\mathbb{U}$ with the set *TaggedTuple* of elements of the form $\langle \mathtt{r}\!:\!u\rangle$ and $\langle \mathtt{s}\!:\!v\rangle$ with $u \in \mathit{Tuple}_{AB}$ and $v \in \mathit{Tuple}_{CD}$. A tagged tuple encodes an element and its origin. For example, the stream of tagged tuples

$$\langle \mathtt{r}\!:\!(1,2)\rangle\langle \mathtt{s}\!:\!(2,3)\rangle\langle \mathtt{s}\!:\!(3,4)\rangle \dots$$

is a representation of the interleaving of the tuple (1,2) arriving in the first stream, followed by the tuples (2,3) and (3,4) arriving in the second stream, and so on. Furthermore, we add the predicates R and S to the universe $\mathbb{U}$ to test whether an element is of the form $\langle \mathtt{r}\!:\!u\rangle$ or $\langle \mathtt{s}\!:\!v\rangle$, respectively. Finally, we add a function *strip*: *TaggedTuple* $\to$ $Tuple_{AB} \cup Tuple_{CD}$ that removes the tag of a tagged tuple. Static functions return $\bot$ when one of the arguments is $\bot$.

Assume for simplicity that the window size is 2. We then equip the sASM with 4 nullary dynamic functions reg_i^R, and reg_i^S for $i = 1, 2$. The following is now a program for an sASM computing the sliding window join described above.

```
par
  if R(in) then
    par
      reg_1^R = in
      reg_2^R = reg_1^R
      out_1 = join_{B=C}(strip(in), strip(reg_1^S))
      out_2 = join_{B=C}(strip(in), strip(reg_2^S))
    endpar
  endif
  if S(in) then
    par
      reg_1^S = in
      reg_2^S = reg_1^S
      out_1 = join_{B=C}(strip(reg_1^R), strip(in))
      out_2 = join_{B=C}(strip(reg_2^R), strip(in))
    endpar
  endif
endpar
```

□

8 Bounded-Memory and $o(n)$-Bitstring sASMs

Due to the extreme generality of the ASM model, one should not expect that restricting attention to stream queries that are computable by an sASM would imply any limitation. Indeed, the only restriction that comes from our sASM model is that at each step in the computation of the stream query, only a constant number of elements can be output. More concretely, since the background structure of an sASM could, a priori, be anything, we have the following proposition and corollary (which in itself are philosophically entirely uninteresting):

Proposition 22. *Let k be a fixed natural number and let K: finStream $\to$ finStream be any kernel function such that the length of $K(\mathbf{s})$, for any finite stream* **s**, *is at most k. Then the stream query* Repeat(K) *is computable by some sASM.*

Proof (sketch). It is an easy matter for an sASM to compute Repeat(K) if it has 1) a background structure containing a) the set of all finite streams *finStream*, b) the append function of sort *finStream* $\times\ \mathbb{U} \to$ *finStream*, c) the function K, and d) functions $element_i$ for $i = 1, \ldots, k$ to extract elements out of a finite stream; and 2) a nullary dynamic function s containing at each step the part of the stream that has already arrived.

At each step, the sASM uses the append function to update the dynamic function s; it applies K to the stream s; and it uses the extraction functions $element_i$ to update the output registers. □

Corollary 23. *Every SAC query is abstract computable by an sASM.*

In order to formulate a relevant complexity limitation on stream queries, we propose "bounded-memory sASMs".

Definition 24. *A bounded-memory sASM is an sASM with the following restrictions: 1) no output register can ever be used as an argument to a function; 2) all dynamic functions are nullary; and 3) non-nullary (static) functions can only be applied in rules of the form* $out := t_0$*, with* out *an output register and* t_0 *a term over the vocabulary.*

Example 25. The sASM computing the sliding window join in Example 21 is a bounded-memory sASM. The obvious sASM for computing the running average query from Example 3, however, is not bounded-memory (but see later, when we introduce bitstring sASMs). □

Every CQL-query where a finite window is applied to the input streams ([2]) is computable by a bounded-memory sASM. Indeed, let $\mathcal{Q}$ be such a CQL-query. Then, $\mathcal{Q} = \text{Repeat}(K_M)$, where M is the following sASM. For each window of $\mathcal{Q}$ of size n, the sASM M has n dynamic constants. When M receives a new input element, say with tag $\langle \mathtt{r}\!: \rangle$, the sASM simulates the sliding of the window(s) on input stream $\mathbf{r}$ by updating the corresponding dynamic constants accordingly. In each step, the output is computed in a brute-force way. This technique was already illustrated in Example 21.

Moreover, every duplicate-eliminating SPJ-query computable in bounded memory in the sense defined by Arasu et al. is computable by a bounded-memory sASM [1].

Bounded-memory sASMs also have some limitations: even the very simple stream query that checks whether two streams intersect, is not computable by a bounded-memory sASM. Let $\mathbb{E}$ be an infinite set of data elements and let *TaggedElement* be the set of elements of the form $\langle \mathtt{r}\!:u \rangle$ and $\langle \mathtt{s}\!:u \rangle$ with $u \in \mathbb{E}$. A stream over *TaggedElement* then represents the interleaving of two streams over $\mathbb{E}$ (see Example 21). Let $\mathbb{U}$ be the set *TaggedElement* extended with the boolean values `true` and `false`. The query INTERSECT is defined on streams over $\mathbb{U}$ and checks whether a common element has been seen in the interleaved streams over $\mathbb{E}$. Concretely, the result of INTERSECT on a stream $\mathbf{s}$ over $\mathbb{U}$ is the stream $\mathbf{s}'$ such that the n-th element of $\mathbf{s}'$ is `true` if and only if for some $i, j \in \mathbb{N}_0$ with $i, j < n$ and for some $u \in \mathbb{E}$, we have $s_i = \langle \mathtt{r}\!:u \rangle$ and $s_j = \langle \mathtt{s}\!:u \rangle$.

Proposition 26. INTERSECT *is not computable by a bounded-memory sASM.*

Proof. Let M be a bounded-memory sASM such that INTERSECT is equal to $\text{Repeat}(K_M)$.

Let Ω be the set of predicates of M. Then for each predicate $p \in \Omega$ of arity k and for each k-sequence α of elements in $\{\mathtt{r}, \mathtt{s}\}$, define the predicate p^α on $\mathbb{E}$ to be true of a tuple $(u_1, \ldots, u_k)$ iff p is true of $(\langle \alpha_1 : u_1 \rangle, \ldots, \langle \alpha_k : u_k \rangle)$. Let $\Omega' := \{p^\alpha \mid p \in \Omega \text{ and } \alpha \in \{\mathtt{r}, \mathtt{s}\}^k \text{ where } k = \text{arity}(p)\}$.

Without loss of generality, we assume that $\mathbb{E}$ is totally ordered by a predicate $<$. Using Ramsey's theorem, we can find an infinite set $V \subseteq \mathbb{E}$ over which the truth of the predicates in Ω' on tuples of elements in $\mathbb{E}$ only depends on the way these data elements compare w.r.t. $<$ (details on this can be found, e.g., in Libkin's textbook [13, Section 13.3]). Now choose $2n$ elements in V, for n large enough, satisfying $v_1 < v_1' < \cdots < v_n < v_n'$. Let $\mathbf{s}$ be the input stream $\langle \mathtt{r} : v_1 \rangle \ldots \langle \mathtt{r} : v_n \rangle$ and consider the run of M on $\mathbf{s}$. After the step where $\langle \mathtt{r} : v_n \rangle$ is processed there will be at least one element $\langle \mathtt{r} : v_\ell \rangle$ that M has not stored in its registers. Then, consider the streams $\mathbf{s}'$ and $\mathbf{s}''$ of length $n + 1$ that have $\mathbf{s}$ as a prefix, and with $s'_{n+1} = \langle \mathtt{s} : v_\ell \rangle$ and $s''_{n+1} = \langle \mathtt{s} : v'_\ell \rangle$. The runs of M on $\mathbf{s}'$ and $\mathbf{s}''$ will be identical to the run of M on $\mathbf{s}$ until right after the step where $\langle \mathtt{r} : v_n \rangle$ is processed. In the next step, the machine receives either $\langle \mathtt{s} : v_\ell \rangle$ or $\langle \mathtt{s} : v'_\ell \rangle$. Because v_ℓ and v'_ℓ have the same relative order with respect to the other v-elements, each tuple of elements from the set $\{v_1, \ldots, v_\ell, \ldots, v_m\}$ satisfies the same predicates in Ω' as the tuple obtained by replacing v_ℓ by v'_ℓ. By definition of Ω', also each tuple of elements from the set $\{\langle \mathtt{r} : v_1 \rangle, \ldots, \langle \mathtt{s} : v_\ell \rangle, \ldots, \langle \mathtt{r} : v_m \rangle\}$ satisfies the same predicates in Ω as the tuple obtained by replacing $\langle \mathtt{s} : v_\ell \rangle$ by $\langle \mathtt{s} : v'_\ell \rangle$. Therefore, the output of M on $\mathbf{s}'$ will be identical to the output of M on $\mathbf{s}''$. As a consequence, Repeat$(K_M)(\mathbf{s}')$ and Repeat$(K_M)(\mathbf{s}'')$ are equal while INTERSECT$(\mathbf{s}')$ and INTERSECT$(\mathbf{s}'')$ are different. Thus, M is wrong. □

This result can also be obtained via a reduction from a result on Finite Cursor Machines (FCMs) in our earlier work with Grohe, Schweikardt and Tyszkiewicz [8]. An FCM works by moving one-way cursors over a number of input lists using an internal memory consisting of a finite number of modes, finitely many element registers containing input elements, and finitely many registers containing bitstrings. To manipulate its internal memory, an FCM has a number of functions and predicates, with the restriction that the output of a function is always a bitstring. It has been shown [8, Theorem 12] that no matter how rich the background is, an FCM can not check whether two sets intersect using bitstring registers of size $o(n)$, where n is the size of the input.

The proof we gave here is more direct and therefore provides more insight on the limitations of bounded memory stream processing. The reduction argument, however, can easily be generalized to accommodate for bitstring registers of size $o(n)$. A *bitstring sASM* is an sASM defined as in Definition 24 with the following relaxation of restriction 3: non-nullary (static) functions can be used also to update non-output registers, as long as those functions produce bitstrings. An $o(n)$-sASM then is a bitstring sASM such that on each stream $\mathbf{s}$ and for each step n in the run on $\mathbf{s}$, the sASM stores bitstrings of length $o(n)$.

Example 27. We can model a version of the running average query (Example 3) using $o(n)$-bitstring sASMs. Indeed, consider streams of natural numbers such that the value in the n-th position of the stream (for any n) is at most $2^{\text{polylog}(n)}$.

Then with a static function from natural numbers to their binary representations, and the addition and division function on binary numbers, we can compute the running average with an $o(n)$-sASM. □

Proposition 28. *The query* INTERSECT *is not computable by an $o(n)$-sASM.*

Proof. Let M be an $o(n)$-sASM M working on a stream of tagged elements such that INTERSECT is equal to Repeat(K_M). From M, we can then construct an $o(n)$-FCM M' working on two lists of elements in $\mathbb{E}$ that checks whether they have a common element. The FCM M' has the same number of bitstring registers as M, and has an element register for every dynamic constant of M. For every element in an element register, M' remembers from which input list the element was copied, using its internal mode. Furthermore, let Ω be the set of predicates of M, including the predicates naturally corresponding to M's boolean output functions. Then the set of predicates of M' is the set Ω' as defined in the proof of Proposition 26. Finally, if $\mathcal{F}$ is the set of functions of M, then the set of functions $\mathcal{F}'$ of M' is similarly constructed from $\mathcal{F}$ as Ω' is constructed from Ω.

Consider the input lists R and S. The FCM M' has a single cursor on R and a single cursor on S. Now, M' computes as follows. At each odd step, M' moves its cursor on R to the next element u, updating the (element and bitstring) registers as M would do when receiving the element $\langle \mathtt{r} : u \rangle$ from the stream. The internal mode is changed so that it contains the origin of each element in the registers. At each even step, M' moves its cursor on S to the next element v, updating the registers as M would do when receiving the element $\langle \mathtt{s} : v \rangle$ from the stream. The internal mode is again changed accordingly. M' can simulate this behaviour using the functions in $\mathcal{F}'$, or the predicates in Ω' together with its internal mode. For example, if M applies a predicate p to an element in a dynamic constant *reg* — i.e., an element of the form $\langle \mathtt{r} : u \rangle$ or $\langle \mathtt{s} : v \rangle$ — the FCM M' would use its internal mode to obtain the origin of the element in the register corresponding to *reg* and then apply the right predicate p^r or p^s to the element in that register — i.e., to u or v. Once M outputs true, M' enters the accept state and halts. As long as M outputs false, M' continues until it has detected the ends of the input lists. In that case, M' enters the reject state and halts. Note that M' can use the predicates corresponding to the boolean functions of M to obtain the output M produces. Because M works correctly, it will also work correctly on this particular interleaving. Therefore, M' correctly checks whether R and S intersect. Hence the contradiction. □

We conclude by pointing out that on finite streams, finite cursor machines are indeed more powerful than bounded-memory sASMs: Consider the query SORT-INTERSECT that given two finite streams A and B, checks if they are both sorted and if so, outputs their intersection; if the inputs are not sorted, SORT-INTERSECT, outputs false. Then,

Proposition 29. *The query* SORT-INTERSECT *is computable by an FCM but not by a bounded-memory sASM.*

Proof. An FCM would compute the query SORT-INTERSECT using one cursor on each list to check if they are sorted and another cursor on each list to do a synchronized scan of both list to search for common elements. Inspection of the proof of Proposition 26 reveals that a bounded-memory sASM can not even check whether two finite sorted streams intersect. □

9 Conclusion

An interesting open problem is to relax the definition of bounded-memory sASM in other ways than with using $o(n)$-length bitstrings.

References

1. Arasu, A., Babcock, B., Babu, S., McAlister, J., Widom, J.: Characterizing memory requirements for queries over continuous data streams. ACM TODS 29(1), 162–194 (2004), Includes an electronic appendix `http://doi.acm.org/10.1145/974750.974756`
2. Arasu, A., Babu, S., Widom, J.: The CQL continuous query language: semantic foundations and query execution. The VLDB Journal 15(2), 121–142 (2006)
3. Arasu, A., Widom, J.: A denotational semantics for continuous queries over streams and relations. SIGMOD Record 33(3), 6–11 (2004)
4. Ayres, F., Mendelson, E.: Schaum's Outline of Calculus. McGraw-Hill, New York (1999)
5. Babcock, B., Babu, S., Datar, M., Motwani, R., Widom, J.: Models and issues in data stream systems. In: PODS 2002, pp. 1–16 (2002)
6. Balakrishan, H., Balazinska, M., Carney, D., Çetintemel, U., Cherniack, M., Convey, C., Galvez, E.F., Salz, J., Stonebraker, M., Tatbul, N., Tibbetts, R., Zdonik, S.B.: Retrospective on Aurora. The VLDB Journal 13(4), 370–383 (2004)
7. Golab, L., Özsu, M.T.: Processing sliding window multi-joins in continuous queries over data streams. In: Aberer, K., Koubarakis, M., Kalogeraki, V. (eds.) Databases, Information Systems, and Peer-to-Peer Computing. LNCS, vol. 2944, pp. 500–511. Springer, Heidelberg (2004)
8. Grohe, M., Gurevich, Y., Leinders, D., Schweikardt, N., Tyszkiewicz, J., Van den Bussche, J.: Database query processing using finite cursor machines. In: Schwentick, T., Suciu, D. (eds.) ICDT 2007. LNCS, vol. 4353, pp. 284–298. Springer, Heidelberg (2006)
9. Gurevich, Y.: Evolving algebra 1993: Lipari guide. In: Börger, E. (ed.) Specification and Validation Methods, pp. 9–36. Oxford University Press, Oxford (1995)
10. Gurevich, Y.: Sequential abstract-state machines capture sequential algorithms. ACM TOCL 1(1), 77–111 (2000)
11. Hocking, J.G., Young, G.S.: Topology. Dover Publications, Mineola, NY (1988)
12. Law, Y.-N., Wang, H., Zaniolo, C.: Query languages and data models for database sequences and data streams. In: VLDB 2004, pp. 492–503 (2004)
13. Libkin, L.: Elements of Finite Model Theory. Springer, Heidelberg (2004)
14. Madden, S.R., Franklin, M.J., Hellerstein, J.M., Hong, W.: TinyDB: An acquisitional query processing system for sensor networks. ACM TODS 30(1), 122–173 (2005)
15. Terry, D., Goldberg, D., Nichols, D., Oki, B.: Continuous queries over append-only databases. In: SIGMOD 1992, pp. 321–330 (1992)
16. Weihrauch, K.: Computable Analysis: An Introduction. Springer, Heidelberg (2000)

Querying Structural and Behavioral Properties of Business Processes*

Daniel Deutch ** and Tova Milo

School of Computer Science, Tel Aviv University
{danielde,milo}@post.tau.ac.il

Abstract. BPQL is a novel query language for querying business process specifications, introduced recently in [5,6]. It is based on an intuitive model of business processes as rewriting systems, an abstraction of the emerging BPEL (Business Process Execution Language) standard [7]. BPQL allows users to query business processes visually, in a manner very analogous to the language used to specify the processes. The goal of the present paper is to study the formal model underlying BPQL and investigate its properties as well as the complexity of query evaluation. We also study its relationship to previously suggested formalisms for process modeling and querying. In particular we propose a query evaluation algorithm of polynomial data complexity that can be applied uniformly to queries on the *structure* of the process specification as well as on the potential *behavior* of the defined process. We show that unless P=NP the efficiency of our algorithm is asymptotically optimal.

1 Introduction

A Business Process (BP for short) consists of a group of business activities undertaken by one or more organizations in pursuit of some goal. It usually depends upon various business functions for support (e.g. personnel, accounting, inventory), and interacts with other BPs/activities carried out by the same or other organizations. Consequently, the implementations of such BPs typically operate in a cross-organization, distributed environment.

It is a common practice to use XML for data exchange between BPs, and *Web Services* for interaction with remote processes [26]. Complementarily, the recent BPEL standard (Business Process Execution Language [7]) allows description not only of the interface between the participants in a process, but also of the *full operational logic* of the process and its *execution flow.*

Since BPEL has a fairly complex syntax, commercial vendors offer systems that allow design of BPEL specifications via a visual interface. These systems use a conceptual, intuitive representation of the process, as a graph of activity

* The research has been partially supported by the European Project EDOS and the Israel Science Foundation.

** Supported by the Deutsch Institute.

M. Arenas and M.I. Schwartzbach (Eds.): DBPL 2007, LNCS 4797, pp. 169–185, 2007.

nodes, connected by control and data flow edges. The designs are automatically converted to BPEL specifications, which in turn can be automatically compiled into executable code implementing the BP [23].

Already in 2002, the importance of query languages for business processes had been recognized by BPMI (the Business Process Management Initiative) [8], yet no draft standard has been published since.

To answer this need, we have recently developed BPQL, a novel query language for querying business process specifications [5,6]. BPQL is based on the same graph-based view of processes, used by vendors for the specification of BPs. It allows users to query BPs visually, in an intuitive manner, very analogous to how such processes are typically specified. In this paper we present a thorough study of the formal model underlying BPQL, suggest a generic algorithm for query evaluation on BPs, and analyze its complexity and relationship with common formalisms for processes modeling and querying.

Next, we give the intuition behind our formalisms. The exact definitions are given in the next section.

Data Model. Intuitively, we model the specification of a BP system as a set of directed, possibly recursive *nested graphs*, including a unique *root* graph that serves as the entry point for the specification. Each graph has a single 'start' and 'end' nodes and represents the execution flow of some function (i.e. a process). A graph may contain (possibly recursive) calls to other functions (processes), which in turn are also represented by flow graphs. Upon an invocation of a call to a function f, appearing in the graph of a function g, the graph of (the implementation of) f is 'plugged-in' into g's graph, replacing the node that represents the call to f. Each graph obtained from g's graph by a sequence of such replacements is called a *refinement* of g.

Query language. At the core of the BPQL language are *BP patterns*, which generalize the tree patterns of XML to nested BP graphs and enable users to describe the patterns of activities/data flow that are of interest. In particular, the patterns allow navigation along two axes: (1) the standard path-based axis, which navigates paths in process graphs, and (2) a novel zoom-in axis, that allows to navigate (transitively) inside the process functions, at any depth of nesting, and query their refinements. Many data models which are all equivalent[1] to this simple model of nested graphs appear in the literature. Among them one can find restricted versions of Rewriting Systems (e.g. [25]), Recursive State Machines (RSMs) [4], Context Free Graph Grammars [14], and others. Each of these works relates to some query language which is evaluated over the data model. We identify two main branches of query languages, as follows. In the Databases area, the query languages are *structural*. Namely, they allow users to ask questions about the structure of a specification (graph). In contrast, in the Verification area, the query languages are *behavioral*. These queries relate to the possible runs of the process defined by specification, and are used to identify invariants, execution patterns, etc. The models considered for the structural

[1] The definition of *models equivalence* is given in section 3.

Database queries are typically 'flat' graph models, without nesting. Verification-related works query include both flat and nested graph models.

While our model for BP specifications is quite standard, we emphasize the uniqueness of our *query language* with respect to common query languages (see Section 3 for an overview). The main features of the query language are given next.

1. BPQL is a unified environment for querying structural as well as behavioral properties of business processes. Specifically, this work is the first to suggest a query language for structural queries over nested graphs.
2. BPQL allows queries with flexible granularity. Users can ask *coarse-grained* queries that consider certain process components as black boxes and allow a high level abstraction, as well as *fine-grained* queries that "zoom-in" on all (or some of) the process components, possibly recursively.
3. BPQL is a graphical query language, with the query being similar to the specification, thus allowing intuitive formulation of the queries parallel to the specification development.

BPQL enables a flexible and intuitive formulation of queries on BPs. We will see, however, that this makes the evaluation of queries somewhat intricate. First, the nested shape of the BP graphs/patterns causes the query evaluation to be computationally more expensive than that of similar queries on flat graphs. Indeed, we show that while the data complexity of BPQL queries is polynomial, the combined complexity is NP-complete w.r.t. the size of the query, even for simple classes of queries that can be evaluated on flat graphs in polynomial time (combined complexity). Second, the need to support both structural and behavioral interpretations for BP patterns required the design of a query evaluation algorithm which can be parameterized by the desired semantics. We propose here such a query evaluation algorithm and show that, unless $P = NP$, a more efficient algorithm does not exist. Moreover, thanks to the modular nature of our algorithm, the complexity of query evaluation over nested BPs is parameterized by the complexity of query evaluation for flat graphs. This allows identification of restricted classes of queries and specifications for which the performance can be further improved.

The BPQL query language was originally introduced in [5] where a first prototype of the BPQL system was demonstrated. There, and in a follow-up work [6] the focus was on the graphical query interface and the system implementation. The model that had been considered was limited to structural queries. The formalization presented here is new, and so are the results. Since BPs in general, and BPEL specifications in particular, are promised such a brilliant future, we believe it is very important to develop a formal foundation for modeling and querying such specifications, so that this technology can be better understood and used. Querying the behavior of a system is essentially a *verification problem* [12] and is typically of very high complexity (from NP-hard for very simple specifications to undecidable in the general case [12]). To guaranty a complexity that is polynomial in the size of the data, BPQL ignores the run-time semantics of certain BPEL constructs such as conditional execution and variable values, and focuses on the given specification flow. We believe that this approach offers a reasonable balance between expressibility and complexity. Clearly, the general problem is more complex, and further work is needed.

The paper is organized as follows. Section 2 describes the BPQL data model and query language and its semantics. Section 3 compares BPQL to related models. Section 4 describes the query evaluation algorithm and Section 5 studies its complexity. We conclude in Section 6.

2 Preliminaries

In this section we present the formal model underlying BPQL. We start with the motivation for our work, and then proceed to the formal definitions.

2.1 Motivation

The following questions may rise from the introduction: Why are structural queries over nested graphs interesting? What are the advantages of a generic framework for multiple query semantics? Why is it important to have a graphical query language, similar to the specification? We give here intuitive answers to these questions, using some examples.

Figure 1 depicts a partial specification of a travel agency system. The rectangle-shaped nodes represent function calls. *BP*1 is the root BP and contains a single node, AlphaTours, that serves as an entry point for the travel agency. *BP*2 describes the implementation of the AlphaTours function, where a user can choose between searching for a trip and reserving one. *BP*3 is the implementation of the *SearchTrip* function used in *BP*2. A user can request for a specific search (for flights, cars, etc.) or can go back to the AlphaTours trip reservation process. Note that this definition establishes recursive dependencies between the processes, as *BP*2 may call *BP*3, which in turn, if the user decides to reset (implemented in the BP as a call to AlphaTours), calls *BP*2.

An example query is depicted in Figure 2. It is formulated graphically in a manner very similar to the specification. This is an important feature of the query language, as (a) it allows faster learning curve of the language and (b) it allows simultaneous formulation, by the specification designer, of a specification and verification queries over it.

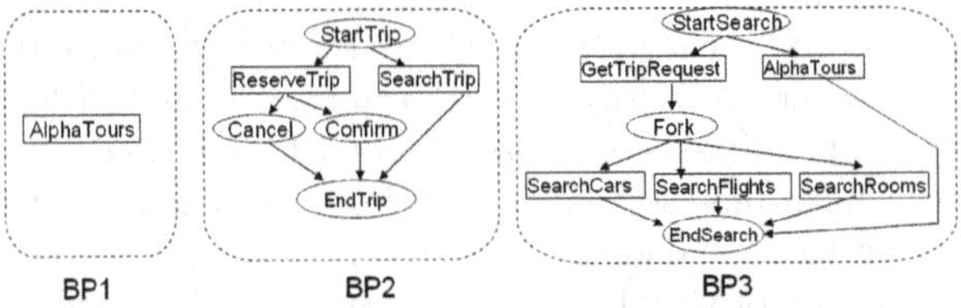

Fig. 1. A BPQL Specification

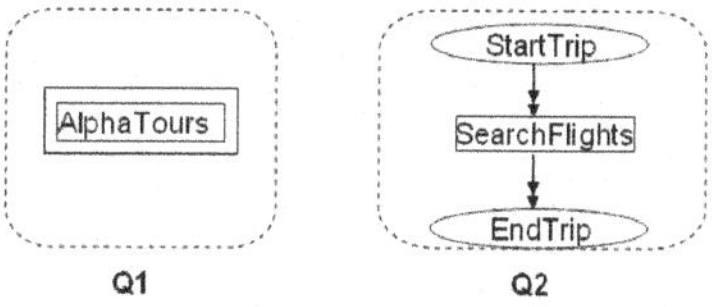

Fig. 2. A BPQL Query

To answer a query, we seek for occurrences of the described patterns within the specification. Intuitively, the query in Figure 2 searches the AlphaTours BP, and the processes that it uses, for execution paths leading to/from a SearchFlights operation. $Q2$ here describes an *implementation pattern* for the AlphaTours function. The double-headed arrows indicate that we are looking for execution paths of arbitrary length. The double bounding of the AlphaTours rectangle denotes an *unbounded zoom-in*; we search for the $Q2$ pattern inside the implementation of AlphaTours and (recursively) the functions that it invokes. In general, when matching a (double-bounded) function node n of the query to a function node n' in the specification, we require that the implementation pattern of n, as given in the query, is matched to (a refinement of) the implementation of n' in the specification. Such matching is called an *embedding*.

Some variants of the answer to a query are suggested. The first distinction is between *boolean* and *explanatory* answers. The former answers whether or not some embedding exists, while the latter is a new BP, consisting of the specification parts that contributed to some possible embedding. To continue with our example, the explanatory answer for the query in Figure 2 when applied on the system in Figure 1 is depicted in Figure 3. The answer here is a 'projection' of the travel agency system over the parts relevant to the query, and so it contains the SearchTrip function in $BP2$ and the path in its implementation, $BP3$, that leads to SearchFlights. It also contains the AlphaTours function call node in $BP3$, as this call allows to invoke $BP2$ and recursively reach (by calling SearchTrip) $BP3$ and SearchFlights, via another execution path (in fact, an infinite number of such recursive calls, hence paths, are possible).

Another distinction concerns the type of embedding (of the query in the specification) sought for. We look at two common approaches for such embeddings, referred to as *structural* and *behavioral*. Consider the query (BP pattern) depicted

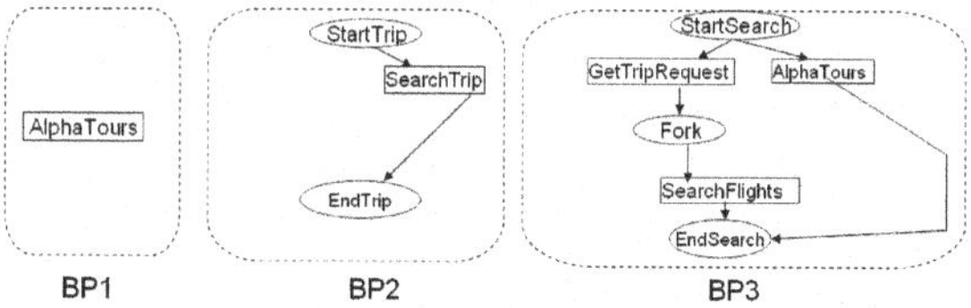

Fig. 3. Explanatory Query Answer

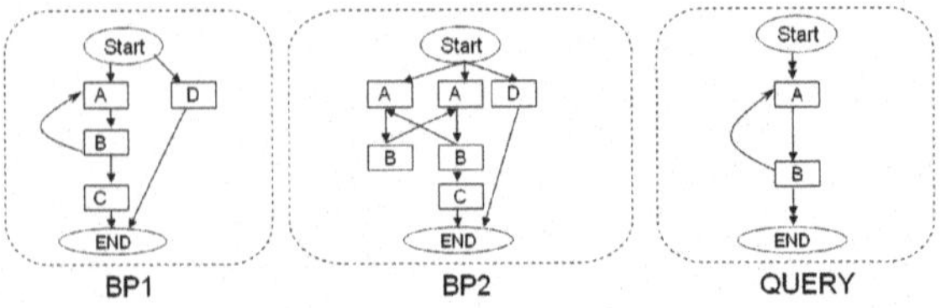

Fig. 4. Structural vs. Behavioral

in Figure 4. Interpreted as a query over the *structure* of a process specification, this query searches for BPs whose "code" contains a loop of the shape depicted by the query. BP1 in Figure 4 is an example for such BP. The same query, interpreted as a query over the *behavior* of the BPs, will look for processes containing execution paths of form similar to the one specified in the query, namely an unbounded sequence of A,B's. This is satisfied by both BP1 and BP2. The key point is that here, unlike the structural interpretation, the use of distinct occurrences of A and B is allowed.

In previous query languages for querying process specifications, typically only the behavioral approach was taken, with modal (and specifically temporal) logics being used as the basis for the query language. The dichotomy between the two approaches is established by the fact that subgraph isomorphism/homomorphism cannot be expressed by any bisimulation-invariant language [12], and thus, in particular, by any temporal logic (as these are bisimulation-invariant [12]). Thus, structural queries cannot be formulated using the previous works, but are still of great interest, as explained next. Continuing with the example above, code reuse is a common programming policy. This policy would probably impose loops of the structure depicted in BP1 rather than the structure in BP2. The query in Figure 4, when interpreted as structural query, enforces this policy, in a manner not possible using behavioral queries. In general, structural queries are of high importance for any purpose that is interested also in the code itself, and not only in its executions. Such purposes may include coding conventions, profiling and optimizations.

2.2 Definitions

We now give the formal definitions of the specification and query languages. To simplify the presentation we first consider a basic data model and query language, and then enrich them to obtain the full fledged model.

BPs and BP systems We assume the existence of two infinite domains: a domain $\mathcal{N}$ of nodes and a domain $\mathcal{L}$ of node labels, containing a sub-domain $\mathcal{F}$ of function names. We model a BP as a directed labeled graph. Formally,

Definition 1. *A* business process *(BP) is a quadruple* $p = (G, \lambda, \texttt{start}, \texttt{end})$, *where* $G = (N, E)$ *is a connected directed graph in which* $N \subset \mathcal{N}$ *is a finite set of nodes,* E *is a set of edges with endpoints in* N; $\lambda : N \rightarrow \mathcal{L}$ *is a labeling function* *for the nodes;* `start`, **end** *are two distinguished nodes in G and every node in G resides on a path from* `start` *to* **end**. *Nodes labeled by function names from* $\mathcal{F}$ *are called* function calls.

A *system* is a collection of BPs, and a mapping of function names to implementations.

Definition 2. *A* system *s of BPs is a triple* (S, s_0, τ)*, where S is a finite set of BPs,* $s_0 \in S$ *is a distinguished BP, called the* root process, *and* $\tau : \mathcal{F} \rightarrow 2^S$ *is a (possibly partial) function, called the* implementation function, *mapping function names in S to sets of BPs in S.*

W.l.o.g we assume that the nodes in the graphs have distinct identifiers. This will be utilized below in the construction of the explanatory answer to a query. A function name can be mapped, through the implementation function, to a set of BPs. These represent alternative possible implementations for the function (one of which will be chosen at run time as the actual implementation). The implementation function is partial if the internal implementation structure of some functions is unknown (e.g. since their providers do not wish to expose their specification). Given a BP p and a function call n in p, a more detailed description of p can be obtained by replacing n by one of the function's possible implementations. A result of such replacements is called a *refinement.*

Definition 3. *Given a system* $s = (S, s_0, \tau)$*, a BP p, and a node n in p labeled by a label l for which* τ *is defined, we say that* $p \xrightarrow{n} p'$ *(w.r.t.* τ*) if* p' *is obtained from p by replacing n in p by one of its possible implementations* $g \in \tau(l)$*. [Namely, n is deleted from p, and a copy of g is plugged in its place, with the incoming/outgoing edges of n now connected to the start/end node of g, resp.]*

If $p \xrightarrow{n_1} p_1 \xrightarrow{n_2} p_2 \ldots \xrightarrow{n_k} p_k$*, we say that* p_k *is a* refinement *of p, and name the sequence of node replacements a* refinement sequence.

We say that a node $v \in p_k$ depends *on a node* n_i *in the sequence if* $v \in p_i$ *but* $v \notin p_{i-1}$*. v* depends transitively *on* n_i *if it either depends on* n_i *or depends on some node* n_j *transitively depending on* n_i*.*

Queries We now consider queries and their answers. Queries are modeled using *BP patterns.* These generalize BPs similarly to the way tree patterns generalize XML trees. Formally,

Definition 4. *A BP* pattern *is a tuple* $\hat{p} = (p, I_e, I_f)$*, where p is a BP and* I_e*,* I_f *are distinguished sets of edges and function names in p, resp. These are the* indirect *edges and functions of* $\hat{p}$*.*
A query *q is a system of* BP patterns (Q, q_0, τ)*, where Q is a set of BP patterns,* q_0 *is the root BP pattern, and* τ *is an implementation function.*

Embeddings. To evaluate a query, its patterns are embedded into the system BPs. Generally speaking, every type of relation over (finite) flat graphs may be generalized to an embedding type. We suggest here the usage of three main types of graph relations - homomorphism, isomorphism, and bisimulation. These are generalized to *homomorphic-* and *isomorphic-embeddings* (which capture the structural query interpretation) and *bisimilar-embedding* (capturing behavioral interpretation). We define these next. We consider first the embedding of a single BP pattern, then of full queries.

Definition 5. *Let $\hat{p}$ be a BP pattern and let p be a BP. An* homomorphic (resp. isomorphic)-embedding *of $\hat{p}$ into p is a homomorphism (isomorphism) ψ from the nodes of $\hat{p}$ to the nodes of p s.t.*

1. **(nodes)** *each node of $\hat{p}$ is mapped to a node of p having the same label; the start (resp. end) node of $\hat{p}$ is mapped to the start (resp. end) node of p.*
2. **(edges)** *for each (indirect) edge of $\hat{p}$ from a node m to a node n there is an edge (path) in p from $\psi(m)$ to $\psi(n)$.*

Definition 6. *Let $\hat{p}$ be a BP pattern and let p be a BP. A* bisimilar-embedding *of $\hat{p}$ into p is a binary relation R between the nodes of $\hat{p}$ and the nodes of some subgraph p' of the transitive closure [2] of p s.t.*

1. **(nodes')** *for each node $n \in \hat{p}$ [resp. each $n' \in p'$] there exists some node $n' \in p'$ [$n \in \hat{p}$] s.t. $R(n, n')$ holds; whenever $R(n, n')$ holds, n and n' have the same label and if one is a start/end node then so is the other.*
2. **(edges')** *for each (indirect) edge from a node n to a node m in $\hat{p}$, [resp. from n' to m' in p'] there exists a (indirect) edge from some node n' to some m' in p' [resp. from some n to some m in $\hat{p}$] s.t. $R(m, m')$ and $R(n, n')$ hold.*

In the sequel, when some definition/result applies to all homomorphic, isomorphic, and bisimilar embeddings we will denote all by *X-embedding.*

We now consider the embedding of a query consisting of a set of such BP patterns into a specification.

Definition 7. *Let $q = (Q, q_0, \tau_q)$ be a query and let $s = (S, s_0, \tau_s)$ be a system of BPs. An* X-embedding *of q into s consists of*

1. *An homomorphism h from the BP patterns in Q to the BPs in S and their refinements that (i) maps the root pattern q_0 of q to the root BP s_0 of s, and (ii) maps, for each (indirect) function name c in q, the BPs in $\tau_q(c)$ to (refinements of) the BPs in $\tau_s(c)$.*
2. *An X-embedding for each $\langle BPpattern, BP \rangle$ pair in the homomorphism.*

To conclude, we need to define the query semantics. We distinguish between *boolean* and *explanatory* answers for a query. The boolean X-answer to a query q on a system s is positive if such X-embedding exists and is negative otherwise. The explanatory X-answer consists of s's components participating in such X-embeddings, as defined formally below.

[2] The transitive closure of a graph is obtained by adding edges (specially marked as 'indirect') between any two nodes n, m such that m is reachable from n.

Definition 8. *The nodes and edges of a system s that are* relevant *to a given X-embedding include*

1. *the nodes of s in the ranges of the mappings (ψ or R, depending on the embedding type)*
2. *the edges and nodes of s appearing on paths between these nodes and which could be used to verify requirement* `(edges)` *(resp.* `(edges)'`*) for the embedding.*
3. *the nodes on which any of the above depend on, transitively (see Definition 3).*

The explanatory *X-answer of a query q on a system s, denoted $q_X(s)$, is a restriction of s to those nodes and edges that are relevant to some X-embedding of q in s. (Empty BPs are removed and the domain of τ is restricted to the relevant functions).*

In the sequel, we will refer to BPQL, under isomorphic, homomorphic, and bisimilar embeddings, as isoBPQL, homBPQL, and bisBPQL, resp. One may also consider combinations, allowing the user to specify different interpretations for various BP patterns in the query, and our results will still hold.

3 Related Models and Languages

Before presenting our query evaluation algorithm, we first set the background by looking at some closely related models and languages. We compare our work to relevant works in three areas, namely Model Checking, Formal Models and Databases. We classify the works according to the structural/behavoiural dichotomy, and discuss their relationships. Due to space constraints, we cannot give the formal definitions of each model we discuss, and the reader is referred to the literature. In the following, we use $BPQL_{spec}$, and $BPQL_{query}$ to denote the specification and query parts of BPQL, respectively. We start by formally defining the notion of model and query languages containment for models that define sets of finite graphs. In the following, $\equiv$ denotes graph isomorphism, and $\simeq$ denotes query equivalence (where two boolean queries Q_1, Q_2 over graphs are considered equivalent if a graph satisfies Q_1 iff it also satisfies Q_2).

Definition 9. *For two models M_1, M_2, $M_1 \subseteq M_2$ if for all $m_1 \in M_1$ there exists $m_2 \in M_2$ s.t. m_1, m_2 represent respectively (possibly infinite) sets of graphs S_1, S_2, and $\forall G_1 \in S_1\ \exists G_2 \in S_2$ s.t. $G \equiv G'$. Also, $|m_2|$ is required to be linear in $|m_1|$.*

$M_1 \sim M_2$ if $M_1 \subseteq M_2$ and $M_2 \subseteq M_1$.

For two (boolean) query languages L_1, L_2 over some domain D, $L_1 \subseteq L_2$ if for all $Q_1 \in L_1$ there exists $Q_2 \in L_2$ s.t. $Q_1 \simeq Q_2$, and $|Q_2|$ is linear in $|Q_1|$.

$L_1 \sim L_2$ if $L_1 \subseteq L_2$ and $L_2 \subseteq L_1$.

Model Checking. Several models similar to our model of nested graphs appear in works related to model checking. A common model that captures this semantics is named Recursive State Machines (RSM) [4]. This model naturally extends Finite State Machines (FSM), by allowing some states to be *call* states, invoking other FSMs. A call is simulated by replacing the call state by its implementation. Each FSM has some entry and exit states. The simplest form of RSM is Single Entry Single Exit RSM (SERSM), where each FSM has unique start and exit nodes. It is straightforward to prove the following proposition.

Proposition 1. $BPQL_{spec} \sim SERSM$

By their nature, works in the area of Model Checking use *behavioral* query languages, being interested in properties of the process's possible executions rather than its exact structure. *Temporal logics* are used to capture such properties. The most common of these are LTL, CTL*, and the more powerful alternation-free μ-calculus. These logics consider the behavior of programs over time, and differ in their quantifiers. CTL^* allows queries over branching execution paths, and supply corresponding quantifiers; LTL considers the time as linear, and does not allow branching; μ-calculus is the most general temporal logic, containing fix-point operators (μ and ν), that allow recursive iterations over the queried process. A particular fragment of μ-calculus, called 'alternation-free', is the one consisting of formulas that contains no μ operator depending on ν or vice versa. The exact definitions can be found in [12]. We can show the following:

Proposition 2. $bisBPQL_{query} \subset$ *alternation-free* μ*-calculus*

Specifically, using [10] one can easily obtain an evaluation algorithm for alternation-free μ-calculus over SERSM, of complexity $poly(|spec|){*}2^{|query|}$. This algorithm can be used to answer $bisBPQL$ queries with the same complexity.

Formal Languages. There is rich literature on Context Free Processes in the area of Formal Models. A main branch of this research concerns *Context Free Graph Grammars*, first introduced in early works such as [24]. These grammars generalize the common model of context free grammars over strings. Similarly, the grammar consists of a set of non-terminals and derivation rules. Each non-terminal derives labeled graphs, which in turn contain objects (nodes, edges, etc.) labeled by non-terminals. The rules are accompanied by instructions on how to connect the new graphs to the original graph. These instructions are called the *connection relation.* The literature (e.g. [20]) considers mainly two particular cases of context free graph grammars: Hyperedge Replacement (HR) grammars, where the non-terminals in the graph are hyperedges, and Vertex Replacement (VR) grammars, where the non-terminals are graph *nodes.* By [20], $HR \subset VR$.

The following proposition establishes the connection between our specification model and context free graph grammars.

Proposition 3. *$BPQL_{spec} \subset HR \subset VR$*

The work on these models is mostly theoretic, and uses, for query formalism, formal logics such as $FO(TC)^3$ or MSO^4. The following theorem from [14] shows decidability of MSO over HR graph grammars.

Theorem 1. *[14] It is decidable whether a given MSO formula is satisfied by any graph generated by a given HR graph grammar*

As FO(TC) and MSO are *structural* query languages, it is suitable to compare the structural variants of BPQL to these logics. It is easy to see that

Proposition 4. *$isoBPQL_{query}$,$homBPQL_{query} \subset FO(TC) \subset MSO$*

Using Prop. 3, 4 and Thm. 1, we obtain:

Theorem 2. *isoBPQL, homBPQL are decidable*

Where bisBPQL is decidable as well, as implied from the discussion above. However, though the proof of theorem 1 is constructive, i.e. provide a decision procedure, it is unfeasible for practical use, as its complexity is non-elementary in the size of the query.

Databases. Works in the Database world typically consider the representation of data as *flat* graphs (e.g. [13,1]). Models that consider nested relations [3], actually consider flat trees . One exception that does consider nested graphs (trees) is *Active XML* (AXML) [2]. AXML is an extension of XML where the XML trees may contain nodes that represent calls to Web services. When invoked, the calls return new AXML trees that replace the call element. AXML data is queried using standard XML query languages like XQuery [11]. However, the semantics relates only to the full (possibly infinite) refinement of the document and does not allow queries of finer granularity. For this purpose, the model presented here can be adapted.

4 Query Evaluation for BPQL

To evaluate a query q on a system s, we need to embed the BP patterns in q within (refinements) of the BPs in s. We assume first the existence of some oracle, denoted *X-match*, that given a single BP pattern $\hat{p}$ and some BP p, computes the X-embeddings of $\hat{p}$ into p. (We will consider the implementation of such an oracle later). We start by showing how to use this oracle to find X-embeddings of $\hat{p}$ into *refinements* of p. Later, we use this to derive an evaluation algorithm for the full query.

Our algorithm is inspired by the original BPQL query evaluation algorithm presented in [6]. However, unlike that algorithm, which is applicable only to

[3] First Order logic augmented by a Transitive Closure operator.

[4] Monadic Second Order Logic.

structural queries, the present algorithm is designed in a modular manner that can be parameterized by the required type of embedding. This is achieved by modeling the queries as logic formulas – FO(TC) formulas for structural queries and μ-calculus formulas for behavioral ones – and using a similar formula decomposition method for both, as described below. We sketch here an intuitive description for the boolean version of our algorithm, and then explain how to obtain its explanatory version. A full description of the algorithm, as well as its correctness proof, can be found in the full version of the paper [17].

Embedding a single pattern. We start by explaining how to find, given a system s, a BP p and a BP pattern $\hat{p}$, X-embeddings of $\hat{p}$ into refinements of p. Our algorithm first constructs (1) a graph grammar G_p that describes the possible refinements of p (w.r.t s), and (2) an FO(TC) or μ-calculus formula, depending on the embedding type, $F_{\hat{p}}$ that represents the pattern $\hat{p}$. It then uses the two to compute a new graph grammar that encodes the X-embeddings of $\hat{p}$ into refinements of p. The boolean query answer will be positive iff the constructed grammar is not empty. We explain each of these steps below.

Grammar. We first construct a graph grammar for the system s, as explained in the previous section. We use the result of [22] stating that an HR graph grammar can be translated into a normal form, where each graph includes only two non-terminals. We assign to the normal-formed grammar a new root non-terminal R that derives the BP p, and denote the resulting grammar by G_p. It is easy to see that the set of graphs derived from R in G_p corresponds precisely to the set of possible refinements of p w.r.t s.

Formula. The formula for $\hat{p}$ uses two types of predicates: $L_A(n)$ holds iff the given BP contains a node n having a label A. $Path(n,m)$ holds iff there is a path from node n to node m. In general, each pattern $\hat{p}$ can be expressed as a conjunction of these predicates.

The distinction between the different embeddings sought for is expressed in the formula construction: For homBPQL and isoBPQL, variables are interpreted over individual nodes, while for bisBPQL they are interpreted over sets of nodes. Also, *isoBPQL* formulas contain additional clauses representing inequalities between the node variables.

Algorithm. We use the graph grammar G_p and the formula $F_{\hat{p}}$ described above to construct a new graph grammar that encodes the embeddings of $\hat{p}$ in refinements of p. The basic idea is similar to the one used in verification algorithms, e.g. [4]. We try all splits of the formula $F_{\hat{p}}$ up into 3 parts, each of which is 'not larger' then the original formula. Each part is then handled separately, as follows. The first part is embedded directly within p, where the other two parts are embedded recursively within the implementations of p's function call nodes. To capture this recursive embedding, we replace within (the grammar representation of) p its two non-terminals N_1,N_2, that represent the function calls, by (N_1, F_{N_1}) and (N_2, F_{N_2}), (where F_{N_1}, F_{N_2} are the above mentioned parts of $F_{\hat{p}}$) and we continue recursively to finding embeddings of F_{N_1} (F_{N_2}) within the implementation of N_1 (N_2). Intuitively, we find the fix-point of the set of constraints generated.

Formula Decomposition. To complete the algorithm description, we only need to describe the split of a formula F. For a BP g with two function call nodes (grammar non-terminals) N_1, N_2, we define the *split* F into three formulas denoted F_g, F_{N_1} and F_{N_2}. This is done by considering all possible splitting of the node predicates of F into three sets [5] f_g, f_{N_1}, f_{N_2} (representing the nodes to be embedded in g, N_1, and N_2, resp.) and then splitting the remainder of F based on this nodes split. The node predicates in F_g, F_{N_1}, F_{N_2} are trivially f_g, f_{N_1}, f_{N_2}, respectively. We further need to consider the paths connecting the nodes. The splitting of the path formulas depends upon the nodes split - path predicates with both end-nodes in f_{N_1} (resp. f_{N_2}) are added [6] to F_{N_1} (resp. F_{N_2}). The treatment of path predicates with one end-node in f_{N_1} and the other in f_{N_2} is similar: these are split into three parts s.t. one describes the sub-path to be embedded in N_1 (the corresponding path predicate is added to F_{N_1}), the second describes the sub-path to be embedded in g, connecting N_1 to N_2 (added to F_g), and the third describes the sub-path to be embedded in N_2 (added to F_{N_2}). We can show the following theorem, used in the algorithm correctness proof.

Theorem 3. *(informal) A pattern $\hat{p}$ can be X-embedded within a BP p, containing call nodes N_1 and N_2 labeled l_{N_1} and l_{N_2} resp., if and only if there exists a split of $F_{\hat{p}}$ into F_1, F_2, F_3 (as described in the algorithm) such that F_1 can be X-embedded into p without matching N_1 and N_2, F_2 and F_3 can be X-embedded into the implementations of l_{N_1} and l_{N_2} respectively.*

Evaluating a full query. The algorithm above constructs a graph grammar that encodes the embedding of a single BP Pattern. Extending it to handle a full BPQL query is fairly straightforward. For each indirect function call node in the query, we use the algorithm above to compute the graph grammar rules representing the embeddings of the function's implementation into refinements of the corresponding call node in the system. If any of the computed grammars happens to be empty, we stop and return an empty graph grammar. For the direct call nodes in the query, as well as for the query root BP pattern, we use directly the X-match oracle to obtain grammar rules describing their possible (direct) embedding into the corresponding system BPs. Here again, if any of these embeddings fail, we stop and return an empty grammar.

The following theorem states the correctness of the algorithm. The proof appears in the full version of the paper [17].

Theorem 4. *The grammar constructed by the algorithm is not empty iff an embedding exists*

The explanatory query answer can also be easily obtained from the above algorithm, as it maintains the unique identifiers of all nodes and edges being used.

---

[5] For structural queries the sets are required to be disjoint.

[6] Note that all formulas are conjunctive, so whenever we refer to 'adding' a formula f_1 into a formula f_2 we mean generating the conjunction $f_1 \bigwedge f_2$.

These can be extracted from the constructed graph grammar and used to generate the explanatory answer.

5 Complexity

The complexity of the algorithm presented in the previous section depends on the complexity of the X-match oracles. We first examine the complexity of such oracles for isomorphic, homomorphic and bisimilar embeddings. Next we analyze the complexity of the full algorithm, parameterized by the oracle's complexity.

X-match oracles. Given a BP pattern $\hat{p}$ and some BP p, X-match computes the X-embeddings of $\hat{p}$ into p. For the three types of embedding, the problem of testing for the existence of an embedding is NP-complete w.r.t the size of the query pattern, but polynomial in the data size. (The proof follows immediately from the NP-completeness of subgraph isomorphism/homomorphism/bisimulation [16,18]). A worst case complexity for the oracles is thus $O(p^{\hat{p}})$. However, using optimization techniques, this is typically much lower in practice [21].

The overall algorithm. For a given X-match oracle, we use O(X-match(n,m)) to denote the worst case time complexity of the oracle when embedding a query pattern of size m into a BP of size n.

Theorem 5. *Given a BP system s and a query q, the time complexity of (the Boolean and Explanatory versions of) the query evaluation algorithm presented in the previous section is* $O(\mid s \mid^2 \times c^{|q|} \times O(X\text{-}match(\mid s \mid, \mid q \mid)))$*, where c is a constant.*

Thus, the algorithm is polynomial in the size of the system s [7] and in the complexity of the X-match oracle, but is exponential in the size of the query. Since testing for the existence of isomorphic-, homomorphic-, and bisimilar-embeddings is NP-hard in the size of the query, it is evident that testing if the answer to a iso-,hom-, and bisBPQL is empty is also NP-hard in the query size. Interestingly, we can expose an additional type of hardness that comes from the nested shapes of the system and query graphs, as follows.

Theorem 6. *1. Boolean hom-, iso-, and bisBPQL are NP-hard in the size of the query even when the system BPs and the query patterns belong to a restricted class of graphs for which the X-match can be computed in polynomial time.*

2. For homBPQL and bisBPQL, the above holds if, furthermore, all the call nodes in the system and the query have only one possible implementation. [8]

It is open if (2) holds also for isoBPQL. The proof (appearing in the full version) is by reduction from the problem of testing if a 3NF formula is satisfiable, known

[7] The complexity is quadratic in the size of the system because of the mapping to normal form grammars, resulting in a quadratic size grammar.

[8] In general, the implementation function allows to map each function name to a set of BPs, representing alternative possible implementations for the function.

to be NP-complete. The graphs used in the proof have very simple, almost tree-shaped structure, where all nodes besides the end nodes have a single parent.

To give a lower bound we can show that

Theorem 7. *The Boolean versions of homBPQL and isoBPQL are in NP (combined complexity).*

The main lemma required in order to supply an NP algorithm is the following.

Lemma 1. *For every BPQL system s and homBPQL (isoBPQL) query q, exactly one of the following holds:*

1. *There is no homomorphic (isomorphic) embedding of q into s.*
2. *There is at least one homomorphic (isomorphic) embedding that maps nodes of q only to nodes of refinements obtained by a* polynomial *number of refinement steps.*

The correctness of this lemma stems from the correctness of the analogous lemma for context free *string* grammars. (The proof is in the full version). Interestingly, when the query is viewed as a logic formula, this property can also be viewed as an instance of the *Small Model Property.* It is open if the same holds for bisBPQL.

A different kind of analysis is obtained through *parameterized complexity*, where the size of one of the inputs which is typically small (the query size, in our case) is considered as a parameter k, and the size of the rest of the input is denoted n. A parameterized complexity class corresponding to $PTIME$ is FPT [19], which is the class of all problems solved with time complexity $O(f(k) * P(n))$, P being a polynomial and f being any computable function. An important hardness class, namely W[1]-hard [19], contains problems which are likely not to be in FPT, and thus is analogous to the class of NP-hard problems. We can show the following proposition.

Proposition 5. *If X-match is in FPT (resp. is W[1]-hard) then so is X-BPQL.*

Note the difference from conventional complexity analysis, where even for X-matches that are in $PTIME$, X-BPQL is NP-hard (See theorem 6(1)).

6 Conclusion

This paper studied the formal model underlying BPQL, a novel query language for BP specifications. We investigated its properties as well as the complexity of query evaluation, showed how queries on the structure and behavior of BPs can be processed in a uniform manner, and analyzed the relationship to previously suggested formalisms for processes modeling and querying. Because of space constraints, we have discussed only parts of the full BPQL model and query language, which include extensions such as regular path expressions, joins, and negation. Our results extend to this setting as well, as shown in [17].

To guaranty a complexity that is polynomial in the size of the data, BPQL ignores the run-time semantics of certain BPEL constructs such as conditional execution and variable values. Identifying semantic constructs that can nevertheless be incorporated without increasing the complexity is a challenging future research task. It would be interesting, following e.g. [15], to consider the data manipulated by BPs and the messages passed from one process to another. One may also consider a setting where calls are possibly asynchronous, or where the knowledge of the implementation of some (remote) processes may be partial [9]. It would also be interesting to combine our algorithm with some existing verification techniques, e.g. [21].

References

1. Abiteboul, S., Abrams, Z., Haar, S., Milo, T.: Diagnosis of asynchronous discrete event systems: datalog to the rescue! In: Proc. of PODS 2005 (2005)
2. Abiteboul, S., Benjelloun, O., Milo, T.: Positive active xml. In: Proc. of PODS 2004 (2004)
3. Abiteboul, S., Fischer, P.C., Schek, H.J.: Nested Relations and Complex Objects in Databases. LNCS, vol. 361. Springer, Heidelberg (1989)
4. Alur, R., Benedikt, M., Etessami, K., Godefroid, P., Reps, T., Yannakakis, M.: Analysis of recursive state machines. ACM Trans. Program. Lang. Syst. 27(4) (2005)
5. Beeri, C., Eyal, A., Kamenkovich, S., Milo, T.: Querying Business Processes with BP-QL (demo). In: Proc. of VLDB (2005)
6. Beeri, C., Eyal, A., Kamenkovich, S., Milo, T.: Querying business processes. In: Proc. of VLDB (2006)
7. Business Process Execution Language for Web Services. `http://www.ibm.com/developerworks/library/ws-bpel/`
8. BPMI. Business process management initiative: Business process: Business process query language (bpql). `http://www.service-architecture.com/web-services/articles/business_process_query_language_bpql.html`
9. Buneman, P., Cong, G., Fan, W., Kementsietsidis, A.: Using partial evaluation in distributed query evaluation. In: Proc. of VLDB (2006)
10. Burkart, O., Steffen, B.: Model checking for context-free processes. In: Cleaveland, W.R. (ed.) CONCUR 1992. LNCS, vol. 630, Springer, Heidelberg (1992)
11. Chamberlin, D.: Xquery: a query language for xml. In: Proc. of SIGMOD (2003)
12. Clarke, E.M., Grumberg, O., Peled, D.A.: Model checking. MIT Press, Cambridge (1999)
13. Consens, M., Mendelzon, A.: The g+/graphlog visual query system. In: Proc. of SIGMOD (1990)
14. Courcelle, B.: The monadic second-order logic of graphs. Inf. Comput. 85(1) (1990)
15. Deutsch, A., Sui, L., Vianu, V., Zhou, D.: Verification of communicating data-driven web services. In: Proc. of PODS (2006)
16. Dovier, A., Piazza, C.: The subgraph bisimulation problem. IEEE Trans. Knowl. Eng. 15(4) (2003)
17. Querying structural and behavioral properties of business processes - full version. `http://www.cs.tau.ac.il/~danielde/BPQLFull.pdf/`
18. Garey, M.R., Johnson, D.S.: Computer and Intractability: A Guide to the Theory of NP-Completeness. W. H. Freeman, New York (1979)

19. Grohe, M.: Parameterized complexity for the database theorist. SIGMOD Rec. 31(4) (2002)
20. Janssens, D., Rozenberg, G.: Graph grammars with node-label controlled rewriting and embedding. In: Proc. of COMPUGRAPH (1983)
21. Lam, M.S., Whaley, J., Livshits, V.B., Martin, M.C., Avots, D., Carbin, M., Unkel, C.: Context-sensitive program analysis as database queries. In: Proc. of PODS (2005)
22. Lengauer, T., Wanke, E.: Efficient decision procedures for graph properties on context-free graph languages. J. ACM 40(2) (1993)
23. Oracle BPEL Process Manager 2.0 Quick Start Tutorial. `http://www.oracle.com/technology/products/ias/bpel/index.html`
24. Pavlidis, T.: Linear and context-free graph grammars. J. ACM 19(1) (1972)
25. Schurr, A.: Logic based programmed structure rewriting systems. Fundam. Inf. 26(3-4) (1996)
26. The World Wide Web Consortium. `http://www.w3.org/`

Efficient Evaluation of HAVING Queries on a Probabilistic Database

Christopher Ré and Dan Suciu

Department of Computer Science and Engineering
University of Washington
{chrisre,suciu}@cs.washington.edu

Abstract. We study the evaluation of positive conjunctive queries with Boolean aggregate tests (similar to HAVING queries in SQL) on probabilistic databases. Our motivation is to handle aggregate queries over imprecise data resulting from information integration or information extraction. More precisely, we study conjunctive queries with predicate aggregates using MIN, MAX, COUNT, SUM, AVG or COUNT(DISTINCT) on probabilistic databases. Computing the precise output probabilities for positive conjunctive queries (without HAVING) is $\sharp\mathcal{P}$-hard, but is in $\mathcal{P}$ for a restricted class of queries called safe queries. Further, for queries without self-joins either a query is safe or its data complexity is $\sharp\mathcal{P}$-Hard, which shows that safe queries exactly capture tractable queries without self-joins. In this paper, for each aggregate above, we find a class of queries that exactly capture efficient evaluation for HAVING queries without self-joins. Our algorithms use a novel technique to compute the marginal distributions of elements in a semiring, which may be of independent interest.

1 Introduction

We study the complexity of evaluating aggregate queries on probabilistic databases. Our motivation is managing data resulting from integration applications, e.g. object reconciliation [15,30,31] and information extraction [5,14,17,19]. Standard approaches require that we eliminate all uncertainty before any querying can begin, which is expensive in both man-hours to perform the integration and in lost revenue due to down time. An alternative approach where data are allowed to be uncertain but we capture uncertainty using probabilities has attracted renewed interest [6,7,9,10,22,29]. In such systems, individual tuples are allowed to be incorrect, but aggregations of tuples still provide meaningful information.

In SQL, aggregates come in two forms: *value aggregates* that are returned to the user in the SELECT clause (e.g. the MAX price) and *predicate aggregates* that appear in a HAVING clause (e.g. is the MAX price greater than \$10.00?). In this paper, we focus on positive conjunctive queries with a single predicate aggregate which we call HAVING queries. Prior art [4,16] has defined a semantic for *value aggregation* that returns the expected value of an aggregate query (e.g. the expected MAX price) and have demonstrated its utility for Decision Support or OLAP style applications. In this paper, we propose a complementary semantic for predicate aggregates inspired by HAVING (e.g. what is the *probability* that the MAX price is bigger than \$10.00?). We illustrate the difference between the approaches with a simple example:

M. Arenas and M.I. Schwartzbach (Eds.): DBPL 2007, LNCS 4797, pp. 186–200, 2007.

Example 1. Consider a probabilistic database with a `Profit` relation that contains the profit forecasted for each item if we continue to sell it:

Item	Forecaster	Profit	P
Widget	Alice	$-99K	0.99
	Bob	$100M	0.01
Whatsit	Alice	$1M	1

`Profit`(Item;Forecaster,Profit;P)

```
SELECT SUM(PROFIT)
FROM PROFIT
WHERE ITEM='Widget'
```

(a) Expectation Style

```
SELECT ITEM
FROM PROFIT
WHERE ITEM='Widget'
HAVING SUM(PROFIT) > 0.0
```

(b) HAVING Style

`Profit` is an example of BID relation which captures our uncertain about contradictory and incompatible forecasts. Here, we trust Alice's forecast (probability 0.99) more than Bob's (0.01). Prior art [16] considered aggregate queries in the SELECT clause such as (a). Their semantic computes the *expected profit*. Using linearity of expectation, the value of query (a) is $100M * 0.01 + -99K * 0.99 \approx 900K$. This large value suggests that we should continue selling widgets because we expect to make money. However, if we asked the HAVING style query (b), which says: What is the chance that we will make a profit? The answer is only 0.01, which tells us that we should immediately stop selling widgets or risk going out of business.

Prior work [7,11,21] has shown that for Boolean conjunctive queries without HAVING, computing a query's probability is $\sharp\mathcal{P}$-Complete[1]. Although in general evaluating conjunctive queries on a probabilistic database is hard, there are a class of queries that can be computed efficiently called *safe queries* [7,21]. In this paper, for each aggregate α, we find a class of HAVING queries called **α-safe** that can be evaluated efficiently. Further, we show that there is a dichotomy for queries without self-joins: Either Q is α-safe, and has an algorithm in $\mathcal{P}$, or Q is not α-safe and is $\sharp\mathcal{P}$-Hard.

Our starting observation is that evaluating a query with a value aggregate with aggregate α on a traditional database can be computed by annotating the database with values from some semiring, S_α, then computing the annotations returned by a the query by evaluating any algebra plan P over the semiring, using the rules in [12]. Therefore the output of an aggregate function α on a probabilistic database is described by a random variable s_Q with values in S_α, and a HAVING query Q whose predicate is, say, COUNT($*$) $< k$, can be computed over the probabilistic database in two stages: first compute the random variable s_Q, second apply some *recovery function* that computes the probability $s_Q < k$. The cost of this algorithm depends on the space required to represent random variables s_Q, which is proportional to the set of possible worlds of the probabilistic database and hence is prohibitively high. Our key technical insight is that if the plan P is a *safe plan* then the random variable s_Q can be computed using a much more concise representation called a *marginal vector*, because P can guarantee that the random variables being combined are either independent or disjoint. In addition we need to impose an extra condition on P to ensure that the recovery function can be computed from the marginal vector representation of s_Q, and we call this condition plus the safety condition for the plan P, which depends on α, α-safety.

[1] $\sharp\mathcal{P}$ defined by Valiant [28] is the class of functions that contains the problem of counting the number of solutions to $\mathcal{NP}$-Hard problems (e.g. #3-SAT).

Contributions and Overview. We study conjunctive queries with HAVING predicates where the aggregation function is given by MIN, MAX, COUNT, SUM, AVG or COUNT(DISTINCT) and the aggregate test is one of $=, \neq, <, \leq, >,$ or $\geq$ on common representations of probabilistic databases [3,22,29]. In Sec. 2, we formalize HAVING queries, our choice of representation and define efficient evaluation. In Sec. 3, we review the relevant technical material (e.g. semirings and safe plans). In Sec. 4, we give our main results: For each aggregate α, we find a class of HAVING queries, called α-safe, such that for any Q using α:

- If Q is α-safe then Q's data complexity is in $\mathcal{P}$.
- If Q has no self-joins and is not α-safe then, Q has $\sharp\mathcal{P}$-hard data complexity.
- It can be decided in polynomial time in the size of Q if Q is α-safe.

2 Formal Problem Description

We first define the syntax and semantics of HAVING queries on probabilistic databases and then define the problem of evaluating HAVING queries.

Semantics. We consider the aggregates MIN, MAX, COUNT, SUM, AVG and COUNT(DISTINCT) as functions on multisets with the obvious semantics.

Definition 1. *A Boolean conjunctive query is a single rule $q = g_1, \ldots, g_m$ where each g_i is a positive EDB predicate. A Boolean HAVING query is a single rule:*

$$Q[\alpha(y)\ \theta\ k] \ :\!-\ g_1, \ldots, g_n$$

where for each i, g_i is a positive EDB predicate, $\alpha \in$ {MIN, MAX, COUNT, SUM, AVG, COUNT(DISTINCT)}, y is a single variable[2], $\theta \in \{=, \neq, <, \leq, >, \geq\}$ and k is a constant. The set of variables in the body of Q is denoted **var**(Q). *We assume that $y \in$* **var**(Q). *The conjunctive query $q = g_1, \ldots, g_n$, is called the* **skeleton** *of Q, denoted* **sk**$(Q) = q$. *We call θ the* **predicate test**, *k, the* **predicate operand** *and a pair (α, θ) an* **aggregate test**.

Fig. 1(a) shows a SQL query with a HAVING predicate, that asks for all movies reviewed by at least two distinct reviewers. A translation of this query into an extension of our syntax is shown in Fig. 1(b). The translated query is not a Boolean HAVING query be-

```
SELECT m.Title
FROM MovieMatch m, Reviewer r
WHERE m.ReviewTitle = r.ReviewTitle
GROUP BY m.Title
HAVING COUNT(DISTINCT r.reviewer) ≥ 2
```

(a) SQL Query

$Q(m)$[COUNT(DISTINCT y) ≥ 2] :-
MovieMatch$^p(t, m)$,
Reviewer$^p(-, r, t)$

(b) Extended Sytanx (Non Boolean)

Q[COUNT(DISTINCT y) ≥ 2] :-
MovieMatch^p('Fletch', m),
Reviewer$^p(-, r, t)$

(c) Syntax of this paper

Fig. 1. A translation of the query "Which moviews have been reviewed by at least 2 distinct reviewers?" into SQL and the syntax of this paper.

[2] For COUNT, we will omit y and write the more familiar COUNT(∗) instead.

cause it has a head variable (d). In this paper, we discuss only Boolean HAVING queries. However, as is standard, to study the complexity of non-boolean queries, we can substitute constants for head variables. For example, if we substitute 'M. Ritchie' for d, then the result is Fig. 1(c) which is a Boolean HAVING query.

Definition 2. *Given a* HAVING *query* $Q[\alpha(y)\ \theta\ k]$ *and a relational instance* W*, let*

$$\mathcal{Y} = \{\!|\ v(y) \mid v \text{ is a valuation for } Q \text{ and } \mathbf{im}(v) \subseteq W\ |\!\}$$

i.e. $\mathcal{Y}$ *is the multiset of all valuations of* Q *applied to* y*. We say that* Q *is satisfied on* W *and write* $W \models Q[\alpha(y)\ \theta\ k]$ *(or simply* $W \models Q$*) if* $\mathcal{Y} \neq \emptyset$ *and* $\alpha(\mathcal{Y})\ \theta\ k$ *holds.*

Probabilistic Databases. In this paper, we will use probabilistic databases described in the block-independent disjoint (BID) representation [22,24] which generalizes many representations in the literature including p-?-sets and p-or-sets [13], ?- and x-relations [26] and tuple independent databases [7,18] and is similar to [3].

Syntax. A **BID schema** has relational schemas of the form $R(\boldsymbol{K}; \boldsymbol{A}; P)$ with its attributes partitioned into three classes separated by semicolons: the **possible worlds key** ($\boldsymbol{K}$), the **value attributes** ($\boldsymbol{A}$), and a single distinguished probability attribute P taking values in $(0, 1]$. The corresponding **possible worlds schema** has relations of the form $R(\boldsymbol{K}; \boldsymbol{A})$, i.e. the same schema without the attribute P.

Semantics. Let J be an instance of a BID schema. We denote by $t[KAP]$ a tuple in J, emphasizing its three kinds of attributes, and call $t[KA]$, its projection on the KA attributes, a *possible tuple*. Define a *possible world*, W, to be any instance consisting of possible tuples s.t. K is a key in W. Note that the key constraints do not hold in J, but do hold in any possible world. Let $\mathcal{W}_J$ be the set of all possible worlds. We define the semantics of BID instances only for *valid* instances, which are instances J s.t. for every tuple $t \in R^J$ in any BID relation $R(\boldsymbol{K}; \boldsymbol{A}; P)$ the inequality $\sum_{s \in R: s[\boldsymbol{K}]=t[\boldsymbol{K}]} s[P] \leq 1$ holds. For a valid instance J its semantics is a finite probability space $(\mathcal{W}_J, \mu_J)$. First note that any possible tuple $t[KA]$ can be viewed as an event in the probability space $(\mathcal{W}_J, \mu_J)$, namely the event that a world contains $t[KA]$. Then we define the semantics of J to be the probability space $(\mathcal{W}_J, \mu_J)$ s.t. (a) the marginal probability of any possible tuple $t[KA]$ is $t[P]$, (b) any two tuples from the same relation $t[KA]$, $t'[KA]$ s.t. $t[K] = t'[K]$ are *disjoint events* (a.k.a. exclusive events), and (c) for any set of tuples $\{t_1, \ldots, t_n\}$ s.t. all tuples from the same relation have distinct keys, the events defined by these tuples are independent.

Example 2. The data in Fig. 2 shows an example of a BID representation that stores data from integrating extracted movie reviews (e.g. from USENET) with a movie database (e.g. IMDB). The MovieMatch table is uncertain because it is the result of an automatic matching procedure. For example, the probability a review title 'Fletch' matches a movie titled 'Fletch' is very high 0.95, but not 1 because the title is extracted from text and so may contain errors: For example, from 'The second Fletch movie', our extractor will likely extract just 'Fletch' although this review actually refers to 'Fletch 2'. The review table is uncertain because it is the result of *information extraction* and so

Title	Matched	P	
'Fletch'	'Fletch'	0.98	m_1
'Fletch'	'Fletch 2'	0.9	m_2
'Fletch 2'	'Fletch'	0.4	m_3
'The Golden Child'	'The Golden Child'	0.95	m_4
'The Golden Child'	'Golden Child'	0.8	m_5
'The Golden Child'	'Wild Child'	0.2	m_6

MovieMatch(CleanTitle,ReviewTitle;P)

ReviewID	Reviewer	Title	P	
231	'Ryan'	'Fletch'	0.7	t_{231a}
		'Spies Like Us'	0.3	t_{231b}
232	'Ryan'	'European Vacation'	0.90	t_{232a}
		'Fletch 2'	0.05	t_{232b}
235	'Ben'	'Fletch'	0.8	t_{235a}
		'Wild Child'	0.2	t_{235b}

Reviews(Reviewer,ReviewTitle;Rating;P)

Fig. 2. Sample Data arising from integrating automatically extracted reviews from a movie database. MovieMatch is a probabilistic relation, we are uncertain which review title matches with which movie in our clean database. Reviews is uncertain because it is the result of *information extraction* and *sentiment analysis*.

we have extracted the title from free text (e.g. 'Fletch is a great movie, just like Spies Like Us'). Notice that $t_{232a}[P] + t_{232b}[P] = 0.95 < 1$, which indicates that there is some probability reviewid 232 is actually not a review at all.

Remark 1. Recall that two distinct possible $t[KA]$ and $t'[KA]$ are disjoint if $t[K] \neq t'[K]$ and $t[A] = t'[A]$. But what happens if $A = \emptyset$, i.e. all attributes are part of the possible worlds key ? In that case all possible tuples become independent, and we sometime call a table $R(K;;P)$ a *tuple independent table* [7] or a *?-table* [20] or a *p-?-table* [13].

Queries are posed over the possible worlds schema. For clarity, we denote such relations with a superscripted p (e.g. $\texttt{Reviews}^p$).

Definition 3 (Query Semantics). *The marginal probability of a* HAVING *query Q on BID database J is denoted $\mu_J(Q)$ (or simply $\mu(Q)$) and is defined by:*

$$\mu_J(Q) = \sum_{W \in \mathcal{W}_J : W \models Q} \mu_J(W)$$

We also make use of $\mu_J(q)$ where q is a Boolean conjunctive query with the standard semantics.

Example 3. Fig. 1(c) shows a query which asks for all movies that were reviewed by at least 2 different reviewers. The movie 'Fletch' is present when the formula is satisfied $(m_1 \wedge t_{231a}) \vee (m_2 \wedge t_{232b}) \vee (m_1 \wedge t_{235a})$ and the multiplicity of tuples is exactly the number of disjuncts satisfied. Thus, $\mu(Q)$ is the probability that at least two of these disjuncts are true, which semantically can be computed by summing over all possible worlds.

Notions of complexity for HAVING queries. In the database tradition, we would like to measure the data complexity [1], i.e. treat the query as fixed, but allow the data to grow. This assumption makes sense in practice because the running time for query evaluation can be $O(n^{f(|Q|)})$ where $|Q|$ is the size of a conjunctive query Q. This exponential running time is considered to be tenable in practice, because database queries are generally small. However, in our setting this introduces a problem. By fixing a HAVING query q we also fix k, which means that we should accept a running time n^k as efficient. Clearly this is undesirable: because k can be large. For example, $Q()[\texttt{SUM}(y) > 200] \coloneq R(x, y)$. For that reason we consider in this paper an alternative definition of the data complexity of HAVING queries, where both the database and k are port of the input.

Definition 4. *Fix a skeleton q, an aggregate α, and a comparison operator θ. The **query evaluation problem** is: given as input the encoding of a BID representation J,* and *a binary representation of $k > 0$, calculate $\mu_J(Q)$, where $Q[\alpha\ \theta\ k]$ is such that* $\mathbf{sk}(Q) = q$.

The technical problem we address in this work is the complexity of query evaluation. We shall see for the query in Ex. 3, that the query evaluation problem is hard for $\sharp\mathcal{P}$. And moreover, this is the general case for all HAVING queries.

3 Preliminaries

We review here some basic facts on semirings (mostly from [12] and introduce random variables over semirings.

3.1 Background: Random Variables on Semirings

Definition 5. *A **monoid** $(S, +, 0)$ is a set S and $+$ is an associative binary operation with identity,* 0. *A **semiring** is a structure $(S, +, \cdot, 0, 1)$ where $(S, +, 0)$ is a commutative monoid with identity* 0, *$(S, \cdot, 1)$ is a monoid with identity* 1, *$\cdot$ distributes over $+$ and* 0 *annihilates S. A commutative semiring is one in which $(S, \cdot, 1)$ forms a commutative monoid. We abbreviate either structure with the set S when clear from the context.*

We shall consider only commutative semirings in this paper.

Example 4. For integer $k \geq 0$, let $\mathbb{Z}_{k+1} = \{0, 1, \ldots, k\}$ then for every such k, $(\mathbb{Z}_k, \max, \min, 0, k)$ is a semiring. In particular, $k = 2$ is the Boolean semiring. Another set of semirings we consider, $\mathbb{S}_k = (\mathbb{Z}_k, +_k, \cdot_k, 0, 1)$ where $+_k(x, y) = \min(x + y, k)$ and $\cdot_k = \min(xy, k)$ where addition and multiplication are in $\mathbb{Z}$.

For the rest of this section fix a BID instance J, and denote $(\mathcal{W}, \mu) = (\mathcal{W}_J, \mu_J)$ the probability space induced by J on possible worlds.

Definition 6. *Given a semiring $(S, +_S, \cdot_S)$, an S**-random variable**, r, is a function $r : \mathcal{W} \to S$. Given two random variables r, s then $r +_S s$ and $r \cdot_S s$ are random variables defined as $(r +_S s)(W) = r(W) +_S s(W)$ and $(r \cdot_S s)(W) = r(W) \cdot_S s(W)$.*

In the sequel, we make use of the following fact:

Fact 1 . *The set of S-random variables on a fixed BID instance J induces a semiring, denoted S^J, with the operations in Def. 6.*

Definition 7. *Given a semiring S and a set of random variables $R = \{r_1, \ldots, r_n\}$ on S, R is **independent** if $\forall N \subseteq 1, \ldots, n$ and any set $k_1, \ldots, k_n \in S$, we have $\mu(\bigwedge_{i \in N} r_i = k_i) = \prod_{i \in N} \mu(r_i = k_i)$. We say that R is **disjoint** if for any $i \neq j$ we have $\mu((r_i \neq 0) \wedge (r_j \neq 0)) = 0$.*

To represent a single random variable we need space as large as $|\mathcal{W}|$, which is exponential in the size of the J and thus prohibitive for most applications. However, there exists an alternative representation in terms of *marginal vectors*, which only takes size S.

Definition 8. *Given a random variable r on S, the* **marginal vector** *(or simply, the marginal) of r is denoted $\boldsymbol{m}^r$ and is a vector indexed by S defined by $\forall s \in S\, \mu(r = s) = \boldsymbol{m}^r[s]$. Given a monoid $(S, +_S, 0)$, the* **monoid convolution** *is a binary operation on marginals denoted $\otimes^{+_S}$, and for any marginals $\boldsymbol{m}^r$ and $\boldsymbol{m}^t$ is defined by*

$$\forall s \in S\ (\boldsymbol{m}^r \otimes^{+_S} \boldsymbol{m}^t)[s] \stackrel{\text{def}}{=} \sum_{\substack{i +_S j = k \\ i,j \in S}} \boldsymbol{m}^r[i]\boldsymbol{m}^t[j]$$

The disjoint operation for $(S, 0)$ is denoted $\boldsymbol{m}^r \perp \boldsymbol{m}^s$ and is defined by

$$\text{if } s \neq 0\ (\boldsymbol{m}^r \perp \boldsymbol{m}^s)[s] \stackrel{\text{def}}{=} \boldsymbol{m}^r[s] + \boldsymbol{m}^s[s] \text{ else } (\boldsymbol{m}^r \perp \boldsymbol{m}^s)[0] \stackrel{\text{def}}{=} (\boldsymbol{m}^r[0] + \boldsymbol{m}^s[0]) - 1$$

The next proposition tells us when the operations defined in the previous definition yield the correct results:

Proposition 1. *If r and s are random variables on the monoid $(S, +_S, 0)$ with marginal vectors $\boldsymbol{m}^r$ and $\boldsymbol{m}^s$ then let $\boldsymbol{m}^{r+_S s}$ denote the marginal of $r +_S s$. If r and s are independent then $\boldsymbol{m}^{r+_S s} = \boldsymbol{m}^r \otimes^{+_S} \boldsymbol{m}^s$. If r and s are disjoint then $\boldsymbol{m}^{r+_S s} = \boldsymbol{m}^r \perp \boldsymbol{m}^s$. Further, the n-fold convolution can be computed in time $O(n|S|^2)$ and the n-fold disjoint operation can be computed in $O(n|S|)$.*

The importance of this proposition is that if the semiring is small, then each operation can be done efficiently.

Example 5. Consider the Boolean semiring, and two random variables r and s with marginal probabilities (of truth) p_r and p_s. Then $\boldsymbol{m}^r = (1 - p_r, p_r)$ and $\boldsymbol{m}^s = (1 - p_s, p_s)$. If r and s are independent then, the distribution of $r \vee s = r +_S s$ which can be computed using $r \otimes^+ s$. This satisfies $(r \otimes^+ s)[1] = p_r(1 - p_s) + (1 - p_r)p_s + p_r p_s$ or in a more familiar form, $\boldsymbol{m}^r \otimes^+ \boldsymbol{m}^s = ((1 - p_r)(1 - p_s), 1 - (1 - p_r)(1 - p_s))$.

3.2 Background: Queries on Databases Annotated from a Semiring

In this section, we review material from [12] on computing queries on databases annotated with semiring elements. A slight twist on prior art is that we allow the query to induce the annotations as a first step, rather than being part of the data.

Definition 9. *Given a commutative semiring S and a Boolean conjunctive query $q = g_1, \ldots, g_n$, an annotation is a set of functions indexed by subgoals, such that for $i = 1, \ldots, n$, τ_{g_i} is a function on tuples that unify with g_i to S. We denote the set of annotation functions with τ.*

As in [12], we compute the annotation using a modified relational algebra which we define below:

Definition 10.

- *a* **plan** *P is inductively defined as (a) a single subgoal (b) $\pi_{-x}P_1$ if P_1 is a plan (b) $P_1 \bowtie P_2$ if P_1, P_2 are plans.*
- **var**(P), *the variables output by P, is defined as* **var**(g) *if* $P = g$, **var**($\pi_{-x}P$) = **var**(P) $- \{x\}$ *and* **var**($P_1 \bowtie P_2$) = **var**(P_1) $\cup$ **var**(P_2).
- **goal**(P), *the set of subgoals in P, is defined as (a)* **goal**(g) $= \{g\}$, *(b)* **goal**($\pi_{-x}P_1$) = **goal**(P_1) *(c)* **goal**($P_1 \bowtie P_2$) = **goal**(P_1) $\cup$ **goal**(P_2).

The **value** of a plan P on a standard instance W is a set of tuples with attributes corresponding to the variables in **var**(P) each annotated with a semiring element, denoted $\omega_P^W(t)$, which is defined inductively below. Concurrently, we define the support of a tuple $\mathbf{supp}_{P,V}(t) = \{t' \mid \forall y \in V\ t[y] = t'[y] \ \wedge\ \omega_P^W(t') \neq 0\}$ where P is a plan, V is a set of variables such that $V \subseteq \mathbf{var}(P)$, t is a tuple with attributes corresponding to V and t' is a tuple with attributes corresponding to **var**(P).

- If $P = g$ then if t unifies with g then $\omega_P^W(t) = \tau_g(t)$ else $\omega_P^W(t) = 0$.
- If $P = \pi_{-x}P_1$, then $\omega_{\pi_{-x}P_1}^W(t) = \sum_{t' \in \mathbf{supp}^W_{P_1,\mathbf{var}(P)}(t)} \omega_{P_1}^W(t')$.
- else $P = P_1 \bowtie P_2$ and for $i = 1, 2$ let t_i be t restricted to **var**(P_i) then $\omega_{P_1 \bowtie P_2}^W(t) = \omega_{P_1}^W(t_1) \cdot \omega_{P_2}^W(t_2)$

A result of [12] shows that ω_P^W is independent of the choice of plan P, which justifies the notation $s_{\tau,W,q}$, the value of a conjunctive query q on a determinsitic instance W under annotation τ defined as $s_{\tau,W,q} \stackrel{\text{def}}{=} \omega_P^W()$ where P is any plan for q where and ω_P^W is applied to the empty tuple.

4 Approaches for HAVING

In this section, we define the α-safe HAVING queries for $\alpha \in$ {MIN, MAX, COUNT} in Sec. 4.3, for α = COUNT(DISTINCT) in Sec. 4.4 and $\alpha \in$ {AVG, SUM} in Sec. 4.5.

4.1 Aggregates and Semirings

We explain the details of computing HAVING queries using semirings on deterministic databases, which immediately generalizes to probabilistic databases. Since HAVING queries are Boolean, we use a function ρ, the **recovery function**, which maps semiring values to true if that value would satisfy the HAVING query. Fig. 3 lists the (commutative) semirings for the aggregates in this paper, their annotations τ and a Boolean recovery function ρ. EXIST is similar to the safe plan algebra of [7,8,21].

Example 6. Consider the query Q[MIN(y) $\geq$ 10] :– $R(y)$ where $R = \{t_1, \ldots, t_n\}$. Fig. 3 tells us to use the semiring ($\mathbb{Z}_3$, max, min). We first apply τ: $\tau(t_i) = 1$ represents that $t_i[y] > 10$ while $\tau(t_i) = 2$ represents that $z_i[y] \leq 10$. Let $s = \sum^S_{i=1,\ldots,m} \tau(t_i) = \max_{i=1,\ldots,m} \tau(t_i)$. $\rho(s)$ is satisfied only when s is 1, i.e. all $z_i[y]$ are greater than 10.

HAVING Predicate	Semiring	Annotation $\tau_{g^*}(t)$	Recovery $\rho(s)$
EXISTS	$(\mathbb{Z}_2, \max, \min)$	1	$s = 1$
MIN(y) $\{<, \leq\}$ k	$(\mathbb{Z}_3, \max, \min)$	if $t\ \theta\ k$ then 2 else 1	$s = 2$
MIN(y) $\{>, \geq\}$ k	$(\mathbb{Z}_3, \max, \min)$	if $t\ \theta\ k$ then 1 else 2	$s = 1$
MIN(y) $\{=, \neq\}$ k	$(\mathbb{Z}_4, \max, \min)$	if $t < k$ then 3 else if $t = k$ then 2 else 1	if = then $s = 2$ if ≠ then $s \neq 2$
COUNT(*) θ k	$\mathbb{S}_{k+1}$	1	$(s \neq 0) \wedge (s\ \theta\ k)$
SUM(y) θ k	$\mathbb{S}_{k+1}$	$t[y]$	$(s \neq 0) \wedge (s\ \theta\ k)$

Fig. 3. Semirings for the operators MIN, COUNT and SUM. Let g^* be the lowest indexed subgoal such that contains y. For all $g \neq g^*$, $\forall t$, $\tau_g(t)$ equals the multiplicative identity of the semiring. Let $\mathbb{Z}_{k+1} = \{0, 1, \ldots, k\}$ and $+_k(x, y) \stackrel{\text{def}}{=} \min(x + y, k)$ and $\cdot_k \stackrel{\text{def}}{=} \min(xy, k)$, where $x, y \in \mathbb{Z}$. Let $\mathbb{S}_k \stackrel{\text{def}}{=} (Z_{k+1}, +_k, \cdot_k, 0, 1)$. MAX and MIN are symmetric. AVG and COUNT(DISTINCT) are omitted.

More generally, we have the following proposition:

Proposition 2. *Given a HAVING query Q, let $q = \mathbf{sk}(Q)$ and S, ρ and τ be chosen as in Fig. 3, then for any deterministic instance W and $s_{\tau,W,q}$ (Sec. 3.2):*

$$W \models Q \iff \rho(s_{\tau,W,q})$$

In probabilistic databases, we want to compute the random variable $s_{\tau,q}$ defined as $s_{\tau,q}(W) \stackrel{\text{def}}{=} s_{\tau,W,q}$. A simple corollary of Prop. 2 is the following generalization to probabilistic databases:

Corollary 1. *Given Q, let q, S,ρ and τ be as in Prop. 2 then for any BID instance J we have the following equalities:*

$$\mu_J(Q) = \mu_J(\rho(s_{\tau,W,q})) = \sum_{k\,:\,\rho(k)} \boldsymbol{m}^{s_{\tau,q}}[k]$$

Cor. 1 tells us that examining the entries of the marginal vector at index s such that $\rho(s)$ is true is sufficient to answer Q. Hence our goal is to compute $\boldsymbol{m}^{s_{\tau,q}}$.

4.2 Computing Safely in Semirings

We now extend safe plans to compute a marginal vector instead of a Boolean value. Specifically, we compute $\boldsymbol{m}^{s_{\tau,q}}$, the marginal vector for $s_{\tau,q}$ using the operations defined in Sec. 3.1.

Definition 11. *An extensional plan for a Boolean conjunctive query q is a subgoal g and if P_1, P_2 are extensional plans then so are $\pi^I_{-x}P_1$, $\pi^D_{-x}P_1$ and $P_1 \bowtie P_2$. An extensional plan P is **safe** if P_1 and P_2 are safe then*

- $P = g$ *is safe*
- $P = \pi^I_{-x} P_1$ *is safe if* $x \in \mathbf{var}(P_1)$ *and* $\forall g \in \mathbf{goal}(P_1)$ *then* $x \in \mathbf{key}(g)$
- $P = \pi^D_{-x} P_1$ *is safe if* $x \in \mathbf{var}(P_1)$ *and* $\exists g \in \mathbf{goal}(P_1)$, $\mathbf{key}(g) \subseteq \mathbf{var}(P)$, $x \in \mathbf{var}(g)$.
- $P = P_1 \bowtie P_2$ *is safe if* $\mathbf{goal}(P_1) \cap \mathbf{goal}(P_2) = \emptyset$
  - *and for* $i = 1, 2$ $\mathbf{var}(\mathbf{goal}(P_1)) \cap \mathbf{var}(\mathbf{goal}(P_2)) \subseteq \mathbf{var}(P_i)$

An extensional plan P is a safe plan for q if P is safe and $\mathbf{goal}(P) = q$.

Proposition 3. *If P is a safe plan for q, then for* $x \in \mathbf{var}(q)$ *there is exactly one of* π^I_{-x} *or* π^D_{-x} *in P.*

At least one of the two projections must be present, because we must remove the variable x (q is boolean). If there were more than one in the plan, then they cannot be descendants of each other because $x \notin \mathbf{var}(P_1)$ for the ancestor and they cannot be joined afterward because of the join condition for $i = 1, 2$ $\mathbf{var}(\mathbf{goal}(P_1)) \cap \mathbf{var}(\mathbf{goal}(P_2)) \subseteq \mathbf{var}(P_i)$.

Definition 12. *Given a BID instance J. Let P be an safe plan, then denote the* ***extensional value*** *of P in S on J as* $\hat{\omega}^J_{P,S}$ *which is a marginal vector on S defined inductively:*

- $\hat{\omega}^J_{g,S}(t) = \hat{\tau}_g(t)$ *where* $\hat{\tau}_g(t)$ *is the marginal vector* $\boldsymbol{m}^t$ *given by* $\boldsymbol{m}^t[0] = 1 - t[P]$ *and* $\boldsymbol{m}^t[\tau_g(t)] = t[P]$, *i.e. the (probabilistic) image of* τ.
- $\hat{\omega}^J_{\pi^I_{-x}P_1,S}(t) = \otimes^{+S}_{t' \in \mathbf{supp}_{P_1,\mathbf{var}(P)}(t)} \hat{\omega}^J_{P_1,S}(t)$.
- $\hat{\omega}^J_{\pi^D_{-x}P_1,S}(t) = \perp_{t' \in \mathbf{supp}_{P_1,\mathbf{var}(P)}(t)} \hat{\omega}^J_{P_1,S}(t)$.
- $\hat{\omega}^J_{P_1 \bowtie P_2}(t) = \hat{\omega}^J_{P_1,S}(t_1) \otimes^{\cdot} \hat{\omega}^J_{P_2,S}(t_2)$ *where for* $i = 1, 2$ t_i *is t restricted to* $\mathbf{var}(P_i)$

The next lemma uses the observation that an operator in a safe plan and the operator used to compute the value have the same correlation assumptions. For example, π^I assumes independence, which is required for $\otimes^+$.

Lemma 1. *If P is a safe plan for a Boolean query q then for any* $s_i \in S$ *on any BID instance J, we have* $\hat{\omega}^J_P()[s_i] = \mu_J(s_{\tau,q} = s_i)$.

Remark 2. A safe plan is not necessarily efficient for any S (Def. 4). In particular, the operations in a safe plan on S take time polynomial in $|S|$. Thus, if the size of S grows super-polynomially in $|J|$, the size of the BID instance, the plan will not be efficient.

4.3 MIN, MAX and COUNT-Safe

We can now formalize the class of queries which are efficient for MIN, MAX and COUNT.

Definition 13. *If* $\alpha \in \{MIN, MAX, COUNT\}$ *and* $Q[\alpha(t)\ \theta\ k]$ *is a HAVING query, then Q is* ***α-safe*** *if the skeleton of Q is safe.*

Theorem 1. *If* $Q[\alpha(y)\ \theta\ k]$ *is a HAVING query for* $\alpha \in \{MIN, MAX, COUNT\}$ *and Q is* α*-safe then the exact evaluation problem for Q is in polynomial time.*

Correctness is straightforward from Lem. 1. Efficiency follows because the semiring is of polynomial size. Hence the translation and each operation in the evaluation is of polynomial size for each aggregate in the theorem. In particular, S is constant for MIN and MAX and upper bounded by n for COUNT.

Remark 3. We remark that for SUM, we can only guarantee that $|S| = O(k)$, which implies a running time of $O(kn^{|Q|})$, which is not efficient (Def. 4).

The results of [7,8,21] show that either a conjunctive query without self-joins has a safe plan or it is $\sharp\mathcal{P}$-hard. It is not hard to see that each aggregate has at least one test so that a HAVING query Q is satisfied only when the skeleton of Q is satisfied. It is then straightforward to extend to all predicate tests. Formally, we have:

Theorem 2. *If $\alpha \in \{MIN, MAX, COUNT\}$ and $Q[\alpha(y)\ \theta\ k]$ does not contain self-joins, if Q is α-safe then Q has data complexity in $\mathcal{P}$ else Q has $\sharp\mathcal{P}$-hard data complexity. Further, we can find an α-safe plan in $\mathcal{P}$.*

The algorithm to find a safe plan is identical to [8,21].

4.4 COUNT(DISTINCT)-Safe Queries

Intuitively, we compute COUNT(DISTINCT) in two stages: proceeding bottom-up, we first compute the probability a y value appears (i.e. DISTINCT), we then count the number of distinct values (i.e. COUNT) using the techniques of the previous section. However, one caveat is that the representation is lossy: We do not know *which* values are present, only the distribution of their count. This implies that not all operations on these lossy marginal vectors are correct, which restricts the class of allowable plans:

Definition 14. *A query $Q[COUNT(DISTINCT\ y)\ \theta\ k]$ is* ***COUNT(DISTINCT)-safe*** *if there is a safe plan P for the skeleton of Q such that π^I_{-y} or π^D_{-y} is in P and no proper ancestor is π^I_{-x} for any x.*

Example 7. Fix a BID instance J. Consider $Q[\text{COUNT(DISTINCT } y) > 2]$:– $R(y,x)$, $S(y)$, a safe plan for the skeleton of Q is $P = \pi^I_{-y}((\pi^I_{-x}R(y,x)) \bowtie S(y))$. For the subquery $P_1 = (\pi^I_{-x}R(y,x)) \bowtie S(y)$, calculate the probability that each value EXISTS in the subplan P_1, i.e. for each t, $\hat{\omega}^J_{P,\text{EXISTS}}(t)$. Intuitively, all tuples returned by the plan are independent because π^I_{-y} is correct, and all y values are trivially distinct.

Intuitively, we map each EXISTS marginal vector to a vector suitable for computing COUNT, i.e. a vector in $\mathbb{Z}_k$ where $k = 2$, in this problem. In other words, $(1-p, p) = \hat{\omega}^J_{P,\text{EXISTS}}(t) = \boldsymbol{m}^t$ is mapped to $\hat{\tau}(\boldsymbol{m}^t) = (1-p, p, 0)$. Thus, the correct distribution is given by $\otimes_{t' \in \mathbf{supp}_P(())} \hat{\tau}(t')$. To compute the final result, use the recovery function, ρ defined by $\rho(s) \iff s > 2$.

The proof of the following theorem is a generalization of Ex. 7, whose proof is in the full paper [23]:

Theorem 3. *If Q is COUNT(DISTINCT)-safe then its evaluation problem is in $\mathcal{P}$.*

Complexity. We now establish that for COUNT(DISTINCT) queries without self-joins, COUNT(DISTINCT)-safe captures efficient computation. We first show the canonical hard patterns for COUNT(DISTINCT) and then extend this to show that the evaluation of any COUNT(DISTINCT) query without self-joins that is not COUNT(DISTINCT)-safe can be reduced to one of these hard patterns.

Proposition 4. *The following HAVING queries are $\sharp\mathcal{P}$-hard for $i \geq 1$:*
$Q_1[\mathit{COUNT(DISTINCT}\, y)\, \theta\, k]$:- $\mathrm{R}^p(x), \mathrm{S}(x, y)$ *and* $Q_{2,i}[\mathit{COUNT(DISTINCT}\, y)\, \theta\, k]$:- $\mathrm{R}_1^p(x; y), \ldots, \mathrm{R}_i^p(x; y)$

Proof (Sketch). To see that Q_1 is hard, we reduce from counting the number of independent sets in a graph (V, E). We let k be the number of edges, intuitively Q is satisfied only when all edges are present. For each node $u \in V$, create a tuple $\mathrm{R}(u)$ with probability 0.5. For edge $e = (u, v)$ create two tuples $\mathrm{S}(e, u), \mathrm{S}(e, v)$, each with probability 1. For any set $V' \subseteq V$, let $W_{V'}$ denote the world corresponding where the tuples corresponding to V' are present. For any subset of nodes, N, we show that if N is an independent set if and only if W_{V-N} satisfies Q_1. Since $f(N) = V - N$ is one-to-one, the number of possible worlds that satisfy Q_1 are exactly the number of independent sets. If N is independent, then for any edge (u, v), it must be the case that at least one of u or v is in $V - N$, thus every edge is present and Q is satisfied. If N is not independent, then there must be some edge (u, v) such that $u, v \in N$, hence neither of u, v is in $V - N$. Since this edge is missing, Q_1 cannot be satisfied. The hardness of Q_2 is based on a reduction from counting the set covers of a fixed size and is in the full paper [23].

There is some work in generalizing the previous theorem, we show in the full paper [23]:

Theorem 4. *If Q is not COUNT(DISTINCT)-safe and does not contain self-joins, then Q has $\sharp\mathcal{P}$-hard data complexity.*

Proof (Sketch). We sketch the proof in the simpler case when only tuple independent probabilistic tables are used in Q. Assume the theorem fails, let Q be the minimal counter example in terms of subgoals; this implies we may assume that Q is connected and the skeleton of Q is safe. Since there is no safe plan projecting on y and only independent projects are possible, the only condition that can fail is that some subgoal does not contain y. Thus, there are at least two subgoals $R(\boldsymbol{x})$ and $S(\boldsymbol{z}y)$ such that $y \notin \boldsymbol{x} \cup \boldsymbol{z}$ and $\boldsymbol{x} \cap \boldsymbol{z} \neq \emptyset$. Given a graph (V, E), we then construct a BID instance J exactly as in the proof of Prop. 4. Only the R relation is required to have probabilistic tuples, all others can set their probabilities to 1.

Extending to tuple-disjoint databases requires slightly more work, because adding multiple tuples with probability 1 may violate a possible world key constraint. The proof appears in the full paper [23]. It is straightforward to decide if a plan is COUNT(DISTINCT)-safe, the safe plan algorithm of [8,21] simply tries only disjoint projects and joins until it is able to project away y or it fails.

4.5 SUM-Safe and AVG-Safe Queries

To find SUM- and AVG-safe queries, we further restrict the class of allowable plans. Intuitively, if each value for y is present disjointly, then computing the multiplicity of each value is sufficient to compute the query, which we accomplish using the COUNT algebra of Sec. 4.3. Since computing SUM and AVG for a HAVING query with a single tuple independent table is already $\sharp\mathcal{P}$-Hard, our safe plans we must not contain an independent project for y (π^I_{-y}).

Definition 15. *A* HAVING *query* $Q[\alpha(y)\ \theta\ k]$ *for* $\alpha \in \{SUM, AVG\}$ *is* α*-safe, if there is a safe plan* P *for the skeleton of* Q *such that* π^D_{-y} *in* P *and no proper ancestor of* π^D_{-y} *is* π^I_{-x} *for any* x.

Theorem 5. *If* $Q[\alpha(y)\ \theta\ k]$ *for* $\alpha \in \{SUM, AVG\}$ *is* α*-safe, then* Q*'s evaluation problem is in* $\mathcal{P}$.

Proof (Sketch). Since Q is α-safe, there is a plan P satisfying Def. 15. We may assume without loss of generality that $P = \pi^D_{-y}(P_1)$. We compute P_1 using the algebra for COUNT, $\hat{\omega}^J_{\mathrm{COUNT},P_1}(t)$, which is correct because P_1 is safe. We then have the following equation which can be computed efficiently:

$$\mu(Q) = \sum_{t \in \mathbf{supp}_{P_1}()} \ \sum_{s : s * t[y]\ \theta\ k} \hat{\omega}^J_{P_1,\mathrm{COUNT}}[s]$$

Example 8. Consider $Q[\mathrm{SUM}(y) > 10]$:– R('a'; y), S(y, u). This query is SUM-safe, with plan $\pi^D_{-y}(\mathrm{R}(\text{'a'}; y) \bowtie \pi^I_{-u}\mathrm{S}(y, u))$.

Complexity. We show that if a HAVING query without self-joins is not SUM-safe then, it has $\sharp\mathcal{P}$-data complexity. AVG follows by essentially the same construction.

Proposition 5. *If* $\alpha \in \{SUM, AVG\}$ *and* $\theta \in \{\leq, <, =, >, \geq\}$ *then* $Q[\alpha(y)\ \theta\ k]$:– $R^p(y)$ *has* $\sharp\mathcal{P}$*-data complexity.*

Proof (Sketch). Consider when θ is =. An instance of $\sharp$SUBSET-SUM is a set of integers $x_1, \ldots, x_n$ and our goal is to count the number of subsets $\emptyset \neq S \subseteq 1, \ldots, n$ such that $\sum_{s \in S} x_i = B$. We create the representation with schema $R(X; ; P)$ satisfying $\mathrm{R} = \{(x_1; 0.5), \ldots, (x_n; 0.5)\}$, i.e. each tuple present with probability 0.5. Thus, $\mu(Q) * 2^n$ is number of such S. Showing hardness for other aggregate tess is straightforward.

Theorem 6. *If* $\alpha \in \{SUM, AVG\}$ *and* $\theta \in \{=, \neq, \leq, <, >, \geq\}$ *then let* $Q[\alpha(y)\ \theta\ k]$ *be a* HAVING *query if* Q *does not contain self-joins and is not* α*-safe, then* Q *has* $\sharp\mathcal{P}$*-data complexity. Further, there is an algorithm to decide if* Q *is* α*-safe in* $\mathcal{P}$.

If Q's skeleton is unsafe, then it is straightforward that Q has $\sharp\mathcal{P}$-hard data complexity. So we may assume that Q is safe, but not SUM-safe. Given any set of constants $y_1, \ldots, y_n$, let $q = \mathbf{sk}(Q)$ and for $i = 1, \ldots, n$, q_i be $q[y \to y_i]$. We construct an instance J such that the q_i are satisfied independently with multiplicity 1[3]. This allows us to construct the reduction above. A formal proof is in the full paper [23].

[3] By multiplicity, we mean that for any $W \in \mathcal{W}_J$ and any q_i there is at most one valuation v such that $\mathbf{im}(v) \subseteq W$.

5 Related Work

Probabilistic relational databases have been discussed by Barbara et. al [3] and more recently Dalvi and Suciu [7], Ré et. al [22], Sen et. al [27] and Widom [29], though all omit HAVING style aggregation. Cheng et al. [6] and Desphande et. al [9] consider probabilistic databases resulting from sensor networks and handle continuous distributions with more general correlations, while we handle only the discrete case. In their settings, aggregate queries are effectively value aggregates over a singe relation.

In the OLAP setting [4] and streaming setting [16] give efficient algorithms for *value aggregation* in a model which is equivalent to the single table model and focuses on scaling such computation (e.g. using streaming techniques). In contrast, computing the AVG for predicate aggregates on a single table is already $\sharp\mathcal{P}$-Hard. Ross et al. [25] describe an approach to computing aggregates on a probabilistic database, by computing bounding intervals (e.g. the AVG is between [5600, 5700]). For more aggregate functions than we discuss, they show computing bounding intervals exactly is $\mathcal{NP}$-Hard but do not offer any results on the boundary of hardness.

A closely related work is Arenas et. al, [2] which considers the complexity of aggregate queries, similar to HAVING queries, over data which violates functional dependencies. Their semantic is greatest lower bound or least upper bound on the set of all minimal repairs, i.e. not probabilistic. They consider multiple predicates, which we do not. In this paper, we deal with more general types of value inconsistency.

6 Conclusion

In this paper we have examined the complexity of evaluating positive conjunctive queries with predicate aggregates over probabilistic databases. For each aggregate, we discussed a novel method based on computing the distribution of elements in a semiring to evaluate such queries. We proved that for conjunctive queries without self-joins our methods are optimal.

Acknowledgements. This work was partially supported by NSF Grants IIS-0428168 and IIS-0454425.

References

1. Abiteboul, S., Hull, R., Vianu, V.: Foundations of Databases. Addison-Wesley, Reading (1995)
2. Arenas, M., Bertossi, L., Chomicki, J., He, X., Raghavan, V., Spinrad, J.: Scalar aggregation in inconsistent databases. Theoretical Computer Science (2003)
3. Barbara, D., Garcia-Molina, H., Porter, D.: The management of probabilistic data. IEEE Trans. Knowl. Data Eng. 4(5), 487–502 (1992)
4. Burdick, D., Deshpande, P.M., Jayram, T.S., Ramakrishnan, R., Vaithyanathan, S.: Olap over uncertain and imprecise data. VLDB J. 16(1), 123–144 (2007)
5. Cafarella, M.J., Ré, C., Suciu, D., Etzioni, O.: Structured querying of web text data: A technical challenge. In: CIDR, pp. 225–234 (2007), http://www.crdrdb.org
6. Cheng, R., Kalashnikov, D., Prabhakar, S.: Evaluating probabilistic queries over imprecise data. In: Proceedings of ACM SIGMOD Conference, ACM Press, New York (2003)

7. Dalvi, N., Suciu, D.: Efficient query evaluation on probabilistic databases. In: VLDB, Toronto, Canada (2004)
8. Dalvi, N., Suciu, D.: Management of probabilisitic data: Foundations and challenges. In: PODS, pp. 1–12 (2007)
9. Deshpande, A., Guestrin, C., Madden, S., Hellerstein, J., Hong, W.: Model-driven data acquisition in sensor networks (2004)
10. Fuxman, A., Miller, R.J.: First-order query rewriting for inconsistent databases. In: ICDT, pp. 337–351 (2005)
11. Gradel, E., Gurevich, Yu., Hirch, C.: The complexity of query reliability. In: Symposium on Principles of Database Systems, pp. 227–234 (1998)
12. Green, T., Karvounarakis, G., Tannen, V.: Provenance semirings. In: PODS (2007)
13. Green, T.J., Tannen, V.: Models for incomplete and probabilistic information. IEEE Data Engineering Bulletin 29 (2006)
14. Gupta, R., Sarawagi, S.: Curating probabilistic databases from information extraction models. In: Proc. of the 32nd Int'l. Conference on Very Large Databases (VLDB) (2006)
15. Hernandez, M.A., Stolfo, S.J.: The merge/purge problem for large databases. In: SIGMOD Conference, pp. 127–138 (1995)
16. Jayram, T.S., Kale, S., Vee, E.: Efficient aggregation algorithms for probabilistic data. In: SODA (2007)
17. Jayram, T.S., Krishnamurthy, R., Raghavan, S., Vaithyanathan, S., Zhu, H.: Avatar information extraction system. IEEE Data Engineering Bulletin 29(1) (2006)
18. Lakshmanan, L., Leone, N., Ross, R., Subrahmanian, V.S.: Probview: A flexible probabilistic database system. ACM Trans. Database Syst. 22(3) (1997)
19. Mansuri, I., Sarawagi, S.: A system for integrating unstructured data into relational databases. In: Proc. of the 22nd IEEE Int'l. Conference on Data Engineering (ICDE), IEEE Computer Society Press, Los Alamitos (2006)
20. Parag, A., Benjelloun, O., Sarma, A.D., Hayworth, C., Nabar, S., Sugihara, T., Widom, J.: Trio: A system for data uncertainty and lineage. In: VLDB (2006)
21. Ré, C., Dalvi, N., Suciu, D.: Query evaluation on probabilistic databases. IEEE Data Engineering Bulletin 29(1), 25–31 (2006)
22. Ré, C., Dalvi, N., Suciu, D.: Efficient top-k query evaluation on probabilistic data. In: Proceedings of ICDE (2007)
23. Ré, C., Suciu, D.: Efficient evaluation of having queries on a probabilistic database. Technical Report TR2007-06-01, University of Washington, Seattle, Washington (June 2007)
24. Ré, C., Suciu, D.: Materialized views in probabilsitic databases for information exchange and query optimization. In: VLDB (2007)
25. Ross, R., Subrahmanian, V.S., Grant, J.: Aggregate operators in probabilistic databases. J. ACM 52(1), 54–101 (2005)
26. Sarma, A.D., Benjelloun, O., Halevy, A.Y., Widom, J.: Working models for uncertain data. In: Liu, L., Reuter, A., Whang, K.-Y., Zhang, J. (eds.) ICDE, p. 7. IEEE Computer Society Press, Los Alamitos (2006)
27. Sen, P., Deshpande, A.: Representing and querying correlated tuples in probabilistic databases. In: Proceedings of ICDE (2007)
28. Valiant, L.G.: The complexity of enumeration and reliability problems. SIAM J. Comput. 8(3), 410–421 (1979)
29. Widom, J.: Trio: A system for integrated management of data, accuracy, and lineage. In: CIDR, pp. 262–276 (2005)
30. Winkler, W.E.: Improved decision rules in the fellegi-sunter model of record linkage. Technical report, Statistical Research Division, U.S. Census Bureau, Washington, DC (1993)
31. Winkler, W.E.: The state of record linkage and current research problems. Technical report, Statistical Research Division, U.S. Bureau of the Census (1999)

Succinctness of Pattern-Based Schema Languages for XML

Wouter Gelade* and Frank Neven

Hasselt University and Transnational University of Limburg
School for Information Technology
{firstname.lastname}@uhasselt.be

Abstract. Martens et al. defined a pattern-based specification language equivalent in expressive power to the widely adopted XML Schema definitions (XSDs). This language consists of rules of the form (r, s) where r and s are regular expressions and can be seen as a type-free extension of DTDs with vertical regular expressions. Sets of such rules can be interpreted both in an existential or universal way. In the present paper, we study the succinctness of both semantics w.r.t. each other and w.r.t. the common abstraction of XSDs in terms of single-type extended DTDs. The investigation is carried out relative to three kinds of vertical pattern languages: regular, linear, and strongly linear patterns. We also consider the complexity of the simplification problem for each of the considered pattern-based schema's.

1 Introduction

In formal language theoretic terms, an XML schema defines a tree language. The for historical reasons still widespread Document Type Definitions (DTDs) can then be seen as context-free grammars with regular expressions at right-hand sides which define the local tree languages [1]. XML Schema [10] extends the expressiveness of DTDs by a typing mechanism allowing content-models to depend on the type rather than only on the label of the parent. Unrestricted application of such typing leads to the robust class of unranked regular tree languages [1] as embodied in the XML schema language Relax NG [3]. The latter language is commonly abstracted in the literature by extended DTDs (EDTDs) [9]. The Element Declarations Consistent constraint in the XML Schema specification, however, restricts this typing: it forbids the occurrence of different types of the same element in the same content model. Murata et al. [8] therefore abstracted XSDs by single-type EDTDs. Martens et al. [7] subsequently characterized the expressiveness of single-type EDTDs in several syntactic and semantic ways. Among them, they defined an extension of DTDs equivalent in expressiveness to single-type EDTDs: ancestor-guarded DTDs. An advantage of this language is that it makes the expressiveness of XSDs more apparent: the content model of an element can only depend on regular string properties of the string formed

* Research Assistant of the Fund for Scientific Research - Flanders (Belgium).

M. Arenas and M.I. Schwartzbach (Eds.): DBPL 2007, LNCS 4797, pp. 201–215, 2007.

Table 1. Overview of complexity results for translating pattern-based schema's into other schema formalisms. For all non-polynomial complexities, except the ones marked with a star, there exist examples matching this upper bound. Theorem numbers are given between brackets.

	other semantics	EDTD	EDTDst	DTD
$\mathcal{P}_\exists$(Reg)	2-exp (14(1))	exp (14(2))	exp (14(3))	exp* (14(5))
$\mathcal{P}_\forall$(Reg)	2-exp (14(6))	2-exp (14(7))	2-exp (14(8))	2-exp (14(10))
$\mathcal{P}_\exists$(Lin)	\ (16(1))	exp (16(2))	exp (16(3))	exp* (16(5))
$\mathcal{P}_\forall$(Lin)	\ (16(6))	2-exp (16(7))	2-exp (16(8))	2-exp (16(10))
$\mathcal{P}_\exists$(S-Lin)	poly (19(1))	poly (19(2))	poly (19(3))	poly (19(6))
$\mathcal{P}_\forall$(S-Lin)	poly (19(7))	poly (19(8))	poly (19(9))	poly (19(12))
$\mathcal{P}_\exists$(Det-S-Lin)	poly (19(1))	poly (19(2))	poly (19(3))	poly (19(6))
$\mathcal{P}_\forall$(Det-S-Lin)	poly (19(7))	poly (19(8))	poly (19(9))	poly (19(12))

by the ancestors of that element. Ancestor-based DTDs can therefore be used as a type-free front-end for XML Schema. As they can be interpreted both in an existential and universal way, we study in this paper the complexity of translating between the two semantics and into the formalisms of DTDs, EDTDs, and single-type EDTDs.

In the remainder of the paper, we use the name pattern-based schema, rather than ancestor-based DTD, as it emphasizes the dependence on a particular pattern language. A pattern-based schema is a set of rules of the form (r, s), where r and s are regular expressions. An XML tree is then existentially valid w.r.t. a rule set if for each node there is a rule such that the path from the root to that node matches r and the child sequence matches s. Furthermore, it is universally valid if each node vertically matching r, horizontally matches s. The existential semantics is exhaustive, fully specifying every allowed combination, and more DTD-like, whereas the universal semantics is more liberal, enforcing constraints only where necessary.

Kasneci and Schwentick studied the complexity of the satisfiability and inclusion problem for pattern-based schemas under the existential ($\exists$) and universal ($\forall$) semantics [6]. They considered regular (Reg), linear (Lin), and strongly linear (S-Lin) patterns. These correspond to the regular expressions, XPath-expressions with only child (/) and descendant (//), and XPath-expressions of the form $//w$ or $/w$, respectively. A snapshot of their results is given in the third and fourth column of Table 2. These results indicate that there is no difference between the existential and universal semantics.

We, however, show that with respect to succinctness there is a huge difference. Our results are summarized in Table 1. Both for the pattern languages Reg and Lin, the universal semantics is exponentially more succinct than the existential one when translating into (single-type) extended DTDs and ordinary DTDs. Furthermore, our results show that the general class of pattern-based schemas is ill-suited to serve as a front-end for XML Schema due to the inherent exponential or double exponential size increase after translation. Only when resorting to S-Lin patterns, there are translations only requiring polynomial size increase.

Table 2. Overview of complexity results for pattern-based schema's. All results, unless indicated otherwise, are completeness results. Theorem numbers for the new results are given between brackets.

	SIMPLIFICATION	SATISFIABILITY	INCLUSION
$\mathcal{P}_\exists$(Reg)	EXPTIME (14(4))	EXPTIME [6]	EXPTIME [6]
$\mathcal{P}_\forall$(Reg)	EXPTIME (14(9))	EXPTIME [6]	EXPTIME [6]
$\mathcal{P}_\exists$(Lin)	PSPACE (16(4))	PSPACE [6]	PSPACE [6]
$\mathcal{P}_\forall$(Lin)	PSPACE (16(9))	PSPACE [6]	PSPACE [6]
$\mathcal{P}_\exists$(S-Lin)	PSPACE (19(4))	PSPACE [6]	PSPACE [6]
$\mathcal{P}_\forall$(S-Lin)	PSPACE (19(10))	PSPACE [6]	PSPACE [6]
$\mathcal{P}_\exists$(Det-S-Lin)	in PTIME (19(5))	in PTIME [6]	in PTIME [6]
$\mathcal{P}_\forall$(Det-S-Lin)	in PTIME (19(11))	in PTIME [6]	in PTIME [6]

Fortunately, the practical study in [7] shows that the sort of typing used in XSDs occurring in practice can be described by such patterns. Our results further show that the expressive power of the existential and the universal semantics coincide for Reg and S-Lin, albeit a translation can not avoid a double exponential size increase in general in the former case. For linear patterns the expressiveness is incomparable. Finally, as listed in Table 2, we study the complexity of the simplification problem: given a pattern-based schema, is it equivalent to a DTD?

Outline. The paper is further organized as follows. In Section 2, we recall the necessary definitions concerning regular expressions, schema languages, and pattern-based schemas. We define the decision problems we consider and introduce a notation for succinctness. In Section 3, 4, and 5, we study pattern-based schemas with regular, linear, and strongly linear expressions, respectively. We conclude in Section 6. A version of this paper containing all proofs is available from the authors' webpages.

2 Preliminaries

In this section, we recall the necessary definitions and results concerning regular expressions, schema languages for XML and pattern-based schemas. We also formally define the problems we address.

2.1 Regular Expressions

For the rest of the paper, Σ always denotes a finite alphabet. A *Σ-symbol* (or simply symbol) is an element of Σ, and a *Σ-string* (or simply string) is a finite sequence $w = a_1 \cdots a_n$ of Σ-symbols. We define the length of w, denoted by $|w|$, to be n. We denote the empty string by ε. The set of *positions of* w is $\{1, \ldots, n\}$ and the *symbol of w at position i* is a_i. By $w_1 \cdot w_2$ we denote the *concatenation* of two strings w_1 and w_2. For readability, we usually denote the concatenation of w_1 and w_2 by w_1w_2. The set of all strings is denoted by Σ^* and the set of all non-empty strings by Σ^+. A *string language* is a subset of Σ^*. For two string languages $L, L' \subseteq \Sigma^*$, we define their concatenation $L \cdot L'$ to be the set $\{w \cdot w' \mid w \in L, w' \in L'\}$. We abbreviate $L \cdot L \cdots L$ (i times) by L^i.

The set of *regular expressions* over Σ, denoted by RE, is defined in the usual way: $\emptyset$, ε, and every Σ-symbol is a regular expression; and when r_1 and r_2 are regular expressions, then $r_1 \cdot r_2$, $r_1 + r_2$, and r_1^* are also regular expressions. The language defined by a regular expression r, denoted by $L(r)$, is inductively defined as follows: $L(\emptyset) = \emptyset$; $L(\varepsilon) = \{\varepsilon\}$; $L(a) = \{a\}$; $L(r_1 r_2) = L(r_1) \cdot L(r_2)$; $L(r_1 + r_2) = L(r_1) \cup L(r_2)$; and $L(r^*) = \{\varepsilon\} \cup \bigcup_{i=1}^{\infty} L(r)^i$. The *size* of a regular expression r over Σ, denoted by $|r|$, is the number of Σ-symbols and operators occurring in r. By $r?$, r^+, and r^k, with $k \in \mathbb{N}$, we abbreviate the expression $r + \varepsilon$, rr^*, and $rr \cdots r$ (k times), respectively. For a set $S = \{a_1, \ldots, a_n\} \subseteq \Sigma$, we denote by S^* the regular expression $(a_1 + \cdots + a_n)^*$. The sets of prefixes and suffixes of strings defined by r are $\text{Prefix}(r) = \{w \mid \exists v \in \Sigma^*, wv \in L(r)\}$ and $\text{Suffix}(r) = \{w \mid \exists v \in \Sigma^*, vw \in L(r)\}$.

A non-deterministic finite automaton (NFA) A is a 4-tuple (Q, q_0, δ, F) where Q is the set of states, q_0 is the initial state, F is the set of final states and $\delta \subseteq Q \times \Sigma \times Q$ is the transition relation. We write $q \Rightarrow_{A,w} q'$ when w takes A from state q to q'.

We use the following theorem of Glaister and Shallit [5].

Theorem 1 ([5]). *Let $L \subseteq \Sigma^*$ be a regular language and suppose there exists a set of pairs $M = \{(x_i, w_i) \mid 1 \leq i \leq n\}$ such that*

- *$x_i w_i \in L$ for $1 \leq i \leq n$; and*
- *$x_i w_j \notin L$ for $1 \leq i, j \leq n$ and $i \neq j$.*

Then any NFA accepting L has at least n states.

We make use of the following results on transformations of regular expressions. Theorem 2(3-4) are from [4].

Theorem 2. *1. Let $r_1, \ldots, r_n, s_1, \ldots, s_m$ be regular expressions. A regular expression r, with $L(r) = \bigcap_{i \leq n} L(r_i) \setminus \bigcup_{i \leq m} L(s_i)$, can be constructed in time double exponential in the sum of the sizes of all r_i, s_j, $i \leq n$, $j \leq m$.*

2. Let $r_1, \ldots, r_n$ be regular expressions. A regular expression r, with $L(r) = \bigcap_{i \leq n} L(r_i)$, can be constructed in time double exponential in the sum of the sizes of all r_i, $i \leq n$.

3. For every $n \in \mathbb{N}$, there are a linear number of regular expressions $r_1, \ldots, r_m$ of size linear in n such that any regular expression r with $L(r) = \bigcap_{i \leq m} L(r_i)$ must be of size at least double exponential in n.

4. For every $n \in \mathbb{N}$, there is a regular expression r_n of size linear in n such that any regular expression r defining $\Sigma^* \setminus L(r_n)$ is of size at least double exponential in r.

5. For any regular expressions r and alphabet $\Delta \subseteq \Sigma$, an expression r^-, such that $L(r^-) = L(r) \cap \Delta^*$, can be constructed in time linear in the size of r.

2.2 Schema Languages for XML

The set of *unranked* Σ*-trees*, denoted by $\mathcal{T}_\Sigma$, is the smallest set of strings over Σ and the parenthesis symbols "(" and ")" such that, for $a \in \Sigma$ and $w \in (\mathcal{T}_\Sigma)^*$, $a(w)$ is in $\mathcal{T}_\Sigma$. So, a tree is either ε (empty) or is of the form $a(t_1 \cdots t_n)$ where each t_i is a tree. In the tree $a(t_1 \cdots t_n)$, the subtrees $t_1, \ldots, t_n$ are attached to the root labeled a. We write a rather than $a()$. Notice that there is no a priori bound on the number of children of a node in a Σ-tree; such trees are therefore *unranked.* For every $t \in \mathcal{T}_\Sigma$, the *set of nodes* of t, denoted by Dom(t), is the set defined as follows: *(i)* if $t = \varepsilon$, then $\text{Dom}(t) = \emptyset$; and *(ii)* if $t = a(t_1 \cdots t_n)$, where each $t_i \in \mathcal{T}_\Sigma$, then $\text{Dom}(t) = \{\varepsilon\} \cup \bigcup_{i=1}^{n} \{iu \mid u \in \text{Dom}(t_i)\}$. For a node $u \in \text{Dom}(t)$, we denote the label of u by $\text{lab}^t(u)$. By $\text{anc-str}^t(u)$ we denote the sequence of labels on the path from the root to u including both the root and u itself, and $\text{ch-str}^t(u)$ denotes the string formed by the labels of the children of u, i.e., $\text{lab}^t(u1) \cdots \text{lab}^t(un)$. In the sequel, whenever we say tree, we always mean Σ-tree. Denote by $t_1[u \leftarrow t_2]$ the tree obtained from a tree t_1 by replacing the subtree rooted at node u of t_1 by t_2. By $\text{subtree}^t(u)$ we denote the subtree of t rooted at u. A *tree language* is a set of trees.

We make use of the following definitions to abstract from the commonly used schema languages [7]:

Definition 3. *Let $\mathcal{R}$ be a class of representations of regular string languages over Σ.*

1. *A* DTD($\mathcal{R}$) *over Σ is a tuple (Σ, d, s_d) where d is a function that maps Σ-symbols to elements of $\mathcal{R}$ and $s_d \in \Sigma$ is the start symbol. For notational convenience, we sometimes denote (Σ, d, s_d) by d and leave the start symbol s_d implicit.*
   A tree t satisfies *d if* (i) *$lab^t(\varepsilon) = s_d$ and,* (ii) *for every $u \in Dom(t)$ with n children, $lab^t(u1) \cdots lab^t(un) \in L(d(lab^t(u)))$. By $L(d)$ we denote the set of trees satisfying d.*
2. *An* extended DTD *(EDTD($\mathcal{R}$)) over Σ is a 5-tuple $D = (\Sigma, \Sigma', d, s, \mu)$, where Σ' is an alphabet of* types, *(Σ', d, s) is a DTD($\mathcal{R}$) over Σ', and μ is a mapping from Σ' to Σ.*
   A tree t then satisfies *an extended DTD if $t = \mu(t')$ for some $t' \in L(d)$. Here we abuse notation and let μ also denote its extension to define a homomorphism on trees. Again, we denote by $L(D)$ the set of trees satisfying D. For ease of exposition, we always take $\Sigma' = \{a^i \mid 1 \leq i \leq k_a, a \in \Sigma, i \in \mathbb{N}\}$ for some natural numbers k_a, and we set $\mu(a^i) = a$.*
3. *A* single-type EDTD *(EDTDst($\mathcal{R}$)) over Σ is an EDTD($\mathcal{R}$) $D = (\Sigma, \Sigma', d, s, \mu)$ with the property that for every $a \in \Sigma'$, in the regular expression $d(a)$ no two types b^i and b^j with $i \neq j$ occur.*

We denote by EDTD, and EDTDst the classes EDTD(RE), and EDTDst(RE), respectively. As explained in [7,8], EDTDs and single-type EDTDs correspond to Relax NG and XML Schema, respectively. Furthermore, EDTDs correspond to the unranked regular languages [1], while single-type EDTDs form a strict subset thereof [7].

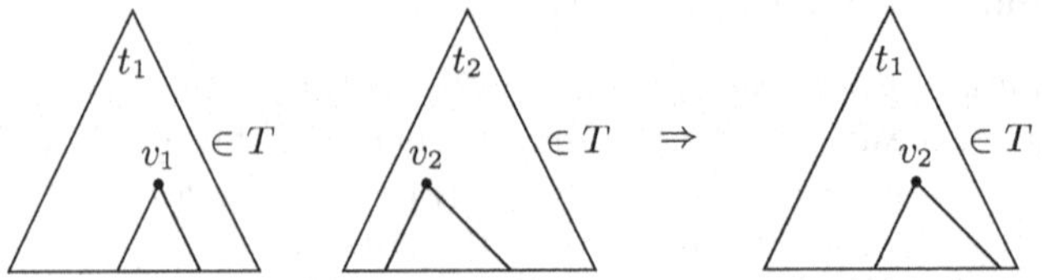

Fig. 1. Closure under label-guarded subtree exchange

A regular tree language $\mathcal{T}$ is closed under *label-guarded subtree exchange* if it has the following property: if two trees t_1 and t_2 are in $\mathcal{T}$, and there are two nodes v_1 in t_1 and v_2 in t_2 with the same label, then $t_1[v_1 \leftarrow \text{subtree}^{t_2}(v_2)]$ is also in $\mathcal{T}$. This notion is graphically illustrated in Figure 1.

Lemma 4 ([9]). *A regular tree language is definable by a DTD iff it is closed under label-guarded subtree exchange.*

An EDTD $D = (\Sigma, \Sigma', d, s_d, \mu)$ is *trimmed* if for for every $\mathsf{a}^i \in \Sigma'$, there exists a tree $t \in L(d)$ and a node $u \in \text{Dom}(t)$ such that $\text{lab}^t(u) = \mathsf{a}^i$.

Lemma 5. *[7]*

1. *For every EDTD D, a trimmed EDTD D', with $L(D) = L(D')$, can be constructed in time polynomial in the size of D.*
2. *Let D be a trimmed EDTD. For any type $\mathsf{a}^i \in \Sigma'$ and any string $w \in L(d(\mathsf{a}^i))$ there exists a tree $t \in L(d)$ which contains a node v with $lab^t(v) = \mathsf{a}^i$ and $ch\text{-}str^t(v) = w$.*

We give another schema formalism equivalent to single-type EDTDs. An *automaton-based schema* D over vocabulary Σ is a tuple (A, λ), where $A = (Q, q_0, \delta, F)$ is a DFA and λ is a function mapping states of A to regular expressions. A tree t is accepted by D if for every node v of t, where $q \in Q$ is the state such that $q_0 \Rightarrow_{A,\text{anc-str}(v)} q$, $\text{ch-str}(v) \in L(\lambda(q))$. Because the set of final states F of A is not used, we often omit F and represent A as a triple (Q, q_0, δ).

Remark 6. *Because DTDs and EDTDs only define tree languages in which every tree has the same root element, we implicitly assume that this is also the case for automaton-based schema's and the pattern-based schema's defined next. Whenever we translate among pattern-based schema's, we drop this assumption. Obviously, this does not influence any of the results of this paper.*

Lemma 7. *Any automaton-based schema D can be translated into an equivalent single-type EDTD D' in time at most quadratic in the size of D, and vice versa.*

2.3 Pattern-Based XML Schemas

We recycle the following definitions from [6].

Definition 8. *A* pattern-based schema P *is a set* $\{(r_1, s_1), \ldots, (r_m, s_m)\}$ *where all* r_i, s_i *are regular expressions.*

Each pair (r_i, s_i) of a pattern-based schema represents a schema rule. We also refer to the r_i and s_i as the vertical and horizontal regular expressions, respectively. There are two semantics for pattern-based schemas.

Definition 9. *A tree* t *is* existentially valid *with respect to a pattern-based schema* P *if, for every node* v *of* t*, there is a rule* $(r, s) \in P$ *such that* $\text{anc-str}(v) \in L(r)$ *and* $\text{ch-str}(v) \in L(s)$*. In this case, we write* $P \models_\exists t$*.*

Definition 10. *A tree* t *is* universally valid *with respect to a pattern-based schema* P *if, for every node* v *of* t*, and each rule* $(r, s) \in P$ *it holds that* $\text{anc-str}(v) \in L(r)$ *implies* $\text{ch-str}(v) \in L(s)$*. In this case, we write* $P \models_\forall t$*.*

Denote by $P_\exists(t) = \{v \in \text{Dom}(t) \mid \exists(r, s) \in P, \text{anc-str}(v) \in L(r) \wedge \text{ch-str}(v) \in L(s)\}$ the set of nodes in t that are existentially valid. Denote by $P_\forall(t) = \{v \in \text{Dom}(t) \mid \forall(r, s) \in P, \text{anc-str}(v) \in L(r) \Rightarrow \text{ch-str}(v) \in L(s)\}$ the set of nodes in t that are universally valid.

We denote the set of Σ-trees which are existentially and universally valid with respect to P by $\mathcal{T}_\exists^\Sigma(P)$ and $\mathcal{T}_\forall^\Sigma(P)$, respectively. We often omit the existential or universal quantifier if it is clear from the context which semantics is meant. Likewise, we usually drop Σ.

When for every string $w \in \Sigma^*$ there is a rule $(r, s) \in P$ such that $w \in L(r)$, then we say that P is *complete.* Further, when for every pair $(r, s), (r', s') \in P$ of different rules, $L(r) \cap L(r') = \emptyset$, then we say that P is *disjoint.*

In some proofs, we make use of unary trees, which can be represented as strings. In this context, we abuse notation and write for instance $w \in \mathcal{T}_\exists(P)$ meaning that the unary tree which w represents is existentially valid with respect to P. Similarly, we refer to the last position of w as the leaf of w.

Lemma 11. *For a pattern-based schema* P*, a tree* t *and a string* w

1. $t \in \mathcal{T}_\forall(P)$ *iff for every node* v *of* t*,* $v \in P_\forall(t)$*.*
2. *if* $w \in \mathcal{T}_\forall(P)$ *then for every prefix* w' *of* w *and every non-leaf node* v *of* w'*,* $v \in P_\forall(w')$*.*
3. $t \in \mathcal{T}_\exists(P)$ *iff for every node* v *of* t*,* $v \in P_\exists(t)$*.*
4. *if* $w \in \mathcal{T}_\exists(P)$ *then for every prefix* w' *of* w *and every non-leaf node* v *of* w'*,* $v \in P_\exists(w')$*.*

Lemma 12. *For any complete and disjoint pattern-based schema* P*,* $\mathcal{T}_\exists(P) = \mathcal{T}_\forall(P)$*.*

2.4 Problems

We give an overview of the problems studied by Schwentick and Kasneci [6] and the ones studied in this paper. We define all problems for the existential semantics, and leave the identical definitions for the universal semantics implicit.

Definition 13. *Given pattern-based schemas P, P'*

- SATISFIABILITY *for P: Is there a non-empty tree t such that $t \in \mathcal{T}_\exists(P)$?*
- INCLUSION *for P, P': Is $\mathcal{T}_\exists(P) \subseteq \mathcal{T}_\exists(P')$?*
- SIMPLIFICATION *for P: Does there exist a DTD D with $\mathcal{T}_\exists(P) = L(D)$?*

2.5 Succinctness

We introduce some additional notation to characterize the complexity of translating pattern-based schema's into DTDs and (single-type) EDTDs.

For a class $\mathcal{S}$ and $\mathcal{S}'$ of representations of schema languages, and F a class of functions from $\mathbb{N}$ to $\mathbb{N}$, we write $\mathcal{S} \xrightarrow{F} \mathcal{S}'$ if there is an $f \in F$ such that for every $s \in \mathcal{S}$ there is an $s' \in \mathcal{S}'$ with $L(s) = L(s')$ which can be constructed in time $f(|s|)$. This also implies that $|s'| \leq f(|s|)$. By $L(s)$ we mean the set of trees defined by s.

We write $\mathcal{S} \overset{F}{\Rightarrow} \mathcal{S}'$ if $\mathcal{S} \xrightarrow{F} \mathcal{S}'$ and there is an $f \in F$, a monotonically increasing function $g : \mathbb{N} \to \mathbb{N}$ and an infinite family of schema's $s_n \in \mathcal{S}$ with $|s_n| \leq g(n)$ such that the smallest $s' \in \mathcal{S}'$ with $L(s) = L(s')$ is at least of size $f(g(n))$. By poly, exp and 2-exp we denote the classes of functions $\bigcup_{k,c} cn^k$, $\bigcup_{k,c} c2^{n^k}$ and $\bigcup_{k,c} c2^{2^{n^k}}$, respectively.

Further, we write $\mathcal{S} \not\rightarrow \mathcal{S}'$ if there exists an $s \in \mathcal{S}$ such that for every $s' \in \mathcal{S}'$, $L(s') \neq L(s)$. In this case we also write $\mathcal{S} \overset{F}{\not\rightarrow} \mathcal{S}'$ and $\mathcal{S} \overset{F}{\not\Rightarrow} \mathcal{S}'$ whenever $\mathcal{S} \xrightarrow{F} \mathcal{S}'$ and $\mathcal{S} \overset{F}{\Rightarrow} \mathcal{S}'$, respectively, hold for those elements in $\mathcal{S}$ which do have an equivalent element in $\mathcal{S}'$.

3 Regular Pattern-Based Schema's

In this section, we study the full class of pattern-based schema's which we denote by $\mathcal{P}_\exists(\text{Reg})$ and $\mathcal{P}_\forall(\text{Reg})$. The results are shown in Theorem 14. We only give sketches of some proofs.

Theorem 14. *1.* $\mathcal{P}_\exists(Reg) \overset{2\text{-}exp}{\Rightarrow} \mathcal{P}_\forall(Reg)$
2. $\mathcal{P}_\exists(Reg) \overset{exp}{\Rightarrow}$ *EDTD*
3. $\mathcal{P}_\exists(Reg) \overset{exp}{\Rightarrow}$ *EDTD*st
4. SIMPLIFICATION *for* $\mathcal{P}_\exists(Reg)$ *is* EXPTIME-*complete.*
5. $\mathcal{P}_\exists(Reg) \overset{exp}{\not\rightarrow}$ *DTD*
6. $\mathcal{P}_\forall(Reg) \overset{2\text{-}exp}{\Rightarrow} \mathcal{P}_\exists(Reg)$
7. $\mathcal{P}_\forall(Reg) \overset{2\text{-}exp}{\Rightarrow}$ *EDTD*
8. $\mathcal{P}_\forall(Reg) \overset{2\text{-}exp}{\Rightarrow}$ *EDTD*st
9. SIMPLIFICATION *for* $\mathcal{P}_\forall(Reg)$ *is* EXPTIME-*complete.*
10. $\mathcal{P}_\forall(Reg) \overset{2\text{-}exp}{\not\Rightarrow}$ *DTD*

Proof. (1) We first show $\mathcal{P}_\exists(\text{Reg}) \overset{\text{2-exp}}{\rightarrow} \mathcal{P}_\forall(\text{Reg})$. Let $P = \{(r_1, s_1), \ldots, (r_n, s_n)\}$. We show that we can construct a complete and disjoint pattern-based schema P' such that $\mathcal{T}_\exists(P) = \mathcal{T}_\exists(P')$ in time double exponential in the size of P. By Lemma 12, $\mathcal{T}_\exists(P') = \mathcal{T}_\forall(P')$ and thus $\mathcal{T}_\exists(P) = \mathcal{T}_\forall(P')$.

For any non-empty set $C \subseteq \{1, \ldots, n\}$, denote by r_C the regular expression which defines the language $\bigcap_{i \in C} L(r_i) \setminus \bigcup_{1 \leq i \leq n, i \notin C} L(r_i)$ and by $r_\emptyset$ the expression defining $\Sigma^* \setminus \bigcup_{1 \leq i \leq n} L(r_i)$. That is, r_C defines any word w which is defined by all vertical expressions contained in C but is not defined by any vertical expression not contained in C. Denote by s_C the expression defining the language $\bigcup_{i \in C} L(s_i)$. Then, $P' = \{(r_\emptyset, \emptyset)\} \cup \{(r_C, s_C) \mid C \subseteq \{1, \ldots, n\} \wedge C \neq \emptyset\}$. Now, $\mathcal{P}_\exists(\text{Reg}) \overset{\text{2-exp}}{\rightarrow} \mathcal{P}_\forall(\text{Reg})$ follows from the facts that $\mathcal{T}_\exists(P) = \mathcal{T}_\exists(P')$ and that P' can be constructed from P in time double exponential in the size of P.

To show that $\mathcal{P}_\exists(\text{Reg}) \overset{\text{2-exp}}{\Rightarrow} \mathcal{P}_\forall(\text{Reg})$, we slightly extend Theorem 2(4).

Lemma 15. *For every $n \in \mathbb{N}$, there is a regular expressions r_n of size linear in n such that any regular expression r defining $\Sigma^* \setminus L(r_n)$ is of size at least double exponential in r. Further, r_n has the property that for any string $w \notin L(r_n)$, there exists a string u such that $wu \in L(r_n)$.*

Now, let $n \in \mathbb{N}$ and let r_n be a regular expression over Σ satisfying the conditions of Lemma 15. Then, define $P_n = \{(r_n, \varepsilon), (\Sigma^*, \Sigma)\}$. Here, $\mathcal{T}_\exists(P_n)$ defines all unary trees w for which $w \in L(r_n)$.

Let P be a pattern-based schema with $\mathcal{T}_\exists(P_n) = \mathcal{T}_\forall(P)$. Define $U = \{r \mid (r, s) \in P \wedge \varepsilon \notin L(s)\}$ as the set of vertical regular expressions in P whose corresponding horizontal regular expression does not contain the empty string. Finally, let r be the disjunction of all expressions in U. Then, since $L(r) = \Sigma^* \setminus L(r_n)$, the size of P must be at least double exponential in n.

(4) For the upperbound, we combine a number of results of Kasneci and Schwentick [6] and Martens et. al [7]. In the following, an NTA(NFA) is a non-deterministic tree automaton where the transition relation is represented by an NFA. A DTD(NFA) is a DTD where content models are defined by NFAs.

Given a pattern-based schema P, we first construct an NTA(NFA) A_P with $L(A_P) = \mathcal{T}_\exists(P)$, which can be done in exponential time (Proposition 3.3 in [6]). Then, Martens et. al. [7] have shown that given any NTA(NFA) A_P it is possible to construct, in time polynomial in the size of A_P, a DTD(NFA) D_P such that $L(A_P) \subseteq L(D_P)$ and $L(A_P) = L(D_P)$ iff $L(A_P)$ is definable by a DTD. Summarizing, D_P is of size exponential in P, $\mathcal{T}_\exists(P) \subseteq L(D_P)$ and $\mathcal{T}_\exists(P)$ is definable by a DTD iff $\mathcal{T}_\exists(P) = L(D_P)$.

Now, construct another NTA(NFA)$A_{\neg P}$ which defines the complement of $\mathcal{T}_\exists(P)$. This can again be done in exponential time (Proposition 3.3 in [6]). Since $\mathcal{T}_\exists(P) \subseteq L(D_P)$, $\mathcal{T}_\exists(P) = L(D_P)$ iff $L(D_P) \cap L(A_{\neg P}) \neq \emptyset$. Here, D_P and $A_{\neg P}$ are of size at most exponential in the size of P, and testing the non-emptiness of their intersection can be done in time polynomial in the size of D_P and $A_{\neg P}$. This gives us an EXPTIME algorithm overall.

For the lower bound, we reduce from SATISFIABILITY of pattern-based schema's, which is EXPTIME-complete [6].

(6) The proof of $\mathcal{P}_\forall(\text{Reg}) \overset{\text{2-exp}}{\rightarrow} \mathcal{P}_\exists(\text{Reg})$ is along the same lines as that of Theorem 14(1).

We show that $\mathcal{P}_\forall(\text{Reg}) \overset{\text{2-exp}}{\Rightarrow} \mathcal{P}_\exists(\text{Reg})$. Let $n \in \mathbb{N}$. According to Theorem 2(2), there exist a linear number of regular expressions $r_1, \ldots, r_m$ of size linear in n such that any regular expression defining $\bigcap_{i \leq m} L(r_i)$ must be of size at least double exponential in n. For brevity, define $K = \bigcap_{i \leq m} L(r_i)$.

Define P_n over the alphabet $\Sigma_a = \Sigma \uplus \{a\}$, for $a \notin \Sigma$, as $P_n = \{(a, r_i) \mid i \leq m\} \cup \{(ab, \varepsilon) \mid b \in \Sigma\} \cup \{(b, \emptyset) \mid b \in \Sigma\}$. That is, $\mathcal{T}_\forall(P_n)$ contains all trees $a(w)$, where $w \in K$.

Let P be a pattern-based schema with $\mathcal{T}_\forall(P_n) = \mathcal{T}_\exists(P)$. For an expression s, denote by s^- the expression defining all words in $L(s) \cap \Sigma^*$. According to Theorem 2(5), s^- can be constructed from s in linear time. Define $U = \{s^- \mid (r, s) \in P \wedge a \in L(r)\}$ as the set of horizontal regular expressions whose corresponding vertical regular expressions contains the string a. Finally, let r_K be the disjunction of all expressions in U. Then, $L(r_K) = K$, and thus must the size of P be at least double exponential in n. □

4 Linear Pattern-Based Schema's

In this section, following [6], we restrict the vertical expressions to XPath expressions using only descendant and child axes. For instance, an XPath expression $\backslash\backslash a \backslash\backslash b \backslash c$ captures all nodes that are labeled with c, have b as parent and have an a as ancestor. This corresponds to the regular expression $\Sigma^* a \Sigma^* bc$.

Formally, we call an expression *linear* if it is of the form $w_0 \Sigma^* \cdots w_{n-1} \Sigma^* w_n$, with $w_0, w_n \in \Sigma^*$, and $w_i \in \Sigma^+$ for $1 \leq i < n$. A pattern-based schema is *linear* if all its vertical expressions are linear. Denote the classes of linear schema's under existential and universal semantics by $\mathcal{P}_\exists(\text{Lin})$ and $\mathcal{P}_\forall(\text{Lin})$, respectively.

Theorem 16 lists the results for linear schema's. The complexity of SIMPLIFICATION improves slightly, PSPACE instead of EXPTIME. Further, we show that the expressive power of linear schema's under existential and universal semantics becomes incomparable, but that the complexity of translating to DTDs and (single-type) EDTDs is in general not better than for regular pattern-based schema's.

Theorem 16. *1.* $\mathcal{P}_\exists(Lin) \not\rightarrow \mathcal{P}_\forall(Lin)$
2. $\mathcal{P}_\exists(Lin) \overset{exp}{\Rightarrow} EDTD$
3. $\mathcal{P}_\exists(Lin) \overset{exp}{\Rightarrow} EDTD^{st}$
4. SIMPLIFICATION *for* $\mathcal{P}_\exists(Lin)$ *is* PSPACE-*complete.*
5. $\mathcal{P}_\exists(Lin) \overset{exp}{\not\rightarrow} DTD$
6. $\mathcal{P}_\forall(Lin) \not\rightarrow \mathcal{P}_\exists(Lin)$
7. $\mathcal{P}_\forall(Lin) \overset{2\text{-}exp}{\Rightarrow} EDTD$
8. $\mathcal{P}_\forall(Lin) \overset{2\text{-}exp}{\Rightarrow} EDTD^{st}$
9. SIMPLIFICATION *for* $\mathcal{P}_\forall(Lin)$ *is* PSPACE-*complete.*
10. $\mathcal{P}_\forall(Lin) \overset{2\text{-}exp}{\not\Rightarrow} DTD$

Proof. (1) First, consider the following simple lemma. Given an alphabet Σ, and a symbol $b \in \Sigma$, denote $\Sigma \setminus \{b\}$ by Σ_b.

Lemma 17. *There does not exist a set of linear regular expression* $r_1, \ldots, r_n$ *such that* $\bigcup_{1 \leq i \leq n} L(r_i)$ *is an infinite language and* $\bigcup_{1 \leq i \leq n} L(r_i) \subseteq L(\Sigma_b^*)$.

Now, let $P = \{(\Sigma^* b \Sigma^*, \varepsilon), (\Sigma^*, \Sigma)\}$. Then, $\mathcal{T}_\exists(P)$ defines all unary trees containing at least one b. Suppose that P' is a linear schema such that $\mathcal{T}_\exists(P) = \mathcal{T}_\forall(P')$. Define $U = \{r \mid (r,s) \in P' \text{ and } \varepsilon \notin L(s)\}$ as the set of all vertical regular expressions in P' whose horizontal regular expressions do not contain the empty string. We show that the union of the expressions in U defines an infinite language and is a subset of Σ_b^*, which by Lemma 17 proves that such a schema P' can not exist.

First, to show that the union of these expressions defines an infinite language, suppose that it does not. Then, every expression $r \in U$ is of the form $r = w$, for some string w. Let k be the length of the longest such string w. Now, $a^{k+1}b \in \mathcal{T}_\exists(P) = \mathcal{T}_\forall(P')$ and thus by Lemma 11(2) every non-leaf node v of a^{k+1} is in $P'_\forall(a^{k+1})$. Further, $a^{k+1} \notin L(r)$ for all vertical expressions in U and thus the leaf node of a^{k+1} is also in $P'_\forall(a^{k+1})$. But then, by Lemma 11(1), $a^{k+1} \in \mathcal{T}_\forall(P')$ which leads to the desired contradiction.

Second, let $w \in L(r)$, for some $r \in U$, we show $w \in \Sigma_b^*$. Towards a contradiction, suppose $w \notin \Sigma_b^*$, which means that w contains at least one b and thus $w \in \mathcal{T}_\exists(P) = \mathcal{T}_\forall(P')$. But then, for the leaf node v of w, $\text{anc-str}(v) = w \in L(r)$, and by definition of U, $\text{ch-str}(v) = \varepsilon \notin L(s)$, where s is the corresponding horizontal expression for r. Then, $v \notin P'_\forall(w)$ and thus by Lemma 11(1), $w \notin \mathcal{T}_\forall(P')$, which again gives the desired contradiction.

(2-3) First, $\mathcal{P}_\exists(\text{Lin}) \stackrel{\text{exp}}{\rightarrow} \text{EDTD}^{\text{st}}$ follows immediately from Theorem 14(3). We show $\mathcal{P}_\exists(\text{Lin}) \stackrel{\text{exp}}{\Rightarrow} \text{EDTD}$, which then implies both statements. Thereto, we first characterize the expressive power of EDTDs over unary tree languages.

Lemma 18. *For any EDTD D for which $L(D)$ is a unary tree language, there exists an NFA A such that $L(D) = L(A)$. Moreover, A can be computed from D in time linear in the size of D.*

Now, let $n \in \mathbb{N}$. Define $\Sigma_n = \{\$, \#_1, \#_2\} \cup \bigcup_{1 \leq i \leq n} \{a_i^0, a_i^1, b_i^0, b_i^1\}$ and $K_n = \{\#_1 a_1^{i_1} a_2^{i_2} \cdots a_n^{i_n} \$ b_1^{i_1} b_2^{i_2} \cdots b_n^{i_n} \#_2 \mid i_k \in \{0,1\}, 1 \leq k \leq n\}$. It is not hard to see that any NFA defining K_n must be of size at least exponential in n. Indeed, in Theorem 1, define $M = \{(x,w) \mid xw \in K_n \wedge |x| = n+1\}$ which is of size exponential in n, and satisfies the conditions of Theorem 1. Then, by Lemma 18, every EDTD defining the unary tree language K_n must also be of size exponential in n. We conclude the proof by giving a pattern-based schema P_n, such that $\mathcal{T}_\exists(P_n) = K_n$, which is of size linear in n. It contains the following rules:

- $\#_1 \rightarrow a_1^0 + a_1^1$
- For any $i < n$:
  - $\#_1 \Sigma^* a_i^0 \rightarrow a_{i+1}^0 + a_{i+1}^1$
  - $\#_1 \Sigma^* a_i^1 \rightarrow a_{i+1}^0 + a_{i+1}^1$

  - $\#_1\Sigma^* a_i^0 \Sigma^* b_i^0 \to b_{i+1}^0 + b_{i+1}^1$
  - $\#_1\Sigma^* a_i^1 \Sigma^* b_i^1 \to b_{i+1}^0 + b_{i+1}^1$
- $\#_1\Sigma^* a_n^0 \to \$$
- $\#_1\Sigma^* a_n^1 \to \$$
- $\#_1\Sigma^* \$ \to b_1^0 + b_1^1$
- $\#_1\Sigma^* a_n^0 \Sigma^* b_n^0 \to \#_2$
- $\#_1\Sigma^* a_n^1 \Sigma^* b_n^1 \to \#_2$
- $\#_1\Sigma^* \#_2 \to \varepsilon$

(4) For the lower bound, we reduce from UNIVERSALITY of regular expressions. That is, deciding for a regular expression r whether $L(r) = \Sigma^*$. The latter problem is known to be PSPACE-complete [11]. Given r over alphabet Σ, let $\Sigma^P = \{a, b, c, d\} \uplus \Sigma$, and define the pattern-based schema $P = \{(a, b + c), (ab, e), (ac, e), (abe, \Sigma^*), (ace, r)\} \cup \{(abe\sigma, \varepsilon), (ace\sigma, \varepsilon) \mid \sigma \in \Sigma\}$. We show that there exists a DTD D with $L(D) = \mathcal{T}_\exists(P)$ iff $L(r) = \Sigma^*$.

If $L(r) = \Sigma^*$, then the following DTD d defines $\mathcal{T}_\exists(P)$: $d(a) = b + c$, $d(b) = e$, $d(c) = e$, $d(e) = \Sigma^*$, and $d(\sigma) = \varepsilon$ for every $\sigma \in \Sigma$.

Conversely, if $L(r) \subsetneq \Sigma^*$, we show that $\mathcal{T}_\exists(P)$ is not closed under label-guarded subtree exchange. From Lemma 4, it then follows that $\mathcal{T}_\exists(P)$ is not definable by a DTD. Let w, w' be strings such that $w \notin L(r)$ and $w' \in L(r)$. Then, $a(b(e(w))) \in L(D)$, and $a(c(e(w'))) \in L(D)$ but $a(c(e(w))) \notin \mathcal{T}_\exists(P)$.

For the upper bound, we again make use of the closure under label-guarded subtree exchange property of DTDs. Observe that $\mathcal{T}_\exists(P)$, which is a regular tree language, is not definable by any DTD iff there exist trees $t_1, t_2 \in \mathcal{T}_\exists(P)$ and nodes v_1 and v_2 in t_1 and t_2, respectively, with $\text{lab}^{t_1}(v_1) = \text{lab}^{t_2}(v_2)$, such that the tree $t_3 = t_1[v_1 \leftarrow \text{subtree}^{t_2}(v_2)]$ is not in $\mathcal{T}_\exists(P)$. It can be shown that if there exist such trees t_1, t_2 then there also exist such trees t_1', t_2' of polynomial depth, which allows us to give a PSPACE algorithm for the problem.

(6) Let $\Sigma = \{a, b, c\}$ and define $P = \{(\Sigma^* b \Sigma^* c, b)\}$. Then, $\mathcal{T}_\forall(P)$ contains all trees in which whenever a c labeled node v has a b labeled node as ancestor, ch-str(v) must be b. We show that any linear schema P' defining all trees in $\mathcal{T}_\forall(P)$ under existential semantics, must also define trees not in $\mathcal{T}_\forall(P)$.

Suppose there does exist a linear schema P' such that $\mathcal{T}_\forall(P) = \mathcal{T}_\exists(P')$. Define $w_\ell = a^\ell c$ for $\ell \geq 1$ and note that $w_\ell \in \mathcal{T}_\forall(P) = \mathcal{T}_\exists(P')$. Let $(r, s) \in P'$ be a rule matching infinitely many leaf nodes of the strings w_ℓ. There must be at least one as P' contains a finite number of rules. Then, $\varepsilon \in L(s)$ must hold and r is of one of the following forms:

1. $a^{n_1} \Sigma^* a^{n_2} \Sigma^* \cdots \Sigma^* a^{n_k} c$
2. $a^{n_1} \Sigma^* a^{n_2} \Sigma^* \cdots \Sigma^* a^{n_k} c \Sigma^*$
3. $a^{n_1} \Sigma^* a^{n_2} \Sigma^* \cdots \Sigma^* a^{n_k} \Sigma^*$

where $k \geq 2$ and $n_k \geq 0$.

Choose some $N \in \mathbb{N}$ with $N \geq |P'|$ and define the unary trees $t_1 = a^N b a^N cb$ and $t_2 = a^N b a^N c$. Obviously, $t_1 \in \mathcal{T}_\forall(P)$, and $t_2 \notin \mathcal{T}_\forall(P)$. Then, $t_1 \in \mathcal{T}_\exists(P')$ and since t_2 is a prefix of t_1, by Lemma 11(4), every non-leaf node v of t_2 is in $P'_\exists(t_2)$. Finally, for the leaf node v of t_2, anc-str$(v) \in L(r)$ for any of the three expressions given above and $\varepsilon \in L(s)$ for its corresponding horizontal expression. Then, $v \in P'_{\exists}(t_2)$, and thus by Lemma 11(3), $t_2 \in \mathcal{T}_{\exists}(P')$ which completes the proof. □

5 Strongly Linear Pattern-Based Schema's

In [7], it is observed that the type of a node in most real-world XSDs only depends on the labels of its parents and grand parents. To capture this idea, following [6], we say that a regular expression is *strongly linear* if it is of the form w or $\Sigma^* w$, where w is non-empty. A pattern-based schema is *strongly linear* if it is disjoint and all its vertical expressions are strongly linear. Denote the class of all strongly linear pattern-based schema's under existential and universal semantics by $\mathcal{P}_{\exists}$(S-Lin) and $\mathcal{P}_{\forall}$(S-Lin), respectively.

In [6], all horizontal expressions in a strongly linear schema are also required to be deterministic or one-unambiguous [2], as is the case for DTDs and XML Schema. The latter requirement is necessary to get PTIME SATISFIABILITY and INCLUSION which would otherwise be PSPACE-complete for arbitrary regular expressions. This is also the case for the SIMPLIFICATION problem studied here, but not for the various translation problems. Therefore, we distinguish between strongly linear schema's, as defined above, and strongly linear schema's where all horizontal expressions must be deterministic, which we call *deterministic strongly linear schema's* and denote by $\mathcal{P}_{\exists}$(Det-S-Lin) and $\mathcal{P}_{\forall}$(Det-S-Lin).

Theorem 19 shows the results for (deterministic) strongly linear pattern-based schema's. First, observe that the expressive power of these schema's under existential and universal semantics again coincides. Further, all considered problems become tractable, which makes strongly linear schema's very interesting from a practical point of view.

Theorem 19. *1.* $\mathcal{P}_{\exists}(\text{S-Lin}) \overset{poly}{\rightarrow} \mathcal{P}_{\forall}(\text{S-Lin})$ *and* $\mathcal{P}_{\exists}(\text{Det-S-Lin}) \overset{poly}{\rightarrow} \mathcal{P}_{\forall}(\text{Det-S-Lin})$

2. $\mathcal{P}_{\exists}(\text{S-Lin}) \overset{poly}{\rightarrow} \text{EDTD}$ *and* $\mathcal{P}_{\exists}(\text{Det-S-Lin}) \overset{poly}{\rightarrow} \text{EDTD}$
3. $\mathcal{P}_{\exists}(\text{S-Lin}) \overset{poly}{\rightarrow} \text{EDTD}^{st}$ *and* $\mathcal{P}_{\exists}(\text{Det-S-Lin}) \overset{poly}{\rightarrow} \text{EDTD}^{st}$
4. SIMPLIFICATION *for* $\mathcal{P}_{\exists}$*(S-Lin) is* PSPACE*-complete.*
5. SIMPLIFICATION *for* $\mathcal{P}_{\exists}$*(Det-S-Lin) is in* PTIME.
6. $\mathcal{P}_{\exists}(\text{S-Lin}) \overset{poly}{\not\rightarrow} \text{DTD}$ *and* $\mathcal{P}_{\exists}(\text{Det-S-Lin}) \overset{poly}{\not\rightarrow} \text{DTD}$
7. $\mathcal{P}_{\forall}(\text{S-Lin}) \overset{poly}{\rightarrow} \mathcal{P}_{\exists}(\text{S-Lin})$ *and* $\mathcal{P}_{\forall}(\text{Det-S-Lin}) \overset{poly}{\rightarrow} \mathcal{P}_{\exists}(\text{Det-S-Lin})$
8. $\mathcal{P}_{\forall}(\text{S-Lin}) \overset{poly}{\rightarrow} \text{EDTD}$ *and* $\mathcal{P}_{\forall}(\text{Det-S-Lin}) \overset{poly}{\rightarrow} \text{EDTD}$
9. $\mathcal{P}_{\forall}(\text{S-Lin}) \overset{poly}{\rightarrow} \text{EDTD}^{st}$ *and* $\mathcal{P}_{\forall}(\text{Det-S-Lin}) \overset{poly}{\rightarrow} \text{EDTD}^{st}$
10. SIMPLIFICATION *for* $\mathcal{P}_{\forall}$*(S-Lin) is* PSPACE*-complete.*
11. SIMPLIFICATION *for* $\mathcal{P}_{\forall}$*(Det-S-Lin) is in* PTIME.
12. $\mathcal{P}_{\forall}(\text{S-Lin}) \overset{poly}{\not\rightarrow} \text{DTD}$ *and* $\mathcal{P}_{\forall}(\text{Det-S-Lin}) \overset{poly}{\not\rightarrow} \text{DTD}$

Proof. (1) We show $\mathcal{P}_{\exists}(\text{S-Lin}) \overset{\text{poly}}{\rightarrow} \mathcal{P}_{\forall}(\text{S-Lin})$. The key of this proof lies in the following lemma:

Lemma 20. *For each finite set R of disjoint strongly linear expressions, a finite set S of disjoint strongly linear regular expressions can be constructed in* PTIME *such that* $\bigcup_{s\in S} L(s) = \Sigma^*\setminus\bigcup_{r\in R} L(r)$.

We show how this lemma implies the theorem. For $P = \{(r_1,s_1),\ldots,(r_n,s_n)\}$, let S be the set of strongly linear expressions for $R = \{r_1,\ldots,r_n\}$ satisfying the conditions of Lemma 20. Set $P' = P \cup \bigcup_{s\in S}\{(s,\emptyset)\}$. Here, $\mathcal{T}_\exists(P) = \mathcal{T}_\exists(P')$ and since P' is disjoint and complete it follows from Lemma 12 that $\mathcal{T}_\exists(P') = \mathcal{T}_\forall(P')$. This gives us $\mathcal{T}_\exists(P) = \mathcal{T}_\forall(P')$. By Lemma 20, the set S is polynomial time computable and therefore, P' is too.

(3) We show $\mathcal{P}_\exists(\text{S-Lin}) \overset{\text{poly}}{\rightarrow} \text{EDTD}^{\text{st}}$. Given P, we construct an automaton-based schema $D = (A,\lambda)$ such that $L(D) = \mathcal{T}_\exists(P)$. By Lemma 7, we can then translate D into an equivalent single-type EDTD in polynomial time. Let $P = \{(r_1,s_1),\ldots,(r_n,s_n)\}$. We define D such that when A is in state q after reading w, $\lambda(q) = s_i$ iff $w \in L(r_i)$ and $\lambda(q) = \emptyset$ otherwise. The most obvious way to construct A is by constructing DFAs for the vertical expressions and combining these by a product construction. However, this would induce an exponential blow-up. Instead, we construct A in polynomial time in a manner similar to the construction used in Proposition 5.2 in [6].

First, assume that every r_i is of the form $\Sigma^* w_i$. The following construction can be extended to also handle vertical expressions of the form w_i. Define $S = \{w \mid w \in \text{Prefix}(w_i), 1 \le i \le n\}$. Then, $A = (Q, q_0, \delta)$ is defined as $Q = S \cup \{q_0\}$, and for each $a \in \Sigma$,

- $\delta(q_0,a) = a$ if $a \in S$, and $\delta(q_0,a) = q_0$ otherwise; and
- for each $w \in S$, $\delta(w,a) = w'$, where w' is the longest suffix of wa in S, and $\delta(w,a) = q_0$ if no string in S is a suffix of wa.

For the definition of λ, let $\lambda(q_0) = \emptyset$, and for all $w \in S$, $\lambda(w) = s_i$ if $w \in L(r_i)$ and $\lambda(w) = \emptyset$ if $w \notin L(r_i)$ for all $i \le n$. Note that since the vertical expression are disjoint, λ is well-defined. □

6 Conclusion

In this paper, we studied the succinctness of pattern-based schema's under existential and universal semantics with respect to each other and the common schema formalisms: DTDs, EDTDs, and single-type EDTDs. This is done for regular, linear, and strongly linear pattern-based schema's. The main observation is that schema's under existential semantics behave at least as good or better than the corresponding schema's under universal semantics. In some translations a double exponential blow-up can even not be avoided. However, almost all problems for the class of strongly linear schema's turn out to be tractable, which makes this class very interesting from a practical point of view.

As our main motivation comes from using pattern-based schema's as a front-end to more traditional schema languages like XSDs, we only studied the translation of pattern-based schema's to these formalisms. However, it would also be interesting to see results for translations in the other direction. We leave open the exact complexity of translating from regular and linear schema's under existential semantics to DTDs, and of the transformation of linear schema's between the two semantics.

References

1. Brüggemann-Klein, A., Murata, M., Wood, D.: Regular tree and regular hedge languages over unranked alphabets. Technical report, The Hongkong University of Science and Technologiy (April 3, 2001)
2. Brüggemann-Klein, A., Wood, D.: One-unambiguous regular languages. Information and Computation 142(2), 182–206 (1998)
3. Clark, J., Murata, M.: RELAX NG Specification. OASIS (December 2001)
4. Gelade, W., Neven, F.: Succinctness of the complement and intersection of regular expressions. Manuscript (2007)
5. Glaister, I., Shallit, J.: A lower bound technique for the size of nondeterministic finite automata. Inf. Process. Lett. 59(2), 75–77 (1996)
6. Kasneci, G., Schwentick, T.: The complexity of reasoning about pattern-based XML schemas. In: PODS, pp. 155–163 (2007)
7. Martens, W., Neven, F., Schwentick, T., Bex, G.: Expressiveness and complexity of XML schema. ACM Trans. Database Syst. 31(3), 770–813 (2006)
8. Murata, M., Lee, D., Mani, M., Kawaguchi, K.: Taxonomy of XML schema languages using formal language theory. ACM Trans. Internet Techn. 5(4), 660–704 (2005)
9. Papakonstantinou, Y., Vianu, V.: DTD inference for views of XML data. In: PODS, pp. 35–46 (2000)
10. Sperberg-McQueen, C.M., Thompson, H.: XML Schema (2005), `http://www.w3.org/XML/Schema`
11. Stockmeyer, L.J., Meyer, A.R.: Word problems requiring exponential time: Preliminary report. In: STOC, pp. 1–9 (1973)

Analysis of Imperative XML Programs

Michael G. Burke[1], Igor Peshansky[1], Mukund Raghavachari[1], and Christoph Reichenbach[2,⋆]

[1] IBM T. J. Watson Research Center
{mgburke,igorp,raghavac}@us.ibm.com
[2] University of Colorado at Boulder
reichenb@colorado.edu

Abstract. The widespread adoption of XML has led to programming languages that support XML as a first class construct. In this paper, we present a method for analyzing and optimizing imperative XML processing programs. In particular, we present a program analysis, based on a flow-sensitive type system, for detecting both redundant computations and redundant traversals in XML processing programs. The analysis handles declarative queries over XML data and imperative loops that traverse XML values explicitly in a uniform framework. We describe two optimizations that take advantage of our analysis: one merges queries that traverse the same set of XML nodes, and the other replaces an XPath expression by a previously computed result. We show the effectiveness of our method by providing performance measurements on XMark benchmark queries and XLinq sample queries.

1 Introduction

XML processing applications in imperative languages such as Java and C# use runtime APIs such as DOM [18], or language-based approaches such as XLinq [2], XJ [5], or XAct [7]. In either case, the programmer is provided with an XML data model and navigational constructs. The XML data model is typically an object view, where each element in an XML document is instantiated as an object. The navigational constructs range from library routines that access children of a node in an XML tree, to comprehensions, to queries in declarative query languages such as XPath [17].

The imperative nature of systems such as XLinq and XJ poses challenges that differ from those in declarative languages such as XQuery. Consider the program in Figure 1 written in a language based on XJ. Assume that in Line 1, x is set to refer to some XML value. The XPath expression on Line 2 can be interpreted as computing the set of all descendants of the root of the tree referred to by x such that each member of the result is labeled book and has an attribute author with value 'Poe'. Similarly, the XPath expression on Line 5 can be interpreted as computing the set of all publisher descendants of x. Some challenges in the optimization of such programs are:

- **Query identification:** Queries may be latent in a program where programmers combine imperative traversals (with variable assignment) with declarative queries.

⋆ This work was supported in part by NSF Career Grant CCR-0133457.

M. Arenas and M.I. Schwartzbach (Eds.): DBPL 2007, LNCS 4797, pp. 216–230, 2007.

```
1  x = ...;
2  y = $x//book[@author='Poe'];
3  u = $x//book;
4  v = $u[@author='Poe'];
5  z = $x//publisher;
6  k = ∅;
7  foreach i in u {
8      System.out.println(i);
9      if ($i[@author='Poe'])
10         k ⇐ i
11 }
```

Fig. 1. Example demonstrating redundant computations

Consider the loop that begins on Line 7 of Figure 1. The statement on Line 10 can be interpreted as k = k ∪ {i}—the accumulate operator "⇐" models the invocation of a method such as add on an instance of the Set class in Java. Observe that at the end of the loop, k is guaranteed to contain the same value as y. While the loop itself is not redundant (it has effects), the computation of k certainly is.

- **Optimizations across Multiple Queries:** The detection of two queries (or subqueries) that return the same results could be used to remove redundant computation. The complication in this analysis is that there are many ways of writing equivalent queries (including as explicit loops), which precludes the use of syntactic techniques such as value numbering [1,6]. In all executions of the program of Figure 1, the variable v on Line 4 will refer to the same value as y—the computation of v is redundant.

  Further, two different computations over an XML tree may not produce the same value, but visit the same set of nodes in performing the computations. The two computations could be combined to return the two results in one traversal of the tree. This transformation is called *tupling*. Consider the expressions in Lines 2 and 5. They traverse the same set of nodes (the subtree rooted at x), but filter these sets in different ways—both sets of results can be produced efficiently in one traversal.

This paper studies the analysis of imperative XML processing programs, where traversals over data may be specified in many ways—as explicit loops over data and in terms of XPath expressions. We present a program analysis, based on a flow-sensitive type system, for detecting both redundant computations and redundant traversals in XML processing programs. The analysis handles both loops that traverse XML values explicitly and declarative query expressions in a uniform framework. For exposition, we focus on a core language for XML processing based on the XJ programming language. Our techniques are applicable to other languages with XML support, such as XLinq, to imperative derivatives of XQuery, such as XQueryP [3], and also to invocations of runtime APIs such as DOM (if the compiler detects invocations of XPath expressions on DOM objects as special operations).

The contributions of this paper are an analysis, based on a flow-sensitive type system, that computes a symbolic representation of the values assumed by each XML expression or variable in a program, a description of transformations enabled by the analysis, and experiment results demonstrating the effectiveness of the optimizations.

Structure of the Paper. Section 2 introduces the XML processing language that we use as the basis of the exposition of our analysis. In Section 3 we describe the types that track the values of expressions and variables in programs, and formally define correctness criteria for our analysis. In Section 4 we present a flow-sensitive type system for detecting redundant computations and traversals. We describe the transformations enabled by the analysis in Section 5. Section 6 describes our implementation and experimental results. Section 7 presents related work, and we conclude in Section 8.

2 Syntax and Semantics

We model XML documents as ordered, labeled trees. $\mathfrak{T}$ refers to the set of all such trees, and $\mathcal{N}$ is the (infinite) set of all nodes used in trees in $\mathfrak{T}$. Each node n in each XML tree has unique identity and a label, $\text{LABEL}(n)$, drawn from an infinite alphabet Σ (we use uppercase characters (A, B, C) to represent members of Σ).

For exposition, we focus on a fragment of XPath 1.0 [17], whose (somewhat non-standard) syntax is listed in Figure 2. The evaluation of an XPath expression is always with respect to a set of nodes in XML trees (the nodes could belong to different XML trees) and the result is a set of nodes. The operators $\downarrow$ and $\downarrow^+$ represent the *child* and *descendant* traversals, that is, they return the union of the set of children and the set of descendants of the nodes in the input node set, respectively. In the syntax, s ranges over Σ and it represents a node test, which filters its inputs with respect to s. The semantics of these expressions is standard and is also provided in Figure 2.

$$Xp ::= \epsilon \mid \downarrow \mid \downarrow^+ \mid s \mid Xp/Xp \mid Xp[Xp] \mid Xp[\neg Xp]$$

$$[\![\cdot]\!] : \mathcal{P}(\mathcal{N}) \rightarrow \mathcal{P}(\mathcal{N})$$

$$\begin{aligned}
&[\![\epsilon]\!](N) = N\\
&[\![\downarrow]\!](N) = \bigcup\{child(n) \mid n \in N\}\\
&[\![\downarrow^+]\!](N) = \bigcup\{descendant(n) \mid n \in N\}\\
&[\![s]\!](N) = \{n \in N \mid \text{LABEL}(n) = s\}\\
&[\![Xp_1/Xp_2]\!](N) = [\![Xp_2]\!]([\![Xp_1]\!](N))\\
&[\![Xp_1[Xp_2]]\!](N) = \{n \in [\![Xp_1]\!](N) \mid [\![Xp_2]\!](\{n\}) \neq \varnothing\}\\
&[\![Xp_1[\neg Xp_2]]\!](N) = \{n \in [\![Xp_1]\!](N) \mid [\![Xp_2]\!](\{n\}) = \varnothing\}
\end{aligned}$$

Fig. 2. Syntax and semantics of XPath-like expressions

We describe a core imperative language for XML processing that serves as the domain for our static analysis. The syntax for the language is provided in Figure 3. For simplicity, we have not included XML literal-based construction, XML updates, effects (such as I/O or Java-like constructs), a more expressive XPath fragment, or schema information in our core language. The handling of these constructs is mostly orthogonal to the central ideas of this paper. We discuss the extension of our analysis to support these issues in Section 4.4.

In the language, there are three disjoint, finite sets of variables—*Id*, *IndexVar*, and *DocVar*. *IndexVar* may only appear in foreach statements, where each foreach statement has a unique *IndexVar*. The *DocVar* represents some input XML document or XML construction. Only *Id* variables may be on the left-hand side of assignments or accumulations. *IndexVar* are updated implicitly by loops and *DocVar* remain constant through the program.

$$
\begin{aligned}
\mathit{Var} &::= \mathit{Id} \mid \mathit{IndexVar} \mid \mathit{DocVar} \\
\mathit{Expr} &::= \mathit{Var} \mid \$\mathit{Var}\ /\ \mathit{Xp} \mid \varnothing \\
\mathit{Stmt} &::= \mathit{Id} = \mathit{Expr} \\
&\mid\ \mathit{Id} \Leftarrow \mathit{Expr} \\
&\mid\ \textsf{if}\ (\mathit{Expr})\ \textsf{then}\ \mathit{Stmt}\ \textsf{else}\ \mathit{Stmt} \\
&\mid\ \textsf{foreach}\ \mathit{IndexVar}\ \textsf{in}\ \mathit{Expr}\ \mathit{Stmt} \\
&\mid\ \mathit{Stmt}\ ;\ \mathit{Stmt} \\
&\mid\ \textsf{skip}
\end{aligned}
$$

Fig. 3. Language syntax

The semantics of program execution is provided in Figure 4. A value in the language is a subset of $\mathcal{N}$. A store σ maps each program variable to such a value. $\langle S, \sigma\rangle \Downarrow \sigma'$, where σ, σ' are *stores*, represents that the evaluation of statement S takes the program from store σ to σ'. $\langle \mathit{Expr}, \sigma\rangle \models \mathit{value}$ states that expression *Expr* evaluates to value, given store σ.

A program is a *Stmt*. In the inital store, each *Id* variable used in the program is mapped to $\varnothing$, and each *DocVar* variable used in the program is mapped to the root node of some tree in $\mathfrak{T}$. The expression $*Var/Xp* evaluates the XPath expression Xp with respect to the set of nodes specified by *Var*. We refer to *Var* as the *context variable* of the XPath expression.

The foreach loop iterates over the value denoted by its *Expr*, which we call the loop's *iteration space*; for each node in this set, it binds the *IndexVar* to a singleton set consisting of that node, and then evaluates the *Stmt* in the new store. Since an index variable is only defined within a loop, it is removed from the result store of the loop. The execution of foreach is non-deterministic (the elements are visited in some unspecified order). The statement skip has no effect on the store. The accumulate statement, $x \Leftarrow y$, sets x to the equivalent of $x \cup y$. Observe that one can express general union operations, *i.e.*, $x = y \cup z$, with a pattern like $x = y;\ x \Leftarrow z$.

Consider the code sample in Figure 5. Line 1 sets x to the singleton set containing the root of some XML tree that is refered to by the *DocVar* d. The foreach loop on lines 3–7 iterates over an XPath expression evaluated with respect to the value referred to by x. This expression returns a set of nodes containing all B descendants of the root node of the tree referenced in Line 1. In each iteration of the loop, if a particular B node has a C child, then the B node is added to y. At the end of the loop, y will refer to the equivalent of the expression $\$x/{\downarrow^+}/B[\downarrow/C]$.

$$\text{VAR}\ \frac{N = \sigma(x)}{\langle x, \sigma\rangle \models N} \qquad \text{XPATH}\ \frac{N = \sigma(x), N' = [\![Xp]\!](N)}{\langle \$x/Xp, \sigma\rangle \models N'} \qquad \text{EMPTY}\ \frac{}{\langle \varnothing, \sigma\rangle \models \varnothing}$$

$$\text{ASSIGN}\ \frac{\langle Expr, \sigma\rangle \models N}{\langle \mathsf{x} = Expr, \sigma\rangle \Downarrow \sigma[x \mapsto N]} \qquad \text{ACCUM}\ \frac{\langle Expr, \sigma\rangle \models N \qquad N' = \sigma(x) \cup N}{\langle x \Leftarrow Expr, \sigma\rangle \Downarrow \sigma[x \mapsto N']}$$

$$\text{IF-THEN}\ \frac{\langle Expr, \sigma\rangle \models N, N \neq \varnothing \qquad \langle S_1, \sigma\rangle \Downarrow \sigma'}{\langle \mathsf{if}(Expr)\ \mathsf{then}\ S_1\ \mathsf{else}\ S_2, \sigma\rangle \Downarrow \sigma'} \qquad \text{IF-ELSE}\ \frac{\langle Expr, \sigma\rangle \models \varnothing \qquad \langle S_2, \sigma\rangle \Downarrow \sigma'}{\langle \mathsf{if}(Expr)\ \mathsf{then}\ S_1\ \mathsf{else}\ S_2, \sigma\rangle \Downarrow \sigma'}$$

$$\text{FOREACH}\ \frac{\begin{array}{c}\langle Expr, \sigma\rangle \models \{x_1, x_2, \ldots, x_k\} \\ \langle S, \sigma[i \mapsto \{x_1\}]\rangle \Downarrow \sigma_1 \\ \vdots \\ \langle S, \sigma_{k-1}[i \mapsto \{x_k\}]\rangle \Downarrow \sigma_k\end{array}}{\langle \mathsf{foreach}\ i\ \mathsf{in}\ Expr\ S, \sigma\rangle \Downarrow \sigma_k \backslash i} \qquad \text{COMPOSE}\ \frac{\langle S, \sigma\rangle \Downarrow \sigma' \qquad \langle S', \sigma'\rangle \Downarrow \sigma''}{\langle S; S', \sigma\rangle \Downarrow \sigma''} \qquad \text{SKIP}\ \frac{}{\langle \mathsf{skip}, \sigma\rangle \Downarrow \sigma}$$

Fig. 4. Semantics of language

```
x = d;
y = ∅;
foreach i in $x/ ↓+ /B
  if ($i/ ↓ /C) then
    y ⇐ i
  else
    skip
```

Fig. 5. Sample program

3 Types

The types in our type system are the "don't know" type or ξ; the "empty" type or $\varnothing$, which denotes that a variable or expression evaluates to an empty set; types of the form $(\$\mathsf{x}, Xp, \Psi)$, where Ψ is a set $\{\psi_1, \ldots, \psi_k\}$ and each ψ_i is of the form τ or $\neg\tau$, and union types, $\tau_1 \cup \tau_2$.

$$\tau ::= \xi \mid \varnothing \mid (\$\mathsf{x}, Xp, \Psi) \mid \tau \cup \tau'$$

$$\Psi = \{\psi_1, \ldots, \psi_k\}, \text{where } \psi_i ::= \tau \mid \neg\tau$$

In a type $(\$\mathsf{x}, Xp, \Psi)$, x is either a *DocVar* or an *IndexVar* and Xp is an XPath expression. For such a type, we refer to x as the *context variable* of the type, and Ψ as the *filter* of the type. If a variable has the type $(\$\mathsf{d}, \epsilon, \varnothing)$, under all executions, the variable refers to the node to which the store maps d. The type $(\$\mathsf{d}, \epsilon, \Psi)$ is equivalent to $(\$\mathsf{d}, \epsilon, \varnothing)$ if the denotation of each $\psi \in \Psi$ is non-empty, and to $\varnothing$ otherwise.

More precisely, the denotation of a type τ is defined in terms of a store σ. The denotation, $[\![\tau]\!]_\sigma$, is a subset of $\mathcal{N}$ or a distinguished set ξ. The semantics of the types is defined as:

$$[\![\xi]\!]_\sigma = \xi \qquad [\![\varnothing]\!]_\sigma = \varnothing \qquad [\![\tau_1 \cup \tau_2]\!]_\sigma = [\![\tau_1]\!]_\sigma \cup [\![\tau_2]\!]_\sigma$$

$$[\![(\$\mathsf{x}, Xp, \Psi)]\!]_\sigma = \begin{cases} [\![Xp]\!](\sigma(\mathsf{x})) & \mathsf{satisfied}(\Psi) = true \\ \xi & \mathsf{satisfied}(\Psi) = \xi \\ \varnothing & \text{otherwise} \end{cases}$$

The definition of **satisfied** relies on a notion of *equivalence* between two types τ and τ', denoted $\tau \equiv \tau'$, if for all σ, $[\![\tau]\!]_\sigma = [\![\tau']\!]_\sigma$. The function $\mathsf{satisfied}(\Psi)$ is a three-valued logic function:

$$\mathsf{satisfied}(\Psi) = \begin{cases} \xi & \exists \tau \in \Psi \vee \neg\tau \in \Psi, [\![\tau]\!]_\sigma \equiv \xi. \\ true & \forall \tau \in \Psi, [\![\tau]\!]_\sigma \not\equiv \varnothing \wedge \forall \neg\tau \in \Psi, [\![\tau]\!]_\sigma \equiv \varnothing \\ false & \text{otherwise} \end{cases}$$

A typing environment, Γ, maps program variables to types. Our goal is a type system that ensures that if two variables x and y are assigned equivalent types at a program point, then in all executions of the program, x and y refer to identical values at that program point. More formally, a store σ is *consistent* with a typing environment Γ, if for all $\mathsf{x} : \tau \in \Gamma$, $\tau \equiv \xi$ or $[\![\tau]\!]_\sigma = \sigma(\mathsf{x})$. With this definition of consistency, the soundness property is defined as follows:

Property 1 (Statement Typing Soundness). If a store σ is consistent with Γ, and $\Gamma\,\{S\}\,\Gamma'$ and $\langle S, \sigma\rangle \Downarrow \sigma'$, then σ' is consistent with Γ'.

By $\Gamma\,\{S\}\,\Gamma'$, we mean that if the type system starts in environment Γ, the environment at the end of S is Γ'. It should be clear that if a store σ is consistent with Γ and $\Gamma(\mathsf{x}) \equiv \Gamma(\mathsf{y})$, and $\Gamma(\mathsf{x}) \not\equiv \xi$, then x and y contain the same value at that point.

4 A Flow-Sensitive Type System

We first consider a type system for detecting when variables must refer to the same value in programs *without* loops. We then extend this type system to support loops. The typing judgments for expressions (Figure 6) are of the form $\Gamma \vdash \mathit{Expr} : \tau$.

It is straightforward to show that if a store σ is consistent with respect to an environment Γ, and $\langle \mathit{Expr}, \sigma\rangle \models N$, then $\Gamma \vdash \mathit{Expr} : \tau$ implies that $\tau \equiv \xi$ or $[\![\tau]\!]_\sigma = N$.

4.1 Analyzing Programs Without Loops

Figure 7 lists the judgments of our type system for statements other than foreach. The judgments are of the form $\Gamma\,\{S\}\,\Gamma'$. A program S is well typed if $\Gamma_\emptyset\,\{S\}\,\Gamma'$ is derivable, where $\Gamma_\emptyset$ assigns the $\varnothing$ type to each *Id*, and $(\$\mathsf{d}, \epsilon, \varnothing)$ to each *DocVar* d.

$$\frac{}{\vdash \varnothing : \varnothing} \qquad \frac{\mathsf{x} : \tau \in \Gamma}{\Gamma \vdash \mathsf{x} : \tau} \qquad \frac{\Gamma \vdash \mathsf{x} : \tau}{\Gamma \vdash \$\mathsf{x}/Xp : \tau \circ Xp}$$

$$\xi \circ Xp = \xi \qquad \varnothing \circ Xp = \varnothing \qquad (\$\mathsf{x}, Xp_1, \Psi) \circ Xp_2 = (\$\mathsf{x}, Xp_1/Xp_2, \Psi)$$

$$(\tau \cup \tau') \circ Xp = (\tau \circ Xp) \cup (\tau' \circ Xp)$$

Fig. 6. Expression type system

$$\text{ASSIGN}\ \frac{\Gamma \vdash \mathit{Expr} : \tau}{\Gamma\{x = \mathit{Expr}\}\ \Gamma[x \mapsto \tau]} \qquad \text{ACCUM}\ \frac{\Gamma \vdash \mathit{Expr} : \tau \qquad \Gamma \vdash x : \tau'}{\Gamma\{x \Leftarrow \mathit{Expr}\}\ \Gamma[x \mapsto \tau' \cup \tau]}$$

$$\text{SEQ}\ \frac{\Gamma\ \{S_1\}\ \Gamma' \qquad \Gamma'\ \{S_2\}\ \Gamma''}{\Gamma\ \{S_1; S_2\}\ \Gamma''} \qquad \text{IF}\ \frac{\Gamma \vdash \mathit{Expr} : \tau \qquad \Gamma\ \{S_1\}\ \Gamma' \qquad \Gamma\ \{S_2\} \Gamma'' \qquad \Gamma_f = \mathsf{merge}(\Gamma', \Gamma'', \tau)}{\Gamma\ \{\mathsf{if}\ \mathit{Expr}\ \mathsf{then}\ S_1\ \mathsf{else}\ S_2\}\ \Gamma_f}$$

$$\text{SKIP}\ \frac{}{\Gamma\ \{\mathsf{skip}\}\ \Gamma}$$

Fig. 7. Type system for programs without loops

The rule for accumulation reflects the set-based semantics of the operation—the resulting type is the union of the types of the two expressions in the accumulation.

The IF rule is designed to handle cases such as the following statement:

if c **then** y = \$c/Xp_2 **else** y = ∅

If the type of the variable c is $(\$\mathsf{d}, Xp_1, \varnothing)$, then ideally, the analysis should derive the type $(\$\mathsf{d}, Xp_1/Xp_2, \varnothing)$ for y at the end of the conditional. In any execution of the program, the store would either map c to ∅ or to a non-empty set of nodes. In the first case, the else branch would be taken, and $[\![(\$\mathsf{d}, Xp_1/Xp_2, \varnothing)]\!]_\sigma = \varnothing$, which is sound. If c is non-empty, then, again, $(\$\mathsf{d}, Xp_1/Xp_2, \varnothing)$ would be an appropriate type according to the \$x/Xp rule in Figure 6.

The typing rule evaluates the then and else branches of an if statement independently. The merge function is used to unify the environments obtained in the two branches. Its definition depends on that of the type constructor, $\tau[\psi]$. For a type τ and ψ, where ψ is of the form τ' or $\neg\tau'$, $\tau[\psi]$ is defined as follows:

$$\tau[\psi] = \begin{cases} \xi & \tau = \xi \vee \tau' = \xi \\ \varnothing & \tau = \varnothing \\ (\$\mathsf{d}, Xp, \Psi \cup \{\psi\}) & \tau = (\$\mathsf{d}, Xp, \Psi) \end{cases}$$

Definition 1. *The* merge$(\Gamma', \Gamma'', \tau)$ *function is a new environment* Γ_f *such that:*

$$\mathsf{merge}(\Gamma', \Gamma'', \tau) = \begin{cases} \Gamma'(\mathsf{x}) & \Gamma'(\mathsf{x}) \equiv \Gamma''(\mathsf{x}) \\ \Gamma'(\mathsf{x})[\tau] \cup \Gamma''(\mathsf{x})[\neg\tau] & \text{otherwise} \end{cases}$$

In short, the **merge** function encodes the control dependency in the type of a variable to ensure greater precision. In our example, the resulting type for y would be $(\$\mathsf{d}, Xp_1/Xp_2, \varnothing)$ in Γ', and $\varnothing$ in Γ''. The **merge** function would generate the type $(\$\mathsf{d}, Xp_1/Xp_2, \{(\$\mathsf{d}, Xp_1, \varnothing)\}) \cup \varnothing$, which can be simplified to $(\$\mathsf{d}, Xp_1/Xp_2, \varnothing)$, which is equivalent to $\Gamma_f(\mathsf{c}) \circ Xp_2$.

4.2 Handling Foreach Loops

In this section, we provide the rule for analyzing foreach loops. The rule is non-constructive—we discuss in the next section how the types can be assigned to statements in a foreach loop to satisfy this rule. To support accurate and precise handling of loops, we modify the operational semantics of loops to include two pseudovariables i^- and i^+, where i is the index of the loop. i^+ corresponds to the set of all nodes over which the loop has iterated, including the current iteration. i^- is similar, but does not include the current iteration. The types corresponding to i^- and i^+ are used to distinguish between the types of y = i (which will have the type $(\$\mathsf{i}, \epsilon, \varnothing)$) and y $\Leftarrow$ i (which will have type $(\$\mathsf{i}^+, \epsilon, \varnothing)$) in the scope of a loop, where i is the index variable.

FOREACH

$$\frac{\begin{array}{c}\langle \mathit{Expr}, \sigma\rangle \models \{x_1, x_2, \ldots, x_k\} \\ \langle S, \sigma[\mathsf{i} \mapsto \{x_1\}, \mathsf{i}^- \mapsto \varnothing, \mathsf{i}^+ \mapsto \{x_1\}]\rangle \Downarrow \sigma_1 \\ \vdots \\ \langle S, \sigma_{k-1}[\mathsf{i} \mapsto \{x_k\}, \mathsf{i}^- \mapsto \bigcup_{j=1}^{k-1}\{x_j\}, \mathsf{i}^+ \mapsto \bigcup_{j=1}^{k}\{x_j\}]\rangle \Downarrow \sigma_k\end{array}}{\langle \mathsf{foreach\ i\ in}\ \mathit{Expr}\ S, \sigma\rangle \Downarrow \sigma_k - \{\mathsf{i}, \mathsf{i}^+, \mathsf{i}^-\}}$$

Let Γ_s and Γ_f be the type environments at the start and end of the loop body, respectively. Let Γ_0 be the type environment at the statement immediately preceding the loop body. In a loop body, the typing rule for foreach should ensure that variables are assigned types that are consistent in any iteration of the loop. The typing rule for foreach is as follows:

FOREACH

$$\frac{\begin{array}{c}\Gamma_0 \vdash \mathit{Expr} : \tau \\ \mathsf{match}(\Gamma_0, \Gamma_s) \qquad \Gamma_s\{S\}\Gamma_f \\ \mathsf{valid}(\Gamma_s, \Gamma_f)\end{array}}{\Gamma_0\{\mathsf{foreach\ i\ in}\ Expr\ S\}\ \mathsf{promote}_\tau(\Gamma_f)}$$

$\mathsf{valid}(\Gamma_s, \Gamma_f)$ constrains the start and end environments of the loop body. Let $\mathsf{subst}(\tau)$ be the type derived from τ by replacing all instances of i^- in τ by i^+.

Definition 2. valid(Γ_s, Γ_f) *is satisfied if:*

1. *For each variable* x*, either* $\Gamma_s(\mathsf{x}) \equiv \Gamma_f(\mathsf{x})$ *or* $\Gamma_f(\mathsf{x}) \equiv \mathsf{subst}(\Gamma_s(\mathsf{x}))$.
2. *The type of no variable in* Γ_s *other than* i *can refer to* i*. Similarly, the type of no variable in* Γ_s *other than* i^+ *can refer to* i^+.

The rationale behind the first condition is that by the operational semantics, at the start of a new iteration of a loop, i^+ and i^- are modified so that i^- is equivalent to i^+ at the end of the previous iteration of the loop. Since the operational semantics of a foreach loop modifies the value of i at the head of a loop to contain a new value, it would be unsound for any other variable to be based on i or i^+. In any execution, the contents of that variable must have been based on the previous value of i or i^+. It is safe, however, for a type to refer to i^- since i^- at the head of a loop is equivalent to i^+ at the end of a loop. The valid function ensures that the types at the start and end of the loop match up. The existence of environments that satisfy the definition of valid requires the ability to convert types based on i^- to those based on i^+. Observe that the type $(\$\mathsf{i}^-, Xp, \Psi) \cup (\$\mathsf{i}, Xp, \Psi)$ is equivalent to $(\$\mathsf{i}^+, Xp, \Psi)$. Our algorithm for type assignment implements such rewritings when deriving appropriate types in a loop body.

The variables i, i^+, and i^- are not visible outside the body of the loop. The match (promote) function supports the composition of the type environment at the start (end) of a loop with preceding (following) statments by allowing these loop-based variables to be eliminated.

Definition 3. match(Γ_0 , Γ_s) *is true if for each variable* x*,* $\Gamma_0(\mathsf{x})$ *contains no references to* i*,* i^+*, and* i^-*, and either (1)* $\Gamma_0(\mathsf{x}) \equiv \Gamma_s(\mathsf{x})$ *or (2)* $\Gamma_0(\mathsf{x}) \equiv \varnothing$ *and* $\Gamma_s(\mathsf{x}) = (\$\mathsf{i}^-, Xp, \Psi)$.

Observe that the soundness of this composition relies on the fact that i^- is equivalent to $\varnothing$ at the start of the loop. The definition of promote at the end of the loop is dual — it converts instances of i^+ to types involving the iteration space of the loop.

Definition 4. $\mathsf{promote}_\tau(\tau')$*, where* $\tau = (\$d, Xp_1, \Psi_1)$ *and* τ' *is a type, is defined as*

$$\begin{cases} \xi & \tau' = \xi \\ \varnothing & \tau' = \varnothing \\ (\$d, Xp_1/Xp_2, \Psi_1 \cup \mathsf{promote}_\tau(\Psi_2)) & \tau' = (\$\mathsf{i}^+, Xp_2, \Psi_2) \\ (\$x, Xp, \mathsf{promote}_\tau(\Psi)) & \tau' = (\$x, Xp, \Psi) \end{cases}$$

$\mathsf{promote}_\tau(\Psi)$ *implies applying the function to each* τ*, where* τ *or* $\neg\tau$ *is in* Ψ*. We lift the* promote *function to environments by applying it to each binding in the environment.*

Finally, we introduce a subsumption rule to support the widening of the type of a variable.

$$\text{SUB}\quad \frac{\Gamma_1\,\{S\}\,\Gamma_1'}{\Gamma_2\,\{S\}\,\Gamma_2'} \quad \Gamma_1 \sqsubseteq \Gamma_2, \Gamma_2' \sqsubseteq \Gamma_1'$$

where $\Gamma \sqsubseteq \Gamma'$ if for all x, $\Gamma(x) \equiv \xi$ or $\Gamma(x) \equiv \Gamma'(x)$.

4.3 Assigning Types

The algorithm for assigning types to variables according to the typing rules depends on efficient mechanisms for detecting the equivalence of types, for simplifying union types, and for deriving an appropriate typing for loops.

There are several algorithms for determining the equivalence of XPath expressions [10,4]. Our analysis is orthogonal to the equivalence algorithm used; an appropriate algorithm could be chosen depending on the fragment of XPath supported. In our implementation, we use a straightforward algorithm based on matching the syntactic structure of types. Two types ($\$\mathsf{x}, Xp_1, \Psi_1$) and ($\$\mathsf{x}, Xp_2, \Psi_2$) are equivalent if Xp_1 is equivalent to Xp_2 and one can match each element in Ψ_1 with an element in Ψ_2. Xp_1 and Xp_2 are equivalent if the tree representations of Xp_1 and Xp_2 are identical modulo commutativity of predicates, that is, $\tau[\tau_1][\tau_2]$ is equivalent $\tau[\tau_2][\tau_1]$. While this syntactic matching is incomplete, it allows us in practice to detect equivalences in the presence of data value comparisons, count, and other functions that more complete algorithms do not handle [4].

For union types, we simplify types using straightforward rewriting rules where possible so that the equivalence heuristic mentioned previously can find matches. The rewriting rules are sound but incomplete. Specifically, for $\tau' = \tau_1 \cup \tau_2$, if $\tau_1 = \varnothing$, then $\tau' = \tau_2$, and vice-versa. Furthermore, if $\tau_1 = (\$\mathsf{x}, Xp, \{\tau_3\})$ and $\tau_2 = (\$\mathsf{x}, Xp, \{\neg\tau_3\})$, then $\tau' = (\$\mathsf{x}, Xp, \varnothing)$ is a valid rewriting. Also, as mentioned before, the type $(\$\mathsf{i}^-, Xp, \Psi) \cup (\$\mathsf{i}, Xp, \Psi)$ is converted to $(\$\mathsf{i}^+, Xp, \Psi)$. Finally, the type $(\$\mathsf{d}, Xp, \{(\$\mathsf{d}, Xp_1, \Psi)\})$ can be flattened to $(\$\mathsf{d}, Xp[Xp_1], \Psi)$, if d is known to always refer to a singleton set (a *DocVar* or *IndexVar*).

For loops, assume that we wish to derive an appropriate type environment Γ_s according to the foreach rule, given a Γ_0. We will sketch how we incrementally arrive at a Γ_s'' that will satisfy the conditons of the FOREACH typing rule.

Consider the typing rule for foreach. For a Γ_0 to *match* Γ_s, only variables that are $\varnothing$ in Γ_0 can have a different type in Γ_s. Let us call these variables *accumulators*. Observe that according to the definition of match, in Γ_s, the context variable for any accumulator must be i^-, where i is the index variable of the loop. We now sketch the algorithm for assigning types to these accumulators—the types of the accumulators must either be $\varnothing, \xi$, or a type with context variable i^-.

We start with $\Gamma_s = \Gamma_0$ and recursively assign types to the body of the loop. Let Γ_f be the type environment at the end of the body of the loop. We modify Γ_s to create a new typing environment Γ_s' as follows. If the type for an accumulator in Γ_f is $\varnothing$, its type in Γ_s' is $\varnothing$. If the type for an accumulator in Γ_f is $(\$\mathsf{i}, Xp, \Psi)$ or $(\$\mathsf{i}^+, Xp, \Psi)$, we set its type in Γ_s' to be $(\$\mathsf{i}^-, Xp, \Psi)$. Otherwise, we set its type to be ξ in Γ_s'. If any non-accumulator variable has a different type in Γ_s and Γ_f, we set its type to be ξ as well in Γ_s'.

Starting in Γ_s', we run the typing algorithm recursively for the body of the loop. Assume that the environment at the end of the loop is Γ_f'. We now create a final version of Γ_s, Γ_s''. Γ_s'' is essentially the same as Γ_s'. If for any accumulator in Γ_s' of the form $(\$\mathsf{i}^-, Xp, \Psi)$ that variable has type $(\$\mathsf{i}^+, Xp, \Psi)$ in Γ_f', then we leave it unchanged. Otherwise, we set its type to ξ. For any other variable, if the types of that variable are different in Γ'_s and Γ'_f, we set its type in Γ''_s to be ξ. Observe that Γ''_s is guaranteed by construction to satisfy all the conditions on Γ_s in the typing rule for foreach.

The above algorithm can be viewed as an iterative data flow algorithm, with the type environment representing the fixed point data flow solution. The worst-case complexity of the iterative algorithm is $3nv$, where n is the number of statements in the program, and v is the number of variables.

4.4 Extensions

For simplicity, we have focused on a core fragment of an XML-based language. We expect the extension of our analysis to the richer set of constructs available in an imperative language such as XJ to be straightforward. Since the interaction between XML values and non-XML values occurs in a constrained manner, traditional alias analyses or value numbering algorithms could be applied to the non-XML (Java) subset of the imperative language prior to the execution of our analysis. Updates to Java variables do not directly affect our analysis. Updates to XML values would require the detection of the values that are killed by an update statement. Existing algorithms for read-write conflict detections [12] can be adapted to this end.

The type system that we have described is mostly orthogonal to the fragment of XPath used — the framework depends essentially on an efficient algorithm for detecting the equivalence of XPath expressions. Recently, Geneves *et al.* [4] have presented an engine that in practice can detect equivalences between XPath expressions efficiently. We could adapt our analysis to support a larger fragment by taking advantage of their equivalence checker. XML Schema information can be incorporated into our analysis by performing a preprocessing pass, where XPath expressions are rewritten using schema information. For example, $(\$\mathsf{a}, \downarrow^+ /A, \Psi)$ could be rewritten into $(\$\mathsf{a}, \downarrow /B/ \downarrow /A, \Psi)$ if appropriate schema information states that A elements only occur as children of B elements.

5 Transformations

The analysis described in the previous section computes a symbolic representation of all possible values assumed by each XML expression or variable in the program. This section describes how this symbolic representation is used to optimize programs. We describe three transformations enabled by our analysis. The first is *common subexpression elimination* [6], which replaces an XPath expression by a previously computed result. The second, *XPath extraction* allows for the treatment of loops as XPath expressions; while it is not an optimization in itself, it enables other optimizations. The third, *common traversal elimination* is an optimization across multiple queries; if two XPath evaluations are likely to traverse a common set of nodes (though they might return different results), the XPath engine could optimize the computation by evaluating both queries in parallel. We provide a brief overview of these transformations below.

Common Subexpression Elimination (CSE): The symbolic representation resulting from our analysis provides a basis for applying traditional CSE algorithms to XPath expressions. For example, given a statement "y = $\$\mathsf{x}/XP$", if the analysis were to discover that the type of some variable z after the statement is equivalent to that of y, then we could replace the statement with "y = z".

XPath Extraction: This transformation extracts XPath expressions out of loops that accumulate values. It consists of two steps: *loop splitting* and *XPath conversion*. If, using algorithms such as loop reordering analysis [11], we can detect that splitting a loop preserves semantics, then we can isolate accumulate operations by splitting the loop. The essence of the transformation can be described through the following example:

```
                                    // Loop 1
foreach i in $x/XP {                foreach i in $x/XP {
    y ⇐ $i/...;                         y ⇐ $i/...
    ...                     ⇝       }
}                                   foreach i in $x/XP {
                                        ... // y ⇐ ... removed
                                    }
```

The XPath conversion step replaces loops of the form of Loop 1 in the previous example with the statement "y = $x/XP/...". Such a transformation may enable further optimizations such as CSE and common traversal elimination.

Common Traversal Elimination: Consider two XPath expressions over the same document and whose evaluation would traverse the same set of nodes. The analysis results described in Section 4 implicitly encode the sets of nodes traversed by XPath evaluations. Common traversal elimination, or *tupling*, merges XPath expressions that traverse the same set of XML nodes. Intuitively, the tupling optimization represents simultaneous computation of multiple results over the same data set. For example, consider two XPath expressions a = $x/\downarrow/B/\downarrow/C$ and b = $x/\downarrow/B/\downarrow/D$. The tupling transformation takes advantage of the fact that the evaluation of both XPath expressions would visit the B children of x and all the children of those nodes. Rather than evaluating the two XPath expressions separately, one could compute the two solutions in parallel. To support this optimization, we add a new operator "$\otimes$" to our XPath syntax. In our XPath engine, the two XPath expressions would be represented as x$/\downarrow/B/\downarrow/(C \otimes D)$. The denotation of the $\otimes$ operator, $[\![\tau \otimes \tau']\!](N)$ is defined to be the tuple $([\![\tau]\!](N), [\![\tau']\!](N))$. Consider a statement of the form y = x/XP_1/XP_2$. If some variable z at that statement has type ($x, $XP_1/XP_3, \Psi$), we follow the definition of z to see if the computation of z and y are amenable to common traversal elimination. The transformation detects whether the computation of y can be safely hoisted to the point where z is computed.

For example, consider the following instance of the transformation:

```
// ∃ e : x = e/XP1;              // ∃ e : (x,y) = e/(XP1 ⊗ XP2);
foreach i in e/XP2 {             // let y = e/XP2;
    ...                   ⇝      foreach i in y {
    y ⇐ i;                           ... // y ⇐ ... removed
    ...                              ...
}                                }
```

In this example, we first perform XPath extraction to move the assignment to y out of the loop. We can then tuple the computation of x and y. If $\Gamma(x) = (\$\mathsf{d}, XP_1/XP'_1, \Psi_1)$

and $\Gamma(y) = (\$\mathsf{d}, XP_2/XP'_2, \Psi_2)$, our implementation searches for an expression e, where e is a "common prefix" of x and y. Specifically, $\Gamma \vdash e : \tau'$, where

$$\tau' \equiv (\$\mathsf{d}, XP_1, \Psi_1) \equiv (\$\mathsf{d}, XP_2, \Psi_2)$$

The implicit encoding of traversals in the analysis results provides the information needed to find a common traversal for x and y. More elaborate matching is possible, but it would require a more complex transformation than the tupling described above.

6 Experiments

We compare the runtimes achieved by code emitted by our AXIL backend [13] with and without the transformations described in the paper. The benchmarks for our experiments are based on programs drawn from the XMark XML Benchmark project [14] and the XLinq [2,9] 101 samples. In all cases, the benchmarks were transcribed in a straightforward manner as XJ programs. Our compiler implements the type assignment algorithm from Section 4.3 and the tupling optimization from Section 5.

We provide the performance comparisons for the tupling optimization on XLinq34, XLinq35, XLinq36, XLinq38 (from the XLinq samples) and XMarkQ7 and XMarkQ20 (from the XMark benchmark suite).

Our experiments were run on the data sets provided by the XMark benchmarks and the XLinq samples. We measured the runtimes using the with and without the tupling optimization on an IBM Intellistation with 3.0 GHz processor and 3GB of memory, running the IBM J9 VM 1.5.0 on top of a GNU/Linux 2.6.15-28 system. We ran each query 10 times, picking the best result for each query. Before measuring, we removed all text output from the benchmarked code. Our results are summarized in Table 1. The results of the tupling optimization are shown in the column "Tupling". For the queries testing tupling, the introduction of tupling produces an improvement of 19.7% to 49.9%.

Table 1. Performance results, in microseconds, best out of 10 consecutive executions

Benchmark	Unopt	Tupling
XLinq34	4096	2050 / 49.9%
XLinq35	3206	2554 / 20.3%
XLinq36	2718	2182 / 19.7%
XLinq38	2503	1779 / 28.9%
XMark7	16390	11688 / 28.7%
XMark20	1227	846 / 31.1%

The CSE optimizations were implemented by-hand using the analysis results. We provide results for XMarkQ3 and XMarkQ20. We manually modified *XMark20.xj* into *XMark20opt.xj*, eliminating the same redundant traversal as the tupling optimization as well as manual CSE of an XPath expression. *XMark3opt.xj* is a manual modification of *XMark3.xj*, which eliminates the redundant computation of two XPath expressions. The improvements on other applications that have the same pattern is similar.

XMark20opt.xj achieves a 51.0% reduction in the runtime of *XMark20.xj* , while the tupling optimization achieves a 31.1% reduction. This difference is due to the hand-coding of XPath expression CSE in *Xmark20opt.xj*. *XMark3opt.xj* achieves an 8.5% reduction in runtime with respect to *XMark3.xj* by eliminating the redundant computation of two XPath expressions.

7 Related Work

The problem studied in this paper is similar to the inference of relational queries and optimizations from imperative programs. For example Lieuwen and Dewitt [8] analyze database programming languages to detect whether optimizations such as reordering loops can improve performance. Recently, Wiedermann and Cook studied the inference of queries in a language with orthogonal persistence [16]. The motivation in this paper is similar — understanding accesses to a different data model in the scope of an imperative language. We, however, focus on the XML data model, and the XPath querying language, with the incident challenges these bring. In terms of XML static analysis, previous work has mostly focused on typechecking [7], where types are used to verify statically that constructed XML data satisfy a specified schema.

Genevès *et al.* have developed a framework for analyzing XPath expressions (with our without schema information). They provide a uniform representation capable of answering questions such as equivalence, containment, and satisfiability of XPath expressions. Our types fit well into their framework, and it would be interesting to use their engine as the underlying basis of our analysis.

The problem we study in this paper is closely related to that of value numbering [1,6], which attempts to discovers those expressions that are Herbrand equivalent: *i.e.*, use the same operator applied to equivalent operands, where the operators are treated as uninterpreted functions. In our context, however, it is necessary to take advantage of known algorithms for detecting equivalences of XPath expressions, and not treat them as uninterpreted functions. Moreover, we wished to be able to deduce the values computed by loops in the same framework.

Steensgard [15] presents an interprocedural flow-insensitive points-to analysis for a small imperative pointer language based on type inference methods. He uses types to model how storage is used in a program at runtime, where typing rules specify when a program is well-typed. In some sense, the problem addressed in this paper can be considered a points-to analysis problem. We wish to derive some notion of the relationships between nodes in a tree when the tree is accessed using complex "pointer" expressions such as XPath expressions.

8 Conclusions

In this paper, we have studied the analysis of embedded XPath queries in an imperative language. We have described a flow-sensitive type system that takes into account the equivalence properties of XPath expressions and that can detect when a loop produces values equivalent to XPath expressions. While we have motivated this analysis using the example of redundant computation removal, such an analysis is essential for many purposes — for example, if we can infer that the values computed by a loop are equivalent to an XPath expression, then, in certain circumstances we can replace a loop with a direct invocation to an XPath engine that could implement the query more efficiently (in a sense, performing strength reduction).

References

1. Alpern, B., Wegman, M.N., Zadeck, F.K.: Detecting equality of variables in programs. In: Proceedings of the 15th Symposium on Principles of Programming Languages, pp. 1–11 (January 1988)
2. Calvert, C.: Linq samples update (2007), `http://blogs.msdn.com/charlie/archive/2007/03/04/samples-update.aspx`
3. Chamberlin, D., Carey, M., Florescu, D., Kossman, D., Robie, J.: XQueryP: Programming with XQuery. In: XIME-P (2006)
4. Genevès, P., Layaida, N., Schmitt, A.: Efficient static analysis of XML paths and types. In: Conference on Programming Language Design and Implementation (June 2007)
5. Harren, M., Raghavachari, M., Shmueli, O., Burke, M., Bordawekar, R., Pechtchanski, I., Sarkar, V.: XJ: Facilitating XML processing in Java. In: Proceedings of World Wide Web (WWW), pp. 278–287 (May 2005)
6. Kildall, G.A.: A unified approach to global program optimization. In: Proceedings of the 1st Symposium on Principles of Programming Languages, pp. 194–206 (1973)
7. Kirkegaard, C., Møller, A., Schwartzbach, M.: Static analysis of XML transformations in Java. IEEE Transactions on Software Engineering 30(3), 181–192 (2004)
8. Lieuwen, D.F., DeWitt, D.J.: Optimizing loops in database programming languages. In: DBPL, pp. 287–305 (1991)
9. Meijer, E., Beckman, B.: XLinq: XML Programming Refactored (The Return of the Monoids). In: XML 2005 Proceedings (2005)
10. Miklau, G., Suciu, D.: Containment and equivalence for a fragment of XPath. J. ACM 51(1), 2–45 (2004)
11. Moon, S.-M., Ebcioğlu, K.: Parallelizing nonnumerical code with selective scheduling and software pipelining. ACM Transactions on Programming Languages and Systems 19(6), 853–898 (1997)
12. Raghavachari, M., Shmueli, O.: Conflicting XML updates. In: Ioannidis, Y., Scholl, M.H., Schmidt, J.W., Matthes, F., Hatzopoulos, M., Boehm, K., Kemper, A., Grust, T., Boehm, C. (eds.) EDBT 2006. LNCS, vol. 3896, Springer, Heidelberg (2006)
13. Reichenbach, C., Burke, M., Peshansky, I., Raghavachari, M., Bordawekar, R.: AXIL: An XPath Intermediate Language. IBM Research Report RC24075 (2006)
14. Schmidt, A., Waas, F., Kersten, M., Carey, M., Manolescu, I., Busse, R.: Xmark: A benchmark for XML data management. In: Bressan, S., Chaudhri, A.B., Lee, M.L., Yu, J.X., Lacroix, Z. (eds.) CAiSE 2002 and VLDB 2002. LNCS, vol. 2590, pp. 974–985. Springer, Heidelberg (2003)
15. Steensgaard, B.: Points-to analysis in almost linear time. In: Proceedings of the 23rd Symposium on Principles of Programming Languages, pp. 32–41 (1996)
16. Wiedermann, B.A., Cook, W.R.: Extracting queries by static analysis of transparent persistence. In: Proceedings of the 34th Symposium on Principles of Programming Languages (January 2007)
17. World Wide Web Consortium. XML Path Language (XPath) Version 1.0 (1999)
18. World Wide Web Consortium. Document Object Model Level 2 Core (2000)

Efficient Inclusion for a Class of XML Types with Interleaving and Counting

Giorgio Ghelli[1], Dario Colazzo[2,*], and Carlo Sartiani[1]

[1] Dipartimento di Informatica - Università di Pisa - Italy
{ghelli,sartiani}@di.unipi.it
[2] Université Paris Sud, UMR CNRS 8623, Orsay F-91405 - France
dario.colazzo@lri.fr

Abstract. Inclusion between XML types is important but expensive, and is much more expensive when unordered types are considered. We prove here that inclusion for XML types with interleaving and counting can be decided in polynomial time in presence of two important restrictions: no element appears twice in the same content model, and Kleene star is only applied to disjunctions of single elements.

Our approach is based on the transformation of each such type into a set of constraints that completely characterizes the type. We then provide a complete deduction system to verify whether the constraints of one type imply all the constraints of another one.

1 Introduction

XML schemas are an essential tool for the robustness of applications that involve XML data manipulation, transformation, integration, and, crucially, data exchange. To solve any static analysis problem that involves such types one must first be able to reason about their inclusion and equivalence.

XML schema languages are designed to describe ordered data, but they usually offer some (limited) support to deal with cases where the order among some elements is not constrained. These "unordered" mechanisms bring the language out of the well-understood realm of tree-grammars and tree-automata, and have been subject to little foundational study, with the important exception of a recent work by Gelade, Martens, and Neven [1]. Here, the authors study a wide range of schema languages, and show that the addition of interleaving and counting operators raises the complexity of inclusion checking from PSPACE (or EXPTIME, for Extended DTDs) to EXPSPACE. These are completeness results, hence this is really bad news. A previous result in [2] had already shown that the inclusion of Regular Expressions with interleaving alone is complete in EXPSPACE, hence showing that counting is not essential for the high cost. The paper [1] concludes with: "It would therefore be desirable to find robust subclasses for which the basic decision problems are in PTIME". Such subclasses could be used either to design a new schema language, or to design adaptive algorithms, that use the PTIME algorithm when possible, and resort to the full algorithm when needed. To this aim, it is important that (i) the subclass covers large classes of XML types used in practice, (ii) it is easy to verify whether a schema belongs to the subclass.

* Work of this author was partially funded by the French ACI young researcher project "WebStand".

M. Arenas and M.I. Schwartzbach (Eds.): DBPL 2007, LNCS 4797, pp. 231–245, 2007.

Our Contribution. In this paper we define a class of XML types with interleaving and numerical constraints whose inclusion can be checked in polynomial time. These types are based on two restrictions that we impose on the Regular Expressions (REs) used to the define the element content models: each RE is conflict-free (or *single occurrence*) meaning that no symbol appears twice, and Kleene star is only applied to elements or to disjunctions of elements. These restrictions are severe, but, as shown in [3] and [4], they are actually met by most of the schemas that are used in practice.

Our approach is based on the transformation of each type into an equivalent set of constraints. Consider, for instance, the following string type $T = (a\,[1..3] \cdot b\,[2..2]) + c\,[1..2]$, and the following properties for a word w in T:

1. lower-bound: at least one of a, b and c appears in w;
2. cardinality: if a is in w, it appears 1, 2 or 3 times; if b is there, it appears twice; if c is there, it appears once or twice;
3. upper-bound: no symbol out of $\{a, b, c\}$ is in w;
4. exclusion: if one of a, b is in w, then c is not, and if c is in w then neither of a, b is in w;
5. co-occurrence: if a is in w, then b is in w, and vice versa;[1]
6. order: no occurrence of a may follow an occurrence of b.

It is easy to see that every w in T enjoys all of them. We will prove here that the opposite implication is true as well: every word that satisfies the six properties is indeed in T, i.e., that constraint set is *complete* for T.

We will generalize this observation, and will associate a complete set of constraints, in the six categories above, to any conflict-free type (we will actually encode exclusion constraints as order constraints.) We will then define a polynomial algorithm to verify whether, given T and U, the constraints of T imply those for U, so that T is included in U. We will formalize the constraints using a simple ad-hoc logic. We will describe the constraint implication algorithm by first giving a sound and complete constraint deduction system, and then giving an algorithm that exploits the deduction system.

The ability to transform a type into a complete set of constraints expressed in a limited variable-free logic is used here to design an efficient inclusion algorithm. We believe that it can also be exploited for many related tasks, such as PTIME membership checking (which is NP-complete for REs with interleaving), and path containment under a DTD. Quite surprisingly, binary type intersection, which is usually simpler than type inclusion, turns out in this case to be NP-hard; the constraint-based approach was important in our discovery of the proof that we present here.

Paper Outline. The paper is structured as follows. Section 2 describes the data model, the type language, and the constraint language we are using. Section 3 shows how types can be characterized in terms of constraints, and how inclusion can be encoded in terms of constraint implication. Section 4 describes a deduction system for type constraints. Section 5, then, sketches a polynomial time algorithm for deciding type inclusion based on the deduction system of Section 4. In Section 6 we show that intersection is NP-hard. In Sections 7 and 8, finally, we briefly revise some related works and draw our conclusions.

[1] The term *co-occurrence constraint* has an unrelated meaning in [5]; we use it as in [6].

2 Type Language and Constraint Language

2.1 The Type Language

Gelade, Martens, and Neven showed that, if inclusion for a given class of regular expressions with interleaving and numerical constraints is in the complexity class $\mathcal{C}$, and $\mathcal{C}$ is *closed under positive reductions* (a property enjoyed by PTIME), then the complexity of inclusion for DTDs and single-type EDTDs that use the same class of regular expressions is in $\mathcal{C}$ too [7,1]. Hence, we can focus our study on a class of regular expression over strings, and our PTIME result will immediately imply the same complexity for the inclusion problem of the corresponding classes of DTDs and single-type EDTDs. Single-type EDTDs are the theoretical counterpart of XML Schema definitions (see [1]).

We adopt the usual definitions for string concatenation $w_1 \cdot w_2$, and for the concatenation of two languages $L_1 \cdot L_2$. The *shuffle*, or *interleaving*, operator $w_1 \& w_2$ is also standard, and is defined as follows.

Definition 1 ($v\&w$, $L_1\&L_2$). *The shuffle set of two words $v, w \in \Sigma^*$, or two languages $L_1, L_2 \subseteq \Sigma^*$, is defined as follows; notice that each v_i or w_i may be the empty string ϵ.*

$$\begin{aligned} v\&w &=_{def} \{v_1 \cdot w_1 \cdot \ldots \cdot v_n \cdot w_n \\ &\qquad \mid v_1 \cdot \ldots \cdot v_n = v,\ w_1 \cdot \ldots \cdot w_n = w,\ v_i \in \Sigma^*,\ w_i \in \Sigma^*,\ n > 0\} \\ L_1\&L_2 &=_{def} \textstyle\bigcup_{w_1 \in L_1,\ w_2 \in L_2} w_1\&w_2 \end{aligned}$$

Example 1. $(ab)\&(XY)$ contains the permutations of $abXY$ where a comes before b and X comes before Y:

$$(ab)\&(XY) = \{abXY, aXbY, aXYb, XabY, XaYb, XYab\}$$

When $v \in w_1\&w_2$, we say that v is a shuffle of w_1 and w_2; for example, $w_1 \cdot w_2$ and $w_2 \cdot w_1$ are shuffles of w_1 and w_2.

We define $\mathbb{N}_* = \mathbb{N} \cup \{*\}$, and extend the standard order among naturals with $n \leq *$ for each $n \in \mathbb{N}_*$. We consider the following type language for strings over an alphabet Σ, where $a \in \Sigma$, $m \in \mathbb{N} \setminus \{0\}$, $n \in \mathbb{N}_* \setminus \{0\}$, and $n \geq m$ (please notice the specific domains for m and n):[2]

$$T ::= \epsilon \mid a\,[m..n] \mid T + T \mid T \cdot T \mid T\&T$$

Note that expressions like $a\,[0..n]$ are not allowed due to the condition on m; of course, the type $a\,[0..n]$ can be equivalently represented by $a\,[1..n] + \epsilon$.

Our type system generalizes Kleene star to counting, but it only allows symbols to be counted, so that, for example, $(a \cdot b)*$ cannot be expressed. However, it has been found that DTDs and XSD schemas use Kleene star almost exclusively as $a*$ or as $(a + \ldots + z)^*$ (see [3]), which can be easily expressed in our system as: $(a^* \& \ldots \& z^*)$, where a^* abbreviates $(a\,[1..*] + \epsilon)$. The *simple expressions* studied in [3] are a subclass of what can be expressed with our approach, and [3] measured a 97% fraction of XSD schemas with simple expressions only.

[2] We call them "types" because of our background, but they are actually a specific family of REs with interleaving, counting, and some restrictions.

Moreover, most of the non-simple expressions that they present are also easy to express in our system. Chain Regular Expressions [4] can also be expressed with our approach (see Section 7).[3]

Definition 2 **($S(w), S(T), Atoms(T)$).** *For any string w, $S(w)$ is the set of all symbols appearing in w. For any type T, $Atoms(T)$ is the set of all atoms $a\,[m..n]$ appearing in T, and $S(T)$ is the set of all symbols appearing in T.*

Semantics of types is defined as follows.

$$\begin{aligned}
[\![\epsilon]\!] &= \{\epsilon\} \\
[\![a\,[m..n]]\!] &= \{w \mid S(w) = \{a\},\ |w| \geq m,\ |w| \leq n\} \\
[\![T_1 + T_2]\!] &= [\![T_1]\!] \cup [\![T_2]\!] \\
[\![T_1 \cdot T_2]\!] &= [\![T_1]\!] \cdot [\![T_2]\!] \\
[\![T_1 \& T_2]\!] &= [\![T_1]\!] \& [\![T_2]\!]
\end{aligned}$$

We will use $\otimes$ to range over $\cdot$ and & when we need to specify common properties, such as, for example: $[\![T \otimes \epsilon]\!] = [\![\epsilon \otimes T]\!] = [\![T]\!]$.

In this system, no type is empty. Some types contain the empty string ϵ, and are characterized as follows ($\mathrm{N}(T)$ is read as "T is nullable").

Definition 3. $\mathrm{N}(T)$ *is a predicate on types, defined as follows:*

$$\begin{aligned}
\mathrm{N}(\epsilon) &= \mathit{true} \\
\mathrm{N}(a\,[m..n]) &= \mathit{false} \\
\mathrm{N}(T + T') &= \mathrm{N}(T)\ \mathit{or}\ \mathrm{N}(T') \\
\mathrm{N}(T \otimes T') &= \mathrm{N}(T)\ \mathit{and}\ \mathrm{N}(T')
\end{aligned}$$

Lemma 1. $\epsilon \in [\![T]\!]$ *iff* $\mathrm{N}(T)$.

We can now define the notion of *conflict-free* types.

Definition 4 (Conflict-free types). *Given a type T, T is* conflict-free *if for each subexpression $(U + V)$ or $(U \otimes V)$: $S(U) \cap S(V) = \emptyset$.*

Equivalently, a type T is conflict-free if, for any two distinct subterms $a\,[m..n]$ and $a'\,[m'..n']$ that occur in T, a is different from a'.

Example 2. Consider the following type: $(a\,[1..1]\,\&b\,[1..1]) + (a\,[1..1]\,\&c\,[1..1])$. This type generates the language $\{ab, ba, ac, ca\}$. This type is not conflict-free, since $S(a\,[1..1]\,\&b\,[1..1]) \cap S(a\,[1..1]\,\&c\,[1..1]) = \{a\} \neq \emptyset$.

Consider now $a\,[1..1]\,\&(b\,[1..1] + c\,[1..1])$; it generates the same language, but is conflict-free since $a\,[1..1]$ and $(b\,[1..1] + c\,[1..1])$ have no common symbols.

Conflict-free DTDs have been considered many times before, because of their good properties and because of the high percentage of actual schemas that satisfy this constraint (see Section 7).

Hereafter, we will silently assume that every type is conflict-free, although some of the properties we specify are valid for any type.

[3] We are only discussing here our Kleene-star restriction, ignoring conflict-freedom for a moment.

2.2 The Constraint Language

We verify inclusion between T and U by translating them into constraint sets C_T and C_U and by then verifying that C_T implies C_U. Constraints are expressed using the following logic, where $a, b \in \Sigma$ and $A, B \subseteq \Sigma$, $m \in \mathbb{N}\backslash\{0\}$, $n \in \mathbb{N}_*\backslash\{0\}$, and $n \geq m$:

$$F ::= A^+ \mid A^+ \Rightarrow B^+ \mid a?[m..n] \mid \text{upper}(A) \mid a \prec b \mid F \wedge F' \mid \mathbf{true}$$

Satisfaction of a constraint F by a word w, written $w \models F$, is defined as follows.[4]

$$\begin{aligned}
w \models A^+ &\Leftrightarrow S(w) \cap A \neq \emptyset, \text{ i.e. some } a \in A \text{ appears in } w \\
w \models A^+ \Rightarrow B^+ &\Leftrightarrow w \not\models A^+ \text{ or } w \models B^+ \\
w \models a?[m..n]\ (n \neq *) &\Leftrightarrow \text{if } a \text{ appears in } w, \\
&\quad\ \text{then it appears at least } m \text{ times and at most } n \text{ times} \\
w \models a?[m..*] &\Leftrightarrow \text{if } a \text{ appears in } w, \text{ then it appears at least } m \text{ times} \\
w \models \text{upper}(A) &\Leftrightarrow S(w) \subseteq A \\
w \models a \prec b &\Leftrightarrow \text{there is no occurrence of } a \text{ in } w \text{ that follows} \\
&\quad\ \text{an occurrence of } b \text{ in } w \\
w \models F_1 \wedge F_2 &\Leftrightarrow w \models F_1 \text{ and } w \models F_2 \\
w \models \mathbf{true} &\Leftrightarrow \text{always}
\end{aligned}$$

We will also use $A^+ \Rightarrow \mathbf{true}$ as an alternative notation for **true**. This should not be too confusing, since the two things are logically equivalent, and will simplify the notation for one crucial definition.

The atomic formulas are best understood through some examples.

$dab \models \{a,b,c\}^+$	$ca \models \{a,b,c\}^+$	$\epsilon \not\models A^+$	$w \not\models \emptyset^+$
$dab \not\models \text{upper}(\{a,b,c\})$	$ca \models \text{upper}(\{a,b,c\})$	$\epsilon \models \text{upper}(A)$	$\epsilon \models \text{upper}(\emptyset)$
$ca \models b?[2..*]$	$cba \not\models b?[2..*]$	$cbab \models b?[2..*]$	$bcbab \models b?[2..*]$
$ca \models a \prec b$	$caba \not\models a \prec b$	$aacb \models a \prec b$	$\epsilon \models a \prec b$

Observe that A^+ is monotone, i.e. $w \models A^+$ and w is a subword of w' imply that $w' \models A^+$, while upper(A) and $a \prec b$ are anti-monotone.

We use the following abbreviations:

$$\begin{aligned}
a^+ &=_{def} \{a\}^+ \\
a \prec\succ b &=_{def} (a \prec b) \wedge (b \prec a) \\
A \prec B &=_{def} \bigwedge_{a \in A, b \in B} a \prec b \\
A \prec\succ B &=_{def} \bigwedge_{a \in A, b \in B} a \prec\succ b
\end{aligned}$$

[4] Notice that $A^+ \Rightarrow b^+$ differs from the sibling constraint $A \Downarrow b$ of [8], since $A^+ \Rightarrow b^+$ means "if one symbol of A is in w then b is in w", while $A \Downarrow b$ means "if *all* symbols of A are in w then b is in w".

The next propositions specify that $A \prec\succ B$ encodes mutual exclusion between sets of symbols.

Proposition 1. $w \models a \prec\succ b \;\Leftrightarrow\;$ *a and b and are not both in* $S(w)$

Proposition 2. $w \models A \prec\succ B \;\Leftrightarrow w \not\models A^+ \wedge B^+$

Definition 5. $a \in S(F)$ *if one of the following is a subterm of* F: $a?[m..n]$, $a \prec b$, A^+, $A^+ \Rightarrow B^+$, $\mathrm{upper}(A)$, *where, in the last three cases,* $a \in A$ *or* $a \in B$.

The atomic operators are all mutually independent: only A^+ can force the presence of a symbol independently of any other, only $A^+ \Rightarrow B^+$ induces a positive correlation between the presence of two symbols, only $a?[m..n]$ can count, only $\mathrm{upper}(A)$ is affected by the presence of a symbol that is not in $S(F)$, and only $a \prec b$ is affected by order. However, combinations of the atomic operators can be mutually related (see Proposition 2, for example).

3 Characterization of Types as Constraints

3.1 Constraint Extraction

We first extend satisfaction from words to types, as follows.

Definition 6. $T \models F \;\Leftrightarrow\; \forall w \in [\![T]\!].\ w \models F$

To each type T, we associate a formula $S^+(T)$ that tests for the presence of one of its symbols, as follows.

Definition 7. $S^+(T) \;=\; (S(T))^+$

The $S^+(T)$ formula allows us to express the exclusion constraints associated with the type $T_1 + T_2$: if $S(T_1) \cap S(T_2) = \emptyset$ and $w \in [\![T_1 + T_2]\!]$, then $w \models S^+(T_1)$ is sufficient to deduce that $w \models \neg S^+(T_2)$, i.e. $T_1 + T_2 \models \neg(S^+(T_1) \wedge S^+(T_2))$ (which we actually express as $T_1 + T_2 \models S(T_1) \prec\succ S(T_2)$).

We would like to have a dual constraint for $T_1 \cdot T_2$, such as $T_1 \cdot T_2 \models S^+(T_1) \Rightarrow S^+(T_2)$, but this does not hold in case T_2 contains the empty string; we will prove that this weaker constraint holds: $T_1 \cdot T_2 \models$ if not $\mathrm{N}(T_2)$ then $S^+(T_1) \Rightarrow S^+(T_2)$.

The condition "if not $\mathrm{N}(T)$ then ..." will be expressed using the $\mathit{SIf}(T)$ notation that we define below.

We can now endow a type T with five sets of constraints. We start with the lower-bound, cardinality, and upper-bound constraints (we introduced this terminology in Section 1).

Definition 8 (Flat constraints).

$$
\begin{array}{rrll}
\textit{Lower-bound:} & \mathit{SIf}(T) =_{def} & S^+(T) & \textit{if not } \mathrm{N}(T) \\
 & \mathit{SIf}(T) =_{def} & \mathbf{true} & \textit{if } \mathrm{N}(T) \\
\textit{Cardinality:} & \mathrm{ZeroMinMax}(T) =_{def} & \bigwedge_{a[m..n] \in Atoms(T)} a?[m..n] & \\
\textit{Upper-bound:} & \mathrm{upperS}(T) =_{def} & \mathrm{upper}(S(T)) & \\
\textit{Flat constraints:} & \mathcal{FC}(T) =_{def} & \mathit{SIf}(T) \wedge \mathrm{ZeroMinMax}(T) \wedge \mathrm{upperS}(T) &
\end{array}
$$

We can now add co-occurrence, order, and exclusion constraints, whose definition is inductive over the type structure. Exclusion constraints are actually encoded as order constraints.

Definition 9 (Nested constraints).

Co-occurrence:

$$\begin{aligned} \mathcal{CC}(T_1 + T_2) &=_{def} \mathcal{CC}(T_1) \wedge \mathcal{CC}(T_2) \\ \mathcal{CC}(T_1 \otimes T_2) &=_{def} (S^+(T_1) \Rightarrow \mathit{SIf}(T_2)) \wedge (S^+(T_2) \Rightarrow \mathit{SIf}(T_1)) \wedge \\ &\qquad \mathcal{CC}(T_1) \wedge \mathcal{CC}(T_2) \\ \mathcal{CC}(\epsilon) =_{def} \mathcal{CC}(a\,[m..n]) &=_{def} \mathbf{true} \end{aligned}$$

Order and exclusion:

$$\begin{aligned} \mathcal{OC}(T_1 + T_2) &=_{def} (S(T_1) \prec\!\succ S(T_2)) \wedge \mathcal{OC}(T_1) \wedge \mathcal{OC}(T_2) \\ \mathcal{OC}(T_1 \& T_2) &=_{def} \mathcal{OC}(T_1) \wedge \mathcal{OC}(T_2) \\ \mathcal{OC}(T_1 \cdot T_2) &=_{def} (S(T_1) \prec S(T_2)) \wedge \mathcal{OC}(T_1) \wedge \mathcal{OC}(T_2) \\ \mathcal{OC}(\epsilon) =_{def} \mathcal{OC}(a\,[m..n]) &=_{def} \mathbf{true} \end{aligned}$$

Nested constraints:

$$\mathcal{NC}(T) =_{def} \mathcal{CC}(T) \wedge \mathcal{OC}(T)$$

Notice that, when $\mathrm{N}(T_2)$ is *true*, $S^+(T_1) \Rightarrow \mathit{SIf}(T_2)$ is just **true**, because $(A^+ \Rightarrow \mathbf{true})$ is **true**, by definition. This notation is helpful to visualize, for example, the fact that $S^+(T_1)$ and $S^+(T_1) \Rightarrow \mathit{SIf}(T_2)$ imply $\mathit{SIf}(T_2)$.

3.2 Correctness and Completeness of Constraints

We plan to prove the following theorem, that specifies that the constraint system completely captures the semantics of conflict-free types.

Theorem 1. *Given a conflict-free type T, it holds that:*

$$w \in [\![T]\!] \;\Leftrightarrow\; w \models \mathcal{FC}(T) \wedge \mathcal{NC}(T)$$

We first prove that constraints are complete, i.e., whenever w satisfies all the five groups of constraints associated with T, then $w \in [\![T]\!]$.

Proposition 3 (ZeroMinMax(T))**.**

$$\begin{aligned} w &\models \mathrm{ZeroMinMax}(T_1 + T_2) \Rightarrow w \models \mathrm{ZeroMinMax}(T_1) \wedge \mathrm{ZeroMinMax}(T_2) \\ w &\models \mathrm{ZeroMinMax}(T_1 \otimes T_2) \Rightarrow w \models \mathrm{ZeroMinMax}(T_1) \wedge \mathrm{ZeroMinMax}(T_2) \end{aligned}$$

Definition 10. *We define $w|_{S(T)}$ as the string obtained from w by removing all the symbols that are not in $S(T)$.*

We can now prove the crucial completeness theorem.

Theorem 2 (Completeness of constraints).

$$w \models (\mathcal{FC}(T) \wedge \mathcal{NC}(T)) \;\Rightarrow\; w \in [\![T]\!]$$

Proof. For the sake of convenience, we will use ZMM-SIf(T) as a shortcut for ZeroMinMax(T) $\wedge$ *SIf*(T), so that we can rewrite the thesis to prove as

$$w \models (\text{upperS}(T) \wedge \text{ZMM-SIf}(T) \wedge \mathcal{NC}(T)) \quad \Rightarrow \quad w \in [\![T]\!]$$

We prove the following fact, by case inspection and structural induction on T.

$$w \models (\text{ZMM-SIf}(T) \wedge \mathcal{NC}(T)) \quad \Rightarrow \quad w|_{S(T)} \in [\![T]\!]$$

The theorem follows because $w \models \text{upperS}(T)$ implies that $w = w|_{S(T)}$.

We first observe that $w|_{S(T)} = \epsilon$ and $w \models SIf(T)$ imply the thesis $w|_{S(T)} \in [\![T]\!]$. Indeed, $w|_{S(T)} = \epsilon$ implies that $w \not\models S^+(T)$, hence, the hypothesis $w \models SIf(T)$ implies that N(T) is true, which in turn implies that $\epsilon \in [\![T]\!]$, i.e. $w|_{S(T)} \in [\![T]\!]$.

Having dealt with the $w|_{S(T)} = \epsilon$ case, in the following we assume that $w|_{S(T)} = a_1 \cdot \ldots \cdot a_n$, where $n \neq 0$.

T $= \epsilon$ **:**
Trivial, as $w|_{S(\epsilon)} = \epsilon$ and $\epsilon \in [\![\epsilon]\!]$.

T $=$ **a [m..n] :**
Since N(T) is false, $w \models$ ZMM-SIf(T) implies that $w \models$ ZeroMinMax(T) $\wedge$ $S^+(T)$, i.e., $w \models$ ZeroMinMax($a\,[m..n]$) $\wedge\, a^+$, i.e., $w \models a?[m..n] \wedge a^+$, hence $w|_{S(a[m..n])} \in [\![a\,[m..n]]\!]$.

$\mathbf{T = T_1 + T_2}$ **:**
Let $w|_{S(T)} = a_1 \cdot \ldots \cdot a_n$, and assume,without loss of generality, that $a_1 \in S(T_1)$.

By hypothesis we have that $w \models$ ZMM-SIf($T_1 + T_2$) $\wedge$ $(S(T_1) \prec\!\succ S(T_2)) \wedge \mathcal{NC}(T_1) \wedge \mathcal{NC}(T_2)$. As $w|_{S(T)} = a_1 \cdot \ldots \cdot a_n$ with $a_1 \in S(T_1)$, we also have that $w \models S^+(T_1)$.

This implies that $w \models SIf(T_1)$ (by definition of *SIf*()) and that $w \not\models S^+(T_2)$ (by Proposition 2). This, in turn, implies $w|_{S(T_1+T_2)} = w|_{S(T_1)}$ (*). By Proposition 3 and by $w \models$ ZMM-SIf($T_1 + T_2$) we obtain that $w \models$ ZeroMinMax(T_1). Putting all together, $w \models$ ZMM-SIf(T_1) $\wedge\, \mathcal{NC}(T_1)$.

By induction we have that $w|_{S(T_1)} \in [\![T_1]\!]$; hence, by (*), we get $w|_{S(T_1+T_2)} \in [\![T_1]\!]$, which, in turn, implies that $w|_{S(T_1+T_2)} \in [\![T_1 + T_2]\!]$.

$\mathbf{T = T_1 \cdot T_2}$ **:**
We have two possible cases:

1. $w|_{S(T)} = a_1 \cdot \ldots \cdot a_n$ and $a_1 \in S(T_1)$;
2. $w|_{S(T)} = a_1 \cdot \ldots \cdot a_n$ and $a_1 \in S(T_2)$.

Case 1 ($w|_{S(T)} = a_1 \cdot \ldots \cdot a_n$ and $a_1 \in S(T_1)$).
By hypothesis we have that:

$$\begin{aligned} w \models \text{ZMM-SIf}(T_1 \cdot T_2) &\wedge (S^+(T_1) \Rightarrow SIf(T_2)) \\ &\wedge (S^+(T_2) \Rightarrow SIf(T_1)) \\ &\wedge (S(T_1) \prec S(T_2)) \\ &\wedge \mathcal{NC}(T_1) \wedge \mathcal{NC}(T_2) \end{aligned}$$

Since $w|_{S(T)} = a_1 \cdot \ldots \cdot a_n$ with $a_1 \in S(T_1)$, we have that $w \models S^+(T_1)$, which implies that $w \models SIf(T_1)$ (by definition of *SIf*()) and that $w \models SIf(T_2)$ (by hypothesis). By Proposition 3 we conclude that $w \models$ ZMM-SIf(T_1)$\wedge$ZMM-SIf(T_2).

Let us define $w_1 = w|_{S(T_1)}$ and $w_2 = w|_{S(T_2)}$. As $w \models \mathcal{NC}(T_1) \wedge \mathcal{NC}(T_2)$, by induction we obtain that $w_1 \in [\![T_1]\!]$ and $w_2 \in [\![T_2]\!]$.

By conflict-freedom, w_1 and w_2 do not contain any common symbols, hence, from the constraint $S(T_1) \prec S(T_2)$ we obtain that each symbol of w_1 precedes each symbol of w_2 in w. As a consequence, $w|_{S(T_1 \cdot T_2)} = w|_{S(T_1)} \cdot w|_{S(T_2)} = w_1 \cdot w_2$. Thus, $w|_{S(T_1 \cdot T_2)} \in [\![T_1 \cdot T_2]\!]$.

Case 2 ($w|_{S(T)} = a_1 \cdot \ldots \cdot a_n$ and $a_1 \in S(T_2)$).
By hypothesis we have that:

$$\begin{aligned} w \models \text{ZMM-SIf}(T_1 \cdot T_2) &\wedge (S^+(T_1) \Rightarrow \mathit{SIf}(T_2)) \\ &\wedge (S^+(T_2) \Rightarrow \mathit{SIf}(T_1)) \\ &\wedge (S(T_1) \prec S(T_2)) \\ &\wedge \mathcal{NC}(T_1) \wedge \mathcal{NC}(T_2) \end{aligned}$$

Since $w|_{S(T)} = a_1 \cdot \ldots \cdot a_n$ and $a_1 \in S(T_2)$, we obtain that $w \models S^+(T_2)$, which implies that $w \models \mathit{SIf}(T_1)$ (by hypothesis) and that $w \models \mathit{SIf}(T_2)$ (by definition). By Proposition 3 we conclude that $w \models \text{ZMM-SIf}(T_1) \wedge \text{ZMM-SIf}(T_2)$. As $w \models \mathcal{NC}(T_1) \wedge \mathcal{NC}(T_2)$, by induction we obtain that $w|_{S(T_1)} \in [\![T_1]\!]$ and $w|_{S(T_2)} \in [\![T_2]\!]$.

$w \models (S(T_1) \prec S(T_2))$ and $a_1 \in S(T_2)$ imply that $w \not\models S^+(T_1)$, i.e., $w|_{S(T_1)} = \epsilon$. Hence, $w|_{S(T_1 \cdot T_2)} = w|_{S(T_2)} = \epsilon \cdot w|_{S(T_2)} = w|_{S(T_1)} \cdot w|_{S(T_2)}$. Hence, by $w|_{S(T_1)} \in [\![T_1]\!]$ and $w|_{S(T_2)} \in [\![T_2]\!]$, we conclude that $w|_{S(T_1 \cdot T_2)} \in [\![T_1 \cdot T_2]\!]$.

$\mathbf{T = T_1 \& T_2}$: similar, but simpler. □

In order to prove soundness, we use the following lemma that specifies that the value of any formula F over w does not change if any letter a that is not in $S(F)$ is added or deleted from w, provided that F does not contain the upper(A) operator. Recall that upper(A) is only used to express upper-bound constraints.

Soundness is stated by Theorem 3 below; for reasons of space, we omit the proof and refer the reader to [9] for further details.

Theorem 3 (Soundness).

$$w \in [\![T]\!] \Rightarrow w \models \mathcal{FC}(T) \wedge \mathcal{NC}(T)$$

Corollary 1. *For any conflict-free type T:*

$$w \in [\![T]\!] \Leftrightarrow w \models \mathcal{FC}(T) \wedge \mathcal{NC}(T)$$

4 Deduction System

We introduce here a deduction system as a first step for the formalization of a constraint implication algorithm. The system is partitioned into two separate judgements, $\vdash_{cc}$ and $\vdash_{oc}$, for deducing co-occurrence and order constraints, This deduction system is not complete in general, but is powerful enough to decide type inclusion (Theorem 10).

Each judgement $\vdash_x$ will be defined, by a set of deduction rules with shape $F_1 \wedge \ldots \wedge F_n \vdash_x F$; the notation $F_1 \wedge \ldots \wedge F_m \vdash_x F'_1 \wedge \ldots \wedge F'_n$ also means that $F'_1 \ldots F'_n$ can be deduced from $F_1 \ldots F_m$ through the repeated application of the corresponding deduction rules.

From now on, we will often identify a set formula A^+ with the symbol set A; the use will clarify the distinction. Hence, we will use metavariables A and B to range over subsets of Σ and also over set-formulas.

For reasons of space, we omit the proofs of the results of this section and refer the reader to [9] for further details.

4.1 Co-occurrence Deduction

We start by defining a deduction system that will be used for co-occurrence constraints of the form $A^+ \Rightarrow B^+$. The *R-T-A* rules correspond to the *Armstrong system* used to deduce functional constraints [10], after left-hand-sides are switched with right-hand-sides. We will denote set union as juxtaposition: $AB =_{def} A \cup B$ and $aA =_{def} \{a\} \cup A$. The *False* rule specifies that, if an upper-bound constraint excludes a, then we can deduce any B from the impossible presence of a.

$$
\begin{array}{rll}
R: & & \vdash_{cc} A \Rightarrow AB \\
T: & (A \Rightarrow B) \wedge (B \Rightarrow C) & \vdash_{cc} A \Rightarrow C \\
A: & A \Rightarrow B & \vdash_{cc} AC \Rightarrow BC \\
False: a \notin A: & \text{upper}(A) & \vdash_{cc} a \Rightarrow B
\end{array}
$$

The backward correspondence between the *R-T-A* rules and Armstrong axioms can be easily explained: a functional dependency $X_1, \ldots, X_n \Rightarrow Y_1, \ldots, Y_m$ over a relation R is an implication of conjunctions $\forall t, u \in R.(P(X_1) \wedge \ldots \wedge P(X_n)) \Rightarrow (P(Y_1) \wedge \ldots \wedge P(Y_m))$, where $P(X)$ is $t.X = u.X$. An implication $\{a_1, \ldots, a_n\}^+ \Rightarrow \{b_1, \ldots, b_m\}^+$ is an implication of disjunctions $\forall w.(a_1 \in S(w) \vee \ldots \vee a_n \in S(w)) \Rightarrow (b_1 \in S(w) \vee \ldots \vee b_m \in S(w))$, that becomes a backward implication of conjunctions by contraposition: $(Q(b_1) \wedge \ldots \wedge Q(b_m)) \Rightarrow (Q(a_1) \wedge \ldots \wedge Q(a_n))$, where $Q(a)$ is $a \notin S(w)$. Hence, co-occurrence constraints can be manipulated as functional dependencies, after the two sides have been switched.

From these rules we can derive some additional rules, shown below.

$$
\begin{array}{rll}
Down: A' \subseteq A: & A \Rightarrow B & \vdash_{cc} A' \Rightarrow B \\
Up: B \subseteq B': & A \Rightarrow B & \vdash_{cc} A \Rightarrow B' \\
Union: & (A \Rightarrow C) \wedge (B \Rightarrow C) & \vdash_{cc} AB \Rightarrow C \\
Decomp: & AB \Rightarrow C & \vdash_{cc} A \Rightarrow C
\end{array}
$$

These rules are trivially sound.

Theorem 4 (Soundness of co-occurrence deduction). *If $w \models F$ and $F \vdash_{cc} F'$, then $w \models F'$. If $T \models F$ and $F \vdash_{cc} F'$, then $T \models F'$.*

The following lemma contains the core of the completeness proof.

Lemma 2. *For each type T and for each symbol $a \in S^+(T)$, if $T \models a \Rightarrow B$, then $\mathcal{CC}(T) \vdash_{cc} a \Rightarrow B$, using the R-T-A rules only.*

Theorem 5 (Completeness of co-occurrence deduction for subtypes). *If $[\![T_1]\!] \subseteq [\![T_2]\!]$, then* $\text{upperS}(T_1) \wedge \mathcal{CC}(T_1) \vdash_{cc} \mathcal{CC}(T_2)$.

4.2 Order Deduction

Order constraints can be deduced from upper bounds, as follows.

$$\begin{array}{ll} FalseL : b \notin A : & \text{upper}(A) \vdash_{oc} b \prec b' \\ FalseR : b \notin A : & \text{upper}(A) \vdash_{oc} b' \prec b \end{array}$$

Theorem 6 (Soundness of order deduction). *If* $w \models F$ *and* $F \vdash_{oc} F'$, *then* $w \models F'$. *If* $T \models F$ *and* $F \vdash_{oc} F'$, *then* $T \models F'$.

Lemma 3 (Completeness of order deduction). *If* $a \neq b$ *and* $\{a, b\} \subseteq S(T)$ *and* $T \models a \prec b$, *then* $\mathcal{OC}(T) \vdash_{oc} a \prec b$.

Theorem 7 (Completeness of order deduction for subtypes). *If* $[\![T_1]\!] \subseteq [\![T_2]\!]$, *then* $\text{upperS}(T_1) \wedge \mathcal{OC}(T_1) \vdash_{oc} \mathcal{OC}(T_2)$.

4.3 Flat Constraints Deduction

Flat constraints are manipulated with a different approach. In this case, we check them together, and we directly discuss their soundness and completeness with respect to a pair of types. We first introduce a system to deduce whether the flat constraints of T_1 imply all the flat constraints of T_2.

Definition 11 $(T_1 \vdash_{flat} T_2)$

$$\begin{array}{ll} T_1 \vdash_{flat} T_2 \Leftrightarrow_{def} & \\ \quad (a?[m..n] \in Atoms(T_1) & \Rightarrow \exists m' \leq m, n' \geq n.\ a\,[m'..n'] \in Atoms(T_2)) \\ \quad \wedge\ (\text{N}(T_1) & \Rightarrow \text{N}(T_2)) \end{array}$$

Checking all flat constraints together makes sense because the three of them, in a sense, just check inclusion of $Atoms(T_1)$ into $Atoms(T_2)$. But there is another strong reason: the design of a sound and complete deduction system for $SIf(T)$ alone is actually much trickier than expected, while the holistic check is simple, sound, and complete, for the three of them, as formalized below.

Theorem 8 (Soundness of $\vdash_{flat}$). *If* $T_1 \vdash_{flat} T_2$, *then:*

1. $T_1 \models SIf(T_2)$;
2. $T_1 \models \text{upperS}(T_2)$;
3. $T_1 \models \text{ZeroMinMax}(T_2)$.

Theorem 9 (Completeness of $\vdash_{flat}$). *If* $[\![T_1]\!] \subseteq [\![T_2]\!]$, *then* $T_1 \vdash_{flat} T_2$.

4.4 Correctness and Completeness of Inclusion Deduction

We can now state the final theorem.

Theorem 10 (Correctness and completeness of inclusion deduction).

$$\begin{array}{lll} [\![T_1]\!] \subseteq [\![T_2]\!] & \Leftrightarrow & \text{upperS}(T_1) \wedge \mathcal{CC}(T_1) \vdash_{cc} \mathcal{CC}(T_2) \wedge \\ & & \text{upperS}(T_1) \wedge \mathcal{OC}(T_1) \vdash_{oc} \mathcal{OC}(T_2) \wedge \\ & & T_1 \vdash_{flat} T_2 \end{array}$$

5 Inclusion Checking

Theorem 10 proves that language inclusion among conflict-free string types can be decided through the deduction systems presented in the previous section. From this theorem we can derive an inclusion checking algorithm. The algorithm first verifies whether $T \vdash_{flat} U$, in time $O(n)$ in the size of T and U. The algorithm, then, verifies the deduction of co-occurrence constraints by a simple extension of the Beeri and Bernstein algorithm for functional constraints implication [10] (Section 5.1). The deduction for order constraints is much simpler: we essentially verify that each constraint of $\mathcal{OC}(U)$ either is in $\mathcal{OC}(T)$ or it involves a symbol that is not in $S(T)$ (Section 5.2).

In the following we will only sketch the basic principles of our algorithm; for more details, see [9].

5.1 Co-occurrence Constraints

We present here an algorithm to verify whether upperS$(T) \wedge \mathcal{CC}(T) \vdash_{cc} \mathcal{CC}(U)$. To this aim, it invokes a "backward closure" algorithm for the U_i argument of each $S^+(U_j) \Rightarrow S^+(U_i)$ constraint generated by the occurrence of an $\otimes$ operator inside U. The "backward closure" of $S(U_i)$ with respect to $F = \mathcal{CC}(T)$ (TBackwardClose($S(U_i)$)) is defined as the maximal $R \subseteq S(T)$ such that $F \vdash_{cc} R \Rightarrow S(U_i)$, and is computed using a reversed version of the standard Beeri-Bernstein algorithm, which is correct and complete for deduction rules R, T, and A [10]. By Lemma 2, and by rules *Union* and *Decomp*, upperS$(T) \wedge \mathcal{CC}(T) \vdash_{cc} S^+(U_j) \Rightarrow S^+(U_i)$ iff $(S(U_j) \cap S(T)) \subseteq$ TBackwardClose($S(U_i)$).

By a standard argument [10], the backward closure algorithm is linear in the total size of the rules. Since no symbol can appear in more than $2 * d_\otimes$ co-occurrence rules, where $d_\otimes$ is the nesting level of $\otimes$ operators, each closure invocation is in $O(n * d_\otimes)$. Backward closure is invoked once, or less, for each argument of each $\otimes$ inside U, which means that the co-occurrence constraint algorithm is in $O(n * n * d_\otimes)$, i.e. in $O(n^3)$.

In practice, we traverse U bottom up and we compute the T-closure of U subterms that are bigger and bigger. We can easily use dynamic programming in order to reuse the results of closure on the subterms to speed up the closure of a superterm. We do not study this optimization here.

5.2 Order Constraints

Order constraints correspond to the concatenation and union type operators. For each pair of leaves $a\,[m..n]$ and $b\,[m'..n']$ in the syntax tree of T, let $LCA_T[a, b]$ be their common ancestor that is farthest from the root (the *Lowest Common Ancestor*). For each a and b in $S(T)$, $a \prec\succ b \in \mathcal{OC}(T)$ iff $LCA_T[a, b]$ is labeled by $+$: the if direction is clear; for the only if direction, observe that any $+$ that is lower than the LCA is not a common ancestor, and any $+$ that is higher has both a and b below the same child. Similarly, $a \prec b \in \mathcal{OC}(T)$ iff $LCA_T[a, b] = +$ or a precedes b in T and $LCA_T[a, b] = \cdot$. As a consequence, upperS$(T) \wedge \mathcal{OC}(T) \vdash_{oc} \mathcal{OC}(U)$ iff, for each a and b in $S(U)$, such that a precedes b in U:

- if $LCA_U[a,b] = +$ then either $a \notin S(T)$ or $b \notin S(T)$ or $LCA_T[a,b] = +$;
- if $LCA_U[a,b] = \cdot$ then either $a \notin S(T)$ or $b \notin S(T)$ or $LCA_T[a,b] = +$ or ($LCA_T[a,b] = \cdot$ and a precedes b in T).

Hence, we can verify whether upperS$(T) \wedge \mathcal{OC}(T) \vdash_{oc} \mathcal{OC}(U)$ via the following algorithm. We first build an array $LCA_T[a,b]$ which associates each a and b in $S(T)$ with the operator that labels the LCA of a and b in T, and similarly for U; this can be done in linear time [11]. We then scan all the ordered pairs a, b of $S(U)$, checking the condition above, which can be done with $O(n^2)$ constant-time accesses to $LCA_T[\_,\_]$ and $LCA_U[\_,\_]$, which gives a $O(n^2)$ algorithm.

This inclusion-checking algorithm is presented here to prove that inclusion is in PTIME, but we do not expect it to be optimal. Specifically, in the crucial case of co-occurrence constraints, the set $\mathcal{CC}(T)$ has a very regular structure. For example, for any two constraints $L \Rightarrow R$ and $L' \Rightarrow R'$, if $R \cap R' \neq \emptyset$ then either $R \subset R'$ or $R' \subset R$, and similarly for L and L'. It seems plausible that better solutions could be achieved by exploiting this regularity.

6 Complexity of Intersection

Intersection for subclasses of RE corresponds to automata product, while inclusion corresponds to automata complement plus product, hence intersection is in general cheaper than inclusion. We show here that, for conflict-free types, things are quite different: while inclusion is in PTIME, intersection of two confict-free expressions is NP-hard. This result is quite surprising, and it suggests that it makes sense to study such types with an approach that is not based on automata.

Interestingly, NP-hardness does not depend on counting or Kleene star, but our proof depends crucially on the & operator.

Theorem 11. *Emptyness of the intersection of two conflict-free types is NP-hard, even if the types do not use counting and concatenation.*

Proof. (Hint) Consider m boolean variables $x_1, \ldots, x_m$ and a formula $\phi = (a_1^1 \vee a_1^2 \vee a_1^3) \wedge \ldots \wedge (a_n^1 \vee a_n^2 \vee a_n^3)$ where each literal a_j^i is either a variable x_l or a negated variable $\neg x_l$; Satisfiability of ϕ can be encoded as the intersection of two conflict-free types T_1 and T_2 as exemplified below. Both types have one symbol for each occurrence of a literal in ϕ, hence their size is linear in $|\phi|$.

$$
\begin{aligned}
\phi &= (x_1 \vee x_2 \vee x_3) \wedge (\neg x_1 \vee x_3 \vee x_4) \wedge (\neg x_2 \vee \neg x_3 \vee \neg x_4) \wedge (\neg x_1 \vee \neg x_3 \vee x_4) \\
T_1 &= (a_1^1 + a_1^2 + a_1^3) \mathbin{\&} (a_2^1 + a_2^2 + a_2^3) \mathbin{\&} (a_3^1 + a_3^2 + a_3^3) \mathbin{\&} (a_4^1 + a_4^2 + a_4^3) \\
T_2 &= ((a_1^1?) + (a_2^1? \mathbin{\&} a_4^1?)) \mathbin{\&} ((a_1^2?) + (a_3^1?)) \\
&\quad \mathbin{\&} ((a_1^3? \mathbin{\&} a_2^2?) + (a_3^2? \mathbin{\&} a_4^2?)) \mathbin{\&} ((a_2^3? \mathbin{\&} a_4^3?) + (a_3^3?))
\end{aligned}
$$

ϕ is satisfiable iff it has a *witness*, i.e. a choice of literal instances, one from each factor, such that not two instances are contradictory, i.e. if x_i is chosen in a factor then $\neg x_i$ is not chosen in any other factor.

Any element of T_1 corresponds to a choice of literal instances, one from each factor. If the same list also belongs to T_2, then it is not contradictory. Hence, words in $[\![T_1]\!] \cap [\![T_2]\!]$ correspond to witnesses for ϕ.

7 Related Work

The properties of unordered XML types have been studied in several recent papers. In [12], the authors discuss the techniques and heuristics they used in implementing a type-checker, based on sheaves automata with Presburger arithmetic, for unordered XML types. The type language is an extension of the language we are considering here, and shares a similar restriction on the use of repetition types. The main purpose of the paper is to address scalability problems that naturally arise when working on XML types; as a consequence, they describe effective heuristics that improve scalability, but do not affect computational complexity.

Restrictions to RE languages that are similar to ours have been proposed many times. For example, conflict-free REs appear as "conflict-free DTDs" in the context of well-typed XML updates in [13], as "duplicate-free DTDs" in the context of path inclusion in [8], and as "single occurrence REs" in the context of DTD inference in [4]. The same restriction that we pose on Kleene-star can be found, for example, in [12]. Chain Regular Expressions (CHARE's) [4,1] are also strictly related. They are defined as concatenations of factors, where each factor has a shape $(a_1 + \ldots + a_n)$, $(a_1 + \ldots + a_n)?$, $(a_1 + \ldots + a_n)^*$ or $(a_1 + \ldots + a_n)^+$. As we discussed in Section 2.1, the first three classes of factors can be easily expressed in our language, using counting and interleaving. Factors like $(a_1 + \ldots + a_n)^+$ cannot be expressed in our languages, but we could add them as a third class of base types $\{a_1, \ldots, a_n\}[1..*]$, besides $a\,[m..n]$ and ϵ, with $\mathcal{FC}(A[1..*]) = (A^+ \wedge \text{upper}(A))$ and $\text{N}(A[1..*]) = \mathit{false}$. We did not consider these base types just for minimality. Simple expressions [3] have a more general syntax than CHAREs but the same expressive power, hence can still be managed through our approach.

We have cited many times paper [1], where the complexity of type inclusion is studied for many different dialects of REs with interleaving and/or counting, showing that inclusion complexity is almost invariably EXPSPACE-complete. In particular, this is shown to hold for chain-REs with counting, which are concatenations of CHARE factors, as defined above, and counting factors $(a_1 + \ldots + a_k)[m..n]$ (with $n \neq *$ and $m \geq 0$), with no interleaving operator. In a sense, this hints that the conflict-free restriction, rather than the Kleene-star restriction, is crucial for our PTIME result. In the same paper, the authors introduce a sublanguage of CHAREs with PTIME inclusion, but that fragment is quite trivial, since it only includes counting factors $(a_1 + \ldots + a_k)[m..n]$, with the further restriction that $m > 0$ and $n \neq *$, hence cannot express neither optionality nor unbounded repetition (neither * nor $^+$).[5]

8 Conclusions

Inclusion for REs with interleaving, counting, or both, is EXPSPACE-complete, even if we consider the restricted subclass of CHAREs (with counting) [2,1]. This result easily extends to XML types featuring these operators. We have introduced

[5] Observe that our language can express optionality and repetition, but cannot express counting factors $(a_1 + \ldots + a_k)[m..n]$ with $k > 1$, unless $m = 0$ and $n = *$.

here a restricted class of REs with interleaving and counting. Our restriction is severe, but it seems to match reasonably well the measured features of actual DTDs and XSDs found on the web, and is extremely easy to define and verify. For this class of REs, we have proved that inclusion is in PTIME, a complexity that is surprising low, and trivially extends to DTDs and XSDs that use REs of this class for their content models. We have shown how to use classical algorithms to get a $O(n^3)$ upper bound, but we feel that this could be easy lowered. We also proved that intersection of two conflict-free types has not the same complexity as inclusion (unless P=NP) but is, quite surprisingly, NP-hard.

Our result is based on the transformation of our REs into sets of constraints which completely characterize the expressions and are easy to manipulate. We believe that this constraint-based approach could be fruitfully used for other analysis tasks, such as, for example, type normalization, path minimization under a DTD, or a polynomial membership algorithm.

Acknowledgments. We thanks the anonymous referees for their constructive comments and suggestions.

References

1. Gelade, W., Martens, W., Neven, F.: Optimizing schema languages for XML: Numerical constraints and interleaving. In: Schwentick, T., Suciu, D. (eds.) ICDT 2007. LNCS, vol. 4353, Springer, Heidelberg (2006)
2. Mayer, A.J., Stockmeyer, L.J.: Word problems-this time with interleaving. Inf. Comput. 115, 293–311 (1994)
3. Bex, G.J., Neven, F., den Bussche, J.V.: DTDs versus XML schema: A practical study. In: Amer-Yahia, S., Gravano, L. (eds.) WebDB, pp. 79–84 (2004)
4. Bex, G.J., Neven, F., Schwentick, T., Tuyls, K.: Inference of concise DTDs from XML data. In: Dayal, U., Whang, K.Y., Lomet, D.B., Alonso, G., Lohman, G.M., Kersten, M.L., Cha, S.K., Kim, Y.K. (eds.) VLDB, pp. 115–126. ACM Press, New York (2006)
5. Amer-Yahia, S., Cho, S., Lakshmanan, L.V.S., Srivastava, D.: Minimization of tree pattern queries. In: SIGMOD Conference, pp. 497–508 (2001)
6. Thompson, H.S., Beech, D., Maloney, M., Mendelsohn, N.: XML Schema Part 1: Structures Second Edition. Technical report, World Wide Web Consortium, W3C Recommendation (2004)
7. Martens, W., Neven, F., Schwentick, T.: Complexity of decision problems for simple regular expressions. In: Fiala, J., Koubek, V., Kratochvíl, J. (eds.) MFCS 2004. LNCS, vol. 3153, pp. 889–900. Springer, Heidelberg (2004)
8. Wood, P.T.: Containment for XPath fragments under DTD constraints. In: Calvanese, D., Lenzerini, M., Motwani, R. (eds.) ICDT 2003. LNCS, vol. 2572, pp. 300–314. Springer, Heidelberg (2002)
9. Ghelli, G., Colazzo, D., Sartiani, C.: Efficient inclusion for a class of XML types with interleaving and counting. Technical report, Dipartimento di Informatica - Università di Pisa (2007)
10. Beeri, C., Bernstein, P.A.: Computational problems related to the design of normal form relational schemas. ACM Trans. Database Syst. 4, 30–59 (1979)
11. Bender, M.A., Farach-Colton, M.: The LCA problem revisited. In: Gonnet, G.H., Viola, A. (eds.) LATIN 2000. LNCS, vol. 1776, pp. 88–94. Springer, Heidelberg (2000)
12. Foster, J.N., Pierce, B.C., Schmitt, A.: A logic your typechecker can count on: Unordered tree types in practice. In: PLAN-X, informal proceedings (2007)
13. Barbosa, D., Mendelzon, A.O., Libkin, L., Mignet, L., Arenas, M.: Efficient incremental validation of XML documents. In: ICDE, pp. 671–682. IEEE Computer Society Press, Los Alamitos (2004)

Towards Practical Typechecking for Macro Tree Transducers

Alain Frisch[1] and Haruo Hosoya[2]

[1] INRIA Rocquencourt
alain@frisch.fr
[2] The University of Tokyo
hahosoya@is.s.u-tokyo.ac.jp

Abstract. Macro tree transducers (mtt) are an important model that both covers many useful XML transformations and allows decidable exact typechecking. This paper reports our first step toward an implementation of mtt typechecker that has a practical efficiency. Our approach is to represent an input type obtained from a backward inference as an alternating tree automaton, in a style similar to Tozawa's XSLT0 typechecking. In this approach, typechecking reduces to checking emptiness of an alternating tree automaton. We propose several optimizations (Cartesian factorization, state partitioning) on the backward inference process in order to produce much smaller alternating tree automata than the naive algorithm, and we present our efficient algorithm for checking emptiness of alternating tree automata, where we exploit the explicit representation of alternation for local optimizations. Our preliminary experiments confirm that our algorithm has a practical performance that can typecheck simple transformations with respect to the full XHTML in a reasonable time.

1 Introduction

Static typechecking for XML transformations is an important problem that expectedly has a significant impact on real-world XML developments. To this end, several research groups have made efforts in building typed XML programming languages [10,3] with much influence from the tradition of typed functional languages [2,12]. While this line of work has successfully treated general, Turing-complete languages, its approximative nature has resulted in an even trivial transformation like the identity function to fail to typecheck unless a large amount of code duplicates and type annotations are introduced [9]. Such situation has led us to pay attention to completely different approaches that have no such deficiency, among which *exact typechecking* has emergingly become promising. The exact typechecking approach has extensively been investigated for years [14,22,18,25,28,26,13,17,1,15,20,16], in which *macro tree transducers* (mtt) have been one of the most important computation models since they allow decidable exact typechecking [6], yet cover many useful XML transformations [6,13,5,21]. Unfortunately, these studies are mainly theoretical and their practicality has never been clear except for some small cases [25,28].

M. Arenas and M.I. Schwartzbach (Eds.): DBPL 2007, LNCS 4797, pp. 246–260, 2007.

This paper reports our first step toward a *practical* implementation of typechecker for mtts. As a basic part, we follow an already-established scheme called *backward inference*, which computes the preimage of the output type for the subject transformation and then checks it against the given input type. (This is because, as is well known, the more obvious, forward inference does not work since the image of the input type is not always a regular tree language and can even go beyond context-free tree languages.[1]) However, our proposal is, on top of this scheme, to use a representation of the preimage by an *alternating tree automaton* [23], extending the idea used in Tozawa's typechecking algorithm for XSLT0 [25]. In this approach, typechecking reduces to checking emptiness of an alternating tree automaton.

Whereas normal tree automata use only disjunctions in the transition relation, alternating tree automata can use both disjunctions and conjunctions. This extra freedom permits a more compact representation (they can be exponentially more succinct than normal tree automata) and make them a good intermediate language to study optimizations. Having explicit representation of transitions as Boolean formulas (with disjunctions and conjunctions) allows us to derive optimized versions of the rules for backward inference, such as Cartesian decomposition and state partitioning (Section 4), from which we obtain a typechecking algorithm that scales to large types. Also, in our emptiness algorithm for alternating tree automata, we exploit various simple facts on Boolean formulas (e.g., a formula $\phi_1 \wedge \phi_2$ denotes an empty set if ϕ_1 does so) to perform efficient shortcuts—these exploited facts are not immediately available in normal tree automata (our emptiness algorithm is omitted from this abstract for lack of space; see our technical report [8]).

For preliminary experiments on our implementation, we have written several sizes of transformations and verified against the full XHTML type automatically generated from its DTD. (In reality, transformations are often small, but types that they work on are quite big in many cases; excellent statistical evidences are provided in [19].) The results show that, for this scale of transformations, our implementation has successfully completed typechecking in a reasonable time (about 1 second or less on a stock PC) even with XHTML, which is considered to be quite large. We have also compared the performance of our implementation with Tozawa and Hagiya's [28] and confirmed that ours has comparable speed for their small examples that are used in their own experiments.

Related work. Numerous techniques for exact typechecking for XML transformations have been proposed. Many of these take their target languages from the tree transducer family. Those include techniques for macro tree transducers [14,5], for macro forest transducers [22], for k-pebble tree transducers [18,5], for subsets of XSLT [25,28], for high-level tree transducers [26], and a tree transformation

[1] Special thanks to Sebastian Maneth providing a simple proof for this: a macro (or even a top-down) tree transducer can produce the tree language over $\{a, b, c\}$ that consists of trees $a(t, t')$ where t' is identical to t except that every symbol b in t is replaced with c in t', but this language is not in context-free tree languages according to [4].

language TL [13]. Other techniques treat XML query languages in the select-construct style [17,1,15] or even simpler transformations [20,16]. Most of the above mentioned work provides only theoretical results; the only exceptions are [25,28], where some experimental results are shown though we have examined much bigger examples (in particular in the size of types).

Several algorithms in pragmatic approaches have been proposed to address high complexity problems related to XML typechecking. A top-down algorithm for inclusion test on tree automata has been developed and used in XDuce typechecker [11]; an improved version is proposed in [24]. A similar idea has been exploited in the work on ℂDuce on the emptiness check for alternating tree automata [7]; the emptiness check algorithm in our present work is strongly influenced by this. Tozawa and Hagiya have developed BDD-based algorithms for inclusion test on tree automata [27] and for satisfiability test on a certain logic related to XML typechecking [28].

Lastly, another relevant piece of work is on static typechecking for XSLT programs by Møller, Olesen, and Schwartzbach [19]. They employ a context-sensitive flow analysis and have experimentally proved its high precision by using a number of style sheets taken from real applications. However, their technique is, in a sense, based on a forward inference and, in theory, cannot be exact (even if we exclude obscure features such as complex conditionals and external function calls). Whether or not the lack of exactness can be problematic in practice is yet to be seen. (A remark worthwhile here is that their analysis is precise enough to typecheck a trivial identity function with respect to a given type.)

Overview. This paper is organized as follows. In Section 2, we recall the classical definitions of macro tree transducers (mtt), bottom-up tree automata (bta), and alternating tree automata (ata). In Section 3, we present a basic construction of our backward type inference that produces an ata from an mtt and a deterministic bta. In Section 4, we revisit this construction from a practical point of view and describe important optimizations and implementation techniques. In Section 5, we report the results of our experiments with our implementation of the typechecker for several XML transformations. In Section 6, we conclude this paper with future research directions.

Our accompanied technical report [8] describes, in addition to proofs of theorems and our emptiness check for atas, our theoretical contributions omitted from this abstract for lack space. Namely, we establish an exact relationship with two major existing algorithms for mtt typechecking, a classical algorithm based on "function enumeration" [5] and an algorithm proposed by Maneth, Perst, and Seidl [14]. In this, we show that each of these algorithms can be retrieved from ours by composing it with a known algorithm.

2 Preliminaries

2.1 Macro Tree Transducers

We assume an alphabet Σ where each *symbol* $a \in \Sigma$ is associated with its arity; often we write $a^{(n)}$ to denote a symbol a with arity n. We assume that there is a symbol ϵ with zero-arity. *Trees*, ranged over by $v, w, \ldots$, are defined as follows: $v ::= a^{(n)}(v_1, \ldots, v_n)$. We write ϵ for $\epsilon()$ and $\vec{v} = (v_1, \ldots, v_n)$ to represent a tuple of trees. Assume a set of *variables*, ranged over by $x, y, \ldots$. A *macro tree transducer* (mtt) $\mathcal{T}$ is a tuple (P, P_0, Π) where P is a finite set of *procedures*, $P_0 \subseteq P$ is a set of *initial procedures*, and Π is a set of *(transformation) rules* each of the form $p^{(k)}(a^{(n)}(x_1, \ldots, x_n), y_1, \ldots, y_k) \to e$ where each y_i is called *(accumulating) parameter* and e is a (n, k)-expression, defined below. We will abbreviate the tuples $(x_1, \ldots, x_n)$ and $(y_1, \ldots, y_k)$ to $\vec{x}$ and $\vec{y}$. Note that each procedure is associated with its arity, i.e., the number of parameters; we write $p^{(k)}$ to denote a procedure p with arity k. An (n, k)-*expression* e is defined by the following grammar

$$e ::= a^{(m)}(e_1, \ldots, e_m) \mid p^{(l)}(x_h, e_1, \ldots, e_l) \mid y_j$$

where only y_j with $1 \le j \le k$ and x_h with $1 \le h \le n$ can appear as variables. We assume that each initial procedure has arity zero.

We describe the call-by-value semantics of an mtt (P, P_0, Π) by a denotation function $[\![\cdot]\!]$. First, the semantics of a procedure $p^{(k)}$ takes a tree $a^{(n)}(v_1, \ldots, v_n)$ and parameters $\vec{w} = (w_1, \ldots, w_k)$ and returns the set of trees resulting from the evaluation of p's body expressions.

$$[\![p^{(k)}]\!](a^{(n)}(\vec{v}), \vec{w}) = \bigcup_{(p^{(k)}(a^{(n)}(\vec{x}), \vec{y}) \to e) \in \Pi} [\![e]\!](\vec{v}, \vec{w})$$

Then, the semantics of an (n, k)-expression e takes a current n-tuple $\vec{v} = (v_1, \ldots, v_n)$ of trees and a k-tuple of parameters $\vec{w} = (w_1, \ldots, w_k)$, and returns a set of trees. It is defined as follows.

$$\begin{aligned}
[\![a^{(m)}(e_1, \ldots, e_m)]\!](\vec{v}, \vec{w}) &= \{a^{(m)}(v'_1, \ldots, v'_m) \mid v'_i \in [\![e_i]\!](\vec{v}, \vec{w}), \text{ for } i = 1, \ldots, m\} \\
[\![p^{(l)}(x_h, e_1, \ldots, e_l)]\!](\vec{v}, \vec{w}) &= \{[\![p^{(l)}]\!](v_h, (w'_1, \ldots, w'_l)) \mid w'_j \in [\![e_j]\!](\vec{v}, \vec{w}), \\
&\qquad\qquad\qquad\qquad\qquad\qquad\qquad\qquad \text{ for } j = 1, \ldots, l\} \\
[\![y_j]\!](\vec{v}, \vec{w}) &= \{w_j\}
\end{aligned}$$

Note that an mtt is allowed to inspect only the input tree and never a part of the output tree being constructed. Also, parameters only accumulate subtrees that will potentially become part of the output and never point to parts of the input.

The whole semantics of the mtt with respect to a given input tree v is defined by $\mathcal{T}(v) = \bigcup_{p_0 \in P_0} [\![p_0]\!](v)$. An mtt $\mathcal{T}$ is *deterministic* when $\mathcal{T}(v)$ has at most one element for any v; also, $\mathcal{T}$ is *total* when $\mathcal{T}(v)$ has at least one element for any v. We will also use the classical definition of *images* and *preimages*: $\mathcal{T}(V) = \bigcup_{v \in V} \mathcal{T}(v)$ and $\mathcal{T}^{-1}(V') = \{v \mid \exists v' \in V'. v' \in \mathcal{T}(v)\}$.

2.2 Tree Automata and Alternation

A *(bottom-up) tree automaton* (bta) $\mathcal{M}$ is a tuple (Q, Q_F, Δ) where Q is a finite set of *states*, $Q_F \subseteq Q$ is a set of *final states*, and Δ is a set of *(transition) rules* each of the form $q \leftarrow a^{(n)}(q_1, \ldots, q_n)$ where each q_i is from Q. We will write $\vec{q}$ for the tuple $(q_1, \ldots, q_n)$. Given a bta $\mathcal{M} = (Q, Q_F, \Delta)$, acceptance of a tree by a state is defined inductively as follows: $\mathcal{M}$ *accepts* a tree $a^{(n)}(\vec{v})$ by a state q when there is a rule $q \leftarrow a^{(n)}(\vec{q})$ in Δ such that each subtree v_i is accepted by the corresponding state q_i. $\mathcal{M}$ accepts a tree v when $\mathcal{M}$ accepts v by a final state $q \in Q_F$. We write $[\![q]\!]_{\mathcal{M}}$ for the set of trees that the automaton $\mathcal{M}$ accepts by the state q (we drop the subscript $\mathcal{M}$ when it is clear), and $\mathcal{L}(\mathcal{M}) = \bigcup_{q \in Q_F} [\![q]\!]$ for the set of trees accepted by the automaton $\mathcal{M}$. Also, we sometimes say that a value v *has type* q when v is accepted by the state q. A bta (Q, Q_F, Δ) is *complete and deterministic* when, for any symbol $a^{(n)}$ and n-tuple of states $\vec{q}$, there is exactly one transition rule of the form $q \leftarrow a^{(n)}(\vec{q})$ in Δ. Such a bta is called *deterministic bottom-up tree automaton* (dbta). For any value v, there is exactly one state q such that $v \in [\![q]\!]$. In other words, the collection $\{[\![q]\!] \mid q \in Q\}$ is a partition of the set of trees.

An *alternating tree automaton* (ata) $\mathcal{A}$ is a tuple (Ξ, Ξ_0, Φ) where Ξ is a finite set of *states*, $\Xi_0 \subseteq \Xi$ is a set of *initial states*, and Φ is a function that maps each pair $(X, a^{(n)})$ of a state and an n-ary symbol to an n-formula, where *n-formulas* are defined by the following grammar.

$$\phi ::= \downarrow_i X \mid \phi_1 \vee \phi_2 \mid \phi_1 \wedge \phi_2 \mid \top \mid \bot$$

(with $1 \leq i \leq n$). In particular, note that a 0-ary formula evaluates naturally to a Boolean. Given an ata $\mathcal{A} = (\Xi, \Xi_0, \Phi)$, we define acceptance of a tree by a state. $\mathcal{A}$ *accepts* a tree $a^{(n)}(\vec{v})$ by a state X when $\vec{v} \vdash \Phi(X, a^{(n)})$ holds, where the judgment $\vec{v} \vdash \phi$ is defined inductively as follows: $\vec{v} \vdash \phi_1 \wedge \phi_2$ if $\vec{v} \vdash \phi_1$ and $\vec{v} \vdash \phi_2$; $\vec{v} \vdash \phi_1 \vee \phi_2$ if $\vec{v} \vdash \phi_1$ or $\vec{v} \vdash \phi_2$; $\vec{v} \vdash \top$; $\vec{v} \vdash \downarrow_i X$ if $\mathcal{A}$ accepts v_i by X. That is, $\vec{v} \vdash \phi$ intuitively means that ϕ holds by interpreting each $\downarrow_i X$ as "v_i has type X." We write $[\![X]\!]$ for the set of trees accepted by a state X and $[\![\phi]\!] = \{\vec{v} \mid \vec{v} \vdash \phi\}$ for the set of n-tuples accepted by an n-formula ϕ. We write $\mathcal{L}(\mathcal{A}) = \bigcup_{X_0 \in \Xi_0} [\![X_0]\!]$ for the language accepted by the ata $\mathcal{A}$. Note that a bta $\mathcal{M} = (Q, Q_F, \Delta)$ can be seen as an ata with the same set of states and final states by defining the function Φ as $\Phi(q, a^{(n)}) = \bigvee_{(q \leftarrow a^{(n)}(\vec{q})) \in \Delta} \bigwedge_{i=1,\ldots,n} \downarrow_i q_i$, and the definitions for the semantics of states and the language accepted by the automaton seen as a bta or an ata then coincide. We will use the notation $\simeq$ to represent semantical equivalence of pairs of states or pairs of formulas.

3 Typechecking

Given a dbta $\mathcal{M}_{\text{out}}$ ("output type"), a bta $\mathcal{M}_{\text{in}}$ ("input type"), and an mtt $\mathcal{T}$, the goal of typechecking is to verify that $\mathcal{T}(\mathcal{L}(\mathcal{M}_{\text{in}})) \subseteq \mathcal{L}(\mathcal{M}_{\text{out}})$. It is well known that $\mathcal{T}(\mathcal{L}(\mathcal{M}_{\text{in}}))$ is in general beyond regular tree languages and hence the forward inference approach (i.e., first calculate an automaton representing $\mathcal{T}(\mathcal{L}(\mathcal{M}_{\text{in}}))$ and check it to be included in $\mathcal{L}(\mathcal{M}_{\text{out}})$) does not work. Therefore an approach usually taken is the backward inference, which is based on the observation that $\mathcal{T}(\mathcal{L}(\mathcal{M}_{\text{in}})) \subseteq \mathcal{L}(\mathcal{M}_{\text{out}}) \iff \mathcal{L}(\mathcal{M}_{\text{in}}) \cap \mathcal{T}^{-1}(\mathcal{L}(\mathcal{M})) = \emptyset$, where $\mathcal{M}$ is the complement automaton of $\mathcal{M}_{\text{out}}$. Intuitively, if the intersection

$\mathcal{L}(\mathcal{M}_{\text{in}}) \cap \mathcal{T}^{-1}(\mathcal{L}(\mathcal{M}))$ is not empty, then it is possible to exhibit a tree v in this intersection; since this tree satisfies that $v \in \mathcal{L}(\mathcal{M}_{\text{in}})$ and $\mathcal{T}(v) \not\subseteq \mathcal{L}(\mathcal{M}_{\text{out}})$, it means that there is a counter-example of the well-typedness of the mtt with respect to the given input and output types. Algorithmically, the approach consists of computing an automaton $\mathcal{A}$ representing $\mathcal{T}^{-1}(\mathcal{L}(\mathcal{M}))$ and then checking that $\mathcal{L}(\mathcal{M}_{\text{in}}) \cap \mathcal{L}(\mathcal{A}) = \emptyset$. Since the language $\mathcal{T}^{-1}(\mathcal{L}(\mathcal{M}))$ is regular and indeed such automata $\mathcal{A}$ can effectively be computed, the above disjointness is decidable.

The originality of our approach is to compute $\mathcal{A}$ as an alternating tree automaton. Let a dbta $\mathcal{M} = (Q, Q_F, \Delta)$ and an mtt $\mathcal{T} = (P, P_0, \Pi)$ be given. Here, note that the automaton $\mathcal{M}$, which denotes the complement of the output type $\mathcal{M}_{\text{out}}$, can be obtained from $\mathcal{M}_{\text{out}}$ in a linear time since $\mathcal{M}_{\text{out}}$ is deterministic. From $\mathcal{M}$ and $\mathcal{T}$, we build an ata $\mathcal{A} = (\Xi, \Xi_0, \Phi)$ where

$$\begin{aligned}
\Xi &= \{\langle p^{(k)}, q, \vec{q}\rangle \mid p^{(k)} \in P,\ q \in Q, \vec{q} \in Q^k\} \\
\Xi_0 &= \{\langle p_0, q\rangle \mid p_0 \in P_0,\ q \in Q_F\} \\
\Phi(\langle p^{(k)}, q, \vec{q}\rangle, a^{(n)}) &= \bigvee_{(p^{(k)}(a^{(n)}(\vec{x}), \vec{y}) \to e) \in \Pi} \mathrm{Inf}(e, q, \vec{q}).
\end{aligned}$$

Here, the function Inf is defined inductively as follows.

$$\begin{aligned}
\mathrm{Inf}(b^{(m)}(e_1, \ldots, e_m), q, \vec{q}) &= \bigvee_{(q \leftarrow b^{(m)}(\vec{q'})) \in \Delta} \bigwedge_{j=1,\ldots,m} \mathrm{Inf}(e_j, q'_j, \vec{q}) \\
\mathrm{Inf}(p^{(l)}(x_h, e_1, \ldots, e_l), q, \vec{q}) &= \bigvee_{\vec{q'} \in Q^l} \left(\downarrow_h \langle p^{(l)}, q, \vec{q'}\rangle \wedge \bigwedge_{j=1,\ldots,l} \mathrm{Inf}(e_j, q'_j, \vec{q}) \right) \\
\mathrm{Inf}(y_j, q, \vec{q}) &= \begin{cases} \top \ (q = q_j) \\ \bot \ (q \neq q_j) \end{cases}
\end{aligned}$$

Intuitively, each state $\langle p, q, \vec{q}\rangle$ represents the set of trees v such that the procedure p may transform v to some tree u of type q, assuming that the parameters y_i are bound to trees w_i each of type q_i. Formally, we can prove the following invariant

$$\forall \vec{w} \in [\![\vec{q}]\!].\ v \in [\![\langle p^{(k)}, q, \vec{q}\rangle]\!] \iff [\![p^{(k)}]\!](v, \vec{w}) \cap [\![q]\!] \neq \emptyset \qquad (1)$$

where $\vec{w} \in [\![\vec{q}]\!]$ means $w_1 \in [\![q_1]\!], \ldots, w_k \in [\![q_k]\!]$. Note that this invariant implies that whether the right-hand side holds or not does not depend on the specific choice of the values w_i from the sets $[\![q_i]\!]$. From this invariant, the initial states Ξ_0 represent the set of trees that we want. Then, the function $\mathrm{Inf}(e, q, \vec{q})$ infers an n-formula representing the set of n-tuples $\vec{v}$ such that the expression e may transform $\vec{v}$ to some tree of type q, assuming that the parameters y_i are bound to trees w_i each of type q_i. Each case can be understood as follows.

- In order for a tree u of type q to be produced from the constructor expression $b^{(m)}(e_1, \ldots, e_m)$, first, there must be a transition $q \leftarrow b^{(m)}(\vec{q'}) \in \Delta$. In addition, u's each subtree must have type q'_i and must be produced from the corresponding subexpression e_i.

- In order for a tree u of type q to be produced from the procedure call $p(x_h, e_1, \ldots, e_l)$, first, a tree w'_j of some type q'_j must be yielded from each parameter expression e_j. In addition, the h-th input tree must have type $\langle p, q, (q'_1, \ldots, q'_l)\rangle$ since the result tree u must be produced by the procedure p from the h-th tree with parameters $w'_1, \ldots, w'_l$ of types $q'_1, \ldots, q'_l$.
- In order for a tree of type q to be produced from the variable expression y_j, this variable must have type q.

Theorem 1. $\mathcal{L}(\mathcal{A}) = \mathcal{T}^{-1}(\mathcal{L}(\mathcal{M}))$.

Finally, it remains to check $\mathcal{L}(\mathcal{M}_{\text{in}}) \cap \mathcal{L}(A) = \emptyset$, for which we first calculate an ata $\mathcal{A}'$ representing $\mathcal{L}(\mathcal{M}_{\text{in}}) \cap \mathcal{L}(A)$ (this can easily be done since an ata can freely use intersections) and then check the emptiness of $\mathcal{A}'$. For lack of space, we give our emptiness checking algorithm in [8].

Note that the size of the ata $\mathcal{A}$ is polynomial in the sizes of $\mathcal{M}_{\text{out}}$ and of $\mathcal{T}$. The size of $\mathcal{A}'$ is thus polynomial in the sizes of $\mathcal{M}_{\text{in}}$, $\mathcal{M}_{\text{out}}$, and $\mathcal{T}$.

4 Optimization Techniques

In this section, we describe some optimization techniques for speeding up the backward inference presented in Section 3.

A simple algorithm to compute the input type as an alternating tree automaton is to follow naively the formal construction given in Section 3. A first observation is that it is possible to build the automaton lazily, starting from the initial states, producing new states and computing $\Phi(\_)$ only on demand. This is sometimes useful since our emptiness check algorithm [8] works in a top-down way and will not always materialize the whole automaton.

The defining equations for the function Inf as given in Section 3 produce huge formulas. We will now describe new equations that produce much smaller formulas in practice. Before describing them, it is convenient to generalize the notation $\text{Inf}(e, q, \vec{q})$ by allowing a *set of states* $\overline{q} \subseteq Q$ instead of a single state $q \in Q$ for the output type. Intuitively, we want $\text{Inf}(e, \overline{q}, \vec{q})$ to be semantically equivalent to $\bigvee_{q \in \overline{q}} \text{Inf}(e, q, \vec{q})$. We obtain a direct definition of $\text{Inf}(e, \overline{q}, \vec{q})$ by adapting the rules for $\text{Inf}(e, q, \vec{q})$:

$$
\begin{aligned}
\text{Inf}(b^{(m)}(e_1, \ldots, e_m), \overline{q}, \vec{q}) &= \bigvee_{(q \leftarrow b^{(m)}(\vec{q'})) \in \Delta, q \in \overline{q}} \; \bigwedge_{j=1\ldots,m} \text{Inf}(e_j, \{q'_j\}, \vec{q}) \\
\text{Inf}(p^{(l)}(x_h, e_1, \ldots, e_l), \overline{q}, \vec{q}) &= \bigvee_{\vec{q'} \in Q^l} \left(\downarrow_h \langle p^{(l)}, \overline{q}, \vec{q'}\rangle \wedge \bigwedge_{j=1,\ldots,l} \text{Inf}(e_j, \{q'_j\}, \vec{q}) \right) \\
\text{Inf}(y_j, \overline{q}, \vec{q}) &= \begin{cases} \top \; (q_j \in \overline{q}) \\ \bot \; (q_j \notin \overline{q}) \end{cases}
\end{aligned}
$$

We have used the notation $\downarrow_h \langle p^{(l)}, \overline{q}, \vec{q'}\rangle$. Intuitively, this should be semantically equivalent to the union $\bigvee_{q \in \overline{q}} \downarrow_h \langle p^{(l)}, q, \vec{q'}\rangle$. Instead of using this as a definition, we prefer to change the set of states of the automaton:

$$\begin{aligned}
\Xi &= \{\langle p^{(k)}, \overline{q}, q_1, \ldots, q_k\rangle \mid p^{(k)} \in P,\ \overline{q} \subseteq Q, \vec{q} \in Q^k\}\\
\Xi_0 &= \{\langle p_0, Q_F\rangle \mid p_0 \in P_0\}\\
\Phi(\langle p^{(k)}, \overline{q}, \vec{q}\rangle, a^{(n)}) &= \bigvee_{(p^{(k)}(a^{(n)}(\vec{x}), \vec{y}) \to e) \in \Pi} \mathrm{Inf}(e, \overline{q}, \vec{q}).
\end{aligned}$$

In theory, this new alternating tree automaton could have exponentially many more states. However, in practice, and because of the optimizations we will describe now, this actually reduces significantly the number of states that need to be computed.

The sections below will use the semantical equivalence $\bigvee_{q \in \overline{q}} \mathrm{Inf}(e, \{q\}, \vec{q}) \simeq \mathrm{Inf}(e, \overline{q}, \vec{q})$ mentioned above in order to simplify formulas.

Cartesian factorization. The rule for the constructor expression $b^{(m)}(e_1, \ldots, e_m)$ can be rewritten:

$$\mathrm{Inf}(b^{(m)}(e_1, \ldots, e_m), \overline{q}, \vec{q}) = \bigvee_{\vec{q'} \in \Delta(\overline{q}, b^{(m)})} \bigwedge_{j=1\ldots,m} \mathrm{Inf}(e_j, \{q'_j\}, \vec{q})$$

where $\Delta(\overline{q}, b^{(m)}) = \{\vec{q'} \mid q \leftarrow b^{(m)}(\vec{q'}) \in \Delta, q \in \overline{q}\} \subseteq Q^m$. Now assume that we have a decomposition of this set $\Delta(\overline{q}, b^{(m)})$ as a union of l Cartesian products:

$$\Delta(\overline{q}, b^{(m)}) = (\overline{q}_1^1 \times \ldots \times \overline{q}_m^1) \cup \ldots \cup (\overline{q}_1^l \times \ldots \times \overline{q}_m^l)$$

where the $\overline{q}_j^i$ are sets of states. It is always possible to find such a decomposition: at worst, using only singletons for the $\overline{q}_j^i$, we will have as many terms in the union as m-tuples in $\Delta(\overline{q}, b^{(m)})$. But often, we can produce a decomposition with fewer terms in the union. Let us write $\mathrm{Cart}(\Delta(\overline{q}, b^{(m)})$ for such a decomposition (seen as a subset of $(2^Q)^m$). One can then use the following rule:

$$\mathrm{Inf}(b^{(m)}(e_1, \ldots, e_m), \overline{q}, \vec{q}) = \bigvee_{(\overline{q}_1, \ldots, \overline{q}_m) \in \mathrm{Cart}(\Delta(\overline{q}, b^{(m)}))} \bigwedge_{j=1,\ldots,m} \mathrm{Inf}(e_j, \overline{q}_j, \vec{q})$$

State partitioning

Intuition. The rule for procedure call enumerates all the possible states for the values of parameters of the called procedure. In its current form, this rule always produces a big union with $|Q|^l$ terms. However, it may be the case that we don't need fully precise information about the value of a parameter to do the backward type inference.

Let us illustrate that with a simple example. Assume that the called procedure $p^{(1)}$ has a single parameter y_1 and that it never does anything else with y_1 than copying it (that is, any rule for p whose right-hand side mentions y_1 is of the form $p^{(1)}(a^{(n)}(x_1, \ldots, x_n), y_1) \to y_1$). Clearly, all the states $\langle p, \overline{q}, q'_1\rangle$ with $q'_1 \in \overline{q}$ are equivalent, and similarly for all the states $\langle p, \overline{q}, q''_1\rangle$ with $q''_1 \notin \overline{q}$. This is because whether the result of the procedure call will be or not in $\overline{q}$ only depends on the input tree (because there might be other rules whose right-hand side doesn't involve y_1 at all) and on whether the value for the parameter is itself in $\overline{q}$ or not. In particular, we don't need to know exactly in which state the accumulator is. So the rule for calling this procedure could just be:

$$\begin{aligned}
&\mathrm{Inf}(p(x_h, e_1), \overline{q}, \vec{q}) \\
&= \bigvee_{q_1' \in Q} \downarrow_h \langle p, \overline{q}, q_1' \rangle \wedge \mathrm{Inf}(e_1, \{q_1'\}, \vec{q}) \\
&= \left(\bigvee_{q_1' \in \overline{q}} \downarrow_h \langle p, \overline{q}, q_1' \rangle \wedge \mathrm{Inf}(e_1, \{q_1'\}, \vec{q}) \right) \\
&\quad \vee \left(\bigvee_{q_1'' \in Q \backslash \overline{q}} \downarrow_h \langle p, \overline{q}, q_1'' \rangle \wedge \mathrm{Inf}(e_1, \{q_1''\}, \vec{q}) \right) \\
&= (\downarrow_h \langle p, \overline{q}, q_1' \rangle \wedge \mathrm{Inf}(e_1, \overline{q}, \vec{q})) \vee (\downarrow_h \langle p, \overline{q}, q_1'' \rangle \wedge \mathrm{Inf}(e_1, Q \backslash \overline{q}, \vec{q}))
\end{aligned}$$

where in the last line q_1' (resp. q_1'') is chosen arbitrarily from $\overline{q}$ (resp. $Q \backslash \overline{q}$).

A new rule. More generally, in the rule for a call to a procedure $p^{(l)}$, we don't need to consider all the l-tuples $\vec{q'}$, but only a subset of them that capture all the possible situations. First, we assume that for given procedure $p^{(l)}$ and output type $\overline{q}$, one can compute for each $j = 1, \ldots, l$ an equivalence relation $E\langle p^{(l)}, \overline{q}, j \rangle$ such that:

$$(\forall j = 1, \ldots, l.\ (q_j', q_j'') \in E\langle p^{(l)}, \overline{q}, j \rangle) \Rightarrow \langle p^{(l)}, \overline{q}, \vec{q'} \rangle \simeq \langle p^{(l)}, \overline{q}, \vec{q''} \rangle \quad (*)$$

Let us see again the right-hand side of the definition for $\mathrm{Inf}(p^{(l)}(x_h, e_1, \ldots, e_l), \overline{q}, \vec{q})$:

$$\mathrm{Inf}(p^{(l)}(x_h, e_1, \ldots, e_l), \overline{q}, \vec{q}) = \bigvee_{\vec{q'} \in Q^l} \left(\downarrow_h \langle p^{(l)}, \overline{q}, \vec{q'} \rangle \wedge \bigwedge_{j=1,\ldots,l} \mathrm{Inf}(e_j, \{q_j'\}, \vec{q}) \right)$$

Let us split this union according to the equivalence class of the q_j' modulo the relations $E\langle p^{(l)}, \overline{q}, j \rangle$. If for each j, we choose an equivalence class $\overline{q}_j$ for the relation $E\langle p^{(l)}, \overline{q}, j \rangle$ (we write $\overline{q}_j \lhd E\langle p^{(l)}, \overline{q}, j \rangle$), then all the states $\langle p^{(l)}, \overline{q}, \vec{q'} \rangle$ with $\vec{q'} \in \overline{q}_1 \times \ldots \times \overline{q}_l$ are equivalent to $\langle p^{(l)}, \overline{q}, \mathrm{C}(\overline{q}_1 \times \ldots \times \overline{q}_l) \rangle$, where C is a choice function (it picks an arbitrary element from its argument). We can thus rewrite the right hand-side to:

$$\bigvee_{\overline{q}_1 \lhd E\langle p^{(l)}, \overline{q}, 1 \rangle, \ldots, \overline{q}_l \lhd E\langle p^{(l)}, \overline{q}, l \rangle} \left(\begin{aligned} &\downarrow_h \langle p^{(l)}, \overline{q}, \mathrm{C}(\overline{q}_1 \times \ldots \times \overline{q}_l) \rangle \\ &\wedge \bigvee_{\vec{q'} \in \overline{q}_1 \times \ldots \times \overline{q}_l} \bigwedge_{j=1,\ldots,l} \mathrm{Inf}(e_j, \{q_j'\}, \vec{q}) \end{aligned} \right)$$

The union of all the formulas $\bigwedge_{j=1,\dots,l} \mathrm{Inf}(e_j, \{q'_j\}, \vec{q})$ for $\vec{q'} \in \overline{q}_1 \times \ldots \times \overline{q}_l$ is equivalent to $\bigwedge_{j=1,\dots,l} \mathrm{Inf}(e_j, \overline{q}_j, \vec{q})$. Consequently, we obtain the following new rule:

$$\mathrm{Inf}(p^{(l)}(x_h, e_1, \dots, e_l), \overline{q}, \vec{q}) = \bigvee_{\overline{q}_1 \lhd E\langle p^{(l)}, \overline{q}, 1\rangle, \dots, \overline{q}_l \lhd E\langle p^{(l)}, \overline{q}, l\rangle} \left(\downarrow_h \langle p^{(l)}, \overline{q}, \mathrm{C}(\overline{q}_1 \times \ldots \times \overline{q}_l)\rangle \wedge \bigwedge_{j=1,\dots,l} \mathrm{Inf}(e_j, \overline{q}_j, \vec{q}) \right)$$

In the worst case, all the equivalence relations $E\langle p^{(l)}, \overline{q}, j\rangle$ are the identity, and the right-hand side is the same as for the old rule. But if we can identify larger equivalence classes, we can significantly reduce the number of terms in the union on the right-hand side.

Computing the equivalence relations. Now we will give an algorithm to compute the relations $E\langle p^{(k)}, \overline{q}, j\rangle$ satisfying the condition $(*)$. We will also define equivalence relations $E[e, \overline{q}, j]$ for any (n,k)-expression e (with $j = 1, \dots, k$), such that:

$$(\forall j = 1, \dots, k.(q'_j, q''_j) \in E[e, \overline{q}, j]) \Rightarrow \mathrm{Inf}(e, \overline{q}, \vec{q'}) \simeq \mathrm{Inf}(e, \overline{q}, \vec{q''})$$

We can use the rules used to define the formulas $\mathrm{Inf}(e, \overline{q}, \vec{q})$ in order to obtain sufficient conditions to be satisfied so that these properties hold. We will express these conditions by a system of equations. Before giving this system, we need to introduce some notations. If E_1 and E_2 are two equivalence relations on Q, we write $E_1 \sqsubseteq E_2$ if $E_2 \subseteq E_1$ (when equivalence relations are seen as subsets of Q^2). The smallest equivalence relation for this ordering is the equivalence relation with a single equivalence class. The largest equivalence relation is the identity on Q. For two equivalence relations E_1, E_2, we can define their least upper bound $E_1 \sqcup E_2$ as the set-theoretic intersection. For an equivalence relation E and a set of states $\overline{q}$, we write $\overline{q} \lhd E$ if $\overline{q}$ is one of the equivalence class modulo E. Abusing the notation by identifying an equivalence relation with the partition it induces on Q, we will write $\{Q\}$ for the smallest relation and $\{\overline{q}, Q \backslash \overline{q}\}$ for the relation with the two equivalence classes $\overline{q}$ and its complement. The system of equations is derived from the rules used to define the function Inf:

$$\begin{array}{ll}
E[b^{(m)}(e_1, \dots, e_m), \overline{q}, i] & \sqsupseteq \bigsqcup \{E[e_j, \overline{q}_j, i] \mid (\overline{q}_1, \dots, \overline{q}_m) \in \mathrm{Cart}(\Delta(\overline{q}, b^{(m)})), \\
& \qquad\qquad\qquad\qquad\qquad\qquad\qquad\qquad \text{for } j = 1, \dots, m\} \\
E[p^{(l)}(x_h, e_1, \dots, e_l), \overline{q}, i] & \sqsupseteq \bigsqcup \{E[e_j, \overline{q}_j, i] \mid \overline{q}_j \lhd E\langle p^{(l)}, \overline{q}, j\rangle, \text{ for } j = 1, \dots, l\} \\
E[y_j, \overline{q}, i] & \sqsupseteq \begin{cases} \{\overline{q}, Q \backslash \overline{q}\} & (i = j) \\ \{Q\} & (i \neq j) \end{cases} \\
E\langle p^{(k)}, \overline{q}, j\rangle & \sqsupseteq \bigsqcup \{E[e, \overline{q}, j] \mid p^{(k)}(a^{(n)}(\vec{x}), \vec{y}) \to e) \in \Pi\}
\end{array}$$

Let us explain why these conditions imply the required properties for the equivalence relation and how they are derived from the rules defining Inf. We will use an intuitive induction argument (on expressions), even though a formal proof actually requires an induction on trees. Consider the rule for the procedure call. The new rule we have obtained above implies that in order to have $\mathrm{Inf}(p^{(l)}(x_h, e_1, \ldots, e_l), \overline{q}, \vec{q'}) \simeq \mathrm{Inf}(p^{(l)}(x_h, e_1, \ldots, e_l), \overline{q}, \vec{q''})$, it is sufficient to have $\mathrm{Inf}(e_j, \overline{q}_j, \vec{q'}) \simeq \mathrm{Inf}(e_j, \overline{q}_j, \vec{q''})$ for all $j = 1, \ldots, l$ and for all $\overline{q}_j \lhd E\langle p^{(l)}, \overline{q}, j\rangle$, and thus, by induction, it is also sufficient to have $(q'_i, q''_i) \in E[e_j, \overline{q}_j, i]$ for all i, for all $j = 1, \ldots, l$ and for all $\overline{q}_j \lhd E\langle p^{(l)}, \overline{q}, j\rangle$. In other words, a sufficient condition is $(q'_i, q''_i) \in \bigcap\{E[e_j, \overline{q}_j, i] \mid \overline{q}_j \lhd E\langle p^{(l)}, \overline{q}, j\rangle,\ j = 1, \ldots, l\}$, from which we obtain the equation above (we recall that $\sqcup$ corresponds to set-theoretic intersection of relations). The reasoning is similar for the constructor expression. Indeed, the rule we have obtained in the previous section tells us that in order to have $\mathrm{Inf}(b^{(m)}(e_1, \ldots, e_m), \overline{q}, \vec{q'}) \simeq \mathrm{Inf}(b^{(m)}(e_1, \ldots, e_m), \overline{q}, \vec{q''})$, it is sufficient to have $\mathrm{Inf}(e_j, \overline{q}_j, \vec{q'}) \simeq \mathrm{Inf}(e_j, \overline{q}_j, \vec{q''})$ for all $(\overline{q}_1, \ldots, \overline{q}_m) \in \mathrm{Cart}(\Delta(\overline{q}, b^{(m)}))$ and $j = 1, \ldots, m$.

As we explained before, it is desirable to compute equivalence relations with large equivalence classes (that is, small for the $\sqsubseteq$ ordering). Here is how we can compute a family of equivalence relations satisfying the system of equations above. First, we consider the CPO of functions mapping a triple $(e, \overline{q}, i)$ to an equivalence relation on Q and we reformulate the system of equation as finding an element x of this CPO such that $f(x) \sqsubseteq x$, where f is obtained from the right-hand sides of the equations. To compute such an element, we start from x_0 the smallest element of the CPO, and we consider the sequence defined by $x_{n+1} = x_n \sqcup f(x_n)$. Since this sequence is monotonic and the CPO is finite, the sequence reaches a constant value after a finite number of iterations. This value x satisfies $f(x) \sqsubseteq x$ as expected. We conjecture that this element is actually a smallest fixpoint for f, but we have no proof of this fact (note that the function f is not monotonic).

Sharing the computation. Given the rules defining the formulas $\mathrm{Inf}(e, \overline{q}, \vec{q})$, we might end up computing the same formula several times. A very classical optimization consists in memoizing the results of such computations. This is made even more effective by hash-consing the expressions. Indeed, in practice, for a given mtt procedure, many constructors have identical expressions.

Complementing the output. In the example at the beginning of the section on "state partitioning," we have displayed a formula where both $\mathrm{Inf}(e, \overline{q}, \vec{q})$ and $\mathrm{Inf}(e, Q\backslash\overline{q}, \vec{q})$ appear. One may wonder what the relation is between these two sub-formulas. Let us recall the required properties for these two formulas:

$$[\![\mathrm{Inf}(e, \overline{q}, \vec{q})]\!] = \{v \mid [\![p]\!](\vec{v}, \vec{w}) \cap [\![\overline{q}]\!] \neq \emptyset\}$$

$$[\![\mathrm{Inf}(e, Q\backslash\overline{q}, \vec{q})]\!] = \{v \mid [\![p]\!](\vec{v}, \vec{w}) \cap [\![Q\backslash\overline{q}]\!] \neq \emptyset\}$$

(for $\vec{w} \in [\![\vec{q}]\!]$). Note that $[\![Q\backslash\overline{q}]\!]$ is the complement of $[\![\overline{q}]\!]$. As a consequence, if $[\![p]\!]$ is a total deterministic function (that is, if $[\![p]\!](\vec{v}, \vec{w})$ is always a singleton), then $[\![\mathrm{Inf}(e, Q\backslash\overline{q}, \vec{q})]\!]$ is the complement of $[\![\mathrm{Inf}(e, \overline{q}, \vec{q})]\!]$. If we extend the syntax of formula in alternating tree automata with negation (whose semantics is trivial to define), we can thus introduce the following rule:

$$\mathrm{Inf}(e, \overline{q}, \vec{q}) = \neg\mathrm{Inf}(e, Q \backslash \overline{q}, \vec{q})$$

to be applied e.g. when the cardinal of $\overline{q}$ is strictly larger than half the cardinal of Q. In practice, we observed a huge impact of this optimization: the number of constructed states is divided by two in all our experiences, and the emptiness algorithm runs much more efficiently. Also, because of the memoization technique mentioned above, this optimization allows us to share more computation. That said, we don't yet have a deeper understanding of the very important impact of this optimization.

The rule above can only be applied when the expression e denotes a total and deterministic function. We use a very simple syntactic criterion to ensure that: we require all the reachable procedures $p^{(k)}$ to have exactly one rule $p^{(k)}(a^{(n)}(x_1, \ldots, x_n), y_1, \ldots, y_k) \to e$ for each symbol $a^{(n)}$.

5 Experiments

We have experimented on our typechecker with various XML transformations implemented as mtts. Although we did not try very big transformations, we did work with large input and output tree automata automatically generated from the XHTML DTD (without taking XML attributes into account). Note that because this DTD has many tags, the mtts actually have many transitions since they typically copy tags, which requires all constructors corresponding to these tags to be enumerated. They do not have too many procedures, though. The bottom-up deterministic automaton that we generated from the XHTML DTD has 35 states.

Table 1 gives the elapsed times spent in typechecking several transformations and the number of states of the inferred alternating tree automaton that have been materialized. The experiment was conducted on an Intel Pentium 4 processor 2.80Ghz, running Linux kernel 2.4.27, and the typechecking time includes the whole process (determinization of the output type, backward inference, intersection with the input type, and emptiness check). The typechecker is implemented in and compiled by Objective Caml 3.09.3.

We also indicate the number of procedures in each mtt, the maximum number of parameters, and the minimum integer b, if any, such that the mtt is syntactically b-bounded copying. Intuitively, the integer b captures the maximum number of times the mtt traverses any node of the input tree. This notion has been introduced in [14] where the existence of b is shown to imply the polynomiality of the algorithm described in that paper (see [8]). Here, we observe that even unbounded-copying mtts can be typechecked efficiently.

Unless otherwise stated, transformations are checked to have type `XHTML`→`XHTML` (i.e., both input and output types are `XHTML`). Transformation (1) removes all the `<b>` tags, keeping their contents. Transformation (2) is a variant that drops the `<div>` tags instead. The typechecker detects that the latter doesn't have type `XHTML`→`XHTML` by producing a counter-example:

```
<html><head><title/></head><body><div/></body>
```

Table 1. Results of the experiments

Transformation:	(1)	(2)	(3)	(4)	(5)	(6)	(7)
# of procedures:	2	2	3	5	4	6	6
Max # of parameters:	1	1	1	1	2	2	2
Bounded copying:	1	1	2	∞	∞	2	1
Type-checking time (ms):	1057	1042	0373	0377	0337	0409	0410
# of states in the ata:	147	147	43	74	37	49	49

Indeed, removing the `<div>` element may produce a `<body>` element with an empty content, which is not valid in XHTML. This kind of error is quite common in XML transformations but it is difficult to find with testing or with a simple type system. Transformation (3) copies all the `<a>` elements (and their corresponding subtrees) into a new `<div>` element and prepends the `<div>` to the `<body>` element. Transformation (4) groups together adjacent `<b>` elements, concatenating their contents. Transformation (5) extracts from an XHTML document a tree of depth 2 which represents the conceptual nesting structure of `<h1>` and `<h2>` heading elements (note that, in XHTML, the structure among headings is flat). Transformation (6) builds a tree representing a table of contents for the top two levels of itemizations, giving section and subsection numbers to them (where the numbers are constructed as Peano numerals), and prepends the resulting tree to the `<body>` element. Transformation (7) is a variant that only returns the table of contents.

We have also translated some transformations (that can be expressed as mtts) used by Tozawa and Hagiya in [28] (namely `htmlcopy`, `inventory`, `pref2app`, `pref2html`, `prefcopy`). Our implementation takes between 2ms and 6ms to typecheck these mtts, except for `inventory` for which it takes 22 ms. Tozawa and Hagiya report performance between 5ms and 1000ms on a Pentium M 1.8 Ghz for the satisfiability check (which corresponds to our emptiness check and excludes the time taken by backward inference). Although these results indicate our advantages over them to some extent, since the numbers are too small and they have not undertaken experiments as big as ours, it is hard to draw a meaningful conclusion.

6 Conclusion and Future Work

We have presented an efficient typechecking algorithm for mtts based on the idea of using alternating tree automata for representing the preimage of the given mtt obtained from the backward type inference. This representation was useful for deriving optimization techniques on the backward inference phase such as state partitioning and Cartesian factorization, and was also effective for speeding up the subsequent emptiness check phase by exploiting Boolean equivalences among formulas. Our experimental results confirmed that our techniques allow us to typecheck small sizes of transformations with respect to the full XHTML type.

The present work is only the first step toward a truly practical typechecker for mtts. In the future, we will seek for further improvements that allow typechecking larger and more complicated transformations. In particular, transformations with upward axes can be obtained by compositions of mtts as proved in [13] and a capability to typecheck such compositions of mtts in a reasonable time will be important. We have some preliminary ideas for the improvement and plan to pursue them as a next step. In the end, we hope to be able to handle (at least a reasonably large subset of) XSLT.

Acknowledgments. This work is partly supported by Japan Society for the Promotion of Science and by The Okawa Foundation for Information and Telecommunications. We are grateful to Sebastian Maneth for useful discussions.

References

1. Alon, N., Milo, T., Neven, F., Suciu, D., Vianu, V.: XML with data values: Typechecking revisited. In: Proceedings of Symposium on Principles of Database Systems (PODS) (2001)
2. Appel, A.W., MacQueen, D.B.: Standard ML of New Jersey. In: Third Int'l. Symp. on Prog. Lang. Implementation and Logic Programming, pp. 1–13. Springer, Heidelberg (1991)
3. Benzaken, V., Castagna, G., Frisch, A.: CDuce: An XML-centric general-purpose language. In: Proceedings of the International Conference on Functional Programming (ICFP), pp. 51–63 (2003)
4. Engelfriet, J., Filé, G.: The formal power of one-visit attribute grammars. Acta Informatica 16, 275–302 (1981)
5. Engelfriet, J., Maneth, S.: A comparison of pebble tree transducers with macro tree transducers. Acta Informatica 39(9), 613–698 (2003)
6. Engelfriet, J., Vogler, H.: Macro tree transducers. J. Comput. Syst. Sci. 31(1), 146–710 (1985)
7. Frisch, A.: Théorie, conception et réalisation d'un langage de programmation adapté à XML. PhD thesis, Universit Paris 7 (2004)
8. Frisch, A., Hosoya, H.: Towards practial typechecking for macro tree transducers. Technical report, INRIA (2007)
9. Hosoya, H.: Regular expression filters for XML. Journal of Functional Programming 16(6), 711–750 (2006) Short version appeared. In: Proceedings of Programming Technologies for XML (PLAN-X), pp.13–27, (2004)
10. Hosoya, H., Pierce, B.C.: XDuce: A typed XML processing language. ACM Transactions on Internet Technology 3(2), 117–148 (2003). In: Suciu, D., Vossen, G. (eds.) WebDB 2000. LNCS, vol. 1997, pp. 226–244. Springer, Heidelberg (2001)
11. Hosoya, H., Vouillon, J., Pierce, B.C.: Regular expression types for XML. ACM Transactions on Programming Languages and Systems, 27(1), 46–90 (2004). Short version appeared. In: Proceedings of the International Conference on Functional Programming (ICFP), pp. 11–22 (2000)
12. Leroy, X., Doligez, D., Garrigue, J., Vouillon, J., Rémy, D.: The Objective Caml system. Software and documentation available on the Web (1996), `http://pauillac.inria.fr/ocaml/`

13. Maneth, S., Perst, T., Berlea, A., Seidl, H.: XML type checking with macro tree transducers. In: Proceedings of Symposium on Principles of Database Systems (PODS), pp. 283–294 (2005)
14. Maneth, S., Perst, T., Seidl, H.: Exact XML type checking in polynomial time. In: Schwentick, T., Suciu, D. (eds.) ICDT 2007. LNCS, vol. 4353, pp. 254–268. Springer, Heidelberg (2006)
15. Martens, W., Neven, F.: Typechecking top-down uniform unranked tree transducers. In: Proceedings of International Conference on Database Theory, pp. 64–78 (2003)
16. Martens, W., Neven, F.: Frontiers of tractability for typechecking simple XML transformations. In: Proceedings of Symposium on Principles of Database Systems (PODS), pp. 23–34 (2004)
17. Milo, T., Suciu, D.: Type inference for queries on semistructured data. In: Proceedings of Symposium on Principles of Database Systems, Philadelphia, pp. 215–226 (May 1999)
18. Milo, T., Suciu, D., Vianu, V.: Typechecking for XML transformers. In: Proceedings of the Nineteenth ACM SIGMOD-SIGACT-SIGART Symposium on Principles of Database Systems, pp. 11–22. ACM, New York (2000)
19. Møller, A., Olesen, M.Ø., Schwartzbach, M.I.: Static validation of XSL Transformations. Technical Report RS-05-32, BRICS, Draft, accepted for TOPLAS (October 2005)
20. Murata, M.: Transformation of documents and schemas by patterns and contextual conditions. In: Nicholas, C., Wood, D. (eds.) PODDP 1996 and PODP 1996. LNCS, vol. 1293, pp. 153–169. Springer, Heidelberg (1997)
21. Nakano, K., Mu, S.-C.: A pushdown machine for recursive XML processing. In: Kobayashi, N. (ed.) APLAS 2006. LNCS, vol. 4279, pp. 340–356. Springer, Heidelberg (2006)
22. Perst, T., Seidl, H.: Macro forest transducers. Information Processing Letters 89(3), 141–149 (2004)
23. Slutzki, G.: Alternating tree automata. Theoretical Computer Science 41, 305–318 (1985)
24. Suda, T., Hosoya, H.: Non-backtracking top-down algorithm for checking tree automata containment. In: Farré, J., Litovsky, I., Schmitz, S. (eds.) CIAA 2005. LNCS, vol. 3845, pp. 83–92. Springer, Heidelberg (2006)
25. Tozawa, A.: Towards static type checking for XSLT. In: Proceedings of ACM Symposium on Document Engineering, ACM Press, New York (2001)
26. Tozawa, A.: XML type checking using high-level tree transducer. In: Hagiya, M., Wadler, P. (eds.) FLOPS 2006. LNCS, vol. 3945, pp. 81–96. Springer, Heidelberg (2006)
27. Tozawa, A., Hagiya, M.: XML schema containment checking based on semi-implicit techniques. In: Ibarra, O.H., Dang, Z. (eds.) CIAA 2003. LNCS, vol. 2759, pp. 213–225. Springer, Heidelberg (2003)
28. Tozawa, A., Hagiya, M.: Efficient decision procedure for a logic for XML (unpublished manuscipt, 2004)

Author Index

Acar, Umut A. 138
Ahmed, Amal 138

Björklund, Henrik 66
Bravo, Loreto 97
Brenes, Sofía 48
Burke, Michael G. 216

Cheney, James 97, 138
Cohen, Sara 32
Colazzo, Dario 231

Deutch, Daniel 169

Fan, Wenfei 1
Fletcher, George H.L. 48
Frisch, Alain 246
Fundulaki, Irini 97

Geerts, Floris 127
Gelade, Wouter 201
Ghelli, Giorgio 81, 231
Gil, Joseph (Yossi) 32
Götz, Michaela 17
Gurevich, Yuri 153
Gyssens, Marc 48

Hosoya, Haruo 246

Koch, Christoph 17

Leinders, Dirk 153

Martens, Wim 17, 66
Milo, Tova 169

Neven, Frank 201

Onose, Nicola 81

Paredaens, Jan 48
Peshansky, Igor 216

Raghavachari, Mukund 216
Ré, Christopher 186
Reichenbach, Christoph 216
Rose, Kristoffer 81

Sartiani, Carlo 231
Schwentick, Thomas 66
Siméon, Jérôme 81
Suciu, Dan 186

Van den Bussche, Jan 127, 153
Van Gucht, Dirk 48

Wijsen, Jef 112
Wu, Yuqing 48

Zarivach, Evelina 32

Lecture Notes in Computer Science

Sublibrary 3: Information Systems and Application, incl. Internet/Web and HCI

For information about Vols. 1–4312
please contact your bookseller or Springer

Vol. 4797: M. Arenas, M.I. Schwartzbach (Eds.), Database Programming Languages. VIII, 261 pages. 2007.

Vol. 4796: M. Lew, N. Sebe, T.S. Huang, E.M. Bakker (Eds.), IEEE Workshop on Human Computer Interaction. X, 157 pages. 2007.

Vol. 4777: S. Bhalla (Ed.), Databases in Networked Information Systems. X, 329 pages. 2007.

Vol. 4761: R. Obermaisser, Y. Nah, P. Puschner, F.J. Rammig (Eds.), Software Technologies for Embedded and Ubiquitous Systems. XIV, 563 pages. 2007.

Vol. 4740: L. Ma, M. Rauterberg, R. Nakatsu (Eds.), Entertainment Computing – ICEC 2007. XXX, 480 pages. 2007.

Vol. 4730: C. Peters, P. Clough, F.C. Gey, J. Karlgren, B. Magnini, D.W. Oard, M. de Rijke, M. Stempfhuber (Eds.), Evaluation of Multilingual and Multi-modal Information Retrieval. XXIV, 998 pages. 2007.

Vol. 4723: M. R. Berthold, J. Shawe-Taylor, N. Lavrač (Eds.), Advances in Intelligent Data Analysis VII. XIV, 380 pages. 2007.

Vol. 4721: W. Jonker, M. Petković (Eds.), Secure Data Management. X, 213 pages. 2007.

Vol. 4718: J. Hightower, B. Schiele, T. Strang (Eds.), Location- and Context-Awareness. X, 297 pages. 2007.

Vol. 4717: J. Krumm, G.D. Abowd, A. Seneviratne, T. Strang (Eds.), UbiComp 2007: Ubiquitous Computing. XIX, 520 pages. 2007.

Vol. 4715: J.M. Haake, S.F. Ochoa, A. Cechich (Eds.), Groupware: Design, Implementation, and Use. XIII, 355 pages. 2007.

Vol. 4714: G. Alonso, P. Dadam, M. Rosemann (Eds.), Business Process Management. XIII, 418 pages. 2007.

Vol. 4704: D. Barbosa, A. Bonifati, Z. Bellahsène, E. Hunt, R. Unland (Eds.), Database and XMLTechnologies. X, 141 pages. 2007.

Vol. 4690: Y. Ioannidis, B. Novikov, B. Rachev (Eds.), Advances in Databases and Information Systems. XIII, 377 pages. 2007.

Vol. 4675: L. Kovács, N. Fuhr, C. Meghini (Eds.), Research and Advanced Technology for Digital Libraries. XVII, 585 pages. 2007.

Vol. 4674: Y. Luo (Ed.), Cooperative Design, Visualization, and Engineering. XIII, 431 pages. 2007.

Vol. 4663: C. Baranauskas, P. Palanque, J. Abascal, S.D.J. Barbosa (Eds.), Human-Computer Interaction – INTERACT 2007, Part II. XXXIII, 735 pages. 2007.

Vol. 4662: C. Baranauskas, P. Palanque, J. Abascal, S.D.J. Barbosa (Eds.), Human-Computer Interaction – INTERACT 2007, Part I. XXXIII, 637 pages. 2007.

Vol. 4658: T. Enokido, L. Barolli, M. Takizawa (Eds.), Network-Based Information Systems. XIII, 544 pages. 2007.

Vol. 4656: M.A. Wimmer, J. Scholl, Å. Grönlund (Eds.), Electronic Government. XIV, 450 pages. 2007.

Vol. 4655: G. Psaila, R. Wagner (Eds.), E-Commerce and Web Technologies. VII, 229 pages. 2007.

Vol. 4654: I.-Y. Song, J. Eder, T.M. Nguyen (Eds.), Data Warehousing and Knowledge Discovery. XVI, 482 pages. 2007.

Vol. 4653: R. Wagner, N. Revell, G. Pernul (Eds.), Database and Expert Systems Applications. XXII, 907 pages. 2007.

Vol. 4636: G. Antoniou, U. Aßmann, C. Baroglio, S. Decker, N. Henze, P.-L. Patranjan, R. Tolksdorf (Eds.), Reasoning Web. IX, 345 pages. 2007.

Vol. 4611: J. Indulska, J. Ma, L.T. Yang, T. Ungerer, J. Cao (Eds.), Ubiquitous Intelligence and Computing. XXIII, 1257 pages. 2007.

Vol. 4607: L. Baresi, P. Fraternali, G.-J. Houben (Eds.), Web Engineering. XVI, 576 pages. 2007.

Vol. 4606: A. Pras, M. van Sinderen (Eds.), Dependable and Adaptable Networks and Services. XIV, 149 pages. 2007.

Vol. 4605: D. Papadias, D. Zhang, G. Kollios (Eds.), Advances in Spatial and Temporal Databases. X, 479 pages. 2007.

Vol. 4602: S. Barker, G.-J. Ahn (Eds.), Data and Applications Security XXI. X, 291 pages. 2007.

Vol. 4601: S. Spaccapietra, P. Atzeni, F. Fages, M.-S. Hacid, M. Kifer, J. Mylopoulos, B. Pernici, P. Shvaiko, J. Trujillo, I. Zaihrayeu (Eds.), Journal on Data Semantics IX. XV, 197 pages. 2007.

Vol. 4592: Z. Kedad, N. Lammari, E. Métais, F. Meziane, Y. Rezgui (Eds.), Natural Language Processing and Information Systems. XIV, 442 pages. 2007.

Vol. 4587: R. Cooper, J. Kennedy (Eds.), Data Management. XIII, 259 pages. 2007.

Vol. 4577: N. Sebe, Y. Liu, Y.-t. Zhuang, T.S. Huang (Eds.), Multimedia Content Analysis and Mining. XIII, 513 pages. 2007.

Vol. 4568: T. Ishida, S. R. Fussell, P. T. J. M. Vossen (Eds.), Intercultural Collaboration. XIII, 395 pages. 2007.

Vol. 4566: M.J. Dainoff (Ed.), Ergonomics and Health Aspects of Work with Computers. XVIII, 390 pages. 2007.

Vol. 4564: D. Schuler (Ed.), Online Communities and Social Computing. XVII, 520 pages. 2007.

Vol. 4563: R. Shumaker (Ed.), Virtual Reality. XXII, 762 pages. 2007.

Vol. 4561: V.G. Duffy (Ed.), Digital Human Modeling. XXIII, 1068 pages. 2007.

Vol. 4560: N. Aykin (Ed.), Usability and Internationalization, Part II. XVIII, 576 pages. 2007.

Vol. 4559: N. Aykin (Ed.), Usability and Internationalization, Part I. XVIII, 661 pages. 2007.

Vol. 4558: M.J. Smith, G. Salvendy (Eds.), Human Interface and the Management of Information, Part II. XXIII, 1162 pages. 2007.

Vol. 4557: M.J. Smith, G. Salvendy (Eds.), Human Interface and the Management of Information, Part I. XXII, 1030 pages. 2007.

Vol. 4541: T. Okadome, T. Yamazaki, M. Makhtari (Eds.), Pervasive Computing for Quality of Life Enhancement. IX, 248 pages. 2007.

Vol. 4537: K.C.-C. Chang, W. Wang, L. Chen, C.A. Ellis, C.-H. Hsu, A.C. Tsoi, H. Wang (Eds.), Advances in Web and Network Technologies, and Information Management. XXIII, 707 pages. 2007.

Vol. 4531: J. Indulska, K. Raymond (Eds.), Distributed Applications and Interoperable Systems. XI, 337 pages. 2007.

Vol. 4526: M. Malek, M. Reitenspieß, A. van Moorsel (Eds.), Service Availability. X, 155 pages. 2007.

Vol. 4524: M. Marchiori, J.Z. Pan, C.d.S. Marie (Eds.), Web Reasoning and Rule Systems. XI, 382 pages. 2007.

Vol. 4519: E. Franconi, M. Kifer, W. May (Eds.), The Semantic Web: Research and Applications. XVIII, 830 pages. 2007.

Vol. 4518: N. Fuhr, M. Lalmas, A. Trotman (Eds.), Comparative Evaluation of XML Information Retrieval Systems. XII, 554 pages. 2007.

Vol. 4508: M.-Y. Kao, X.-Y. Li (Eds.), Algorithmic Aspects in Information and Management. VIII, 428 pages. 2007.

Vol. 4506: D. Zeng, I. Gotham, K. Komatsu, C. Lynch, M. Thurmond, D. Madigan, B. Lober, J. Kvach, H. Chen (Eds.), Intelligence and Security Informatics: Biosurveillance. XI, 234 pages. 2007.

Vol. 4505: G. Dong, X. Lin, W. Wang, Y. Yang, J.X. Yu (Eds.), Advances in Data and Web Management. XXII, 896 pages. 2007.

Vol. 4504: J. Huang, R. Kowalczyk, Z. Maamar, D. Martin, I. Müller, S. Stoutenburg, K.P. Sycara (Eds.), Service-Oriented Computing: Agents, Semantics, and Engineering. X, 175 pages. 2007.

Vol. 4500: N.A. Streitz, A.D. Kameas, I. Mavrommati (Eds.), The Disappearing Computer. XVIII, 304 pages. 2007.

Vol. 4495: J. Krogstie, A. Opdahl, G. Sindre (Eds.), Advanced Information Systems Engineering. XVI, 606 pages. 2007.

Vol. 4480: A. LaMarca, M. Langheinrich, K.N. Truong (Eds.), Pervasive Computing. XIII, 369 pages. 2007.

Vol. 4473: D. Draheim, G. Weber (Eds.), Trends in Enterprise Application Architecture. X, 355 pages. 2007.

Vol. 4471: P. Cesar, K. Chorianopoulos, J.F. Jensen (Eds.), Interactive TV: A Shared Experience. XIII, 236 pages. 2007.

Vol. 4469: K.-c. Hui, Z. Pan, R.C.-k. Chung, C.C.L. Wang, X. Jin, S. Göbel, E.C.-L. Li (Eds.), Technologies for E-Learning and Digital Entertainment. XVIII, 974 pages. 2007.

Vol. 4443: R. Kotagiri, P. Radha Krishna, M. Mohania, E. Nantajeewarawat (Eds.), Advances in Databases: Concepts, Systems and Applications. XXI, 1126 pages. 2007.

Vol. 4439: W. Abramowicz (Ed.), Business Information Systems. XV, 654 pages. 2007.

Vol. 4430: C.C. Yang, D. Zeng, M. Chau, K. Chang, Q. Yang, X. Cheng, J. Wang, F.-Y. Wang, H. Chen (Eds.), Intelligence and Security Informatics. XII, 330 pages. 2007.

Vol. 4425: G. Amati, C. Carpineto, G. Romano (Eds.), Advances in Information Retrieval. XIX, 759 pages. 2007.

Vol. 4412: F. Stajano, H.J. Kim, J.-S. Chae, S.-D. Kim (Eds.), Ubiquitous Convergence Technology. XI, 302 pages. 2007.

Vol. 4402: W. Shen, J.-Z. Luo, Z. Lin, J.-P.A. Barthès, Q. Hao (Eds.), Computer Supported Cooperative Work in Design III. XV, 763 pages. 2007.

Vol. 4398: S. Marchand-Maillet, E. Bruno, A. Nürnberger, M. Detyniecki (Eds.), Adaptive Multimedia Retrieval: User, Context, and Feedback. XI, 269 pages. 2007.

Vol. 4397: C. Stephanidis, M. Pieper (Eds.), Universal Access in Ambient Intelligence Environments. XV, 467 pages. 2007.

Vol. 4380: S. Spaccapietra, P. Atzeni, F. Fages, M.-S. Hacid, M. Kifer, J. Mylopoulos, B. Pernici, P. Shvaiko, J. Trujillo, I. Zaihrayeu (Eds.), Journal on Data Semantics VIII. XV, 219 pages. 2007.

Vol. 4365: C.J. Bussler, M. Castellanos, U. Dayal, S. Navathe (Eds.), Business Intelligence for the Real-Time Enterprises. IX, 157 pages. 2007.

Vol. 4353: T. Schwentick, D. Suciu (Eds.), Database Theory – ICDT 2007. XI, 419 pages. 2006.

Vol. 4352: T.-J. Cham, J. Cai, C. Dorai, D. Rajan, T.-S. Chua, L.-T. Chia (Eds.), Advances in Multimedia Modeling, Part II. XVIII, 743 pages. 2006.

Vol. 4351: T.-J. Cham, J. Cai, C. Dorai, D. Rajan, T.-S. Chua, L.-T. Chia (Eds.), Advances in Multimedia Modeling, Part I. XIX, 797 pages. 2006.

Vol. 4328: D. Penkler, M. Reitenspiess, F. Tam (Eds.), Service Availability. X, 289 pages. 2006.

Vol. 4321: P. Brusilovsky, A. Kobsa, W. Nejdl (Eds.), The Adaptive Web. XII, 763 pages. 2007.

Vol. 4317: S.K. Madria, K.T. Claypool, R. Kannan, P. Uppuluri, M.M. Gore (Eds.), Distributed Computing and Internet Technology. XIX, 466 pages. 2006.